British Diplomacy and Swedish Politics, 1758-1773

Jag känner icke så noga alla då varande omständigheter, men hvar och en bör känna, at omständigheter mycket verka och göra mycket intryck: ty att sitta uti lugnet och derifrån utfärda hårda domar öfver dem, som seglat uti svallande haf och imellan fördolde bränningar, utmärker liten kunskap om sakernas lopp här i verlden, liten om människans krafter emot lycka och olycka, liten billighet och kärlek . . .

A. J. von Höpken, *Äre-Minne öfver . . . Tessin*, 1771

Published with assistance
from the
David H. Willson Fund

British Diplomacy and Swedish Politics, 1758-1773

Michael Roberts

University of Minnesota Press
Minneapolis

Published by the University of Minnesota Press,
2037 University Avenue Southeast,
Minneapolis, Minnesota 55455
Printed in the United States of America

Library of Congress Cataloging in Publication Data

Roberts, Michael, 1908-
British diplomacy and Swedish politics, 1758-1773.
Bibliography: p.
Includes index.
1. Great Britain—Foreign relations—Sweden.
2. Sweden—Foreign relations—Great Britain.
3. Sweden—Politics and government—1718-1772.
4. Goodricke, John, Sir. I. Title.
DA47.7.R62 327.410485 80-11499
ISBN 0-8166-0910-1

for

Michael Metcalf

THE NORDIC SERIES

Volume 1

Other Titles in the Series

Volume 2	Henrik Ibsen, *Peer Gynt,* translated by Rolf Fjelde. A thoroughly revised version of Fjelde's translation, with new appendixes.
Volume 3	*The Finnish Revolution, 1917-1918* by Anthony F. Upton
Volume 4	*To the Third Empire: Ibsen's Early Drama* by Brian Johnston
Volume 5	*Scandinavian Literature since 1870* by Sven Rossel
Volume 6	*Viking Art* by David M. Wilson and Ole Klindt-Jensen

THE NORDIC SERIES

In carrying out general plans for this series, the University of Minnesota Press is advised on various aspects by the following scholars:

Contents

Preface

This book has been a spare-time occupation for many (too many) years, attended to only in intervals between other and more immediate demands. It was Sir Herbert Butterfield who long ago remarked to me that "all historians should at some time or other try to write diplomatic history: it is a discipline," and thereby launched me on what at the time seemed a rash enterprise. Once begun, it could not have been continued without generous assistance, for which I now make grateful acknowledgment: to the Senate of The Queen's University, Belfast, for grants for research; to The Leverhulme Trust, which elected me to a European Faculty Fellowship; to Svenska Institutet för kulturellt utbyte, Stockholm, for repeated kindness and financial help, as so often in the past; to Professor Sten Carlsson and Historiska Institutionen at Uppsala University, who gave me a warm welcome and a base from which to work; to Professor Jeff Opland, Director of the Institute for Social and Economic Research, Rhodes University, Grahamstown, who provided me with an ideal milieu in which to write, and made generous typing assistance available to me; to Mrs. R. Vroom and Mrs. V. Ochtman, for the patience and accuracy with which they undertook the task of typing and retyping; to Dr. Roger Bartlett, for help with translations from the Russian.

But my most important obligation is to Professor Michael Metcalf. Professor Metcalf not only excerpted for me from the manuscripts of

Russian diplomatic correspondence now preserved in microfilm in Riksarkivet, Stockholm; he generously permitted me to read his own book on a closely related subject, chapter by chapter as it was written; and he gave me the advantage of his comment and criticism at every stage as I proceeded. In stimulating conversations, and in correspondence extending over the last five or six years, he provided a challenge (at times a corrective) to my own interpretations; and it is proper that this book should be dedicated to him.

M. R.

Introduction

The Tranquillity of the North

The language of diplomacy, as it developed and achieved consistency from the seventeenth century onwards, acquired a precision appropriate to the binding character of the international agreements toward which its efforts are directed; but it combined this (at least until our own time) with a highly stylized diction, designed to give dignity and weight to trifling dispatches, to put a gloss of amenity upon protests which might otherwise appear unduly sharp, and to clothe even menace in the decent forms of courtesy. Diplomacy, in short, like other professions, has created its own jargon. And one useful and timesaving element in that jargon has been the employment of a kind of international shorthand to describe concepts too familiar to need explanation, or problems too complex to be set out at length. The men of the seventeenth century knew quite well what was meant by *partes principales paciscentes*, or *libertates Germaniae*, and they bequeathed to their successors the notions of the Dutch Barrier and the Maritime Powers. The eighteenth century saw the emergence of such conveniently elastic phrases as the Balance of Power, or the *systeme copartageant*. In the nineteenth, the Principle of Legitimacy covered a multitude of sins, and the Eastern Question a congeries of problems. And the twentieth, for whom a classical orotundity has in any case little charm, satisfies its compulsive urge to save time by the invention of an international vocabulary of acronyms.

It is to this type of locution that is to be referred that deceptively reassuring expression "the Tranquillity of the North," which, in most of the languages of Europe—"Die Ruhe des Nordens," "La Tranquillité du Nord," "Nordens ro"—was an internationally current verbal counter in the chancelleries throughout the period which lies between the Peace of Utrecht and the first partition of Poland.

The phrase expressed not so much a state of affairs as an aspiration, an objective: the desire, shared at one time or another by all the major European powers, to prevent the outbreak of war in the Baltic region, and in particular between the Scandinavian states. In the seventeenth century this had been a part of the world where the peace had been notoriously fragile, and where, thanks to the eruptive force of Swedish military might, disturbances had too often entailed wider involvements on the Continent, besides producing recurrent disruptions of the trade between Eastland and the West. After 1713, and especially after 1721, there was a strong feeling that it would be better for all parties if it could be arranged that the North be somehow politically frozen in its native ice; and it seems in fact that it was just in this period that the phrase "the Tranquillity of the North" first became current among statesmen. However, this laudable objective proved easier to formulate than to attain. Between 1721 and 1790 the Tranquillity of the North was thrice shattered by war (in 1741, 1757, 1788), and it was in addition seriously threatened in 1726-27, 1743-44, 1749-51, and 1772-73.

For much of the period, the slow-burning fire which defeated efforts to keep the region cool was generated by friction within the Oldenburg dynasty. Indeed, the idea of the Tranquillity of the North arose in the first instance out of the formidable complexities of what a later age would call the Schleswig-Holstein question; and its original purpose was to prevent, if that were possible, the involvement in that question of the non-Scandinavian powers. In course of time this limited objective came to embrace other and larger issues. It was not only to avert trouble about ducal Schleswig that the major powers were anxious to keep the North at peace. Their interpretations of what constituted the Tranquillity of the North differed from time to time and case to case; but when they intervened in the North, as occasionally happened, their interventions arose from much weightier causes and much broader considerations than a concern for the fate of a handful of Danish territories. Moreover, there were limits to the desire of some of them to keep the region in a state of perfect political passivity. When in 1741, in a misguided moment, Sweden launched an unprovoked attack on Russia, that attack was the work of a political party which was heavily dependent on French financial support; when Sweden intervened in the Seven Years War in 1757, she did so in response to French promises and persuasions. And on the other hand it was probably only the marked disapproval of Russia's allies that restrained the Empress Elizabeth from beginning hostilities against Sweden in 1750. French and Russian statesmen might talk of the Tranquillity of the North, but what was really in their minds was how to maintain (or alternatively to produce) a situation in which Scandinavia should be so firmly bound to the interests of one or other of them as to ensure that policies to which they attached much greater importance could be pursued without their attention's being distracted by Baltic complications. In relation to the great issues of the day—the historic duel of Bourbon and Hapsburg, the rise of Prussia, the decay of Poland—the political stances of Sweden and Denmark, though not unimportant, were secondary considerations; and if the major powers meddled in Scandinavia, it was in order to forward their strategies on the Continent, or their objectives beyond the seas. From this wider angle, intervention in the North was seen, in Paris and St. Petersburg, as a measure essentially conservative and defensive; and even actions which might bear a superficially aggressive appearance were felt to be dictated by prudential motives, and by the necessity to deny the command of Scandinavia to a hostile or potentially hostile power.

With one short fortuitous interval, France and Russia were overt or covert adversaries throughout the whole period 1721-72. For most of that period it was a consistent object of French diplomacy to block any Russian intervention in the affairs of Europe: Lionne and Torcy in their day had found the conduct of diplomacy quite sufficiently difficult without the intrusion of a new power from beyond the confines of the Continent. But there were all too many signs that Russia was impinging upon the old world to which French diplomacy had grown accustomed: Russian troops in Mecklenburg in the time of the Regent Orleans; the succession of alliances which, from 1726 onwards, bound Russia to Austria, and which, taken together with the Anglo-Russian alliance of 1742, made Russia virtually a member of that Old System which William III had called into being to redress the balance of Europe; successful Russian intervention (and French diplomatic humiliation) in Poland, in the mid-thirties and mid-sixties; 30,000 Russian troops on the Rhine in 1748; Russian plans to annex East Prussia in 1759, which only French firmness had defeated. It was no wonder if France, in the face of these evidences of Russian activity, developed a deep-seated fear of the Russian Colossus; no wonder either that she strove as best she could to check the growth of Russian influence in the North, and to exclude it from Stockholm and Copenhagen. Despite French attempts from time to time to negotiate a commercial treaty with Russia—attempts which were not successful until as late as 1785—France's trading connections with that country were not sufficiently significant to offset these political considerations. And this in part explains why it was that France, much earlier than England, saw the threat to the old European system posed by the emergence of Russia as a great power. Her traditional interest in Poland—a country to which England, in contrast, was almost indifferent before the late eighties—sharpened her perception in this regard: already in 1772 d'Aiguillon would vainly seek England's aid in forming a bloc to resist the *système copartageant*. Not until the time of the Oczakow crisis would an English statesman be prepared to admit that in this matter Paris had been more prescient than London. And to support a policy of erecting a barrier against the Russian advance France was prepared to pay, and to pay liberally, by subsidies in peacetime to Denmark and Sweden, by bribes to Swedish and Polish politicians, by clandestine military aid to Polish Confederations.

In the face of the growing power of Russia, the instinctive reaction of French statesmen was to try to reanimate their classical Eastern System—that chain of alliances in eastern Europe which had long included Sweden, Poland, and the Turks. But whereas in the seventeenth century this had been a device to tip the balance against the Hapsburgs by threatening them with a stab in the back, in the eighteenth its essential purpose was to interpose an effective barrier between Russia and central Europe. An alternative policy was indeed conceivable: a policy of seeking Russia's friendship and relying upon her to discharge the same sort of function as had been performed by Sweden in the old days of that country's greatness: Choiseul is said to have contemplated adopting it, and Louis XV's secret correspondence with the Empress Elizabeth perhaps pointed in the same direction. But after the Franco-Austrian alliance of 1756 such a policy would have been meaningless, and in any case the blunders of French diplomats at St. Petersburg made it impracticable. But undeniably the old Eastern System was crumbling fast: Poland drifted rapidly out of the French and into the Russian orbit; and though the Turks (despite the shock of Bernis's Austrian alliance) remained staunch to France, and on three occasions achieved an unexpected measure of success in wars against Russia, the barrier was visibly weakening. All the more important, then, to prevent Russian influence establishing itself in Sweden and Denmark.

Yet the course of French policy in Sweden makes it clear that it will not do to see that policy as simply defensive. The French fostered the birth and nourished the growth of a parliamentary party in Sweden—the party of the Hats—which among its original objects undoubtedly included a war of revenge against Russia which should lead to the recovery of some or all of the lands lost at the peace of Nystad in 1721. The war of 1741, launched against Russia in an access of hubris, but with French connivance, proved, indeed, a humiliating fiasco; the Empress Elizabeth in 1743 dictated peace at Åbo on terms which compelled the Swedes to accept Adolf Fredrik of Holstein-Eutin as Fredrik I's successor. But though this particular venture turned out ill, it illustrates the fact that for France Sweden was not merely one element in a defensive cordon, but an available springboard from which to mount an attack.

It is therefore not surprising that the Tranquillity of the North had a very different meaning for Russia from that which it had for France. Russia saw herself, with some justice, as ringed round by French client states waiting their chance to do her a mischief with the aid of French gold. The French incited the Turks and the Swedes to attack her; their agents were forever stirring up trouble in Poland. And once Russia had lost her Austrian ally to France, a strong Poland, if Panin had his way, would have taken Austria's place as the natural coadjutor in resistance to the Turkish danger. But the most imminent peril, it seemed, came from Sweden: neither Russia nor Denmark could easily forget Karl XII. Whereas in the case of Poland Russian domination was seen first as opening the gateway to Europe, and then as ensuring help against the Turks, neither of these considerations played any part in Russia's attitude to Sweden. Here the main purpose was to make sure that Sweden should be too weak to be a serious danger. For on this side Russia was highly vulnerable: even after the peace of Åbo, St. Petersburg was within easy striking-distance from the Finnish frontier. In 1741 and 1788 only military ineptitude and bad organization stood in the way of the Swedish armies' attempting a stroke at Peter's capital; and when Russia was deeply involved in a Turkish war (as from 1768 to 1774) Catherine had good grounds for feeling how exposed that capital was. Russia accordingly sought in various ways to keep Sweden in a state in which she would be incapable of doing much harm. The hope that Adolf Fredrik would be a pliable instrument in her hands proved delusive; but other means were possible. One of them was to create a pro-Russian party in Sweden to balance the pro-French party of the Hats. By 1740 the rule of the Hats had in fact provoked the emergence of an opposition, the party of the

Caps; and though that party preferred to seek a counterpoise to French influence in England rather than in Russia, the bitter parliamentary struggles of the mid-forties drove it unwillingly to accept Russian patronage too. The other way of keeping Sweden weak was to uphold, by every available means, the Swedish constitution of 1720. That constitution, as it evolved during the succeeding half-century, gave a near-sovereign authority to the four Estates of the Diet; it effectively emasculated the executive power; and it opened the way to the corruption of the Diet by foreign bribery. Resolute action and quick decisions in the field of foreign policy, in particular, became increasingly difficult and hazardous to those who took them; attention was increasingly concentrated on struggles for jobs and promotion, parliamentary battles, and domestic affairs generally, while faction and maladministration played havoc with the effectiveness of the country's armed forces. By a clause in the peace of Nystad Russia had promised to respect Sweden's constitutional arrangements, and by a strained interpretation of this clause (which, however, was expressly disavowed at the peace of Åbo) she claimed a right to veto any attempt to amend the constitution in a sense adverse to Russian interests—which meant in fact any attempt to prune it of the ranker abuses which were debilitating Sweden's national efficiency, and above all any attempt to strengthen the powers of the executive. Thus for Russia the maneuvers and intrigues of Swedish party politics, the controversies over the Swedish constitution and its interpretation, became a major factor in a foreign policy which was aimed—despite all appearances to the contrary—at preserving the Tranquillity of the North, as that phrase was understood by Russia's rulers.

The interest of England in the Baltic region was of a very different character from that of France or Russia. George II no doubt shared with Kristian VI of Denmark an anxiety to keep Hanover insulated as far as possible from the shock of the great wars in Germany; but Englishmen were not in general much concerned about the problem of ducal Schleswig, and it may be doubted whether they would have honored the guarantee of 1720, if a situation had arisen in which they were called upon to do so. They viewed Scandinavia neither as a counterscarp which must not be left in enemy hands, nor as a base from which to launch diversionary attacks. They did not think of it either in offensive or defensive terms. They thought of it primarily in terms of the navy, and in terms of trade. Britain's position as a great power was based on her fleet, and the Navy Board depended upon the naval stores which it received from the Baltic region: Swedish iron and pitch, Russian hemp and flax, Riga masts. Britain's commercial supremacy required the maintenance of a great mercantile marine; and for that such commodities were not less essential. If hostile powers were to close the Sound to British shipping, as had happened in 1652, the great East Indiamen might be unable to sail, and the navy be crippled by lack of sailcloth, masts and rigging: the crucial failure to press home the advantage at Ushant in 1778—a failure which was one of the turning points in the American war—depended precisely on shortages of this sort. It was therefore an obvious British interest to prevent naval stores from becoming the monopoly of any one supplier: the attempt of the Swedish Tar Company in the early years of the War of the Spanish Succession to corner the market had been a warning which was not forgotten. In the second decade of the century it had therefore been the object of Secretaries of State to rescue Karl XII from his catastrophic predicament on tolerable terms, in the interests of preserving some sort of Baltic balance. This policy had lain behind the hectic diplomatic activity of Carteret in the months immediately preceding the peace of Nystad. But the success of such a policy depended in the last resort on whether Englishmen would be willing to fight in order to carry it through, and by 1721 it was clear that the British public had no intention of allowing itself to be dragged into a war against Russia for the sake of salving such wreckage of the Swedish empire as might still be recoverable. It was the same situation as Pitt was to confront in regard to Oczakow, seventy years later.

From that moment the policy of a Baltic balance was as good as dead. Russia was undisputed political mistress of the Baltic, and she had a virtual monopoly of most (though not quite of all) of the strategic materials which were vital to Great Britain. It took a whole decade for this unpalatable truth to sink into the minds of English statesmen: the old hankering for a balance remained, and the sign of it was the dispatch of English fleets, in 1726 and 1727, to protect Sweden against the threat of Russian-Holstein aggression. For almost a decade (1719-28) Britain registered her refusal to look the situation in the face by breaking off all diplomatic relations with Russia. All this, however, was in the palmy days of the Anglo-French entente of the 1720s. After 1731 the situation was altered. The entente with France was rapidly dissolving, as Fleury took his revenge for the second treaty of Vienna. And in 1734 Walpole, facing the facts with characteristic common sense, concluded a commercial treaty with Russia which is one of the great landmarks in the history of British foreign policy in this century. For over fifty years Anglo-Russian relations were influenced or determined by it. For that treaty was a recognition of the fact that the trade with Russia was so valuable—to both countries—that its preservation must take precedence over purely political questions. This had become apparent even in the 1720s, when despite the acute tension between the two countries Peter I had declared that commercial relations must not be permitted to be affected; and it received still more striking illustration during the Seven Years War, when Russia and England, though fighting on opposite sides, took care to remain at peace with one another.

Before the thirties came to an end the Family Compact and the Spanish war had made France once again England's archenemy, and the great maritime-colonial struggle which was to fill the middle years of the century had begun. In the face of this development England revived the Old System of King William, but this time she reinforced it by association with the Austro-Russian alliance which had triumphed in the War of the Polish Succession. Eight years after Walpole's commercial treaty came the first Anglo-Russian alliance of 1742.

In these circumstances, what meaning had the Tranquillity of the North for an English statesman? It meant, first, security for the vital trade with Russia, and therefore the careful cultivation of Russian goodwill. It meant that neither England nor Russia could afford to stand tamely by and see both the Scandinavian powers in hostile—that is, in French—hands, able to close the Sound in wartime to the passage of naval stores, or at least to enforce the sending of a British squadron to keep the passage open. In the War of the Austrian Succession the British navy was fully extended, and not until its close could the Admiralty feel able to reckon on an adequate margin of superiority over the combined fleets of Spain and France: the detachment of a Baltic squadron would have been a serious embarrassment. Moreover, the navies of the two Scandinavian powers, small though they might be, might in such a situation of near-equipoise be just sufficient to tip the balance in favor of the Bourbons.

As a consequence of all this, the maintenance of the Tranquillity of the North now imposed the requirement of vigorous British diplomatic action in Stockholm and in Copenhagen. In Copenhagen the requirement was not met. Denmark was a pure absolutism run by a small council of state: she possessed no parliamentary institutions corruptible by English guineas. With the generality of the Danish public England seems to have been popular; and successive kings of Denmark were ready enough to espouse English princesses; but in fact England had no inducement to offer which could tempt Denmark from her alliance with France.

All the more important, therefore, to come to grips with the French system in Sweden. And here, in fact, English diplomacy in the forties was vigorously aggressive. The anti-French party of the Caps needed a patron and a paymaster; and they found them first in England and subsequently in Russia. Colonel Guydickens, the energetic British minister, worked hand in glove with his Russian colleague, Baron Korff, and their collaboration was only terminated when an awkward diplomatic incident in 1747 led to Guydickens's recall, and this in turn to an interruption of Anglo-Swedish diplomatic relations which lasted for no less than sixteen years. However, neither this incident nor the Diplomatic Revolution of the fifties really affected the basic principles of British policy in the North. For England, Sweden's attack on Prussia in 1757 provided one more illustration of the danger of French ascendancy in Stockholm; and the Swedish-Danish Armed Neutrality of 1759 underlined yet again the possible implications of their fleets for the maintenance of British naval superiority over the Bourbon powers.

For if in the first place the Tranquillity of the North meant for England the safeguarding of her trade to Russia, with the appropriate political corollaries, in the second place it was an application (and an increasingly important one) of the general principle that French influence must be fought wherever it prevailed. The task of British diplomacy in Sweden was therefore to provide, by support of the Caps, a workable alternative to the francophil Hats. And by doing this England would at the same time be making a contribution to cementing that friendship with Russia which was the other basic assumption of her statesmanship.

The ending of the Seven Years War was not at once seen in England as marking the close of the period of the grand European conflicts of the midcentury. The new imperial acquisitions no doubt made naval considerations loom even larger than before; but 1763 did not mean that England would turn her back on Europe, still less that she wished to do so. But since the Old System now appeared to be dead, and since relations with Prussia had become envenomed as a result of Bute's peace, ministers found themselves, by a puzzling paradox, in a state of diplomatic isolation which seemed to them extraordinary on the morrow of the most triumphant war their country had ever waged. Some of them still hoped that Austria might be regained; others, that Frederick the Great might somehow be mollified; but all were agreed that the natural solution to their difficulty lay in an alliance with the Russia of Catherine II. And for the next ten years the search for such an alliance became the will o' the wisp of English diplomacy.

After 1763 Russia became increasingly preoccupied in Poland; and just for that reason the preservation of the Tranquillity of the North became more important to her than ever. And hence also to Russia's would-be ally, England. The more the French strove to hold on to their position in Stockholm, the more they bolstered up the sagging energies and damaged reputations of the Hats, the more obvious it seemed to British diplomats that a position to which France apparently attached so much importance, and which Russia was prepared to spend so much money to capture, must inevitably be an objective of British policy. As seen from London, it did not appear that France could reasonably have anything to fear from a Russian-dominated Scandinavia. But French control of Scandinavia, and especially of Sweden, was a different matter. It could scarcely be construed, even by the most credulous and benevolent Bedfordite, as a legitimate defensive measure. It could be rationally motivated only by offensive intentions; and as such both Russia and England had reason to fear it. By the Tranquillity of the North, France could only mean a Scandinavia sufficiently strong to be able both to act as a threat to Russia and to provide France with a small but possibly crucial reinforcement of her shattered navy. For Russia and England, on the other hand, the Tranquillity of the North meant a Denmark in a condition of amiable somnolence; and a Sweden which should have her freedom to act so firmly tied by the complex knots of her constitution, and her impulse to act so safely channeled into party management and the exposure of the accumulated scandals of Hat rule, that she would be incapable of being a danger to anybody, except possibly to herself.

The state of affairs in Sweden, therefore, had become of crucial interest, both to England and to Russia. Upon success or failure there depended a whole series of issues: the consolidation of the Tranquillity of the North, the prospect of forming some sort of countersystem to what Lord Chatham was in the habit of referring to as "the formidable League of the South," and the chance of persuading Catherine to agree to an alliance on terms which Parliament could accept. In all these respects the years from 1764 to 1772 form a kind of watershed in British foreign policy. It is the purpose of this book to try to illuminate the dilemmas which confronted British statesmen, and the doubts and vacillations that beset them; to attempt some explanation of why in the end the search for the Russian alliance lost its impetus, and finally petered out; and to suggest why, after interminable procrastinations, London came to prefer the advantages of an entente with Russia to the disadvantages of an alliance on such terms as Russia was prepared to entertain. As the negotiation dragged on, year after year, it became increasingly clear that whichever option was chosen one possible key to the problem lay in Stockholm. In Denmark Russia had no need of British assistance, and in any case the obliquity of British handling of Danish affairs made it unlikely that she would receive any: it was not in Copenhagen that Anglo-Russian friendship would be cemented. As to Poland, all British ministries quite rightly were clear that they were not prepared, even for the sake of Russian goodwill, to involve themselves in the confused politics of that distressful country. But whether Britain opted for an alliance or settled for an entente Sweden provided the easiest, and perhaps the only, approach to the goal. If the British government really desired the Russian alliance, a preliminary alliance with Sweden might well provide the bridge to it. And if they came to the conclusion that an entente would give them all the security they needed, it was in Stockholm, and in Stockholm only, that constant, day-to-day practical collaboration would furnish the means of laying a basis of confidence and goodwill firm enough to withstand the shock of an international crisis. Sweden thus became, in Russian eyes, something of a touchstone. Against British actions in Stockholm they would appraise the strength of purpose and the sincerity of the professions of successive British administrations. Here deeds spoke louder than words; here a reasonable openhandedness or a Grenvillian parsimony provided an index to the real intentions of the British government. And conversely, as Secretaries of State blew hot or cold about the Russian alliance, as they were fired or repelled by Panin's vision of a comprehensive Northern System, as their alarm at French recovery and French designs waxed or waned, so their participation in Swedish affairs grew heartier or more apathetic.

Thus any judgment of British foreign policy in the postwar decade (and so far no attempt seems to have been made to survey it as a whole) necessarily involves the Swedish dimension. The intense political life of Stockholm, the party struggles of Hats and Caps, with their dramatic reversals of fortune, the parliamentary crises and maneuvers—these things formed the medium in which British policy operated, the material with which it had to work: victory or defeat in a critical division, misjudgment or delay in the distribution of bribes, might have repercussions extending all over Europe, since they might mean the triumph of the Hats and the restoration of French ascendancy. Controversies about the amendment or integrity of the Swedish constitution were directly relevant to the Tranquillity of the North. In short, Swedish domestic affairs, by an odd combination of circumstances, became for the first and only time a constituent element in British foreign policy. Secretaries of State would be continually faced with the question whether an alliance with Russia was worth the cost of a party triumph in Stockholm. And the final demonstration of the impact of Swedish domestic affairs came on 19 August 1772, when by a revolution which was very largely the outcome of internal factors Gustav III at a blow shattered the Anglo-Russian system and transformed the whole position in the North.

In these circumstances, very much depended upon the character and ability of Britain's representative in Stockholm, on his knowledge of Swedish politics, his capacity to handle men, his ability to cooperate with his Russian colleague—and, not least, upon his readiness to risk the censure of his masters in Whitehall by exceeding his instructions, or acting in the absence of instructions, when confronted with a local emergency. Throughout the whole of the period covered by this study the legation in Stockholm was in the hands of Sir John Goodricke. It was his first post on the permanent establishment, and also his last. He was over fifty when he arrived in Sweden, and before his appointment to Stockholm he had no knowledge of Swedish affairs. The generality of English historians know nothing of him (though Swedish historians are better informed), and the importance of his mission has never been appreciated by the historians of British foreign policy. He was in all essential respects ideally qualified for the work he had to do. Few English diplomats can have been more completely master of the politics (and, incidentally, the language) of their place of residence, nor have used that mastery more to the advantage of their country. Thick-skinned, buoyant, shrugging off official disapproval, he flung himself into the task of destroying French influence in Sweden with unmistakable zest and sustained energy. For eight years he worked in the closest harmony with his Russian colleague, Count Osterman. He traversed the murkier byways of Swedish parliamentary politics with easy familiarity and a complete absence of squeamishness, and his influence reached middle-class circles which were beneath the notice of his aristocratic French adversaries. For himself, he had no doubt that the right policy for England was a Russian alliance, and he became convinced that the easy road to that objective lay through Stockholm. His masters in Whitehall, with their endless "ifs" and "buts," their fear of British public opinion, their maddening half-volitions, their untimely preoccupation with Namierite politics to the temporary exclusion of the destinies of Europe, and (above all) their almost total inexperience of the conduct of diplomacy—such masters might have discouraged a less resilient or more sensitive man. Goodricke took with equal sangfroid their vacillations, their silences, and their thunderbolts. When at last British policy more or less resolved itself into a decision for an entente rather than an alliance, he accepted that decision cheerfully; and he made it a reality. The Anglo-Russian entente as it existed around 1770 was the work of Goodricke more than of any one man, for it rested largely on the confidence he inspired in the Russian government on the basis of his exertions in Stockholm.

Thus in his own person Goodricke linked together the central problem of British foreign policy and the dramatic and violent decade of Swedish history which ended abruptly on 19 August 1772. And so this book is necessarily not only a study of the one and the other; it is also a piece of political biography, the history of one man's mission. For, as Northern Secretaries flitted in and out, ignorant when they took office and scarcely wiser when they quitted it, it was the ministers abroad—Macartney, Harris, Sir Joseph Yorke, Goodricke—who gave to British policy such firmness and consistency of purpose as it possessed, or at least labored to present it in such a light to the foreign ministers with whom they had to deal. In this matter the legation in Stockholm was the key post: the only place in Europe where British professions were from time to time transmuted into effective action. And the alchemist who brought off that difficult feat was Sir John Goodricke.

British Diplomacy and Swedish Politics, 1758-1773

CHAPTER I

The Road to Stockholm, 1758–1764

(i)

March 1758. The Seven Years War ablaze in three continents; the outcome everywhere uncertain. No decision upon the high seas: England must wait a year yet for Lagos and Quiberon. No decision in America, where Fort William Henry had lately fallen to the French, and the stolid Abercromby was making heavy weather of the preparations for this summer's campaign. The French flag still flew over Louisburg, and while that bastion remained untaken England could boast no trophy which might serve to buy back Minorca, if it should come to negotiations for a peace: Admiral Boscawen, sailing westward with reinforcements, could not divine that he carried with him, in the person of James Wolfe, the man who would decide the destiny of the New World. In India, despite the miracle of Plassey, the issue dubious still. In Germany, the balance no better than even: the twin victories of Rossbach and Leuthen had effaced the memory of Kolin; the Convention of Klosterzeven had been disavowed as disgracefully as it was made; Ferdinand of Brunswick was thrusting westwards across the rivers, so that Frederick the Great, hardly sensible as yet of the impending shock of Russian manpower, had room to breathe again; but the Anglo-Prussian alliance was creaking under the strain, and that still more fortuitous coalition of Pitt and Newcastle creaked in sympathy.

Against this stormy background of great events and high politics, "that chit Lord Holdernesse" (to borrow the duke of Newcastle's unkind description of the Secretary of State for the Northern Department) on 10 March 1758 put his signature to a letter addressed to Arnold Wynantz, chargé d'affaires at the Swedish legation in London.[1] Its contents intimated, curtly enough, that it was the intention of the British government to proceed at once to the nomination of a minister to the court of Stockholm. No great matter, this, it might be supposed, at a moment when the fate of Europe and America hung in the balance. Yet, little as Lord Holdernesse may have realized it, his signature to that letter was a minor turning point in British foreign policy; and from his action would spring consequences which would outlast for more than a decade those great struggles that for the moment obscured it.

In 1758 England had for ten years been without diplomatic representation in Sweden, and Sweden had been represented in England only by a chargé d'affaires. This unusual state of things had arisen out of a somewhat scandalous intermezzo in the autumn of 1747. It had revolved round the person of one Christopher Springer. Springer was a Stockholm merchant who had made himself obnoxious to the Swedish government as a suspected Russian agent, and also as a vocal champion of the right of constitutents to call members of the Estates to account for their actions.[2] The latter offence was especially heinous in the eyes of a Diet which assumed the powers, if not the name, of a sovereign body; and Springer, after a highly political trial, had been sentenced to imprisonment for life. Contriving before very long to escape from jail, he had taken refuge in the house of the British minister, Colonel Guydickens, whence he hoped to make his way to that of Guydickens's Russian colleague, Baron Korff. Before he was able to do so, his hiding place was betrayed, and Guydickens was constrained under threat of force to surrender him to the authorities. The Swedish government showed no disposition to apologize for this violation of diplomatic immunities; Guydickens, a man of warm and truculent temper, made matters worse by trumpeting his resentments in the public prints of Europe; and in February 1748 Lord Chesterfield forestalled a Swedish request for his recall by ordering him to quit Stockholm at once without taking leave.[3] His departure was followed by the transfer of the Swedish minister in London to another post; and though the Swedish government twice proposed replacements, the names they put forward were those of persons so notoriously hostile to the Hanoverian dynasty that there could be no question of receiving them.[4]

Affairs thus reached a deadlock; and for years no British government showed any great anxiety to break it. For some years after 1748 there seemed indeed no particular reason why formal relations should be restored to the old footing. A. J. von Höpken, who as chancery-president had charge of Sweden's foreign affairs, expected the situation to last for George II's lifetime, and did not seem unduly concerned at the prospect.[5] In England, the closing of the Stockholm legation did not appear to make much difference: British commercial interests could apparently get along in Sweden well enough without diplomatic assistance.[6] In the early fifties ministers had at best but a tepid interest in Sweden and Swedish politics; and that interest was more than adequately satisfied by the considerable volume of information which reached them through unofficial or semiofficial channels.

One such channel was provided by Christopher Springer himself, who had escaped from prison at the second attempt and eventually made his way to London, where he became a trusted and popular member of the Swedish colony there, much to the chagrin of Wynantz and his government.[7] From London Springer kept up an extensive correspondence with members of the opposition in his native country;[8] and in return for a modest pension of £100 a year[9] passed on a good deal of information to the British government. Another regular source of information was Baron Karl Gedda. Gedda was the young son of a former Swedish diplomat (himself a pensioner of England);[10] he moved in the best Stockholm society; he was chronically impecunious; and he aspired eventually to some regular diplomatic employment, whether in the service of his own country or another was a matter of relative indifference.[11] Experience was to prove him to be a zealous, intelligent, and tolerably discreet pensioner. He possessed, in short, a liberal selection of the qualities which might be considered desirable in a British secret agent. Guydickens had recruited him already in 1746,[12] and when he left Sweden two years later recommended that he be continued in the service upon a permanent basis.[13] The recommendation was accepted: Gedda was furnished with a cipher, was provided with the reassuringly English alias of "Wilkinson," and was promised an annual salary of £200,[14] paid through the canal of successive Dutch ministers to Sweden, who also obligingly undertook the care of Gedda's correspondence. Of these Dutch ministers one, van Marteville, was a good deal more than a mere paymaster and postmaster. For van Marteville dabbled in Swedish politics; he was himself a paid agent of the British government;[15] and in return for his pension he sent reports to London on his own account.

There was thus plenty of intelligence coming in to London about the state of Swedish politics—more, perhaps, than British ministers had leisure or inclination to digest—though not all of it was equally trustworthy. Gedda, undoubtedly, was the best of the three. He sent over great masses of material, much of which had at least the merit of being accurately reported. In order to obtain it he posed as a zealous supporter of the French system of foreign policy; and he must have played his part with considerable skill, for he secured easy access to ministers and diplomats, and they seem to have talked freely to him. Every time the Diet met, moreover, he compiled, and transmitted to London, a massive "Journal of the Diet," which provides a day-by-day account of parliamentary proceedings and a summary of debates. It may be doubted whether anybody in the Secretary's office took the trouble to wade through these formidable dossiers; but for historians they provide useful information of a kind which is not always to be found in any other source.[16]

Gedda was always nervous of discovery (as well he might be, with the fate of Springer in mind); and at intervals besieged the British government with appeals to be allowed to retire to England so that he might be out of the way when the Diet met. In the long run, indeed, it proved impossible for the secret of his activities to be preserved. By the end of the fifties it was pretty well known in Stockholm that he was a British agent; and the method by which he transmitted his reports was correctly surmised.[17] Gedda himself seems not to have been aware that he was discovered, but the British government realized it very well. This did not mean, however, that he had ceased to be useful: indeed, he began to be useful in a new way; for Swedish politicians now used him as a convenient means of letting London know what they wished London to hear, and what they told him was by no means always designed to mislead.

Since the disintegration of the Anglo-French entente in the years after 1731, England's essential interest in Sweden had been to prevent that country's becoming a satellite of France; and in the late 1730s and early 1740s Stockholm had been one of the minor diplomatic battlefields in the perennial struggle between the two countries. The enemies of Arvid Horn, the rising young politicians who were to found the Hat party upon the ruins of Horn's system, had turned to France for aid, and had won their victory with the assistance of French money. It was natural enough, therefore, that their adversaries, the vanquished of 1739, who in time would also be driven to constitute themselves as a party—the party of the Caps—should seek the assistance of France's enemy, England: an orientation which was the less difficult for them since friendship with England had been an important element in Horn's statesmanship.[18] But direct English involvement in Swedish domestic politics had not been very important before the mid-1740s. However, with the conclusion in 1747 of alliances between Sweden, France, and Prussia, England was drawn more deeply than before into Swedish politics, as the coadjutor of her ally the Empress Elizabeth. Whereas in the preceding years both Hats and Caps had looked to England as offering a possible escape from dependence upon Russia, that way was now barred to them. The Hats, recovering their moral authority as the champions of Sweden's independence against Russian blackmail, were now once more committed to France; the Caps, threatened with party persecutions and political justice, were driven ruefully for self-protection into the arms of Russia. It was not what they would have preferred. A Russian party in Sweden was always felt to be unnatural, even by those who had sufficient political realism to acknowledge to themselves that the hope of reversing the verdict of Nystad was a dangerous illusion. What they would have liked was the support of England: an English party was really what the Caps felt themselves to be—not merely because English backing and English gold would give them resources to fight their domestic battles against the Hats, without involving them in a dependence on Russia which to most Swedes had about it an unpleasant whiff of treason, but also because the Caps by temperament felt an affinity to England. They tended to be sympathetic to English ways of thought, English political systems, English preoccupation with peace and prosperity, and were not much moved by quixotic and chevaleresque notions of national honor or prestige.[19] Their practical, materialist outlook on politics had much in common with Sir Robert Walpole's, and not a little with that of the Tory country gentlemen. And this was odd, since those elements in Swedish society which were most closely connected with England—the ironmasters, the exporters, the East India merchants—were mostly Hats. But, odd or not, the fact was so; and for the Caps it was a real misfortune that England in the late forties should have been content to be no more than Russia's auxiliary. During the Diet of 1746-47 the English and Russian ministers pooled their resources and established a common purse for the purpose of bribing Swedish politicians;[20] but if at that Diet their efforts had been successful, if the Caps had got the better of their adversaries, the victory would have led to a Russian, far more than to an English, ascendancy.

There were, however, limits to this collaboration. When, after Guydickens's recall, Russian attempts to bully Sweden reached such a pitch that it seemed that they might issue in a Russian onslaught on

Finland, British ministers did what they could to restrain their ally. The sequel showed that the Russians had overplayed their hand. In 1749 and 1750 French diplomacy secured the alliance of Sweden with Denmark, sealed by the Swedish crown prince's renunciation of the succession to Holstein and the engagement of his son to a Danish princess: the Franco-Prussian system had acquired a solid Baltic buttress. In 1750 the Swedes called Russia's bluff, defied the last of a series of ultimata, and got away with it. Russia's Swedish policy collapsed in the face of general international disapproval. And in that collapse the Caps, whose commitment to Russia had taken them to the brink of treason, if not beyond it, were necessarily involved.

The removal of the threat from Russia, and the unchallengeable domination which the Hats now seemed to have secured as the party of patriotism and national independence, so far from inaugurating a period of domestic calm in fact prepared the way for an internal crisis which appeared to threaten civil war. The constitution of 1720 had in the succeeding thirty years evolved in such a way that the prerogatives of the crown had been eroded to the point of extinction. Power now lay in the hands of the sovereign Estates; the Senate, of sixteen members, was (together with the king, who sat on it, and had two votes) nominally the executive power, although only the chancery-president was a true minister holding a specific portfolio; but it was, in effect, the obedient servant of the Diet, when it was sitting, and its fiduciary agent, when it was not. King Adolf Fredrik, who succeeded to the throne in 1751, was not the man to translate his resentment of this situation into effective action;[21] but his queen, Lovisa Ulrika, had spirit and energy for two.[22] She was the sister of Frederick the Great, brought up in a country which put no shackles on the sovereign; she was restless and ambitious, and to her enemies seemed faithless, hypocritical, and an inveterate intriguer. She had undoubtedly legitimate grievances; and she had plenty of rancor to keep them warm. She had also a clear sense of what she wanted: a revision of the constitution which would give the king an effective share in appointments and in the shaping of policy; in a longer perspective, perhaps, the establishment of a benevolent despotism on the Prussian model.[23] At her first coming to Sweden she had allied herself with the Hats, and from them had certainly received assurances that they would in due time introduce a reform of the constitution which should correct its imbalance and give more power to the crown. As long as the threat from Russia remained, the alliance between them held firm; for Russia menaced not only Sweden's independence but Adolf Fredrik's succession. But when that threat was dissipated, and when Adolf Fredrik was safely crowned, the ties between the queen and the Hats rapidly loosened. The Hats, comfortably enjoying their ascendancy, conveniently forgot their promises of reform; and Lovisa Ulrika, at first impatient, then embittered, incensed them by prodding her husband into provocations which were sometimes of dubious legality, and not seldom decidedly petty. Within a year or two of Adolf Fredrik's accession relations between king and ministers had become intolerably strained. In 1756 came a violent crisis: the monarchy was accused of plotting a coup d'état; eight of its supporters were sent to the scaffold, including the premier nobleman in Sweden; the king and queen were personally humiliated, and might consider themselves lucky to escape deposition; the power of the crown was still further reduced. The Hats could now pose as the saviors of the nation's liberties; the remnants of the old Caps, whose reputations had barely recovered from their compromising connection with Russia, found themselves stigmatized anew as the allies of those who sought to subvert the constitution—a charge with much less substance than the other. They were now a disorganized remnant, harried by delations and proscriptions, and certainly incapable of giving England a secure foothold in Sweden, even if such a foothold had been desired. Ministers in London could congratulate themselves that they had politely rejected an urgent appeal for financial aid which Lovisa Ulrika had sent to them, through van Marteville, on the eve of the attempted coup d'état.[24]

What concern, then, had England with Sweden on the morrow of the crisis of 1756? The Diplomatic Revolution, and the coming of war in Europe, certainly altered the situation. England had no longer any need to be anxious about the possibility of a Swedish attack on Russia, as in 1741, for Sweden and Russia were now both in league with France: one of the reasons for British intervention in Stockholm thus fell away. But considerations of a similar kind now applied to England's new ally, Prussia. It was certainly a British interest to protect Frederick from a stab in the back from Swedish Pomerania, and by the beginning of August 1757 the British government had certain information that a Swedish attack on Prussia was impending.[25] It occurred to Lord Holdernesse that it might still be possible to avert it, if a minister were sent promptly to Stockholm. He was determined, however, not to expose himself to a diplomatic snub: his envoy should go as a private individual, with instructions to reveal that he was accredited only if it appeared that the Swedes would be prepared to receive him. For this delicate mission Holdernesse selected a certain Lieutenant-Colonel Robert Campbell. Campbell had no diplomatic experience; but he had a father who lived in Sweden, and who might be made an excuse for a visit; he had himself been born in that country, and had spent some of his youth there;[26] his sister was a favorite of Lovisa Ulrika;[27] and Holdernesse seems to have counted on the queen's influence to secure Campbell's reception.

On 16 August 1757 Campbell received his instructions;[28] on 8 September he arrived in Stockholm; shortly before Christmas he took his departure, never having ventured to produce his credentials; on 27 February he was back in London. His mission had been a fiasco notable even in the annals of British diplomacy. In spite of the instruction to use all possible discretion the secret of his journey reached Stockholm almost as soon as Campbell himself; which was the less surprising, since not only had Campbell talked freely about it in London, but Holdernesse himself had revealed it to Wynantz.[29] Campbell's denials that he came in any official capacity thus served only to discredit him with the Swedish ministers, who knew better. His personal connections in Sweden discommended him to Gedda on the one hand and to the Swedish ministry on the other; in particular his sister's favor at court was enough to wreck the enterprise from the beginning. To crown all, he left his cipher behind, and had great difficulty in communicating with his government at all.[30] The Swedish Senate, through Wynantz, let Holdernesse know that if Campbell produced his credentials he would not be received, on the ground that both he and his father were Swedish subjects. The truth of this allegation was at least doubtful, and it was certainly no more than a pretext. The real reasons were given by Höpken, the chancery-president. Already in April Höpken had shown that he wished to avoid anything which could lead to a resumption of diplomatic relations: an English minister, he wrote, "multiplieroit infiniment les soubçons, les intrigues et les embarras."[31] He now told Gedda that he considered the whole enterprise to be an intrigue of the queen, who wanted an English minister in Stockholm for her own nefarious purposes.[32] Holdernesse had thus contrived to give precisely the sort of impression which he should have taken every care to avoid. He had compromised his objectives by connecting them with the one person in Sweden whose goodwill was damning in the eyes of the Swedish ministry; he had put his country in the position of taking sides in a domestic quarrel which was none of its business; and he had treated his Swedish agents with a nonchalance which was hardly calculated to stimulate them to zeal in the service. As to stopping the war, Campbell had not been in Sweden a fortnight before hostilities broke out in Pomerania.

Nevertheless, it might still be possible for Britain to do good offices for Frederick in Stockholm. An English minister might persuade the Swedes to think better of it and call off the campaign. He might provide them with a convenient channel for putting out feelers for peace, if the war should go badly for them. Frederick would certainly find it useful to have a reliable observer in Stockholm who could report on Swedish troop movements, give information on the state of the Swedish finances, record any possible change for the better in the political climate, and provide an additional link between Lovisa Ulrika and himself. In the existing state of the Anglo-Prussian alliance anything which might act as an emollient was worth trying, for relations between the two countries had become uncomfortably strained. Frederick demanded English reinforcements in Germany, and a naval squadron in the Baltic; Pitt declined to provide either. Frederick refused to sign a convention pledging himself not to make a separate peace; Pitt insisted that it should be a quid pro quo for British subsidies, and suspected (quite wrongly) that Sir Andrew Mitchell, his minister in Berlin, was encouraging Frederick's intransigence. He decided, therefore, to send a special envoy to Berlin, in the hope of bringing Frederick to a better mind.[33]

The envoy he selected was Sir Joseph Yorke, his minister at the Hague. Yorke was summoned home to receive his instructions, and arrived in London on 28 February,[34] just one day after Colonel Campbell reported the failure of his mission to Lord Holdernesse; and perhaps it was this coincidence which led to the determination to make another attempt in Stockholm, and to the instruction to Yorke to inform Frederick of that decision. And so it happened that within a fortnight of Campbell's presenting himself in the Secretary's office, Holdernesse had taken steps to replace him. This time there was to be no affectation of secrecy. The insult of 1747 was to be overlooked, a duly accredited minister appointed. Despite the failure with Campbell, Holdernesse does not seem to have doubted that this more straightforward approach would be successful, and that his envoy would be received. When the Swedish troops had first invaded Prussia, the Swedish government had issued a declaration promising that they would not violate Hanoverian territory; and this Holdernesse chose to regard as "une ouverture amicale."[35] No doubt he was well aware that it was no such thing; but it might serve to save England's face. But perhaps it was because there was the possibility of yet another rebuff that he chose as Campbell's successor an obscure member of the diplomatic service who had never hitherto filled any established post. If the Swedes should once again prove uncivil, their incivility would not blight the career of anyone that mattered.

The expendable pawn thus boldly pushed forward was Sir John Goodricke.

(ii)

Sir John Goodricke, fifth baronet, of Ribston in Yorkshire, was born on 20 May 1708, and succeeded to the baronetcy at the age of thirty.[36] Of his early life we know almost nothing; but we do know that in September 1731 he married Mary Johnson, the illegitimate daughter of a Yorkshire peer, Lord Bingley. The marriage was nicely timed; for Lord Bingley died in the same year, leaving "large sums" to his bastard.[37] But however large her fortune, it proved insufficient to keep Goodricke afloat. It may be that he succeeded to a heavily encumbered estate; for what we know of his later career does not suggest a reckless or spendthrift character, rather the contrary. At all events, by the late 1740s his affairs had become so embarrassed that he was compelled to put the Channel between himself and his creditors.[38] In the autumn of 1747 we find him in the Netherlands, or at Liège, acting as a spy for the British government, and reporting to Colonel John Selwyn.[39] He had at this stage no public character, and it is not even certain that he had regular emolument. His wife he was forced to leave behind in England: one gets the impression that she may not have been very presentable; at all events she spent only a few months with him during his mission to Stockholm. At the end of the 1740s she was living with her half-sister and brother-in-law at Bingley House in Cavendish Square.[40] It happened that Lord Bingley's only son had died before his father; and the greater part of the family fortune, with all the estates including his Yorkshire seat of Bramham Park, passed upon his death to this daughter, as his only surviving legitimate child. She was thus a great matrimonial catch, with £100,000 in cash and £7,000 a year from land; and just two months before her half-sister married Goodricke she was quickly snapped up by George Fox, afterwards known as George Fox Lane.[41] Thus was established a connection which was twice to have a decisive influence on Goodricke's fortunes.

Meanwhile he was trying to make interest, through his Yorkshire friends and neighbors, to obtain a position as secretary of legation—at the Hague, perhaps, or at Aix; and he also had his eye on the post of resident at Liège. An approach seems to have been made to Sandwich; and Henry Pelham is said to have promised to recommend him. June 1748 found him in Amsterdam, whence on the news of the suspension of arms he wrote to the government inquiring what he was to do next. At Selwyn's suggestion he came home, and by September was back at Ribston. We do not know how long he stayed there; but we do know that a Yorkshire friend lent him money (presumably to stave off his creditors), and it seems likely that he and his friends used the opportunity to press his claims to employment. At all events, in August 1750 he could write from the Hague announcing that Pelham had approved his appointment to the post of resident at Brussels.

It might now seem that he was at last fairly launched. He had gone to the Hague, as he was later to inform Fox Lane, "to instruct myself in the affairs of the Barrier and of the trade of the Austrian Netherlands": very necessary information, no doubt, for a resident at Brussels. But before he had a chance to apply it he found his career abruptly cut short. As the result of "a dark intrigue" his appointment as resident was revoked before he had even arrived at his place of residence; and it was not much consolation that "the strongest promises were made me of being otherwise provided for."[42] So the prospect of going to Brussels vanished for ever, and all that remained was some arrears of salary and appointments due to him; and even these were not paid until four years later.[43]

The scanty details of this disheartening experience are to be found in a letter from Goodricke to Fox Lane, written in January 1757, and now preserved among the Chatham Papers in the Public Record Office,[44] in which Fox Lane was asked to do what he could to recommend Goodricke to Pitt. From this letter we learn that in 1752 Newcastle had given him orders to remain at the Hague, and to confer with the Dutch "upon the affairs of the Barrier etc."—with which inspiriting topic we can hardly suppose he succeeded in filling his time for the next six years. However, he made use of his enforced leisure to establish his footing in Dutch society.[45] Of the contacts he made there, much the most important for his future career was Sir Joseph Yorke, minister (afterwards ambassador) to the Dutch Republic; and it may have been through Yorke that he was brought into touch with Lord Royston, the heir of Lord Chancellor Hardwicke. Both of these became lifelong friends; and with both he maintained a copious, familiar, and informative correspondence.

Sir Joseph Yorke's attempt to get Goodricke appointed secretary of legation at the Hague came to nothing; but it was probably to the influence of the Yorkes, reinforcing Fox Lane's application to Pitt, that Goodricke owed his selection by Holdernesse for the post at

Stockholm in 1758. He was certainly not chosen on account of his familiarity with Swedish affairs, for of these he seems to have had no previous knowledge. His qualifications were of a different kind; and they did not appear particularly relevant to the immediate object of his mission. From an early stage in his attempt to carve out a niche for himself in the diplomatic service Goodricke seems to have decided to specialize on commerce, finance, and economic affairs generally. In the summer of 1747 he sent Henry Pelham a calculation of the public debt of France.[46] After the peace of Aix-la-Chapelle he seems to have had a discussion with him in which he tried to convince him of the expediency and practicability of reducing the national debt:[47] it argues some self-assurance in a private individual thus to attempt to teach the first lord of the treasury his business. About the same time he drew up a memorandum entitled "Considerations on the Linen Duties in England," which urged the raising of duties on imported linen in order to protect the native industry against Silesian competition.[48] He seems to have left in Lord Royston's hands an unfinished account of the Dutch fiscal system; and we know that he later contemplated preparing a similar survey for Denmark. He was also the author of a general treatise on the principles of taxation,[49] which he presented to Sir Joseph Yorke. As might have been expected, Goodricke's views on this subject were very much those of the typical country gentleman: he was opposed to the Malt Tax, and thought that the imposition of an excise on tobacco would be "an odious shame"—though he had foresight enough to remark that it was not improbable that both wine and tobacco might be excised within the next twenty years. He lived long enough to see his prediction fulfilled.

Such was the man whom Holdernesse now decided to send to Sweden. Before 1758 the fragmentary nature of our knowledge leaves him a somewhat shadowy figure; but it is perhaps already possible to infer those qualities of enterprise, self-confidence, and determination to succeed which were to stand him in good stead when dealing with rapacious Swedish politicans and costive or vacillating Secretaries of State. He had had to fight hard for his foothold, and the experience had given him toughness and resilience. He had already learned that he could expect little unless he worked for it, and that his fortune was not likely to be made by sitting still. Perhaps in the toughening process he had shed some scruples too: Lord Rochford was later reported to have said that he was not to be trusted in money matters.[50] One has the impression that he was by nature a little coarse in the grain; but he was a good-humored fellow on the whole. He had a stock of philosophy sufficient to carry him through the chagrins and disappointments which lay in wait for all British diplomats in this period; and he had the additional asset of an uncommonly thick skin. Yet he was very far from being the typical provincial squire; for though his manners may have lacked French polish, his mind was alert and keen, and he was by no means without cultural interests: in his letters to Royston he reveals himself as an informed bibliophile; he was acquainted with Greek; and his judgments on Hume and Voltaire as historians are satisfactorily astringent.[51] The French party in Sweden, when there was still a danger that he might be received, depicted him as an impoverished fortune-hunter, encumbered with a wife and a large family, who had hitherto been employed only in petty intrigues. There was a modicum of truth in this; but when they added that he was "sec et pedant" they were drawing too freely upon their imaginations.[52] On the contrary, he seems to have been a convivial companion: Macartney found him so, when he visited Sweden; and he had the gift of forming strong and lasting friendships. His dispatches show him to have been eminently sensible and clearheaded; with none of Macartney's literary ebullience, or the interminable verbiage of Lord Cathcart, they are vigorous, pithy, and unadorned.

So, somehow or other, by natural quality or intelligent application to the business of self-improvement, he emerged from the *coulisses* of diplomacy to take a conspicuous part in the center of the stage.

(iii)

On Goodricke's appointment to Stockholm he was furnished with two sets of instructions. One was purely formal, except that it enjoined him to seek audience with the queen, and to give her an assurance of "the particular Regard we have for her"; and further directed him to hold a good correspondence with the Dutch minister.[53] The "Additional and Private Instructions" of the same date were more explicit. He was to apply upon arrival to van Marteville for any lights upon Swedish politics. If "Wilkinson" should present himself, he was to give him his confidence; but to make no inquiries about him if he did not. He was to report on Sweden's military and financial position; and if he found any chance of inclining the Swedes to seek peace with Prussia was to assure them of British readiness to help them. The main object of his mission was firmly defined as being to give assistance to Frederick; and hence he was directed to keep in close touch with such persons as might seem to be trusted by Lovisa Ulrika, who was clearly considered to be the most hopeful nucleus of a peace party. But it was realized that the objects of the mission were not likely to be advanced if it were compromised from the start (as had been the case with Campbell) by being identified in the minds of the Swedish ministers with a faction in Sweden which was committed to the alteration of the constitution. Goodricke was accordingly instructed to take the utmost care to avoid offending the Hat Senate.[54] Something, at least, had been learned from the fate of Campbell's mission.

Goodricke was appointed minister to Sweden on 10 March 1758. Seven days later, Sir Joseph Yorke left London on his mission to Frederick: he reached Frederick's headquarters at Griessau in Silesia on 10 April.[55] He did not arrive alone; for somewhere on the road, in circumstances which are not wholly clear, he picked up his friend Goodricke. Six years later Yorke reproached himself with having "obliged Goodricke, for the sake of his company," to go with him.[56] Certainly no instruction to Goodricke to take Silesia on his way seems to have survived; but the fact that he reported on his visit to Holdernesse without explanation or apology suggests that Yorke must have obtained Holdernesse's verbal approval for the excursion. And indeed, if there were to be any chance of bringing Sweden to consider a peace with Prussia, it would be well that Goodricke should know in advance what kind of terms Frederick would be prepared to accept; and the most expeditious and surest method of finding out was probably to get that information from his own lips. Goodricke was accordingly presented to the great man by Sir Andrew Mitchell (who plainly regarded him as Sir Joseph's toady);[57] and endured a dinner at the royal table which lasted four hours, during which time Frederick did most of the talking.[58] We do not know what impression Frederick made upon Goodricke; but six years later Frederick summed up the impression Goodricke made upon him in the words, "C'est un homme sans monde"[59] —a verdict which at that stage of Goodricke's career may have been better based and less malicious than many of Frederick's judgments. However, in the intervals of royal table-talk Goodricke did elicit the terms upon which Frederick was willing to make peace; and with these in his mind, and a letter to Lovisa Ulrika in his pocket, he made his way to Copenhagen.[60]

He had hardly arrived there before he was met by the most mortifying intelligence. The Swedish government, he was informed, would not receive him. And when, in obedience to his instructions, he continued his preparations for departure, he was told that orders had been given to stop any vessel he might embark in, and see that it did not approach within a hundred miles of Stockholm. Even Goodricke was halted by this; and after consultation with other members of the diplomatic corps he resigned himself to remaining for the moment in Copenhagen, pending further orders from home. They were not long in coming. Holdernesse's reaction to this renewed insult was immediate: Wynantz was ordered to leave London forthwith; Goodricke was bidden to stay in Copenhagen until further orders. And in Copenhagen he was destined to remain, kicking his heels on Sweden's doorstep, for almost six years.[61] Having at last got his foot on the diplomatic ladder, he was now prevented from climbing it.

The reason offered by the Swedish government for what Holdernesse termed "un procédé violent et insensé" was that Goodricke, by visiting the camp of a monarch with whom they were at war, and conferring with him, had become to all intents and purposes an enemy agent—a reason which to Holdernesse seemed "as extraordinary and offensive, as the Thing itself."[62] Perhaps it was; but it was certainly not the true reason, as Holdernesse himself perceived. The real reason was almost certainly given by Höpken, who justified the refusal on the ground that at the time of the alleged royalist plot of 1756 the Court had hoped to overthrow the constitution with aid from England and Russia, to which the reception of an English minister would have been the first step.[63] The Hat Senate, in short, saw Goodricke as they had seen Campbell—as the ally or agent of the queen; and they declined to receive him, not on any grounds of foreign policy, still less on a point of ceremony, but because they feared English meddling in matters which were of purely domestic concern. There is nothing to suggest that their fears were justified; but in 1758 it was still too early for any Swedish minister to forget the crisis of 1756.

(iv)

For Goodricke, thus arrested within sight of his objective, the prospects must have appeared discouraging. All the signs seemed to show that he could look forward to a prolonged period of idleness in Copenhagen, with no defined character at the court, no obvious duties, and no great expectation of much in the way of instructions from home. And Copenhagen was not, perhaps, the most enlivening of European capitals: when Ralph Woodford went there as minister in 1772, he found the social perspectives profoundly depressing.[64] Goodricke, however, could not afford this blasé attitude. He took good care to turn his sojourn to profitable use. He came to Copenhagen as a person almost unknown, except perhaps at the Hague; by the time he left for Sweden he had begun to count for something in the world of diplomacy. For after all there were things to be done in Copenhagen; and he made it his business to do them.

He could, in the first place, assist the English minister on the spot, Walter Titley; or at least could supplement him. Titley, who had been stationed in Copenhagen for almost thirty years, was a genial humanist, a scholar, a man who loved his ease. He was also a martyr to gout, and lived much of the year at his country house forty miles from the capital, where he received visitors only by appointment.[65] He had long since resigned himself to Denmark's being politically a French satellite: there was at least a soothing stability about the situation. An able minister he may once have been; an active minister he was no longer. It happened therefore that when Titley was laid up with gout the Danish ministers found it convenient to talk to the more accessible (and livelier) Goodricke; and increasingly they continued to talk to him after Titley was on his legs again.[66] Moltke and Bernstorff had much to say to him on such things as the Armed Neutrality, or the grievances arising from the action of British privateers. On these matters Goodricke soon became well-informed; and he was able to ram home to Holdernesse the not unimportant point that it was not so much privateering, as the intolerable delays of the admiralty courts, that were putting a strain on Anglo-Danish relations.[67] He also transmitted a good deal of naval intelligence; he collected information about the state of English trade with the Scandinavian countries; he furnished Lord Holdernesse with useful facts about the important Danish trade in smuggled tea.[68] And he undoubtedly managed to win the trust of the Danish ministers, and the esteem of the Danish court. He was on good terms, for instance, with St. Germain, and also with Reventlow, who had a high opinion of him.[69] He won the respect of Bernstorff; who later recommended him to a Danish minister as "homme judicieux, rempli de connoissances et rompu dans les affaires."[70] When at last he was on the point of leaving for Sweden, "some leading persons" let it be known that they regretted that he was not to be Titley's successor.[71] Certainly before his departure he had become very much at home in Danish society and knowledgeable about a wide range of Danish affairs, from the history of the Thott family in the fifteenth century to the intricacies of the Schleswig-Holstein question, of which he sent a lucid digest to Lord Royston.

Goodricke's interests in Denmark were not all political or commercial. In the absence of Lady Goodricke (still, one must presume, either at Ribston or at Bingley House), he took to himself a mistress. The lady was of some celebrity, and was familiarly known in Copenhagen by the name of "Jackboot Kate" (Stövlet Katrine). She is said to have been the illegitimate daughter of Prince George of Brunswick-Bevern; but her mother was married off to a maker of jackboots, and after Prince George's death she was in the habit of delivering orders to her father's customers. From this useful occupation she passed to the corps de ballet, and it was from this point of vantage that she captivated Goodricke. Her association with him was sufficiently notorious to bring her a change of sobriquet: henceforward she would be known as "Mylady"; and as Mylady she became, after Goodricke's departure, successively the mistress of the Austrian ambassador, and then of Kristian VII.[72]

It was not only with Danish affairs that Goodricke busied himself during his enforced residence in Copenhagen. Quite soon after his arrival he hired a master to teach him Swedish.[73] By the end of 1760 he was able to read a Swedish book; a year later we find him engaged upon a Swedish pamphlet on the rates of exchange.[74] Now this was certainly very unusual in a century when social intercourse, as well as diplomacy, was mainly in French; and one may well wonder whether there was any other foreign diplomat, apart from the Danish ministers, who was similarly equipped at his first going to Stockholm. Goodricke's command of Swedish must have given him important advantages, not least in dealing with members of the three lower Estates in the Diet, whose French would be something less than fluent; and it may account for the contemptuous references by Breteuil to the low sort of people with whom Goodricke consorted in Stockholm.[75] Apart from his study of the language, he also immersed himself in the recent history of Anglo-Swedish relations.[76] But the key to success in Sweden lay not so much in a knowledge of past diplomacy as in the mastery of the intricacies of the Swedish constitution, and a grasp of how those intricacies could be manipulated to secure political advantages. There is no doubt that before ever Goodricke left Denmark he had acquired a thorough understanding of these matters; and when at last he arrived in Stockholm he was able to plunge into the battle, at a moment when parties were in an unusually labile state, with an assurance which is at first sight surprising. Few foreigners can have come to Sweden for the first time with such a command of Swedish politics, or such insight into Swedish affairs.[77]

Much of his information, of course, came through those canals which the British government had been keeping open since 1748. But he was able to supplement these sources of information. He very early recruited agents of his own—typically enough, among the commercial community.[78] His good standing with the Danish ministers gave him access to Danish sources: on more than one occasion he was allowed to read the dispatches of the Danish minister in Stockholm.[79] He developed a confidential intercourse with the Swedish minister to Denmark, Ungern-Sternberg, who was no friend to the ruling Hat Senate, and benevolently disposed towards England. And by choice, no less than as a matter of duty, he was on intimate terms with Baron Borcke, from 1761 the Prussian minister to the court of Denmark. This was a very special contact, closely connected with the object of his mission, for it put him in touch with the channel of communication which led from Lovisa Ulrika, through her secretary Count C. W. von Düben, or through van Marteville, to Frederick the Great. Goodricke was here able to render useful services; for the channels through which he received secret information from Sweden were so much safer than those available to the Prussians that they were on more than one occasion forced to turn to him to arrange for the transmission of messages or money to the queen.[80]

(v)

Thus armed with information about Swedish conditions; well dug in at Copenhagen, and having the confidence of the Danish ministers; strategically situated at a vital point on the line of communications between Lovisa Ulrika and her brother, Goodricke was in a better position than might have been expected to try to help Frederick by encouraging those elements in Sweden that were working for peace. The problem was how to do this without getting himself, and still worse his government, involved in the purely domestic controversies of that country. This was particularly difficult to avoid in dealings with Lovisa Ulrika. It was not to be wondered at that she saw the situation primarily in terms of the opportunities it might offer to the crown to strengthen its prestige and confound its enemies, to wipe out the humiliations she had suffered, and to recover the prerogatives that had been lost: insulted, lectured, menaced in 1756, she saw herself with royal magnanimity giving peace to the country which had ill-treated her, and collecting a substantial dividend of loyalty and gratitude as her reward. The party of the Court would become a popular party, a national party, as men turned in disillusionment from the politically bankrupt Hats; and with its aid she would reform (her enemies would have said, overturn) the constitution.

This was a program which had no interest for an English statesman. If England should help to overthrow the enemies of the crown, it would not be from any hostility to constitutional principles; it would be because the Hats, who were for the moment the constitution's defenders, were the pensioners and allies of France. The establishment of an absolutism, or even the strengthening of the prerogative, was for ministers a matter of indifference, at best, and certainly held no attraction for them. On the contrary, if England were to lend aid to any such enterprise, one consequence would be the alienation of the remnants of that old Cap party which had always considered itself "English"; for at bottom, as experience was to show, the Caps were at least as committed to the defense of the constitution as were their rivals.

Goodricke very soon ran up against this complication. In November 1758 he was approached by a Court supporter who had fled from Sweden, and who suggested that England put up £2,000 to finance a lunatic scheme for kidnapping the members of the Senate.[81] To this, of course, he had nothing to say; but soon more official appeals were reaching him, by way of van Marteville, from Lovisa Ulrika; appeals for money to overthrow the Hats, to "throw off the yoke". They were couched in urgent terms: this, he was told, was a chance England could not afford to miss. But they were notably lacking in precision, either as to the means to be employed, or the objectives to be aimed at; and the financial demands were large: van Marteville was asking for £20,000-£25,000.[82] Goodricke was coolly skeptical; and Holdernesse, who might have been prepared to take a ticket in this political lottery when it seemed that the price was only £2,000,[83] jibbed immediately when he learned the true amount. To van Marteville's fervid exhortations Goodricke drily replied that the object of his mission was simply peace; that he knew Frederick's terms, and believed them to be acceptable; and that he was prepared to discuss them with the Swedish minister in Copenhagen, or any other duly authorized person.[84] Van Marteville's argument that it was desirable that peace should be made through Lovisa Ulrika because the crown would therefore be strengthened evoked no response from Goodricke:[85] when Lovisa Ulrika pressed him to ask Holdernesse for money, he sent her a polite refusal.[86]

No doubt the queen was the obvious choice as peacemaker; but others were at least conceivable. One such possibility was the chancery-president himself. Höpken was a man of splendid attainments, strong prejudices, and little political courage: a classic stylist but an indifferent statesman. He had privately disapproved the war against Prussia, but had characteristically tried to take as inconspicuous a part in the decision as possible; and he was sufficiently clear-sighted to realize at an early stage that the gamble was not going to come off. He was, and perhaps felt himself to be, the representative of a system that had outlived itself, and was now breaking, and he was much concerned that he should not break with it. He was tired of being France's client; bitterly hostile to Sweden's ally (and France's other client) Denmark, who had contrived under Bernstorff's more skillful leadership to remain neutral, very much to her advantage. He perceived the abuses and the corruption which were discrediting his party, and which were among the consequences of its having been too long in power;[87] and in common with many men of all shades of opinion he had begun to be uneasy at the imbalance in the constitution which had resulted from the success of himself and his friends in crushing the monarchy, and from the consequent engrossment of power by the Senate: of that engrossment the war itself, unconstitutionally begun, was not the least flagrant example. With some of his colleagues in the Senate—notably with C. F. Scheffer, the friend and confidant of Bernstorff—he was on terms of smoldering hostility. Höpken was therefore beginning to speculate on ways of getting out of the war, ways of loosening (though not yet of breaking) Sweden's ties with France, ways of drawing a little closer to Russia—and perhaps to England.[88] A Diet was due to meet in 1760, and it was beginning to appear likely that when it did the Senate could expect rough handling for the failure of the war and the disastrous state of the economy. It was already a question whether they would be able to weather that storm, if it came, without splitting. A prudent statesman might think the time had come to prepare alternative options; a timid one would be casting around for friends against the evil day that might come upon him. An approach to England, a hint in good time of willingness to talk peace, could do no harm—provided that it were kept secret.

Höpken had indeed been in contact with England, off and on, since 1752, when he had made tentative approaches to Newcastle through Gedda.[89] But now there was more reason to believe him serious. In 1759 Choiseul propounded his great plan for a concerted invasion of England and Scotland, the Scottish half of which was to be based on Swedish ports and carried out by Swedish forces. Höpken had no intention of going to war with England if he could help it: the Swedish economy depended largely on exports of iron, and of these much the largest proportion went to the British Isles. By skillful procrastination he effectively sabotaged the invasion project, without provoking France by a direct refusal.[90] But the affair had illustrated the risks which Sweden might run if she continued to be a belligerent. At the end of May 1759, therefore, Höpken sent a long and careful letter to Ungern-Sternberg, his minister in Copenhagen, instructing him to contrive private talks with Goodricke with a view to ascertaining what peace terms Sweden might expect from Prussia. He was not to take any ministerial initiative; the conversations were to be strictly secret; and Ungern-Sternberg predicted that if the news of them leaked out he would be made a scapegoat; for after all he was not one of Höpken's political adherents.[91] Goodricke doubted if the talks would lead anywhere; Frederick the Great surmised that they were designed only to put pressure on France for bigger subsidies.[92]

But the approach was renewed in September, reinforced by the revelation of Choiseul's plan of invasion (which the British knew all about already), for whose failure Höpken now claimed the credit.[93] To both Goodricke and Holdernesse this persistence (not unrelated, perhaps, to the flood of British victories this year) suggested that Höpken might after all mean what he said. It occurred to them that any movement for peace would gain added impetus if Höpken and Lovisa Ulrika could somehow be got to collaborate.[94] Holdernesse accordingly decided that Höpken was to be informed that he could count on British support and assistance "if he will engage himself sincerely and heartily in a new system"; his jealousy of C. F. Scheffer was fed by the information (undoubtedly derived from intercepted French dispatches) that France and Denmark would support Scheffer against him if it came to a struggle between them; and Goodricke was even authorized to say that England would be glad of a Swedish alliance—which was something no British minister had said for a generation.[95] But the bait was dangled in vain; for it was dangled too soon. Höpken was not yet ready to commit himself so far. Irritated though he might be with France, he dared not yet break the connection by an overt move for peace. Sweden's finances were certainly wretched, but without French subsidies they would undoubtedly be even worse. So the reciprocal insinuation of 1759 got no further; and the idea of peace was put into cold storage for a year or more.

Nevertheless, the year 1760 saw a significant change of scene in Sweden. The Diet met in the autumn, and though the elections had seemed to give the Hats a secure majority, and the initial parliamentary struggles appeared to confirm that impression, the ground was in fact already crumbling beneath their feet. Members found themselves confronted with "an unexpected war, a measureless confusion in the currency, an intolerable rate of exchange, a shameless luxury, a crushing cost of living."[96] The war had never been popular, the economic situation was chaotic, the scandals of Hat rule in the way of jobbery and corruption were notorious. Within a few weeks of the Diet's meeting the Senate was under heavy attack. The onslaught was led by Colonel Carl Fredrik Pechlin. Pechlin was one of the most remarkable figures in Swedish public life, and certainly one of the most repellent.[97] It may be granted that he was in his own way an idealist, in that he devoted his political life to championing that "liberty" which the constitution was considered to enshrine: he was to close his career as the patron and fomenter of regicide. But liberty might well blush for her champion. For if he was an idealist, he was an idealist whose perfidies would have tainted any cause. A powerful and inflammatory parliamentary orator, despite his imperfect command of the Swedish language;[98] an expert parliamentary tactician; tough, coarse, and formidable, resolute and ruthless; he had an extensive knowledge of the underground sewers of corruption which ran beneath the elegant classical façade of Swedish parliamentarism. It would be difficult to decide whether he was more dangerous as a friend or as an enemy: certainly those who sought to enlist him as an ally had need to look sharp about them. Among them was destined to be Goodricke, whose career was on more than one occasion to bring him into close touch with this political profligate.

Pechlin had made up his mind that the Hats must be relieved of some of the odium which now attached to them, by the removal of the more vulnerable of their leaders. He collected around him a body of Adullamites which for a short time went under the name of the Country Party (*lantpartiet*): a casual coalition of old Caps, supporters of the Court, friends of the constitution, disillusioned Hats, ambitious *frondeurs*, whose only common ground was hostility to the Hat Senate.[99] By the end of 1760 their attacks had been so successful that it seemed as though nothing could prevent the removal of at least some of the Senators; and even that the "French system" which had prevailed so long in Sweden might be on the point of being overthrown.

At the beginning of January 1761 Goodricke received information of the appointment of an extraordinary committee of 250 to inquire into the circumstances of Sweden's attack on Prussia; and his informants were of opinion that a majority of its members would be in favor of bringing the war to an end.[100] The situation now looked so hopeful that even Frederick the Great was prepared to open his purse strings. Already in November 1760 he promised Lovisa Ulrika financial assistance; and in January 1761 successive installments of money found their way to Stockholm through the Prussian minister in Copenhagen.[101] To England, too, the queen sent urgent appeals for money; and this time Goodricke gave them his support. The duke of Newcastle was moved to unusual expedition; on 23 January 1761 he agreed to make £10,000 available in the form of a credit on the Hamburg house of Hanbury and Halsey.[102] But this promptitude availed nothing; for the supposed opportunity had indeed been no more than an optical illusion. Pechlin had no wish at this stage either to overthrow the Hats, as a party, or to change the system of foreign policy: he was rather concerned to strengthen both by driving some conspicuous scapegoats from power, and by reducing the Senate to a proper sense of its subordination to the Estates. The Country Party was no more than the instrument for achieving these purposes. And among the Hat leaders he found one—Fredrik Axel von Fersen—who was willing to go along with him in lightening the ship of a handful of political rivals. By the middle of December Fersen and Pechlin had reached an agreement: Höpken, C. F. Scheffer, and Palmstierna were to be evicted from the Senate; Pechlin in return would deflect attacks upon the others, and while seeming to oppose would secretly support the Hats. On 8 January 1761 this bargain was successfully sold to the French ambassador, d'Havrincour, who accepted it without enthusiasm but was probably relieved that it was no worse: it did, after all, leave the French system intact. Thus long before English or Prussian money could reach Stockholm, the situation to which it had been designed to apply no longer existed.[103]

Pechlin duly carried out his bargain. Höpken was frightened into retiring, and was succeeded as chancery-president by the estimable but undynamic Claes Ekeblad;[104] Scheffer and Palmstierna were voted out of office by a procedure (roughly akin to impeachment) known as *licentiering*; by the end of February 1761 all three were gone.[105] Soon afterwards Pechlin, to the fury of some sections of the Country Party, openly rejoined the Hats. The comedy was over. Even Lovisa Ulrika, sanguine as she so often was, hesitated to draw on Messrs. Hanbury and Halsey: by the end of May she had collected only half the money available to her.[106]

Nevertheless, the success of Pechlin's maneuvers had one good effect: it brought Höpken and the Court together. Moreover, the weight of defeat was driving France herself to think of peace: in February d'Havrincour gave Ekeblad a memorial announcing Choiseul's intention to open negotiations.[107] In the early summer the opposition to Fersen and Pechlin slowly began to get the upper hand in the Diet. In July, the Estates voted that Höpken should be invited to resume his place on the Senate; in August, after parliamentary battles of unprecedented duration and violence, Pechlin was expelled from the House of Nobility by a single vote.[108]

These events really marked the end of the long domination of the Hats. They might make temporary recoveries, but only through tactical alliances, or proposals for a party truce: not until 1769 would they again sit secure in the seats of power. But the French system was not to be dismantled overnight (French subsidies were too important); nor, indeed, was the war to be ended just yet. Nevertheless, to Goodricke, viewing the prospects in mid-September, it seemed that the goal he had aimed at was already in sight: "The point I have been labouring, ever since I came to this place, is now effected, and I hope it will make a great alteration in the Swedish system. The Union of M. Höpken with the Court is complete."[109] It may be doubted whether Goodricke's laboring had had any great influence on the progress of events; but at least he was right in thinking that without a coalition between the queen and some respectable body of outside support the French system at this stage was unlikely to be seriously shaken. As it was, he reckoned without Höpken's irresolution and timidity. That he should have been invited to resume office was gratifying to his self-esteem; that he should once more shoulder the burden of responsibility was more than his courage was equal to. After long wavering, he at last decided to decline the invitation. But at least the harmony between Höpken and the queen lasted long enough to produce the long hoped-for (and, as it proved, decisive) initiative for peace. On 28 September 1761 Lovisa Ulrika could inform Goodricke that she had transmitted Höpken's draft peace-terms to Berlin. By the beginning of December she had received a satisfactory reply from her brother, and reported that a proposition for ending the war was to be made to the Diet almost immediately.[110]

The will to peace was now undoubted: in February 1762 the House of Nobility, in March the Secret Committee (a body of 100 members drawn from the three upper Estates, which acted for the Diet in all matters deemed to be secret, and was the real center of political power when the Diet was in session), pronounced in favor of ending the war. The death of the Empress Elizabeth in January, the accession of Peter III, and above all the Russo-Prussian peace, news of which reached Stockholm in March, all reinforced the trend. It was essential, however, to be sure that Prussia would agree to tolerable terms before any formal negotiation was engaged in.[111] Even to the queen's enemies it was now clear that the nation urgently needed her assistance; for only she could provide Sweden with the means of informal negotiation with Frederick. It was no doubt infinitely sweet to her to be able triumphantly to inform Goodricke that her enemies and persecutors had "interceded" with her to use her good offices with her brother.[112] All now went smoothly; before the end of April 1762 the commanders in Pomerania had signed an armistice; formal peace negotiations began at Hamburg in May; peace was signed on the twenty-second; and it was ratified in November.[113]

(vi)

Peace, then, was made at last; and Frederick was relieved of the military embarrassment of Swedish operations in Pomerania. What had been defined as the main object of Goodricke's mission had been attained, and attained by the means which from the beginning had been envisaged as most likely to succeed. What object now remained? Goodricke was still shut out of Sweden: was it worth England's while to press for his admission, or even to keep him in Copenhagen? Had England now any ends to gain in Sweden which made diplomatic representation, if not essential, then at least desirable? The dealings with Lovisa Ulrika had already demonstrated how easily the pursuit of peace could slide into that "meddling" with Sweden's internal affairs which Goodricke, in the first flush of his appointment, had promised Holdernesse to abjure.[114] It was no decisive argument for sending a minister to Stockholm to say that the old Caps wanted him to come. Of course they did: they wanted English money.

On the other hand, the Hats were now obviously in disarray; disgraced, divided, politically and morally bankrupt: it was as though the Whigs had lost the Seven Years War instead of winning it. And the shake administered to the Hats had shaken the French system too. For the first time for more than a decade and a half there seemed a fair chance of taking Sweden out of French hands and putting it into the hands of a set of men who by tradition and political descent could be at least nominally accounted "English." The Diet of 1760-62 might seem to have ended in a draw;[115] but the next one, it was possible to hope, might see the Hats defeated. And what if financial stringency should force the Senate to call an Extraordinary Diet, ahead of time? The efforts they made to avoid having to do so, and the anxiety of friends of the French system such as Bernstorff that they should succeed,[116] must make its summons desirable for England; for it might be England's opportunity. But if that opportunity should come, not much use could be made of it if there were no English minister in Stockholm. France's defeat in the war, and the extreme fluidity of international alignments after the peace, might likewise suggest that if England were disposed to resume the old policy of backing a faction in Sweden, this might be as good a time to choose as any. And a faction could scarcely be supported without a minister on the spot.

Considerations such as these occurred intermittently to British Secretaries of State, who were periodically reminded by Goodricke's dispatches that they still had a minister to Sweden stationed in Copenhagen. But their attitude to the question was slow to crystallize. Until peace was made they had more important things to think of. Whatever the arguments for persisting in the attempt to place a minister in Stockholm, there was one great obstacle that must first be removed. Until the Swedes had shown a decent contrition for the events of 1747, and the aggravations of insult thereafter, the king could not compromise his dignity by another initiative. Soon after the opening of the Diet in 1760 Goodricke had dropped the remark that the enemies of France in Stockholm were feeling the need of a foreign minister to coordinate them.[117] But Holdernesse at once made it clear that there could be no question of his going to Sweden until some reparation had been made for past offenses. Nevertheless, he added what was clearly intended as a hint: "a natural opportunity" for such an *amende*, he observed, was afforded by the accession of George III. Goodricke was at liberty to insinuate that the sending of a compliment to the new king would be well taken, and the envoy who brought it be assured of a gracious reception. "The natural consequence" would be Goodricke's departure for Stockholm.[118] This, all things considered, was a sufficiently modest requirement. But the Swedes declined to take the hint: after all, no British envoy had congratulated Adolf Fredrik on his accession in 1751.[119]

From time to time the opponents of the Hats alarmed their adversaries with rumors that Goodricke was really coming;[120] and in the summer of 1761, when their side was doing well in the Diet, reports more than once reached Goodricke that the Secret Committee had debated whether they should not take the initiative and send a minister to London.[121] The demand of public opinion for an end to the war, and the increasingly obvious fact that the Hats would be driven to ask the queen to help them, led Lord Bute to think that perhaps the moment was ripe for Goodricke to go. On 5 January 1762 he instructed him to sound Lovisa Ulrika on the chances of his being received, and sent credentials for him to use at his discretion.[122] But Bute's move depended on the queen's being able to persuade or influence the Senate, and was based on an estimate of the strength of her political position which was still much too sanguine; and it was compromised before it got under way by leaks in London for which Christopher Springer seems to have been responsible. It thus repeated most of the mistakes of the Campbell fiasco.[123] Goodricke himself had plainly little faith in its success; and Lovisa Ulrika's reception of it justified his skepticism. She did indeed assure him that she would make him welcome if he came, but she told him frankly that she could not guarantee that his arrival would at once be followed by the nomination of a Swedish minister to London, nor even that he could count on an honorable reception by the Senate. In view of this there was nothing to be done; and on 23 February 1762 Bute instructed Goodricke to take no action until further orders.[124]

There for a year or so the situation remained. Peace came to Sweden, and then to Europe, without doing anything for Goodricke. The Swedish factions walked warily around each other, sniffing at the notion of a "Composition"—that is, of a party truce and a bipartisan Senate; but Goodricke appeared as immovably stuck in Copenhagen as ever. In February 1763, however, came a new development. France had tempted Sweden into the war with the promise of liberal subsidies, in return for which Sweden was to put a specified number of troops in the field. Both sides cheated on their bargain. The Swedish army never reached the stipulated strength; the French government was remiss or tardy in its payments. At the end of the war the Swedes had a long account for arrears, and Choiseul appeared in no hurry to settle it. The patience of the Senate began to wear thin, for they desperately needed the money. The general crisis which shook the European banking houses in the summer of 1763 was felt in Sweden with particular severity, for it entailed the ruin of no less than three of the agents upon which the Swedish government relied—the Stenglins and the Boués of Hamburg, and the Grills of Amsterdam.[125] It was no wonder that in this situation Claes Ekeblad should confess that he dreamed of nothing but subsidies.[126] At last the Senate began to canvass expedients to bring Choiseul to a proper sense of his obligations. Early in February Goodricke had word from "my Court correspondent" (who was probably Count C. W. von Düben) that it had been decided to make one more attempt to obtain payment, and if that failed to send a minister to England.[127] How far this attempt at blackmail would have succeeded is impossible to say; for before it really had time to bite, the patience of British government, which had appeared to be inexhaustible, suddenly snapped.

On 9 September Lord Halifax wound up his brief tenure of the Northern Secretaryship (Lord Sandwich succeeded him the same day) by peremptorily ordering Goodricke to terminate his mission and return home, "upon consideration of the very neglectful and in all respects improper Behaviour of the Court of Sweden towards His Majesty since his Accession to the Throne."[128] It is unlikely that the failure of the Swedish government to compliment George III on his accession (or on his marriage, or on the birth of the Prince of Wales) was really seen as sufficient justification of this step. It was probably rather that the cabinet had grown tired of paying for an apparently interminable diplomatic anomaly: the hand was the hand of Halifax, but one may suspect that the voice was the voice of George Grenville.

This thunderbolt struck Goodricke on 19 September.[129] His reaction was immediate, vigorous, and typical of the man. His first step was a measure of precaution: he wrote to Halifax, and also to Sandwich, urgently soliciting another post.[130] But he had no intention of abandoning his Swedish mission without a struggle. What he needed was evidence to persuade Sandwich that the deadlock in Anglo-Swedish relations was showing signs of breaking. The best he could do in this line, for the moment, was to relay to him reports from Stockholm that an Extraordinary Diet was likely to be summoned shortly. This was not much, perhaps; but it gave him a rather thin pretext for deferring his departure, since if such a Diet should in fact meet (he argued) it would be useful to have him, if not in Stockholm, then at least in Copenhagen.[131] And this gave him time, pending Sandwich's reply, to take his measures for providing a more solid reason for remaining. Those measures he set in train at once. On the day after the arrival of Halifax's instructions, Goodricke put himself in touch with Faxell, who had been left in charge of the Swedish legation in Copenhagen during the absence of the minister on leave. To Faxell he revealed, in confidence, that he was recalled; but added, artlessly enough, that he supposed he should not be able to get away much before the middle of October. He thus gave plenty of time for Faxell to communicate the news to the Swedish government, and for their reaction to it to reach Copenhagen.[132]

Having done all that could be done (and perhaps more than he ought) Goodricke sat back to await the effects. The response from England was speedy, uncompromising, and disheartening. Sandwich was not in the least impressed by vague stories of the imminence of an Extraordinary Diet, and curtly reiterated his orders of recall.[133] Before this letter reached him, however, Goodricke had collected heavier ammunition. His dispatch to Sandwich of 1 October reported that the controversy about France's subsidy arrears had reached a crisis. The French had offered, by way of settlement, a new treaty of alliance, to last for ten years, and payment of the arrears at the rate of a million livres in 1764, and a million and a half annually thereafter; and they had asked in return that Sweden should make six ships of the line and six frigates available to France in the event of war. The Senate received these proposals with indignation, and on 6 September unanimously rejected them. They refused to consider any proposals until France had paid four million on account; and they decided, in the event of a French refusal, to summon an Extraordinary Diet.[134] Goodricke had now a double-barreled argument for Sandwich: either the French would pay the four million, and thus be free to negotiate for the Swedish warships (a matter to which Sandwich, of all ministers, was unlikely to be indifferent); or they would refuse, and by refusing precipitate an Extraordinary Diet which would probably see the ruin of the Hats and the collapse of the French system. In the event (though this was to have no effect on the question of Goodricke's going to Sweden) Choiseul was shaken by the Senate's firm attitude. He dropped the talk of a new treaty, and offered a million for 1763 and two million for 1764, on condition that no Extraordinary Diet was summoned. This proposal the Senate accepted, ad interim, leaving a full settlement of the arrears to be negotiated with the new French ambassador, Breteuil, who was expected before the end of the year.

Meanwhile Goodricke's broad hint to Stockholm was producing gratifying results. The Senate was obviously taken aback by Faxell's report. They had no wish for an overt breach with England at a moment when they had already sufficient difficulties on their hands. On 3 October, accordingly, they approved orders to Faxell to intimate verbally to Goodricke, as from himself, that he was confident that a Swedish minister to England would be appointed if Goodricke came to Stockholm.[135] On 11 October Goodricke was able to report that Faxell had spoken to him as a result of a letter from Ekeblad; had assured him that Sweden would look upon a renewal of diplomatic relations as a happy event; had told him that he would be welcome in Stockholm, and that his arrival would at once be followed by the nomination of a minister to England. Though Faxell had refused to give anything in writing, he had permitted Goodricke to make a note of his remarks, and had confirmed its accuracy. Goodricke seems to have felt (or at least he affected to feel) that this was as much as any Secretary of State could require; and he did not fail to point out to Sandwich that Bute's orders of 5 January 1762 would have authorized him at this point to proceed to Stockholm, if they had not been superseded by the order for his recall.[136] The game seemed in his hands. Once more he ignored his instructions, deferred his departure, and awaited Sandwich's reply.

Lord Sandwich did not share this euphoric view of the position. His letter of 29 October was distinctly chilly.[137] No attention, in his opinion, was to be given to "loose verbal Declarations, made with so much precaution of not giving anything in writing." There would be no change in the order for recall without "some authentick overture, in writing, on the part of Sweden, and the immediate nomination of such a minister to reside at this Court as shall be acceptable to the King, and not the proposing persons whom there may be reasons to suppose beforehand his Majesty must object to." Indeed, he more than half suspected that the hint of readiness to receive an English minister might be no more than a device to put the screw on France to pay more arrears.[138] If Faxell should give hopes of an acceptance of Sandwich's terms within a reasonable time, Goodricke might remain in Copenhagen to await it; but if not, or if the Swedish reply when it came should be unsatisfactory, he was to leave at once, without further instructions, and without transmitting any other proposals.

At this stage came a weighty intervention from quite another quarter. On 8 November Sandwich received a dispatch from Lord Buckinghamshire, his ambassador to the court of Catherine II. It transmitted information, which had been passed on to Buckinghamshire by the Russians, about the French proposals for paying off their arrears to Sweden (already, of course, known to Sandwich); it pointedly drew his attention to the naval implications; it suppressed the information that the Swedish Senate had provisionally rejected the plan; and it strongly urged the sending of an English minister to Stockholm to collaborate with his Russian colleague in defeating the machinations of France.[139] The question then arises, what effect (if any) this dispatch may have had upon Goodricke's chances of getting to Sweden.

Relations between England and Russia at this time were officially excellent. Though the two countries had fought on opposite sides in the war, they had been very careful to avoid a breach: as with England and Sweden, commercial considerations made the preservation of peace highly desirable to both. England had naturally been careful to propitiate Peter III, as the friend and rescuer of Frederick the Great; but had also established a long credit with Catherine, who had received English assistance in the difficult closing years of Elizabeth's reign, and was in any case anglophil in sympathy. After the peace, a Russian alliance was undoubtedly the main objective of English foreign policy. Secretaries of State were willing to go to considerable lengths to please Russia. Since 1762 Buckinghamshire had been at the Russian court, charged to renew the commercial treaty of 1734 and the political alliance of 1742. The Russians were willing enough in principle, though they had their own ideas about the terms; but Catherine had her hands full in the opening months of her reign; her tenure of the throne seemed precarious; and she was increasingly preoccupied with the problem of the Polish succession, since the life of Augustus III was unlikely to be prolonged.[140] For these reasons she had dragged her feet about the renewal of the treaties; or so at least it seemed in London.[141] Halifax felt that he had gone as far as could reasonably be expected of him when he assured Catherine that England would concur with her plans in Poland—as soon as she announced what they were.[142] But Russian dilatoriness about the treaties annoyed him; and in June 1763 he gave unmistakable signs of his displeasure.[143] The Russians took the point. At the beginning of August the Russian ministers produced a draft treaty of alliance; on 22 August they presented it to Buckinghamshire; on 13 September it reached Sandwich in London—four days after the dispatch of the order recalling Goodricke.[144] The draft proposed common action in Poland, with financial aid from England to the tune of 500,000 rubles; it envisaged the sending of an English minister to Stockholm, instructed to collaborate with his Russian colleague in counteracting the French system; it omitted the "Turkish clause"—that is, that clause which in the previous treaty had exempted England from the obligation to give assistance in the event of Russia's becoming involved in war with the Turks. And, finally, it postponed consideration of the commercial treaty until the political alliance should have been concluded.

To Sandwich and his colleagues these seemed outrageous proposals. On 16 September a unanimous cabinet rejected them;[145] a week later Sandwich wrote to Buckinghamshire that the articles dealing with Poland and Sweden were "wholly inadmissible."[146] Thus the Russian plea that an English minister be sent to Stockholm had already been implicitly rejected. But now, on 8 November, Sandwich found himself confronted with it again. His temper cannot have been improved by the knowledge that Catherine's ambassador in London, A. R. Vorontsov, was deep in intrigues with members of the opposition (including Pitt), and was sending derogatory reports of the Grenville administration to his court.[147] Sandwich's reply to Buckinghamshire, dated 11 November, was therefore by no means forthcoming.[148] He was ready, he said, to "oblige" Catherine by sending a minister to Stockholm; but only if the necessary conditions were fulfilled: "the loose and insufficient manner" in which the Swedes had hinted their readiness to renew relations did not, he thought, suggest sincerity. He had no intention of exposing his court to a snub in Stockholm simply to placate Catherine. In the next two years Sandwich was to hammer away at the point that England had sent Goodricke to Sweden only because Russia had requested it. He never tired of claiming it as a kind of moral credit upon which he was entitled to draw.[149] But this was tactics rather than truth. If the Swedes had not more or less complied with Sandwich's preconditions, no amount of Russian pleading would have made any difference.

All now depended on whether Goodricke could bring his negotiations with Faxell within the scope of the terms which Sandwich had laid down. The great difficulty was the insistence on an overture in writing. This Faxell refused to give, arguing that Goodricke's insinuation had not been written but verbal. Goodricke countered on 10 November by permitting him to make an agreed minute of their conversation, and promising to give him a note if a satisfactory answer should come from Stockholm.[150] The Swedish Senate and Chancery had now to consider their attitude. They did so with unusual speed: on 29 November Faxell read to Goodricke a note which referred to the "ouvertures aimables qui annoncent la nomination" of an English minister, and promised that Sweden would "incessament" choose a minister to London, should Goodricke be authorized to "prendre la même caractère." And as a token of their sincerity Faxell was able to inform him that nominations for the post were already under consideration. In return for all this, Goodricke now gave Faxell the note which he had earlier promised.[151] Both parties were nervous of incurring the censure of their courts;[152] and it took a long discussion before agreement could be reached on a text of Goodricke's note of 29 November which was acceptable to each of them.[153] Faxell thought that the final version left the diplomatic advantage on Sweden's side, and he was probably right: the Swedish note could scarcely be described as "an authentick overture," for it was so phrased as rather to have the appearance of a response to an overture from England.[154] No doubt it was true that there was not much reason any longer to doubt the Senate's sincerity: though Goodricke could not know it, the Swedish minister to London had not been merely nominated but actually appointed as early as 22 November.[155] But the question had become one of diplomatic "face"; and Goodricke, well aware that his country was the thrice-injured party, was conscious that he had given ground. Nevertheless, he took the risk, as he was to take risks so often in the course of his ministry: partly, no doubt, because his own future was at stake; but partly too because he judged that it was not worth contending for the minutiae of ceremony. The risk came off. His luck was in. Sandwich was prepared to bury the hatchet, with only a mild obligatory grumble; and on 20 December he sent Goodricke his credentials, though with strict orders that he was not to use them until a Swedish minister had been appointed, and a time set for his departure from Stockholm.[156]

There remained one possible obstacle. It was still conceivable that the minister whom the Senate would appoint might be unacceptable to the British government. Their choice had fallen on Baron Gustaf Adolf von Nolcken. Nolcken seems to have been a man of no very strongly marked political color: at all events, the friends of England, as well was those of France, considered that he inclined to their side. What is truly remarkable is that Sandwich, despite his stringent caveat to Goodricke, never seems to have raised the question of his acceptability at all, or to have manifested the slightest interest in the character and disposition of the man who was now to repair a breach of sixteen years. In the event, Nolcken proved to be a most fortunate choice, and a minister of great ability. Whatever his political predilections, he soon made himself at home in England: he was to live there for most of the rest of his life. At quite an early stage of his mission he acquired an insight into English politics comparable with Goodricke's insight into the politics of Sweden, and almost certainly superior to that of any of his diplomatic colleagues. The surveys of English affairs which he sent home to successive Diets are remarkable for their ability to penetrate below the surface of English politics to the realities beneath; and they can still be read with profit by an English historian.

But however happy the choice of the Senate, Goodricke could not move from Copenhagen until he was sure that Nolcken had started for London; and Nolcken's departure was unaccountably delayed. So much so, that it began to be rumored that Goodricke would not go to Sweden at all, but was destined for another post.[157] It was not until 16 April that Nolcken left Stockholm.[158] Schack, the Danish minister to Sweden, guessed that this long postponement might be a device to keep Goodricke away until the decision had been taken upon whether or not to summon an Extraordinary Diet.[159] But this was mere speculation: the true explanation was very different. It was not Nolcken, but Goodricke, who was responsible for the delay. No doubt his private affairs required time for settling: he had a house to dispose of, for one thing, and some arrangement had presumably to be made for Mylady. But he may well have felt some embarrassment about pleading with Lord Sandwich for delay, after urging so forcibly the importance of his presence in Sweden. From this little difficulty he extricated himself with an adroitness which reflects more credit on his skill than on his honesty. He contrived to let the chancery-president know that he would be glad of a couple of months' respite before leaving, and asked therefore that Nolcken's departure might be deferred for so long. Ekeblad made no difficulty about obliging him.[160] Luckily for Goodricke, Sandwich never seems to have raised the question, or even to have expressed the mildest astonishment that a mission which had been represented as being so necessary had still failed to get under way four months after it was authorized. However, there was always the possibility that he might be revolving the question in his mind; and Goodricke prudently took care to provide him with an explanation before he asked for one: the delay, he informed him, arose in all probability from Nolcken's wish to have two or three months' salary and appointments in hand before taking up his post. The impudence of the lie sheds some light upon the character of its inventor.[161]

On 10 April 1764 Goodricke had his farewell audience of Fredrik V; on the eighteenth he quitted Copenhagen; on the twenty-fifth he at last arrived in Stockholm.[162] The Swedish wits observed that Nolcken could hardly be said to have started first, for Goodricke had been six years on his journey. Before he left Denmark he had received fresh instructions from Sandwich, written this time in the expectation of his immediate departure. They were for the most part of a quite general nature; but they included one passage of some significance. It ran:

> The distrest state of the finances in that Kingdom, their total want of Resources; and the inability of France, in the present juncture, to supply those Defects; throw so many Difficulties in the way of the leading Senators among the French Party, that there could hardly be a more favourable opportunity for a British Minister to resume his Functions at the Court of Sweden, after so many Years' interruption.[163]

It was an intimation, as plain as could be desired, of what was now expected of him. For a generation Sweden had been a French pocket borough. It was now to be considered as a marginal constituency. And it was Goodricke's business to capture the seat. With what allies, at what cost, for what purpose, had hardly yet been considered in London; still less what the possible consequences of success might be. If the French system could be overturned, that was program enough for the present: time enough to think when victory had been won. In the meantime, they had a man on the spot who knew what he was about. Which perhaps was more than could be said for Lord Sandwich.

CHAPTER II

A Diplomatic Revolution, 1762–1764

The coming of peace at the beginning of 1763 inaugurated, for most of the combatants, a period of painful readjustment. Wartime partnerships dissolved when the war was over; and statesmen groped their way to new connections to meet the changed perspectives which the peace had brought. The international landmarks were altering their shape and shifting their position; old patterns were dissolving, new ones had not yet come into focus.

Nowhere was the change more evident than in the microcosm of Swedish affairs. Whether in regard to domestic politics or international groupings, all was labile, uncertain, and confused. In the 1740s and 1750s the political situation in Sweden, from the point of view of those foreign powers who were interested in it, had been comparatively stable and predictable. France and Russia had contended for supremacy, with England as Russia's auxiliary; and each side had stood patron and paymaster to one or other of the two parties in the state. To this rivalry the reshuffling of European alliances in 1756 had put a temporary stop, since France and Russia were now, if not allies, then at least belligerents on the same side. After 1756, moreover, the total eclipse of the Caps had left no party in Sweden which could be used to oppose the French system, even if any foreign power had been available to organize it. It might have been foreseen, however, that this was an abnormal state of affairs. The rule of the Hats would not last forever. The Court, with care and patience, might expect one day to make at least a partial recovery from disaster. The alignments of 1756 were unlikely to prove permanent; and once the war was over France and Russia would probably revert to their former attitudes of covert hostility—as Choiseul, for one, clearly foresaw.[1]

And in fact, for the three foreign powers who had taken an especial interest in Sweden—France, Russia, Denmark—there had now come a moment when the validity of the old assumptions began to appear doubtful. One after the other they were being driven to a reexamination of their Swedish policies; and as a result of that reexamination each was modifying its tactics and reconsidering its objectives. The movement was not uniform in speed for each; and as it proceeded it dragged along with it, for a considerable time, the rags and remnants of old attitudes and old friendships. In 1763 the change was nowhere complete; but the general trend was already unmistakable. When Goodricke arrived in Stockholm he found himself in the middle of a scene-shifting operation whose final outcome was still a matter for conjecture, but whose most palpable immediate result was no inconsiderable quantity of dust.

(i)

For a quarter of a century France had exerted herself to attach Sweden to her system; with such success that her ascendancy in Stockholm had now continued virtually unbroken for two decades. It rested on close alliance with the Hats. A natural alliance; for the Hats were the heirs of Sweden's Age of Greatness, they embodied the aspirations of the patriots, the romantics, the Hotspurs, the half-pay officers—in short, of all those who dreamed of recovering for their country its reputation in arms and at least a portion of its former Baltic empire.[2] But the link with the Hats, though based essentially on considerations of foreign policy, had entailed a commitment to the support of other aspects of their political program. It had made France the upholder of their constitutional ideas, the protector of the quasi-republican régime which emerged from the humiliation of the monarchy in 1756. This in turn had had the consequence that it had turned the king and queen into France's enemies. It was a consequence far from inevitable, if foreign policy had been the only consideration; for Lovisa Ulrika, at all events, was at heart as disposed to foreign adventures, and as sensitive to considerations of prestige, as were the Hats themselves.[3]

Since the time of Richelieu and Mazarin French statesmen had found their relations with the two Scandinavian powers bedeviled by the perennial hostility between them. They had striven to mitigate that hostility by submerging it in a general French system of the North in which both countries should be included as France's allies. It was certainly a French interest to relieve Sweden of any anxiety about a possible attack across the Sound. But it was also important to keep Denmark, as the possessor of the most efficient navy in the Baltic, out of the orbit of England.[4] France's aim, then, was a Swedish-Danish bloc under French protection; a bloc strong enough, perhaps, to close the Sound to Britain, and so interrupt the supply of naval stores and iron upon which the British navy depended: a design which came near to realization in 1781. This policy had the unforeseen consequence of entangling France in the great dynastic quarrel between the two branches of the house of Oldenburg: that branch which sat on the throne of Denmark; and that which ruled in ducal Holstein, and which considered itself to have been despoiled in 1720 of territories which rightly belonged to it. For if Karl Peter Ulrich, the young duke of Holstein, were to die without heirs, his lands and pretensions would pass to Adolf Fredrik of Sweden; and the Hats had no wish to see Adolf Fredrik's position strengthened by succession to such an inheritance. France did not desire it either, since it would have entailed the engrafting upon Sweden of Holstein's hereditary feud with Denmark. With French encouragement and assistance, therefore, the Hats in 1749 forced Adolf Fredrik to conclude an agreement with Fredrik V of Denmark whereby he undertook, if the succession to Holstein should fall in to him, to exchange it for the outlying Danish territories of Oldenburg and Delmenhorst;[5] and they followed this up in 1750 by extorting his reluctant acquiescence in the engagement of his infant son (afterwards Gustav III) to the Danish princess Sofia Magdalena, as a prophylactic against dynastic quarrels in the future.[6] The constraint thus put upon the Swedish royal pair in matters which they felt to be peculiarly personal was never forgotten or forgiven; and their implacable hostility to Denmark, which they transmitted in some measure to their son,[7] remained a constant factor in politics thereafter. It began their alienation from the Hats; it reinforced their hostility to France; and in its turn this committed France still more firmly to the support of the "republican" constitution, as it developed after 1756. For it was reasonably certain that if ever that constitution should be overthrown, if ever the monarchy should emancipate itself from the fetters in which it was now confined, one of Adolf Fredrik's first acts would be to denounce the agreements of 1749 and 1750, and thus shatter the Scandinavian harmony which France had labored to preserve.

Nevertheless, despite these complications, France might until 1757 congratulate herself upon pursuing a Swedish policy which was coherent, logical, and successful. Sweden and Denmark were both her clients, bound to Louis XV by subsidy treaties which their extenuated finances effectively restrained them from repudiating. The Hats sat firmly in the saddle in Stockholm. The English had vanished from the scene. The Russians were for the moment neutralized, and had no longer a party of their own. Under France's inspiration, Denmark and Sweden were cooperating with Russia in an Armed Neutrality which in intention, and to some extent in fact, was directed against Great Britain.[8] In 1757 Sweden discharged the function which was expected of her by attacking France's enemy Prussia. But within a very short time these gratifying appearances proved delusive. The Armed Neutrality turned out to be an insidious solvent of Scandinavian amity.[9] Sweden's intervention in the war was neither creditable to her government nor useful to her ally. The large sums which France paid out to her in subsidies, whether in war or peace, began to look like money thrown away. To Praslin, who directed France's foreign policy during the concluding period of the war, it became increasingly clear that Sweden's usefulness as an ally was much diminished by the abuses of her system of government and the corruption of her politicians.[10] The rule of the Hats, the triumph of "liberty," seemed to have produced a nation of factious soldiers, slippery politicians, and parliamentarians whose zeal for the constitution was a cloak for party vendettas and shameless greed.[11]

By 1761 it was possible to foresee that the long domination of the Hats was coming to an end: the internal splits in the party, the parliamentary successes of their adversaries in the summer of that year, announced the imminence of change. It was now a question for France whether it was any longer worthwhile to spend money on retaining Sweden's fidelity; or at least whether that end could best be achieved by squandering bribes to keep the Hats in office. The days were now over when France could afford to be indifferent to how much she lavished on her protégés and pensioners in northern Europe: French finances were deeply embarrassed, and Choiseul was to initiate a policy of heavy cuts in foreign office expenditure.[12] If resources were now short, they must be husbanded for other ends than Swedish corruption. Already in 1761 and 1762 France had suspended supplies; when Sweden withdrew from the war they were cut off altogether.[13] Once peace was made France had her eyes fixed upon the next war against England; and Choiseul had no intention of allowing that war to be mixed up, as the war just ended had been, with European issues peripheral to French interests. It was to be a war for colonies and commerce, a naval war, a war to end that upsetting of the balance of power which Choiseul believed arose from England's maritime and commercial "tyranny";[14] and hence the rebuilding and expansion of the French navy was a more urgent matter even than the maintenance of France's historic Northern System.[15] For that system had been designed to divert pressure from France in the event of war in Europe; and Choiseul and Praslin did not intend that there should be another war in Europe if they could help it. The alliance with Austria survived both war and peace precisely because it was France's insurance against accidents in Germany; and the Family Compact, despite a certain cynical skepticism on the part of both partners,[16] became the linchpin of French policy just because its concern was mainly with oceanic and colonial issues.

This did not mean, however, that France was ready to allow her Northern System simply to wither away. Choiseul, for all his concentration on the imperial theme, continued to regard its maintenance as a necessity. But he was sure that France could no longer afford the luxury of an ally who was a burden rather than an asset;[17] and this might suggest a doubt whether after all France, in choosing Sweden, had chosen the best instrument for her purposes. For years it had been a French maxim that Sweden should be the "active" ally in the North, Denmark the "inactive": the Swedes were to be kept ready to launch at their neighbors when it suited France's book; the Danes were to be paid to remain neutral—an arrangement which accorded happily with their interests. It was at least a question worth considering, whether Denmark could not do France's business more effectively than Sweden. This not only because of the efficiency of the Danish navy in comparison with the Swedish, but because of the stability and strength of the Danish system of government. Denmark was a pure absolutism, run on its king's behalf by a small council of devoted and (on the whole) disinterested ministers; one of whom, at least—J. H. E. Bernstorff—was a statesman of impressive stature, and (incidentally) the old friend of Choiseul. Compared with the solidity and dependability of the Danish régime, Swedish "liberty" appeared in a more disadvantageous light than ever. Before 1763 there were moments when the attractions of the Danish option must have presented themselves forcibly to Choiseul; and Höpken, for all his bitter hatred of Denmark, believed that France would best consult her own interests by adopting it.[18] But if the option was ever really open,

Choiseul and Praslin threw it away by their neglect of Danish interests and their contempt for Danish susceptibilities. By the time Goodricke arrived in Stockholm this question, at least, had been decided; and French policy had fallen back into its old groove of reliance upon Sweden as the active ally in the North.

Nevertheless, the debate on how best to ensure that such activity should be effective was by 1764 producing visible shifts in French tactics. D'Havrincour had left Sweden in October 1762, disillusioned with the Hat régime. His successor, the Baron de Breteuil, who did not arrive until December 1763 (an interval whose length was significant of French ill-humor), came to Stockholm indoctrinated with d'Havrincour's misgivings. In two memoranda written in September 1763 d'Havrincour had suggested that France needed a stronger and more untrammeled government in Sweden; and that the correct line might be to aim at a revision of the constitution which would sweep away all the modifications which had been introduced since the accession of Adolf Fredrik in 1751. This would mean restoring to the crown some of the rights and prerogatives which it had lost in 1756. It by no means implied, however, that France ought to engage herself to support the supposed designs of Lovisa Ulrika, or to work for the establishment of an unlimited monarchy; but it would be a step towards curbing the irresponsibility of the Diet and achieving a greater concentration of power in the executive organs of government. The best hope for the kind of government France needed in Stockholm seemed in fact to lie in increasing the power of the Senate and liberating it from harassment by the Estates; and this, essentially, was what d'Havrincour recommended. The advantages which might be expected were double. It would make Sweden a more effective ally; and at the same time would give France's friends the Hats a chance of arresting the decline in their fortunes which had evidently set in since 1760. It presupposed, no doubt, a reconciliation between the Hats and the Court; but in the existing situation the Hats' best hope of retaining their grip on the government might well lie in detaching the Court from its alliance with the Caps, and recruiting fresh strength from its supporters. The price to be paid by way of concessions to the prerogative was not so great as to be alarming; and it would in any case be more than offset by the increase in the Senate's authority.

Such was the new French policy; and as far as it went it met the needs of the moment. The time would come when Choiseul would recognize that after all it had been a half-measure; that France's need for strong government in Sweden could be satisfied by nothing less than a monarchical coup d'état. But for the moment it served. Breteuil arrived in Sweden instructed to work for a revision of the constitution and a reconciliation with the Court.[19] It was not a program to be proclaimed from the housetops. It involved a major readjustment in the attitudes, not only of the Hat leaders and of Lovisa Ulrika, but also—and this was much more difficult— of the ordinary members of the Hat party who had grown up with a set of mental attitudes and political stereotypes which were not to be suddenly jettisoned or brusquely turned upside down. The process of re-education would require time and delicate handling. But the ground was preparing; and in the first six months of 1764 the process was already in operation.

(ii)

The shift in French policy was matched by an analogous shift in the policy of Russia. In the years between the peace of Nystad and the peace of Paris two main considerations influenced Russia's attitude to Sweden. The one was strategic; the other, dynastic. Strategically, Russia's concern was to protect herself against the possibility of a Swedish military resurgence. No doubt it was true that the Russia of Peter I and his successors was now a power so formidable that it stood in no great danger from Sweden, provided the conflict were limited to a straight fight between them. But the case would be altered if the Swedes were to attack at a moment when Russia should happen to be involved in a major war in central Europe, or a struggle with the Turks which necessitated the denuding of her northwestern frontiers of troops, or if (as happened on several occasions in this century) the empire were distracted by some domestic crisis. It was therefore a cardinal point of Russian policy to keep Sweden weak; and this, it was felt, could best be done by ensuring that the Swedish monarchy was subjected to the control of the Estates. The constitution of 1720 appeared to do this; and hence Russia felt obliged to uphold it. In the application of this general principle Russia supported the Caps, since they were the party which opposed the policy of adventure and revenge which had carried the Hats to power; but also because party strife in itself, in virtue of its debilitating effects on the national energies, was a Russian interest.

These unexceptionable considerations of national interest, however, had latterly become somewhat blurred by dynastic issues. In 1743 the Empress Elizabeth forced the Swedes, as the price of an easy peace, to accept Adolf Fredrik as heir to the throne. She thus prepared the way for a dynastic tie between the two countries; for Karl Peter Ulrich of Holstein, whom Elizabeth designated as her own heir, and who did in fact succeed her as Peter III, was Adolf Fredrik's second cousin. It is true that she soon came to regret having sent Adolf Fredrik to Stockholm, once it became clear that he was not willing to be her puppet; but the dynastic connection none the less produced crosswinds which at times seemed likely to blow Russian policy off course. There were not a few observers, in Sweden and Denmark, who feared that it might one day lead a tsar to support the attempts of Adolf Fredrik to recover his lost prerogatives. Dynastic interest, in short, might contradict the tradition of Russian policy: instead of being directed to maintaining the Swedish constitution intact, with all the political weakness which sprang from it, Russia might be committed to the establishment of a strong monarchy on the constitution's ruins.

In 1762 this seemed very likely to happen. Peter III showed decided sympathy with the plight of his relative in Stockholm. He made it quite clear that he was prepared to give active support to Lovisa Ulrika's aspirations to restore the crown's authority;[20] and he asked pressingly, though in vain, for Swedish assistance in the war against Denmark which he was preparing at the moment of his deposition.[21] It was no wonder that Peter's fall was felt by Lovisa Ulrika as a bitter blow, or that the Swedish court ostentatiously went into mourning when the news came of his demise.[22] No doubt Peter's reign was no more than a brief and eccentric episode; but it was an episode which sent shivers down the backs of the Hat Senate. And it was not forgotten. Who could tell whether Catherine too might not feel that the cause of monarchs everywhere required that she do something for her oppressed connections in Stockholm? She was, after all, Adolf Fredrik's niece, as well as the widow of his cousin. For full two years after Peter's deposition it seemed possible that Russia might reverse her traditional policy, and apply military pressure to extort concessions to the crown. The Court in Sweden was still closely linked to the old Caps—that is, to the former pensioners of Russia. When Adolf Fredrik sent A. R. Durietz to St. Petersburg to congratulate Catherine on her accession, the warmth of his welcome and the duration of his stay seemed ominous to the pensive friends of "liberty."[23] It was long suspected that Catherine and Lovisa Ulrika were conducting a secret correspondence of sinister import.[24] That there was such a correspondence was undeniably true; that Lovisa Ulrika tried to enlist the empress's support was true likewise; but in fact she had no success: what she received from Catherine was not a promise of political support, but gifts of choice tea and presents of Ukrainian horses, and into such amenities even the most sanguine royalist could hardly read very much.[25] Nevertheless, the enemies of the Court found the situation disquieting. In October and November 1763 Bernstorff and C. F. Scheffer were making each other's flesh creep with rumors of concentrations of Russian troops on the Finnish frontier—designed, as was supposed, to given countenance and aid to some undefined royalist *démarche* in Stockholm.[26]

These alarms had little basis in reality. There was no love lost between Catherine and Lovisa Ulrika (who had not scrupled, in private, to call the empress a murderess);[27] and in any case Catherine was not to be diverted from the pursuit of Russia's interests by dynastic considerations.[28] Within a few days of her accession Peter's orders to Osterman (his minister in Stockholm) were canceled, and the policy of supporting Adolf Fredrik abandoned.[29] This did not mean, however, that affairs would simply resume their former aspect. The decay of the Hats, and the sharp deterioration in Franco-Russian relations which became apparent after the death of Elizabeth, had paved the way for the revival of Russian patronage of the Caps: for the first time for more than a decade a Russian party in Sweden became conceivable. By August 1762 it was apparent that Catherine was rethinking her Swedish policy. A rescript to Osterman pointed out that the existing constitutional situation was not in Russia's interests. An absolutism in Stockholm would certainly be bad; but the predominance of the Senate might well be worse. Just what could happen when the Senate became too powerful had been made clear by its unconstitutional action in beginning war with Prussia in 1757 in defiance of the king's opposition, and by the dubiously legal measures which it had employed thereafter to finance it. An untrammeled monarch, a senatorial dictatorship, might no doubt be equally acceptable to France, for either might serve her purposes; but they would not do for Russia. The best guarantee against them lay in the preservation of those parts of the constitution which reserved to the Estates the control of taxation and the decision upon peace or war. Catherine for the present had her hands too full with other business to give much attention to Sweden, and Osterman was therefore ordered only to try to secure a balance of parties, and to cultivate good relations with all, pending the moment when the empress should be ready to take Swedish problems seriously in hand.[30]

That moment came in October 1763; and it coincided with the final victory of Panin in his contest with Bestuzhev for the direction of foreign affairs. Panin's success meant that Russia would seek the friendship of Prussia rather than of Austria; and it meant also that her Swedish policy would be shaped by a man whose twelve years' mission to Stockholm (1748-60) had given him unrivaled insight into Swedish affairs. The change was reflected in the decisions of the so-called October Conference, and the rescripts which flowed from it.[31] Osterman's reports from Stockholm had by this time convinced Panin that the constitution had become odious to the nation, and that there was a real danger that an absolutism might be established on a basis of popular approval. Some reform had therefore become necessary, as the only means of preserving it. What was needed, he thought, was a return to something like the original text of 1720, but with a guarantee that in future the fundamentals should not be capable of change at the whim of a single Diet. No doubt the constitution had been declared immutable from the beginning; but it had also included a fatally elastic clause which permitted the Estates to "interpret," and even to "improve" it, provided that such improvements were consonant with its spirit.[32] Abuse of this clause had made it possible to upset that constitutional balance which it had been the intention of the men of 1720 to secure. The crown had been stripped of too much power; the Senate had enlarged its authority at the expense both of crown and Estates. Only if a proper balance were restored could Sweden be relied upon to be an inoffensive neighbor. The remedy, perhaps, was some act of state which would entrench the fundamentals, and make it impossible to alter them by snap majorities: the Estates should "once for all" be deprived of their supposed right to interpret and improve. No doubt such a reform would restore some measure of power to the crown, particularly in the matter of appointment to offices; but this was preferable to running the risk of permitting existing malpractices to continue until a revolution of popular indignation swept the constitution away. The real gainers, in the long run, would be the Estates, rather than the monarchy; the real losers, the Senate.

Thus by the end of 1763 Russia, like France, had determined to work for a revision of the constitution; and both were seeking to remove the accretions of 1756. But for very different ends; and therefore also upon very different lines. France aimed at making possible a strong government, capable of ensuring that Sweden should be a serviceable weapon in her hands; Russia aimed at a system of checks and balances which should ensure that no such government was possible. France sought above all to strengthen the Senate at the expense of the Estates; Russia, to strengthen the Estates at the expense of the Senate, but at the same time to preserve the constitution by making it less easy to alter. Both had necessarily to offer some crumbs of comfort to the Court, for both needed the help of the Court's partisans for the success of their program; and both had come to realize that the impotence of the monarchy was a mistake. As it was the aim of French policy to draw Hats and Court into alliance, so it was the aim of Russian policy to preserve and strengthen the alliance of Court and Caps which had been in existence since 1755.

The new line in Russia's Swedish policy had scarcely been adumbrated before efforts were made to enlist the cooperation of other powers in pursuing it. The first attempt was made with England. The draft treaty of alliance which Buckinghamshire sent home in August 1763 included a secret article which would have pledged England to collaborate with Russia in maintaining a balance between the Hats and their opponents.[33] This was to phrase Panin's intentions so cautiously as to be positively misleading; but even so the cabinet in London would have none of it. Very different was the case in regard to Prussia. Frederick's relationship to Lovisa Ulrika certainly enlisted his interest in the fate of the Swedish monarchy; more than once he had given his sister advice as to how she might improve her position, and had even made some effort to assist her on his own account.[34] But he was the last man to allow family feeling to come between himself and the interests of his country. The opening of negotiations for a Russo-Prussian alliance gave Catherine an opportunity to find out how strong the ties of blood really were; and she speedily discovered that they would not be permitted to stand in the way of Frederick's desire for an alliance with Russia. When she suggested that they cooperate against the French party in Sweden Frederick agreed without hesitation;[35] he did his best to persuade his sister that Panin was her friend;[36] and when the fateful treaty of alliance was concluded, on 11 April 1764, it included a secret article which bound the two contracting parties to work together against that party in Sweden (*sc*. the Hats) which had upset the "equilibrium" of the original constitution, and against the foreign powers which supported them. They agreed further that "dans le cas où l'on auroit à craindre un renversement *totale* [my italics] de la forme du gouvernement de la Suede," they would consider themselves free "de se concerter plus particulièrement sur les moyens de détourner un événement si dangéreux et de maintenir la susdite forme du gouvernement en son entier afin de conserver par là la tranquillité générale et principalement celle du Nord."[37] By which there is no doubt that they intended the maintenance of the constitution as it stood in the Form of Government of 1720.

(iii)

Among the rescripts sent out to Russian diplomats after the October Conference was one to Korff in Copenhagen. To Panin it might well seem a reasonable assumption that his new line in Sweden would commend itself to Bernstorff. Denmark, after all, viewed Sweden very much as Russia did—as a potential aggressor; it was a prime principle of Danish politics to keep Sweden innocuous; and in order to make sure of that, Denmark pinned her faith, as Russia did, to the maintenance of the Swedish constitution. Nevertheless, Panin's approach was cautious. Korff was instructed only to try to persuade Denmark to cooperate to save the Swedish constitution, which might be considered to be in danger from internal discontent, from the demand for an Extraordinary Diet, and from the insidious proposals of France. Panin perhaps hoped that the cooperation of Bernstorff in these matters might open the way to Denmark's inclusion later in some sort of Northern League; but of these larger hopes he for the present said nothing.[38] Even this, however, was to take altogether too much for granted.

Bernstorff's policy was rooted in conviction and experience; it was no light matter for him to direct it at short notice into new courses. It rested on two basic principles.[39] One was to keep Denmark at peace; the other was to put an end to the constant threat from Holstein (a threat which had acquired terrifying force from the moment Elizabeth adopted Karl Peter Ulrich as her heir) by arranging an agreed exchange of ducal Holstein for Oldenburg and Delmenhorst—a project to which it will be convenient henceforward to refer by its Danish name of *Mageskiftet*. An absolutism in Sweden would challenge both these principles: the former, because an absolute monarch would be free to declare war on Denmark, uncontrolled by his Estates; the latter, because he might be expected to denounce the agreements which the Hats and France had forced upon Adolf Fredrik in 1749. Bernstorff therefore erected the preservation of every letter of the Swedish constitution into a major Danish interest; though he had no word to say against the king-yoking additions which had been made to it in 1756: rather the contrary.[40] The slightest concession to the crown, the slightest relaxation of the restrictions which had been imposed on the monarchy, presented itself to his alarmed imagination as the opening of the floodgates of disaster. For Panin's ideas of a rebalanced constitution he had therefore at first no understanding; and any suggestion that the changes of 1756 be swept away would have appalled him.

Moreover, strong practical and sentimental reasons made him regard Panin's approach with surprise and suspicion. For Denmark, after all, was the ally of France, and with a short interval in the late 1740s, had been a French supporter since 1742. Danish finances relied heavily on French subsidies, and Denmark had lived in comfortable security as the inactive partner in France's Northern System. In Sweden, too, no less than in Europe, France appeared to Bernstorff as the necessary friend; for France was the patron of the Hats, the guardian of the constitution, and (not least) the enemy of Lovisa Ulrika, for whom Bernstorff entertained a hatred which amounted to an obsession. On the other hand, Russia in Danish eyes appeared as a dangerously expansive power, whose alarming designs on East Prussia had been thwarted only with great difficulty, and whose rulers were ominously linked with Holstein.[41] The deposition of Peter III, which appeared as a species of divine intervention in answer to the anguished prayers of Fredrik V,[42] had come only in the very nick of time to save Denmark from a Russian onslaught which (on land, at all events) she was in no condition to withstand. Bernstorff was in general a placable man; he was ready enough for friendly relations with Russia—as he was, indeed, for friendly relations with anybody, except Lovisa Ulrika; he had during the Armed Neutrality shown his willingness to collaborate with the Russian fleet; above all, he desired an agreement with Catherine on *Mageskiftet*. But historically he felt himself on the side of France. Certainly he was no French puppet: his policy, as he truly said, was neither "French" nor "English"; it was Danish.[43] Under his leadership Denmark retained, in great measure, her independence; but undeniably she had hitherto stood with her feet in the French camp. In the conditions that developed after 1763 she could hardly collaborate with Russia in Sweden without quitting it. Not that Bernstorff felt any great inclination to quit it for the sake of winning Catherine's friendship. He was far from sure that she had abandoned the policies of her late husband, and he had at first no great respect for her character or abilities. He thought her lacking in those solid qualities which he admired; inclined (no recommendation, this) to ape Frederick the Great; worst of all, too sympathetic to her relative in Stockholm.[44] In an analysis of Russian policy written as late as 15 November 1763—a mere fortnight before Panin's initiative reached him—Bernstorff expressed the opinion that Catherine's object was to reduce Sweden to the status of a vassal kingdom, with Adolf Fredrik as a constitutionally unlimited Russian viceroy.[45] Ten days after that he could write that only the death of Augustus III of Poland had saved Sweden from subjection to Russia.[46]

Bernstoff's attitude to the internal politics of Sweden reflected these principles and prejudices. He had certainly no desire to see an unduly powerful neighbor to the north of him; but equally he could not wish that Sweden should be so enfeebled as to fall under Russian domination. From Denmark's point of view it perhaps did not greatly matter whether the Senate in Stockholm were Hat or Cap, provided Sweden preserved her liberty and her constitution; but in practice he was the unwavering supporter of the Hats. He might lament their decrepitude and be disgusted by their tergiversations; but with characteristic magnanimity he was ready to overlook what he could not help: Denmark, he wrote, "leur pardonnera d'être ingrats, pourvu qu'ils soient libres."[47] Close ties of friendship, dating back to 1752, bound him to C. F. Scheffer; and Scheffer was Denmark's warmest and steadiest friend in Stockholm: if ever there were to be a Danish party in Sweden, Scheffer would inevitably be its nucleus.[48] This Bernstorff never forgot. He felt towards Scheffer, and in less degree towards a handful of other leading Hats who shared Scheffer's views (Ekeblad, Palmstierna, C. O. Hamilton) a sense of personal obligation; and even when things were most difficult, and when he and Scheffer had politically drifted apart, he was chivalrously prepared to risk compromising himself and his policies in order to give them assistance and rescue them from their enemies.[49]

Such, then, were Bernstorff's political axioms; and such they had remained, without important modification, since his accession to office in 1750. At first sight it might seem that Panin had therefore but a slender chance of obtaining a hearing for his overture. But in fact the chance was better than it seemed. The rock of principle upon which Bernstorff took his stand was already showing cracks and fissures; the day was not far distant when it would crumble beneath his feet. Whether Panin knew it or not, all was not well between Bernstorff and Choiseul. Temperamentally they were an ill-assorted pair: Choiseul's impatience, arrogance, and rashness contrasted forcibly with Bernstorff's sober wisdom and dignified self-control;[50] and during the war his snubs and reproaches had stretched Bernstorff's forbearance to the limit. In 1759 Bernstorff had written "Il n'y a que la France seule qui puisse le [Fredrik V] détacher de la France";[51] but by 1763 Choiseul and Praslin between them had very nearly done it. Both treated Denmark as France's pawn; both showed a wounding indifference to Danish interests and Danish feelings. In the great crisis of 1762, when it seemed that Denmark might be overwhelmed by Peter III, Choiseul had responded to Bernstorff's desperate appeals for help by vague assurances and the promise of a trivial cash contribution to be paid by driblets too late to be of any use. Bernstorff felt he had been let down.[52] There were large arrears of subsidy due from France, of which the Danish treasury stood in urgent need: Choiseul and Praslin attempted, with transparent sophistries, to repudiate the obligation.[53] It was scarcely possible, by 1763, to believe that any effective support from France was to be expected in the matter of *Mageskiftet*. If this was so, nothing remained but to reach, somehow or other, an amicable settlement with Catherine, and the sooner the better.[54] Thus on many accounts Bernstorff was deeply dissatisfied with his ally. But more disturbing than all the rest were the reports which kept coming in from Schack in Stockholm; reports which indicated that France was no longer sound on the question of the Swedish constitution. The prospect of a change in French policy on this issue moved him to utter a solemn warning: the maintenance of the Swedish constitution, he wrote, was the strongest tie which bound France to Denmark; if Choiseul were to weaken on this issue, if it should seem that he was prepared to countenance absolutism in Sweden, Denmark would not hesitate to do her utmost to oppose him.[55] And this warning was followed by another: in the event of France's continued refusal to pay Denmark's arrears, that refusal would be resented, "and might have far-reaching consequences."[56]

Panin's overture thus arrived at a moment when Denmark's relations with France were under considerable strain. As yet there was no breach; and when the alliance ran out in March 1764 Bernstorff still "asked nothing better" than its renewal on the old terms.[57] Even when Praslin, in response to this insinuation, offered only alliance without subsidies (an offer which was rejected) Bernstorff could say, and probably mean, that he would never oppose France while she defended the Swedish constitution.[58] But it was just here that the shoe pinched. If Breteuil were really engaged in talks with Lovisa Ulrika, where now could Denmark look for help in preserving Swedish "liberty"? No longer, perhaps, to her old friends the Hats, of whom strange reports were coming in to Copenhagen. France's defection seemed to be accompanied (or preceded) by that of her Swedish protégés. If this was so, there was something to be said for taking a look at Panin's proposals, which at least professed to be designed for the constitution's preservation; and there was a great deal to be said for it, if somehow it could be used to pave the way for a bargain which would give Denmark *Mageskiftet*. For the sake of that enormous gain, even a risk in Sweden might be worth taking.

Nevertheless, when early in December 1763 Korff broached Panin's proposals, Bernstorff would say no more than that he would consider them in consultation with his "associates." By this expression it turned out that he meant his friend C. F. Scheffer. Scheffer showed neither surprise nor resentment that Bernstorff should contemplate discussions with his party's most dangerous enemy: on the contrary, he encouraged Bernstorff to continue the talks, as a means of keeping the Hats informed of Catherine's plans.[59] But what finally decided Bernstorff to enter into serious negotiations with the Russians was probably not Scheffer's approval, but rather the conviction, borne in upon him by Schack's recent dispatches, that the Hat leaders, and Scheffer himself, were no longer to be relied upon to defend the constitution in its integrity. And so on 7 January 1764 the order went out to A. S. von der Osten, the Danish minister in St. Petersburg, to begin talks with Panin.[60] Three days before the Franco-Danish alliance lapsed, on 12 March 1764, Osten was ordered to propose to Panin a treaty based on a renewal of the alliance of 1746 and the guarantee of the Swedish constitution; to which was added, by way of a *bonne bouche* for the empress, a promise of support in the forthcoming Polish election.[61] More than a year would elapse before the negotiations crystallized into a formal alliance; but from the spring of 1764 Denmark was plainly halting uneasily between two systems, old animosities and old friendships contradicting the new realities, deeply ingrained habits of thought obstructing the slow set of the political current. It would be almost two years before Schack adapted himself to the new ways of thinking and ceased to flavor his dispatches from Stockholm with their customary seasoning of Hat-inspired gall.

(iv)

However much Bernstorff might lament it, the stories of the Hats' defection were true: his friends in Sweden had drifted from their old moorings. A sense of the defects and abuses of the constitution had never been peculiar to the partisans of the Court and the ministers of foreign powers. The old Caps had long lamented the glosses which the Hats had put upon the letter of the law in order to buttress their control of the state. Among the Hats themselves, many of the leaders had been expressing disquiet, off and on, for the last twenty years.[62] In the late forties, during their political honeymoon with Lovisa Ulrika, they had even promised reforms; though since Adolf Fredrik's accession they had chosen to forget about it. By 1760, however, it was impossible for thinking men to close their ears to the clamorous complaints about the way the constitution was abused: the success of Pechlin's attack upon the Senate rammed home the lesson. Patriots of different opinions were at one in longing for an end to bribery, party strife, and foreign intervention, and in a desire for honest government and disinterested leadership on a bipartisan basis. The trend of opinion was reinforced by the self-interest of party politicians. To Fersen, for instance, some kind of party truce, or even a bipartisan government, offered a hope—perhaps the best hope—of escaping the political nemesis which now overhung the Hats. It would, of course, involve a reconciliation with the Court, which in 1760-62 was virtually the leader of a powerful opposition. But this too might be a measure of prudence. In 1762 the crown prince was seventeen; and already he seemed to many, for good or for ill, to be the man of the future. Patriots and idealists could see in him the country's best hope of extricating itself from the political slough in which they were laboring; friends of the constitution looked forward with dread to the prospect of his accession, judging him a much more formidable enemy than either his passionate and capricious mother or his harmless necessary father.[63] A settlement with the Court in good time, while Adolf Fredrik still lived, might be worth a few sacrifices.

From this complex of origins arose the idea of a "Composition." At an early stage it comprised not only a party truce and bipartisan government, not only the ending of corruption and some measure of "economical reform," but also a revision of the constitution on lines acceptable to both parties, and therefore also to the Court. No one wished—or at least, no one avowed a wish—to give the crown powers which might open the way to absolutism. Even the queen professed to have abandoned any such ideas. Her professions may well have been sincere; for she felt the shadow of her son falling across her shoulders. The crown prince had already begun to emancipate himself from his mother's political leading-strings. He disliked her friends the Caps, whom he considered unpatriotic, and he had disliked her temporary alliance with Pechlin still more. For her foreign policy he had no sympathy; he detested England and adored France. He saw the remedy for Sweden's ills in a large increase in the powers of the crown; and so far he and his mother were at one. But Lovisa Ulrika knew herself too well not to be sure that her haughty and domineering temper would never suffer gracefully the relegation to political insignificance which would be her lot if she should survive her husband; and in the conflict with her son which she already foresaw she had no wish to give him more advantages than she need. Absolutism had few attractions for her if it were not to be she who would wield it; fewer still, if it were to be exerted against herself.[64]

Such, at least, were the reasons which she avowed in private for the relatively moderate attitude which she adopted towards the various initiatives for a Composition.[65] In effect, she asked no more than the destruction of that Act of State which in 1756 had rehearsed the misdeeds of herself and her husband, the payment of the debts of the crown, and a return to the letter and spirit of 1720. Negotiations with the Hat leaders began, on Fersen's initiative, in January 1762. In February, and again in May, the talks were broadened to include some Cap leaders; and their first result was an agreement to bring the Diet to an early close. But this was not all: it was agreed also that there should be an end of party strife; that a reasonable number of Caps be admitted to seats on the committees of the Diet; that the Act of State be destroyed; that both sides would abjure corruption in future. The question of Sweden's foreign policy was to be deferred until peace with Prussia should be made; the revision of the constitution was to be discussed once the Diet was over.

The Act of State was duly destroyed; the Senate, when the Diet ended, was nearly evenly balanced between Hats and their opponents; and in July 1762, in strict secrecy, talks on the constitution began: there were too many fanatical defenders of "liberty," too many men of the cast of Pechlin, too many members of the Diet who had a vested interest in abuses and corruption, for the negotiations to bear the light of day. Even among the participants there seems to have been a certain doubt and hesitation. Perhaps this was more true of the Caps than of the Hats;[66] for as the talks proceeded it looked increasingly possible that their upshot might be the defection of the queen to the Hat side. Their political principles allowed the Hats to make a rather better bid than their rivals; and that bid might well prove sufficiently tempting to induce Lovisa Ulrika to swallow a French system in foreign policy.

Even on the Hat side the negotiations were not entered into with uniform alacrity. C. F. Scheffer, in particular, was at first reluctant to engage in an agreement with the Court. For years he had been Bernstorff's constitutional watchdog. He had expounded the unadulterated doctrine of constitutional orthodoxy in a textbook specially written for his royal pupil;[67] and though he had also on one occasion committed himself to the view that what Sweden needed was a Diet which would undertake to defend liberty against the Estates themselves,[68] and though he had himself been one of Pechlin's victims in 1761, he found it difficult to surmount the distrust of the queen which had struck such deep root in 1756. Perhaps, too, the increasing esteem which he and the crown prince felt for each other may have made reconciliation with Lovisa Ulrika more difficult.

Yet, difficult or not, it took place. Throughout the autumn of 1763 Scheffer drew steadily closer to the Court. On 13 December Osterman reported that Fersen hoped to use him to persuade Denmark to accept the negotiators' plan of constitutional revision. A fortnight later Schack informed Bernstorff that Scheffer had told him that he hoped to achieve a full reconciliation between the Court and the Hats; that the queen had promised adherence to their policies at home and abroad; and that it was expected that she would collaborate with them in forwarding an agreed program of measures to be introduced at the next Diet, the object of which would be to limit the arbitrary power of the Estates.[69] By the beginning of 1764 such progress had been made that Fredrik Sparre could note in his journal that Fersen and Hermansson were in high favor at court, and remark that society no longer seemed to be split between Hats and Caps, but all lived well with each other.[70] An optimist might be forgiven for thinking that the next Diet would see a reform of the constitution by common consent of both parties. To Bernstorff, these developments were of course profoundly alarming; and in April 1764 his last constitutional anchor dragged, when Scheffer, with something less than perfect tact, and perhaps a good seasoning of author's vanity, forwarded to him for his comments (and, he seems to have hoped, for his approval) the plan of constitutional reform which he had drawn up in collaboration with the other Hat leaders.[71]

Scheffer's plan[72] began with a lengthy exordium which Bernstorff must have found disagreeable reading, and which amounted in fact to a broad indictment of the evils for which the Form of Government had been responsible. Invoking the authority of Montesquieu to justify the principle of separation of the legislative from the executive power, as necessary to avoid a tyranny, Scheffer declared for some form of balanced constitution. Some counterpoise must be found to the excessive power of the Estates; but it would be dangerous to seek it in the monarchy alone, nor could it simply be entrusted to the Senate, for they too might abuse their powers. The remedy seemed rather to be a triangular balance. The monarchy should be strengthened by giving it full control over all appointments save membership of the Senate. The Senate would have the right to refuse to execute decisions of the Estates which violated the constitution. King and Senate would have reciprocal vetoes upon proposals which trenched on the rights of the one or the other. The Senate's approval would be required before the Diet could consider any matter affecting the nation as a whole. And the Diet would be precluded from making any change in the "loix fondamentales" on the pretext of "correction ou d'explication" unless with the previous assent of king and Senate.

It will be seen that this plan embraced the ideas both of d'Havrincour and of Panin. On the one hand, the strengthening of the authority of the Senate was the central point of France's program; on the other, the preventing of a constant fiddling with the constitution for party purposes was a salient feature of the reforms desired by Russia. To the Court it offered real and solid advantages, advantages which might well be sufficient to secure the queen's adhesion.

It was doubtful whether the Caps could do as much. They do not at this stage seem to have digested their ideas into any formal scheme which could be weighed against Scheffer's; but they had given some indication of the lines upon which their leaders were thinking in a couple of memoranda which they had sent to Catherine in December 1763, the authorship of which has been conjecturally assigned to Senator C. G. Löwenhielm and Colonel T. G. Rudbeck, respectively.[73] Löwenhielm's memorandum (if indeed it was his) after emphatically listing all the things the king might not do, conceded the point that the explanations, alterations, and abridgments of the prerogative which had occurred since 1720, if repugnant to the spirit of the constitution, might be swept away. Rudbeck's suggested more significant alterations: the executive power would lie with the king; the Senate would be reduced to an advisory and informative body. But the constitutional center of gravity was clearly to be in the Estates, whose extensive functions would include, in particular, sole control over taxation, and over peace and war.

Thus both the Hat and Cap leaders were thinking in terms of a return to 1720; and both were disposed towards some system of constitutional checks and balances. Both offered some inducements to the crown; neither gave any opening for the establishment of an absolutism. The Cap scheme looks almost like a prescription for a clash between king and Diet, with the Senate in no position to act as a buffer between them; the Hat scheme would have tamed the Diet, and might have turned Adolf Fredrik into a monarch not too different from George III. But these after all were no more than plans excogitated in secret by a handful of leading politicians. Neither had as yet any sanction or authority from the broad mass of party members, who were still ignorant that there were any negotiations at all. It was very uncertain how far the leaders could count on the adherence of their supporters on such matters as the ending of corruption, the intermission of party strife, the sharing of power—to say nothing of any project for constitutional reform. The commingling of the old Caps with the Court by no means reflected any necessary community of ideas: it was a mere accident of history; and this was to the full as true of the more recent cooperation of the Hat leaders with Lovisa Ulrika. As to the queen herself, contemporaries were divided in their opinions as to whether she was moved by a genuine desire to end party strife, and sincere in her disavowal of absolutist aims, or whether after all she was only an ambitious and capricious intriguer, upon whose word no reliance was to be placed. Since the surviving evidence, though extensive, is incomplete and capable of differing interpretations, a similar lack of unanimity has manifested itself among later historians.[74]

(v)

Whatever the answer to these questions, one great fact confronted Goodricke on his arrival. Since the day in 1758 when he was first appointed minister to Stockholm, Swedish politics had undergone a major transformation. The identity of Court and Caps could no longer be assumed. The constitution had become a central issue in politics. Bernstorff might cling nostalgically to the hope that Denmark could stand where she had always stood in relation to Swedish domestic affairs, and to international alignments; but he was mistaken. Russia, France, and even Prussia now looked on Swedish politics with new eyes: their objectives might remain substantially unchanged; their tactics had altered. The inescapable initial question for Goodricke (and for Sandwich) was therefore to define the attitude of Great Britain to these developments.

Goodricke's original instructions had been directed narrowly to one specific end: the rendering of assistance to Prussia. It was not intended that he should allow himself to be diverted from it by speculating in Swedish party struggles. On his way to Sweden he had been warned against "meddling": by Holdernesse, by Knyphausen, by Frederick himself.[75] Yet it was perhaps only human that as he observed the Swedish political scene at short range he should have felt the itch to meddle after all. It did not take him long to realize that those in Sweden who professed English sympathies were not uninfluenced by the prospect of being able to tap supplies of English gold, and that the prospects of an effective return for any such outlay were very uncertain.[76] Yet if the French party in Stockholm were ever to be overthrown and an English party put in its place, that could hardly be done simply by sitting still. The creation and management of such a party would certainly be expensive: more expensive than an English Secretary of State might be willing to approve.[77] Nevertheless he could not help toying with the idea: in June 1759 he wrote to Lord Royston that if he had £20,000-£25,000 at his disposal he would undertake to break the French system without even quitting Copenhagen.[78] In March 1762, no doubt under the influence of the impression caused by the parliamentary reverses of the Hats, he risked proposing to Bute the formation of "a party that should be properly British at all events, composed of several well-intentioned persons . . . who are against the French, and also against an absolute government, who are neither attached to our enemies, nor to the Court"—an undertaking which might entail (as he modestly added) "some small expense."[79] He was perhaps not unduly surprised when no reply was vouchsafed to this suggestion.

By 1762, there can be no doubt, Goodricke had been bitten by Swedish politics, and looked forward with pleasurable anticipation to the day when he should be able to play the part of party manager, vote-manipulator, and distributor of judiciously placed bribes. Already he grasped the fact that there was a real distinction between Lovisa Ulrika and her friends (whom his original instructions bade him cultivate) and the remnants of the old English party of the Caps. In January 1759 he distinguished between the hot partisans of the Court and "the sensible men of the anti-senatorial party" who did not share the Court's desire for political confusion, but who did hope to see the power of the Senate reduced, and did not wish to see an absolutism.[80] It was these "sensible men," the survivors of the old Cap party, who had been the old English party and with their heirs would be the basis for a new. Occasional dispatches from Goodricke give us the names of those whom he considered to be the leaders of this group: Löwenhielm, Rudbeck, Adam Horn, Lagerberg, Wrangel, Liewen, and the two veterans of 1739, Counts Bonde and Bielke, now triumphantly restored (in December 1761) to their places on the Senate.[81] The distinction between Court and Caps was revealed in the autumn of 1763, when the old Caps tried to persuade Goodricke that the Court (as against themselves) no longer desired his coming to Stockholm.[82] In 1761 an old Cap such as Adam Horn could indeed still write of himself and his friends as being known as "the King's party";[83] but in fact they had little in common with the Court except fear of Hat persecution and a desire to be revenged upon their enemies. The Court had never, until its breach with the Hats at the beginning of the fifties, been an English party; and only then because its oppressors were the friends of France. For the economic and constitutional ideals of the old Caps it had little understanding, and still less for those of the new generation of Caps which was waiting in the wings; and to Lovisa Ulrika the Caps' Walpolean ideas on foreign policy certainly made no appeal.

Already, then, Goodricke had realized that it would not do to lump Court and Caps together;[84] and it would be surprising if he had not also perceived that he might have to choose between them. To the cultivation of the queen prescribed in his original instructions there could of course be no objection, provided she remained constant in her hostility to France; but if she did not, England would be driven to turn to the "sensible men of the anti-senatorial party" if there were to be an English party at all. This would mean, almost inevitably, a greater or less commitment to their domestic programs: in particular, to economical reform, the reduction of the power of the Senate, and resistance to the aggrandizement of the crown.

Goodricke had no great opinion of the Swedish constitution. He did indeed succeed in inducing Bernstorff to believe that he was an "admirateur si passioné de la Liberté que je crois qu'il ne se laissera jamais employer à la faire perdre à une Nation";[85] but if his conduct in Sweden in the end turned out to be eminently satisfactory from Bernstorff's point of view, that was not because he had any special predilection for "liberty" as the Swedes understood it: on the contrary. "If there be a government in Europe where the people are equally free and happy as in England," he wrote, "it is certainly not the Swedish one."[86] But their freedom and happiness were not his business. When Bernstorff spoke forebodingly to him about the danger of absolutism, he had enough sense and discernment to reply that an absolutism seemed more likely to come from the nation's disgust at the Diet's abuse of its powers than from a royalist coup d'état.[87] Whether Sweden was an absolutism or an anarchy it was enough for him that it should not be "French." He knew that the question of the constitution was likely to be an issue in Swedish politics; he knew that the old Caps had views about the constitution which did not square with those of the Court; he reported, not without concern, that the Hat leaders seemed to be trying to establish good relations with the queen.[88] But there is nothing to suggest that he had before his arrival any idea of the negotiations for a Composition, and still less of the changed posture of France and Russia in regard to the Swedish system of government.

Lord Sandwich was no better informed. Of the change in French policy inaugurated by d'Havrincour's memoranda he seems to have known nothing; of Panin's new course the only hints had come in the Russian draft of an alliance of August 1763, and in a dispatch from Buckinghamshire of 6 April 1764; and both of these were misleading, since both spoke of Russia's aims as being to achieve a balance between the French party and its opponents, whereas what Panin was really after was a balance, not only of parties, but of constitutional powers. Perhaps if Lord Sandwich had realized that his information was defective he would not have felt that it made much difference. For indeed it is very unlikely that he intended taking any active part in the Swedish imbroglio. No doubt broader considerations of policy suggested that cooperation with Russia in Stockholm would be a useful way of building up a credit in St. Petersburg; but this was something which seemed far from urgent in the spring of 1764, when Anglo-Russian relations tended to be rather wintry than otherwise. The negotiations for an alliance had come to a dead stop, and Sandwich professed to think them at an end.[89] The negotiations for a commercial treaty were stopped likewise. Neither, it seemed, had much hope of coming to life again as long as Lord Buckinghamshire remained ambassador. Panin's obvious assumption that Russia held all the trumps,[90] and that England had no option but to beg for an alliance on such terms as Catherine might think proper to offer, had in January produced from Sandwich a vehement retort which by no means exhausted a feeling of irritation which had been banking up for some time.[91] Ministers were exasperated by Panin's reiterated observation that Russia would be taking risks by engaging in an alliance in view of the probability that an Anglo-French war could hardly be long delayed.[92] And if they were piqued by Panin's attitudes and assumptions, they can hardly have been mollified or convinced by the arguments he put forward to inveigle England into Swedish domestic affairs. In September 1763 Panin had told Buckinghamshire

> That when England proposed to enter into an alliance with Russia, it must be with a View of interesting herself in the affairs of the North, . . . for unless we secured Russia against the attacks of her neighbours, she would be very little able, upon any emergency, to assist us.[93]

But Sandwich and his colleagues could raise no more than a tepid interest in the affairs of the North, least of all if it meant involving the hard-pressed exchequer in large disbursements. Buckinghamshire told Panin frankly that "it was not to be expected that she [England] would engage in a further expense, especially in a cause where her interests were not concerned." To this Panin answered that "surely it was an object to England to prevent Sweden from becoming an absolute monarchy, and that if Russia was not easy with regard to the state of that country and Poland her alliance would be of very little consequence to any European power."[94] But this was an argument which was both disingenuous and unperceptive. "An absolute monarchy. . . "? What Panin was afraid of was not an absolute monarch, but a too-powerful Senate. He understood very little of the way the minds of the English ministry worked if he supposed that he would make their blood run cold with his talk of an absolutism. In the first place, an absolutism looked improbable in 1764; in the second, it was by no means so obvious as Panin assumed that it was "an object to England" to prevent it. Any effect which Panin's argument about Sweden might have made was certainly compromised by his linking Sweden with Poland: once admit that the domestic affairs of Sweden called for action by England, and it would be difficult to resist the application of the argument to Poland also. And upon that, at any rate, ministers were unshakable; though here too Panin deluded himself into thinking that they might be cajoled or browbeaten.[95] In itself, absolutism in Sweden was to England a thing indifferent: what mattered was whether the absolute sovereign was, or was not, "French." And to the best of Sandwich's knowledge in the spring of 1764 Lovisa Ulrika was not.

Goodricke therefore began his ministry under considerable disadvantages. He found a political situation which he cannot have foreseen, and of which it was impossible that he should have informed himself. He was responsible to a Secretary of State to whom these complex tangles had to be patiently explained, and to whom (in the beginning, at all events) they must have seemed only marginally relevant. Above all, in a situation in which he would of necessity be acting in more or less close accord with the Russian minister in Stockholm, he was hampered by the fact that Anglo-Russian relations were compromised by a fundamental lack of understanding between the two countries. That lack of understanding in the end ensured the failure of all attempts to conclude an Anglo-Russian alliance. But in Stockholm, and perhaps in Stockholm only, the distrust and suspicion which it engendered was mitigated or masked by harmonious cooperation in dealing with day-to-day problems, and participation in a common struggle. It is true that this proved insufficient to remove the differences which divided London from St. Petersburg; but it was nevertheless a considerable achievement. And it depended, for such success as it enjoyed, very largely upon the character and talents of Sir John Goodricke.

CHAPTER III

The Overthrow of the "French System," April 1764–January 1765

If foreign ministers looked upon Copenhagen as a social desert, they did not make similar complaints about Stockholm. There the trouble was not tedium, but rather the hectic pace of life and the high cost of living.[1] By the middle of the eighteenth century Stockholm had grown to be a city of perhaps 70,000 inhabitants. For more than a century it had been expanding beyond the confines of the old town, huddled on the islands which separate the Mälar from the tidewater: to the north, and more recently to the south, extensive new urban areas had come into existence, climbing the steep banks of Söder and the rocky obstacle of Brunkeberg. Nature had endowed the place with charms to which Copenhagen could offer no competition: the romantically broken terrain, still almost unviolated by the leveling activities of the town planners, the scatter of islands and islets, the pines and the birches, water everywhere—stretching wide and blue to the west under the pale Swedish sunlight, pouring tumultuously in spring floods through Slussen and Norrströmmen, malodorously stagnant in Nybroviken during the dog days, icebound for many a mile in winter. It was still an acceptable poetic license for Carl Michael Bellman to imagine Naiads in Brunnsviken. Despite the respectable size of its population, the open country still lay very close to the doors of its citizens, and was indeed plainly visible to most of them. Solna was a village well beyond the city limits when Bellman's Naiads spouted festive cascades over its church tower; Årsta to the south, Täby to the north, where today an egalitarian society plants building complexes of terrifying immensity—these were deep in the country. The long perspective of Drottninggatan was closed by rocks and copses; and the northern customs-post at the city limits stood where today Wenner-Gren's Helicon provides a wellspring and a hospice for the visiting researcher.

Nature had indeed done more for Stockholm than man, whose contributions to the environment were not impressive. The old town was picturesque enough, but it was crowded and insanitary; Södermalm was in the spotty adolescent stage of urban development;[2] Norrmalmstorg,[3] having lost most of the architectural ornaments of the age of Queen Kristina, and not yet having acquired those of the age of Gustav III, offered little to impress the visitor. A single bridge connected Norrmalm with the old town: for the rest, movement from shore to shore depended upon the exertions of a corps of Amazonian boatwomen, whose muscular development and resourceful vocabulary perhaps evoked, for an English traveler, nostalgic memories of Covent Garden porters. A fair proportion of the houses were still of wood; and recurrent fires raged through the city, despite the constant vigilance of the municipal fire service: when Goodricke came to Stockholm he must certainly have seen traces of the great conflagration of 1759, which laid waste great tracts of Södermalm; and perhaps there were still visible signs of that other outbreak which in 1751 had swept through St. Klara's parish and destroyed most of the scientific collections of Daniel Tilas. Architecturally, Stockholm had little to compare with the glories of Copenhagen. Tessin's Royal Palace, now complete after being half a century a-building, dominated the city; overtopping its only rival, the House of the Nobility, and confronting, with historical propriety, the palaces of Fersen and Pechlin on Blasieholm. Across the elbow of Strömmen they glared at each other, symbols of the latent clash between monarchy and aristocracy. The high pomps of aristocratic baroque architecture had by this time paled into a common (and often commonplace) classicism: of the splendors displayed in Erik Dahlberg's *Suecia Antiqua et Hodierna* little remained, and of that little most has now been turned into government offices. Much has vanished altogether: of Fersen's house, as of Pechlin's, no trace remains—though to Pechlin, at least, the Grand Hotel may be esteemed no unworthy successor. As in politics, so in architecture, the monarchy has proved to have a higher survival value than the aristocracy; and Stockholm is still ringed—as it then was—by a semicircle of small royal palaces within easy reach of the city center: Karlberg, Svartsjö,

Ulriksdal, with Haga soon to be added to the list, and Rosendal to follow after that. Above all Drottningholm, exquisite in its park, mirrored in the waters, speaking French with a Swedish accent, still evoking the brittle culture of the court of Lovisa Ulrika. Thither, on many occasions in the future, Goodricke would go, as all the polite world then went, by water: in a sloop in summer, or by sledge when the Mälar was frozen.

Whether at Drottningholm or in the city, whether at Court or in private society, Stockholm in the 1760s was not a place where a diplomat was likely to be dull. Rapid inflation, financial crises, national misfortunes, the uncertainty of the domestic political situation, gave it a tense and feverish quality, and drove men to enjoy themselves as they might until the crash came. It came for some in the autumn of 1763, when great financial houses tottered, and humble civil servants who had lived fashionably beyond their means went bankrupt, or sought refuge from their creditors in Norway. Despite sumptuary ordinances and restrictions upon imported luxuries, men lived lavishly, partly perhaps from a sound instinct to put their money into realizable durables, partly at the bidding of fashion, partly in a spirit of reckless fatalism. The upper ranks of society, and above all the Court, were thoroughly permeated with French culture. They read the latest French publications, they attended performances—in Bollhuset, or in the little theatre at Drottningholm—of the French theatrical company which Lovisa Ulrika had imported; they went once a fortnight to the *ridotto* or the *bal masqué*; they promenaded in the Royal Garden on Norrmalm. Some of their diversions had an endearing quality of arcadian innocence, characteristic of the age: their delight in picnics, sledge parties, fireworks, illuminations and transparencies, festive salvos on name-days, garlanded arches with floral devices, leafy arbors, occasional verses, "surprises." But many diversions were less reputable: beneath the veneer of French culture the coarse grain of the native timber showed through; at the highest levels polite conversation demanded *équivoques* which might have shocked Queen Caroline. Lower down the social scale, where the veneer was absent, amusement tended to rely on the basic constituents of food, drink, and women. It was the age of *brännvin* (the Swedish snapps), as in contemporary England it was the age of gin. One ate inordinately, one drank frenetically, one spewed, slept it off in the gutter, and drank again. No Swedish Hogarth produced a "Gin Lane"; but on the other hand no English Bellman produced a *Fredmans epistlar.* In England, the flood of gin provoked the artist's reprobation; in Sweden, the greatest poet in the language floated his genius on a tide of liquor. It is no accident that the Swedish tongue is enviably rich in the vocabulary of drinking. In the eighteenth century the worship of Bacchus became a literary cult; and much poetic ink was spilled upon the nice question as to whether it was to Bacchus or to Venus that the preference should be given. In the cellars of the old town, in a dozen city taverns made famous by Bellman's lyrics—*Lokatten, Altona, Rostock, Tre Remmare,* and the rest—at rustic pubs just outside the city limits such as *Stallmästaregården* (which still survives), the men of the sixties, harassed and unhopeful, forgot the uncertainties of the present in carousals, and celebrated the delights of oblivion in anacreontic verse.

But one thing they could never forget: politics. The charged atmosphere of life in the capital, the restless fever of pleasure seeking, the vaguely fin-de-siècle feeling, no doubt derived in part from economic uncertainties of a kind with which our own age is familiar; but also, certainly, from politics. As the Hat régime began to crack and crumble, the forces of repression which it had used so ruthlessly weakened in its hands. The spies and delators, the extraordinary parliamentary commissions—their day was over, at least for the present; and the opposition, the Caps and the Court, liberated from the restraints of actual bodily fear, began publicly to attack the principles and methods of their former oppressors. From 1764-65 dates a strife of parties of extraordinary vehemence: to find a parallel in English history one must go back to the Exclusion Crisis, or at least to the closing years of Queen Anne. Party politics seemed now to permeate the whole of life, from pothouse to pulpit. Stockholm was soaked in politics; the air was tainted with it. When the Diet was sitting it developed a febrile intensity in the brawling taverns where parliament men foregathered according to their party color, where party leaders mapped out parliamentary maneuvers, debated the purchase of votes, and fortified their backwoodsmen's ardor for "liberty" by liberal infusions of *brännvin* at the expense of the ministers of France or Russia. A more violent contrast with the contented, apolitical torpor of Copenhagen, dozing peacefully in the arms of absolutism, could scarcely be imagined.

(i)

Such was the capital which was to be Goodricke's home, with only one brief interval of leave, for the next nine years. The constant eddy of intrigue made navigation hazardous for a newcomer, and Goodricke might be thankful that his instructions enjoined him to act in close association with Count Osterman—a pilot who had already had four years' experience of these tricky waters.[4] Goodricke lost no time in making himself known to him;[5] and luckily for both of them they got on well together from the beginning. It was essentially a business partnership: it would be impossible, from Osterman's dispatches, to form any idea of what Goodricke was like; and personal traits are almost as rare on Goodricke's side. Contemporaries, and some subsequent historians, have dismissed Osterman as an insignificant personage, without initiative or talent; but this is certainly not the impression produced by the record of his mission to Stockholm. From that record he appears as a shrewd, skillful, and resourceful minister, adept in the arts of party management. At all events, they made a good team: Osterman was able to give initial guidance, and he found in Goodricke the only minister (at least for a couple of years) upon whose cooperation he could rely with certainty; Goodricke on his side was able to pass on to Osterman the invaluable secret intelligence intercepted by the Hanoverian post office in Nienburg.[6] But while Osterman had by this time the advantage of a good general notion of his country's policy in Sweden, Goodricke as yet hardly knew whether England had a Swedish policy or not: it was part of his task to help to decide that question. Of Russia's intentions he certainly knew almost as little: nothing of Catherine's attitude to the Composition, nothing of her views on the constitution. But at all events he knew that Russia was the enemy of the French system which it was his business to destroy, and that was enough: on that basis he could without a qualm assume a certain community of aim, and engage in concerted action with his colleague.

Goodricke began his mission with energy and *brio*: the dammed-up impatience of six years of waiting was released; and a flood of dispatches—sixteen of them by the end of June—recorded his obvious enjoyment of his new situation. His instructions had ordered him to produce an analysis of Swedish politics and the state of Swedish parties: within little more than a fortnight after his arrival he had sent off a lengthy, detailed, and acute report to the office.[7] Sandwich, in spite of himself, was impressed: on 22 May he wrote commending his envoy's zeal and activity;[8] on 19 June he conveyed to him His Majesty's "highest appreciation of the good use you have made of your time in gaining such an insight into the affairs of Sweden, as well as of the many judicious reflections you have given in your account of them."[9] The tribute was unusually cordial, and it was well merited; but Goodricke could scarcely have earned it unless he had also made good use of his time in Copenhagen.

Nevertheless, he found the situation more complex at close range than it had seemed at a distance. At the moment of his arrival the great issue demanding decision was whether or not to summon an Extraordinary Diet. The alarming state of the finances certainly made an early meeting of the Estates urgently necessary; and the Court desired it in order that the promises which Lovisa Ulrika had received from the Hats might be implemented without delay. Lovisa Ulrika certainly believed that the Hat leaders, and especially C. F. Scheffer, had pledged themselves that when the question was debated by the Senate (as it was due to be, at the beginning of May) they would come to a firm decision. But from the point of view of the Hats there were arguments why a decision should in fact be postponed. It was always possible that France might come forward with an offer in regard to the arrears due from her which might obviate the need for an Extraordinary Diet, and thus assure them of a continued tenure of power at least until the Diet should meet at its normal time in the autumn of 1765. They clung to delusive estimates which made the financial position appear less disastrous than it really was; they persisted in hoping that something might turn up; some of them would not have been sorry to postpone—and by postponing ultimately to evade—the fulfillment of the promises which in their weakness they had felt bound to give to the Court.[10] Considerations such as these prevailed; and almost the first of Goodricke's dispatches reported that Scheffer had broken his word to the queen on this issue: at the meeting of the Senate on 1 May the Hats had agreed to defer a decision until 1 September. Lovisa Ulrika was understandably annoyed; and Goodricke could report with satisfaction a check to that *rapprochement* between Court and Hats which had already aroused his anxiety.[11]

This was the situation in which he produced for Sandwich his analysis of Swedish parties and politics.[12] Of parties he saw three:

> first, that of the Court, in which are included our Friends, and those of Russia; Secondly, the French Party; in which I reckon the Friends of Denmark . . . ; and lastly, Mr. Hopken's Party; consisting of the Malecontents and disobliged of all sides, who have, as yet, adopted no system in foreign affairs, but appear, secretly, well-inclined to Us; The difficulty will be to reconcile them with the Court. . . .

But party lines had recently become blurred as a result of the Composition, of whose origins and purposes Goodricke now furnished the first account to reach London. He made the point that though the Composition passed over foreign affairs in silence, it was not therefore irrelevant to England's objectives in Sweden; for though it was known only to a few, it nevertheless disgusted some of the Court party "who call themselves the English party"—by which he clearly meant the old Caps. Thus the distinction between "our Friends" and the party of the Court, which he had already drawn in Copenhagen, was found on a closer view to be valid. And the personalities fitted satisfactorily into the categories to which he had already assigned them: "the chief of our Friends in the Senate," he reported, was Count Löwenhielm, who would probably break with the Court if Lovisa Ulrika should turn to France.[13] Other members of the Senate of similar views were Bonde, Horn, Lagerberg, and Friesendorff. There were thus five English partisans in the Senate, against nine for France and one for the Court; so that if it were possible to count on the two votes of the king, the winning over of only one of the nine would deprive the pro-French party of its majority. The Composition had at least been of service in that it had made possible the giving of offices to the enemies of France: there were now twice as many of them in post as three years ago. Of these the most important was Colonel T. G. Rudbeck, "who is very remarkable by his constant refusal to accept money from either side"; "a firm and sensible Man, and has as much influence in the Assembly of the States as any man can command without money." As to Höpken, the feud between him and C. F. Scheffer was still a polarizing influence; and the Hat leaders did their best to poison Lovisa Ulrika's mind against him. "Our Friends," it appeared, could not make up their minds about Höpken, though clearly he was a possible ally if they should break with the Court; and they suspected that his support for the summoning of an Extraordinary Diet might well be attributable to his hope of recovering his place on the Senate.

By the time Goodricke had reached this point in his analysis, the three parties with which he had started had insensibly become four; or at least, he could see four leaders, each with different aims: "One seeks for more power to the Crown"—by which he meant Colonel F. C. Sinclair, who had now the chief place in the queen's confidence; "another to preserve his own influence, and the French system"—Fredrik Axel von Fersen; "a third to re-establish himself at the head of affairs"—the would-be revenant A. J. von Höpken; and "a fourth to espouse our interest and to govern by that"—which was a slightly tendentious way of describing Löwenhielm. From the very beginning, then, the question Goodricke had to resolve was whether he ought, or ought not, to encourage the formation of an "English party," distinct from that of the Court. Its nucleus, if it came into existence, would obviously be the old Caps: those Senators, headed by Löwenhielm, whom he had listed as "our Friends," together with Rudbeck and some lesser lights whom he also named. For a time, at least, the hope of recruiting Höpken and his associates remained alive; and it would die hard. But it proved as delusive in 1764-65 as in 1761-62. Goodricke soon found that the queen had put an absolute ban upon collaboration with Höpken;[14] and the behavior of his following during the elections of the coming autumn was to confirm the old Caps in their suspicions of him.[15] Höpken in fact was to prove, as he had proved before, a political *cul de sac*.[16]

The crucial question, then, was the relations between the Court and the old Caps. The vital distinction between them had been clearly pointed out in that *Pro Memoria* which had been given to Goodricke either just before or just after his arrival, and which seems to have been drawn by a member of the Court party (perhaps by Lovisa Ulrika herself);[17] for it had there been admitted, by implication, that the queen's desire for a strong monarchy was not shared by the Caps, who still clung (more pertinaciously, perhaps, than the Hats themselves) to the constitution as by law established. No doubt a man like old Count Bonde, who "thanked God that he had lived to see an English minister again in Stockholm," was "English."[18] But was the queen "English" in the same sense? And even if she were, would she be prepared to tone down her ambitions in deference to Cap susceptibilities? Goodricke realized very well that it was a French object to drive a wedge between Court and Caps; just as it was a Russian object to keep Court and Hats apart. But Osterman's approach to the problem could not be Goodricke's. For Osterman one determinant was the attitude of either to the constitution. For Goodricke the only determinant was their stance on foreign affairs. For the Hats, the French system and their own political survival were ultimately more important than the preservation of the constitution in its integrity. For the Caps, emancipation from France was a precondition for power, and was thus the prime, but by no means the only consideration. As to the queen, her essential objective was an increase in the power of the crown, and (whatever her professions) a French or an English system was of subordinate importance. What no one could be sure of was how far the queen's professed desire for domestic tranquillity, constructive reform, and an end to the corroding strife of factions, was genuine or not. On the whole, they thought not. She was obviously a highly intelligent woman; but it required some faith to believe her honest. As a politician, even giving her generous credit for good intentions, she was clearly too clever by half. But because they doubted her sincerity they made it difficult for themselves to assess her actions fairly and objectively: too often they were disposed to put the worst construction on maneuvers which might quite as easily have arisen from embarrassment, or from the hope of saving what was best in the Composition, as from the ambition and the propensity to intrigue which they were inclined to assume underlay everything that she did.

Goodricke had his first meeting with the king and queen on 7 May.[19] Lovisa Ulrika had certainly more serious reasons for looking forward to the encounter than those which she had communicated to Frederick in a characteristically flippant letter of 6 January:

> J'ai une très grande [curiosité] de voir Goodricke. Je voudrais pour la rareté qu'il fût étourdi et pétillant comme les Français, ce qui ferait l'opposite de notre ambassadeur de France, qui véritablement a les avis et les manières de Jacques Roastbeef.[20]

It is to be feared that Goodricke did not conform to these specifications; but at least he came with warm personal recommendations from his friend Borcke, whom he had employed as a canal through which to pay his homage in advance.[21] We have no direct evidence of the initial impression they made on each other; but it seems probable that Goodricke distilled some of his into the survey of the political situation contained in his dispatch of 11 May. By the end of the month he had certainly reached the conclusion that France's bid to capture the queen must be taken seriously: Rudbeck, in whom he was placing increasing trust, warned him of the danger.[22] Outwardly, no doubt, she appeared ostentatiously favorable to France's enemies;[23] but these appearances might well be calculated to deceive. If Breteuil's attempts to secure Lovisa Ulrika were to be parried, England would need to produce a counterbid, and what that counterbid should be, what advantages should be held out in order to retain her, must depend in large measure upon how much Russia was prepared to tolerate in the way of inducements. It was essential to have this information, essential to be clear about Catherine's intentions in Sweden: English policy there would probably depend upon it. If the bid were inadequate, Goodricke's only resource would be the old Caps: already he was beginning to think that England would have to form a party of her own.[24] But in such a case the Caps themselves would look to England and to Russia for rewards and compensations. What advantages could be offered them if they should be victorious? What precisely was Russia's policy in Sweden? Osterman apparently could give no satisfactory answer to these questions; which is not surprising, for in truth he did not know what the answer was, except in very general terms: from 14 May to 8 November he received not a single rescript from Panin, for Panin was preoccupied with the affairs of Poland, and subsequently with the conspiracy of Mirovich in favor of the imprisoned Ivan VI.[25] Goodricke therefore asked Sandwich to put specific questions to the Russian government: (i) "who the Persons are whom Russia proposes either to exclude, or to push forward?"; (ii) what Russia wished England "to propose to Sweden, or endeavor to lead them into?"; (iii) "what advantages they would be willing should be granted to the Court in the next Diet?" Some advantages there must certainly be, if the Court were to be retained, and perhaps the price need not be, from Russia's point of view, prohibitive; for his information was that "they ask no more, than that the King's crown should be placed upon the same footing as it was between 1720 and 1738, [and] that whatever the Queen might have thought formerly, Her Majesty did not now . . . seek the Government absolutely, for certain family reasons"—a discreet circumlocution for her jealousy of the crown prince.[26]

A fortnight later he was able to transmit to Sandwich a memorial from Lovisa Ulrika herself, in which she professed her predilection for England, related the genesis and progress of the Composition, outlined her aims, emphasized their moderate character, and asked for English money in order to attain them.[27] On 1 July she reinforced this appeal. In a secret interview at Karlberg, after renewing her protestations of attachment to England, she revealed to Goodricke that France was making attractive offers of constitutional reform, and would shortly be proposing a settlement of the subsidy arrears based upon a reciprocal undertaking by Sweden to provide warships for the French navy in time of war. In response to this barely disguised threat Goodricke went so far as to ask how much money she would expect England to provide. The queen referred him to Sinclair for an estimate. A fortnight later Sinclair provided it, and it did not err on the side of modesty: £15,000, it appeared, would be needed to do the queen's business—or to prevent France from doing it for her. It is perhaps not surprising that Goodricke neglected, for some time to come, to pass on this formidable figure to his government.[28] Nevertheless, he was not discouraged: rather the contrary. To Buckinghamshire he wrote on 13 July: "The more I get acquainted with the affairs of this country, the more I see of the practicability of changing its system in foreign affairs, provided we do not want money to bestow on those who are willing to take it."[29] A not insignificant proviso. It remained to be seen what view Lord Sandwich would take of it.

(ii)

On 6 November 1764 Baron von Nolcken sent a dispatch to his government from London summing up his impressions of the development of British policy in Sweden since the time of Goodricke's arrival there. He reported that when he first came to London he found that Goodricke was quite unknown: he had not at that time the confidence of his minister, and was considered to have exceeded his instructions, especially in regard to the negotiations with Faxell which led to his being given leave to proceed to Stockholm. Sandwich had almost excused himself for not sending a person of more distinction as Britain's representative. "And at that time," Nolcken added, "I am positive that Sandwich did not intend to meddle in Sweden's internal affairs." But Goodricke, who felt he must enlist his masters' interest, had made his reports so full as to induce the British government to think that Sweden might really be detached from the French system; and he was now praised for the detailed and precise information which he sent home. It was still doubtful how far the ministry might be prepared to allow itself to be involved; but it was at least probable that they would provide against the possibility of a change of system by maintaining a party in Sweden.[30]

It is difficult to resist the impression that this was a shrewd and accurate account of what really happened. On Goodricke's standing with his government at the time of his departure from Copenhagen it is obviously right: how should a man who had been out of England since 1750 be known at home? What interest had this obscure Yorkshire baronet at his command, other than that of Sir Joseph Yorke? How could Sandwich forget that he had been virtually confronted by Goodricke with a *fait accompli* in the negotiations with Faxell? Goodricke himself must have been well aware how the land lay. He came to Sweden with a lively sense of the need to justify his appointment, and a strong determination to interest Sandwich in the business of his mission: hence the remarkable energy of his beginnings, and the fullness and vigor of his early dispatches. Within a couple of months of his arrival it is clear that he had modified Sandwich's ideas about Sweden, and greatly altered his opinion of his envoy. By the middle of June, at latest, Sandwich had become aware that he had in Stockholm a minister whose dispatches would repay perusal, and whose suggestions were worth attending to. On 22 May, in reply to Goodricke's remark that if there were to be an English system in Sweden money would have to be forthcoming, he had written in terms so general that it is clear that he had not yet really brought his mind to bear on the question as to what England's relations with Sweden were to be:[31] he urged caution, deprecated any loose schemes, and added an ill-considered remark to the effect that British promptitude in providing £10,000 for Lovisa Ulrika in 1761 should be evidence that his government would not be backward in supporting a good cause. Of the broader aims of English policy he then said no more than that it was "the intention of this Court to concur in whatever may effectually establish such a System, as may preserve a true Balance of Powers in the North, and from thence, extend itself to the rest of Europe." But under the impression of the dispatches which reached him from Stockholm in the next few weeks he rapidly brought his view of Swedish affairs into sharper focus. He began to realize that something more might be required than merely to "concur" in some as yet undisclosed line of action which would "preserve a true Balance of Powers in the North"; and also to see that even if British action should be confined to concurring, it would be as well to get some idea of what he was likely to be asked to concur in. Goodricke was reporting that the French were putting money into Swedish corruption;[32] Buckinghamshire was expressing the view that Catherine, owing to her Polish commitments, might be so short of money as to have none to spare for Stockholm.[33] The underlying implication that the British government might have to foot the bill was not pleasant. Then, on 15 June, arrived Goodricke's dispatch of 1 June, with its three specific questions about Russian policy and objectives in Sweden. They must have appeared to Sandwich peculiarly pertinent. That same dispatch also contained the very disquieting news of France's probable attempt to secure a treaty with Sweden which would put Swedish warships at her disposal. This was a possibility which in 1763 had left Sandwich comparatively unmoved, though he might perhaps have remembered that one of the objects of the Convention of St. Petersburg in 1755 had been to prevent Sweden's lending warships to France. But by the summer of 1764 the situation had altered. Europe was now buzzing with rumors that Austria was to be invited to join the Family Compact: a preliminary, perhaps, to France's renewal of the struggle with England.[34] To the still-unresolved disputes about the Manila ransom and the expenses of French prisoners of war were now added more serious causes of tension: Spain's action against the logwood-cutters in Honduras; D'Estaing's provocative attack on Turks Island.[35] All Europe knew that the French navy was rapidly recovering from the losses it had sustained during the war: Frederick the Great in February had been retailing a report that France had just bought twenty warships from the Swedish government at a high price.[36] The first lord of the admiralty, Lord Egmont, was certainly not happy about the position; and in April he had demanded alterations in the king's speech, on the ground that the provision for the navy was not, as the king was made to say, "ample."[37] His objections beat ineffectually on the adamantine parsimony of George Grenville; but on Sandwich, who had once been an active first lord himself, and for whom the navy was a hereditary interest, they may well have made an impression.

Nevertheless, Sandwich still regarded the prospect of becoming involved in Swedish politics with distaste. He seems to have had a deeply rooted fear of being overreached. He believed that England and France had been equally the dupes of adroit Swedish politicians, who played on their reciprocal fears and used them to line their own pockets.[38] Even after receiving Goodricke's report that France was preparing a naval treaty he could not resist the reflection that England's "friends" in Sweden might be privily encouraging the idea so that they might be in a better position to put pressure upon him to give them money for their party funds.[39] He could still on 19 June write nebulously that it would be useful if Goodricke, "in forming your Plan, . . . can begin it before a Variety of interests at present subsisting in Sweden, can have Time to understand each other, and insensibly to adhere, and gain a consistence which would, afterwards, be difficult to dissolve"—a sentence from which Goodricke must have been hard put to it to extract any precise meaning, other than that Sandwich was prepared to accept that there must be a plan of some sort.[40] Still, he was clearly impressed by Goodricke's dispatch of 1 June; and four days after its arrival in the office he wrote urgently to Buckinghamshire at St. Petersburg, asking him to extract from Panin explicit answers to Goodricke's interrogatories on Russian policy.[41]

It was to be a very long time before he received any satisfactory answer to this inquiry; and in the meantime he had to steer his Swedish policy by such lights as Goodricke afforded him. Of these, to be sure, there was no lack. By the end of June he was in possession of the substance of the queen's Memorial. His reply was virtually silent on the topic upon which Goodricke could have done with some guidance, for he said nothing of England's attitude to the relations of Court and Caps: that, he obviously considered, was a problem of minor tactics for the expert on the spot.[42] But it was typically morose on the financial aspects. "There is no doubt," he wrote sourly, "but that Great Britain, as usual, will be looked upon as the Power which is to be charged with the Whole of that Burthen," and that her friends would take care to make it as large as possible. Goodricke was therefore ordered to "engage in nothing whatever without further instructions from hence." To this stark directive there was, however, a qualifying corollary: if Sandwich was still skeptical about the value of spending money, at least Goodricke had convinced him of the necessity of activity of some sort. So the letter went on:

> But you are not, upon this account, to quit the Field, without trying your whole Strength, and Judgment, in defeating the Intentions of the Enemy. If a thorough change of System in the Swedish Councils . . . cannot be obtained, without engaging this Country in Expence which She can, by no means, undertake, consistent with Her Interests, You will throw every Difficulty in the Way, which may perplex the Designs of the Opposite Party, and make the Purchase of the Swedish Alliance as burthensome to France as possible; for, next to overturning the French system, it is the Interest of Great Britain that France should continue her subsidies to Sweden, provided they exceed (as frequently has been the case) the Utility and Value of such an alliance.

Which was tantamount to an instruction to do nothing, but to take care to be successful.

Still, Sandwich was at least beginning to think of where a Swedish policy might lead him. He wanted to know how "those who will take the lead" (whether old Caps or partisans of the Court was in this context evidently a matter of indifference to him) proposed to live after they had won their victory at the expense of the hard-pressed Civil List. Sweden, after all, had barely remained solvent with the aid of French subsidies. A defeat of the French system would naturally entail the end of French financial support. What then? Did they suppose that England could somehow be relied upon to fill the gap? This was indeed to touch the tender spot, and Goodricke can have had no difficulty in taking the point. But he must have found it extraordinary that his circumstantial account of his secret interview with the queen, with its combination of appeals for unspecified sums and thinly veiled threats of seeking the aid of France, had not provoked even so much as a passing comment from the Secretary of State. Perhaps Sandwich was waiting for Goodricke to let him know just how high Sinclair would pitch his financial demands. At all events, he refrained from committing himself on a basis of incomplete information. On 3 August he was asking for a more explicit account of what "those persons" who looked to England for assistance would require in the way of monetary aid, and (equally important) what they might be expected to do for England in return—if, indeed, they were likely to be strong enough to do anything.[43] Would they be likely to ask for an Anglo-Swedish treaty of alliance? Would they clamor—intolerable thought!—for a subsidy? Would they expect to be indemnified for forfeited French arrears?

This wary disinclination to buy a pig in a poke might perhaps have inhibited the efforts and damped the ardor of any minister less buoyant than Goodricke. But Goodricke increasingly came to believe that the French system could be broken; and he was too hardheaded not to appreciate Sandwich's reluctance to be inveigled into a bad bargain. His masters in Whitehall had asked, reasonably enough, for estimates. By 28 July he was in a position to provide them. He had already warned Sandwich that if money were provided he must have a reserve always in hand, "to purchase half a dozen votes in the Secret Committee, at half an hour's warning;"[44] and he had cautioned him, as he was to caution Sandwich's successors at intervals for the next seven years, that to embark on a campaign of corruption, and then to be forced to stop short in the middle for lack of funds, was a mere waste of money. But now he moved from these minor points and general considerations to actual figures.[45] It was undoubtedly the case, he conceded, that "our Friends" at first had counted on receiving a substantial subsidy from England in the event of a victory at the elections. But he believed that he had convinced them that they had no hope of getting it. They would be content, he thought, with bribery at the Diet; they would take the line that France's subsidies, even if they had been honestly paid, were not worth the risk of being involved in a new war, and that Sweden's resources, if properly managed, were adequate to support her in time of peace without foreign aid. So far, Sandwich could feel reassured. But Goodricke's estimates for corruption were anything but reassuring. Sinclair's figure, it appeared, was £20,000; Löwenhielm's, £40,000, "to be quite sure"; Osterman believed that £30,000 would be the minimum.[46] On the other hand "my confidant, who is the only person upon whom I can perfectly rely in these money matters" (by which Goodricke undoubtedly meant Rudbeck) thought that England might manage on half what France gave, whatever that might be.[47] Some indication of its possible amount was provided by the report that the Hats had asked Breteuil for a credit of 300,000 livres before 1 September, and as much again before the Diet met.[48] As to the method of supply, Goodricke suggested a credit upon Hamburg, to be drawn on piecemeal, in small parcels only, so that the operation could at any time be stopped without great loss if it showed no chance of success.

These alarming figures arrived in Sandwich's office on 24 August, and excited his lively indignation. He bottled it up for nearly three weeks; and when at last he gave vent to it, on 11 September (after having taken the opinion of the duke of Bedford),[49] his objections turned out to be not so much to the general principle of investing in Swedish corruption, as to the exorbitancy of the demand and the possibility that England might be left to bear more than her fair share.

No reply had as yet been received from Panin to his request for an answer to Goodricke's questions, and he was beginning to suspect that it was Catherine's intention to shuffle off the financial burden on to English shoulders. His reaction was to slip back into his former negative attitude. He was not prepared, he wrote, to "charge the Nation with a Load of Expence, in support of continental Measures, suggested to us by another Nation, who, tho' their Interest is much more nearly concerned, seems as yet no ways inclined to take a forward Part either in the Trouble or Charge of this Undertaking." Goodricke therefore was to confine himself to causing the maximum of embarrassment to the French, and to make them pay as dearly as possible "for any imaginary advantage they may wish to obtain."[50]

Nevertheless, Sandwich was more concerned about the situation than these orders might suggest. It was all very well to write as though Sweden was a Russian rather than an English interest; but even for Sandwich that was not the whole truth. For not long before Goodricke's estimates arrived in London, Sandwich had received an intercept of a letter from Praslin to Breteuil which made it certain that the reports of a projected naval treaty were true.[51] And this made a great deal of difference. So much so, that on 29 August he wrote to George Grenville a letter which makes it plain that he had begun to give serious consideration to substantial expenditure in Stockholm.

> It is absolutely necessary for me to give soon a final answer, whether any money should be given for the support of what is called our party in Sweden; it is very plain that France means, if they carry their point in the approaching Diet, to engage part of their fleet for future occasions, and if they should execute that scheme (considering the lowering aspect of our affairs both with France and Spain), should not we be justly blamed for not having used every means in our power to obstruct their measures? Turn this matter in your thoughts, and let me know your determination when we next meet.[52]

Grenville replied two days later that he would think of it. Whether he did so, and to what effect, seems not to be recorded; but it may perhaps be inferred that he was not wholly intransigent. For Sandwich's instructions of 11 September, discouraging as they were, did contain the intimation that if only he could be assured of Russia's bearing a fair share of the expense, he would be prepared to review his decision.

But from St. Petersburg came only cloudy answers, which were no answers at all; and it was in fact Goodricke who made up Sandwich's mind for him. In a dispatch of 31 August, received in London on 15 September, Goodricke filled in the detail of the estimates of 28 July.[53] On the assumption that the coming Diet would last six months, Goodricke estimated for a total expenditure of somewhere in the region of £25,000. This sum he broke down into nine different heads, divided into two categories: a preliminary expenditure, up to and including the elections to the Secret Committee, which always took place soon after the opening of the Diet; and "keeping the party together" thereafter. If the friends of England should be unsuccessful in the elections to the Secret Committee, they had agreed with Goodricke that no more expense should be incurred; but once again Sandwich was warned that if they gained early successes it would be a waste of money to cut off supplies thereafter. Much of the cost of keeping the party together was attributable to the need to subsidize the members from Finland, who were "so poor, that they are neither able to pay their journey, nor to maintain themselves here, sometimes not even to buy a Coat to appear in, without help." To all these expenses there must probably be added the cost of a present to the queen. The total cost of the preliminary expenditure he estimated at £8,000; so that if Russia could be assumed to pay a half share, England would have to find £4,000 initially, and perhaps a further £9,000 after the Diet had begun.

There was an appearance of solidity about these calculations which must have impressed Sandwich favorably. He had asked for exact figures, and on the whole he had got them. He had got something else too. For at the end of his dispatch Goodricke slipped in a sentence or two of ground-bait. If the friends of England should be successful, he wrote, he confidently hoped to gain from them commercial concessions so valuable as easily to outweigh the expenditure upon corruption, even if the whole amount were to be borne by Great Britain. This was a hint to make an English minister's eyes glisten. Here at last was the prospect of a quid pro quo, and a particularly tempting one. If Sandwich's Swedish policy should ever have to be debated in Parliament, if its issue should be a treaty of some sort, nothing would be better calculated to make it go down with MPs than the prospect of commercial advantages. For the balance of trade with Sweden was notoriously unfavorable, and for half a century no British statesman had been able to do anything to improve it.[54]

Whether for this reason or for some other, the effect of Goodricke's dispatch upon Sandwich was immediate. Within three days of its arrival he had congratulated Goodricke on the precision of his estimates, foreshadowed an alteration in his instructions, and eagerly urged him to send details of what commercial concessions he had in mind.[55] Considerations of trade, it now appeared, must form the "constant Tenour" of his instructions, no less than the preservation of Sweden's navy from the clutches of France.[56] It would seem then that England had after all very real interests to defend or advance in Sweden, apart from the axiomatic principle of foreign policy that French influence was to be combated wherever it might be met with. This, it is worth recalling, was by no means the position from which Sandwich had started; and it was wholly irreconcilable with the argument, which he was to develop passionately in the months that followed, that Sweden was essentially a Russian interest rather than an English; that Goodricke had been sent to Sweden simply to oblige Catherine; that any English exertions in Stockholm arose purely from goodwill towards Russia; and that Russia might therefore fairly be expected to bear a much heavier share of the expense than England.[57] The fear that England might be left committed to bearing the whole expense, or the major portion of it, was exaggerated; but with Sandwich it soon became almost an obsession. He was reluctant squarely to face the question whether the Swedish navy, or possible trade concessions, or the winning of Sweden from France, were not in themselves a sufficient justification for spending money. Nor, apparently, did it occur to him that if they were indeed British interests, then the Russians might fairly claim that by supporting the Caps they were paying to secure those interests, as well as their own.

(iii)

Hitherto, the question of what share of expense England was to bear had been hypothetical, or at least not immediate; for it was not yet certain that there would be an election before the autumn of 1765. The situation was transformed by the meeting of the Senate which took place on 3 September. Osterman has left a vivid description of how the Hats tried to the very last to escape acknowledging the truth which stared them in the face, and how argument raged high among members of the Senate even in the sloop which was carrying them to Drottningholm for the meeting.[58] But in truth there was no escape from their predicament. The French had cut off subsidies when Sweden made a separate peace with Prussia, and were only now tardily resuming them; the arrears which Sweden claimed were being used by France as a lever to extort political advantages; the treasury was almost empty; the Bank would advance no more money; the value of the Swedish daler was falling every day on the international exchanges. Whatever the consequences for their party, an Extraordinary Diet could no longer be avoided. The Hats had met parliament in worse situations than this in the past, and had managed to wriggle out of them; and some of their leaders believed they could do it again. There were even optimists who believed in a victory at the elections, a short Diet, and the rapid implementation of some of the reforms foreshadowed in the Composition with the Court.[59]

At all events, there was to be an Extraordinary Diet. The Estates were convoked for 15 January; the election campaign began at once. The decision for an election in its turn imposed a decision on Sandwich as to how large a share in that campaign he was prepared to engage for. The news reached him on 22 September, a week after Goodricke's detailed estimates of 31 August.[60] Those estimates, as we have seen, convinced him that some expenditure in Sweden was a British interest; but the question now was, the immediate question, what share of the election expenses could England reasonably be expected to bear? How was he to be sure that he was not being cheated? How could he be certain that the king was not being asked to dive into his pocket for what were really Russia's concerns?

Goodricke had very early provided him with two guidelines in this matter. He had suggested (4 May)[61] that any expenditure should be by carefully regulated installments, so that in the event of ill-success it could be cut off at any moment with the minimum of wastage. He had at the same time observed, in a somewhat casual sentence, that he supposed that Russia would pay an equal share. On both these points Goodricke remained consistent: he told Osterman in May that England would probably be prepared to go halves;[62] he wrote to Buckinghamshire in June that the prospects were encouraging, on the assumption that Russia paid a half share.[63] The plan for expenditure by installments was twice approved—and once, indeed, advised—by Rudbeck;[64] though on the latter of these occasions Goodricke commented to Sandwich that the plan might run into difficulties if Russia and England were to pool their financial resources. Nevertheless, it was reiterated in the estimates which he sent home on 31 August.[65]

Sandwich laid fast hold of Goodricke's guidelines. From the moment he made up his mind to spend money in Sweden, he made up his mind also that it must be spent on a 50:50 basis. Having brought himself to accept Goodricke's plan for a preliminary expenditure of £8,000, his immediate concern was to make sure that Russia would make herself responsible for £4,000 of it. Goodricke was ordered to press Osterman for assurance on this point;[66] Buckinghamshire was instructed to extract a promise from Panin;[67] Sandwich himself cross-questioned the Russian minister Gross.[68] Goodricke's confident answer to this all-important enquiry did not arrive until 5 November;[69]

Buckinghamshire's (fortunately for Goodricke) not until twelve days later;[70] but from Gross Sandwich was able to obtain reassuring promises without delay, on the basis of which he magnanimously condoned an unauthorized expenditure of £250 laid out by Goodricke for corruption in the Stockholm elections[71] —the less unwillingly, perhaps, since Goodricke had been careful to inform him that he had personally seen Osterman pay out an equal sum before he had given any money himself.[72] Perhaps Sandwich would not have been quite so ready to oblige if he had known that Goodricke, in his anxiety to persuade his government to be generous, had willfully misled him about the outcome of his discussion with Osterman. In his dispatch of 12 October Goodricke had reported that on the question of the sharing of expenses Osterman had held the same language as Gross. But Osterman informed Panin on the same day that he had requested Goodricke to give no answer at all until he had had a chance of receiving further instructions from St. Petersburg; and to this Goodricke had agreed, promising to keep the King's Messenger some days longer in Stockholm in the expectation of their arrival. By 22 October he had felt he could keep him no longer. The Messenger had accordingly been dispatched; but Goodricke had assured Osterman that the only reply he had sent home was to the effect that Osterman had no instructions, and could thus give no answer to the inquiry.[73]

From Goodricke's point of view, this cavalier disregard for the truth seemed to serve its purpose. On 6 November, the day after Goodricke's reply reached him, Sandwich accepted in principle the plan for a preliminary expenditure of £4,000;[74] on 9 November a draft for that amount was forwarded to Goodricke by Messenger, with an anxious exhortation to make quite sure that Osterman did not cheat him.[75] One day earlier Panin had sent off to Osterman a draft for 50,000 rubles.[76] Since the ruble was then worth about 4/3d,[77] Russia had not merely matched Sandwich's £4,000, but had provided not far short of three times that sum. But of this Sandwich as yet knew nothing; and he was able to relax into a state of magnanimous self-approval: his orders to Goodricke, he felt, should have convinced Panin of England's good faith; our friends in Sweden would be inexcusable if they failed to show a proper appreciation of such generosity.

It was not long, however, before this agreeable complacency was rudely disturbed. First, by Goodricke. If Goodricke had not agreed to hold his Messenger at Osterman's request, his dispatch of 16 October might probably have reached Sandwich before the draft for £4,000 was sent off, instead of eight days afterwards. If so, it would have been in time to prevent the Treasury, in all innocence, from committing a regrettable gaffe. For the draft for £4,000 which was then sent by Sir George Amyand to Goodricke was drawn on the firm of Jennings & Finlay of Stockholm, and a more unsuitable channel of payment could not have been selected. Jennings & Finlay was among the two or three largest exporting firms in Sweden, dealing mainly in the iron trade to Great Britain.[78] Jennings was an Ulsterman, Finlay a Scot; but both had become naturalized Swedes, and neither was prepared to allow his British origin to affect either his business or his politics. For Finlay Goodricke still had some degree of trust;[79] but in Jennings he recognized a political adversary of no small importance.[80] For Jennings was at the very heart of Hat politics. The Hats had ennobled him, as they had ennobled not a few entrepreneurs, and he had become a man to be reckoned with in the House of Nobility.[81] In the last Diet he had been a member of the Secret Committee. He was linked by a spreading web of marriage connections with leading Hat families (he and Pechlin had married sisters);[82] he was a leading light in the Iron Office; he was well in with the Bank, and borrowed heavily from it; and he was closely linked with the consortium of Hat financiers which professed to manage the rates of exchange in Sweden's interest, and certainly managed them in their own. In Goodricke's dispatch of 16 October he had warned Sandwich against sending remittances to him through Jennings & Finlay, and had told him why.[83] But the warning came too late; and when the draft for £4,000 at last reached Stockholm (which was not until 7 December) Goodricke had the mortification of knowing that his political adversaries would within twenty-four hours be exactly informed of the limits of the financial resources at his disposal.[84] In this difficulty there seemed only one thing to do. He had already, it appears, risked spending £1,000 in advance of his instructions (which was just as well, since they failed to turn up at the same time as the draft), so that in fact only £3,000 remained available to him. Of this he drew for £500 on Jennings & Finlay, as a blind, informing them he needed no more; and drew for the remaining £2,500 on another Anglo-Swedish merchant, John Fenwick, who had served as his agent when Goodricke was in Copenhagen, and who was as zealous a partisan of the Caps as Jennings of the Hats.[85] This solved the immediate difficulty; but it was felt that something should be done to put pressure on Jennings to acknowledge the calls of patriotism. The government tried to get at him through his London agent, Robert Macky, and also through Clifford of Amsterdam; and Goodricke himself remonstrated with him on his conduct. But Jennings altogether declined to be intimidated. "He held a pretty high language, saying, he had withdrawn himself entirely out of commerce, being resolved to live upon his estate here, and to act as He thought best for the good of this Country, where He was established"; he had always been pro-British, and would support a connection with Britain whenever she proposed to Sweden the same advantages that France gave, but never until then; adding that "there were a Hundred more in the House of Nobles of his opinion. . . . In short, he spoke as if he was Master of the whole government."[86] Goodricke retired, baffled; comforting himself, no doubt, with the reflection that at any rate a mishap of this kind could not occur again.

On the same day as the arrival of the disconcerting news about Jennings & Finlay, Sandwich received from Buckinghamshire a reply to his questions about what share Panin would be prepared to take in expenditure in Sweden.[87] It by no means bore out the soothing assurances of Gross, or those similar assurances which Goodricke had put into the mouth of Osterman. On the contrary. Panin refused categorically to give any undertaking to bear a half share, and frankly based his refusal on the ground that he was convinced that once the French system in Sweden was overthrown England would have to step in with a subsidy; and he was determined not to put himself in a position in which he might be exposed to a claim for a half share in that: throwing Sweden into England's arms, he explained, was not "an Object of such consequence to [Russia] as to give in to an Idea of paying any Part of the Subsidies which in that Case would be unavoidable." Least of all, since he had heard from Gross that "England was determined to meddle as little as possible with the Affairs of the Continent, which he said was a serious Consideration to Russia, whose Views could only be Continental."[88]

This reply confirmed all Sandwich's worst suspicions. Russia was dragging her feet over the commercial treaty; she was holding up the negotiations for an alliance by insistence either on removing the Turkish clause, or on being given a secret subsidy to assist her in Poland: for some time Sandwich had been of opinion that affairs at St. Petersburg wore "a lowering cast," that Buckinghamshire was getting nowhere, and that any progress must await the arrival of his successor, Macartney.[89] Now came the suggestion that England must give Sweden a subsidy sooner or later, and the repudiation of those assurances from Gross on the faith of which he had already embarked upon expenditure in Stockholm. His ingrained suspicion that England was (as usual) to be cheated returned in full force; and was certainly strengthened by a decisive dispatch from St. Petersburg which reached him at the beginning of December, for in that dispatch Buckinghamshire, in reference to Panin's plan for a great Northern System, wrote: "though he is very desirous of uniting the Powers of the North to overawe the House of Bourbon, yet, he is determined to throw as much of the Expence as possible upon England.'"[90] The effect of this dispatch was never really erased from Sandwich's mind, and undoubtedly influenced the minds of his successors. And up to a point Sandwich was right. Panin never understood, or gave sufficient weight to, the determination of all British governments never again to pay subsidies in peacetime, as in the old days before the war—a determination which applied equally to Sweden and to Russia. Panin was quite prepared to pay out very large sums in bribery and corruption; but the regular financing of Sweden, he considered, must be England's affair. It was England that wanted the French system destroyed; it was England therefore that must take the logical financial consequences. Sandwich refused to admit that the logic was valid. The idea that England would pay a subsidy to Sweden must be smothered at birth: in an angry letter to Buckinghamshire on 20 November he bade him assure Panin that Russia need be under no apprehension of being called upon to pay a half share of a subsidy, since there was not going to be a subsidy at all.[91] His indignation on this point made him incapable of appreciating the magnitude of the financial effort Russia was to make in Stockholm: Panin would pour out money there on corruption to an extent which would never have been sanctioned by an English ministry. Even with the statistics in front of him to prove it, Sandwich's resentments and suspicions were not to be appeased. It was only right, he argued, that Russia should be openhanded: was not Sweden essentially her concern? A political success for Russia in Stockholm would be dearly bought, if it resulted in pressure's being brought to bear upon England to pay Sweden a subsidy! However, it was too late for repining: the draft to Goodricke had already been dispatched; to that "preliminary expenditure" he was already committed. What was to follow it—whether anything was to follow it—must depend, partly on what results that expenditure achieved, but almost more on whether the policy Russia would pursue thereafter had any real relevance to British interests. More urgently than ever, he pressed Buckinghamshire for information about Russia's plans; more emphatically than ever he insisted that Goodricke had been sent to Sweden only for Russia's sake, and in response to Panin's entreaties.[92] Of course it was not true; but in the circumstances it was scarcely surprising if Sandwich persuaded himself that it was.

There followed a prolonged and exasperating silence. Sandwich's demand for information died away echo-less in the corridors of the College of Foreign Affairs. Nothing for it, then, but to accept the situation, insofar as he was committed to it, and watch jealously to insure that he obtained full value (and an equal Russian expenditure) in return for his £4,000. Such, certainly, was the only course open to Goodricke, thus condemned to fight an election campaign without clear instructions, with strictly limited supplies, and with an ally who was still not much better informed of Panin's intentions than Sandwich himself.

(iv)

Both the nature of the struggle which was now to begin, and its outcome, would depend upon whether the Composition held firm in the face of the strains which an election would inevitably impose upon it. By the summer of 1764 the Hats and the Court had reached general agreement on modification of the constitution; and the Cap leaders, though far less definitely, had probably committed themselves to agreeing that some alteration was at least a matter for discussion. All were agreed that there were abuses in the government which the next Diet might be expected to correct, though the identification of those abuses, and the importance attached to them, varied from party to party.[93] There had also been some sort of understanding that at the next election the Court would remain neutral; that Hats and Caps would refrain from corruption, especially with foreign money; and (more vaguely) that Hats and Caps should have equal representation on the committees of the next Diet, and perhaps also (by an implication and extension to which the Caps' leaders did not feel committed) that there should be a sharing of seats in the representation of (e.g.) Stockholm, which returned ten members. Lastly, it was a basic principle of the Composition that it was a purely domestic matter: the divisive issue of foreign policy was to be carefully excluded, pending the carrying through of the work of reform and reconstruction.[94]

The program was difficult and perhaps impossible to realize; for a variety of reasons. First, the return of an English minister to Stockholm necessarily brought considerations of foreign policy into the forefront of politics: Hats and Caps became once again characteristically pro-French or pro-English. Moreover, whatever Lovisa Ulrika may have protested, and the Hat leaders have believed, Breteuil had no intention of giving support to a system which was not clearly committed to France. His pact with the Court, he was to say later, was based on the supposition that the queen accepted the French alliance.[95] Secondly, the Composition was an agreement between leaders, which did not yet bind their followers; and on the Cap side even the leaders had entered into it with hesitation, and would be ready to break it if a breach seemed likely to be to their advantage. Between Hats and Court some sort of a treaty was possible, and seems to have been made; but between Court and Caps the relationship was different, and more complex. Whereas Lovisa Ulrika and Fersen were former enemies who had reached an understanding, Löwenhielm and Rudbeck were regarded by the queen only as prominent members of a party of which she was herself the natural head. Her constant endeavor was to absorb the old Cap party into that of the Court, to tie its hands, to direct its councils. There had been a time when the virtual identity of Court and Caps was a fact. But it was a fact no longer, and a line of action which assumed that it ought to be was likely to lead to disillusionment and bitterness. The Composition therefore confronted the queen with very real difficulties. Each party suspected there was a catch in it; each was at bottom suspicious of the other. If it were to be kept together, Lovisa Ulrika would find herself forced to conciliate—by special attentions, demonstrations of confidence, private conferences, secret communication of information—whichever party seemed for the moment most likely to break away. Inevitably these things, when public, excited remark and raised jealousies; and when secret, all too often leaked out, with results which were even more damaging. The task was not made any easier by her frank avowals, in the course of such maneuvers, of a desire for enlargements of the prerogative considerably exceeding the moderate demands which had formed a basis for the Composition. To keep the fragile bark of Composition properly trimmed would have taxed the skill of the wisest statesman, and was certainly beyond the capacity of an indiscreet, rash, and temperamental woman.

Yet at the time when the decision to call an Extraordinary Diet was finally taken—that is, at the beginning of September—the Composition, on the whole, held firm: certainly so, as far as the Hat leaders were concerned.[96] It was not until the beginning of October that C. F. Scheffer's confidence in the queen was really shaken; and not until three weeks later that Breteuil came to the conclusion that she was not to be trusted. And it was ironical (and typical of her difficulties) that in this particular instance their suspicion that she was playing them false was, as a matter of fact, quite unfounded. It arose out of matters entirely outside her control.

On 22 September Bernstorff sent off to Schack, his minister in Stockholm, an account of an initiative lately made to him by Korff, the Russian minister in Copenhagen.[97] On Panin's orders, Korff had suggested that Denmark should cooperate with Russia, England, and Prussia to remove the additions to the Swedish constitution which had been made in 1756, and restore it to the pristine purity of 1720. It will be remembered that at this time Denmark was engaged in negotiations (by now somewhat protracted) for a Russian alliance, and the prize of success in those negotiations, it was hoped, would be *Mageskiftet*. Bernstorff was, moreover, well aware of the background to the Composition: he knew that Scheffer, in particular, believed that some increase in the power of the crown was a necessary part of the bargain; he knew that the Hats were ready to remove at least some of the humiliations of 1756. In view of all this his reaction to Korff's initiative seems oddly emotional and exaggerated. It did not occur to him, apparently, that Russia might be as much concerned as himself to safeguard Sweden's neighbors from the risk of an absolutism in Sweden. Yet within a very few days of Bernstorff's indignant reception of Korff's suggestions, his minister in St. Petersburg, A. S. von der Osten, was writing a report of an interview with Panin which, if it had arrived in time, would have made his panic unnecessary. For in that interview Panin had clearly explained that Russian policy in regard to the Swedish constitution was "a just equilibrium" between king, Senate, and Diet; and had particularly stressed the point that the power of war and peace, and of taxation, must on no account lie solely in the hands either of king or Senate. And Osten, in his account of the conversation, had recorded his conviction that Panin had no intention of increasing the power of the crown, but really sought only to limit that of the Senate; and had given it as his own opinion that any increase in the Senate's powers, and any decrease in the crown's, would be the quickest way to an absolutist revolution.[98] Osten's report seems to have dissipated Bernstorff's apprehensions immediately. His reply to it, in which he virtually associated himself with Panin's policy, constituted (whether he realized it or not) a turning point in Russo-Danish relations.[99] But in the meantime his letter to Schack had put the cat among the pigeons in Stockholm.

That letter, after expressing horror and alarm at Korff's insinuation, and professing that Denmark would prefer to sacrifice the conclusion of a treaty with Russia rather than agree to any modification of the constitution, had ordered the dread news to be communicated to Scheffer, and had wound up by expressing the opinion that the whole affair was an intrigue engineered by the queen. This wild conclusion was really more an expression of Bernstorff's obsessive fear and hatred of Lovisa Ulrika than a considered political judgment. But in Stockholm it caused extensive damage. Schack, whose views of the queen coincided with Bernstorff's, hastened to obey his orders and inform Scheffer. Scheffer was appropriately shocked, and exclaimed that if the queen should enlist any foreign aid, all was over between them.[100] For him, indeed, the story could hardly have arrived at a more awkward moment; for on 4 October he had issued a private appeal to the Hats to stick by the Composition, arguing that the old Hat party had disintegrated, and that the only hope now was to forget party differences, put a stop to foreign corruption, form a union of All Good Men, and take especial care not to do anything which might drive the queen into the arms of the Caps.[101]

For the moment, Schack's news was strictly confined to the inmost circle of Hat politicians: even Breteuil was not told of it until the end of the month, and as late as 22 October was writing sanguine dispatches on the solidity of the Court's alliance with the Hats.[102] Lovisa Ulrika, tackled directly about it by Fersen, firmly denied complicity, as well she might;[103] but though Scheffer was perhaps anxious to believe her, and though Breteuil was prepared to think that Adolf Fredrik, at least, had had no hand in the business, the matter rumbled on. The chancery-president, by way of putting the Cap members of the Senate at a moral disadvantage, formally reported it to that body on 12 November, the king and queen having again given an explicit denial on the previous day.[104] There the matter rested, overtaken and obscured by more important things; but it left an unpleasant feeling behind it, and it prepared the ground for the disintegration of the Composition which was to follow soon after.

In this situation, Lovisa Ulrika felt obliged to counteract the bad impression left by the Korff affair by showing complaisance to the Hats and to Breteuil. She informed Fersen, for instance, of Goodricke's electioneering activities, and at Breteuil's request undertook to restrain them.[105] This promise she did, indeed, keep; but she kept it in a manner typically ambiguous. On 13 November the Prussian minister Cocceji reported to Frederick that she had been complaining hotly to him that Goodricke "négociait avec la nation, sans aucun concert avec la cour."[106] This was in fact tantamount to accusing him of trying to divide the Court, not from the Hats (which would have been legitimate) but from the Caps. Cocceji was commissioned to relay this complaint to Goodricke, with the threat that "la Cour ne pouvait pas regarder tout cela avec indifférence": the queen did not want to join France, but she must know where she stood, and if she were forced to choose, she would choose the side which offered her the best constitutional advantages. Goodricke replied simply that he had always worked in the interests of the Court, provided it did not range itself on France's side, and that what Lovisa Ulrika called negotiating with the nation "n'était que la nécessité de s'instruire de la façon de penser des gens et de connaître de quel parti ils sont"; adding, with a reasonable approximation to the truth, that he had as yet given out no money, since he had none to give, and that his sole political object was the destruction of the French system.[107] The matter for the moment went no further; but it offered a good example of the queen's devious methods: while she sought to appease the Hats by damping down Goodricke's activities, she used the opportunity to reassert her claim to a monopoly of anti-Hat exertions. She rounded off the performance by confiding to Breteuil on 9 November that Goodricke had received supplies to the amount of £15,000 or £16,000.[108] Within a day or two her story was found to be totally without foundation. Possibly, as Schack conjectured, it was a rumor spread by Goodricke himself;[109] possibly she genuinely believed it, since the sum tallied more or less with the amount Sinclair had asked of Goodricke in July—though if, as Schack reported, she also said that Goodricke had actually offered this amount to Sinclair she was taking liberties with the truth. Whatever the explanation, the episode cannot have done much to reestablish her reputation for reliability.

What finally blasted that reputation was the long-impending affair of the French subsidy arrears. Since the autumn of 1763, when Sweden's reclamation for payment had for a time seemed to threaten the summoning of an Extraordinary Diet, the question had been under negotiation in Paris and in Stockholm. In 1763 France had averted an Extraordinary Diet by the promise to pay 3 million livres; but this was considered as no more than a temporary expedient, pending a more general settlement. Praslin undoubtedly hoped that it might be possible to combine a solution of the controversy over arrears with the conclusion of a treaty which would guarantee to France the assistance of ten Swedish ships of the line in time of war; and to Sandwich and Goodricke (to say nothing of outside observers such as Frederick the Great)[110] it seemed probable that if the arrears question were once settled the whole Swedish navy would de facto henceforward be at France's disposal. Fortunately for England, a settlement proved difficult to reach. France's finances were in poor shape, and Praslin was obliged to inform Ulrik Scheffer, the Swedish ambassador who had been sent to Paris expressly to negotiate the matter, that the Contrôleur-Général had insisted on drastic cuts in the amount available for foreign subsidies, in order that more money might be released for naval rearmament.[111] As a result, France was late with the payment of her regular subsidy installments. Moreover, there were sharp disputes as to the amount of arrears which was really due. Löwenhielm reckoned that Sweden was entitled to as much as 18 million livres; France at first offered no more than 6, to be paid off at the rate of 1.5 million a year until the expiry of the existing Franco-Swedish alliance in 1768.[112] This offer was debated in the Senate two days after the decision to summon an Extraordinary Diet; it was received with indignation; and it was unanimously rejected.[113]

In October, however, Ulrik Scheffer came home on leave, no doubt because his name was being canvassed in certain Hat circles as a possible *lantmarskalk* (i.e., Speaker and leader of the majority party in the House of Nobility) at the forthcoming Diet. He carried with him a new French offer which went a long way to meet the Swedish claim.[114] France now admitted a debt of 12 million, and suggested its payment at the rate of 1.5 million a year, beginning in January 1765, and terminating at the end of 1772. In return, France would expect no more than that Sweden "persistera dans les sentimens où Elle a été jusqu'à présent à l'égard de la France; qu'en toute occasion Elle lui donnera des preuves d'une amitié constante, et que dans toutes les affaires qui pourront survenir, elle se conduira de la manière la plus conforme aux intérêts du Roi ainsi à l'amitié des deux couronnes."[115] Not a word, then, about a quid pro quo in the shape of naval aid. France had changed her tactics. It was now Breteuil's hope that at the forthcoming Diet a Hat-controlled Senate would be given a free hand to negotiate treaties and alliances—perhaps under the disguise of granting additional powers in this matter to the crown[116]—and would thus be in a position to make a deal over the warships. For the moment, Breteuil could be well content if he secured the acceptance of the terms as they stood; for in fact they gave France, in exchange for her financial concessions, one enormous gain. The Franco-Swedish alliance of 1754 was due to expire on 23 July 1768. On that date the repayment of arrears would have totalled only 6 million; and France would be in a position to present Sweden with the alternative of renewing the alliance on (at best) the old terms, or of losing the further 6 million still outstanding. The practical effect would be that Sweden would be tied tightly to the French system, not until 1768, but until the end of 1772. As Goodricke put it, the Swedes were to be bought with their own money.[117] Thus though the threat of a naval treaty was no longer imminent, it might well be implicit. The subsidy agreement might help to save the Hats from financial disaster; it gave them a better hope of winning the election; and if they won it, a Hat Senate might then conclude the naval treaty. Goodricke had early and accurate information of the French proposals, and their defeat was rightly felt to be of crucial importance. Since he had no money at his disposal, his only hope was delay.[118] First, because there was always a chance that Sandwich's draft might arrive in time; but also for another reason. The longer a decision was postponed, the nearer the meeting of the Diet; and for the Senate to proceed to a major political decision of this sort, when the Estates would be assembled within a very few weeks, was to take a risk so great that it might be hoped that they would shrink from it. For the Senate, after all, were no more than the Estates' fiduciary agents, and accountable to them; their executive authority, even when the Diet was not in session, was circumscribed by the instructions which its predecessor had left behind it.[119] The Estates were sovereign in all but name; they were, in the current phrase, "vested with authority" (*maktägande*). A rushed decision on a critical issue, taken on the very eve of the Diet, might well bring retribution from the Senate's parliamentary principals. It had been precisely this charge that had formed the gravamen of the accusations which led to the fall of Horn and the Caps in 1739; and old Senators such as Count Seth could not put the recollection of those events wholly out of their minds.[120] There was, moreover, the attitude of the Court to be considered: if opinion in the Senate were anywhere near evenly split, Adolf Fredrik's two votes might be decisive. So, though Goodricke must have felt that he was fighting with his hands tied, he was not disposed entirely to despair of success.

In mid-November Breteuil formally presented the French offer to Ekeblad, the chancery-president, with the ominous remark that "si cette proposition n'était pas acceptée avec un empressement égal au plaisir que le Roy avoit eu à la faire, je la rétirerois sans balancer."[121] It was considered in the Chancery on 14 November, and by a majority recommended; though Joakim von Düben, Secretary of State, and till recently treasurer to the queen, took the unusual step of entering his protest on the minutes.[122] There followed a tense interval of a fortnight, in which Goodricke did his best to enlist the Court's influence against it, while C. F. Scheffer attempted, without success, to lobby the queen, and Breteuil promised financial help at the next Diet.[123] At last, on 28 November, a bare seven weeks before the Diet was due to meet, the Senate proceeded to a decision. Three Senators, Rosen, Seth, and Liewen (the last generally reckoned as an adherent of the Court) were reported by Goodricke to have wavered to the last; but in the end the Senate voted to agree with C. F. Scheffer's proposed reply to Breteuil accepting France's terms. But the voting had been nine to eight; and the minority included not only six members who could be reckoned as Caps—Löwenhielm (whom Breteuil had vainly endeavored to seduce),[124] Horn, Friesendorff, Lagerberg, Bonde, Törnflycht—but also the two votes of Adolf Fredrik, who appended to the minutes a *diktamen* of protest which had been drawn for him by Joakim von Düben. Goodricke believed, or professed to believe, that if he had had £600 at his disposal he could have secured a majority.[125]

It was a victory big with portents of defeat: after such a decision, so narrowly carried, so publicly opposed by the king, it was inconceivable that the forthcoming Diet would not reopen the issue. The king's *diktamen*, it was said, was tantamount to an invitation to the Estates to proceed to a *licentiering*.[126] The terms of Scheffer's motion of acceptance were such as to reinforce that invitation. The French offer, it appeared, had been accepted, not out of consideration for the embarrassed state of the Swedish treasury, but out of regard for the financial difficulties of France; though they "hoped and expected" that when the position of France's finances should permit, "nouvelles facilités" would be available for furnishing the whole 12 million without waiting for the stipulated term to expire.[127] This was to give hostages to fortune with a vengeance. Ministers in London, feigning ignorance of the outcome, innocently inquired of Nolcken whether it was really conceivable that any new treaty with France could be made at a time when the Diet was to assemble so soon.[128] They could afford this malicious indulgence; for the moral victory was on their side. The Caps could continue their election campaign with increased confidence. But for the Court, and for Lovisa Ulrika in particular, the vote of 28 November was an irreparable disaster.

The delicate balancing act between the parties which was essential if the Composition was to be maintained, and was a precondition for the Court's hopes of enlarging the prerogative, could be carried on only if the shocks to which it was subjected were of no more than moderate force. It could survive, for instance, the Court's support of a Cap candidate for the vacant archiepiscopal see.[129] It could stand up to the Court's advocacy of a candidate for the post of *lantmarskalk* who, though a Cap, was so infirm that his functions were certain to be discharged by a deputy who would be a Hat.[130] The one act aroused Hat resentment, the other raised Cap suspicions; but neither was so serious as to destroy Lovisa Ulrika's credibility. She could even surmount a piece of bad luck such as the Korff insinuation, though only at the cost of hasty compensatory action which undermined confidence. What the Composition could not survive was the necessity that the Court should take an attitude upon a central issue of foreign policy. The question of the French arrears was such an issue. It was no wonder that the Court tried to get it postponed until the Diet should meet.[131] If the decision were made by the Secret Committee, Adolf Fredrik's views need never be known at all; if, on the other hand, it were decided in the Senate, he could not avoid taking sides. It is possible that the queen tried to barter Adolf Fredrik's votes against Anglo-Russian concessions.[132] But on 9 November Goodricke reported Sinclair as being afraid of falling between two stools;[133] and as late as 13 November, Sinclair's conversation with Cocceji suggests that the Court was still hoping against hope to save the Composition.[134] The acerbity of Lovisa Ulrika's attack on Goodricke, which formed a main part of that conversation, may reflect not only her desire to recover some credit with the Hats in view of the impending debate in the Senate, not only her jealousy of any attempt to put the leadership of the Caps in any other hands than her own, but her exasperation at the fatal impact of Anglo-French rivalry upon her policies. Attempts were made in the next ten days or so by C. F. Scheffer to induce her to put pressure on the king to support the French proposals.[135] She refused to intervene. It is just possible that this was one of the rare occasions when Adolf Fredrik manifested a will of his own, and that she knew that he was not to be shaken:[136] they must both have been conscious that in his *diktamen* he stood on strong constitutional ground, and that a vote with the majority would expose the crown, no less than the Senate, to the censure of the approaching Diet. But it seems more likely that she realized that it mattered little how he voted: either way, his action would mean the end of all hope of keeping the monarchy above party, and thus all hope of a consensus upon what was for her the vital question—a reform of abuses, and a modification of the constitution. The Composition perished because in the end it could not be prevented from getting entangled in foreign affairs, and entangled precisely at the moment when foreign affairs were a more potent polarizing agent in Swedish politics than at any time since the project for a Composition was first conceived. C. F. Scheffer, after all was over, still liked to believe that Lovisa Ulrika personally was not to blame for Adolf Fredrik's action; and he was probably right. For the last thing she wanted was that she should be forced to take any stance at all on an issue of this nature.[137]

The consequences were clearly foreseen, and they followed at once. Already on 23 November Sinclair came to Osterman to ask his advice as to whether the inevitable breach with the Hats should be allowed to come from their side, or whether the Court should take the initiative in declaring it.[138] No sooner was the vote in the Senate known than Breteuil wrote to Praslin that no reconciliation with the Court was now possible;[139] and on the same day Schack, with sour satisfaction, informed Bernstorff that "the spell is broken."[140] On 30 November Adolf Fredrik expressed his pleasure with Osterman, and transmitted a request to Catherine that she would recognize his services by some mark of her appreciation.[141] On 7 December Osterman reported that the Hat leaders, Fersen and Hermansson, had called on Sinclair and told him that they could act with him no longer.[142] The swiftness and completeness of the transformation in the political scene was sufficiently illustrated by the publication, early in December, of a joint Cap-Court election manifesto, whose vague phrases about upholding the constitution, strengthening the executive power, and preventing the confusion of executive and legislative functions represented a hastily devised compromise which imperfectly concealed the irreconcilable political programs of the contracting parties.[143] The dream of a Patriot King was shattered; all that remained was the waning hope that the Caps might somehow be cozened into appearing as the King's Friends.

(v)

The collapse of the Composition was not merely fatal to the Court; it also destroyed the Hats' last slim chance of victory at the elections. They had long been conscious of their unpopularity,[144] though they certainly did not realize how widespread, and how bitter, was the feeling against them. They clung to the hope that their pact with the Court would somehow ensure an even balance of parties, and they believed that if only both sides would stick to the agreement to renounce reliance on foreign money—if the election were fought with the Composition intact, and on strictly domestic issues—they might be able to overcome their difficulties when the Diet should meet. In June Osterman reported that the Hats had persuaded Breteuil to take no part in the domestic political struggle as long as the French alliance was not in jeopardy.[145] Early in September C. F. Scheffer was still saying that they would not engage in bribery at the elections unless they were driven to do so, and even then only of the three lower Estates, since experience had shown that attempts to control the Nobility by buying proxies before the Diet was simply money thrown away.[146] When Breteuil offered to provide 100,000 francs for buying up proxies, the Hats turned his offer down.[147] As late as 21 September Schack could report that some Hats fancied they could discern a swing in their favor among the Peasants;[148] and a week later Breteuil had good hopes of an inexpensive victory, at least in the Burghers.[149] A month after that he was sufficiently confident to be able to write to Praslin that he proposed "de laisser à peu prés la providence assembler les Etats,"[150] and that he had agreed with the Hats to employ no corruption of any sort, provided the queen agreed to do the same.

They were egregiously mistaken: Providence was no longer on their side. As autumn drew on they were forced to face about, and to pursue, with such speed as they could now make, the well-beaten path of corruption. In July Fersen had made a pact with Sinclair which he believed had ensured an equal division of the ten Stockholm seats between the two parties; and when it became clear that the tide in Stockholm was running strongly against the Hats, Sinclair had in fact exerted himself in their support.[151] But his efforts could not arrest the progress of an electoral landslide. The final result in Stockholm was not merely defeat but disaster. The Hats won only a single seat;[152] and among the defeated (as the Hats learned to their stupefaction) was Gustaf Kierman, Speaker of the Estate of Burghers in the last two Diets, who for the best part of two decades had been the linchpin of Hat politics in the capital, and who by his dominant position in all those financial and commercial enterprises which had now become a main article of accusation against them was a kind of symbol of the Hat mercantilist philosophy, and the very type of Hat corruption.[153] By 12 October it was all over. Where Stockholm led the way, many other towns followed: for the first time since 1739 the Hats had lost control of the Burghers. The *débâcle* was followed by recriminations: the Hats blamed Fersen for the bargain with Sinclair; Fersen accused Sinclair of not carrying it out;[154] one more strain was added to the tensions already existing between Hats and Court. When at the beginning of November there came premature reports that Goodricke had received large sums of money from home, the shock of that intelligence at last made them feel that they could no longer defer "forming a party":[155] on 16 November Goodricke could report the recent formation of a Noble Club, financed by French money, where the first toast was Axel von Fersen;[156] four days later he was lamenting that French purchases of proxies had pushed the price up from 100 to 150 crowns apiece.[157]

Nevertheless, when the breach with the Court came on 27 November the Hats were divided, without any concerted measures of defense against the attacks of their adversaries, and except in Stockholm almost without plan or organization. Their traditional stronghold in the Burghers had crumbled; the Clergy (in any case inclined to be Cap) would be led by a Cap archbishop; it was too late to squander money in the constituencies. The best they could do was to keep what funds they had in their pockets against the meeting of the Diet, and hope with French assistance to carry the vital election for *lantmarskalk*. They were handicapped by the fact that their information about their adversaries was much inferior to Goodricke's: they had no secret office at Nienburg to reveal the designs of England, as England was able to penetrate those of France. It therefore happened that they fell into strange errors about the respective roles of Goodricke and Osterman, believing that Osterman would be dependent on English money, and that Russian policy would conform to that of London.[158] Hence too their consistently inaccurate information about the money available to Goodricke; hence the absurd story put about among them that Goodricke on his own initiative had sought to please the queen by proposing that the crown prince should marry an English princess, and that his dispatch of a Messenger was to be accounted for on this basis.[159] If they had been able to see the course of correspondence between Goodricke and Sandwich they would have spared themselves some of their apprehensions as to the consequences of a Cap victory: C. F. Scheffer seems seriously to have thought that it would be followed not only by political persecutions, but by an English loan of £500,000 to the crown upon the security of the crown forges; that Gotland would be pawned to England; and Visby become a free port on the model (he thought) of Port Mahon.[160] The Hats made some effort to use England's supposed sinister economic designs as propaganda in the election;[161] but the effect was clearly small or none.

On Goodricke's departure from Copenhagen Sir Joseph Yorke had written to Lord Buckinghamshire: "you will find him active, well informed and well intentioned, and very happy to be of any service."[162] Active he certainly was, as the dispatches of Schack and Breteuil make clear; well informed likewise, as appears from his own. Such a minister meant the end of the usefulness of the unfortunate "Wilkinson." The approach of the Diet now made "Wilkinson" something of a liability. At similar junctures in the past he had regularly appealed to the Secretary of State to be allowed to withdraw to England, at least for as long as the Diet should last, in order to be out of range of the persecution of his enemies. The same consideration applied now.[163] Goodricke felt strongly that Gedda was a kind of hostage to fortune, whose safety might have to be bartered against immunity for some of the financial miscreants whom the

Caps were determined to bring to justice. He decided therefore that he must be got out of the way in good time.[164] In mid-October he slipped off in an English ship, Goodricke having made his departure possible by paying his creditors out of his own pocket. His disappearance caused a flutter in Hat circles: clearly he must have been sent upon a mission of importance. The chancery-president wrote to Nolcken in London to keep his eyes open;[165] he alerted Sprengtporten in Copenhagen;[166] and he was probably not much reassured when Sprengtporten duly reported that Gedda had lain *perdu* on board during the whole time that his ship was wind-bound in Elsinore.[167] These alarms were unnecessary: Gedda had in fact no mission; indeed, he felt that he had been badly treated.[168] On arrival in London he wrote to the chancery-president a letter of apology and excuse; he called on Nolcken, and even induced him to present him at Court.[169] But his attempt to mend his fences was wasted. His part in Sweden was played out, at least for the moment; and for the next few years he lived a retired life, at first in the riverside seclusion of Wapping, and later, less obscurely, at Westminister.[170]

Meanwhile Goodricke and Osterman were doing their best with the means available to them. There is not much sign in Goodricke's correspondence that his efforts extended far beyond Stockholm, though at the end of November he was trying to buy up noble proxies in advance of the meeting of the Diet.[171] Even so, he had plenty of demands on his purse: the Stockholm election, the financing of Cap clubs in the capital. To a great extent he had to rely on sheer bluff; but the Hats were certainly right when they reported that he and Osterman pledged their personal security in advance of supplies from their governments.[172] There were limits to the extent to which this could be risked, however, and they were therefore constantly obliged to have recourse to promises, put-offs, and vague assurances that money was to be expected within the next mail or two. Goodricke had views of his own about the best method of using corruption, and he was by no means convinced that his government was setting about it the right way and getting value for its money—or the promise of its money. As long ago as 1759 he had written: "The best way of securing subsidy Courts is to give large pensions, which can easily be saved again in the subsidy."[173] Even though an English subsidy for Sweden might be out of the question, he still believed in pensions rather than in promiscuous bribery. It was the French method; and he considered it preferable because it bought the best brains.[174] If England were not willing to adopt it, if the policy was to buy a majority in the Estates rather than corrupt the Senate, then he was sure that the best instruction that could be given to a minister in his situation was to define the points which it was essential to carry, and to stop supplies if they were not secured. The worst of all methods was to order him to write home for instructions when the Diet was already assembled.[175]

Yet this last was precisely the line which Sandwich seemed likely to follow. Goodricke had succeeded in persuading the Cap leaders to agree to his plan for dividing expenditure into a preliminary phase up to and including the election of the Secret Committee, and a second stage during which money would be required for "holding the party together." By 11 December he could already foresee that the "preliminary" expenditure of £4,000 which Sandwich had sanctioned would be exhausted by the time the end of the first stage had been reached. He needed now to know what England was willing to do about supplying money thereafter. Sandwich had promised to sound Russia about the additional sum of £9,000 which would be required in terms of Goodricke's estimates of 31 August; but so far there had been no answer. His instructions of 20 November, with their strict orders "never to advance a shilling" without being certain that Osterman made an equal contribution, had an ungracious sound at a time when Osterman's expenditure already exceeded Goodricke's, and when the expectation was that Panin would provide him with supplies in excess of what Goodricke could hope for.[176] Osterman, not unnaturally, was pressing for information on how far England might be expected to go, and pleaded with him to try to persuade Sandwich at least to authorize a further thousand or two.[177] In these circumstances Goodricke took his courage in both hands and intimated to Sandwich that he proposed to act on the assumption that England would proceed to stage 2, and that the full amount of £13,000 would be forthcoming.[178] He understood very well that Panin's refusal to pledge Russia to take a half share arose from his fear of being asked to pay half the cost of a subsidy;[179] but he also believed that the difficulty could have been avoided, and the government in London would have been more amenable to persuasion, if Panin had been willing to state frankly the maximum for which he was prepared to engage himself.[180] But Panin was in some ways as difficult, and as afraid of being overreached, as Sandwich himself. It was not helpful that Panin should insist that there was to be no blending of their adherents: Russia's partisans were to be kept strictly separate from England's; Goodricke and Osterman were each to be responsible for paying his own "tail";[181] there was to be no common treasury, as had been the case in 1747. The inevitable consequence of this arrangement was that solicitants ran from Osterman to Goodricke and back again, telling each of what the other was alleged to have promised, asserting that the offer of the one had been conditional on the other's matching it: in short, playing the one off against the other.[182]

This was conspicuously the case in regard to their relations with Sinclair, which in the six weeks before the opening of the Diet taxed their patience to the uttermost. Sinclair by this time was incontestably first in the confidence of the queen, the regular channel of communication between her and those with whom she negotiated. A somewhat muddy channel, certainly, and one whose devious course baffles the historian, as it baffled contemporaries. More royalist than the king (though not, perhaps, than the queen) he was capable in moments of indiscretion of avowing ambitions for the monarchy which it would have been wiser to conceal. His own ambition was obvious; his scruples much less so. Frederick the Great, who thought him "fin, rusé et amusant," had some time ago warned his sister against him.[183] That she should have selected such a man as her confidant and chief agent is a comment on her own character. He ran busily between one side and the other, retailing to each confidential information which was often inaccurate and not seldom pure invention, and these small services did not endear him to those with whom he had to deal. Breteuil remarked that he was more hated and distrusted by the party with whom he professed to be in alliance than by that which he professed to oppose.[184] Rudbeck seems especially to have detested him; and when Lovisa Ulrika, in what must have been a stormy interview, demanded that Rudbeck should "set him right with the nation"—by which she meant, rehabilitate his battered reputation—she received a blunt refusal.[185]

Such was the man with whom Osterman and Goodricke were now condemned to cooperate. Even before the breach between the Hats and the Court at the end of November they had severally arrived at the determination that they would give him just sufficient money to keep him more or less quiet, but would reserve the greater part of their resources for Löwenhielm, Rudbeck, and the Caps.[186] This policy, however, became difficult to maintain now that Court and Caps had issued a joint election-pamphlet, and were supposed to be fighting the campaign in close alliance. It very soon became obvious that Lovisa Ulrika meant to transform that alliance, if she could, into a real fusion; that she aimed at creating a single party, all sections of which should be subordinate to the Court and directed by herself.[187] In particular, she wanted control of the money which England and Russia would provide, and she intended that Sinclair should have charge of its distribution.[188] To Goodricke and Osterman this was a wholly unacceptable arrangement. The queen was financially irresponsible, Sinclair was dubiously honest. The Court's political objectives were irreconcilable with Osterman's instructions; they were of no interest to Goodricke; and they were directly repugnant to the Caps: even the Hat leaders, in moments of private candor, admitted to themselves that the Caps were not in the least likely to tolerate the subversion of Swedish "liberty."[189] Yet some share of the available money could scarcely be denied to the Court: the problem was how to ensure that it was spent on corrupting the right people for the right purposes. By mid-December the elections were virtually over. It looked as though they had registered a clear victory for the Caps; but until the Diet met no one could be certain: much would depend on the color of the majority in the nonelective House of Nobility. In the weeks before its meeting there would be expenses for buying up the proxies of heads of noble families, or providing them with journey money if they were poor, and in other preparations; but the main expense would come when the Diet met: in subsidizing clubs, paying for food and drink and lodging for members, and above all in the securing the election of a suitable *lantmarskalk*, and afterwards of a favorable majority in the Secret Committee. For these purposes it was essential to reach some watertight agreement with Sinclair about the dispensing of bribery. The only solution seemed to be the setting up of a small council, through whom, and only through whom, expenditure would be channeled. Such a council, consisting initially of three members (one of whom was Sinclair) was accordingly constituted: it was afterwards enlarged to seven, only one of the additional four members being an adherent of the Court, so that the Caps had a firm majority on it of five to two.[190] Up to a point it achieved its object; but the problem of Sinclair remained. He broke undertakings; he tried to play off Osterman against Goodricke; he failed to account to the council for moneys entrusted to him.[191]

Behind this duplicity undoubtedly lay another shift in the attitude of the queen. Her alliance with the Caps had brought her no benefits. It had been concluded because after the break with the Hats it seemed the only road open to her. The more probable it became that the new Diet would be under Cap control, the less likely became her chance of modifying the constitution. Not the least important element in the Composition had been an agreement to forswear party rancor. As the elections assumed more and more the aspect of a Cap landslide, it seemed increasingly probable that the new Diet would see the Caps taking their revenge for 1739, and that one of its main preoccupations would be the persecution of the defeated Hats. It may well be that Lovisa Ulrika was sincere in her feeling that she was bound in honor to oppose anything of that sort.[192] At all events, despite an urgent remonstrance from Panin, which Frederick forwarded to her together with his own advice to remain neutral between the parties,[193] she began to explore the possibility of a reconciliation with Fersen and C. F. Scheffer. She found them, under the impact of electoral disaster, not unwilling to listen to her.[194] Her spokesmen began to proclaim ostentatiously in Cap clubs that on the vital question of the election of the *lantmarskalk* the Court would be neutral.[195] By 11 January Breteuil could report that Sinclair, disgusted at his failure to get control of the means of corruption, had gone over to France; and that he himself had concluded, after consultation with Fersen and Scheffer, an agreement with the queen whereby the Court undertook to declare itself neutral, to support Fersen for *lantmarskalk* and Hat candidates for the Secret Committee, and to commit itself to a French system in foreign policy. In return, Breteuil promised that he would support "agrémens" for the Court—but only if they were proposed by the Caps. From the queen's point of view it could hardly have seemed a very satisfactory bargain.[196]

By this time Osterman had decided that Sinclair's behavior was so suspicious that he must seek an interview with the king in the hope of clearing the air.[197] But he found to his chagrin that Adolf Fredrik refused to receive him.[198] He did succeed, not without difficulty, in transmitting a message through Count Horn: its precise nature is obscure. According to Breteuil's information (and he had it from Adolf Fredrik himself) Osterman demanded, in return for financial aid, the abandonment of the French system, the perpetual exclusion of Fersen from the House of Nobility, and the *licentiering* of six of the leading Hat Senators—demands which Adolf Fredrik rejected "with indignation."[199] It may be so; but it seems extremely improbable. Such a demand would have run clean counter to Osterman's instructions. Those instructions enjoined him not to lend himself to any party-political persecutions and personal attacks, and to avoid alarming the partisans of France for fear of a backlash.[200] So far from ordering him to prescribe terms to Adolf Fredrik, they had bidden him only to urge the Court not to meddle with the business of parliamentary management, but to leave it to the Caps and the experts. By Osterman's own account the communication of Catherine's advice on this point was in fact the sole purport of the message he sent to the king; and to that message Adolf Fredrik did eventually return a satisfactory answer. Nevertheless, is is clear that around 11 January—only four days before the Diet was to open—relations between Osterman and the Court came to a crisis which very nearly issued in a total breach. But with the Diet so close at hand he could not allow himself the luxury of his resentment: Sinclair was reckoned to have 73 votes at his command in the House of Nobility;[201] and in a close-run contest for *lantmarskalk* those votes might well be decisive. A reconciliation was hastily effected; and the Court gave assurances that though it would publicly profess neutrality, it would cast its votes for the Caps.[202]

The Diet was opened on 15 January 1765; and almost immediately it became clear that the worst fears of the Hats were exceeded by the reality. Swedish parliamentary institutions worked in such a way that the Speaker of each Estate exercised a great, and on occasions a decisive, influence upon the outcome of its debates, for it fell to him to frame the question that was to be put to the vote. Elections to these offices were consequently on party lines, though two Speakers were chosen more or less ex officio: the archbishop presided over the Clergy; a burgomaster of Stockholm over the Burghers. Now the archbishop, as we have seen, was a Cap. All save one of Stockholm's representatives were Caps, too; and a Cap was duly chosen as Speaker of that Estate. The Peasants, who often aligned themselves politically with the Clergy, elected a Cap Speaker by a large majority. Thus it was only the election to the *lantmarskalk*'s chair that remained doubtful, as the last hope of the Hats. But there too they were defeated: Rudbeck was elected with 532 votes against Fersen's 415. The old Hat clan of the Gyllenborgs, jealous of Fersen's rise to prominence, are said to have voted, 60 strong, on the Cap side;[203] the old Hat stalwart Carl Gustaf Tessin, lachrymose at the dissensions in his party, stayed away, by way of mending them;[204] and Sinclair for once was true to his word, and led the Court phalanx over to Rudbeck's side.[205] Breteuil believed that the Court had been influenced by threats of Russian military demonstrations on the Finnish frontier.[206] It is true that rumors of such action had been put about on a couple of occasions in the past six months (once on Buckinghamshire's suggestion, and with Sandwich's blessing).[207] It is also true that Panin, in his rescript to Osterman of 9 December, had assured him that Russia would keep sufficient troops near the frontier to convince the Swedes that she did not lack the power to interfere, if it should be necessary.[208] But it is unlikely that Osterman invoked that threat at this juncture: on the contrary, he wrote to Panin that he hoped that Catherine would refrain from using it.[209] The motives which led the Court to vote for Rudbeck cannot be stated with certainty, but they can easily be conjectured: perhaps because Lovisa Ulrika felt her credit would not stand breaking her word within the week; perhaps because she still hoped that the Caps might refrain from party persecutions; perhaps because her agreement with the Hats promised such meager benefits. Whatever the motive, it must have been obvious to her, and to all other observers, that the Caps had been lucky to carry Rudbeck's election: Goodricke confessed that he was disappointed with the figures.[210] It would not take much shifting of allegiance to make the Caps vulnerable in the House of Nobility. In the meantime, they carried all before them. Election of members to committees by the House of Nobility was effected by a complicated procedure whereby each of the fifty-eight benches in the House elected a "benchman," the benchmen elected electors, and they in turn elected members to committees. By good management and good luck all these elections went strongly in the Caps' favor.[211] Breteuil hoped to the last to be able to make a fight for a good Hat representation on the Secret Committee; but in the event, of the hundred members only a handful were Hats.[212] The all-powerful Estates were now firmly under the control of a single party, and that party had a generation of wrong to put right, and a long record of victimization to avenge.

It is unlikely that either Goodricke or Osterman, whatever they may have implied in their dispatches, really believed that this result was due mainly to their activities, or that the issue had been decided by some few thousands of pounds of Russian and English gold.[213] The victory of the Caps had its roots deep in the history of the past two decades. It had looked probable from at least as long ago as 1762. The Hats were defeated because the electorate, and a sizeable section of the Nobility, rejected their policies, detested their practice, and disliked their persons. A quarter of a century's tenure of power had left them split into jealous coteries,[214] bankrupt of ideas, odious to the nation. Their blatant jobbery in favor of sound party men had at last alienated even their most loyal supporters in Stockholm.[215] Their policy of secrecy, their concentration of power in the hands of the Secret Committee, had provoked a reaction which demanded the end of censorship, an administration open to the daylight, the entrusting of decisions not to committees but to the *plena* of the Estates themselves. For years Hats had had the pick of official posts; but now officialdom as such had become unpopular, and in many towns the result of the poll had been influenced by the determination of the burghers to emancipate themselves from the control of their magistrates. The country was suffering from an accumulation of economic ills which personally affected the man in the street, and for which it was necessary to find a scapegoat. All classes were feeling the effects of a sharp rise in prices, unaccompanied by any corresponding increase in wages and salaries. It had begun during the war, and culminated about the end of 1763; and no doubt it was produced by the recklessly liberal policy of the Bank in the matter of credit and loans, by the overissue of paper money, and—in regard to imported articles—by the sharp depreciation of the Swedish currency on the international exchanges. One class of men, and one only, appeared to thrive in this situation: the great exporting firms whose business was mainly in iron, and who had done very well out of the war: the Grills, the Totties, Jennings & Finlay, and their kind—Hats almost to a man. Against the ostentatious prosperity of a handful of wholesale exporters was set the ruin of the importers and the small merchants.

There was, indeed, one other class which was precariously kept going by massive injections of gold: the manufacturers. But their survival was now accounted one of the Hats' demerits. Ever since their coming to power, the Hats had pursued a policy of rigorous protection, designed to foster native industry and render Sweden independent of manufactured imports, particularly of most kinds of textiles. It had proved an uphill struggle; but behind a prohibitive tariff hedge the Swedish textile industry had shot up, somewhat weedy, rather rootless, chronically chlorotic; but still alive. But now the cry for an end of secrecy and censorship was mingled with the cry for an end to privilege, paternalism, and protection. The unprivileged towns clamored for the abolition of the specially favored position of the staple-towns. The old guild regulations were under attack. Trade (it was said) ought to be freed from shackles and restraints; Sweden should not seek to engage in manufactures to which she was ill-suited, but concentrate on those forms of economic activity for which Nature seemed to have designed her.

Against these new notions and new demands the Hats had no other defense than feebly to reiterate maxims which rang hollow, and policies which had failed. Against the assault on privilege they were defenseless, since they lacked the only argument which might have availed them—the argument of success. Defeat therefore drove them, as the party of privilege, to bargain afresh with their old adversary the crown, in the hope that by the crown's aid privilege might still somehow be preserved. It was a reasonable hope to entertain.

But when, seven years hence, the bargain was finally struck, they would find that they had a heavy price to pay.

(vi)

Not much of all this, perhaps, was understood in London; and if it had been, it would probably only have reinforced Lord Sandwich's resentment at having to disgorge so much money for ends which were either undefined or unacceptable. Still, it was undeniable that he had sent Goodricke to Stockholm with exhortations to use the favorable opportunity to overturn the French system, and that he had in fact overturned it. Since 1739 no other British minister had been able to do as much. Certainly Goodricke's adversaries on the spot were forced to give unwilling testimony to the effectiveness of his exertions. It is remarkable that both for Breteuil and for Schack it is Goodricke, rather than Osterman, who is the chief target of their animosity; Goodricke whom Breteuil considers as his principal rival;[216] Goodricke who is "active"; Goodricke who is considered to be inciting the Caps to violent measures.[217] Their reports are a curious mixture of unconscious tributes to his efforts, and denigrations of his methods and of himself. Extraordinary how badly he chooses his agents![218] Remarkable that he should spend so much money among "low people," from whom nothing can be expected![219] In August Breteuil had remarked to Schack that "puisqu'il falloit admettre un Ministre Anglois à cette Cour, on n'aurait jamais pu rencontrer plus heureusement!"[220] A couple of months later, though still contemptuous, he was showing signs of disquiet: "M. Goodricke est un homme fort propre à la petite intrigue et si fort accoutumé aux souterrains les plus obscurs qu'il est impossible à suivre et difficile d'éclaircir sa conduite"—which prompted the uneasy reflection that "Il sera fort incommode pendant la tenue des Etats."[221] But if Breteuil regarded him with a mixture of contempt and apprehension, Schack actively disliked him from the start, and persuaded himself (as he tried to persuade Bernstorff) that everybody else disliked him too. As early as July he was reporting that Goodricke was unpopular even with the Caps;[222] and he continued to harp on this string. He was therefore a good deal taken aback when Bernstorff, who had seen Goodricke at close quarters for a matter of six years, gently but firmly corrected his ideas: "Je puis vous dire mais en grande Confidence que le Ch: Goodricke agit en homme de bien et de sens, qu'il parle vrai à sa Cour, et que ne partageant point les haines et les fureurs de ceux qui voudroient que tout peut, pourvu que l'authorité fut arraché des mains des Amis de France . . ."—he was on the whole a man to be relied on.[223] Schack swallowed this with a wry face; but he did not change his opinion. His reply, while professing to bow to his chief's superior judgment, adroitly buttressed his former observations with moral considerations calculated to shock Bernstorff's sense of propriety:

> je l'avoue, que je ne l'ai pas cru si bien disposé comme je suis persuadé a cette heure qu'il l'est effectivement, et si en quelque façon je l'ai regardé jusques ici comme un Homme peu dangéreux, ce n'a pas été que je lui ai supposé incapable des sentiments équitables et modérés, mais parceque dans tout le Public de Stockholm il passe pour un Homme enclin à de certains Vices et par là peu propre à faire le Mal que j'ai cru qu'il désiroit faire aux bien intentionnés dans ce Pays-ci et c'est aussi à cette Raison-là que l'on a attribué les Mécontentements des Bonnets contre lui. Je suis donc enchanté d'être tiré de mon Erreur à son égard.[224]

That Goodricke, as Schack suggested, was somehow disabled from doing his job effectively, was disproved by the whole history of his mission. That he was unpopular with his own side appears unlikely, and certainly does not emerge from the—admittedly rather scanty—evidence which the Cap leaders have left behind them. That he was a homosexual is an allegation which seems to rest solely on this dispatch: otherwise it is wholly unsubstantiated; though it may well be that the story was put about in Hat circles in an attempt to discredit him. No more was heard, indeed, of Goodricke's alleged homosexuality; but Bernstorff was informed that he devoted himself to the pleasures of the table to such an extent as to be a cause of general remark.[225] This may well be true, for Goodricke seems to have been a convivial fellow, and the moment was doubly propitious: first, because political considerations demanded lavish entertainment, with the Diet just in the offing; and secondly, because the opportunities for good eating had just been notably enlarged: the Swedish cuisine had recently been provided with its Bible, in the form of Cajsa Warg's immortal cookbook; and since 1760 Johan Abraham Nebb had been specializing in the production of those meat pasties whose reputation resembled that of Bellamy's pork pies.[226]

What both Schack and Breteuil failed to appreciate was the strategic insight which led Goodricke to concentrate his efforts in the quarter where they could most easily be made, and where success would be most telling: the Estate of Burghers. Schack might write disdainfully of his constant consorting with "le tanneur Westin";[227] Tessin might note with distaste how the English minister was to be found "now in the clubs, now smoking in company in the homes of Stockholm burghers."[228] It is difficult to imagine how he could have been better employed. Westin was the Caps' political boss in Stockholm; and many a wavering burgher must have been flattered to entertain in his own home a minister who could speak his own language. No doubt Goodricke received important assistance from his banker, John Fenwick, who opened his house and made it a center of Cap politics in Stockholm.[229] No doubt Sir Joseph Yorke was right when he wrote that "our friend Sir John has . . . done wonders; but with[t] the Empress of Russia he would long since have been laid sprawling."[230] But this, after all, referred only to the size of the financial resources which Sandwich and Panin respectively put at the disposal of their ministers. Within the limits of those resources he had indeed done wonders, and official comment in London paid ungrudging tribute to his exertions.[231] And he had succeeded precisely because, unlike the aristocrat Breteuil, he had canvassed that middling sort of men who formed the core of the new Cap party, and who were the real victors in 1765.

Within the space of eight or nine months Goodricke had thus achieved a result which would have seemed sufficiently improbable in the days when he was clinging precariously to an unhopeful mission in Copenhagen. He had persuaded an unenthusiastic government to interest itself in Swedish affairs. He had led it, step by step, into a position in which it could scarcely avoid having a Swedish policy. In the process, he had transformed himself in the eyes of Whitehall from being an unknown, peripheral, expendable person, into a minister with a well-deserved reputation for energy and an undeniable record of success. But he knew enough of the politics of patronage to be aware that a discreet minister would do well to commend himself to the consideration of his chief upon other grounds besides those of public service. No doubt it might now seem that he had at last hacked out for himself a firm foothold in the diplomatic line. But personal experience had taught him how easily such a foothold could crumble beneath him, and how lightheartedly he might be sacrificed to serve the conveniences of domestic political arrangements. He was now a man of fifty-six: too old, if things went ill, to begin the world afresh. He could not afford to neglect any opportunity of ingratiating himself politically with his masters in the Secretary's office. Such an opportunity presented itself in the late autumn of 1764. It seems to have come to his notice that it had been reported to Sandwich that he had said that without Pitt, the Grenville ministry was too weak to stand. Goodricke seized the chance to write privately to Sandwich, denying the view which had been ascribed to him, and assuring him of his political support. The letter seems to have been lost; but its tenor is clear enough from the terms of Sandwich's reply. It happened (as that sharp-eyed observer Nolcken noted)[232] that just about this time the administration was courting the support of the Yorkes. Goodricke may have been aware of this: at all events, his being known to be the friend of Lord Hardwicke, and the protégé of Sir Joseph Yorke, may possibly have added a touch of warmth to Sandwich's answer. For though brief, that answer was decidedly cordial; and it ended by expressing the conviction that "I may depend upon you hereafter not only as an able minister, but as one in whom I place real confidence."[233]

Goodricke's letter had thus achieved its purpose. It had established, as no doubt it was intended to do, a personal relationship between himself and the minister. But whatever weight we ascribe to the influence of the Yorkes, it hardly provides a full explanation of the terms of Sandwich's response. A year ago, we may be confident, not all the Yorkes in England could have induced Sandwich to treat a profession of political support from Goodricke with anything other than indifference. The case was altered now. Yorkes or no Yorkes, he had shown himself in sober truth to be "an able minister." No doubt he hoped that the "real confidence" might be interpreted as referring, not only to his political attachment, but to his conduct of affairs at his place of residence. Certainly he would need all the confidence Sandwich could give him, in the months that lay ahead. For the great victory of January 1765, after the pattern of such electoral triumphs, raised more problems than it solved. And of this Goodricke, even in the exuberance of success, was in some measure aware.

CHAPTER IV

Lord Sandwich in Search of a Policy, 1765

(i)

The election was won; Rudbeck was *lantmarskalk*; benchmen, electors, Secret Committee, were all firmly in the hands of the friends of England. Their success confronted Lord Sandwich with the need to come to a decision on three closely interlinked issues. First: was he to continue to pursue the plan of 31 August, once the "preliminary stage" of that plan had been completed, and to draw on the Civil List for the purpose of "keeping the party together" thereafter? Secondly: what concrete advantage for England should he try to obtain, in exchange for the support which had already been given to the Caps, and might continue to be given to them in the future? And thirdly: how far was he prepared to go in collaborating with Catherine in Stockholm?—a question which involved the much larger one of whether, in the immediate future, an Anglo-Russian alliance was attainable.

The first of these questions seemed, indeed, to have been answered already. Goodricke, as we have seen, had rashly intimated that he proposed to proceed upon the assumption that the money for stage 2 of the plan of 31 August would be forthcoming. The assumption, as he found to his chagrin, proved to be unwarranted. Sandwich lost no time in disabusing him of such ideas. On 4 January 1765 he was informed that he need expect no further supply until Catherine had made clear what her intentions in Sweden might be: some sort of agreement to share the preliminary expenses had no doubt been made, but no proposal for sharing expenses thereafter had come from St. Petersburg. Despite repeated reminders that England would not take the lead in Sweden, Panin had remained silent; and his silence could be construed only as "either a Proof that they are not serious in their Designs, or that they wait to have them brought about, at the Expense of this Crown." Until Sandwich was told what Russia's plan was, there would be no more money; and any future contributions from England must depend upon the acceptability of Panin's proposals, when at last he should think proper to make any.[1]

This cold douche reached Goodricke at a critical moment:[2] the elections for benchmen were impending; the struggle for the Secret Committee was still to come; the great merchants of Stockholm had subscribed £6,000 to get their friends on to the important committees.[3] Yet at the very moment when the creation of a strong party which should be essentially "English" seemed to have become possible, Goodricke was to be cut off from the means of sustaining it, and was to find himself relegated to the position of a spectator, or at best to that of the poor relation of the minister of Russia. It is hardly surprising that he found his orders discouraging.

Sandwich had based his refusal of further supplies upon Panin's failure to produce a plan. Yet within a few hours of writing to Goodricke, that plan was in all essentials in his possession. For on that same day he had an interview with Gross, in which the Russian minister gave him what seems to have been a full account of Panin's intentions.[4] Sandwich perhaps regarded Gross's communication as nonministerial; for though he at once wrote a second letter to Goodricke reporting the interview, he made no change in his instructions, said nothing of what Gross had told him, but informed him simply that he was expecting proposals from Russia shortly.[5] It was not until 15 January that he notified Goodricke of Panin's plan, and he then represented it as having just been delivered to Gross by courier.[6] As it happened, the delay of eleven days made no difference, for Goodricke was given particulars of the plan by Osterman on the same day as Gross first imparted them to Sandwich;[7] but it suggests that Sandwich may have felt the need to consult his colleagues in the cabinet. However that may be, when he wrote to Goodricke on 15 January he was in no doubt about his attitude, and he made his disapproval crystal clear.[8] On the details of the plan he did not trouble himself to comment, contenting himself with the remark that it was pointless to discuss proposals "which Russia has actually adopted, and which they have deferr'd communicating to this Court, 'till it is too late to make any reply." His detailed objections were not sent to Goodricke until a month after that.[9] Six weeks were required, it seems, to give articulate form to his suspicions and his resentments.

Panin's plan, so long and so impatiently awaited by Osterman, had certainly been an unconscionable time in coming–so long a time, that Panin felt called upon to preface it by apologies, excuses, and arguments that the delay did not really matter.[10] Yet when it at last appeared there was little in it which can have caused Osterman much surprise.[11] It made a sharp distinction between what it termed "the Interior" and "the Exterior"–that is, between Sweden's domestic arrangements and her system of foreign policy. On the Interior, the proposals were strictly in line with Panin's thinking as it had developed since the autumn of 1763. The objective here was a revision of the constitution to ensure an equilibrium of forces. The crown was to be given a little more power; the Senate, a good deal less; the Estates were to be left in firm control of taxation, and of the power of peace and war. But the clause in the constitution of 1720 which gave to the Estates the right to "improve and interpret" the constitution was to be removed, and in its place was to be inserted a provision that no constitutional change was permissible unless it had been approved by two successive Diets, with an election in between. As to the Exterior, Panin observed that in Sweden's present state of decline the French system was of no particular danger to Russia, once the constitutional changes which he desired had been effected. It would moreover be a costly business to overthrow it. The destruction of the French system was in any case the task of England, though Russia would give close support to any efforts to effect it. If those efforts proved successful, the moment would then be opportune for reversing the arrangement which France had favored, and making Denmark (whose treaty with Russia would probably soon be concluded) the "active" power in the North, and Sweden the "inactive." For the rest, the Court must be warned to keep out of party politics, and to abandon the idea of forming its own party; the Caps were to be strongly supported, and made if possible to feel themselves a Russian party; but Osterman was to urge them to be moderate, and was to give no encouragement to personal attacks or acts of party vengeance. Russia's only concern with Sweden was that the country should be prosperous, and should remain neutral; though if the Caps showed any willingness to join Panin's Northern System[12] it might be discreetly hinted to some of their leaders that the incorporation of Norway would give Sweden her logical geographical boundaries.

Such was the tenor of Panin's rescript to Osterman, which reached him soon after the New Year. The summary of it which Gross imparted to Sandwich on 4 January was based on a rescript to him of 13/24 November,[13] and differed from the rescript to Osterman mainly in omitting much of the detail about domestic politics and the Court, and in saying nothing of Norway, or of Russian indifference as to which external system a reformed Sweden might adopt. It was also a little more explicit on the role allotted to England. It pointed out that Russia could offer Sweden no compensating advantage for the abandonment of the French system; and that the threat of a naval treaty with France was a matter which was primarily England's concern. It proposed therefore that England should offer Sweden a treaty of alliance, and thereafter make Denmark the active and Sweden the inactive power in the North. And finally it reiterated Panin's rejection of Sandwich's demand for a common purse and a guaranteed equality of expenditure on corruption, on the ground that such an arrangement had always proved ineffective in the past.

In all essentials, then, Sandwich was made fully aware of Russian policy by 4 January 1765. It is not to be denied that this was very late, and he was entitled to complain that it left him with the alternatives of either acquiescing in a plan he had had no time to consider, and which committed him to financial burdens which he had from the beginning declined to bear, or of throwing up the sponge in Stockholm altogether, and thus putting himself in the position of having spent his money for nothing. But his objections went very much further than this. He complained that Panin's proposals not only were late, but also in many respects represented a change of policy, sprung upon him without prior consultation, and put into effect without his being given any opportunity of remonstrance.[14] When on 19 February he at last indicated to Goodricke the precise points to which he took exception, it was this that formed the burden of his complaint. "That Court [Russia]," he wrote, "has deviated from the Original Plan . . . ; they begun by building One System, and suddenly adopted another." Goodricke had been sent to Sweden, England had intervened in Swedish affairs, to please Catherine, and at her request. She had been repeatedly told that England would not "take the lead"; she had been repeatedly invited to communicate her plan. England had risked "a previous and certain expence" on the clear understanding that Russia would provide money *pari passu*; but

> only when our measures had been successful in changing the general disposition of Sweden, did Russia reveal her plan. It separates the two Courts, destroys the project of 31 August, and confronts us with either losing all the money we have so far spent, or undertaking such Burthens, as we have utterly disclaimed from the beginning.[15]

The plan, he told Macartney, was "totally inconsistent with the King's constant declarations." He felt himself to have been the victim of Russian sharp practice; he wrote angrily of Panin's "duplicity."[16]

Much of this was unfair and unreasonable: a self-induced tantrum wholly disproportionate to the provocation offered. It was untrue, for instance, to say that the plan had been produced "only when our measures had been successful": when the plan left St. Petersburg for Stockholm on 9/20 December—and still more when the rescript for Gross left on 13/24 November—the battle for control of the Diet had hardly begun. It by no means followed that the plan would "separate the two Courts," or "destroy the project of 31 August:" Osterman continued to collaborate closely with Goodricke (as Panin had ordered him to do) after supplies from England were cut off; and if "the project of 31 August" was destroyed at all, it was destroyed by Sandwich on 4 January, quite as much as by Panin. And, after all, how much of Panin's plan was really new to Sandwich? The program for the Interior can certainly have come as no surprise, for both Buckinghamshire and Goodricke had already correctly reported it.[17] It was in any case a matter in which Sandwich took little interest, and on this part of the plan he made no comment whatever The idea of making a clear demarcation between Interior and Exterior had long been no less familiar to him. He had drawn this distinction himself, when forwarding Goodricke's interrogatories on Russian policy to Buckinghamshire; for the first of these had concerned Panin's plans for the Interior, and the second had run: "What does Russia want *us* [my italics] to propose to Sweden or endeavour to lead them into?" To which Buckinghamshire had answered that Panin wanted England to enter into a treaty with Sweden of the same tendency as the existing Russo-Swedish treaty.[18] On 8 September Buckinghamshire had given a very plain indication of the lines along which Panin was thinking: "He further insinuated that if England meant hereafter to establish a system in the North, she must take upon her that subsidy which France now pays to Sweden, also that she must secure the Court of Denmark."[19] On 17 October he had reported that Panin did not think the throwing of Sweden into England's hands to be worth a Russian subsidy;[20] on 6 November Goodricke had suggested a defensive alliance with Sweden, to which Russia might then adhere;[21] on 31 December he had given it as his opinion that Panin wished to force Sweden into "our [*sic*] system."[22] And finally, Buckinghamshire, in a dispatch which reached London on 1 February 1765 (that is, long before Sandwich formulated his detailed objections to Goodricke), reported Panin as saying that if England could arrange a defensive alliance with

Sweden, Russia would accede to it.[23] Thus the idea of England's making herself responsible for the Exterior was no new one at the time of Sandwich's reception of Panin's plan, and still less at the time of his letter to Goodricke on 19 February. No doubt Sandwich was entitled to retort that he had consistently taken the line that any change in Sweden's foreign alignments must be dependent on Russia's drawing up a plan to that end, and that he had never committed himself further than to promise that he would *cooperate* with Russia to overturn the French system.[24] In his interview with Gross on 4 January he made it clear that he did not relish the suggestion that England should assume sole responsibility for the Exterior, or take it upon herself to propose an alliance with Sweden.[25] But though it may be granted that Sandwich's attitude was consistent on this point, it cannot be said that Panin's proposal came to him as a novelty, or that it in any sense represented a change in Russia's plans.

The same is true in regard to the proposal to make Denmark the active power. This was an idea which had been in Panin's mind as long ago as September 1763.[26] Already on 8 September 1764 Buckinghamshire had reported him as saying "that as it has been the policy of France to keep Denmark quiet in order to avail herself of the force of Sweden, so hereafter it might be advisable for England to make Sweden passive, that Denmark might be enabled to give her effectual assistance."[27] To Osterman, it seems, the idea was really new: he pointed it out to Goodricke as the only novel feature in Panin's plan, and argued that it would put Denmark, as well as Sweden, into England's pocket.[28] Sandwich regarded Denmark as the mere puppet of France;[29] and it might therefore have been expected that this particular proposal would have little attraction for him. But if we may rely on the accuracy of Gross's reporting (a somewhat dubious assumption).[30] this was the one feature of the plan to which he gave his immediate approval.[31] If so, it was not long before he changed his mind. On 15 January he told Macartney that though he would be glad to see Denmark emancipated from France, and though the keeping of Sweden inactive "seems the most eligible on all accounts," it would still be necessary to maintain a preponderant influence in Stockholm.[32] By 9 April he was writing to Goodricke that

> This [i.e., the inactivity of Sweden and the activity of Denmark], which would be a good Policy with respect to the Interests of Great Britain, if our former Connections with Russia were renewed and strengthened, would be of dangerous tendency, whilst things continue on their present uncertain footing; How much more critical would it be if, by a Change of system, not difficult to be foreseen, the Houses of Austria and Bourbon should

> separate their unnatural Coalition, and the Czarina's aversion to the Court of Vienna, and Predilection for the King of Prussia, should engage her to join that Prince in the part which he would gladly take, that of uniting himself intimately with France. The Activity of Denmark would then be as troublesome to the Interests of this Country as the Inability of Sweden would be a charge.[33]

There was certainly some force in the argument that the situation would be transformed if the hoped-for Anglo-Russian alliance should not be concluded; and Sandwich could fairly contend that since Russia and Denmark were known to be on the point of signing a treaty of alliance (if indeed it was not signed already) Denmark was more Russia's concern than England's. But the hypothetical case which he posited was a mere fantasy without any basis in reality. It was nonsense to suppose that Frederick sought an alliance with France; and it was equally nonsense to suppose that Catherine would be disposed to follow him if he made one. If British policy was to take into account contingencies as improbable as these, it would scarcely be prudent to formulate any policy at all.

It appears, then, that there was no essential part of Panin's plan of which Sandwich had not had ample warning beforehand: in no sense was it new. Nothing was being sprung on him. He might charge Panin with indolence and procrastination, but certainly not with duplicity. What, then, is the explanation for his strongly hostile reaction, and for the sense of pique and chagrin which appears so plainly in his letters of the spring of 1765? One clue to his attitude seems to lie in his inability to understand that even though England were to shoulder the entire burden of reversing Sweden's foreign policy Russia would still be deeply committed to expenditure to "keep the party together." An English alliance for Sweden had become conceivable only because Panin had already spent lavishly (more lavishly than Sandwich) to secure a Cap victory. An English alliance would be attainable only if Russia continued that financial support without which Cap majorities in the Diet would be precarious. Panin's plan, if rigorously interpreted, might have meant that England was free to refuse cooperation in all parliamentary maneuvers which did not bear on foreign affairs. But this would have been a nonsensical interpretation. The Caps must be supported by England on all issues, for only the Caps could and would end the French system. Russian backing for them on questions of domestic concern was thus indirectly a service to England. On foreign affairs Russia could not take the lead; and this because (as Panin himself noted) Russia's position as Sweden's neighbor made any direct interference with her foreign policy too invidious, and therefore too counter-productive, for her to undertake if it could be avoided;[34] and because the Caps whom Russia supported thought of themselves as an "English" rather than as a "Russian" party.[35] It was a Russian aim to make a clean sweep of the Hat members of the Senate, and not least of Claes Ekeblad, the chancery-president, in whose hands the direction of foreign policy lay. A Cap chancery-president would mean a foreign policy orientated towards England. Thus a Russian-sponsored change in the Interior would have direct repercussions on the Exterior; Russian corruption would serve England's purposes: as Goodricke pointed out, Interior and Exterior were interdependent,[36] and Panin's refusal to agree to a common purse and the principle of *pari passu* expenditure, however irritating, in reality made no difference.[37] The course of events would demonstrate how unrealistic were Sandwich's suspicions that Panin hoped to "charge the Nation with an insupportable Burthen of Expence": in the next five or six months by far the larger share in the expenses of corruption would be borne by Russia.

At a deeper level, however, Sandwich's suspicions were the expression of something more than mere Grenvillian parsimony. They revealed ministers' fundamental uncertainty about the pattern of international relationships at which British foreign policy ought now to aim. That uncertainty was reflected in Sandwich's hypothetical conjectures about the possibility of a Russo-Prussian rapprochement with France. It was reflected also in his doubts and reservations about England's relations with Russia. He seems not to have made up his mind as to how far along Russia's road he was prepared to go. Certainly he desired, as all English minsters desired, a Russian alliance; but he was not ready to accept terms which would have committed his country to support of Russia in a Turkish war, or to material assistance in Poland.[38] To garner the fruits of victory in Stockholm (such as they were) would no doubt be satisfactory; but the satisfaction would be dearly bought if it incidentally involved England in commitments wider than she was ready to meet. An alliance with Russia was one thing; membership of Panin's Northern System was another.

The origins of Panin's famous Northern System are still a matter of dispute among historians.[39] Fortunately this is a controversy into which it is unnecessary to enter here: whoever may first have conceived the idea, Panin had certainly embraced it by the spring of 1764, and probably even at the time of the October Conference of 1763. The project was based on the belief that Russia needed peace to put her finances in order and improve her administration; and upon the assumption that the peace of Europe was menaced by the Bourbon-Hapsburg alliance, and that measures must be taken to build up a great coalition of northern powers as a counterpoise to "the formidable League of the South." From the start its logic was vitiated by the falseness of the premise upon which it was built. The Bourbon-Hapsburg alliance was in reality no serious threat to the peace of Europe. It was rather designed to ensure peace in Germany while the Family Compact maneuvered for an opportunity to take revenge upon England in America, India, and on the seas. The danger to Russia, in particular, was grossly exaggerated: the feeble performance of Sweden in the Seven Years War, the humiliating collapse of French diplomacy in Poland after the death of Augustus III, should have been sufficiently reassuring to Russian statesmen; and though French intrigues did indeed lie behind the Turkish war of 1768, that was in no sense the result of the Franco-Austrian alliance. Sabathier de Cabres was not far wrong when he dismissed Panin's Northern System as "un nom pompeux" which added nothing to the effective power of Russia and Prussia.[40]

Nevertheless, whether soundly based or not, the idea was pursued by Panin with great pertinacity. He was too wise to attempt to create a full-blown league from the beginning: his tactics were agglutinative—first one bilateral alliance, then another, expanding by a process of accession, knit tighter by cross-alliances between successive members, and all bound together by common subscription to the principle of maintaining "the Tranquillity of the North." The first stone in the projected edifice was laid with the conclusion of the Russo-Prussian alliance of April 1764; but already Panin had taken his measures for attaching Denmark: they were to come to fruition in the Russo-Danish alliance of March 1765. The election of Stanisław Poniatowski to the throne of Poland, in 1764, was significant not only of the strength of the new link between Prussia and Russia, but of Panin's intention to make Poland an effective member of his system: Poland was to replace Austria as Russia's bulwark against the Turks; and if Panin had had his way the Czartoryski would have been permitted to carry through reforms which would have had the effect of making Poland's alliance a real military asset.[41] The success in Poland was significant in another way also. For when the issue of the denial of rights to the Dissidents began to engage Catherine's attention she received diplomatic support not only from Prussia, but also from Denmark and England.[42] It seemed that the Northern System had begun de facto to operate as a system, even though as yet only in a small way; and that it had acquired, as Panin perhaps intended that it should, something of the aspect of a concert of Protestant or, at least, of anti-Catholic powers. In these circumstances it was not unnatural to conjecture that once it had really taken shape the Dutch would join it;[43] and no less natural to suppose that England and Sweden would be included.

But England and Sweden presented difficulties. There can be little doubt that Panin, despite later disclaimers, had thought of England as one of the founder-members: at the time when the alliance with Prussia was still under negotiation he had inquired of Frederick whether he would have any objection to England's inclusion.[44] Frederick had very decided objections, which were not to be shifted.[45] He chose to hide them behind the rancor he felt at his treatment by Bute; but though the rancor was real enough, his opposition to England's entry into Panin's system was based on reason rather than sentiment. He realized, better than Panin, that England was not a "continental" power, and could not be relied on to take a "continental" view of things; he did all he could to prevent an Anglo-Russian alliance, because he desired to secure a monopoly of Russian friendship for himself, and by thus isolating Russia put a bridle upon the power he most feared;[46] and he refused to commit himself to any Northern System on the very reasonable ground that so far from securing the peace, it might imperil the tacit agreement among the powers to keep Germany neutral in the next Anglo-French war. In the face of this attitude Panin had for the moment dropped the idea of England's adhesion to the Prussian alliance, and had fallen back on that of a series of separate alliances between Russia and the powers he wished to attract.[47] He looked upon the conclusion of an alliance with England as being merely a question of time, and believed that he could wear down English intransigence on such points as the obligation to give assistance in a Turkish war.[48] As to Denmark, he had good reason to be confident, once Bernstorff was convinced that he was really being offered a settlement of the Holstein question. Neither in the case of England nor in that of Denmark did Panin expect to meet with any difficulty which could not be overcome by patience and persistence. It was not surprising that Frederick should have watched both negotiations with growing chagrin.

The case of Sweden was less straightforward. If Denmark should enter the Northern System it would be imperative that Sweden should be a member; for to have the two Scandinavian powers in opposite camps would give France precisely the opening for creating trouble which Panin was anxious to block up. As long as Swedish foreign policy was in the hands of a Hat chancery-president, as long as Swedish finances were propped up by French subsidies, there was nothing to be done in Stockholm. But the Cap victory at the elections, and the storm of indignation at the Senate's hasty acceptance of the French proposals for paying off arrears, offered an opportunity which could not be let slip. Panin knew well enough that a Russian alliance could never be popular in Sweden; but an Anglo-Swedish alliance was a different matter. Such an alliance would be in England's interests, since it would at a stroke break France's long domination, and would remove the threat of a Franco-Swedish naval treaty. Russia, it might be argued, was doing her share by securing, not without some sacrifices, the alliance of Denmark. England might surely be expected to do hers, in the shape of bearing the cost of carrying the negotiations for an alliance to a successful issue. When he suggested to Buckinghamshire that Russia might well be willing to accede to an Anglo-Swedish treaty, he probably believed that he was dangling a bait which Sandwich would find himself unable to decline.

If so, he misunderstood the men with whom he had to deal. The Grenville ministry were deeply concerned at the size of the National Debt, and at what they called the "exhaustion" of England at the end of the war.[49] They felt that a period of recuperation was imperative if the country were to be fit to meet the threat of a French *revanche*: some of them, indeed, believed that the only safe course for the moment was to seek a real reconciliation with France. But on the other hand they had a robust faith in England's inherent strength; they could not forget that they had emerged triumphant from the late war; and it seemed to them that the alliance of England was so desirable an object that they had no need to hawk it round or abate the terms on which they would be prepared to grant it.[50] To Russia, they believed, it was so obviously advantageous that its conclusion was only a matter of waiting until the Russians realized that their extravagant demands could not be accepted: in the meantime, ministers were in no hurry. No doubt even an island power must take care to exercise some influence on the Continent, if the peace on which British commerce throve was to be preserved;[51] but for the present the Continent appeared quiescent,[52] and it looked as though for the foreseeable future the old need for a "continental sword" would be less pressing than before the war. As Nolcken remarked, in the acute analysis of British policy which he sent home early in 1765, ministers calculated that Russia would take care of the North, while Prussia could be relied upon to keep the balance in Germany. If a war should blow up, England would always be able to find allies; and when it came, France would this time leave Germany alone, and direct her sole continental diversion against Portugal.[53] There were, no doubt, a few individuals who were truly and avowedly isolationist, men who would have turned their backs on the Continent and kept clear of all alliances.[54]

But this was not the attitude of Sandwich, nor of most of his colleagues. Sandwich was concerned, as Panin was, for the Tranquillity of the North, and for a proper balance; but he felt that England had no need to allow herself to be stampeded into some system devised elsewhere, as the only means of attaining it.

> The Truth is, that His Majesty, duly weighing wherein the Interest, as well as the strength of this Kingdom principally consists, will not throw away the Advantage of the Situation, by making It a Part of the Continent; but will never lose sight of the great Weight and Influence, which It must always have there, and which It can only maintain, by making a proper Use of Its Power as an Island.[55]

As the qualifying clause shows, Sandwich was not an isolationist, and Gross misled Panin when he reported that he was;[56] but unlike Pitt he was not unduly alarmed by Britain's isolation, for he was confident that it was accidental and temporary. He did not realize how quickly after the peace international relations congealed into fixed patterns, difficult to change. He certainly misjudged the situation in thinking that more than one option was open to him. In common with many of his fellow-countrymen he believed that it might still be possible to restore the old alliance with Austria, whose defection to France was responsible for what Stormont called "the violent and unnatural state" of Europe.[57] In January 1765 he considered the prospects for a renewal of the Old System not unpromising.[58] This was, of course, a delusion: Kaunitz had made his choice, and as long as he lived he would stick to it.[59] But the belief that he might be persuaded to change his mind undoubtedly influenced Sandwich's approach to the question of an alliance with Russia, and also to the larger question of a possible Northern System.

At the end of 1764 the negotiations for that alliance appeared to have stuck fast altogether. The substitution of Macartney for Buckinghamshire did indeed give an opportunity for a fresh start; but Macartney's immediate business in St. Petersburg was the conclusion, not of the alliance, but of the long-pending commercial treaty. There seemed little hope of agreement on the "Turkish clause." The open or secret subsidies which Panin suggested in its place were equally unacceptable.[60] With Russia's close ally, Prussia, relations were severely strained, as a result of the intrigues of Michell, Frederick's minister in London, with members of the Opposition, and his consequent recall at the demand of the British government.[61] Sandwich was as determined to keep clear of any engagements with Prussia as Frederick was to veto English accession to his alliance with Catherine.[62] As to

Russia, the Mirovich affair had lent credibility to Buckinghamshire's prediction that a domestic explosion was not unlikely;[63] and if it came, it might well result in another reversal of Russian foreign policy, as had happened in 1761 and 1762. Lastly, Sandwich could not forget that Buckinghamshire seemed to have been proved right when he foretold that Panin would try to shuffle off the financial burden of creating a Northern System on to England's shoulders.

Considerations such as these do much to explain why Sandwich reacted so unfavorably to Panin's plan. What he had been expecting from Panin was a proposal for shared expenditure in stage 2 of the project of 31 August. What he got was a blueprint for Anglo-Russian strategy in which the *pari passu* principle was conspicuously rejected. He thus disliked the plan not only for what it contained, but for what it omitted. Behind his strained and insubstantial objections lay a real uncertainty about the right course for British foreign policy. The captious and splenetic tone of his letters reflects a feeling that Panin was trying to maneuver him in a game which was not of his choosing, and for purposes whose relevance to England's interests seemed to him at least dubious. Maturer reflection would convince him that one feature of the plan—the Anglo-Swedish treaty—was after all worth pursuing, even from a narrowly English standpoint; but the discovery did not really exorcise the feeling of irritation and resentment which the plan had originally aroused. If England were to be drawn into a Northern System—a prospect which Sandwich cannot have found easy to reconcile with his hankering for an Austrian alliance—it would not be in virtue of directives such as these. He was ready enough to be Russia's friend and ally; but though he might profess willingness to act in Sweden as Russia's not-so-brilliant second, he expected to render that service on his own terms.

(ii)

Meanwhile the position of Goodricke was anything but comfortable. The refusal to send more money was bad enough; the rejection of Panin's plan was worse, since it seemed to forbid any hope that Sandwich would change his mind. Goodricke had reacted to Panin's rescript with frank enthusiasm,[64] and it was depressing to find that his masters at home would neither accept it, nor carry though that other plan of 31 August which it was alleged to have upset. Under these gloomy impressions he predicted that Fersen and the Hats would transfer their allegiance to Russia as soon as Sandwich's decision became known—provided, of course, that Osterman guaranteed to leave the French system undisturbed. In vain he tried to comfort himself with the reflection that all the world would recognize that England had won a moral victory; that the plan of 31 August had been shown to be correctly calculated; that "it was no longer in the power of our enemies to hinder our projects, if we had thought it useful to pursue them":[65] such reflections could neither melt Lord Sandwich nor console their author. The joint efforts of himself and Osterman had contributed to produce a Diet "as perfect as we can desire it . . . our party has not been in the situation they are at present, these thirty years."[66] Was it really conceivable that with so much attained, with the game so nearly decided in England's favor, Sandwich should retire morosely to the sidelines, and leave his partner to finish the match? Goodricke could not reconcile himself to thinking so. Even though Russia was henceforth to find all the money, and England to find none, was it not still possible to reap some sort of political harvest by playing on the fact that whereas the Caps looked to Russia as a paymaster, they looked upon England as a friend, and in some senses as an exemplar? After all, the French system which he had been sent to destroy was still formally intact, and would probably remain so until Sweden proceeded to the decisive step of making an English alliance. Sandwich himself had not so long ago been interested in that possibility. He had reacted with prompt approval to Goodricke's hints of trade concessions. He had defined the main object of Goodricke's mission as the ensuring that the Swedish navy did not fall into French hands. The navy; commerce; an alliance: had all these now become matters of indifference in London?

The outcome of the elections had certainly postponed the naval danger to an indefinite future, since a Cap-dominated Secret Committee would take care to leave behind it a political testament which should tie the hands of the Senate in the interval until the next Diet should assemble. But apart from this, ministers no longer took the naval threat as seriously as had been the case six months before. In August 1764 Sandwich had called for a detailed account of the numbers and condition of the Swedish fleet.[67] The report with which Goodricke furnished him showed a respectable paper force of 26 ships of the line and 10 frigates. Of these, a number of ships of the line, variously estimated at 5 or 12, were fit for service. All had been built before 1758, but they were said to be in good condition, properly rigged, and provided with ammunition for one campaign; though very few had all their stores, and the number of seamen in service was 4,000 less than the full complement.[68] A few days before Goodricke's information reached London, by what was perhaps something more than a coincidence, there was placed in the hands of Lord Egmont, the first lord of the admiralty, a memorandum on the state of the navy of Denmark. It came from the Danish minister, Count Bothmer, and was apparently entirely unsolicited.[69] From this it appeared that Denmark could put to sea some 40 ships of the line and 20 frigates, and would soon raise the number of frigates to 30. This certainly over-trumped Goodricke's statistics; but Sandwich was too old a hand to accept Bothmer's figures without question. He promptly ordered his resident in Denmark, Dudley Cosby, to ascertain not only the numbers but also the date of building, and the date of last repair, of each vessel.[70] Cosby carried out his task with exemplary thoroughness. His report of 23 February 1765 revealed a strength distinctly less than Bothmer had alleged: only 31 ships of the line, and only 14 frigates, both mostly old types, and perhaps designed mainly for service in the Baltic. But on the other hand all save one or two in sound condition, recently repaired, and fit for service, with 4,000 seamen on the payroll, and 20,000-24,000 available at need.[71] Even with Cosby's abatements it was reasonable after this to conclude that it was the Danish rather than the Swedish fleet that should engage England's attention. As far as naval strength was concerned, there could be no doubt that Denmark rather than Sweden was the active power in the North. But long before Cosby's careful investigations reached London Sandwich had decided in his own mind that the Swedish navy was not an object of real importance;[72] and though in February 1765 he could still remark that it was the only thing "which could render that country an object of attention to the Crown *considered separately and unconnected with Russia*,"[73] he was convinced that it was too "debilitated" to be of any service either to England or to her enemies. In which opinion there is every reason to believe that he was right. For in fact the Swedish navy in 1765 had only 11 ships that were serviceable, and even these were old and ill-found. By 1769 the figure had fallen to eight.[74]

There was thus no point in Goodricke's trying to engage Sandwich's interest by conjuring up naval bogeys, and in fact he made no further attempt to do so. But the other baits to which Sandwich had risen in 1764—commercial advantages, alliance without subsidies—these it might be worthwhile to cast again. Four months earlier, in response to Sandwich's eager inquiries as to what trade concessions might be expected from the friends of England, Goodricke had detailed a long list of commodities, at that time totally or virtually prohibited, whose free importation he believed they might be persuaded to concede.[75]

Sandwich passed on Goodricke's dispatch to Lord Hillsborough, the president of the Board of Trade; and it is not surprising that the Board should have shown interest in the prospects it held out. For two generations successive presidents of the Board had shaken their heads over the state of Anglo-Swedish trade without being able to produce any effective measures to correct what they felt to be amiss. That trade had last been regulated by article 12 of the Anglo-Swedish treaty of 1720, which guaranteed most-favored-nation treatment for English merchants, promised that all goods which at that date could be freely imported should continue to be so, and froze duties in both countries at the level of 1720. The treaty had expired in 1738, but the Swedes had made it almost a dead letter soon after it was signed. In 1724 they promulgated their own Navigation Act—the *produktplakat*—which laid it down that no goods might be imported in foreign ships unless they were goods of the country of origin, or of its colonies. In 1722 they introduced a differential tariff in favor of exports in native ships, as a result of which bar-iron exported in foreign bottoms paid as much as 70% more in dues than iron exported in native vessels, while exports of timber in foreign ships paid nearly five times as much.[76] As early as 1728 the Swedes began to raise duties on a wide range of English textiles and hardware; in 1735 they prohibited the import of certain luxury textiles and metal goods; in 1756 they forbade the import of foreign flour, and of various colonial products; in 1759, of oats and malt.[77] These measures hit British shippers no less than British exporters. It might have been supposed that the British government would proceed to reprisals: Great Britain was, after all, by far the best customer that Sweden had. Over half of her exports of bar-iron went to British ports, and bar-iron accounted for three-quarters of her outward trade.[78] In fact no administration after 1720 felt in a position to take retaliatory measures; for although the British market was certainly essential to the Swedish economy, the materials which Sweden provided were indispensable to Great Britain, or at least were thought to be so. Between 1750 and 1759 Britain took 64% of her imported bar-iron from Sweden, as against 27.5% from Russia; and between 1761 and 1770 17% of Swedish tar exports went to the United Kingdom.[79] Alternative sources of supply for both these commodities were no doubt available: iron was increasingly imported from Russia; in the sixties Russia's share of the total imports of bar-iron rose from 27.5% to 44%, and in 1765 for the first time overtook and passed that of Swedish iron. But this competition had little effect on the Swedish iron-exporters, for the total demand for iron in Great Britain was increasing so fast that Swedish exports continued to maintain their level, and even to increase it.[80] What mattered was the peculiarly fine quality of a particular type of Swedish iron—the so-called Oreground iron, which came from a handful of works in Uppland and was shipped from the little port of Öregrund. This was considered to make the best steel; and the Royal Navy would use no other.[81] It is true that the amount involved was relatively small: in 1769 the Navy Board stated it at 700 tons a year in peacetime.[82] But small though the quantity might be, the commodity was felt to be vital to the maintenance of the British navy, and no government was anxious to take steps which might lead to its being cut off.[83] The same was true of the high-quality Swedish tar.[84] In the 1730s, indeed, an attempt was made to force Swedish exporters to lower the price of bar-iron by organizing a temporary boycott by importers; but the government was not involved, and the effects were transient.[85] After 1747 it became difficult to apply pressures of this sort; for in that year the Swedish iron-producers associated themselves into a kind of cartel, operating through the Iron Office (*Jernkontoret*), which had among its other functions that of maintaining a high and steady price for iron by enabling producers to keep it off the market until a satisfactory offer was obtained.[86] Yet in one way the Swedish iron industry was vulnerable. Not through the competition of Russian iron, nor by the actions of aggrieved English importers, but from the fact that the export trade in iron was almost wholly financed by British capital. Iron production was organized on the *Verlag*-system: the wholesale exporter owned the producer's iron before it came to the market, since he had advanced the capital for its production, and the wholesaler himself was no more than a commission-agent for the British importer, and operated with his money.[87] English firms such as Patrick & Robert Macky in London, or Sykes in Hull, were indispensable to the maintenance of production and the marketing of the product. Swedish firms such as Jennings & Finlay, which sent some 90% of their iron to England,[88] were really dependent upon their London importers: in the postwar crisis of 1763 they were saved from bankruptcy only by the support of Macky. In August 1769 the weapon implicit in this arrangement was actually used: the English correspondents of Swedish exporters refused to allow them to draw, as usual, for three-quarters of the value of the iron which they were to deliver.[89]

The means of retaliation were certainly there, but they were used only rarely and halfheartedly, and scarcely ever by the government. Nevertheless, there was a persistent feeling that commercial relations between the two countries were unsatisfactory, and a desire to do something to increase the volume of British exports to Sweden. The

Board of Trade was not happy about the perennial (and increasing) adverse balance in the Swedish trade. It is difficult to establish precise figures, but it seems safe to say that the adverse balance was running at about £170,000 in 1756-57 (the last year of peace) and perhaps £224,000 in 1764.[90] This was mainly attributable to the high protectionist policies of the Hats since 1739. They had spent lavishly in premiums designed to encourage native manufactures; they had laid prohibitive duties, and then absolute prohibitions, on foreign manufactures which competed with domestic products; they had been active in attempting to seduce skilled workmen and technical experts from foreign countries, and sufficiently successful to alarm the Board of Trade.[91] Though successive administrations were from time to time pressed by British iron-producers to take retaliatory action, the leading houses exporting to Sweden seem to have accepted the measures of the Swedish government without audible complaint. After all, many of them had invested capital in the Swedish iron-trade; and even if they had not, the tariff restrictions and prohibitory measures of the Hats hit them less hard than might have been expected. It was true that they found the opportunities for exporting textiles and hardware successively blocked up; but they contrived to make good their losses by changing to the export of other commodities, notably tobacco, coal, and colonial goods. And there was always a large and lucrative smuggler's trade. The latest authority on Anglo-Scandinavian trade comes to the conclusion that in spite of Swedish mercantilist measures, British exports to Sweden were in fact well maintained, and may even have been growing, that the merchants trading to Sweden were doing quite well, and that there was no great demand by them for government intervention.[92]

Nevertheless, the prospect which Goodricke held out of tariff barriers lowered or demolished, of Swedish markets opened to British industry, was bound to interest ministers. The Board of Trade was moved to an examination of Anglo-Swedish commercial relations; and on 10 December 1764 Lord Hillsborough sent a report to Lord Sandwich, together with voluminous statistics and other supporting documents.[93] He was forced to confess that the Board had no information on the subject for any year later than 1735, nor had it a complete collection of the relevant treaties—a confession which is some indication of the very limited importance of the Swedish trade in the totality of British exports and imports: considered merely in terms of the money involved, Sweden was too insignificant to matter very much.[94]

On 14 December Sandwich forwarded Hillsborough's report, with its annexures, to Goodricke.[95] He made no comment upon it, nor did he follow it up with any instructions. It was not until 9 April 1765 that his letters to Goodricke contained any reference to commercial objectives as an element in British policy towards Sweden; and any attempt to argue that such objectives formed a major—or, indeed, the most important—element in his Swedish policy finds little support in the available evidence.[96]

Hillsborough's budget reached Goodricke some time towards the end of January, at a moment when all his attention was engaged in the party struggle in the Diet. Though he was certainly more interested in economic questions than Sandwich, even he did not feel that trade was an immediate issue. On 1 February he asked Sandwich to send him copies of the relevant treaties; but he indicated that he was in no great hurry to receive them: "these matters cannot be brought on till the Diet is far advanced". In the meantime, "I endeavour to inculcate to our Friends such general principles of liberty in Trade and of the Inconvenience of prohibitions as may be most likely to bring about our purposes without the obligation of any engagements on our part."[97] He was still sanguine as to the outcome: it seemed to him that the Cap victory had been so complete that if the appropriate moment were chosen there could be little difficulty in obtaining large concessions. One might, no doubt, offer to put no higher duty upon iron than at present, "or some other advantage that costs us nothing"; but no more would be required. The event was to show that Goodricke was the victim of his own interest in contemporary economic thought. Any reader of the works and speeches of Anders Chydenius, or of the pamphlet literature which took a similar line, might be forgiven for imagining that the Caps were ready to embark with enthusiasm upon an enlightened policy of Free Trade. It was only gradually that Goodricke came to realize that for them, as for others in office, what was intellectually convincing was not necessarily politically possible.

Of more immediate relevance, it seemed, was the second dispatch which Goodricke sent off on 1 February, in which he once more raised the question of an Anglo-Swedish treaty.[98] It seems to have been provoked by a letter from Buckinghamshire, which relayed to him Panin's approval of the idea of an Anglo-Swedish defensive alliance and his promise to accede to it if it were made. Unlike Panin, who remarked that such an alliance was more to be desired than expected, Goodricke had no doubt that it would be feasible. From the outset of his mission he had been confident that it could be had without subsidies, and recent conversations with Löwenhielm had only strengthened him in that opinion. Subsidies, he was to remark a little later, were not only expensive in themselves, and politically impossible for any English ministry in peacetime; they were expensive compared with the alternative method of bribery and corruption. The Russians understood this very well. "They appear to act upon a regular Plan, and upon the Supposition, that Sweden being either to be bought at the Diet, or by a subsidiary Treaty, the least Subsidy, that could be offered, would exceed, in one year, all that is necessary for making Them content without it."[99] This was an argument nicely calculated to apply balm to Sandwich's inflamed feelings. It justified his dislike of subsidies; it explained Panin's loudly proclaimed refusal to take a share in paying them; and at the same time it contrived to ram home the point that Osterman was really spending substantial sums in the common cause. It was nonetheless an argument which Goodricke would be glad to forget in the not-so-distant future.

Meanwhile, his two dispatches arrived in London on 15 February. They came at an opportune moment. For on the previous day the Russian minister, Gross—in response, it appears, to urgent pleas from Osterman[100]—had written to Sandwich appealing to him to send further supplies to Stockholm, pending an answer from St. Petersburg to England's objections to Panin's plan, with a promise that he might rely on Osterman to match any expenditure which Goodricke might incur.[101] Sandwich noted with some complacency that Gross seemed thoroughly to understand and sympathize with the British point of view.[102] But Sandwich was deluding himself: what he took for candor was no more than diplomatic finesse. The Russians were understandably irritated by what they considered to be the mean-spirited parsimony of the Grenville ministry. To Osterman Panin wrote of England's "nasty new escapade,"[103] to Solms, the Prussian minister, he spoke of "la lâche abandon de l'Angleterre."[104] The conclusion he drew from this disillusioning experience was that if it were true that England intended to cut off supplies; if the Caps should prove inaccessible to argument, and should insist that a subsidy was essential; and if, in the absence of such a subsidy from England, they had no resort but to stick to their subsidy from France—why then Osterman must do his best to ensure that any future agreement between France and Sweden for reciprocal assistance should make Sweden's contribution naval rather than military: that is, a threat to England rather than to Russia.[105] Since Sandwich's policy appeared to be dictated by a narrow view of England's interest, Panin would shape his own policy to match it.

As it turned out, by the time Panin was thus giving vent to his irritation, Sandwich was beginning to get the better of his. By the middle of February he was ready to be persuaded into an attitude which was at least not wholly negative. In spite of everything, he retained a disposition to conciliate Catherine, a willingness to give her moral support, and an unwearied readiness to make a merit of doing so. The day after receiving Gross's appeal—but before the arrival of Goodricke's two dispatches—he allowed himself to be coaxed from the corner in which he had been sulking, and gave an assent to Gross's request which was less grudging than might have been expected. Goodricke was informed that he was to receive an additional £2,000 (in terms of the plan of 31 August it should really have been £9,000); and the usual warnings were appended against allowing Osterman to overreach him. But this time the hackneyed phrases were more absolute than usual: Sandwich was covering a partial retreat by heavy fire:

> . . . as His Majesty has taken a part in Sweden, solely to shew his readiness to support the Court of Petersburg in their favorite point, it is not his Intention, in any instance, to take the lead, or to act otherwise than as an assistant in the Measures of Russia.[106]

Whatever the truth of the averment, the verdict could not have been clearer. Or bleaker.

Yet within a few hours of the drafting of this letter the arrival of Goodricke's encouraging prospectus did something to mitigate these rigors: the wind shifted another point or two; the weather showed signs of a partial thaw. For though Sandwich allowed Goodricke's prospective trade bargains to pass without any comment whatever, as a matter not yet ripe for action, he was not proof against the bait of a cheap alliance. On 19 February he replied welcoming the proposal in terms whose cordiality accorded ill with his determination of four days ago not to take the lead "in any instance." There could of course be no question of a parliamentary grant for a subsidy, and the Civil List was certainly in no condition to bear the cost of one; but if a treaty could be had by the expenditure of Goodricke's additional £2,000, together with the "granting a regular easy pension to an able Senator or two," or by "some other expenses of that sort"; then the money might probably be found.[107]

From the Swedish point of view a treaty of the sort Sandwich had in mind was conceivable only because Cap leaders thought it essential to their strategy. The experiences of the next few years would bring it home to Goodricke that he had been too sanguine in supposing that any alliance of substance could be easily obtained without payment of a subsidy. For the moment what the Caps wanted was a treaty of amity upon which a future defensive alliance might be built; and for such a treaty a subsidy was neither necessary to give nor reasonable to ask. As they envisaged it, the treaty must be as simple as possible: they wished, for instance, to exclude any commercial clauses, on the ground that the Swedish tariff system was in any case to be modified in the near future.[108] This was no doubt a mere pretext: the only respect in which the tariff was modified in the spring of 1765 was by the decision of 19 April that henceforth duties were to be paid in silver, which meant in fact a raising of duties against all foreign countries, including England.[109] But a simple treaty suited Sandwich well enough. He too saw it as a base upon which something solid might later be erected. The structure he had in mind, however—if it should ever be raised at all—extended much further than a defensive alliance whose prime object should be the final severance of Sweden from France. It may be that he was encouraged by Goodricke's report that Löwenhielm "still stuck to his plan, and to the System, of setting up a Grand Alliance in the North."[110] At all events, he was beginning to think in terms of a Northern System, not superficially very dissimilar to Panin's, but with important shades of difference. As he put it to Macartney, the full powers sent to Goodricke on 9 April were drawn in such terms

> as by throwing apart all unnecessary and embarrassing points may bring it [the negotiation] to a speedy conclusion, and best answer the Purposes of forming in conjunction with Russia, such a reputable alliance in the North, as will counterbalance the weight which France may throw into the scale from another quarter.[111]

And by "another quarter" it seems that he meant Prussia, whose possible seduction by France was one of his recurrent nightmares. The Northern System as he planned it was to be an insurance against that contingency; if all went well, it was to offer a refuge and a welcome to that repentant political Magdalen, Austria. Russian diplomacy was shrewd enough to realize how Sandwich's mind was working, and to play adroitly upon his fears. On 4 May Goodricke reported a remarkable conversation with "two persons, one well acquainted with his [Panin's] past, and one with his present, views": it is reasonable to suppose that the persons thus thinly disguised were Osterman and his recently arrived coadjutor, Stakhiev. Among other things, they told Goodricke that Panin

> is supposed secretly to wish the revival of the old connexion between England, Russia and Austria, as the most agreeable to his way of thinking, which is entirely anti-Gallican, but that in order to render this system solid, He thinks great management must be used with the King of Prussia to keep him from a reunion with France in case this last should break with the House of Austria, for which reason he judged it necessary that the Court of Berlin should be taken fundamentally into the Grand Alliance of the North, thinking this to be the only means by which, upon the first coolness between Austria and France, the former might be taken into our connexion, without throwing His Prussian Majesty into the arms of the latter.[112]

It is of course possible that some such long-range calculation may have been present in Panin's mind, but as a description of the origins of the Russo-Prussian alliance the version given by the "two persons" was a travesty, and they themselves can hardly have believed it. As a guide to Panin's view of Austria it was grievously misleading.[113] There were, no doubt, matters on which Russia and Prussia did not see eye to eye: Panin was exasperated by Frederick's collection of tolls at Marienwerder, and still more by his intrigues with the Turks.[114] But the cement of Poland held the Russo-Prussian alliance firmly together: in 1765 the historic connection with Austria must have seemed, both at Vienna and St. Petersburg, a thing of the irrevocable past. It would need the Turkish war, the tightening grip of Prussia upon Russian policy, the constrained partition of Poland, and the revival of a forward policy in the Balkans, to resurrect it. But for the moment the idea of a Russo-Austrian rapprochement was excellently well adapted to reconcile Sandwich to England's inclusion in a Northern System; and the "two persons" employed it, with success, as a serviceable lubricant to ease the stiffness of his mental machinery.

So far, then, the simple treaty with Sweden had Sandwich's blessing. We may suspect that he calculated that when it had been completed, when upon its foundation a System of the North had been reared, the financing of Sweden would not fall wholly to Great Britain's charge. Even at this stage he was not without his reservations. There were two points, he insisted, which Goodricke must always bear in mind. One of them was the need for "a general article similar to the 12th article of the treaty of 1720, wherein, without entering into any particular discussions" each party gave most-favored-nation treatment to the other: after Goodricke's promises and assurances Sandwich was entitled to think that this was the least he could expect—and the least parliament could expect also, when it came to be asked to ratify a treaty which in all other respects was intended to be nebulous. The second was the fact that "our treaty with Russia is far from being in that state of forwardness which the King has a right to expect."[115] He took care to make the bearing of this remark quite clear:

> it will be a necessary Part of this defensive alliance, to form it upon such principles that, at all events, His Majesty may not find himself encumbered by a useless ally, nor Russia have that additional reason for suspending her Alliance with this Crown, by availing herself of a Disadvantage, she would then have brought upon us.

In other words, any British undertaking to Sweden must be general rather than precise, if only because there was not much likelihood of Sweden's ever being able to render any effective aid in return: if the Russian alliance failed to mature, England must not be left with sole responsibility for any troublesome commitments. If Macartney's negotiations in St. Petersburg should be successful, Goodricke's treaty might be the beginnings of much greater things; if they were not, he must take care that it be no more than an amiable nothing. To call such an arrangement a defensive alliance (as Sandwich persisted in doing) was to attach a meaning to that expression which was, to say the least, unusual.

The point was well taken. The draft which Goodricke sent home on 4 May, as he remarked, was "better calculated for the state of uncertainty in which our Negotiation at Petersburg remains, than a more regular and particular one would have been."[116] But Goodricke realized, as Sandwich had failed to do, that the using of one negotiation as a lever to operate upon the other was a tactic which could also be employed on the other side; and he passed on a hint that the slow progress of Macartney's commercial treaty might not be unconnected with Panin's determination that England should "take the part they wished us to do in the affairs of Sweden."[117] There proved, moreover, to be real difficulties about the treaty's content, and also about its timing. In 1741 Sweden had concluded a treaty with France which included a clause that could not be reconciled with a general undertaking to give most-favored-nation treatment. That clause accorded to France an exclusive privilege in trading to the Swedish port of Wismar, in north Germany. True, it was a clause of which France made virtually no use; but it also gave to Swedish merchants privileges in French ports which they were unwilling to forgo. England's own trade with Wismar was quite insignificant, and it might be supposed that the matter was too unimportant to constitute a real obstacle; but it involved a question of principle, for the clause of 1741 certainly could not be reconciled with article 12 of the Anglo-Swedish treaty of 1720.[118] It was already becoming clear, moreover, that Goodricke's confident prediction of the ease with which England could obtain commercial concessions was unlikely to be borne out in fact: as he confessed, he had to move cautiously, for "all the French party and half of ours think I have a secret Design to ruin all their Manufactures."[119] The idea of a treaty, and its possible terms, were still a close secret between Goodricke and some of the Cap leaders: the Senate, the Chancery, and the Secret Committee were as yet unaware that anything of the sort was in the wind. But in the middle of May Nolcken, thanks to Sandwich's indiscretion, was able to warn the chancery-president of what was afoot.[120] His report, and others which followed it, caused consternation among the Hat members of the Senate, and the chancery-president lost no time in appealing to Breteuil to help him to organize measures of resistance.[121]

Meanwhile, on 29 May, Sandwich had referred Goodricke's draft to the Board of Trade. He was careful to explain that the purport of the treaty was intended to be "rather to introduce one of a more extensive nature, in case the nature of events should require it, than to carry anything of itself very weighty or conclusive"; but even so he needed their advice as to whether the matter was worth pursuing, in view of the difficulty over Wismar.[122] The Board of Trade duly summoned the merchants trading to Sweden;[123] and on the basis of their opinion advised Sandwich that the treaty would be of great advantage, though they agreed with Goodricke that any exception from the most-favored-nation clause must be expressed in particular and not in general terms.[124] It is clear that the merchants must have been given to understand that the treaty was to restore to them the position they had enjoyed in virtue of article 12 of the treaty of 1720: if it went no further than to guarantee most-favored-nation treatment it would give them nothing of any value. No doubt Sandwich knew this; but for him the importance of the treaty was political rather than economic. If it had been otherwise, he would never have been indifferent—as he plainly said he was—as to whether the treaty were for a limited or unlimited duration; for one of the weaknesses of the treaty of 1720, from the English point of view, was that it expired in 1738. But he needed the approval of the merchants as a protection against criticism in parliament; and there was some virtue in that elastic phrase "similar to the 12th article." At all events, a meeting of the cabinet on 12 June recommended that Goodricke be authorized to conclude a treaty on the lines of the project he had transmitted;[125] and two days later Sandwich sent him his instructions[126]—though not, as Goodricke ruefully noted, any more money.[127]

At this stage he ran into his second difficulty: that of timing. When on 4 May he had sent over his draft, he had expected to be able to make a verbal proposition to the Senate within a week or so.[128] But he soon found that so early an initiative would not suit the tactics of the "friends of England."[129]

> The general intention of our Friends is to govern this whole affair so as that no umbrage can be taken at it now and yet that upon the Foundation of the Treaty the Secret Committee may be able to frame a Testament for the Senate's conduct between the Diets in a way that will break the French system entirely by directing that If France refuses to pay the arrears they must immediately declare all engagements at an end and by tying up their hands in such a manner as may effectively prevent their entering into any new ones with that Crown. [*sic*] [130]

The Cap leaders no doubt realized well enough that once the English treaty was made the chances of France's continuing to pay off the arrears were small indeed. Goodricke must have realized it too. He must have foreseen that if such an instruction to the Senate were drawn up and adhered to, the consequence must probably be an application to England for a subsidy to replace what Sweden had lost. It seems very unlikely that Sandwich, whose disposition was rather to look round too many corners than too few, can have failed to draw the same inference.[131] His decision nevertheless to proceed with the negotiations probably reflects his belief—despite all warnings to the contrary from St. Petersburg[132]—that once the treaty had expanded into some sort of Northern System the Russians would take at least a share of the burden.[133]

In the eyes of Osterman, as well as of the Cap leaders, the English treaty, however desirable, was not a matter of immediate urgency. For them it was much more important to consolidate their electoral successes: the Secret Committee was indeed securely in their hands; with care and sufficient expenditure their ascendancy in the Estates might reasonably be expected to continue; but the Senate had still a majority of Hats. And until the Hat Senators were extruded—and in particular until the post of chancery-president was in Cap hands—the victory would be incomplete. An anti-Gallican foreign policy would always be in danger of dilution or sabotage from within. Panin might try to persuade Macartney that all Russia's objectives in Sweden had been attained, and that what remained was essentially the concern of England;[134] but he did not really think so. The constitutional reforms which Catherine considered essential had not even been begun. The removal of the Hat Senators, which had been a Russian aim since the Diet started, had not yet been attempted. Moreover, they could not, in the prevailing climate of opinion in Stockholm, risk launching a treaty which appeared to menace all those vested interests which the Hats' protective policies had created. Goodricke was wholly mistaken when he judged the moment to be propitious for improving England's trading position in Sweden. The practice of a generation could not be so easily reversed; the convinced free-traders were a doctrinaire handful; the mass of the Cap party could not be relied upon to tolerate a dismantling of tariff barriers:[135] they could not afford, at a moment when they were embarked upon a policy of restricting credit and diminishing the stock of paper money, to risk an unfavorable balance of trade as well. Even though the great iron exporters might be mostly Hats, Sweden could not see without alarm any English proposal to increase the duty on imported bar-iron; and when a motion to that end actually came before the Commons in the spring of 1765, the Grenville administration took care that it should be stifled—though not before the report had caused anxiety among Caps and Hats alike.[136] Löwenhielm and Rudbeck might indeed be ready for a most-favored-nation clause; but hardly anybody in Sweden was prepared to swallow a revival of the whole of article 12 of the treaty of 1720. The Caps had their hands quite full enough, in the spring and summer of 1765, without involving themselves in controversial measures which would alienate their own supporters.

By early July Osterman and the Cap leaders had made it clear to Goodricke that his treaty must wait. First things first; first remove the Hat Senators; then—with a remodeled Senate and a new chancery-president—then open the negotiations for a treaty.[137] As to timing, the best Goodricke could now promise himself was that it should be made "at some favourable opportunity."[138] That opportunity was long in coming. The delay in starting negotiations for the treaty was in fact as good an example as could be desired of the interdependence of Interior and Exterior, and the necessary involvement of England and Russia in both.

It was an example which was lost on Lord Sandwich. Before this dispatch reached London he had ceased to hold office. George Grenville had read the king one lecture too many; and after a month of uncertainty, by the end of which Pitt, like some ageing and temperamental prima donna, had contrived to reduce the producer and the rest of the cast to a state of nervous exhaustion, it had been decided that the play should go on without him. The duke of Cumberland directed the proceedings from the prompter's box, as Bute had done in earlier years; the marquis of Rockingham played the pallid *jeune premier*; and the business of the Swedish treaty passed into the prentice hands of that promising young amateur, the duke of Grafton.

CHAPTER V

The Caps and the Court, 1765

(i)

While Lord Sandwich had been endeavoring to concentrate his mind about the place to be allotted to Sweden in the broad strategy of British foreign policy, Sir John Goodricke had had his hands full with the minor tactics of diplomacy. In these local skirmishes he found an evident satisfaction; and he tried hard to instill into his superiors in London an appreciation of their significance for the general plan of campaign. Despite his familiarity with the local terrain the battle was not without its surprises. The alignment of the forces engaged long remained less than perfectly clear. And it may be doubted whether he always grasped the motivation which lay behind some of his allies' maneuvers, or had much sympathy for some of the objectives at which they aimed.

This was certainly true in regard to the victorious Caps. Nearly forty years later, G. F. Gyllenborg—poet rather than politician, born a Hat, but already in 1765 inclining to royalism—recalled his reactions to the advent of the Caps to power. As he looked back over the immediate past, it seemed to him that the Diet of 1765 was a portentous event. It signalized, he thought, the triumph of frantic democracy: it was "a violent *régime*, distinguished by characteristics similar to those in evidence at the beginning of the French Revolution." It marked the victory of men of a leveling spirit, men who not only broke the crown's contracts with cynical indifference, plundered the state and prepared the ruin of substantial citizens, but were offensive to gentlemen by the vulgarity of their origins and the grossness of their manners.[1]

It was a view which conveniently forgot the delinquencies of the Hats, and oversimplified both the composition of the Cap party and the nature of its program. But it was right insofar as it insisted that they *had* a program. And it was right too in that it made clear that 1765 did indeed mark an era, and that "the younger Caps" stood for something new, something rather different from the Cap policies of the age of Arvid Horn. It would be possible to say of them that they embodied both the best and the worst of those qualities which characterized Swedish political life during the Age of Liberty. For historians such as Lagerroth, who with the eye of optimism and faith saw that age as a period of rich promise, criminally aborted by the fatal coup d'état of 1772—a period when Sweden led the world in the development of parliamentary institutions—the younger Caps are the prophets and forerunners of nineteenth-century liberalism and democracy.[2] But to those historians who take a pessimistic view of the potentialities of the Age of Liberty they appear in a very different light, as men without patriotism and without political morality, prepared to subject their country to Russia to secure themselves in power; men whose rule—in 1771-72, if not in 1765-66—provides the final demonstration of the degradation of Swedish politics, and the final justification for the *douce violence* of Gustav III.[3]

However we judge them, one thing is clear: 1765 was not merely the triumph of one faction over another, not merely the rejection by the political nation of a party which had been in power too long. It was also one of those slow, irregular pulses so typical of Sweden's early modern history. For two and a half centuries that history had swung between two views of Sweden's position in the world, two views also (as a consequence) about the right approach to Sweden's internal affairs. On the one hand, an attitude of mind which was outward looking, dynamic, adventurous, self-confident, willing to meet dangers (real or potential) more than halfway, ready in the name of national security to embark on foreign policies of a magnitude which staggered contemporaries because so disproportionate to the country's limited economic and demographic resources. That attitude of mind had built the Swedish empire: it had set a mark, not easily effaced, upon the Swedish character, upon Swedes' view of themselves and their status among the nations; it had entailed an administration geared to war; it had relied, not in vain, upon patriotism and upon religion to nerve the nation to the sacrifices which it had made necessary. Of that policy Gustav Adolf, Axel Oxenstierna, Karl

X Gustav, and Karl XII had been the illustrious exponents. But there had also been another policy, another view of Sweden's destiny; a view which had continued to be held even during the most brilliantly successful period of the great wars: the view that Sweden must choose a path fitted to her resources, a path capable of being followed without extraneous aid; the view that a commitment to adventure based upon arguments from contingencies must give way to the more important task of internal consolidation, the attainment of economic health, the care for the ordinary subject's well-being. This policy too had had its great names: Gustav Vasa, for one; Karl XI, for another. And, most recently, Arvid Horn. The fall of Horn in 1738 marked a reversion to the attitudes of an earlier day: a generation which had not experienced the disasters of the century's second decade dreamed of a new Narva and an empire reborn. Their faith in Sweden's natural right to be a great power led them to wage two disastrous wars: the first, against Russia; the second, in the hope of pickings in Germany. They would have rejected with indignation (and with justice) the charge that they pursued their foreign adventures indifferent to the country's welfare: they lavished financial support on new industries, they protected Sweden's navigation, they had an enlightened interest in technology, in the arts, in science. Was not Linnaeus himself a stout Hat? But in spite of it all their rule had in fact loaded the state with debt, plunged it into an inflation which bore heavily on the ordinary man, reduced it to ignominious dependence upon subsidies from a foreign power. When they fell in the late autumn of 1764 they left behind them a situation not very dissimilar to that which Karl XI had confronted in 1680.

The coming of the Caps to power thus implied, as the absolutism of Karl XI had implied, a deliberate turning away from a foreign policy which had proved to be the vain pursuit of a mirage, and a return to considerations of plenty rather than considerations of power. The Caps could not, indeed, see themselves simply as Karl XI's political heirs: in a constitutional point of view his absolutism embodied everything which was most abhorrent to them, everything against which the Form of Government of 1720 had been a reaction. But in regard to foreign policy they were the direct inheritors of his tradition; as they were too in regard to many aspects of domestic affairs: at least one contemporary saw a parallel between their proceedings and those of Karl XI's *reduktion*.[4] But if the Cap Diet was thus firmly rooted in one of the great traditions of Swedish history, it opened perspectives towards the future too. It represented, in more than one respect, the first dawning of the new Sweden which would slowly emerge after 1809. The pendulum of Swedish history had now swung heavily to the side of realism and thrift, away from the dangerous memories of Breitenfeld and Klissow; and though Gustav III would for a moment try to revive those memories, he would not succeed. Nevertheless, the type of foreign policy for which the Caps stood did not merely incorporate an old tradition: it developed it far beyond what Gustav Vasa, or Karl XI, or Arvid Horn, would have been willing to accept. All three had had a wary eye open for danger; all had believed that a time might come when Sweden would have no choice but to fight: Horn himself was too much of a Caroline not to keep in mind the possibility of one day reversing Pultava, though he saw plainly that that day was not yet. None had been truly isolationist; all had kept their powder dry. The Caps of 1765 were different: different even from the Swedes of the nineteenth century, for whom the problem of national defense was to be a matter of hot controversy; resembling rather the fatalist men of our own day. Anders Nordencrantz, who most clearly formulated their thinking on these matters, laid it down flatly that Sweden was incapable of fighting a modern war; though he professed to believe in the invincibility of a native militia when fighting in defense of its homeland.[5] For the shreds and remnants of the old empire Nordencrantz cared less than nothing; Pomerania for him was a dangerous liability, whose possession might drag Sweden into European quarrels with which she had no concern—a Hanover from which it was best to cut loose, and the sooner the better; and the Age of Greatness was a disastrous mistake, of which the Swedish people had been the victims.[6] He would have been content to withdraw within the limits of Scandinavia and the inner Baltic, and to leave Europe to execute its diplomatic maneuvering or fight its pointless wars without Swedish participation. As to the Balance of Power, Nordencrantz believed in it as little as did Israel Mauduit.[7] Any alliances must be, not merely defensive, but free from any risk of involving the country in war; and Löwenhielm, at least, professed to believe that Panin's Northern League was not irreconcilable with that stipulation.[8] If they must spend money on fortifications, they would spend it on Landskrona, rather than on the defenses of the Finnish frontier; for if Sweden need expect any attack at all (which they doubted) it was more likely to come from Denmark than from any other quarter. From Russia, they believed, they had nothing to fear, provided no provocation were offered.[9] No doubt they underestimated their neighbor's sensitiveness to the exposed situation of St. Petersburg; but in their attitude to Russia they had, once again, both the past and the future on their side: Erik XIV, Axel Oxenstierna, Karl XI, had all based their policies on good relations with the tsar; and to that tradition the men of 1809 would return. Memories of Karl XII were still strong enough—the old, ingrained fear of Russia was still sufficiently potent, the smell of smoke from the Russian harryings of 1719-20 was still sufficiently pungent in their nostrils—for the Caps of 1765 to be unwilling to advertise themselves as a specifically pro-Russian party; but they believed that it was possible to have Russia for a friend, without therefore reducing Sweden to a Russian satrapy.

Their real enemy was France. And this not only because France had been the financial backer and political protector of the Hats, but for reasons both patriotic and temperamental. It had been France, after all, who had incited the wars of 1741 and 1757—France, therefore, who had been responsible for reducing the country to its present disastrous financial position. France had treated Sweden as a pawn in her own game of power politics; France, finally, had cheated on the payment of those subsidies which she had offered as a bribe. As long as the French connection remained, what had happened in 1741 and 1757 could happen again: of this entanglement, certainly, Sweden must free herself—if only her tottering finances could bear it. Above all, when French policy was in the hands of so restless a troublemaker as Choiseul. These severely practical considerations were reinforced by a strong temperamental distaste for all things French. The Court, the higher aristocracy, the Hats, were no doubt steeped in French culture; the more middle-class Caps were not. This was true even of many of their leaders. Löwenhielm, who was to become their chancery-president, was said by Schack to be entirely ignorant of foreign languages;[10] and of the six Caps who entered the Senate in September 1765 only two (as Breteuil noted disgustedly) could speak French.[11] To the rank and file of the party France was abhorrent (confusingly enough) both as the home of freethinking and as the country of popery; the country, too, from which came those unnecessary luxury goods which helped to upset Sweden's balance of trade.

Very different was the case with regard to England. A connection with England, it seemed to them, was not merely unexceptionable but positively desirable. No danger here, they thought, of dangerous involvement in continental quarrels, least of all in the prevailing temper of British politics. Forgetful of experiences during the Seven Years War, they attached little weight to the charges of maritime tyranny and commercial greed which formed a staple of France's anti-British propaganda. Most of them, as it happened, had little or no connection with those manufacturing ventures into which the Hats had poured money—at Alingsås, at Vedevåg—in an effort to make Sweden independent of the import of English manufactures. Löwenhielm, indeed, was a member of the board of directors of the Iron Office; a few leading Caps—Frietzcky and Nordencrantz among them—were forge owners; but by and large their interests lay with importers rather than exporters, and opposition to England on the economic front was not for them a matter of immediate personal concern. If it were a question of national security, they might well feel that the British navy was a better reassurance than the subsidies and diplomacy of France; above all at a time when good relations with Russia set their minds at rest about Finland. Friendship with England made obvious sense when most men believed that an Anglo-Russian alliance was imminent, and when cooperation between the courts of London and St. Petersburg was so close and cordial. Some of their leaders had long been committed anglophiles: Bishop Serenius had served a spell as pastor of the Swedish church in London, had brought back from his stay there the Anglican rite of confirmation, and was the author of the first important Swedish-English dictionary; Nordencrantz too had spent some time in England, and was deeply read in contemporary English political literature; Claes Frietzcky was an enthusiastic admirer of British business methods. They had the feeling that British politicians were men of political principles similar to their own: pragmatic, sensible, inaccessible to cloudy notions of glory or quixotic ideas of chivalry, governed in the main by enlightened self-interest. It was their misfortune that in the 1760s the men who ruled in London pushed these doubtless estimable qualities to excess, at least from the standpoint of a potential ally. Perhaps they never fairly asked themselves how far England could be expected to take risks and make sacrifices for their sake, how far the increasingly introspective temper of British politics made it likely that English statesmen would seriously concern themselves with the outcome of Sweden's domestic crisis: above all, whether the British taxpayer would ever come in to the idea of putting his hand in his pocket to pay for a mere diplomatic success in a minor court. What the Caps needed was an English ministry equipped with all those ideal qualities which they were disposed to associate with England; but equipped also with a parliamentary strength, a resolute leadership, and a grasp of international affairs which would enable them to play the part for which the Caps had cast them. Not until the very eve of the revolution of 1772 was there much sign that such a ministry could be found; and by then it was too late. No wonder that a party originally essentially English found itself forced deeper and deeper into dependence upon Russia.

Thus the victory of the Caps, and the consequent shift in Swedish foreign policy from a "French" to an "English" system, by no means implied that all was now plain sailing, and that Goodricke would have nothing to do but to wait for the appropriate parliamentary moment to reap the diplomatic harvest of electoral victory. On the contrary, it prepared for him a future in which he would be condemned to attempt to reconcile the very different views of London and Stockholm as to what the nature of England's connection with Sweden was to be. It was a situation which demanded tact and bluff on the one hand, and on the other courage and initiative in the face of the reluctance or disapproval of his masters. Nor was his position made easier by the fact that he could not escape from the need to take into account the domestic consequences of the Caps' accession to power. For after all, in the program with which they had won the election, an altered system of foreign policy had not been the only nor even a conspicuous element.

Insofar as the Swedish political system in the Age of Liberty was responsive to public opinion, the election of 1764 represented the electorate's verdict. The victory of the Caps was a popular victory, as even the friends of the defeated conceded.[12] The Diet of 1765 was a Diet of popular indignation; the Caps were returned to power because they were the champions of reform: economical reform, above all. Some of their objectives had been formulated in the joint program which formed the basis of their brief collaboration with the Court at the time of the election, and which Nils von Oelreich—once the constitutional oracle of the Hats, now the fugleman of their adversaries—elaborated in an anonymous pamphlet.[13] Two general problems seemed to confront the nation: the one expressed in the classic question why Sweden's good laws had had such ill effects;[14] the other, how to end the abuses and financial disorder which had stained the rule of the Hats. Oelreich's pamphlet, for instance, demanded strict economy, stringent measures against luxury, the end of corrupt arrangements which had permitted the plundering of the state for private advantage, the termination of the activities of the Exchange Office. There must be measures also to safeguard and restore the liberties of the subject: a sharp scrutiny of the actions of officials; the trial of all crimes and misdemeanors according to law (and not by those extraordinary parliamentary commissions which had been a favored device of the Hats); a curbing of the tendency of the Secret Committee to engross more and more power to itself, and the restoration of the effective control of the *plena*. One consequence of this would be the dissipation of the thick veil of secrecy in which a great part of the more important affairs of the nation had latterly been involved: government by the Estates (which was the constitutional ideal of Hats and Caps alike) was to be government as far as possible in the full light of publicity. In his Hat days Oelreich had for some years filled the office of censor, and was generally considered to have lined his pockets by granting licenses in order to secure the fees;[15] now he appeared as an advocate of the liberty of printing and the abolition of all preliminary scrutiny. Last, but by no means least, Caps and Court were at one in a determination to try to end that intermixture of legislative and executive functions which had become increasingly evident in the last two decades: a situation in which officials, though constitutionally responsible to the Estates, themselves composed a sizeable proportion of the members.

This was a point which was hammered home again and again, in successive (and voluminous) pamphlets, by Anders Nordencrantz. The relatively moderate program upon which the Cap leaders and the Court had agreed, though it did indeed deal with this matter, in other respects fell far short of what Nordencrantz believed the situation to require.[16] He feared not only that Sweden might fall victim to the creeping tyranny of officialdom, but also that it might become, as he put it, an aristocracy controlled by speculators, debtors, and bankrupts.[17] At the root of the evils of Swedish society he saw a little knot of Hat financiers and merchants, and above all those who had been engaged to manage the exchanges. Against the men who had been responsible for the Exchange Office he had since 1761 conducted a personal vendetta of monomaniac intensity. In the weeks just before the meeting of the Diet he brought out in Hamburg a pamphlet—*Sweden's Finance System*—which the Hat Senate made determined efforts to suppress.[18] Not surprisingly. For it was not merely a criticism of prevailing abuses: it was a cry for vengeance. Though the Hat Senate took such effective measures to suppress it that only one copy seems to have survived, its principles became the program which animated the more fiery spirits of his party; a program which saw the first task of the Caps after their victory as the relentless hunting down of those whom Nordencrantz identified as the architects of the nation's ruin. The Cap leaders might disavow such a program (though Rudbeck, for one, seems to have been instrumental in securing the book's publication), but the rank and file embraced it with enthusiasm.[19]

The Diet of 1765, though far from being composed of the rabble of Gyllenborg's highly colored recollection, was certainly of a slightly different social complexion from those which had preceded it: the middle classes had begun to break in. In the Estate of Clergy, for instance, the unbeneficed seem to have been unusually numerous, and unusually vocal: the most distinguished economist among them, Anders Chydenius, the Swedish forerunner of Adam Smith, belonged to this class.[20] In the Estate of Burghers the members were of a distinctly lower social standing than had been usual in the past: the municipal establishment no longer dominated its debates, and for the first time non-officials were in a majority.[21] There was thus some ground for considering this Diet comparatively "democratic." Many years later, Claes Frietzcky claimed that the Caps as a party were democratic in principle, as against the aristocratic Hats.[22] True democrats no doubt were rare enough, though Chydenius seems to have been one.[23] But Gyllenborg's accusation of leveling principles had at least a grain of truth in it, inasmuch as that the Diet did see a heavy attack upon privileges, including some which had long prescription behind them: social and class antagonisms were not far below the surface, and by the time the Diet ended it had come close to that "strife of Estates" which became explicit in the Diet of 1771-72.

There can be no doubt that the party which came to power in 1765 was animated by a sincere desire to cleanse the abuses of Swedish political life. They had the old-fashioned virtues of thrift and piety, they had a streak of Puritanism which showed itself in their suspicion of the graces and amenities of good society, they had the strength inherent in provincialism. No doubt it is true that the ideals of their leaders did not always penetrate very far down into the rank and file of the party, the majority of whom were too restricted in their outlook, and indeed too ignorant, to appreciate economic arguments or the subtleties of debate on political theory: for them, the Caps' "program" meant little more than the prejudices of the backwoodsman, reinforced by propaganda which had simplified the issues to their understanding, and sometimes had deliberately distorted them. It was hardly surprising that they were often swayed more by passion than by reason. In their hands the state's right too easily became the subject's wrong; in the cause of justice they did not shrink from proceedings which neither law nor equity could justify. They suffered, no doubt, from an inexperience of the problems of administration which was the result of more than a generation of exclusion from power,[24] and in many respects they were politically naive. Against the Hats and their protégés they employed methods as hateful as those which they had condemned, and rightly condemned, when they had been used by Tessin, or Renhorn, or Palmstierna; and their rabid vindictiveness looked all the uglier for being associated with the petty-mindedness and materialism which marked so many of them: in this sense, at least, they were the reverse of an aristocratic party; for they lacked, in great measure, that aristocratic quality of civility which sheds a tempering light over what is in itself exceptionable.

All this might have mattered less, if the Caps had been a firmly disciplined party led by men of outstanding political ability or strong personality. But in fact there was no one among them who could compare in these respects with Axel von Fersen, the leading man on the other side. Rudbeck was generally respected as an honest man whom no foreign diplomat ever succeeded in corrupting—admittedly no small distinction in the Sweden of the 1760s—but he was not a man of independent mind, and he proved a barely competent *lantmarskalk*.[25] Löwenhielm was probably the Caps' ablest head; but he was suspect as a turncoat, his record would show him to be a trimmer, he was thought to be greedy for foreign gold and not too particular as to where he got it. In short, men regarded him as a somewhat slippery customer; and in this instance men were right. Bishop Serenius had the distinction of being most cordially hated by his opponents,[26] but his leadership was in practice confined to the Estate of Clergy. Nordencrantz, though still able to impose his diagnosis of the nation's ills upon his party colleagues, was put out of the question as a political leader by his vanity, touchiness, and utter lack of any sense of proportion. Among the others, some were solid and sensible, as Claes Frietzcky was; many had dangerously sharp tongues, or heads too hot for comfort, or principles which were less than perfectly disinterested or reliable. None had commanding authority. In these circumstances the party from the beginning was split into cliques and factions, and the rank and file increasingly took the bit between its teeth, with the result that the leaders were on occasion forced to conform to the fanaticism or vindictiveness of their back-benchers, when their own inclinations might have been towards caution and compromise. This was a circumstance which directly affected Goodricke; for he, like Osterman, was in some sort one of the chiefs of the Cap party. Like that party's domestic leaders, he sometimes found himself following in the wake of rabid clerics or thickheaded municipal politicians whose support for the English connection it was essential not to forfeit.

At first there were few problems. Confronted with the task of undoing the wrongs of a generation, and at the same time saving the state from the financial harpies, the Caps applied themselves to the work with harmonious enthusiasm, their zeal animated by the brimstone sermon with which Serenius celebrated the opening of the Diet. In accordance with the plan agreed upon beforehand with Goodricke and Osterman they began by the examination in the Secret Committee of the state of the nation, as revealed in the Secret Proposition which the Senate had presented to the Diet as an account of its stewardship.[27] Under the influence (one can only suppose) of some sort of passing deathwish, the Senate had entrusted the drawing of this document to (of all people) Löwenhielm, and Löwenhielm had certainly laid on the colors with an unsparing hand. The size of the deficit, the depressed state of the economy, the decay of the defenses, the alarming debility of the armed forces, as set out in this survey, added up to an indictment of the rule of the Hats which satisfied even their enemies.[28] The Caps lost no time in pursuing the lines of investigation which it suggested. On all hands they found scandals; on all hands they initiated reforms. The Diet's Bank Committee reported malversations and embezzlements by the personnel of the Bank: some of its employees prudently decamped to Norway; and in May 1766 the Estates wound up a drastic reform by the dismissal of all the members of the Bank's Board of Management.[29] Their Mines Committee conducted a protracted and hostile investigation into the Iron Office, long suspect as being dominated by great Hat merchants, and linked by personal ties with the financiers of the Exchange Office. They found no great scandals here, however, and the Iron Office escaped the abolition which was probably originally intended; but it emerged in August 1766 considerably reformed, and provided with stringent regulations for its governance in future.[30] The most urgent financial business, however, was to devise some measures for dealing with inflation. The Caps tackled the problem by ordering the calling in, over the next ten years, of a sizeable proportion of the paper money in circulation.[31] And they embarked upon a heroic attempt—which was ultimately to prove politically fatal to them—to control the rate of exchange for the Swedish daler, first by pegging it for the time being, and then by providing for its gradual appreciation by a fixed amount every year, until after an estimated eight years it should have been restored to parity.[32]

Reform went hand in hand with economy. Swedish diplomats found to their chagrin that they could no longer expect to draw salary and allowances as a matter of course while enjoying lengthy periods of leave at home; and in the name of economy (but partly, no doubt, as a gesture against France, and also to vex Ulrik Scheffer) the status of the Paris mission was reduced from an embassy to a legation—a change which had the not unexpected result of producing Scheffer's resignation.[33] The determination to retrench affected more important matters also. The nation's defenses, reduced to debility by the Hats' financial mismanagement, were still further weakened by the new régime of financial order: the galley fleet was cut down; building work on the fortresses was as good as brought to a standstill. A concern for the balance of trade, reinforced by that spirit of austerity which was typical of the Caps, led to a series of prohibitions, not merely of the importing of such luxury goods as coffee, wine, silks and satins, and so forth, but also of their use: in this matter "Clergy, Burghers and Peasants showed a goodwill which was matched only by their ignorance."[34] It produced some unexpected consequences. The prostitutes of Stockholm, thus denied the sartorial equipment essential to their profession, protested vigorously, and obtained a relaxation in their favor thanks only to their shrewd enlistment of the good offices of their influential patron Joseph Hansson, the Speaker of the Estate of Peasants.[35] But if the Cap enthusiasts failed to see round this particular corner, they made no mistake about the implications of an overzealous proposal to limit or prohibit the domestic distillation of *brännvin*. The suggestion was prompted partly by considerations of social welfare, but much more by the fact that grain was the biggest single item in the list of Swedish imports, and a reduction in the size of that item would have substantially improved the balance of trade.[36] But French luxuries were one thing; *brännvin* was another. *Brännvin*, as Clergy and Peasants united in protesting, was no luxury at all: it was a necessity of life to man, an indispensable source of fodder to beasts, and its distillation conformed to all the best economic theories: it represented the manufacture of a domestic raw material; it accorded with a man's right (increasingly championed by their economists) to do as he liked with his own. Economy was all very well; but there were limits. The assault on poteen was vigorously repelled: it would take a famine and a revolution to force its champions to capitulate.

The most important agency in the work of reform was a formidable body, specially set up for that purpose. On 26 March 1765 the Estates charged the Secret Committee to draw up an instruction for a Grand Committee of 250 members, drawn from all four Estates, whose business it was to be to take three things into consideration:

corruption in the finances, with especial reference to the activities of the Exchange Office; the freedom of the press; and possible modifications in the constitution. Long deliberation eventually produced (in 1766) an ordinance for the liberty of printing which may justly be accounted one of the Cap party's imperishable memorials. It abolished the preliminary censorship and liberated the press, very much on the English model; though it took care to impose savage penalties on any writer who had the hardihood to criticize the constitution, question the wisdom or the good faith of the Estates, or attack the Senate. But these trifling abatements were no more than was to be expected from the idiosyncratic ideas of "liberty" which prevailed in Sweden, and they by no means prevented contemporaries (and subsequent Swedish historians) from pointing to the ordinance with pride as evidence of a progressive and enlightened spirit.[37] As to the constitution, that was a matter so bound up with the relationship of the two parties to the Court that its consideration must for the moment be postponed. The main preoccupation of the Grand Committee, in the months immediately after its appointment, was in fact the operations of the Exchange Office. As long ago as 1747 the Hat Senate had hit on the device of trying to bolster up the daler on the foreign exchange market by the operations of a consortium of financiers: believing as they did that the rate for the daler fell as a result of the operations of speculators, the appropriate countermeasure, they thought, was to employ "good" speculators to fight the "bad."[38] With this end in view the state had concluded contracts with two such consortia successively; one consisting of Kierman, Claes Grill, and Lefebure, the second of Wittfoth, Claesson, and König. Kierman and Grill were prominent members of the Hat party, for whom Grill acted as banker, and Lefebure, though no politician, was closely associated with the Iron Office and the Bank.[39] By 1765 two things had become obvious: first, that the operations of these financiers had failed to achieve their object; and secondly, that the contracts had been extremely profitable to those who undertook them. It was true that the Hat government had accepted their accounts and expressly discharged them from further obligation; but the instruction for the Grand Committee ordered it to take no notice of this, since it had been done without the Estates' knowledge or consent. Kierman, as the leader of the Hats in Stockholm municipal politics and a former Speaker of the Estate of Burghers, would in any case have been especially obnoxious to the Caps; but he was doubly so for his pride, his ostentation, the sharpness of his tongue, and the fact that he had never been a regular merchant, but had made his money by financial operations.[40] For some time Cap propaganda had been directed against him, as one who had become rich at the country's expense. To Nordencrantz, in particular, he appeared as the embodiment of that corruption which it was the task of the Caps to root out. There had been a time when Nordencrantz had believed that the cause of the inflationary situation in Sweden lay in the unfavorable balance of trade.[41] Other Caps held that it was to be explained by the excessive issue of paper money, and the overliberal policy of the Bank in the provision of credit at low rates of interest.[42] It would have been well if they had been content with one or other of these explanations; but under Nordencrantz's influence they increasingly came to think that Sweden's ills were not to be explained simply by the operation of economic forces, but by the actions of designing men. Those men were—naturally—the Hat financiers who had used the Bank's facilities for their own ends, and above all those who had managed the Exchange Office.

The Grand Committee, with the popular clamor against Kierman ringing in its ears, was not likely to bring a dispassionate judgment to the question of Kierman's culpability. It was not, of course, a court of justice, and nobody examining its proceedings could possibly mistake it for one. It differed from the extrajudicial parliamentary commissions which the Hats had employed only in its scrupulousness in publishing all its proceedings, including the pleas for the accused. Still, its resolutions had the force of law provided the Estates accepted them, and this was true even if they amounted in fact to verdicts and sentences upon individuals. Already before the Grand Committee fell to work Kierman's property had been sequestered by the Estates; on 4 May he was arrested.[43] In August, the Committee presented its report. It demanded that Kierman be put on bread and water for a month, imprisoned in the fortress of Marstrand for life, and made to repay six million silver daler to the state.[44] This report the Estates accepted, after debates which caused a deep cleavage between the moderate and extremist wings of the Cap party.[45] Lefebure received a lighter sentence, Grill escaped with a fine, and in February 1766 the sum demanded in repayment was reduced from six millions to four;[46] but Kierman died in prison before the end of 1766. The proceedings against the second exchange-consortium were a shade less stringent: Claesson fled in good time; König was absent abroad, and prudently stayed there; only Wittfoth remained as a victim. But he too (in November 1766) was sent to prison in Marstrand—where he remained until the Hats let him out in 1769—and a fine of 915,000 silver daler was exacted from him.[47]

The proceedings against Kierman and his associates provide a good example of the close relation between the laudable and the disreputable aspects of the Cap régime. There is no need to doubt the honesty of those who pressed home the attack. They were supported by strong popular feeling: the Stockholm mob wrecked Kierman's house, with cries of "What's the exchange rate?"[48] But they were mistaken in attributing to the accused the responsibility for the state of the exchange; and they were almost certainly wrong in trying to pin criminality on them. Kierman had no doubt made the best terms for himself that he could obtain; but though it might be regrettable that he should have preferred his private advantage to his patriotism, his actions could not reasonably be made the basis of a criminal charge. In 1772, when Nordencrantz's undying hatred led him to a renewed attempt to attack the Hat financiers, many of those leading Caps who had been so rabid against them in 1765 now rallied to their defense, and candidly admitted as much.[49] But in the inflamed atmosphere of that year it was too much to expect that the accused should receive a fair trial. In fact, they did not receive a trial at all: all they got was a sentence; a sentence which was too plainly born of party passion and blind vindictiveness not to discredit those who imposed it almost as much as those upon whom it was imposed.

It was in the nature of things inevitable that Goodricke and Osterman should be involved, whether they liked it or not, in these proceedings. They were the Caps' patrons and paymasters; they were responsible to their respective governments for the party's continued tenure of power. Their enemies regarded them, or affected to regard them, as the real rulers of the country,[50] and blamed them in consequence for all the measures of persecution which were undertaken. Schack could seriously report that Osterman and Goodricke intended to put Nordencrantz and Oelreich in the Senate;[51] Fredrik Sparre was told "on unimpeachable authority," that Osterman had threatened Sinclair with permanent exclusion from the Secret Committee and Senate, if he did not conform to Russia's wishes.[52] Schack believed that the attack on Kierman had been incited by Goodricke, or at least was actively supported by him, as part of a deliberate design to destroy those Swedish financiers and merchants who might otherwise have been able to defeat his nefarious plan to subject the Swedish economy to British industrialists and exporters.[53] Osterman, he thought, had allowed himself to be dragged along by Goodricke into collaborating in the operation.[54] If we may believe Breteuil (who had it from the queen), Schack's views on this point were shared by Osterman's own colleague, Stakhiev.[55] Stakhiev's credibility on this particular issue is somewhat diminished by the fact that he himself, in his dispatch to Panin of 2/13 May, admitted the need to "use national fanaticism and hatred of the Hat leaders, and sacrifice the hated Kierman to the present mood."[56] But he certainly complained of what he called Goodricke's "manigances," and asserted that "sans lui Osterman auroit été de plus facile accés";[57] and he is reported to have alleged that Osterman took a more imperious tone—with the Court and with his supporters—than his instructions warranted.[58] There may be something in this: certainly the ultimata which Breteuil believed he had delivered to the Court—the demands for the dismissal of members of the Senate, for the exclusion of this man or that from the Secret Committee—were (to put it no higher) in advance of authorization from home.[59] For some time after the Diet met, official Russian policy continued to preach moderation, since Panin feared that violence might alienate more support than it would attract, and might drive France's friends into supporting the more extreme demands of the queen.[60] It was perhaps indicative of the difference between Panin and Osterman, that when in April a pardon was granted to those who had been sentenced for their part in the events of 1756, Panin was relieved to hear that the exiles would not be allowed to return until after the conclusion of the Diet; while Osterman lamented the postponement.[61] Nevertheless, there were occasions when Osterman intervened to temper the rashness of his party: in February, for instance, he restrained them from summarily expelling Breteuil.[62] And it seems that it was Osterman who first insisted on some sort of practicable composition with Kierman, in place of the intransigence of the more rabid enthusiasts who were determined (in defiance of economic common sense) to squeeze him "till the pips squeaked."[63]

As to Goodricke, there is no doubt that he gave hearty support to the *enragés* of the party;[64] but it is most improbable that in doing so he was moved by any considerations of possible economic advantage to England. His motives were essentially political. The Stockholm merchants, after all, were mostly Hats, and they had invited retaliation.[65] No sense in allowing them to escape with impunity; no more than prudent to use the moment of success to strike terror into those who managed the Hats' finances. At least one banker was effectively terrorized: the renegade Robert Finlay was reduced to coming to Goodricke with an entreaty that he would convey to Messrs Clifford of Amsterdam his assurance that he had in no way been involved in the misdeeds of the Exchange Office.[66] On broader grounds of party tactics, moreover, a policy of violence had much to be said for it: the pack hunted better together with the quarry in sight. The decision to reduce the Paris embassy to the status of a legation, for instance, seems to have been taken in response to the urgings of Goodricke and Osterman to make some sort of demonstration of party strength.[67] Moreover, if there was one section of the party which might be considered as characteristically pro-English, one group which specifically followed Goodricke, it was just that section with whom he had been at such pains to drink and smoke at the time of the elections: that is, the middling sort of Burghers, of whom Westin was the leader and the typical representative. These people included some of those who were hottest in the attack on Kierman and his colleagues. When the assault upon the Exchange Office developed, therefore, Goodricke could hardly have dissociated himself from it if he wished to retain his hold over his following. Neither he nor Osterman were free agents to act as they liked. There were limits to what bribery could effect; and in Goodricke's case those limits were especially strait, since he had so little money at his disposal.

In this matter of party violence, then, whoever called the tune—the briber or the bribed—there seems to have been no great difference between the representatives of England and of Russia. It seems unlikely that Goodricke persuaded Osterman into courses which he would not otherwise have followed. Indeed, Schack himself not long before had taken a diametrically opposite view, which he appeared to have forgotten when discussing the Kierman affair. In March he had been of the opinion that it was a great mistake for England and Russia to allow Osterman to take the lead in Stockholm. His imperiousness, his arrogance, alienated moderate men: if Goodricke had only continued to manage the party, as he had done at the beginning, while Osterman had been kept in the background with the money, most Swedes would have thought that it was a mere question of choosing between France and England, and might have transferred their support to England without too much difficulty, whereas they could hardly be expected to stomach Russia.[68] In Sweden, he insisted, only two real parties were possible: the French and the English.[69] This was, of course, a view to which Panin himself inclined: his refusal to agree to a common party fund, his insistence that England and Russia each preserve a separate following, was based just on this belief, and on his desire to preserve the image of the Caps as a pro-English, and therefore a "patriot" party.[70] As Macartney informed Goodricke, Panin might agree that England and Russia had but one common cause in Sweden, but he thought it "by no means for the Interest of either that the nation should think so."[71] And it is fairly clear that there could be no question of Goodricke's subordination to Osterman, precisely because the

"English" party was still a separate entity, which Goodricke took good care to keep so. In March it was reported that he was giving regular dinners (despite his dislike of lavish expenditure) to his old party cronies; though he had stopped inviting members of the Estate of Peasants to these entertainments since "ce sont des diables à boire."[72] He congratulated himself on keeping his following so well together, at a time when he was unable to satisfy their demands for money.[73] His banker, John Fenwick, acted as one of the organizers of Goodricke's group, and it was to Fenwick's exertions that he attributed the recovery of a majority in the Estate of Burghers in June.[74] In July, after a period of delicate negotiations which had the blessing of Sandwich and the approval of Osterman, he succeeded in persuading a member of the Senate to accept a modest English pension.[75] Certainly he drew a clear distinction between his own followers and Osterman's: he wrote on one occasion that "our friends" had become suspicious of Osterman; and on another that Joakim von Düben was the ablest of "the whole English party."[76]

The truth probably is that both Goodricke and Osterman would have derided any suggestion that the one was subordinate to the other. Their cooperation seems in fact to have been at this stage exceptionally close and harmonious. In August Goodricke sharply rebutted a rumor that all was not well between them: "on the contrary," he wrote, "it is impossible for two Ministers to live better or in more intimate confidence together."[77] From Goodricke's point of view it was fortunate that this was so, since he was for long periods dependent upon his colleague for financial assistance. Sandwich might stick to the principle of *pari passu*, but Catherine had made it clear that "she did not regard a little money, more or less, where an affair of Importance could be effected."[78] The empress, happily untrameled by parliamentary considerations, could afford this attitude. She might and did resent what Macartney called "the system of Frugality," but she could not afford to resent it in Stockholm.[79]

For despite the Caps' great victory at the election, by the summer of 1765 they were far from being in secure command of the parliamentary situation. In the House of Nobility their majority soon became precarious; and from time to time their command of the Clergy and the Burghers was seriously threatened. At the beginning of March Breteuil was reporting that they were beginning to split; and a fortnight later they suffered defeat in the Nobility on the question of crown-peasants' right to buy their holdings—admittedly a class issue which cut across party lines, but still a defeat which Goodricke attributed to unpreparedness and confused leadership.[80] In May the Caps in the Estate of Burghers were said to be so divided on the question of Stockholm's trading privileges that they were organized into three rival clubs.[81] Members were beginning to drift away home, and had to be retrieved in a hurry.[82] In July their majority in the Estate of Burghers had fallen to four, though it had been 40 in March.[83] And on 12 June a critical division in the House of Nobility—and a division precisely on the question whether Kierman's colleagues were to be treated as severely as himself—resulted in a tie, to the great jubilation of the Hats, and the great chagrin of Osterman and Goodricke.[84] This situation had come about—as could have been foreseen from the very beginning of the Diet—by the transference of the votes of the supporters of the Court from the Cap to the Hat side. For in the delicate and uncertain relations between Court and Caps it was just this question of persecution which was one of the most important factors: possibly even the decisive one.

(ii)

On 7 December 1764 the ever-suspicious Schack reported to his government a conversation in which Goodricke had tried to make clear to him his country's attitude to the Court. The principal object of England in Sweden, he had said, was

> to prevent France from conserving or acquiring means to increase further the terrible ascendancy which she had for a number of years enjoyed, whereby she was free to alter the constitution whenever she grew tired—as she certainly would, sooner or later—of spending immense sums yearly to maintain her system, as long as that form of government existed; and secondly that his court, if he rightly understood its principles, would do nothing extraordinary in favour of that of Sweden, and did not propose in any way to attack the constitution of that kingdom, partly because she had no interest in doing so, and partly (and this was the argument he most leaned on) because, linked as she was to the court of Russia, who would never permit an alteration in the constitution, she could not do so without offending that power.[85]

It was a statement obviously calculated to soothe the sensitiveness of Bernstorff to any possibility of an increase in the power of the Swedish crown. It appears to have carried conviction. Whereas before the interview Schack had been warning Bernstorff that Goodricke was planning to subvert the Form of Government,[86] he said no more on that head in subsequent dispatches.[87] And indeed what Goodricke told him was strictly true. It exactly reflected the considerations which determined his attitude to the Court. When Malmström wrote that Goodricke and Osterman had identical instructions in this matter he went beyond the evidence;[88] for in reality Goodricke had no specific orders at all, apart from a paragraph in his original instructions which enjoined him to cultivate those persons trusted by the queen. But that paragraph dated from 1758; and though Lovisa Ulrika's tenacious memory had certainly not forgotten it,[89] so much had changed in the five years which had since elapsed that it could scarcely be considered as a directive in 1765. As things stood in the early months of that year, Goodricke's line was necessarily determined, in the absence of any guidance from home, by local and tactical considerations. He must keep in step with Osterman; he must take the opposite line to Breteuil. He was indeed to some extent committed, though he was not a party, to the Court-Cap electoral pact. It had been phrased with careful vagueness, and was susceptible of more than one interpretation; but it might mean support for a modification of the constitution designed to prevent the legislature's encroachment upon the province of the executive, and perhaps the restoration to the crown of some of the prerogatives lost in 1756. Whether anything was to come of this would depend on whether the agreement with the Court held firm; and in January 1765 that agreement was subjected to severe strains. In the end, despite acute tension between Osterman and Sinclair, the Court had appeared to accept defeat; and Sinclair's following had duly voted for Rudbeck as *lantmarskalk*. Nevertheless, the divergence of aim, the rivalry for control of effective political power (and the finance upon which to base it), which had barely been concealed at the time of the joint manifesto, was bound sooner or later to make itself felt. Whatever changes in the constitution might be agreed to, the Caps would accept them only as strengthening the Form of Government by pruning it of abuses. Certainly not as an installment of a program designed radically to shift the balance of forces in the state. They believed in the constitution; more wholeheartedly, perhaps, than the Hats now did. They believed in rule by the Estates; especially now that they were in power.

On this issue Russian policy remained unchanged, despite the tiresome friction with the queen.[90] Breteuil in February informed Praslin that the constitution of 1720 was safe, since the empress desired no more than to "embellish" it so as to give the king a greater influence on appointments, and a veto on certain measures, leaving to the Estates the control of taxation, foreign policy, and legislation.[91] Provided that the power of the Senate was curbed, provided a sound constitutional balance was secured, Catherine still saw no threat to Russia in a moderate increase in the king's authority. But for this there was one indispensable precondition: the Court must not meddle in *riksdag* politics. The queen must stop her irritating demand to decide how the Russians should spend their money, she must abandon the unacceptable pretension to be the leader of the Cap party, she must accept the political consequences of the election, in the shape of the displacement of the leading Hats from the seats of power.[92] Panin and Osterman deeply distrusted her; but they were not in the least afraid of her, so long as she stood alone. What they feared, what haunted them as a political nightmare, was the possibility that France would irrevocably fix the Court to the French side by undertaking to make the crown absolute.[93] Eighteen months later they would awake to find that the nightmare had become reality.

For the moment, the difficulty was that neither side could be sure what Lovisa Ulrika really wanted, and how far she was playing fast and loose with each. Early in January, despite her pact with the Caps, she concluded a parallel agreement with the Hats. In this she pledged herself to be neutral (a pledge which she had also given to the Caps about the same time); she promised to support Fersen for *lantmarskalk* (a promise which she was unable to keep); and she undertook to stick to the French alliance (which was in any case not due to run out until 1768).[94] In return, she received an assurance that the Hats would support concessions to the crown, provided they emanated from the Caps, but would not themselves take the initiative in proposing them. It was an agreement typical of the queen's tortuous diplomacy. Nevertheless, it had logic behind it. She saw very well that any reform of substance was unlikely, if once the constitution became a party question: there must therefore be reform by bipartisan agreement. That is, by Composition. And this required that party relationships should not be exacerbated: in particular, that there should be no vindictive political persecutions. It is certainly possible that her opposition to persecution arose from a genuine desire to compose the strife of parties, restore national unity and national self-respect, and end the degradation of foreign bribery. It is also possible that she had no other consideration in mind than which tactics would best serve her own ambitions. The nature of the evidence hardly permits a confident pronouncement on this question. But in truth it hardly matters: whichever be the correct explanation, from the queen's point of view it must have seemed that the devious path she trod was the path which the situation dictated. She was moreover a proud woman; and it was natural that she should feel herself humiliated by Catherine's requirement that she should efface herself and leave the direction of affairs to the Russian minister: it was a demand which aroused bitter resentment even in the gentle bosom of Adolf Fredrik.[95] Political persecution might be odious, or merely unwise; but it was intolerable if it was carried out in obedience to the orders of a foreign power. It had been a part of the terms of the original Composition that both sides should forswear revenge; and she professed to regard herself as bound in honor to see that this promise was observed. Was she to stand by and see it violated at the behest of Count Osterman?

These were considerations which had little weight with her brother in Berlin. For nearly twenty years her political fortunes and misfortunes had been a matter of intermittent concern to him, and he had never been sparing of advice—often quite sensible advice—which Lovisa Ulrika had frequently found good reason for not taking. All he wanted of her now was that she should not involve herself in a fresh crisis and then come upon him with a call for assistance. Above all, that her conduct should not compromise him with Catherine: for him, the Russian alliance now took precedence over all other political considerations. It was with increasing alarm and irritation that he watched the queen's political gyrations. Out of consideration for Russia, as he explained to her, he had ordered his minister Cocceji to collaborate closely with Goodricke and Osterman;[96] and Cocceji's reports home were disturbing. Frederick reacted to them by bombarding his sister with letters of criticism, exhortation, and advice, in which fraternal candor was scarcely made more palatable by professions of fraternal affection. She must not be rude to Osterman;[97] she must not advertise her resentment by quitting Stockholm.[98] She was not to commit herself to any party, least of all France;[99] she must not suppose that a great potentate such as Catherine would allow herself to be trifled with; but on the other hand she must keep her friendship with France alive, since in the long run only France would be foolish enough to pay subsidies to Sweden. It was a matter of indifference to him (he explained) whether she were Hat or Cap, provided she stuck to her decision and did not provoke Russia.[100] For Russia, he insisted, could be relied upon to restore the crown to the position it had held before the fatal year 1756.[101] It must be said for Frederick that his actions did something to offset the acid tone of his letters: he made real efforts to put the best possible gloss on the queen's behavior, and to persuade Catherine and Panin that it was not she but Sinclair who was to blame.[102] Lovisa Ulrika, on her side, defended her actions with Hohenzollern obstinacy, considerable debating ability, and (in the end) even with dignity; but she made as little impression on him as he on her. By the summer of 1765 their secret correspondence had reached a point at which each was writing "final" letters to the other.

The Diet had scarcely got down to business before its proceedings were interrupted, and its temperature raised, by the tenebrous affair of Cederhielm's Memorial: an episode of intrinsically trivial interest, which acquired importance because in the prevailing murk of intrigue no one knew whence it emanated, or what its significance. At the beginning of February Baron Carl Josias Cederhielm—a political maverick, sharp-tongued and ambitious—presented to the Estate of Nobility a Memorial in which, with some effrontery, he suggested the establishment of a committee, selected and presided over by himself, to examine the defects of the constitution and propose measures for putting it right.[103] This cool proposal met with a stormy reception; and it was not long before Cederhielm found it wise to ask leave to withdraw it. As to what lay behind it, no one was very sure: accusations were freely bandied about. It was generally supposed that Cederhielm had been put up to it by some supporters of the Court; but opinions differed as to the precise provenance. Breteuil believed that it was concerted between Rudbeck, Goodricke, and Osterman;[104] C. F. Scheffer informed Schack, as a matter of fact, that it was the work of Löwenhielm.[105] Certainly Rudbeck, Löwenhielm, and Lovisa Ulrika all knew about it beforehand; and it seems likely that Rudbeck allowed it to go forward in order to test how much meddling with the constitution his followers might be expected to tolerate. What seems clear is that Goodricke had nothing to do with it; and it would be difficult in any case to see why he should. The Memorial came as a surprise to him, and by his own account he tried to stifle it:[106] he told Macartney that he believed it was concocted by the Court in the hope of splitting the Caps, since the queen calculated that they would damage themselves whether they supported or opposed it.[107]

At all events, whether Cederhielm's Memorial is to be regarded as a *ballon d'essai* or a Trojan horse, the month of February saw the beginning of a shift in the Court's position. Soon after the election of the *lantmarskalk* the queen made a last attempt to put her relations with the Caps on a footing more satisfactory to herself, and made contact with such of their leaders as she considered to be most favorably disposed. The attempt led nowhere. They gave her good words; they gave her assurances that the Caps would do as much for her as the Hats ever could.[108] But they could not offer to turn over to her the direction of their party; and nothing less would have satisfied her. Panin lamented the ambiguity of her attitude; the Caps, embittered, suspected that she had already changed sides.[109] But Breteuil, for his part, was equally disappointed: he "complained heavily" of her duplicity, and wrote ironically that she had maneuvered so well that she found herself equally distrusted by both parties.[110] Cocceji suspected that she was bent on establishing a "third party" under her own control: the unwisest thing, in his opinion, that she could possibly have done.[111]

The event was to prove that Cocceji's conjecture was correct. At the beginning of March came a significant move: in midwinter the Court quitted its comfortable quarters in Stockholm, and retired to Ulriksdal. It was a demonstration, an indication that the dialogue with the Caps was terminated; it was a ceremonious and public fit of the sulks. Goodricke noted that on the night before the move the king and queen had lengthy interviews with the Hat leaders. The implication was plain. It was underlined by the Court's conduct at Ulriksdal: during the seven or eight weeks of its stay there the king and queen conversed only with Hats (which even Ekeblad thought unwise) and relieved their feelings by barbed witticisms on the Diet's proceedings.[112]

Panin did not fail to note the significance of these things.[113] But the behavior of the royal pair, however deplorable, did not affect his judgment on the problem of the constitution, for that problem was independent of personalities. It was in fact just at this juncture that he went further in the direction of strengthening the power of the crown than he had ever done before, or was ever to do again. In a letter to Osterman of 28 March he informed him that he considered that Adolf Fredrik's demand (transmitted through Sinclair) that no amendment to the constitution should be valid without the king's consent, was "as delicate . . . as it is just, being based on the reciprocity of the contract between King and nation, in which any alteration naturally requires the consent of both sides"; and that the further demand that the king's assent be necessary to a declaration of war was "just, and useful to the general interests of all Sweden's neighbours."[114] The reasoning, in part at all events, was based on a contractualist view of the Swedish constitution which the Caps certainly, and many of the Hats also, would have regarded as heretical; but it revealed the cool consistency of his approach to the constitutional problem. It did not prevent him, in another letter of the same day, from alluding to "the wilful delusions of the Queen and her followers."[115] The Caps too, it appeared, were capable of making the same distinction; for three weeks later Goodricke reported that the Grand Committee had appointed a subcommittee of thirty to take amendments to the constitution into consideration—a subcommittee which included Fersen and some other Hats "in order that they shall have their part in any alteration it may be thought proper to make, which they refused the Court to begin, but promised to concur in."[116]

Nevertheless, Catherine was not prepared to break with the Court without making a final effort. She suggested threats;[117] she attempted persuasion; she enlisted the help of Frederick the Great, who showed himself very ready to oblige. At Catherine's request, he wrote to Lovisa Ulrika to warn her that Sinclair was betraying her, and enclosed a copy of the empress's letter.[118] Panin had already sent to Osterman an intercepted dispatch which revealed Lovisa Ulrika's approaches to the Hats, with orders to show it to her as evidence of the Hats' insincerity.[119] But nothing helped. The intercepted dispatch completely failed to shake her. The dry and formal answer which she made to Cocceji, in reply to Catherine's attack upon Sinclair, was in fact concerted with the Hat leaders—which Breteuil rightly considered a signal sign of confidence.[120]

By June, in fact, they had come to the parting of the ways. On 31 May Lovisa Ulrika professed that she would live and die a Hat; and Adolf Fredrik informed Ekeblad that though it was a matter of indifference to him whether Sweden followed a French or an English system, "what is impossible for me, and still more for my children, is to see the Estates subject to the will of Russia, assisting that power to establish its authority over my kingdom, and attempting to dictate laws to it."[121] On 19 June the Court's decision became final. On that day Breteuil could report the conclusion of an agreement for tacit collaboration in the Diet: as in the agreement of January, it was provided that the Hats would wait for the Caps to take the initiative on the constitution, and would judge their proposals on their merits. It was this agreement which led directly to the tie in the Estate of Nobility on the Kierman affair.[122] Limited as its scope appeared to be, and warily as either side engaged in it, it proved to be decisive. It would be untrue to say that thereafter Lovisa Ulrika became a reliable Hat; but she had at least decisively severed her connection with the Caps. Henceforward she would command a party of her own—on the day of the agreement she denied to Cocceji that she had turned Hat[123]—but for the next four years it would be a party committed to the Hat alliance.

Panin for his part had already made up his mind that there was no longer any point in taking the Court's feelings or wishes into consideration: the duties of friendship, he felt, had been fully discharged; the Court must be left to its fate. The Caps alone should do Russia's work; their continued control of power must be the prime objective; any constitutional reform must be at their discretion. They were to be free to do away with anything which they found to be repugnant to the law; no attempt was to be made to constrain them to enlarge the prerogative, if they felt such an enlargement to be against their interests. All that was required of them in this respect was that they should not overstep the bounds which the Form of Government laid down. Later in the session, when the Hat Senate had been hurled from power, when the business of retribution had been completed—then Russia would have a word to say: the Diet must not end without the passage of a law inhibiting too-easy "improvements" of the text of 1720—preferably by making all such improvements conditional on the approval of all four Estates, a majority of the Senate, and the king. Such a law, he thought, would give Russia all the security she could reasonably require.[124] The time might come when the Court, repenting its political aberrations, would once more seek Russia's aid; and for this a door was carefully to be kept open. But for the present, Panin was content to give the Caps their head.[125]

The situation thus seemed to have clarified itself at last. From the point of view of the Cap zealots there could now remain no reason for further delay in attacking the Hats' last stronghold, and proceeding to the *licentiering* of the most obnoxious members of the Senate. Goodricke had long taken it for granted that this would happen:[126] it was, indeed, almost a precondition for the success of his treaty that Ekeblad should be removed from the post of chancery-president. As early as January it had been reported that Osterman was demanding the replacement of six of the leading Hats;[127] and now that the breach with the Court had become definitive Panin gave orders for the attack to begin.[128] On the other side, the queen, in virtue of her pact with Breteuil, and as the professed opponent of political persecution, was bound to use every means available to her to defeat the attempt. It was with this object in view that she now contrived a secret interview with Osterman's coadjutor Stakhiev.

Since Stakhiev's return to Sweden in January as minister with responsibility for commercial affairs he had probably had a sufficiently unsatisfactory time of it. His relations with Osterman were bound to be delicate, his position was anomalous, his social contacts—despite his long experience of Stockholm—appear to have been few.[129] Goodricke and Cocceji seem to have kept their distance, Breteuil apparently despised him, the queen is said to have detested him, and he was not included in the invitations to eat at the royal table which were normally given to foreign ministers.[130] It was therefore not perhaps very difficult for Lovisa Ulrika to tempt him into an indiscretion which at least might give him the feeling that his presence in Stockholm was of some importance. At all events, on 21 June he allowed himself to be persuaded by one of the queen's party to come to a secret meeting with Lovisa Ulrika and Adolf Fredrik in the Chinese pavilion at Drottningholm. He came entirely on his own responsibility: Osterman was not informed until the meeting was over. What passed is not wholly clear: it was on this occasion, according to Lovisa Ulrika's report to Breteuil, that Stakhiev permitted himself to make highly reprehensible comments on Osterman's political behavior.[131] Stakhiev's own account to Panin naturally was silent on these points, and dwelt mainly on the responsibility of Sinclair's "third party" for provoking Cap violence.[132] What seems certain is that one purpose of the meeting, from the queen's point of view, was to drive a wedge between the two Russian ministers in the hope of thereby aborting the attack on the Senate; that in the course of it she urged Stakhiev to agree that the *licentiering* be deferred until after the revision of the constitution; and that Stakhiev at the very least showed some sympathy for this proposal.[133]

The moment was not unpromising for such a suggestion. Some of the more moderate Caps, and notably Rudbeck, appear to have been thinking along the same lines.[134] The subcommittee appointed to consider reform had not as yet got down to serious business, but it certainly had not been designed as window dressing, and the Hats seem really to have expected that the Caps would make specific proposals. The spirit of the Composition still hung faintly in the air, at least at the topmost level of politics. Only ten days before Stakhiev had his meeting with the queen Goodricke had reported that the Cap leaders could not make up their minds whether to take up the constitutional issue before *licentiering* or not.[135] On 24 July, however, Rudbeck paid a courtesy call on Lovisa Ulrika at Drottningholm, and as a result of their discussion he agreed to consult with some of his party about the queen's demands. The result was that Rudbeck undertook that the subcommittee should give immediate attention to the constitutional problem, while the queen on her side seems to have promised to persuade Ekeblad and C. F. Scheffer to offer their resignations from the Senate; and she certainly believed that Rudbeck pledged himself that no further move against any of the other Hat Senators would be taken pending the subcommittee's recommendations.[136] It remained to be seen whether either of the parties to this bargain was able to stand by it.

Certainly nothing could now stop the impending action against some at least of the Senate; and neither Osterman, who was angry at Stakhiev's initiative,[137] nor Goodricke, who believed that to postpone *licentiering* was simply to play the queen's game, was inclined to try to restrain their followers. The attack was directed in the first place at Claes Ekeblad, C. F. Scheffer, and Carl Otto Hamilton; and the main article of accusation against them (as expected) was their share in the decision to accept France's offer in regard to the arrears of subsidy, although at the time a meeting of the Diet was only a few weeks ahead. These were the men who had long been regarded as the especial friends and clients of Denmark. More than once in the past Bernstorff had promised them that he would come to their aid if they should be in danger. No doubt much had altered since that promise had last been given: Scheffer and his friends no longer enjoyed Bernstorff's wholehearted trust and support. But for old times' sake he could not simply look the other way: despite his evident reluctance to meddle in Swedish party quarrels he felt himself bound in honor to do something for them. And so to the already sufficiently protean appearance of Denmark's foreign policy was added another element of confusion.

On 11 March 1765 Denmark had at last concluded her long-pending alliance with Russia.[138] It marked the end of the long association with France; it inaugurated a connection with the Court of St. Petersburg which was destined to outlast the century. In the immediate future, it pledged Denmark to cooperation with Russia in Stockholm. Yet to Bernstorff it did not at the time present itself in the light of a watershed or a turning point. The link with France, after all, could not be snapped immediately, for France still owed arrears of subsidy which it was important not to lose.[139] The attachment to Russia was not seen as exclusive or unconditional: on the contrary, at the very period when the negotiations for the treaty were at a critical stage Bernstorff saw no apparent inconsistency in imperilling them, and exposing himself to the charge of duplicity, by reiterated attempts to dissuade Sandwich from supporting Osterman and the Caps.[140] The essential point in the alliance, in Bernstorff's eyes, lay in that secret article which foreshadowed the opening of negotiations upon the crucial question of the Holstein exchange.[141] He did not feel himself bound to follow Catherine's lead in opposition to Denmark's own interests. Least of all in Sweden, where (as he explained to Borcke) it was now a matter of comparative indifference to him which "system" prevailed, provided the pure word of constitutional orthodoxy were not challenged.[142] At the end of January he had put his position very plainly to his minister in St. Petersburg:

> si le but de la Russie n'est autre que d'avoir un allié fidèle, exact et ponctuel dans le roi, elle peut compter avoir pleine satisfaction . . . ; mais si elle se propose, sous prétexte d'amitié, de dépouiller sa maj. de son indépendance et de sa prudence et de l'assujétir à ses vues et à ses haines non comprises ni exprimées dans l'alliance, elle ne sera pas contente, nul intérêt, nul motif au monde ne pouvant engager sa maj. à oublier ce qu'elle est et ce qu'elle se doit.[143]

This was, undoubtedly, an admirable attitude for a Danish statesman. But it was decidedly unfortunate that it was shortly to be spoiled by Bernstorff's own actions: within a few months of writing this passage he was to offend and irritate his new ally by proceedings which had very little to do with Denmark's essential interests. Bernstorff's reservations about his new connection with Russia at times blinded him to the hard fact that he had in reality swapped horses. For some months after the conclusion of the alliance it was not unusual for Danish diplomatic correspondence to refer to Russia, as in the past, as a power whose designs might be dangerous, and whose motives were prima facie suspect.[144] When Bernstorff wrote that Denmark "ne regarderoit néanmoins jamais avec indifférence qu'une puissance, quelle qu'elle puisse être, sans en excepter aucune sur la terre, voulût invahir hostilement la Suède et la mettre sous sa dépendance,"[145] it was sufficiently clear that he had in mind the ally whose Swedish policy he had now pledged himself to support.

Small wonder if in such circumstances his minister in Stockholm found it a matter of difficulty and delicacy to hit upon the line which circumstances demanded. At the beginning of 1765 Schack had felt himself to be mentally on solid ground. He had his political categories neatly sorted out: the Swedish constitution must not be altered by a single syllable; Russia's attitude towards it was suspect; Breteuil and C. F. Scheffer were Denmark's natural friends and supporters; Goodricke was a bad man, with whom (as he informed Bernstorff) he would not again discuss business except upon express orders.[146] But Bernstorff's instructions of 28 January, with their intimation of the intention to conclude an alliance with Russia, completely disorientated him.[147] Within a few months almost all his familiar landmarks were unaccountably shifted or swept away: only Lovisa Ulrika and A. J. von Höpken remained reassuringly in place as the irreconcilable enemies. It is easy to sympathize with his somewhat dazed reaction. He now found himself engaged in a hopeless attempt to be on good terms with both sides; and his amicable professions were robbed of credibility by the circumstance that the British secret intelligence knew all about his dealings with Breteuil, and took care that St. Petersburg should know them too. Panin, now and for some time to come, thoroughly distrusted him, and in March Korff was ordered to work for his recall.[148] He was faced with the unenviable task of explaining away the Russian alliance to C. F. Scheffer and Breteuil.[149] He found himself expected to "live well," not only with the party which Bernstorff had thrown over, but also with the party which he was so frigidly and conditionally embracing.[150] It proved far from easy to change the social habits of years: as late as September Osterman was drily remarking that all Schack's friends seemed to be Hats.[151]

The alliance with Russia had included, besides the Secret Article about the Holstein exchange, another which guaranteed the Swedish constitution.[152] Just what that might mean was anything but clear. Bernstorff had shown an extraordinary impermeability to the idea that Russia's view of the constitution might conceivably be reconcilable with his own. Over a year before he had given a cautious blessing to a suggested revision, transmitted to him by none other than C. F. Scheffer, which would certainly not have left the sacrosanct fabric of 1756 untouched.[153] Nevertheless, he went on protesting that nothing less than the preservation of the amendments of 1756 would satisfy him. He did indeed construct an interpretation of the Secret Article which no doubt was satisfactory to himself;[154] but either it meant nothing, or he did not stick to it. The unfortunate Schack was obviously at sea as to whether the constitution which was to be guaranteed was that of 1720 *simpliciter*, or whether the additions of 1756 were to be deemed to be included.[155] For some weeks Osterman was no wiser than he.[156] It is true that Bernstorff did make up his mind relatively quickly on this crucial point: on 6 April he nerved himself to accept what was a major modification of his earlier standpoint, and indicated that he was now prepared to forget about 1756.[157] But this did not help Schack; for with curious insensitivity Bernstorff communicated his decision, not to Schack, who desperately needed to have his mind cleared on the point, but to his minister in St. Petersburg: it was not until the end of July that Schack was given the information;[158] and it was not until as late as 20 August that he was able to find an opportunity to pass it on to Osterman.[159] Schack noted that he received the intimation with some astonishment; as well he might. His surprise would perhaps have been exceeded by Schack's, if the haziness of Bernstorff's statesmanship had left that minister with much capacity for being surprised at anything.

The fluttering ambiguities of Danish policy, the nicely balanced reservations of Bernstorff's mind, and the consequent distracted state of Schack's, might well have continued indefinitely, for all that can be seen to the contrary. What put an end to them, what fixed Denmark firmly and finally in the Russian camp, was the fiasco of Bernstorff's intervention in the affair of the *licentiering*. Since the beginning of the year Schack had been pressed at intervals by Breteuil to promise to make financial assistance available in case of need.[160] His stereotyped reply had always been that Denmark would spend money in Sweden only for two purposes: to defend the constitution, and to protect old friends from persecution.[161] As so often happened where Bernstorff was concerned this proved to be a truth with a modification. For there was one other object for which he was prepared to open his purse strings, and that was to secure the completion of the marriage between the Princess Sofia Magdalena and the future Gustav III. The engagement between them, contracted as long ago as 1750, had always been bitterly resented by the Swedish royal pair. Since at least the autumn of 1764 Lovisa Ulrika had been casting about for means to break it;[162] and Bernstorff, who was almost morbidly sensitive on this issue, was troubled by fears that a promise to do so might form part of a bargain between the Court and one or other of the parties in Sweden. His anxiety led him to listen to a suggestion from Breteuil that he should promise to pay Sinclair a handsome bribe if he succeeded in preventing the engagement's being broken off; the money to be handed over on the day the marriage was celebrated.[163] This, whatever its wisdom, was at least not inconsistent with his obligations to Russia under the treaty. But on 21 May C. F. Scheffer, who felt the shadow of *licentiering* darkening around him, came to Schack with a modest proposal of his own. The bribe to Sinclair, he suggested, was unnecessary, since Sinclair's only hope now was to stick to the Hats, and this would ensure that the marriage had his support. If Denmark had money to spend, much better to employ it to buy a majority to defeat the attack upon himself and his two colleagues. The matter was admittedly delicate, in view of Denmark's connection with Russia, but after all it could be kept strictly secret.[164]

Now it is true that in April Bernstorff had received a vague assurance from Panin that Osterman would do his best to restrain his friends in Stockholm from attacking Denmark's protégés.[165] But that was before the Court's alliance with the Hats, and the queen's attempt to seduce Stakhiev, had heightened the political tension; and it is in any case doubtful whether Panin considered *licentiering* in itself to be a measure of persecution. By late June it should have been apparent to Bernstorff that intervention against a *licentiering* which now had Russian backing would be a risky business. Yet with rare imprudence he allowed himself, after a momentary hesitation, to acquiesce in Scheffer's perilous proposition.[166] The 400,000 copper daler which had been destined for Sinclair were diverted to rescuing the three Hat Senators.[167] Every precaution was taken. The money was transmitted to the Danish minister in Paris, and from Paris was sent to Breteuil, to whose care the task of parliamentary bribery was committed. So lightly, so rashly, did Bernstorff jeopardize the results of eighteen months of patient diplomacy, and the great matter of *Mageskiftet*, which that diplomacy had been designed to secure.

Thus armed, Breteuil was ready for the battle in the Diet. It was joined soon after the middle of July,[168] and was fought with great fury. The Caps had lost their majority in the Estate of Nobility, where the "Sinclairians" were said to command more than 200 votes,[169] and they were clinging only with difficulty to their command of the Clergy and Burghers. The expenses on both sides were heavy: Breteuil was reported to have spent 100,000 silver daler in three days, and his final account was for 1,280,000, apart from Denmark's contribution;[170] Osterman fortunately received 60,000 rubles (ostentatiously delivered in barrels) just in time, and by 6 August had expended, accordingly to Goodricke's tally, no less than 200,000;[171] Goodricke himself, with no money at his command, sent off a desperate appeal for £2,000: "This is one of those critical Moments . . . when a Minister who has Money at his disposal can do great Things for his Court without much Expense."[172] In vain an embarrassed Schack, acting on orders from home, appealed to an equally embarrassed Osterman to persuade his friends to drop the proceedings: Osterman could only answer that this was the business of the Swedish nation, in which no foreign power ought to interfere.[173]

By the first week of August Rudbeck's bargain with the queen began to bear fruit. The subcommittee on the constitution was galvanized into a whole week's activity. The queen's party put pressure on Scheffer and Ekeblad; and after an agonizing all-night session with Breteuil they decided to throw in their hands: Ekeblad was so shaken that he protested that he would have a stroke if he were to be dragged before the Secret Committee for questioning.[174] On 2 August they announced their intention; and in view of the drain on Cap party coffers it was thought prudent to accept their resignations. The shock to their friends (and to their reputations) was severe. Breteuil was disgusted; Lovisa Ulrika reported to be in tears.[175] "It is not the

Caps," wrote Schack gloomily, "but the ministers of England and Russia, who direct the Diet now."[176] But there was worse news to come. On the morning after their resignations Schack learned to his fury that the whole amount of Bernstorff's 400,000 copper daler had been spent by Breteuil in preliminary expenses: from Denmark's point of view the money had been simply thrown away. Nor was this all; for it was not very long before Schack was made aware that the close-kept secret was no secret at all. On 20 August he had an acutely uncomfortable interview with Goodricke, who with every profession of disbelief in the story made it perfectly clear that every detail of the transaction was known to the British government.[177] And therefore to Russia. It was hardly surprising. For some months past Goodricke and Sandwich had been aware of the possibility that Bernstorff might intervene;[178] and in due course the Hanoverian secret office in Nienburg intercepted a dispatch in which the whole intrigue was laid bare. To those concerned the leak seemed inexplicable. There were agitated conjectures as to who might be to blame: Schack suspected Breteuil;[179] Bernstorff thought it might have come from careless talk by C. F. Scheffer, and even for a moment seemed inclined to blame the Danish legation in Stockholm—to Schack's great indignation;[180] and two years later a new Danish minister believed he had discovered the secret, and traced it to an "officier" who had left Breteuil's service to enter Goodricke's.[181] But no one had an inkling of the truth.

Whatever the explanation, the episode was both damaging and humiliating. Schack was reduced to enlisting Goodricke's good offices to put things right with Osterman.[182] Bernstorff, though he made an elaborate attempt to justify his action in St. Petersburg,[183] was forced to acquiesce very promptly in a Russian demand for a contribution—considerably in excess of the sum which Breteuil had squandered—which might be used to support Osterman's operations.[184] It was a decisive moment. Before very long Caspar von Saldern was expected to leave St. Petersburg to represent Holstein interests in the impending discussions on a provisional *Mageskifte*. In no circumstances now could Bernstorff permit himself another indiscretion. There must be no more willfulness; there must be an end to the lingering suspicions of Russia's motives, an end to those old ideas which had hung on from the period of the French alliance. The fiasco of the *licentiering* came as a sobering cold douche: henceforward Russia and Denmark must go hand in hand in Stockholm. And this had, indirectly, its effects on Goodricke. For whereas at the beginning of 1765 he and Osterman had formed a working team of two, with assistance available at need from Cocceji, a year later the position had changed: the duo had become a trio, with Schack as its third member. A year after that it would be Osterman and Schack, rather than Osterman and Goodricke, who were most intimately linked in collaboration.

(iii)

For some months now tension had been mounting in Stockholm. The air was charged, passions were rising, acts of violence were not inconceivable, and were indeed apprehended by those of a nervous disposition. Already in March Fersen had confided to Breteuil that it would not surprise him if he were to be arrested.[185] In May, there were tumults in Stockholm which Breteuil believed to be the work of Anglo-Russian agents.[186] In August Osterman fled in panic from a diplomatic dinner party on a rumor that his person was in danger and that Fersen had arrested Rudbeck; and for some nights thereafter he, Goodricke, Cocceji, and Rudbeck set guards upon their houses, and Osterman took the precaution of sleeping away from home.[187] There were ominous hints that the extremists among the Caps were so out of hand that they might turn upon their own leaders: Schack heard stories that they were contemplating an attack on Löwenhielm, as being too lenient with Kierman and his associates.[188]

It might perhaps have been expected that the resignation of Ekeblad and Scheffer would do something to disperse these clouds. In terms of Rudbeck's agreement with the queen, their removal should have been the signal for all parties to address themselves to the work of constitutional reform. But the rank and file of the Caps, especially in the three lower Estates, did not consider themselves bound by his undertaking: indeed, it is unlikely that they were aware of it. They had no intention of allowing themselves to be sidetracked from pursuing the business of *licentiering*: Ekeblad and Scheffer had hardly departed before it was suggested that it might be well to make a clean sweep and impeach the entire Senate;[189] and on 16 August the Secret Committee, having completed its laborious examination of the Senate minutes since 1762, laid its findings before the *plena*, and so brought the political crisis to a climax.

The Committee's report intimated that it had decided that four more Senators were unworthy of the confidence of the Estates, and should therefore forfeit their office. This was not a recommendation: it was rather the communication of a verdict; for the charges against them turned on foreign policy (in effect, on the acceptance of France's offer on subsidy arrears), and since this was a state secret of which only the Committee could take cognizance the *plena* were debarred from discussing it. But the Committee reported also that there were a further three Senators who were less seriously inculpated than the four, and their fate it referred to the *plena* for decision. The debates which now began in each of the four Estates were of course in reality straight party struggles; but formally the issue at stake was whether the Committee's report on the four Senators should simply be accepted without comment, or whether the *plena* were free to debate it. For three successive days (17-19 August) the battle raged with swaying fortunes and much deployment of constitutional learning.[190] Just at this moment, on 16 August, Goodricke was heartened by the arrival of a letter of warm commendation from Grafton, the new Secretary of State.[191] But approval was nothing without money, and both sides were now calling up their last financial reserves in an effort to snatch a victory. Goodricke's pockets were empty, and Osterman was in little better case; but Breteuil was somehow able to spend money freely, although the queen, disheartened and embittered by Rudbeck's inability to keep his promise, told him that it was pointless to try to rescue "des vieilles planches qui manquaient sous nos pieds."[192] Nevertheless, for a moment it seemed that French gold might carry the day. On 17 August the Nobility voted by 394 to 327 to debate the Committee's report; the numbers in the Clergy were equal; though the Burghers approved the report by 80 to 2. The Peasants had not yet considered it, but might probably follow the Clergy's decision, when that should emerge. Even if outright defeat were avoided, it was not impossible that two Estates might stand against two; and if that should happen no decision could be taken, and all seven Senators would escape, at least for the moment. Goodricke's dispatch gives a vivid account of the course of the crisis, and may serve as a typical sample of the nature of a British minister's job in Stockholm:[193]

> This sudden Change in the Disposition of the Diet, was owing to our want of Money, and to the French Ambassador's having spent very near Seven Thousand Pounds between Friday Noon, and Saturday evening; He gave a Supper to Five Hundred People, at the old Town House, which is reckoned to have cost him [blank] Hundred Pounds; His emissaries were employed the whole Night in distributing Money, and laid out three Thousand Pounds among the Clergy alone, besides what they disposed of to the other Orders. On Sunday morning our Friends came to me in the greatest Alarm, and told me the whole Diet was over, that the French Party had regained the Superiority, had declared they would make a new Marshal, break the Secret Committee, restore the two Senators that resigned, and change all we had hitherto done, That this Evil could no ways be prevented but by my fur-

nishing a large sum immediately, for if the Point was lost, of removing the Senators, it was to be feared all the rest would; I desired them not to be discouraged, assured them that there was the greatest Reason to believe they would be supported by those who were at present employed by His Majesty, as His Ministers, and that I had no doubt the very next Post would bring me Instructions from Your Grace upon that Subject, that I would consult with M. Osterman what was to be done in the present Emergency.

I went to him directly and found him also very much afraid that everything was going wrong; He said he had not money enough to carry the Affair through; and pressed me to draw for Five Thousand Pounds, saying, that if our Court did not approve of my Conduct in this Respect, he would repay what I advanced, to which I answered that I did not so much as know what Banker I should have any Credit upon, that I could not draw upon him who had been employed by the last Ministry, without being sure he was continued by the present one, and in short after much Difficulty I prevailed with him to raise about Four Thousand Pounds, promising that I would as soon as I had a new Credit, support the Party as far as I was enabled to do by my Orders without asking him to furnish more.

This had so good an effect that we regained the Clergy that same evening, all the Orders are now debating upon the affair, and I shall acquaint Your Grace to-morrow with the result.

The result proved decisive. On 20 August the three lower Estates accepted the Committee's recommendation dismissing the four Senators; and even in the Nobility the Caps substantially increased the size of their minority.[194] A week later the four handed in their resignations; and once again Goodricke and Osterman advised acceptance, rather than face the political and financial hazards of a debate upon the penal measure of dismissal.[195] The last remaining stronghold of the Hats has thus been stormed: although the case of the three Senators still remained to be decided, the Caps might henceforth count on control of the Senate, as they already had control of the Secret Committee.

New men were now in charge of Sweden's foreign policy. On 2 September the Secret Committee chose Löwenhielm to succeed Ekeblad as chancery-president, and soon after picked on Friesendorff as his vice-president (*rikskanslirád*). Neither choice gave unalloyed pleasure to Goodricke, and Breteuil was able to console himself with the reflection that it might easily have been worse.[196] Goodricke would have preferred Baron Joakim von Düben for chancery-president, as being a firm friend of England; but von Düben refused to be a candidate, lest men say he had deserted the Court for the sake of office.[197] Löwenhielm was no doubt the ablest available candidate; he was in receipt of a pension from Russia which Osterman took care to increase after his appointment,[198] and probably of an English pension also. But he had been bred a lawyer, he had no experience of foreign affairs, and only too much of the darker byways of politics: Schack pronounced him to be of all Swedish politicians "le plus rusé, quoique du reste très grossier dans ses façons."[199] Within a few weeks of his appointment Grafton was warning Goodricke that he was in touch with Breteuil, and was not to be trusted.[200] Still, they must make the best of him; and Goodricke, though he had no illusions, was confident that they could keep him steady so long as the Diet lasted. When it was over, they would take care that his hands should be effectively tied by the instruction which the Secret Committee would leave behind it.[201] Despite this optimistic prediction, they were to have trouble with him before the year was out.

The choice of Löwenhielm as chancery-president undoubtedly took off some of the gilt of victory. It remained to be seen whether its luster would be restored by the six new members who were now to be chosen to fill the vacancies in the Senate. Members of the Senate were picked by the king from a list of three names for each vacancy, a method which thus preserved to him a limited power of selection. But since on this occasion all the candidates were objectionable to him in greater or less degree, his only resource was to damage the Caps as much as possible by choosing the weakest and least competent of those on each list; to which end he sought and obtained the advice of the Hat leader, Axel von Fersen.[202] The result was that Goodricke's candidate von Düben was once again firmly excluded. Goodricke and Osterman did not forget it; and a year later they would take their revenge. The new Senators were not, perhaps, very impressive, and one of them—von Wallwijk—would later turn deserter; but at least they were mostly "Old Caps," long-standing partisans of the English connection, and Goodricke may well have been as satisfied in reality as he claimed to be.[203] The Secret Committee had drawn up its lists without serious difficulty, and apparently without much expense; and that was much. And Goodricke could now boast that of the sixteen members of the Senate, twelve were firmly on his side.[204] The fate of a further three still hung in the balance.

All now seemed clear for the inauguration of the long-delayed negotiation of the English alliance. The initial formal approach had been made by Goodricke as long ago as 6 August, on the last day of Ekeblad's tenure of office,[205] though since then the matter had hung fire pending the choice of his successor. But just at this moment the attention of everybody—including that of Goodricke himself—was diverted to the intricate business of the Danish marriage. It is not very easy to understand why Bernstorff should have pursued this objective with such unrelenting pertinacity. No doubt it had become a question of "face," of prestige. But the political advantages to be expected were at best dubious; and the price of success might well be high, both in political and human terms. Schack had given him the most explicit warning, a year ago, that Gustav was not likely to make a satisfactory husband;[206] and his prediction proved true: for many years the marriage was in fact a very unhappy one. It had originally been arranged in concert with the Hats and France; but now, when the time for it was at hand, Bernstorff found himself dealing with a Cap government backed by Russia, and it was far from certain what their attitude would be. Bernstorff hoped that the conclusion of his Russian alliance might induce Catherine to agree to give him active support on this issue. But Catherine, though she felt that something ought to be done to save her new ally from the humiliation of a refusal, was sensible enough to see that it would be unwise to constrain Gustav to take a bride whom he did not want; and the furthest she would go at first was to promise benevolence.[207] She did indeed suggest to Osterman possible alternatives—Princess Philippine of Schwedt, for instance, or (best of all) George III's sister Louisa.[208] George III, however, had indicated in good time that this was a matter in which he intended to be strictly neutral; and Goodricke therefore took Osterman's hints with all possible reserve.[209] But he could not turn down the idea altogether, since in the early summer of 1765 it seemed that most Caps were opposed to the Danish marriage,[210] and they might well have welcomed the substitution of Louisa for Sofia Magdalena. The rumor of an English candidate got abroad, and it had the predictable effect of strengthening Breteuil's support for the Danish princess, if only to obviate the risk of an English.[211]

It now began to occur to both Hats and Caps (and to the foreign ministers who supported them) that the question of the marriage might be used as a lever in negotiations with the Court. The Hats might promise Lovisa Ulrika constitutional concessions in return for the withdrawal of her opposition; the Caps might offer to throw over Sofia Magdalena if only the queen would sever her connection with the Hats. Goodricke, with painful memories of the heavy financial drain of recent weeks, seems to have come to think that it might be worthwhile to attempt to bargain with her on some such terms as these. He believed (mistakenly) that the alienation of the Court was to be ascribed to the machinations of Sinclair, and that a renewal of the former friendly relations between the queen and the Cap leaders might not be impossible, if only Sinclair could be circumvented.[212] At the end of August he had a long interview with Lovisa Ulrika's grand chamberlain, Nils Philip Gyldenstolpe, which was probably intended as a feeler in this direction. He does not seem to have conducted it very wisely: his tone is said to have been hectoring and threatening; both men seem to have lost their tempers; and the conversation closed in mutual recriminations.[213]

Bernstorff, meanwhile, was quite ready to use either Hats or Caps, as might best serve his purpose, though naturally he would have preferred that the marriage should not become a party issue. In September, as a result of appeals from C. F. Scheffer, he gave the Hats a time limit within which to bring Lovisa Ulrika to reason.[214] It ran out in the third week of October, with nothing effected; but already Schack had been ordered to see what could be done through Goodricke.[215] By this time it had begun to appear probable that the issue would be decided by Gustav himself. He was now being pressed on all sides to give way: his Hat friends represented to him that the Danish marriage was an obligation which could not honorably be evaded, besides being the wish of the nation; the Caps, having made nothing of their attempt to bargain with the queen, were now as anxious for the match as their adversaries.[216] From Gustav's own point of view matrimony, with all its drawbacks, offered him a chance to escape from a maternal tutelage which was becoming increasingly irksome.[217] This, no doubt, was one reason why Lovisa Ulrika opposed it with such uncommon obstinacy. She was now desperate; and in order to wreck the marriage was even ready to throw over the Hats, if they would not stand by her: indeed she was prepared to strike a bargain with anybody who came forward with reasonable terms.

But the forces arrayed against her were now too strong for further resistance to have any prospect of success. On 26 October Schack was ordered to make a formal approach to the chancery-president; on 29 October he did so;[218] on 6 December two members of the Senate who waited on the crown prince with a request that he agree to the marriage received from him an answer which, though couched in terms of decent filial submissiveness, was immediately followed by a private intimation that he desired the match.[219] By Christmas the affair was to all intents and purposes decided, and Bernstorff had attained his objective. On 13 February 1766 the chancery-president was directed to make a formal request to Schack for the hand of Princess Sofia Magdalena.[220]

The closing phases of these tedious negotiations were not without aspects of a more general interest. In the first place, it is clear that it was upon Goodricke's good offices with the Caps that Schack ended by placing his chief reliance. It was Goodricke whom he consulted on questions of timing and procedure; it was Goodricke who appeared as the real friend of Denmark.[221] Bernstorff, of course, was not unduly surprised, and he transmitted through Schack warm expressions of appreciation and esteem.[222] As to Schack, if he was surprised he did not say so: his political world had been turned so completely upside down in recent months that it was best to forget that the man on whose good faith and friendship he now professed to rely was the same man whom he had blackguarded and blacklisted ten months earlier. Secondly, the marriage question afforded an illuminating insight into the change in Catherine's attitude to Swedish politics, and the hardening grip of Russia upon both Sweden and Denmark. Catherine may have begun by being neutral; but she was far from neutral at the end of 1765. She intended to use the marriage to provide an example of her vengeance and a demonstration of her power. At the end of October Osterman was ordered to manage the business in such a way as to make it unmistakably clear that the defeat of the queen was a direct consequence of her opposition to Russia; that Bernstorff's success was a result of not "fawning upon France," but of trusting to the empress; and that the Cap party, with their concern for the national interest, and their principle of peace and friendship with all neighbors, was the "sole instrument" for the discharge of Sweden's obligations to Denmark.[223] Schack had indeed been able to put off Osterman's demands for closer collaboration in *riksdag* affairs by pleading that until the great question was settled he was not free to devote his attention to anything else;[224] but now that it was out of the way he would no longer be able to resist such pressures. The empress had no need henceforward to keep half-measures, either with the Court, the Caps, or her Danish ally: it was appropriately symbolic that when Stockholm celebrated Sofia Magdalena's entry upon half a lifetime of misery, the lavish illuminations of Osterman eclipsed those of any other foreign minister.[225] Money told, and Catherine did not lack for it. And having it, she was prepared to spend it: "in such cases," she wrote proudly, "we are not mean."[226] "Such cases" she was probably prepared to interpret as including Goodricke's long-pending treaty. But if so, she would certainly expect England to produce some sort of equivalent for her services.

CHAPTER VI

The Rockinghams and Goodricke's Treaty, 1765–1766

(i)

The attack on the Hat Senators was just gathering impetus, the party struggle was just moving to a climax, when on 12 July the duke of Grafton succeeded Lord Sandwich as Secretary of State for the Northern Department. After nearly two months of political uncertainty the Rockingham administration had at last been installed in office; and though the king, the nation, and Lord Rockingham himself had all alike been disappointed of the hope of the leadership of Pitt, it was now their business to present as Pittish an appearance as was possible in the great man's absence. The laths must be painted to look like iron. It was not an illusion which it was very easy to make convincing with the personnel at their disposal. Even Burke never seems to have ventured to credit Lord Rockingham with any ideas on foreign policy; and as to the two Secretaries of State—General Conway in the Southern Department, the duke of Grafton in the Northern—the one (as Lord Lyttelton remarked) was a very young man, and the other was new to the business.[1] It was expected, however, that they would be able to count on Pitt for advice, if not for active collaboration;[2] but if Pitt was really behind the curtain, there is little sign that he acted as *souffleur*. All in all, one can sympathize with Grafton's reactions to office, who early in July confessed to Lord Gower that "like a Girl that is going to be married, he felt himself much pleased with the general idea, but much frightened as the Hour drew nigh."[3]

The statesmen of Europe do not appear to have shared either his apprehension or his pleasure. They were interested, they were curious; but no one seems to have expected dramatic developments. It was true, no doubt, that there was a general feeling that British policy might now assume a slightly less negative appearance. In the course of the abortive negotiations in May, Pitt had growled ominously that "a foreign system of affairs . . . had been greatly neglected," and had given it to be understood that he intended to repair that omission,[4] but although he had been ready enough to will the end, he had jibbed at willing the means. As to one feature of his intended policy, at all events, there could be no doubt in the minds of his successors. Pitt had been determined to heal the breach with Prussia, to wipe out the shameful memories of Bute and Bedford, and to coax Frederick, by diplomatic embraces as suffocating as the duke of Newcastle's habitual salutations, to resume that glorious partnership which had won the war and established Pitt's claim to immortality. More than that: England was to ally not only with Prussia but with Russia too. A "counter-system" to the Bourbons was to be created,[5] and England was once more to cast her weight into the scale of Europe. Pitt had made acceptance of these principles a sine qua non for his taking office, and upon his failure to obtain it had made that the ground for his refusal. In vain George III had urged the merits of the Old System, and the danger of "ramming Austria deeper with France"; in vain he had invoked those respectable authorities, his God and his conscience:[6] Pitt had been inexorable. But though he had thus excluded himself from power by his peremptory demand that the king pledge himself in advance to a program whose feasibility had never seriously been examined, and whose merits were at least a matter of opinion, a corner of his mantle now fell upon Grafton's slender shoulders. No doubt of it: the Rockinghams would feel themselves committed to an approach to Frederick. And though they hardly realized it as yet, they would also find themselves constrained to face the problem of Britain's attitude to Catherine II. Macartney's Commercial Treaty was already as good as made, and upon their reception of it much was likely to depend.

Almost the first measure of Grafton after taking office was to write to British diplomats abroad to assure them that the change of administration did not imply any change of policy: there might perhaps in future be a little more concern for His Majesty's dignity, but that was all.[7] No doubt this was designed to soothe the fears of any European monarch who might happen to be trembling at the prospect of a display of British vigor, but in fact it spoke more truly than Grafton perhaps realized. There would indeed be no great change of course, for the excellent reason that the international situation left Britain with very little room for maneuver. The much-abused Lord Sandwich soon appeared to his successors as more sensible than they had expected,[8] and it would not be long before Baron Gross, the Russian minister in London, would be writing that Grafton was Sandwich all over again. Still, there would be differences; and most conspicously in their relations with Prussia. After elaborate safeguards against giving either side an advantage over the other in point of punctilio, the Rockinghams' diplomatic offensive in Berlin achieved the normalizing of relations and the exchange of ministers between the two countries. Sir Andrew Mitchell was to return to Berlin, to Frederick's satisfaction; Count Maltzan was to go to London, to plague successive administrations much as his predecessor had done. His instructions strictly forbade him to do anything but observe and report: all British proposals were to be taken *ad referendum.*[9] The twenty-eighth of April 1766 was at last fixed as the day for the opening of this new era in Anglo-Prussian relations.[10] It was all tolerably satisfactory, as far as it went; but it was hardly the transformation which Pitt had intended.

If in the case of Prussia the policy of the Rockingham administration had been determined for them beforehand by the insistence of Pitt, in regard to Sweden their policy was at least their own, since this was a matter in which Pitt seems to have taken little or no interest. But its originality seems to have consisted mainly in an initial determination to mark a contrast with the attitudes of Lord Sandwich. Lord Sandwich had been suspicious, skeptical, and grudging: Grafton would therefore be responsive, openhanded, and forthcoming. Goodricke, with some imaginative understanding of the difficulties of men new to office, had tried to make things easy for them by sending home in good time a précis of the course of events in Sweden over the last year or so, no doubt with the intention of saving the new Secretary of State the trouble of reading through all the correspondence, and probably also of guiding his thinking on the right lines.[11] But this, it appeared, was lost labor. Before ever it reached the office, Grafton had decided upon his attitude. Within a fortnight of accepting the seals—and, as the event was to prove, without having really familiarized himself with the background—he had determined on his policy. On 26 July he wrote to Goodricke to inform him that "Those who have the honor to be now employed by His Majesty as His Ministers both approve the Plan you have hitherto acted upon, and wish to see it continued in the same spirit."[12]

This encouraging attitude was not contradicted by what followed. The urgent appeal for money which Goodricke sent off on 23 July arrived in London on 10 August, at a moment when Grafton happened to be out of town. It was therefore dealt with by his brother-Secretary Conway; and that notoriously vacillating minister, in a surprising access of decision, "being satisfied that a single hour should not be lost," on that same day obtained the king's consent to the immediate transmission of £2,000 to Stockholm.[13] He did indeed add, in that pallidly sententious strain which Goodricke was to come to know all too well, that "A just medium in our carriage, between too warm a Zeal on the one hand, and an entire Neglect of the Cause, on the other, will probably be the sure Way to engage the Russian Minister in a strong and spirited support of the Common Cause"; but this could be charitably ascribed to the ignorance or caution of a beginner. What mattered, from Goodricke's point of view, was that the money arrived "in the nick of time" to carry the *licentieringar.*[14] On the whole, he might have been forgiven for feeling that for him, at all events, the new ministry inaugurated a new era: Sandwich had not been wont to be so prompt, so understanding, and so openhanded. But in Sweden, as British statesmen were to learn, no victory was ever final; no bribe could bind for long; no call for money could safely be represented as being the last. If Grafton and Conway ever cherished that delusion, they were soon undeceived. The very letter in which Goodricke conveyed his thanks for their timely £2,000 contained a pressing request for more: perhaps as much as £5,000, if that were possible.[15] Dispatch after dispatch transmitted the grumbles of Osterman at British parsimony: it was not, Goodricke tactfully explained, that Panin "attributed the Backwardness . . . to any want of good Dispositions in England," but rather to "a certain Oeconomy in the late Ministry."[16]

Grafton took all this surprisingly well. Goodricke had asked for "a substantial sum," to be concealed from Osterman and held in reserve against a real emergency (so much for the *pari passu* principle); and on 10 September Grafton obliged him to the tune of £3,000, "as a peculiar mark of confidence."[17] Evidently the Rockinghams at this stage felt that money spent on Sweden was well bestowed: their first £2,000 had clinched the fate of the three Hat Senators; the next £3,000, they might fairly hope, would give them a Senate dominated by the friends of England.[18] The outcome seemed to justify the speculation; and on 25 October Grafton sent to Goodricke an acknowledgement of his achievements thus far which could scarcely have been handsomer:

> The first great End, and of the greatest consequence to Great Britain, appears indeed to be compleatly answered, at least for a time; you have prevented the Navy of Sweden falling into the power of France. This one Point

> alone His Majesty considers as a Compensation for what has been disbursed, especially as the King was informed, by the surest Intelligence, that our Rival Nation had formed a Plan of so dangerous a Nature.—I am commanded to say, that this Service to this Crown, has been brought about by your Activity, and will never fail to commend you to His Majesty's favour.[19]

If the duke of Grafton had known as much about navies as Lord Sandwich, he would certainly have modified the phrasing of this tribute. Three months later, after a more attentive perusal of Sandwich's dispatches, he would not have written it at all.

Goodricke had scarcely begun to bask in this unexpected sunshine before the summer weather broke under the impact of a disturbance moving in from Russia. Sir George Macartney, sent to St. Petersburg by Lord Sandwich at the beginning of the year to conclude the commercial treaty which for so long had eluded Lord Buckinghamshire, had overcome Russian dilatoriness, demolished Russian objections, and secured, by urgent and brilliant diplomacy, Russian agreement to terms very much more favorable than the British government had ever hoped to obtain. The treaty which embodied them he had signed and sent home for ratification; and by doing so had landed himself in serious trouble, and his government in prolonged embarrassment. For it contained one article (article 4) which the Rockingham administration, with good reason, felt themselves quite unable to accept; and for the next ten months there followed an intricate crisis, in which the British government tried to extract from Panin an explanatory declaration which should interpret the article in the sense desired in London.[20] This contretemps had immediate and unfortunate consequences for Goodricke. Grafton had duly approved the terms of the declaration which he had given to Ekeblad on 6 August; but Macartney's blunder seems to have made him unduly nervous lest something of the kind should happen again in regard to the Swedish treaty. The news of Macartney's signature reached Whitehall on 16 September; on 29 September, after agitated cabinet consultations and reference to the Russia merchants, Grafton disallowed the article, and severely censured Macartney for rashness and insubordination; on 4 October he followed this up by a dispatch to Goodricke forbidding him to sign any treaty without submitting it to London for approval.[21] It was an order as unexpected as it was embarrassing. The negotiation had always been a delicate question of timing. It must coincide with a favorable parliamentary conjuncture; and Goodricke was bringing it forward at this particular moment because in the judgment of the Cap leaders it was the right moment from their point of view.[22] He had assured them that he would be ready to sign at whatever moment they found appropriate. He believed he was authorized to do so; and there is no doubt that he was justified in that opinion. The terms of the treaty had been laid before the Board of Trade; its acceptance in those terms had been recommended by them; the Cabinet had sanctioned his signature in terms of the project he had sent home; and Sandwich had explicitly given him power to sign, provided he took care that the preamble should not seem to admit that former Anglo-Swedish treaties, concluded without time limit, had expired. The case stood on an entirely different footing from that of Macartney, who had been expressly forbidden to sign any treaty without submitting its text for approval. For two months Goodricke had detained the King's Messenger in Stockholm so that he should be available to take home the signed treaty for ratification; and though prolonged detention of Messengers was usually avoided if at all possible, since the staff of Messengers was small, the Secretary of State's office had raised no objection to this proceeding. As Goodricke saw it, the position was that if he succeeded in obtaining a treaty in accordance with his project, and with the modifications in the preamble which Sandwich had required, he was authorized to sign. If he signed on any other terms than these, he might expect his government to refuse to ratify. It did not seem to him that this in practice gave him so much latitude as to make the scrutiny of the duke of Grafton essential in the interests of the country.

Goodricke's dispatch to Grafton on 28 October, though phrased with all proper respect, was therefore a vigorous protest. And by way of reminding Grafton of what his project had actually contained, he sent him another copy of it. In reply, he received an answer so querulous as virtually to concede the main point; and it was in an evident attempt to provide some sort of justification for his action that Grafton inserted into his dispatch a quite new stipulation. Goodricke's original draft had contained an article (article 4) which stated that the present treaty was not to be deemed to prejudice other treaties and alliances anteriorly concluded, "n'y étant en rien contraire." Grafton now required that this clause be entirely omitted; or, if that were impossible to obtain, that the qualification be phrased "autant qu'ils ne sont pas contraires aux termes et stipulations du présent Traité et nommément à l'article 6e ci-dessous." The article 6 in question contained a very general and quite imprecise undertaking that each party would defend the other's lands, subjects, and free navigation, and would not suffer any prejudice to be done to them. If it should prove impossible to obtain the alteration in the wording which Grafton suggested, he was prepared, as a last resort, to accept the article as Goodricke had drafted it, "tho' I must not conceal from You that this last will not be considered as an adequate Compensation for what His Majesty has granted to recover a fallen Party in Sweden."[23]

It is very difficult to understand why Grafton should have attached so much importance to the omission, or the modification, of article 4. The only treaty with another country which had any relevance in this connection was Sweden's treaty with France of 1738, since twice renewed on virtually identical terms. But that treaty was a simple treaty of amity, differing in nature from that which Goodricke was charged to negotiate only in that it was lavishly gilded with subsidies. The only real obligation it imposed upon Sweden was the obligation not to conclude any treaty or alliance with another power without first notifying France of the intention. There was no clause in it repugnant to Goodricke's draft. The amendment to the wording which Grafton put forward seems to suggest that he assumed that the obligations to England which Sweden would assume under the new treaty—and in particular those in article 6—might conflict with the treaty of 1738. But, first, there was nothing in the treaty of 1738 which precluded Swedish aid to England in the event of England's being attacked; and secondly, the defensive commitment in article 6 really had no practical force. It contained none of the precise specifications as to the number and nature of troops or ships to be made available by the one power to the other, or as to the responsibility for their payment—particulars which were indispensable in any effective defensive alliance. It was precisely because these details were lacking that article 5 of Goodricke's draft provided for the conclusion of a defensive alliance as soon as possible after the signing of the treaty. It might indeed be a question, if or when such a defensive alliance were concluded, how far it was reconcilable with Sweden's obligations to France; but that was not a question which was raised by Goodricke's draft. In short, it is difficult to resist the conclusion that Grafton's intervention proceeded, not from an appreciation of possible complications which Sandwich had failed to notice, but rather from an untimely determination to assert his authority as Secretary of State. How unsure his grasp of affairs really was appeared most ominously from the language in which he pressed these changes upon Goodricke:

> it would be too strong a reflexion [wrote Grafton] on the weight and character of our new ally, if I was to suppose that in the space of three

weeks, the time that you are expecting an answer, you should find their inclinations changed in regard to Great Britain.

Either this was a mere debating point, or it was a sentence which revealed a disturbing incomprehension of the peculiar circumstances within which Goodricke had to work. The Caps' "inclinations" were certainly not likely to change in three weeks, or for that matter in three months; but their prospects of carrying an English treaty without too much difficulty—and that meant, without Goodricke's having to make unacceptable calls on the Secret Service Fund—might vary almost from week to week, as members of the Diet drifted back home, or as Osterman's finances happened to be ample or exiguous, or as Breteuil received fresh supplies from Paris. Grafton's insensitiveness to such considerations of timing was sufficiently illustrated by the dilatory pace at which he handled the affair: between the departure of the Messenger with Goodricke's remonstrance and his arrival in Stockholm with Grafton's approval of the project there elapsed not three weeks, but six, for he had delayed sending an answer for a fortnight.

Nevertheless, despite the petulant tone of Grafton's dispatch of 16 November, it did transmit the final £2,000 of the £13,000 which had been contemplated under the plan of 31 August 1764: nervous irritability had not as yet produced any real change of policy. But thereafter it is clear that Grafton became progressively less well-disposed to Goodricke's activities. Financial support for the campaign in Stockholm came to be considered, not on the merits of Goodricke's arguments, but as a means of influencing Panin's attitude towards Macartney's treaty. If Russia should prove complaisant about Macartney's article 4, there would be more money for Goodricke; if not, the purse strings of the Secret Service Fund would be drawn tighter. Goodricke was ordered to regulate his relations with Osterman according to the nature of the reports which would reach him from Macartney.[24] By the late autumn of 1765 the lively interest in Sweden which Grafton had displayed in the first weeks of his tenure of office had obviously evaporated: no longer did he seem to attach much weight to the destruction of the French system as an end in itself; no longer did he record his satisfaction at the defeat of France's attempt to secure reinforcements from the Swedish fleet. It seems likely that somebody in the office had drawn his attention for the first time to Sandwich's opinion of the feebleness of the Swedish navy, and the superiority of the Danish. And this, perhaps, was one reason why, as his interest in Sweden cooled, his thoughts began to turn to Denmark.

Sandwich had regarded Denmark with contempt; a country whose system was "trifling," and whose only link with England was dynastic.[25] But now Denmark was Russia's ally; and it might be time to take fresh bearings. A closer approach to Denmark might one day give Britain some prospect of assistance from the Danish navy; and (more important) might in the immediate future serve to mollify Russian intransigence on the commercial treaty. Moved, it seems, by some such reasoning as this, Grafton drifted, without any clearly defined objective or coherent thought for the implications, into a limited diplomatic initiative in Copenhagen.

Towards the end of November Walter Titley, the British minister to Denmark, was startled to receive from the office a dispatch dealing with matters of policy, and enjoining positive action. Such a thing had not happened to him for some years. It is true that he was ordered to do no more than to use every effort to strengthen the connection between Denmark and Russia; but he was reminded that an English princess would soon be queen of Denmark (Fredrik V's health was breaking) and he was informed that France considered Denmark as good as lost.[26] Long experience had convinced Titley of the unwisdom of being too busy (he complained on one occasion of one of his diplomatic colleagues that he was "always negotiating"),[27] but the shock of receiving instructions of any but the most formal and trivial nature shook him out of his ordinary comfortable habits, and produced an initiative which those instructions had certainly not enjoined. On 27 November he approached Bernstorff with an inquiry whether Fredrik V had any engagements which would prevent him from contracting an English alliance, if a proposition for such an alliance were made to him. If not, he had orders "peut-être [*sic*!] de Lui offrir une alliance à des Conditions qu'Elle trouveroit avantageuses." To this remarkably phrased (albeit nonministerial) communication Bernstorff replied that Denmark had no such engagements, but had for many years followed a policy designed to keep her from being involved in the wars of other powers; and from that policy he would be reluctant to depart, though he would, of course, take the king's pleasure on the matter. The sequel to this curious overture was almost as odd as the overture itself. Nothing happened. At his next ordinary conference Bernstorff came armed with an appropriate ministerial reply; but to his astonishment no Titley was there to receive it: faithful to the habit of years, he had taken himself off to his country house, forty miles from Copenhagen. By the middle of December Bernstorff had still neither heard nor seen any more of him, and was beginning to speculate about what might lie behind this very unaccountable behavior. Granted that Titley's approach had been no more than tentative; granted (as Bernstorff charitably remarked) that everybody negotiated in his own way; still, he could not help wondering whether Titley had taken umbrage, or whether he had received counter-orders.[28]

The answer, of course, was neither the one nor the other: it was probably only that after this unwonted burst of energy Titley had felt the need for a period of recuperation. Nevertheless, the story got about that there had been an offer of alliance to Denmark: Macartney in St. Petersburg reported that Bernstorff had taken Titley's initiative very well, and had hinted that Denmark might be willing to accede to an Anglo-Russian alliance;[29] von der Asseburg, the Danish minister to Russia, informed Bernstorff that Panin was pleased that Titley's offer had been favorably received.[30] Titley himself, to do him justice, did nothing to feed such fantasies, but correctly informed his chief that Bernstorff was unlikely to enter into any particular engagements, at least until the business of *Mageskiftet* was brought to a conclusion.[31] But long before his report reached London Grafton had of his own accord edged a step nearer to Denmark, and consequently a step away from Sweden. In mid-November a dispatch reached the office from Macartney, with the news that Panin had informed him that he had persuaded Catherine to give Sweden a subsidy of 120,000 rubles a year, and that he hoped that England would make an alliance with Denmark on a similar basis. It is very difficult to believe that this report was correct. On this matter Panin's attitude had been quite consistent, and would remain so: Russia would make her financial effort in Sweden by way of bribes and pensions; it was for England to come forward with a subsidy, if a subsidy should be needed. If such a suggestion as Macartney described was indeed made—if it was not a case of simple misunderstanding—one can only suppose that it was thrown out in order to discover whether England's notorious objection to subsidy treaties applied as strongly to Denmark as to Sweden. It is true that there had been previous information, obtained through intercepted French dispatches, that Russia was ready to pay a subsidy in return for Sweden's abandonment of the French alliance,[32] and perhaps this made Grafton more ready to take Macartney's report at its face value. But Goodricke, to whom Macartney had also communicated Panin's news of a Russian subsidy, was skeptical, as well he might be; and he pointed out to Grafton that even if

Russia were prepared to pay such a subsidy the Cap leaders would certainly be unwilling to accept it.[33] If their negotiations for an English treaty should lead to France's stopping her payment of arrears, it would be to England that they would look for assistance, rather than to Russia. And he did his best to convince Grafton that in the event of the British government's being brought to the point of waiving its objections to all subsidies in peacetime, Sweden, rather than Denmark, would be the more eligible recipient.

But Grafton gave these arguments a distinctly cool reception. No doubt (he conceded) it was natural that Goodricke should urge the prior claims of his own country, if there were to be any question of paying subsidies to anybody; no doubt the Swedes would be glad of an English alliance,

> as every Nation would choose to engage preferably with England, whose good faith in the observance of treaties has ever been so distinguish'd. But you must consider on the other hand, that if any View can tempt His Majesty to depart from the System which has been followed of late years, I mean that of granting no subsidy, it can only be in order to engage in alliance with such a foreign Power, whose fleet joined to ours may still maintain the superiority against all the endeavors of the united forces of the House of Bourbon. Your proposal will also, at the same time, be considered, tho' I think there can be no doubt which of the two is the most desirable Ally of Great Britain.[34]

It was not just the most encouraging of messages for a minister who had for the past six months been led to believe that the main object of his endeavors must be the securing of an Anglo-Swedish alliance.

Whether encouraging or not, it was dubiously honest. There is nothing to suggest that Grafton had any intention of seriously considering the payment of a subsidy either to the one country or to the other. It is even doubtful whether he was sincere in professing his readiness for a Danish alliance, without subsidies. His real feelings were revealed in a dispatch to Macartney on 24 December—six days before he received Titley's frank account of Bernstorff's reception of his initiative. In that dispatch he made it quite clear that any suggestion of an Anglo-Danish alliance was being made solely in the hope of persuading Panin to give way on the disputed point in the Anglo-Russian commercial treaty. Macartney was instructed to keep any professions of Britain's willingness to ally with Denmark as general as possible: that is, they were to be such as could be repudiated without undue embarrassment.[35] In fact, he had no intention of committing himself firmly to Denmark at this juncture. It is easy to see why this should have been so. Incomparably the most important business with which he was concerned was the Russian commercial treaty: important not only to British trade and Britain's marine, but important also as a preliminary hurdle to be surmounted before entering upon negotiations for the much-desired Russian alliance. Compared with this, treaties with Denmark or with Sweden were of wholly subordinate interest, except insofar as they might smooth the way to agreement on Macartney's intractable article 4. He did not realize that it was a delusion to imagine that any British gesture, or even any British concession, was going to alter Panin's stand on the commercial treaty: if Grafton had pledged himself to pay subsidies simultaneously in Stockholm and in Copenhagen, it would have made no difference. Grafton (or, more probably, someone in his office) could in the end claim the credit for breaking the deadlock over article 4;[36] but it was done by direct negotiation in St. Petersburg, and not by bribing Russia to sacrifice her principles and her interests in return for illusory promises of cooperation in Scandinavia. Moreover, if the guiding principle for British policy in the North was now to be the propitiation of Catherine, it might have been thought an essential prerequisite for the success of such a policy that it should be based on a correct understanding of what the objectives of Russia in this region really were. Those objectives, and the methods to attain them, had been outlined clearly enough in Panin's plan, as transmitted to Sandwich; and though Sandwich had found them in some respects objectionable, at least he had taken the trouble to understand them. Not so Grafton. With almost inconceivable carelessness or muddle-headedness he contrived to misconceive them so fundamentally that it is difficult to believe that he had ever read Sandwich's dispatches to Goodricke and Macartney. Panin's plan (as Sandwich had complained) had left England to take care of the Exterior in Sweden, while Russia attended to the Interior, and had made it quite plain that Russia could offer Sweden nothing but bribes, and that England must therefore come forward with a subsidy. It had proposed, no doubt, that Denmark should take Sweden's place as the active power in the North; but this was to be a consequence of, not an alternative to, the securing of Sweden for the anti-Bourbon system. Yet by some ineluctable mental process Grafton convinced himself that Panin's plan had contemplated *Russia's* assuming responsibility for the control of Sweden's foreign relations; and that Panin had intended the securing of Denmark by means of an English alliance.[37] How he reconciled this latter belief with the signature, only a few months earlier, of the Russo-Danish alliance, it is profitless to inquire. From these misconceptions he drew the inference that Goodricke's treaty, if ever it were made, would be an act of magnanimity on England's part, the discharge of a function which it was really Russia's business to perform; and that any help from Osterman in securing that treaty was no more than England had a right to expect, and by no means constituted a claim on English gratitude.[38] In view of this startling mental confusion it was no wonder if, after his initial insistence that Goodricke send home his treaty for approval before signing it (which at least suggested that he considered it to be a matter of some consequence), Grafton came to regard the whole affair with something close to indifference.

However, he was not the only careless reader. For the strained relations which now disturbed his dealings with Goodricke, the envoy no less than the minister must bear his share of blame. On 3 December the Messenger arrived in Stockholm with Grafton's sanction for the drawing of the final £2,000 to carry the treaty, bearing with him a dispatch which to a more wary eye might have suggested that the Secretary of State needed careful handling.[39] But Goodricke, absorbed in Swedish politics, preoccupied with the prospects for his treaty, understandably anxious for the success of his first important negotiation, allowed his enthusiasm to get the better of his discretion. With conspicuous want of tact he proceeded—only seven days after the arrival of the £2,000—to ask for still more money, and to ask for it in terms which were as ill-judged as the request itself. Panin (he wrote) did not doubt that Grafton would give him further supplies if he asked for them; the Russians had certainly been exceptionally openhanded, and would have to face a further expenditure of £12,000 to finish the Diet, but their assistance would be absolutely necessary for carrying the treaty; Breteuil in a similar situation would not have hesitated to draw for £5,000-£6,000 against orders. Goodricke's dispatch proved altogether too much for Grafton's temper. The suggestion that further supplies be sent to Stockholm was rejected with indignation: England had got little enough for the money spent already; and the treaty was so unexceptionable that "any hesitation upon it will very little encourage the King's servants to advise the support of a system which would then bear so unpromising an appearance." And if, as Goodricke implied, the carrying of the treaty was dependent upon Osterman's aid, he might inform that minister that if the negotiation did not succeed, Grafton would draw the appropriate inferences, and regulate his Swedish policy accordingly.[40]

This dispatch really marked the end of the period when Goodricke could count on Grafton's support for his efforts in Stockholm; but any remaining chance that he could recover the favorable consideration with which he had been treated in the early days of the Rockingham administration was destroyed by his failure to realize the strength of Grafton's objections to the payment of any subsidy in peacetime. He allowed himself to believe that Grafton's dispatch of 6 December, in which he weighed the relative advantages of a Swedish or a Danish alliance, was really an indication that he was prepared to consider the payment of a subsidy either to the one or to the other, and that the only question was which of the two to choose.[41] This was to misconceive the situation entirely; and more attentive reading of Grafton's dispatch might have made that clear to him. But on the very day on which that dispatch arrived in Stockholm, Goodricke sent an eager reply in which he reported that the Cap leaders had indicated that they proposed to make a formal request for a subsidy, expressed his own support for such a proposal, and once more argued the case for a subsidy to Sweden rather than to Denmark.[42] Would it not be worthwhile, he pleaded, "to lay out a little money to secure this back door?" At the beginning of the New Year the Caps duly presented their memorandum; and this document Goodricke forwarded to London, with his blessing.[43]

This was altogether too much for Grafton's patience. After a fortnight's silent indignation his anger boiled over in a vehement outburst. From the beginning Goodricke had assured his government that no subsidy would be required to wrest Sweden from the control of France; he had been no less positive that he could carry his treaty without one; the Caps, for their part, must be presumed to have taken into their calculations the possibility that they might lose the French arrears if they embarked on a negotiation with England, and were therefore not entitled to start demands for a subsidy now. The Swedish navy was so inconsiderable, the state of Swedish politics so fluctuating, that it was impossible to foresee any circumstances in which any British government would accede to such a proposal. But if because of the exigencies of the local situation in Sweden it was essential to offer the Caps some countervailing advantage to compensate for the probable loss of French gold,

> It seems on every Account to be the Moment to make Proof of the real intentions of Monsr Panin, and whether he is sincere in that System which he has communicated to Sir George Macartney, and thro' Monsr Osterman to you. [Osterman, therefore, was to be told bluntly of] the Impossibility there will ever be, of forming that system and fulfilling that Plan, if Russia does not at this time, give the Friends of the Party, Assurances that from the Czarina may be expected a Treaty of Subsidy which may make amends for that which they are likely to lose.

Even if Panin, against all expectation, should swallow this cool suggestion, and acquiesce in this highly idiosyncratic interpretation of his famous plan, he need look for no assured quid pro quo from Grafton: Goodricke was directed to be careful "not to engage yourself so as to answer for any Part His Majesty will take in forming the general Plan." Money for bribery, indeed, might perhaps be found; a few pensions in influential quarters were not inconceivable; but that was all.[44] Sandwich had been suspicious of the plan in its original form; Grafton, it appeared, was even more suspicious of it after he had turned it on its head.

It was perhaps fortunate that this broadside did not arrive in Stockholm until the business of the treaty was concluded. To some of it Goodricke never seems to have bothered to reply: perhaps he shrank from the task of correcting Grafton's notions of Panin's plan. To other points in it no defense was really possible; for it was true that Goodricke had misled both Sandwich and Grafton on the matter of the Caps' need for subsidies. The best he could do was to explain that though the Cap leaders continued to be opposed in principle to all foreign subsidies, they had been forced to give way to the clamor of "the Nation as a whole"[45] —a development which it ought not to have been out of his power to foresee, and of which it was his duty to warn his government. Probably he had for some time become convinced that a subsidy would be necessary, though he had refrained from upsetting his government by saying so: in mid-November he had written privately to Macartney that he would like a subsidy for Sweden if he could get it.[46] He had a better case in his answer to Grafton's complaints of the heavy drain on the Secret Service Fund, and the apparent uselessness to England of such expenditure. He reminded Grafton that whereas the original plan of 31 August 1764 had budgeted for a Diet lasting six months, it had already lasted more than twice as long; and though six months was perhaps a sanguine estimate even at the time it was made, a more realistic assessment might have frightened off Sandwich altogether. Moreover, that estimate had been arrived at after consultation with Sinclair,[47] and was based on the assumption that Court and Caps would be in alliance. The defection of the Court, and the consequent need to battle to retain majorities in the four Estates, had thrown all financial calculations out of reckoning; and for this, certainly, neither Goodricke nor the Caps could be held responsible. The consequence had been that by January 1766 pensions given by Britain to Swedish politicians were being paid by Osterman out of his own pocket, with money borrowed on his private credit; and had it not been for the provision of supplies by Russia the friends of England would have deserted the Diet and gone home at the close of 1765. All this was incontrovertible; but Goodricke was on shakier ground when he protested that he had never given his government any other assurances than those contained in the representations made to him by the Cap leaders, and when he denied that he had ever "encouraged" Britain to intervene in Swedish affairs:[48] the whole tenor of his correspondence since his arrival in Stockholm had been in effect, if not always in form, a plea for an active and forward policy. Still, he was entitled to make the point that he could only fulfill the expectations he had held out if "our Friends" were kept together—that is, if they were assured of their regular aliment of foreign corruption; and he could truly urge that having been instructed to destroy the French system in Sweden, he (and Osterman) had in fact destroyed it: it was with justice that he wrote, "I believe, it will be hard to give an Instance of a more total Change of Administration and Measures than has been made here in the Compass of one Year." In that change he had had his share: a share which might well have been larger if he had been more abundantly supplied, and which might fairly be called considerable, once he had carried his treaty.

(ii)

Sweden's need of a subsidy may have done something to undermine Goodricke's credit with Grafton, but at least it had the countervailing advantage of facilitating the opening of negotiations in Stockholm. That this should have been so was the result of the miscalculations of French diplomacy. The agreement upon the payment of subsidy arrears which Breteuil had persuaded the Hat Senate to accept in November 1764 had been made at a moment when it was still possible to hope that the Hats might continue in office during the forthcoming Diet. The victory of the Caps at the election, the attack on the Hat Senate—in which the main article of accusation was precisely their conclusion of the French subsidy agreement—obviously put that agreement in jeopardy. Yet the financial stringency in Sweden was such that it was far from certain that the Caps, however anglophile their sentiments, would bring themselves to repudiate it. It was accepted without serious argument that subsidies, however repugnant to Cap principles, were in practice indispensable, at least for the present. They would not run the risk of taking a subsidy from Russia, even if Catherine had been prepared to give one. They had received ample warning of the unlikelihood of extracting one from England. Whatever their attitude to France, therefore, they might well find themselves constrained to allow the agreement of November 1764 to stand. Provided French statesmen kept their tempers, played their cards adroitly, and did not offer such provocation that the Caps' resentment got the better of their prudence, there was a fair chance that Sweden might remain as firmly in financial bonds to France as in the time of the Hat ascendancy. Breteuil may probably have appreciated this. Praslin, it is clear, did not.

At the beginning of 1765 the then chancery-president, Ekeblad, who already foresaw a Diet dominated by his political enemies, had impressed upon his minister in Paris the need for France to take special care to be punctual in paying the quarterly installments of 375,000 livres, in order not to give a handle to his adversaries.[49] And for the first two quarters of 1765 the installments were in fact paid more or less on time. But there remained an outstanding claim of Sweden for 3 million livres, alleged to be due to her in respect of the year 1763; and on this Praslin was (perhaps willfully) obtuse. He contended that the arrears for 1763 were included in the sum of 12 million which had been agreed as the amount of France's indebtedness; and Breteuil had a difficult job trying to persuade Ekeblad that his attitude arose from mental confusion, and not from ill will.[50] By the end of July, however, this matter had been sorted out, and satisfactory assurances about payment of the 3 million had been duly given. But the episode made a bad impression, even on the Hat Senate (still in office) and a still worse one on the Cap Secret Committee. Moreover, payments of the installments due for the second half of the year were delayed, no doubt as a protest against the obviously anti-French trend of Cap foreign policy; and matters were not helped by the revelation, obtained through British intercepts of French dispatches, that Breteuil had first advised Praslin to delay any payments which fell due till after the end of the Diet, and later had urged him to offer to pay the outstanding installments for 1765 in 1773, with the comment that the Senate would probably agree to any date provided it were precise, and that France could always find a pretext later for repudiating the obligation.[51] But already before this last revelation was known to Sweden the Secret Committee had lost patience. When the installment due on 1 October failed to materialize, it directed the chancery-president to demand a categorical answer from Breteuil as to whether the outstanding 750,000 livres for 1765 were to be paid in time or not, with the rider that they would regard an evasive reply as tantamount to a refusal.[52] When Löwenheim put the question to Breteuil on 2 November his answer was so unsatisfactory that the Senate (typically enough) declined to take responsibility for the next move, and referred the matter to the Secret Committee.[53]

Relations with France, already sufficiently strained by this dispute, were now still further embittered by a provocative *démarche* by Praslin. In a conversation with Friesendorff, the Swedish chargé d'affaires in Paris, he referred to reports that members of the staff of the Chancery seemed in danger of being called to account for their share in the subsidy agreement of 1764.[54] It was true that the staff of the Chancery were almost all Hats, and that they had been behind the decision of the Hat Senate to accept France's proposals for a settlement; and some Caps certainly wished to extend party vengeance from the one body to the other. But Praslin's language, as Friesendorff reported it, implied a threat to suspend payments of arrears altogether if any of the Chancery staff were dismissed. This was so palpable an interference in the domestic arrangements of another country that it is no wonder that it caused deep anger in Stockholm, and that Breteuil made every effort to persuade the Swedish government that Friesendorff had misunderstood what he had heard. It proved in fact to be a slightly less crude threat than he had given them to understand. What Praslin had said, it appeared, was that though France did not pretend to meddle in the internal affairs of Sweden, he was entitled to take cognizance of matters concerning the subsidy agreement, and that Louis XV

> ne verroit qu'avec une douleur égale à sa surprise, qu'un arrangement auquel elle s'est portée par une suite de sa constante amitié pour la Suède, et qui a été authentiquement accepté, devint le sujet et le motif d'une recherche contre les membres de la Chancellerie. Que *dans ce cas*, et si la Suède avoit quelque regret de la conclusion de cette affaire, S. Mjté la regarderoit comme non avenue et les choses resteraient a l'égard des subsides, dans l'état où elles étoient avant la conclusion de l'arrangement des Douze Millions.[55]

This was perhaps a little better, but it was bad enough. The Secret Committee promptly drew up a rasping reply, which the Senate subsequently approved, formally protesting against what they considered to be virtually an attempt to tack to the subsidy agreement a new condition which appeared to infringe Adolf Fredrik's sovereign rights.

As Grafton was to remark, it was reasonable to suppose that the Cap leaders must from the beginning have realized that if they negotiated a treaty of alliance with England they might run the risk of

France's canceling the payment of arrears; but it seems likely that they had for long continued to hope that if they made their treaty innocuous enough, in the first instance, they might contrive to escape this consequence. But France's attitude to subsidy payments had been so unsatisfactory, ever since they came into office, that by the autumn of 1765 not much of that hope can have remained. Praslin's attempted blackmail in the matter of the Chancery staff must have extinguished it entirely. No point now in trying to avoid too open a provocation of France; no point either in delaying an application for a subsidy from England. The hope of obtaining it, and (as they believed) the need to obtain it, gave to their negotiations for the treaty an impetus which had hitherto been wanting.

Even with the initial advantage provided by France's mistakes, the negotiations proved to be not without their difficulties. One of these was inherent in the peculiar arrangements of the Swedish constitution. The Senate, before whom in the first place Goodricke's proposals for a treaty were laid, was not an executive body of the type of a British cabinet. Its members had no seat in any of the Estates, and were consequently in no position to advocate their policies to the members, and so secure the backing of the Diet. Indeed, those policies were only to a very limited extent their own; for in between sessions of the Diet they were tightly bound by the instructions which the previous Diet had bequeathed to them; and if the Diet were sitting they were no more than its agents and functionaries, directly responsible to it for their actions, concerned only to comply with the directives which were sent to them from time to time by their principals, timorous of taking any step which had not the Estates' express authorization. The Senate, in short, was not a ministry in the English sense.

This situation made the conduct of diplomacy a business of more than ordinary complexity; since any negotiation involved at least three bodies—the Senate, the Chancery College, and the Secret Committee of the Diet, to whom (in regard to foreign affairs) the Estates had delegated their sovereign authority; and the views of these three bodies might not coincide. This was in fact the situation at the time when Goodricke began his negotiation. The Secret Committee, now completely dominated by Caps, was on the whole dedicated to the overthrow of the French system and its replacement by an English. The Chancery, on the other hand, was still a citadel of Hat influence. For more than a generation the Hats had systematically filled vacancies in the ranks of its staff by members of their own party; and since it was a principle of the Swedish constitution that office was a property of which no man ought to be deprived unless misconduct could be brought home to him, there was no means of effecting a change of personnel in a hurry. The staff of the foreign office might thus be politically at loggerheads with its official chiefs. The existing Chancery staff had as it were been born into the French alliance; and in that alliance they hoped to live and die. As far as lay in their power—by dragging their feet, by the utterance of alarming warnings, by raising procedural or other difficulties—they would certainly do their best to sabotage a connection with England. Lastly, there was the Senate itself: less irresponsible (because likely to be called to account) than the members of the Secret Committee, and perhaps better informed than they; more alive to the possible consequences of a breach with France; and on this issue by no means at one among themselves. Certainly the Senate was now firmly in Cap hands. But there remained a handful of survivors from the Hat era, upon whom the Caps had as yet failed to pin charges which could be made a plausible ground for *licentiering*. These men would divide the Senate if they saw a chance of doing so, and upon a division they could now rely on the two votes of the king. Indeed, it might even be a question (as we shall see in a moment) whether they could not also count on the collaboration, overt or covert, of the chancery-president and his deputy. In short, the Senate stood in a middle position between the Secret Committee and the Chancery; and the very fact that it was not unanimous reinforced the painful caution—not to say fluttering timidity—with which it was at this period accustomed to act when the Diet was in session and the Secret Committee was breathing down its neck.

This tentative and deferential attitude was evident throughout the whole course of this negotiation. In some ways, it worked to Goodricke's advantage. He took care, for instance, to remind one of the Senators (though it is unlikely that he needed the reminder) that clause 7 of the Constitution of 1720 forbade the Senate to conduct any negotiation for a treaty without reference to the Estates if the Diet was sitting;[56] he "found means" to forestall untimely references to the Chancery.[57] A friend of England in the Senate was able to block the introduction of embarrassing new matter into the negotiations by pointing out that they could not venture to discuss topics not specifically mentioned in the Secret Committee's instructions.[58] It might have been expected also that he would have been helped by the Secret Committee's instruction to the Senate, which enjoined all possible speed;[59] but unfortunately the Senate found difficulty in reconciling obedience to this order with their obligation not to take any step without the Committee's prior authorization. Could they risk drawing up even a draft instruction for the commissioners who were to conduct the negotiation? Dared they authorize the commissioners to meet Goodricke? Ought they to send Goodricke's draft to the Chancery College for its comments? Might they venture to instruct the commissioners to draw a counterproject without submitting it to the Chancery, as was usual in such cases? These were questions which produced agonized, circular debates extending over several days, in the course of which they read and reread the Secret Committee's instructions, in the hope of eliciting from them the correct answer to such difficult problems.[60] But except in one case—when they took their courage in both hands and authorized the commissioners to draw the counterproject themselves[61] —the upshot was invariably a decision to evade responsibility, and to refer the question at issue to the Secret Committee even if this line of procedure meant delaying action for a day or two.[62] The experiences of 1761 and 1765 strongly suggested that it was safer to shift the responsiblity to the shoulders of the Secret Committee, and do nothing, rather than take any action for which they could not show incontrovertible authority. It was not, perhaps, a very convenient or expeditious way of conducting business; but it was the Swedish way.

Most of the decisions of which the Senate made such heavy weather had no more than a domestic significance; but there was one which had real implications for foreign policy, and that one confronted them on the very threshold of negotiations. It was simply the question whether Breteuil ought to be informed of Goodricke's overture. The first thing the Senate had done with that overture had been to pass it to the Chancery College for comment; and the Chancery, strongly francophile in feeling, made the point in its answer that France was entitled to know what was going on, since the Franco-Swedish alliance of 1738 (still in force) had stipulated that each country should give advance notice to the other before concluding any treaty or alliance. The gist of the Chancery's answer had been given to the Senate by Löwenhielm on 13 December, when it was debated at some length.[63] It happened that the next day was the ordinary day for the chancery-president's weekly conference with foreign ministers, and Löwenhielm asked his colleagues whether he was to say anything to Breteuil or not. He added that for his part he was in favor of deferring any communication, and indeed, of postponing the conference altogether on a plea of ill health. The Senate, with a sigh of relief, agreed upon this painless expedient; but the question still remained as to what, if anything, was eventually to be said to Breteuil. On 16 December they returned to this awkward problem; and again, in characteristic fashion, they dodged it; this time by voting to refer the matter to the Secret Committee.[64] The Secret Committee in turn remitted the question to its subcommittee, the Lesser Secret Deputation. Here the ground for its reception had been prudently prepared by Goodricke. The relevant provision of the treaty of 1738 had in fact never been consistently complied with on either side, and least of all by France; and Goodricke had diligently collected, and transmitted to the Deputation, a list of instances of France's neglect to observe it.[65] This had its effect; and the Secret Committee duly instructed the chancery-president to say nothing to Breteuil unless confronted with a direct question, and in that case to return an evasive answer. Goodricke reported the outcome with satisfaction: it represented, he thought, a defeat for the Chancery and the francophiles.[66]

In the event, the prospect which had caused so much pother never materialized; for though early in January Breteuil did indeed mention Goodricke's overture to Löwenhielm, he did not condescend to ask for information, and Löwenhielm (by his own account) did not vouchsafe him any.[67] Which was scarcely surprising; for in fact he had privately told Breteuil all about it a month earlier. When on 13 and 16 December the Senate was floundering over whether to inform Breteuil, when Löwenhielm himself was recommending that any communication should be postponed, the secret was already in Breteuil's possession, and Löwenhielm was the channel through which it had reached him.[68] Goodricke seems to have been very well informed about the course of discussions in the Senate; he certainly regarded the question of communication with Breteuil as a touchstone by which to measure men's attitude to England; and it is clear that he suspected that neither the chancery-president nor his deputy was playing straight with him. Just before Christmas he tackled them about their behavior on this question. There was an apparently frank explanation; and Goodricke, for the time being, allowed himself to be persuaded that his suspicions were groundless: Friesendorff, after all, had made the sensible point that it was stupid to make a mystery of a negotiation too innocent to be exceptionable, and probably well known to France already.[69] But it was not long before his suspicions of Löwenhielm revived. The chancery-president clashed sharply with some of the more extreme anglophiles on the Senate on the question whether they should press ahead with the negotiations without waiting for the next meeting of the Secret Committee, and Goodricke interpreted his advocacy of delay as a sign of covert hostility.[70] He may possibly have been right: at all events, it is certain that Löwenhielm in December and January was in much closer touch with Breteuil than Goodricke realized.

The true state of the case became known to him only after the treaty had been signed. On 11 February Grafton forwarded to him the substance of an intercepted dispatch from Breteuil which revealed the full extent of the chancery-president's duplicity. Löwenhielm, by Breteuil's account, had promised exact information about the course of the negotiations, and had already had confidential intercourse with him.[71] He reported further that since Löwenhielm's suspicious conduct had already shaken his credit with the Caps, he had offered him the support of the Hats if he would join them. In reply to this offer Löwenhielm had condemned Cap policy and professed his willingness to change sides, but had pointed out that it was too dangerous to make the change at present. However, he had promised to do his best to sabotage the English treaty; and Breteuil, by way of testing his sincerity, had suggested that he should embarrass the negotiations by drawing up a list of the losses suffered by Swedish shipping at the hands of the English privateers during the recent war, and should demand indemnity for them as a proof of English goodwill. This he had promised to do. And in fact he had done it, as Goodricke was well aware. The suggestion had indeed been most eagerly pressed in the Senate by Rudenschöld—a remnant of the Hat régime whom Goodricke and Osterman had already marked down for attack—but it had originated in Löwenhielm, though subsequently he had left Rudenschöld to make the running, and himself had recommended that it should not be made a part of the treaty.[72]

Thus there was no room for doubt that throughout the negotiation the chancery-president had been playing a double game. The only question was whether it was Goodricke or Breteuil whom he had been trying to dupe. Goodricke was inclined, in spite of everything, to take an optimistic view.[73] Granting that Löwenhielm was a thoroughly shifty character, understandably concerned to secure his line of retreat in case of accident; still, in this particular instance he was disposed to believe that it was Breteuil, rather than himself, who had been "amused." Osterman thought so too: no doubt it was the most comfortable thing to think, in view of the fact that for some months Russia had been paying the chancery-president a substantial pension.[74] At all events, they agreed that they must make the best of the situation: a handsome present on the exchange of ratifications would probably anchor him firmly to the good cause. Their assessment may well have been correct; but there were probably other explanations for Löwenhielm's behavior than considerations of self-interest. He saw, more clearly than some of his more fanatical Cap colleagues on the Senate, that the treaty involved a real risk of a total breach with France, and the ending of French subsidies; he well understood how difficult it would be to replace them, and already was speculating on the possibility of raising a loan in England; and no doubt he hoped, by a pretense of treachery, and by secret promises to Breteuil, to blunt the edge of French resentment. That he should seriously have contemplated defection to the Hats at this juncture is exceedingly unlikely.

Breteuil, it is clear, did not place his whole reliance on the chancery-president. Within the means at his disposal, he did what he could to impede the progress of the negotiations. Though (as he explained to Praslin) he could not hope to match the "argent prodigieux" which he mistakenly believed to have been distributed on the other side, he did his best with promises: Goodricke believed that he had offered 300,000 daler to some of the Clergy and Burghers.[75] His efforts were seconded by Sinclair, and they seem to have had some effect;[76] at all events, by the middle of January Goodricke began to be seriously concerned. He had already been forced to reduce the amounts paid out in pensions; but now he felt he had no alternative but to buy votes: in the end the treaty was carried in the Secret Committee only after he had put 40,000 daler into the hands of one member, to be distributed at his discretion.[77] That this should have been necessary is at first sight surprising, in view of the fact that the Committee was almost wholly Cap. But it may be that some of them, especially among the Burghers, were not unaffected by the powerful arguments against the treaty put forward by Fersen.[78] Fersen contended that England had only one political interest, namely "commerce and a thirst for gain at the expense of every country she deals with"; that in pursuit of this object her policy was essentially aggressive, since as soon as the French fleet reached a certain stage of perfection, England attacked; that France was a satisfied and pacific nation, anxious for peaceful economic development, and disposed therefore to encourage other trading nations; while "the political system of England at present is founded on a system of war." An alliance with England would lead to the loss of French subsidies, to higher taxation, and probably to the ruin of Sweden's trade to the Mediterranean, which was dependent on France's goodwill; and in return England could offer only the simulacrum of protection, and the reality of reducing Sweden to the position of an English economic colony.

There was just sufficient substratum of truth in all this to make it plausible. It was certainly an object of British policy to secure some lowering of the high tariff walls and total prohibitions with which the Hats had sought to protect their carefully nurtured industrial developments. But the members of the Secret Committee need not really have been uneasy: these long-standing vested interests, these oblations to national pride, were not in any respect menaced by Goodricke's modest negotiations. It is true that Lord Sandwich had informed the Lords of Trade that "the Commerce of Great Britain makes the principal part" of the projected treaty;[79] but in actual fact the share of commerce in the affair was restricted to the clause which revived a most-favored-nation agreement between the two countries, and the positive effects of such an agreement, given the existing Sweden mercantilist system, were likely to be quite insignificant, despite Goodricke's smooth words as to the reciprocal benefits it might be expected to bring.[80] The case might indeed be altered if those tariffs were lowered, or if absolute prohibitions were replaced by duties, however stiff. But as to that he was hardly sanguine. He would have been ready to spend money to influence the Committee's members in favor of British manufactures, if he had seen much chance of a return upon his outlay: in the event, a sum of £40 seems to have been all he thought worth risking.[81] He had long admitted to himself, and tardily confessed to his masters,[82] that the exuberant hopes for British trade which he had expressed in the spring of 1765 were unlikely to be realized; and when Grafton, in the course of his angry letter of 3 January 1766, demanded to know what commercial benefits were to be looked for in return for the drains upon the Civil List, he answered soberly (if not quite truthfully) that "As to commerce, I always said it must be approached with caution; and we have made a beginning."[83] But Grafton's complaint was only a quite minor item in a general jeremiad, and in this matter, at least, he seems to have been a realist: it is significant that he made no objection to the completed treaty on the score of its want of solid commercial advantages. The Rockingham administration, despite its interest in mercantile matters, shrugged its shoulders and accepted the facts as they were.

Goodricke held his first meeting with the Swedish commissioners on 20 January.[84] The subsequent negotiations proved to be as easy and expeditious as might have been expected in regard to a proposal so "innocuous and complimentary."[85] In the draft which Goodricke put to the commissioners he tactfully omitted the special exemption of French trade to Wismar; in order (as he explained to Grafton) that the Swedes should be able to feel that they had secured a substantial point by inserting it. Which, indeed, they promptly did. The need to refer their counterproject to the Secret Committee for approval held up proceedings for a week or so; and when at last they presented it, it included (besides the point about Wismar) significant modifications in the wording of two of the articles as Goodricke had drawn them. The idea of inserting a clause designed to give protection against British privateers, which had been mooted in the Senate, was soon abandoned; though it was decided to make representations and remonstrances on this head when the treaty was signed. The only real difficulty, in fact, arose from Grafton's stipulation that Goodricke try to obtain the omission of that clause in his original draft which had laid down that nothing in the present treaty was to operate to the prejudice of existing treaties and alliances, provided that they were not repugnant to it. It was this alteration which led Goodricke to fear for a moment that the treaty might be defeated in the Secret Committee; it was in order to carry it through that body that he was forced to expend 40,000 daler in bribes.[86] And it was essentially as a quid pro quo for Swedish acceptance of the change that he at last agreed to the altered wording of the two other articles in the Swedish counterproject.

Once this obstacle was surmounted there was no further hitch. On 4 February Goodricke accepted the Swedish draft; at noon on the following day he put his signature to the treaty. Immediately after the agreement had been reached, but before the treaty was signed, Löwenhielm presented a memorial in which he asked for indemnity for losses inflicted by British privateers during the war, and proposed that for the future the two powers should agree not to permit their privateers to molest each other's shipping; to which Goodricke replied that his government would take care that those who had suffered injury received justice, and that in the meantime he would transmit the memorial to his court.[87]

So, after months of waiting, the treaty was signed at last. In announcing the event to Nolcken, the chancery-president was careful to point out, as evidence of Swedish goodwill, that the commissioners had completed their task in only two sittings.[88] He was entitled to make the point, for there was indeed a real desire on both sides to reach agreement quickly; but it must be confessed that the treaty was of such a nature that only an unusually captious or hostile commissioner could have hit on a plausible pretext to delay the proceedings much longer. It was, indeed, no more than a simple treaty of amity.[89] Article 1 was devoted to a declaration of friendship. Article 2 ensured, "now and in the future," most-favored-nation treatment for the commerce of each country, with an exception for the special rights enjoyed by France in Wismar. Article 3 declared that the treaty had no point against any other power, "and least of all against the friends and allies of the High Contracting Parties"; article 4 declared that the parties "se concerteront entre Elles, lorsque le temps et les conjonctures le permettront, sur des engagements ultérieurs, rélatifs à Leurs intérêts respectifs"; and article 5 pledged them in the meantime "comme de fidèles Amis et Alliés, de se prêter reciproquement tous les bons offices que les circonstances pourroient exiger pour la sûreté de Leurs Royaumes . . . en Europe."

It may be conceded that this was not a document likely to disturb the repose of the statesmen of Europe, or to inaugurate a new era in international affairs. The parties bound themselves to behave as allies; yet this was certainly not a defensive alliance in the ordinary acceptance of the word. Whether it might prove the basis for one in the future would no doubt depend on the "times and conjunctures" mentioned in article 4. Nevertheless, such as it was, the treaty conformed closely to the specifications which Sandwich had laid down; and it omitted the clause which Grafton had desired to be omitted. Goodricke was entitled to feel some satisfaction; and entitled also to expect a suitable acknowledgement of his achievement from the Secretary of State. What he certainly neither expected nor deserved was the ungracious reception which Grafton accorded to it.

Grafton received the news of the treaty with a contemptuous indifference which he did not trouble to conceal from the representatives of foreign courts.[90] If Nolcken's report can be believed, he was even malicious enough to hint to him that the only reason for the treaty was Goodricke's ambition to have the honor of making one. To Goodricke himself he wrote: "if this Treaty is all that Monsr Osterman brags his Court has done for the benefit of Great Britain, I am of opinion that it will easily be repaid."[91] He had already expressed the characteristic view that "An Alliance with Great Britain . . . carries too much Honor with it to admit of any publick and avowed Opposition";[92] and that view did not predispose him to any sympathy for Goodricke's difficulties in getting the treaty accepted by the Secret Committee, much less to an acknowledgement that it was his own insistence on the omission of one article that had constrained his envoy to accept the amendments in the Swedish counterproject. On the contrary, Goodricke was sharply rebuked for signing a treaty differing from the tenor of his instructions. "It is impossible but that the Alterations made in the 5th Article must strike you, as greatly wanting the Force which the correspondent Article in the Project approved by His Majesty, carryed with it." However, he intimated, with an epistolary shrug of his shoulders, that he was prepared to ratify, "especially since there can arise no Harm from any Part, whatever real efficacy and Importance the whole may want."[93]

Goodricke's response to these censures was a vigorous and cogent defense of his conduct.[94] The differences between the final treaty and Goodricke's original project reduced themselves to two points. Goodricke's article 4, which had provided for the conclusion of a defensive alliance at some future date, had become much more indefinite: further negotiations were now to depend on "le temps et les conjonctures"; and the original commitment to reciprocal "defence" became in article 5 an undertaking simply to use "good offices" on each other's behalf.[95] As Goodricke pointed out, the new version of article 5 was a logical consequence of the change in article 4: it was obviously sensible not to enter into a commitment to defend Sweden until the content of the proposed defensive alliance had been precisely defined:

> my Reasoning was, that, if the King should resolve to embark further in these Affairs, and enter into the Grand Alliance proposed, this Treaty as it stands would be a sufficient Basis to build, what we please, upon; and if His Majesty should not chuse to adopt the System, then it seemed to me that the more general the Terms of our new Connection with this Crown were, the better, because England's express stipulation of Defence is of much more consequence to Sweden, than Sweden's can be to England . . . .[96]

This was plain common sense; but common sense in itself is no justification for a minister who violates his instructions. It was not his business to reason away disobedience to his orders: Grafton had had this kind of trouble before, with Macartney. But in fact the alterations which Goodricke accepted did not conflict with his orders: they conformed to them. They were strictly in line with the directives which Sandwich had given him before he left office, and nothing in Grafton's instructions thereafter had given any hint that the objectives of British policy had changed in the interim. Sandwich had expressly said that the alliance must be such that "at all events His Majesty may not find himself encumbered by a useless ally": his policy had been to keep British commitments to Sweden general rather than precise. If the defensive commitment in the original version of article 5 had any real force, the change in wording was a change which brought it into line with Sandwich's intentions. If, on the other hand, that commitment was little more than amiable verbiage (as Sandwich presumably believed) then the change had no significance, and it was absurd of Grafton to take exception to it. Goodricke commented privately to Macartney:

> Our Ministers look upon the Treaty I have made here as the most indifferent Thing in the World, and tell me it is of no Importance at all, however they have ratify'd it, and if they would have furnished me with a little more Money I could have extended the Engagements contained in it to whatever they pleased, the terms in it being such as are capable of any interpretation that the two Courts shall think fit to give them which is just the Part England should desire, at least till she is determined whether she will have a sistem or not.[97]

As if Grafton's ungracious reception of his treaty were not enough, there followed a miserable epilogue which Goodricke probably felt as more mortifying than all the rest. It was the custom that the ratification of treaties should be accompanied by the exchange of presents to the principal negotiators on either side. On the Swedish side the recipients were inevitably numerous: the chancery-president, the six commissioners, the staff of the Chancery College. Goodricke was under no illusion as to the attitude of his government to expenses of this sort, and had contrived to block a proposal to increase the number of Swedish commissioners by two; for which important service he had been duly commended by Grafton.[98] Nevertheless, he was understandably anxious that the scale of presents should not fall below that of France and Denmark on recent similar occasions, and he was particularly concerned that the present to Löwenhielm should be sufficiently substantial to secure the goodwill of that greedy and susceptible statesman. But all Grafton was prepared to allow him was £4,000; and of course it was not enough, even after Goodricke had contrived to stretch it by some juggling of the exchanges: by French standards, indeed, it was as much as £1,000 short. In order to pay Löwenhielm an amount equal to that paid by France to his predecessor, Goodricke had no alternative but to contribute 35,000 daler (or nearly £500) out of his own pocket.[99] And there was worse to follow. He had given a present of 35,000 daler to the Chancery College, for distribution among its staff, and in return he received 17,500 daler, which in all innocence he had handed over to his secretary, Charles Tullman: the historian may think he well deserved it, as some return for his exemplary calligraphy. This rash act provoked a *mercuriale* from General Conway (who by this time had succeeded Grafton as Northern Secretary), in which he insisted that the money was the perquisite of the staff of the Secretary's office in London.[100] And when Goodricke, once again dipping into his own pocket (for Tullman had long since spent it) arranged for the money to be sent to Conway, that minister was anything but appeased. In a letter to his old patron Sir Joseph Yorke Goodricke unburdened himself of his troubles:

> You will see that he [Conway] is angry with me, I really do not know for what: He writes me a letter the 3rd of June where he gives me a peremptory order to remit immediately the money given for my secretary, without mentioning to whom I was to remit it, and now he is angry that I have ordered Mr Larpent to pay it to himself saying it implys that he claimed the money as a personal right, and then enters into a long discussion to prove that *Chancellerie* signifies the secretary's office, which it certainly does: His and mine too. I have taken all possible pains to please the D. of G, and Mr Conway, but I find young men are more difficult to please and know much more than the old ones: I had better luck with Lord Sandwich, and yet he passes in the world for a man of parts, which I cannot help believing, at least till I have to do with a more capable one.[101]

No doubt this was the kind of misunderstanding which was liable to occur when a minister negotiating his first treaty had to deal with Secretaries of State who were novices in office. But the whole history of the negotiation suggests that the friction between London and Stockholm arose mainly from the unfortunate circumstance that Grafton had no clear-cut or properly digested policy in regard to Sweden at all. Goodricke, on the other hand, had: it may have been somewhat blinkered, somewhat parochial, and no doubt Grafton might feel that it gave too little weight to those wider perspectives which a Secretary of State could not ignore. But even when so much is conceded, the impression remains that Goodricke knew his own mind, knew where he was going, and had a fair idea of how to reach his objective; while Grafton was equally hazy as to ends and means. To Goodricke, the course to be followed seemed perfectly clear. The overriding consideration for England was the securing of the alliance with Russia; and the best approach to such an alliance was by way of a preliminary treaty with Sweden, which could subsequently be expanded by Russia's adhesion. The ending of French influence in Stockholm was certainly a Russian no less than an English interest; but the best way to achieve it was by the creation of an English party and the conclusion of an English alliance: it was for that reason that Catherine had been willing to spend large sums in order to bolster up the Caps; it was for that reason that Osterman had given assistance in the late negotiations. An Anglo-Swedish alliance might, or might not, eventually bring with it advantages for English commerce; but this, though undoubtedly a consideration, was not the main one. The main consideration, as Goodricke saw it, was to use the defeat of France in Stockholm as a bridge to that Northern System which Panin desired, and which England (he was convinced) ought to embrace. For these advantages there was no doubt a price to be paid: a subsidy to Sweden. To Goodricke the price seemed extraordinarily moderate when set beside the political gains which would follow. The Swedish navy might be somewhat decayed, the Swedish army an irrelevance, but it was not these things which they would purchase with a subsidy: what they would purchase was an end to England's isolation, a continent stabilized, the Family Compact balanced. A subsidy to Sweden could thus be seen as an insurance premium against the risk of a resurgent and vengeful France. It was also, in the micropolitical context of Stockholm, the logical consequence of England's earlier expenditure, which England must accept if she were not prepared to lose the benefits of all that she had so far bestowed. And if this was a program which entailed the slaughtering of that political sacred cow "No Subsidies in Peacetime," so much the worse for the cow.

For Grafton, on the other hand, the sacred cow was one of the few certainties in a world of shifting doubts and weak volitions. From Sandwich he had inherited the doctrine that Goodricke had been sent to Sweden only to please Catherine; and it followed for him that British policy in Stockholm had been guided since Goodricke's arrival there only by the desire to oblige Russia. He conveniently forgot his earlier insistence on the importance of the Swedish navy; he showed at best a tepid and intermittent interest in the prospects for trade; he seems entirely to have lacked Sandwich's concern with laying the basis for a Northern System. Believing as he did that Panin's plan was essentially aimed at a Russo-Swedish alliance, he could not understand why so favorable an opportunity for concluding one should be neglected: obviously the Russians did not know their own business.[102] But this did not prevent him from contending that it was Russia's plain duty to spend money to carry Goodricke's treaty, and subsequently reimburse Sweden for the loss of French subsidies which that treaty would probably entail. Ever since Goodricke arrived in Stockholm Russia had been spending far more than England on the Swedish Interior: now, it appeared, she was spending more on the Exterior also. To Grafton this seemed entirely proper and right, and by no means to be regarded as canceling that debt of gratitude which Russia owed to England for Goodricke's being in Stockholm at all. Grafton did not see Goodricke's treaty as a useful step towards an alliance with Russia, or as the basis for a Northern System: he was far from clear in his own mind whether he wanted a Northern System at all, and an alliance must in any case wait for the resolution of the difficulty over Macartney's commercial treaty. He censured Goodricke because the treaty had no teeth in it; but in the same breath he insisted that Sweden's foreign policy was none of England's business. At one moment he was aggrieved because the treaty gave England so little; at the next, he was astonished that the Russians should not have made it themselves. But if a Swedish alliance were Russia's affair rather than England's, why concern himself whether the treaty meant much or little? And if the object of British policy were to oblige Catherine, he certainly went about it with remarkable clumsiness: his parsimony, his treatment of Goodricke, his sneers at Russian help in Stockholm, his denial of any British concern in Swedish affairs, provoked in St. Petersburg reactions of irritated contempt.[103] As Goodricke truly wrote, "this manner is not engaging."[104] And if he were not, after all, concerned to gain or retain Catherine's friendship, what remained to him in the way of a foreign policy?

Goodricke's reaction to this unhappy state of affairs was much to his credit. He took the snubs and the censures philosophically, and continued unperturbed on his way, obeying his orders, but not relinquishing his opinions. He showed also another more unexpected quality: a capacity for sympathetic understanding of the conditions which produced the ineptitudes of Whitehall, and a pleasant absence of rancor towards those who did not understand or appreciate. Macartney, who had to endure the same kind of treatment, responded to it very differently: he sulked, he was insolent or waspish, he struck epistolary attitudes of exaggerated despair or false humility. But Macartney was a vain and pushing young man, sore from a setback at the outset of his career; while Goodricke was tempered by years and hopes deferred, probably considered himself lucky to have secured a ministerial post, and was above all less temperamental, mellower, and more broken to taking life as it came. And so he could write to Macartney (as Macartney would certainly never have written to him) a letter which discussed their common disappointments with admirable temper:

> With regard to the recompense you or I shall have for our pains, I believe it must come from ourselves, That is in the consciousness of having succeeded in what was thought very hard to perform till it was done . . . as to their finding fault with me at home when I know I don't deserve it, this does not affect me at all; I always attribute it to their not understanding the affairs of the Country where I am employed, which may be very pos-

sible without the least derogation from their ability, since in a course of long experience I have never met with a man who understood perfectly the affairs of a Court where He never resided. It has been Count Osterman's happiness to be under the Direction of a man who had been minister here himself and I am sure if Mr Conway had been also envoy in Sweden, I should have had the same praise, if not the same recompense as Count Osterman.[105]

One may hope, without much confidence, that he was right. It is at all events certain that Grafton was almost alone in dismissing Goodricke's treaty as an event of no importance. Panin did not think so: on the contrary, Grafton's indifference seemed to him typical of England's neglect of her own and her friends' interests.[106] Bernstorff wrote to Count Bothmer, his minister in London: "On fait tort au Chev. Goodricke de faire une Plaisanterie du traité qu'il a conclu en Suède. C'est un très grand service qu'il a rendu à la Gr. Bretagne, et un coup sensible qu'il a porté au crédit et au Pouvoir de la France," adding that Goodricke was very highly esteemed in Denmark, and Bothmer would do his country a service if he could manage to get him sent to Copenhagen instead of Gunning.[107] Breteuil certainly did not take the treaty lightly: if he had, he would hardly have tried so hard to block the negotiations. All of them realized, as Hats and Caps also did, that the importance of the treaty lay not so much in what it contained or did not contain, as in its mere existence. For the Caps on the one hand, for French policy in Sweden on the other, it marked the beginning of a new era. Yet it could mean everything or nothing, according to the nature of the political edifice which should be raised upon it. As to that, and as to the difficulties that lay ahead, the Cap leaders were under no illusions. Goodricke saw the implicit consequences very clearly. The French arrears were now as good as lost: somehow they would have to be replaced. A complete breach with France was highly probable: it must be offset by an Anglo-Swedish defensive alliance. The Caps were facing growing domestic difficulties: economic problems, in particular, were already casting long shadows before. The constitutional reforms which had been Catherine's objective from the beginning must somehow be pushed through before weariness, faction, the quarrels of the Estates, and sheer financial exhaustion enforced the termination of the Diet. Hard parliamentary battles lay ahead before that goal could be attained. The carrying of Goodricke's treaty had been a good example of Anglo-Russian cooperation at the local level: without Osterman's financial support it might well have had a perilous passage. In confronting the problems which lay ahead, in pursuing the initial advantage which the treaty had secured, Panin was therefore entitled to expect that Goodricke would be instructed to reciprocate the services which Russia had rendered in Stockholm. Nothing would have pleased Goodricke better. But it was an expectation which was unlikely to be realized, so long as Grafton continued to hold the seals.

CHAPTER VII

The End of the Cap Diet, 1766

(i)

In the still waters of Whitehall Goodricke's treaty might make no more than a transient ripple; but in more sensitive quarters it produced reactions which belied its innocuous appearance. In vain Löwenhielm gave Breteuil reiterated assurances that there was nothing in it to cause offense to France; in vain he pointed out that it gave no hint of an English subsidy.[1] The French did not mistake its significance. They knew, well enough, that if it did not in itself establish an English system, it was designed to be the basis upon which an English system could be built: once the Diet was over, a Cap Senate, obedient to the instructions which the Secret Committee would leave behind them, would complete the work, and France's long ascendancy in Stockholm would be at an end. The final breach with France would almost certainly entail the loss of the subsidy arrears which France was paying under the arrangement of 1764; but before that moment came Rudbeck and his colleagues counted on persuading the English ministry to open its purse, and they were sanguine enough to hope that in the meantime the payment of installments from Paris would continue.

If the Cap leaders thought they could choose their own tempo for the relaxation of their links with France, and their own time for severing them, Praslin and Choiseul had other ideas. The mere news that negotiations with Goodricke had begun provoked Praslin to issue a warning that he would be justified in repudiating any liability for further payments, on the ground that Sweden was acting in violation of the terms of the alliance of 1738.[2] The first two installments due in 1766 were in fact ominously delayed. The Senate grew uneasy; and in April and May insisted that Löwenhielm (who had been dragging his feet in this matter) should press, both in Stockholm and in Paris, for a "positive and categorical" answer to the question whether France intended to pay, or not.[3]

They could hardly have chosen a worse moment for employing language of this sort. For on 11 April 1766 Choiseul succeeded Praslin at the ministry of Foreign Affairs, and he was the last man to suffer himself to be browbeaten by hectoring inquiries from states of the second order. At the close of 1765 he had submitted to Louis XV a famous memorandum, in which he had chalked out the lines which French foreign policy ought to follow.[4] The ultimate objective must be a reversal of the verdict of 1763, and the restoration of that balance of power which England's maritime and commercial supremacy had upset. French ambitions on Belgium and Holland were by no means to be renounced; but the maritime-colonial struggle must take precedence, and with this end in view Spain was a more important ally than Austria. France's moment for revenge would come with the revolt of the American colonies. That revolt he did not expect to live to see; but in any event there must be no war until France had had time to restore her navy—which meant in fact, no war before 1769. In order to concentrate on this program, there must be drastic cuts in the wasteful and ineffective system of subsidy payments to France's European allies.

Such a program boded ill for the traditional policy of backing the Hats and subsidizing Sweden. Nowhere, indeed, did Choiseul subject his country's political traditions to a more scarifying scrutiny than in regard to Scandinavia. It had been the constant aim of French policy in the North to create a Scandinavian bloc embracing both Sweden and Denmark. By 1766 that bloc had been shattered, and each half of it had passed out of France's control. Sweden was in the hands of France's enemies; Denmark had allied with Russia, and was mistakenly believed to be the client of England.[5] These reverses were only the last in a series of humiliations which had begun with the ignominious chaos of French diplomacy in Poland after 1763, and had been underlined by the Russo-Prussian alliance of 1764. Trenchant action, it seemed, was called for; trenchant action was in any case congenial to Choiseul's impatient and superficial temperament; and Denmark and Sweden were obvious candidates for its exercise.

The impact of Choiseul's new course fell first on Denmark. Within a week of his taking office, Ogier, who had ably upheld the cause of France at Copenhagen for the past thirteen years, had been recalled;[6] and on 15 April Choiseul renewed a correspondence with Bernstorff which had been interrupted since 1763—and renewed it, it seemed, expressly in order to give vent to his contempt for Denmark and his indifference to her reactions.[7] It was a letter finely calculated to wound Bernstorff's feelings; and never had that statesman appeared to more advantage than in the dignity and firmness of his reply to this insulting communication.[8] The instructions subsequently prepared for Blosset, who was to replace Ogier, said flatly that all that France had done for Denmark in the past was absurd: in the future, though outstanding arrears would indeed be paid, Denmark need expect no more French largesse.[9] Denmark was formally written off; French policy here would henceforth be purely passive, France's role be merely that of an indifferent observer. It may be conceded that in the circumstances this was a sensible and realistic conclusion; but its implementation could have been achieved without trampling on the feelings of an old friend or outraging the susceptibilities of a nation which had been faithful to France for twenty years.

However, the alienation of Denmark was an event which Choiseul could take in his stride: he was less concerned, apparently, than his colleagues in Whitehall about the usefulness of the Danish navy in the next war. But the loss of Sweden was not tamely to be borne. The old notion of a French Eastern System—directed, now, not against Hapsburg, but against Russia—was very much in Choiseul's thoughts. Poland, indeed, might be difficult to reestablish as an effective force, but French diplomacy at Constantinople was both active and successful, and the Turks might reasonably be expected to play France's game—as was indeed to happen, two years later. But something must clearly be done about the northern flank of the Eastern System; Stockholm must by hook or by crook be constrained back to the fold. As he surveyed, with a searching and unfriendly eye, the history of Franco-Swedish relations over the past decade Choiseul felt profoundly disillusioned. The whole conception of French policy in Sweden since 1756, he decided—the policy of pumping money into Sweden in order to keep the Hats in power—had been mistakenly conceived and demonstrably futile.[10] The Swedish constitution might indeed seem admirable to a philosophic observer, but it was not the sort of polity to provide France with a useful or reliable ally: "la Suède aristocratique, démocratique et platonique ne serait jamais une alliée utile." France's ally in the past had not, in reality, been Sweden, but rather the "Patriotes"—that is, the Hats—whenever they were in power. And now they were in power no longer. They might, indeed, recover a majority at the next Diet, with the aid of massive injections of French gold; but who could guarantee that they would retain it? What sums would not have to be expended to secure them a transient hold on government? The idea of wasting France's waning resources on a system of instability seemed manifest folly. He had no faith whatever in the prospect of getting the Hats to sponsor a sufficiently far-reaching alteration in the constitution by legal and parliamentary means: both Hats and Caps, as he shrewdly perceived, being equally concerned to maintain the existing political order. No: the only way forward lay through a violent coup d'état, which would leave the executive power—and especially the control of the armed forces and of foreign policy—in the hands of the king, would reduce the Senate to a purely advisory body appointed by the crown, and would strip the Diet of virtually all powers except the right to grant taxes. There was to be no more meddling in the party struggles within the Diet: Breteuil (he pointed out) had already had 1,400,000 livres for such purposes during the current Diet: he was not to spend one sou more. As to subisdies, or arrears of subsidies, there would be no more of them as long as the present system lasted.

Thus France, by a strange reversal of roles, was to commit herself to the kind of coup d'état which ten years before she had assisted the Hats to defeat. It is of course true that the idea of a reform of the constitution to increase the power of the crown was no new thing for French statesmen. Hitherto, however, French policy had contemplated constitutional reform by legal, parliamentary, action, and had relied upon the cooperation and goodwill of the Hat leaders to carry it through. Choiseul's new line represented the rejection of the Hats as instruments of efficient change; it represented a deliberate choice of violence. It was a plan which, for all its apparent logic, revealed the rashness of its author, and his insensitiveness to the obstacles in the way of its execution. It depended for its success upon the assumption that the amiable and timid Adolf Fredrik, anxious only for a quiet life, and devoted to his turning lathe, could somehow be transformed overnight into a man of ruthless resolution and a fit leader for a desperate enterprise; and that Lovisa Ulrika, as rash and impetuous as Choiseul himself (but far more indiscreet), could suddenly acquire qualities of judgment, temper, and steadiness which had hitherto been conspicuously absent from her character.

Nobody who knew the king and queen was likely to swallow such assumptions; and Breteuil knew them (or believed that he knew them) only too well. In Lovisa Ulrika he had not the slightest trust; and Adolf Fredrik he rightly considered as inconceivable in the leading role which Choiseul assigned him. Like d'Havrincour before him, he believed that if France was to operate effectively in Sweden, it must be in conjunction with Fersen, Scheffer, and the other Hat leaders. He therefore made no real effort to obey Choiseul's orders. He could afford to risk this disobedience; for in Sweden, as in some other countries, French policy did not speak with a single voice. What the Ministry of Foreign Affairs commanded was one thing; what Louis XV's secret diplomacy dictated might well be another. Breteuil, like his predecessor and immediate successors in Stockholm, was enrolled in the list of his sovereign's private diplomatic corps: he was a member of "The King's Secret"; and if it came to the pinch he would find means to obey the king's instructions, and evade the minister's. As it happened, on this question of the Swedish constitution the Secret pursued the traditional French policy which Choiseul was resolved to overturn.[11] Louis XV, Broglie, and Tercier were ready to concede that some afforcement of the royal authority was necessary, if Sweden were to be a serviceable ally; but they had no faith at this stage in a coup d'état as the remedy. Fidelity to the Hat party, the forcing of an Extraordinary Diet, a Hat victory at the elections for that Diet, and then reform by agreement with the victors and by regular legal means—this seemed, to the men of the Secret and not least to Breteuil, to be the only available policy for the moment. How it might be when Crown Prince Gustav succeeded his father was another matter.

In the meantime, Breteuil delivered successive cold douches to his ardent chief. Even Sinclair, it appeared, had no faith in the success of a coup at present.[12] And the Hat leaders on 17 August produced some "Reflexions des patriotes suèdois" in which (predictably) they urged that France should back their efforts to force an Extraordinary Diet soon after this one was over, and should provide the monetary support for the elections, in the hope that the Hat rank and file might later be persuaded to give a more or less grudging assent to some minor improvements in the constitution.[13] In the face of this discouragement Choiseul, though with strong initial resistance, was compelled to give way. On 28 September 1766 he informed Breteuil that the coup was off for the present, that the Swedes were for the time being to be left to stew in their own juice, and that Breteuil was to be recalled, leaving affairs ad interim in charge of the secretary of legation, the Abbé Duprat.[14] The Secret had been too strong for him, as on some other occasions; common sense had carried the day against hasty inspiration and unripe projects. French policy fell back into its old courses. And as yet Adolf Fredrik and Lovisa Ulrika had apparently not received even a hint of the role for which their new *régisseur* had cast them.

Though for the time being Choiseul was thus forced to concede defeat, he had at least the satisfaction of being able to relieve his feelings in the matter of the French arrears of subsidy. The Swedish demand for "a positive and categorical answer" produced a response which was at least as categorical as could well be imagined. On 6 June he delivered a fulminating *mercuriale* to Creutz; five days later Breteuil administered an even stiffer dose to Löwenhielm.[15] In the face of these peremptory refusals the Senate debated long and anxiously before finally deciding to try the effect of a reasoned remonstrance, though it coupled with it an intimation that if France rejected its arguments, Sweden would reserve full liberty of action.[16] On this issue it is difficult to deny that Sweden had the better of the argument; but Choiseul was in no mood to trouble himself about that. His reply to Creutz reached the Secret Committee on 4 September, and it was so offensive that the Committee seriously considered Creutz's recall. The verbal communication with which Breteuil accompanied it was still stronger:[17] whereas Choiseul had said that all France's engagements to Sweden were to be considered at an end, Breteuil improved this into "extinguished for ever"; and whereas Choiseul had made Louis XV protest his friendship for the king *and crown* of Sweden, in Breteuil's version that assurance was restricted to Adolf Fredrik personally. The final provocation came when it was learned that the payment of arrears, now canceled in regard to Sweden, had been renewed in the case of Denmark. The Senate and the Secret Committee received these communications with anger; and their reply, though kept within the limits of diplomatic good manners, was not a whit behindhand in acerbity.[18] Short of breaking off diplomatic relations altogether, the two countries had now virtually reached the stage of a total breach. It was no wonder that in November Lovisa Ulrika was in the dumps; or that that veteran friend of France, Tessin, should be heard lamenting the evilness of the times.[19]

Thus Goodricke's treaty had set in motion a chain of events which had ended in the apparent destruction of the French system in Sweden. The violence of Breteuil's language had delighted him:[20] French indiscretion, it seemed, had done his work for him. It depended now, as he clearly saw, upon his masters in Whitehall whether a solid English system could be erected upon the ground which Choiseul had thus cleared for them. But the return of Choiseul had also affected British policy in quite another way. Breteuil's caution or skepticism might deter him from giving his Hat friends any clue to the new policy of working for a coup d'état; but the plan for a revolution did not long remain a secret. The Hanoverian post office was soon in possession of it. On 28 June 1766 Conway was able to transmit to Goodricke an accurate account of Choiseul's intentions; and when that account reached him, on 12 July, Goodricke lost no time in communicating the information to Osterman, and also to Rudbeck.[21]

The effect was to add a quite new dimension to British policy in Sweden. Hitherto the constitutional issue had been of only marginal interest to British Secretaries of State. If they encouraged Goodricke to give assistance to Osterman in working for the kind of constitutional reform which Panin and Catherine desired, that was only because it offered a means of showing goodwill to Russia and strengthening their claim on Catherine's gratitude. But now the case was altered. The establishment of legal despotism had become official French policy, as a means to ensuring to France a reliable ally. It followed that the defeat of any such plan became not only a Russian but a British interest: an affair 'not only of the Interior (which was Russia's business) but of the Exterior also. It does not seem that British intelligence discovered that Choiseul was soon forced to put his plan into cold storage. For the first time, then, the Swedish constitution became a central issue in British policy in the North; and it would remain so until that day in 1772 when Gustav III's successful coup implemented Choiseul's plan and wrecked the position which Goodricke had labored so hard to build up. Conway, it is true, did not at once appreciate the significance of the change which had taken place: his initial reaction was to predict that the plan would run aground on Hat opposition, and that the whole affair would end with the recall of Breteuil. In the autumn of 1766 it seemed that he might be right. But he underestimated Choiseul's determination; and —like Choiseul himself—he did not foresee the effect of the increasing political activity of the crown prince. Osterman, too, did not at first judge the danger to be imminent.[22] Nevertheless, the news of Choiseul's change of course must have stiffened Panin's long-standing determination to strengthen the constitution by reforming it, and may well have done something to make the Cap leaders more willing to accept his proposals.

(ii)

Meanwhile the triumphant Cap majority in the Diet, intoxicated by its successes of 1765, heedless of the warnings of its more moderate members, pressed on with its program of stringent reform and political persecution. Carl Gustaf Tessin has a story to the effect that when some pert individual ventured to ask Lovisa Ulrika how it was that she seemed always to back the losing side, she crisply replied "c'est que le dominant fait toujours des sottises." If so, the course of events seemed to bear her out. As early as May 1765 Daniel Tilas, who had greeted the Cap victory as a liberation from Hat tyranny and a triumph for public opinion, had become alarmed at the spirit he saw prevailing among the victors.[23] As the sittings of the Diet continued for month after month party fanaticism seemed to increase with success, and the appetite for victims to show no signs of diminishing; with the result that by the summer of 1766 the Caps had become as odious to the country at large as ever the Hats had been. Their relentless attacks on the managers of the Bank, and on the Iron Office, alienated many; their ruthless cutting down of salaries, their unfeeling cancelation of pensions to deserving and indigent persons and old wornout civil servants appeared as a cruel measure which was not offset by the relatively trivial saving of 70,000 d.s.m. per annum which these economies effected.[24] Their progressive revaluation of the daler hit one section of the mercantile community; their sumptuary legislation against luxury imports, besides provoking derision, adversely affected another; and a rise in commodity prices was already being felt by the man in the street. The three lower Estates, where the Cap majority remained pretty solid until the end of the Diet, had no hesitation in expelling members who were troublesome, or whose religious orthodoxy was questionable, or whose utterances on public affairs were at variance with the party line: freedom of debate was not one of the palladia of the Swedish constitution. The arbitrary action of the Estate of Peasants, in thrice refusing to allow a certain Hoffman, duly elected for Västergötland, to take his seat, provoked a reaction which might well have made them pause: in May 1766, goaded to desperation by this treatment, Hoffman raised an insurrection among his constituents.[25]

The Västergötland rebellion, as it turned out, was an insignificant affair, involving only a handful of peasants, and it had indeed been suppressed before the news of it reached the capital; but in Stockholm it produced panic among the Caps, and great alarm among the foreign ministers who supported them. Who could tell what might not lie behind it? A Hat intrigue, perhaps; a royalist plot, more probably, with Sinclair as its likely organizer. The constitution might well be threatened, "Our Blessed Liberty" endangered. Osterman, in hasty consultation with Goodricke and Schack, had no difficulty in persuading them to agree that if the constitution seemed likely to be imperiled they would join with him in presenting a formal declaration that the friends of Sweden would not permit it to be overthrown;[26] and in due course their respective governments gave retrospective approval to this precautionary measure.[27] The event proved it to be ludicrously disproportionate to the emergency, and no declaration was in fact ever made; but the collaboration of the three ministers and the solidarity of their courts upon this issue was a portent of things to come, and a useful precedent for later and more serious occasions. And when, a few weeks later, the news of Choiseul's plan for a revolution reached Goodricke, it seemed to him and his two colleagues that there had certainly been more in Hoffman's revolt than had appeared at the time.[28]

The Cap majority in the Diet had thought so from the beginning; and their fear of a plot, reinforcing the obvious unpopularity of their government, hurried them into measures which forfeited the respect of moderate men and produced a major parliamentary crisis. Their reaction to the news from Västergötland was to propose the setting up of two extraordinary tribunals, one on the spot in Västergötland, the other in Stockholm, charged to investigate not only the local background to the rising but also its possible connection with discontented elements in the capital. Now the abuse of extraordinary tribunals, judging arbitrarily on party lines, and subject to no judicial review, had been one of the iniquities of the Hat régime which the Caps had denounced most vigorously when in opposition. They had stood before the country at the recent election as a party concerned to restore the rule of law, and their success had given satisfaction to those to whom the rule of law was precious. They had now, it appeared, thrown consistency, principles, and even decency overboard; partly in panic, but partly also (it could hardly be doubted) in the hope that artful cross-examination, supplemented by the judicious application of torture (for torture too was one of the ingredients of Swedish liberty) would drag to light something which might involve their political enemies and justify the use of still greater rigor.[29] The egregious Baron Cederhielm allowed his malicious tongue to run away with him in reflections upon the shabbiness of their conduct, and was subsequently voted out of the House of Nobility for his pains:[30] "The punishment of Deserters," wrote Goodricke severely, "is a necessary part of Good Discipline."[31] The Hats under Fersen's leadership, conveniently forgetful of their own record, put up a desperate resistance to the extraordinary tribunals. Fersen was indeed careful to make the point that there must be no mercy for rebellious peasants,[32] but he felt bound to fight a proposal which opened the way to inquisitorial investigations of unforeseeable extent. The Hat "operators" accordingly hastily recalled members who had drifted off home; the Caps followed their example; Osterman and Breteuil delved deep into their pockets to secure a majority.[33] The struggle soon took on the aspect of a confrontation between the three lower Estates and the Nobility; for the proposal for setting up the tribunals had passed Peasants, Burghers, and Clergy before the Nobility had had a chance to decide upon it, and the non-noble Estates demanded its immediate promulgation. The Nobility, including Rudbeck and other Cap leaders among them, were outraged at what seemed to them to be an attempt by a reckless democracy to reduce the first Estate to insignificance: here begins a struggle of Estates which was to continue and intensify until the revolution of 1772. The crisis was felt to be the gravest since the Diet assembled, and both sides were anxious for compromise. Fersen and Funck, Osterman and Breteuil, between them managed to negotiate a settlement which each party was prepared to accept:[34] the two tribunals were agreed to; but the scope of their investigation was limited to the actual circumstances of the revolt, and was not to be made the starting point for any general political witch-hunt. In the event, the result of the inquiry did not implicate anybody except Hoffman and his immediate associates: the attempt to pin something on to Sinclair got nowhere. Three persons were executed; thirty were sentenced to flogging and hard labor; but the only lasting result of the affair was to discredit the Caps still further in the eyes of the nation.

The threat to the constitution supposed to be implicit in Hoffman's revolt, the news of Choiseul's alarming change of course, gave added urgency to the question of constitutional reform. From Panin's point of view this was one of the main objectives which he had set before himself ever since 1763, and it was the most important task still remaining if Russia were to reap the full benefit of the Caps' tenure of power. Panin's scheme for reform, as it had been set out in his plan of November 1764, had had two main elements. The first was to secure a better constitutional balance by lessening the power of the Senate so that it would never again be in a position to embark on a war without the consent of king and Diet; and this he had proposed to effect by increasing the control of the Estates and by giving back to the crown some of the rights of which it had been stripped in 1756. The constitution should be restored, by the removal of later accretions, to its original form as it had existed in 1720. The second element was to stabilize the constitution for the future by repealing that clause which permitted the Estates to "interpret and improve" it, and which had thus placed the fundamental laws at the mercy of fluctuating party majorities.

To a considerable extent these ideas found a response in the minds of thoughtful men in each of the Swedish political parties. Rudbeck and the Cap leaders had shown that they took the problem seriously. In the summer of 1765 it had seemed not impossible that they might tackle it in the immediate future. But, as we have seen, Rudbeck's bargain with the queen broke down,[35] partly because Lovisa Ulrika refused to disband her "Third Party,"[36] partly because after the resignation of the two Senators the Cap zealots persisted in their attacks on other members of the former Hat administration. In these circumstances the party leaders had dropped the idea of constitutional reform, and under pressure from their back-benchers had addressed themselves to matters of more immediate advantage to their party.

Though the Caps thus seemed for the moment to have lost all interest in the question, for Panin it was still a major issue.[37] Whatever his resentment at the Court's political activities, he had come to believe that henceforward the consent of the king, no less than of the Senate and the Estates, must be a precondition for any major constitutional change, and he was still determined that the reforms which he considered necessary must be carried through before this Diet came to an end.[38] But he was not prepared to risk moving in the matter until he could be sure of a majority in all four Estates;[39] and that situation did not occur until June 1766, when for the first time for almost a year the Caps recovered control of the Estate of Nobility. Nevertheless, from the early months of 1766 Osterman began to lay his plans and take his measures. He consulted Schack; he consulted the Cap leaders. He did not consult Goodricke; and this for obvious reasons. On the constitutional issue England, in the spring of 1766, was still indifferent, and Grafton was not in the least likely to sanction expenditure on an object which did not particularly concern him. Bernstorff, on the other hand, was even more interested than Panin in preserving the constitution; and though he was a good deal less flexible in his approach to the problem, he was prepared to put his hand in his pocket if Panin should produce a plan which satisfied him. As it happened, he did not prove too easy to satisfy; indeed, it is scarcely too much to say that on three major issues Panin and Osterman were compelled to modify their proposals in the face of a Danish veto: the junior partner in the firm was for the moment dictating the terms. For Bernstorff had by now retracted his concessions of 1765: he was no longer prepared to go back to the constitution of 1720 *simpliciter*. And he was not prepared to agree to a proposal for the setting up of a Commission on Public Law, whose purpose would have been to redefine the fundamentals of the constitution.[40] In one other respect, moreover, the plan which Osterman now put forward differed from that which Panin had outlined in November 1764: instead of providing that all major constitutional changes should require the assent of two successive Diets, with a general election in between, he now proposed that alterations should depend upon the unanimous consent of all four Estates, the Senate, *and the king*:[41] it was a last attempt to salvage something of the original program of improving the balance of the constitution by increasing the crown's authority. But here he ran up against the objections both of Bernstorff and also of the more radical Caps; who pointed out that such a plan implied the participation of the head of the executive in the legislative process, whereas one of the original purposes of any reform had been precisely to avoid for the future that confusion of executive and legislative power which had given rise to abuses in the past.[42] Osterman was thus driven back on Panin's original plan for the approval of changes by two successive Diets. But on one issue, at least, Panin was firm. Since 1756 it had been the rule that any candidate for office who had been thrice included in the list of three names submitted to the king, and thrice passed over by him, should, if his name were put forward again, be the sole nominee, and must be accepted. This principle was now to be extended to nominations for the Senate: the king was to be deprived of his veto upon the choice of ministers. Translated into terms of practical politics, this meant that Panin was determined (as Goodricke was also) that when the next vacancy on the Senate should occur their favorite candidate, Joakim von Düben—thrice rejected by Adolf Fredrik in the past—would automatically be elected.

Early in August 1766 the Grand Deputation took the constitution once more into consideration, after an interval of a year since it had last applied itself to the question. The parliamentary situation was favorable; the Hats in the Estate of Nobility washed their hands of the whole affair, and reserved their position; by 8 September, when the proposals passed the Estate of Peasants, the *Ordinance Concerning the Execution of the Laws* had surmounted its last parliamentary hurdle; and on 12 November it duly became law.[43] Panin was delighted, and is said to have regarded it as the crown of his life's work; Osterman was warmly congratulated by his government;[44] and Goodricke, who seems to have felt no resentment at his exclusion from the Russo-Danish discussions, received the news with enthusiasm.[45] The last great objective of Russia at this Diet seemed to have been attained.

In retrospect, this euphoria seems distinctly excessive. The ordinance did indeed begin with a preamble reciting some of the ways in which existing arrangements were defective,[46] and so far, at least, it earned the approbation of reformers such as C. F. Scheffer;[47] but the diagnosis was wofully inadequate, and the prescription more inadequate still. The greater part of the ordinance was in fact concerned with the correction of purely administrative defects: with the selection process for civil servants, with the speeding up of justice, with the hopeless attempt to curb official verbosity, with the effort to prevent the Estates' wasting their own and the nation's time by listening to the complaints of those who considered that they had been unfairly passed over for promotion. With this last end in view it repealed the greater part of the *Memorandum on the Services* (1756), which had attempted to cure the evil by making seniority the only criterion. But Bernstorff, in opposition to Osterman, had insisted on retaining that section of the *Memorandum* which deprived the king of the nomination to the governorship of Stockholm, and to the three most important military commands: these positions were still to be filled by the Estates.[48] The ordinance also deprived the king of the right to appoint the chancellor of justice (an officer who was something between an attorney-general and an ombudsman): henceforward he was to be appointed afresh by each succeeding Diet.

Thus the ordinance had on the one hand made it possible for the Estates, by persistent nomination, four times repeated, to force into the Senate a man who might be abhorrent to the king; and on the other hand it had purported to abolish, by what might be called a "Parliament Act" procedure, the Estates' right to "interpret and improve" the constitution. These were not insignificant changes, certainly. But except for the last they by no means accorded with the objectives which Panin had set before himself in 1763 and 1764. One of those objectives, as we have seen, had been to achieve a better balance of forces within the constitution. To this laudable design the ordinance made virtually no contribution. Panin had wished to lessen the power of the Senate; he had even for a moment been willing to concede to the king the right to participate in a declaration of war. Of this no trace now remained. The position of the Senate remained in all essentials exactly as before: bound by the instructions of the Secret Committee when the Diet was not sitting; tremulously accountable to its principals when the Diet should meet again. The power of the Estates was certainly increased; but it was increased not at the expense of the Senate, but at the expense of the crown. Of the hopes held out to Adolf Fredrik in the summer of 1765 not a shred remained: no veto on unconstitutional proposals; no right to interfere in foreign policy; influence on appointments curtailed rather than increased; all dangerous notions of the contractual nature of the relationship between king and Estates abandoned. After the ordinance, as before, the king would be denied the right to appeal to his coronation oath, denied the right to have a view of his constitutional duties. The whole idea of balance had been simply thrown overboard: Panin and Osterman had ceased even to pay lip service to it. The explanation of the change is of course a matter of conjecture: it is to be found, perhaps, in Bernstorff's inflexible attitude; or perhaps in the impossibility of carrying the more intransigent friends of liberty among the Caps on the subcommittee; or perhaps again in the fact that the breach between Osterman and the Cap extremists, on the one hand, and Lovisa Ulrika and Sinclair on the other, was now so deep that any policy of balance had become politically impossible.

The other main object of Russian policy seemed, indeed, to have been fully attained: the "Parliament Act" clause might be presumed to stop proposals for change dictated by temporary crises or party political motives. But Panin appears to have been unaccountably blind to the underlying realities of Swedish politics; and this in two distinct ways. First, in a letter to M. I. Vorontsov he observed that when in future a proposal for altering the constitution was made "the nation is to have three years . . . to review it sufficiently and then to give their deputies to the next Diet *strict instructions* either to adopt it or reject it."[49] If Panin really imagined that the issue would be decided by the electorate (and the Estate of Nobility was in any case its own constituents), if he supposed that members would come to the Diet with an imperative mandate, if he believed that this quasi-referendum would necessarily bind those who were elected, he showed a surprising obliviousness to the outcome of one of the great constitutional debates of the forties: the debate on the responsibility of members to their constituents, and the right of those constituents to bind them by instructions. The result of that debate had been that the theory of the delegate and the mandate had been pronounced to be a pernicious heresy, and Christopher Springer was still expiating in England his presumptuous pretension to hold a different opinion. No Diet, no Senate, Hat or Cap, would henceforth risk its neck by admitting the possibility of those "strict instructions" to which Panin so naively pinned his faith. And in the second place, Panin forgot that the Estates were, after all, "invested with authority" (*maktägande*), in all but name sovereign; and a future Diet could as easily repeal the ordinance as the ordinance itself had repealed the *Memorandum on the Services*, or as an English parliament had substituted a Septennial for a Triennial Act.[50]

The plain truth seems to be that Panin and Bernstorff, and those Caps who shared their views on the constitution, in the autumn of 1766 missed their last real chance of saving the constitution by reforming it. The ordinance abated a few nuisances; but it did nothing to reconcile men to those features of the régime about which politicians on both sides had become apprehensive, and which the truest friends of liberty wished to see amended or removed. The constitution was now more, not less, rigid; and therefore more fragile. It was now worse, not better, balanced; and therefore more easily to be overturned. At the very moment when Choiseul's mind was turning to plans for an absolutist coup, Panin and Bernstorff made such a coup more credible by missing the chance to reestablish a balanced polity and a moderate constitutional monarchy, which would have been the best and perhaps the only defense against that "legal despotism" which the crown prince was soon to absorb from the exciting pages of Mercier de la Rivière.[51] Bernstorff, indeed, had always been curiously blind to this danger; but Panin's originally clear perception of it had in the last year or so become obscured. What had obscured it was the breach with Lovisa Ulrika which began with the emergence of her Third Party in July 1765, and became final as a result of her effort to cling to the spirit of the Composition, and save the Hat Senators from *licentiering*. In her negotiations with the Caps at that time she was probably entitled to feel that she had been duped. But whatever the rights or wrongs of the matter it is clear that in August-September 1765 a serious hope of reform by agreement was lost; and that it was lost just as a similar hope was to be lost four years later, on the jagged reefs of party strife. It is perhaps one of the heaviest charges against the Swedish constitution that it engendered, by some malign process, an endogenous poison which in the end corrupted the healthy blood in its veins.

(iii)

One consequence of the *Ordinance for the Execution of the Laws*—and it was a consequence to which Goodricke and Osterman attached great importance—was that it now became possible to secure a seat on the Senate for Joakim von Düben. At the beginning of the year they had still hoped to make a clean sweep of those Senators—Liewen, Hiärne, Rudenschöld—who had contrived to escape the purges of the preceding autumn; and Goodricke was especially anxious for the *licentiering* of Rudenschöld, whose attempts to sabotage his treaty he had neither forgotten nor forgiven.[52] There were, however, difficulties: Rudenschöld happened to be Löwenhielm's son-in-law; and in the early months of 1766 the money available to Osterman was insufficient for the large-scale operation of removing three Senators at once.[53] All that could be effected for the moment was their censure by the Secret Committee,[54] and this relatively mild proceeding encouraged Breteuil to predict that they might now consider themselves safe from further harassment.[55]

In this, however, he proved to be mistaken: on 13 May 1766 Burghers and Clergy voted for the *licentiering* of Rudenschöld (though by narrow majorities), and the Peasants voted to throw out all three.[56] Goodricke had been far from confident of success,[57] and was correspondingly delighted at the outcome: "we have removed," he wrote, "the most powerful enemy England had in that Body"; and the Hat majority in the House of Nobility, no less surprised than he, complained of a snap decision, "alledging that it has been done by surprize, and not by fair war."[58]

But the removal of Rudenschöld, however satisfactory, did not open the way for Düben. His name once again stood first on the list of candidates proposed; but once again, and for the third time running, Adolf Fredrik passed him over,[59] and they had to be content with Baron Fredrik Ribbing. Goodricke made the best of a bad job in his report;[60] but his determination to get von Düben on the Senate remained unshaken. The *Ordinance for the Execution of the Laws* at last provided him with the chance he was seeking. The only difficulty was that the numbers of the Senate were now full; but this was circumvented by voting that Senator Törnflycht's health was now so enfeebled that there was a good case for appointing an additional member. It was a transparent pretext; but it served. On 7 October von Düben's name was sent forward to the king, this time as the solitary nomination, in virtue of the new procedure laid down in the ordinance.[61] This too was a blatant political wangle, since the ordinance, though passed by the Estates, had not yet been promulgated, and did not yet have the force of law; but for such trifling proprieties the reformers of the constitution cared nothing at all. The king, however, cared a good deal; and his refusal to sign Düben's patent of appointment was broken only by the Caps's threat to prolong the Diet until he gave way.[62]

So yet another great object had been achieved. Düben was in the Senate; and the victory was clinched by the nomination to one of the Secretaryships of State—now vacant by Düben's elevation—of Baron Ehrencrona, whom Goodricke described as "my particular friend."[63] As to von Düben, if his imposition upon the king appeared to have been an easy victory, that appearance proved delusive. It was, on the contrary, a costly triumph; as the future would make plain. For it turned out to be the starting point of a hardening royalist resistance, the real beginning of the interference of the crown prince in politics, and the presage of events which two years later would topple the Caps from power.

For the moment, however, Goodricke and Osterman could exchange congratulations, convinced that they might now safely bring this unprecedentedly long Diet to a close.[64] Enough was enough: financially, indeed, it was already too much, and for this reason they had long been anxious to end it. Breteuil, for his part, was no less eager: in July and August he, like Osterman and Goodricke, announced that he proposed to cut off supplies.[65] Goodricke, who could never in the ordinary way hope to match their scale of expenditure, was as it happened in a rather less straitened situation than usual. In June, Mr. Secretary Conway, inspirited by Rudenschöld's removal, gave permission to draw for £4,000 on the express condition that the money was applied to turning out the two remaining Hat Senators; on 1 August, in response to Goodricke's plea, he gave him discretion to use the money as might best serve to bring the Diet to a proper conclusion.[66] Further than that he would not go. When in September Goodricke drew for £300 in an emergency, without authority, he was sharply rebuked; and when he repeated the offense a fortnight later the rebuke was even sharper.[67] Yet, on the whole, Whitehall might well have congratulated itself on achieving so much on such easy terms. The total expenditure to which Sandwich and Grafton had committed themselves, for a Diet estimated to last six months (and this one lasted for twenty-one) had been £13,000; the actual cost to the Civil List had in the end been no more than £17,000, to which was to be added £800 per annum by way of pensions to two Cap Senators.[68] Compared with the sums lavished by Catherine this was modest indeed, and Sandwich's anxiety about ensuring that Russia went *pari passu* in the matter of expense looks singularly misplaced. In August 1766 Panin, in an interview with Macartney,

> looked for some time very steadfastly at me, and then said, "When I tell you, that Denmark has given an hundred thousand roubles, when I tell you, that I have spent half a million on this cursed Dyet, can you seriously speak to me of the efforts of Great Britain?"[69]

It was not only for financial reasons that a speedy end to the Diet had become a matter of urgent concern. The Caps had assumed office burdened by the inexperience and irresponsibility of a generation in opposition; their policies had been stained by the desire for vengeance; and they had fallen victims to the corruption of power. No leader had emerged from their ranks of a stature to compensate these defects. What they needed was a Pitt or a Walpole; what they got was a chancery-president whose reputation resembled Shelburne's, and a *lantmarskalk* who had something of North's amiability without his financial skill or his parliamentary talents. In these circumstances, the pushing, the ambitious, the firebrands of the party successively thrust their way to the front, achieving an ascendancy which was usually short and never unchallenged. Such was Gyllensvan, much detested by honest Daniel Tilas until he found that there were worse men than Gyllensvan after all; such was von Essen, who alienated moderates by his conceit and his opinionated attitudes.[70] In the House of Nobles Nordencrantz quarrelled bitterly with Gyllensvan, whom he charged with trying to protect Finlay & Jennings;[71] in the Clergy, Serenius led a faction of his own, and before the Diet ended was fighting furiously with other members of his party. As time went on the activists of 1765 were themselves outflanked by others of still more reckless temper: by September 1766 a new faction called "the little Mice"[72] was campaigning against Gyllensvan and his associates, and actually succeeded in carrying a vote to reverse a judgment in the ordinary courts—an abuse of parliamentary power which had been rare even in the darkest days of Hat rule. In the closing days of the Diet the Estate of Clergy echoed to invective by Serenius which blasted Gyllensvan, von Essen, Ridderstolpe, and Frietzcky in one comprehensive commination.[73]

Rudbeck's admitted honesty was no specific against party chaos of this order. Violent resolutions by extremist clubs—such as that which demanded that Kierman be sent to the scaffold[74]—could be passed without fear of the application of disciplinary action; members of the Secret Committee could arouse the *lantmarskalk's* impotent rage by proposing to confiscate the property of C. F. Scheffer and Ekeblad, and so violate his promise that they should be immune from further molestation in return for their voluntary resignation of office.[75] Rudbeck's own club in March 1766 pledged its members to work for Löwenhielm's removal from the office of chancery-president, and his *licentiering* from the Senate.[76] The Cap majority in the Peasants defied the united appeals of Rudbeck, von Essen, and Gyllensvan, and voted (as it turned out, in vain) to abolish the Iron Office.[77] The three lower Estates would have renewed the threat to purge the Chancery of French sympathizers, if Goodricke had not peremptorily declined to provide the £1,600 which they estimated as necessary for the success of that operation.[78] As to Löwenhielm, his contribution to party unity was that at least all Caps were agreed in distrusting him.[79]

In short, by the autumn of 1766 the Caps were in a condition of near anarchy, in which the attitude of the three lower Estates could hardly be predicted, nor their conduct controlled: in the last week of the Diet's sitting Clergy and Nobility were at one another's throats about the privileges of their respective orders.[80] It was because the party was visibly tearing itself apart, among other reasons, that its leaders were now as anxious as their foreign paymasters to bring the exhausting campaign to an end. This was a design easier to formulate than to realize. Members of the lower Estates, well settled in to a life in which free board and lodging were provided out of French or Russian funds, their appetite for parliamentary proceedings growing by what it fed on, had no great wish to return home to constituents who (if the economic portents meant anything) might well have awkward questions to ask of them. The rank and file of the party accused their leaders of having sold themselves to Russia because they wanted to bring the Diet to an end; the Estate of Clergy was reported to be uncontrollable even by bribery.[81] In September these enthusiasts submitted a program of twenty-one points which, if they had got it accepted, would have comfortably protracted the session well beyond Christmas.[82] Fortunately this proved too much for the responsible leaders on both sides. At the beginning of October they succeeded in getting all four Estates to agree that the Diet should be "blown out" (as the phrase went) on 11 October; and on 15 October it actually came to an end. Not, however, before the Caps had registered one last victory, to which they attached great importance, when they carried a resolution that the next Diet should meet, not in Stockholm, but in Norrköping.[83] Behind this decision lay the calculation that the permanent civil service establishment (which was in the habit of turning up in numbers to the Diet, and was still, after three decades of

Hat rule, overwhelmingly Hat) would, with any luck, be chained to their office-stools in Stockholm during the session; so that a meeting at Norrköping would probably give the Caps a substantial initial advantage. The course of events in 1769 would reveal the vanity of this simpleminded Machiavellianism.

So it was over at last; with much useful reform effected, if often by odious and invidious methods; with attempts to solve economic difficulties which within two years would prove fatal to their authors; but above all with a real opportunity for constructive statesmanship in the constitutional field resolutely ignored. In terms of parliamentary party warfare, it had been a triumphant success: the Hats had everywhere been swept from the field.[84] In terms of foreign policy, the French system appeared to have been destroyed: the limited commission with which Goodricke had been sent to Stockholm had been handsomely discharged. Shortly before the Diet ended Macartney could write to Goodricke:

> Your services have been such as everyone here acknowledges highly to your Honor; whether the Gentlemen at Home will do you that Justice or not, I can't pretend to say, but I know their idea of foreign ministers is much like that which sour Devines are apt to entertain of *very good* Christians, and that they think that when we have done all that we can, we are unprofitable Servants.[85]

But in this instance the gentlemen at home were not unappreciative: Conway sent warm congratulations on the satisfactory conclusion of the Diet, and transmitted His Majesty's gracious approval of Goodricke's "diligence and activity during this interesting & perplext Scene of business."[86] What he did not say was that it now depended upon the British government to proceed to the logical consequences of Goodricke's endeavors; and what he perhaps did not realize was that if they were not prepared to take that step, all his minister's diligence and activity would prove to have been no more than a vain beating of the air.

CHAPTER VIII

Drift, Deflation, and Defeat, 1766–1768

(i)

By November 1766, then, Goodricke and the Caps stood poised to implement the program which they had laid down in the spring of 1765. The French system was broken, France's payment of arrears was indefinitely suspended, the Senate indignant at the language which Choiseul and Breteuil had latterly seen fit to hold towards them. Goodricke's treaty had provided that negotiations for a regular defensive alliance should start when "time and conjunctures" should be opportune: that time, surely, had now arrived.

The reply of the Estates to the Secret Proposition on foreign affairs which had been laid before them at the beginning of the Diet took a broad survey of Sweden's international position, and drew conclusions which were all that Goodricke could desire.[1] Two points, in particular, seemed to stand out. In the first place, Sweden was now isolated. The alliance with Denmark had expired in 1764; and persistent attempts by Löwenhielm to renew it, in the course of 1766, had elicited only vague and noncommital answers from Copenhagen.[2] Otherwise, Sweden had only her alliance with Russia, concluded by the Hats in highly exceptional circumstances in 1758 as a disagreeable logical consequence of their involvement in the Seven Years War. This too had not long to run; and even for the Caps it was not an alliance which they would seek unless they must. The second feature of the international scene to impress itself upon them bore directly on the first. Europe, it appeared, was on the point of dividing into two blocs of powers: on the one hand the Family Compact, together with France's ally Austria; on the other, an association of Russia, Prussia, and Great Britain, into which it seemed already clear that Denmark would be drawn. Sweden could not afford to be left out of one or other of these groups, least of all if Denmark were included in one of them. The only question, then, was which of the two she should endeavor to join. The aim of her foreign policy must above all be peace; and it followed that she must refuse alliances with powers whose interests might drag her into unnecessary wars. On the other hand she needed an ally upon whom she could rely for swift and effective aid if real danger should threaten; and an ally, if possible, who would be prepared to give financial help, if only on the pretext of improving the efficiency of Sweden's armed forces. The conclusion to be drawn could hardly be in doubt. The only powers who were in a position seriously to threaten Sweden were Russia, Denmark, and (as regards Pomerania) Prussia. No power—certainly not France—could give effective military assistance against attacks of this sort; and only the British navy could offer some sort of protection against Danish descents on Skåne, or Russian landings in Roslagen. Experience in two wars had shown that the French alliance entailed the consequence of involvement in France's quarrels: a consequence the more dangerous now, when Catherine II regarded France as her principal enemy. A British alliance was much less open to this sort of objection, especially if care were taken to exclude colonial wars from its scope. As to Russia, there was no reason to suppose that cordial relations could not be maintained on a basis of goodwill and avoidance of provocations: after all, the example of France and Spain sufficiently refuted the idea that neighbors must necessarily be bad friends. Sweden, then, must join the Northern System. In the event, the Estates proved to be mistaken in their assumption that there was no time to lose if they were to avoid that system's being formed without them; but in the circumstances it was a not unnatural error, and was indeed an opinion widely shared throughout Europe. But by joining the Northern System they meant, in reality, allying with England; and not the least of their reasons for desiring that alliance was their hope that English money would compensate for French arrears. They did not, indeed, forbid the Senate to enter into negotiations except upon the basis of a subsidy: no doubt they realized that if they had done so the negotiations would never have begun at all. All they did was to express their desire for an alliance "especially with a subsidy"; but this left open the possibility of other forms of financial aid, and it meant too that negotiations could be started in the hope that if Sweden went on asking long enough the British government might at last allow itself to be persuaded.

That some financial aid was desirable had become clear to the Caps even before France suspended payment of arrears. The economies they had effected did not go very far; the revenue from increased taxation was inadequate:[3] and though Serenius assured Goodricke that Sweden could balance her budget until the next ordinary *riksdag* in 1770, in the Secret Committee he had been one of those who insisted that a subsidy was a sine qua non.[4] Certainly it was so from the point of view of party politics, whatever the financial position: the Caps must have something to show to offset the loss of French money which their policies had entailed. As early as the spring of 1765 Baron Gross, the Russian minister in London, had put forward the suggestion that Sweden's needs might be met by a loan on the London money market.[5] A year later the idea was revived by Rudbeck, and received strong backing from Goodricke. Since this was a form of assistance which entailed no parliamentary difficulties and imposed no strain on the Civil List, Conway was prepared to be cooperative. Goodricke was informed that His Majesty's government was willing to approve, in principle;[6] and the loan might indeed have been floated, if similar negotiations in Genoa had not in the meantime offered an acceptable alternative. Choiseul did his best to sabotage them by frightening the Genoese government into breaking off the deal; but the British consul on the spot was ordered to use his influence in Sweden's favor, and by June 1767 Löwenhielm could report with satisfaction that a total of 1,400,000 florins had been arranged for, which was considerably more than the figure for which he had originally bargained.[7] But though this was satisfactory as far as it went, it did not remove the urgent political necessity to produce a quid pro quo for the lost gold of Versailles.

It was against this background that in November 1766 Löwenhielm made the first approaches to Goodricke for the conclusion of a defensive alliance.[8] It proved, however, no easy matter to get the negotiations started on a regular basis. The British government's attitude was that though of course there could be no question of a subsidy, it would be happy to receive any proposals the Swedes cared to make. Goodricke was not provided with fresh instructions or full powers, and there could consequently be no question of negotiating with Swedish commissioners in the usual manner. Months elapsed, and some adroit maneuvering by Goodricke was necessary, before the point was reached at which Löwenhielm could be pushed into the position of drawing up a *projet*;[9] and when at last it came to the Senate for approval, the king inserted a *dictamen ad protocollum* protesting against the alliance which was certainly too forcibly argued to have been written by himself: "a most able and dangerous paper," in Goodricke's opinion.[10] But at last, on 28 April 1767, the *projet* was handed to Goodricke for transmission to his government.[11] It was to be based, as he had proposed, on the old alliance of 1720: each party to come to the assistance of the other with 6,000 men, or their equivalent. Wars "in remote places" (*sc.* America or Portugal) were to be excluded. The alliance was to be for ten years, and for five of them Sweden asked a subsidy of £50,000 per annum.

So began some eighteen months of desultory diplomacy which led nowhere and achieved nothing. The Swedish *projet* lay unanswered in the Secretary's office. Conway acknowledged it with the discouraging remark that it was perhaps a pity that Goodricke had ever consented to receive it, since it could only raise false hopes;[12] and thereafter confined himself to occasional unhelpful comments to Nolcken on the futility of expecting a subsidy in peacetime.[13] But the collapse of Chatham's health in 1767 paralyzed all activity; Conway could not make up his mind whether to stay in or go out; and for six weeks during the summer he refused to transact any business at all.[14] Weymouth, who succeeded him in January 1768, ignored the whole affair: during the nine months of his tenure of the seals Goodricke received only four communications from him, all of trivial significance, and none of them dealing with the proposed alliance.[15] By the middle of 1768 it seemed that the negotiation was as good as dead. For more than two years Goodricke had labored to engineer a situation which would present his country with the opportunity to complete the task which he had been sent to Sweden to do. In November 1766 that situation existed, and the opportunity was there. To his chagrin he saw the one neglected, and the other ignored.

The insouciant passivity of ministers is no doubt to be explained in part by the chaotic political situation at Westminster; a weakness which was only partially removed by the replacement of Chatham by Grafton, and by the accession of the Bedfords to the ministry. But in the general context of the times this torpor might nonetheless seem surprising. For when the Rockinghams fell from power in the summer of 1766 the main objective of British foreign policy became more sharply defined than at any time since 1763. Chatham took office in July of that year with one overriding purpose: to effect the alliance with Russia which had for so long been hanging fire. The moment seemed propitious. Macartney's commercial treaty had just been successfully concluded; and that treaty had always been considered in London as the necessary preliminary to serious negotiations for an alliance. Macartney himself was urging that now was the moment for propounding a new *projet*: "all that has hitherto taken place has been meer *pour-parler*".[16] The Russian minister in London, Mussin-Pushkin, was of the same opinion, and was suggesting possible alternatives to the Turkish clause to his government.[17] Chatham himself was determined to show to the world that vigorous action, backed by the personal prestige which he still believed himself to command, could effect what his indolent or incompetent predecessors had failed to accomplish. Sweden and Denmark were powers beneath the dignity of his attention: what was required, he believed, was a triple alliance with Russia and Prussia, which should repair the damage done by Bute's peace, and should ensure that such thunderbolts as might be engendered by that "Great Cloud of Power in the North" should be aimed at the Family Compact. Once that alliance was made, the Scandinavian states, the Dutch, and a scattering of the more reliable small fry of Germany, would inevitably gravitate towards it, until (as Conway was to write) "the whole is consolidated into one solid Mass."[18] A special emissary, Hans Stanley, was accordingly commissioned to perform this piece of diplomatic prestidigitation: he was to proceed to St. Petersburg by way of Berlin, where the magic of the name of Pitt (it could hardly be doubted) would be sufficient to remove any hesitations which Frederick might feel about engaging in this arrangement; and thus fortified would surely find his task in St. Petersburg a simple matter. The problem which had baffled successive Secretaries of State would be solved at a stroke, the Family Compact checkmated, the peace of Europe secured.[19]

It was a program which dealt with difficulties by ignoring them, and which was as blundering in its execution as it was false in its premises. It was one of Catherine's fixed principles neither to appoint ambassadors nor to receive them; and the news that one was now to be wished on her did not predispose her favorably to any new British initiative. The remonstrances of Hans Stanley at last persuaded ministers that it might be well, before sending him off on his mission, to make enquiries through Sir Andrew Mitchell in Berlin as to how Frederick was likely to react to the proposals which were to be made to him. The information Mitchell sent home was shattering; but it took them some months before they could bring themselves to swallow the astounding fact that Frederick was not prepared even to consider their proposals.[20] Hans Stanley thereupon prudently declined the commission; and Catherine was coolly informed that perhaps an ambassador might not be sent at all. Since she had in the meantime swallowed her repugnance to ambassadors and announced the appointment of Ivan Chernyshev as ambassador to the Court of St. James, this did not improve her temper. Thus the whole enterprise petered out in a fiasco of unusual magnitude. The hostility and contempt of Frederick was increased rather than diminished; and so far from opening the way to closer relations with Russia the effect was to produce an understandable irritation which the much-injured Macartney made no effort to gloss over in his dispatches. When Conway at last assented to his appeals to be recalled, he did so on the ground that there seemed no prospect of making progress towards the Russian alliance, and about the same time confessed to Nolcken that it "avance moins que jamais."[21] "I should think," commented Macartney with obvious relish, "a treaty of alliance with the Empress of Russia (during M. Panin's Ministry) as distant and unlikely to be brought about, as a League with Prester John, or with the King of Bantam."[22]

Thus the attempt to form a Northern System on the basis of an Anglo-Russian alliance had come up against a stone wall. But it was at least conceivable that the wall might be circumvented. What if, instead of beginning with a direct negotiation with Russia, the beginning were made at the other end?—if, for instance, an alliance were first concluded with Sweden, or with Denmark, and Russia were then invited to accede to it? This might be a way round the difficulty; and it was a line which Conway was at all events prepared to try. The only question was, which of the two to select for the experiment.

It seems clear that Conway's preference was for trying Denmark; and in this he was following in Grafton's footsteps. It could be argued as a ground for the choice that Denmark had still to be fully separated from France, since in the summer of 1766 Choiseul, however sulkily, was still paying Denmark arrears of subsidy, and the Danish finances were not in a condition to make this a matter of no consequence. It was still true that the Danish navy was better than the Swedish—a new report on its effectiveness was sent to Conway in 1767[23]—and that Denmark, therefore, was more likely to be a useful ally in a war with France: Danish troops, moreover, might be conveniently within reach if it were a question of defending Hanover. Denmark was already Russia's ally, and it might be hoped that Panin would use his influence with Bernstorff to induce him to accept England's terms. In contrast to Sweden, Denmark was an absolute monarchy, and there need therefore be no question of heavy expenditure on parliamentary corruption. And not least, by that misconception of

Panin's plan which Grafton bequeathed to his successors, Denmark was not only destined to be the active power in Scandinavia, but was supposed to be England's responsibility, while Sweden was held to be the responsibility of Russia. It happened that the new king, Kristian VII, was for various domestic reasons most anxious for an English alliance—indeed, he would have liked an offensive alliance if he could get it—since he looked forward, with the naive optimism of youth, to expanding and refurbishing his armed forces at the expense of the British taxpayer.[24]

For at least some of these reasons the initiative for a Danish alliance, which had been taken with questionable sincerity by Grafton, was now renewed on a rather more serious basis by Conway. The English minister in Copenhagen, Walter Titley, had now been provided with a young resident to assist him, in the person of Robert Gunning. They concurred in urging Conway to take advantage of what they represented to be a most favorable opportunity; and they concurred too in pleading that Denmark had special claims to be given a subsidy. Conway was not unimpressed by these arguments. He so far relaxed his normallly intransigent attitude as to assure them that if ever England should deviate from the principle of "no subsidies in peacetime" it would be in Denmark's favor; though he was quick to add that he could not foresee such an occasion's arising.[25] Nevertheless, he gave cordial authorization to his ministers in Copenhagen to open a negotiation, and in January 1767 Titley duly made approaches to Bernstorff.[26] But Bernstorff proved disappointingly unresponsive. His negotiations for a provisional *Mageskifte* treaty were far advanced, and until that treaty was safely concluded he was not interested in any other foreign connection, least of all one which might jeopardize France's payment of arrears.[27] He might indeed have been prepared to listen, if Conway had been willing to guarantee the Holstein exchange: but it could not reasonably be expected of any Secretary of State that he should commit the country to upholding an arrangement of which he knew nothing, and which was still no more than prospective. The situation was not helped by the blunders and prejudices of Robert Gunning, who at an early stage made up his mind that Bernstorff was the tool of France. This fundamental error tempted him to try to meddle in Danish internal politics. He was hand in glove with a set of intriguers who twice tried to engineer Bernstorff's dismissal: on the second of these occasions Bernstorff was saved only by the vigorous intervention of Russia. And (what was much worse) his suspicion of Bernstorff had Conway's full endorsement: Bernstorff, wrote Conway, was "the most able, and therefore to Us and to Russia the most dangerous supporter of the French cause in Denmark"[28]—a judgment which can only be described as fantastic nonsense: in effect Conway was telling the Russians that they were backing the wrong horse in Denmark, and did not know their own business. Thus British diplomacy in Copenhagen, so far from paving the way to a Northern System, did its feeble best to envenom Anglo-Russian relations there; and if Gunning's activities did no permanent damage to Anglo-Russian amity, that was to be attributed to the forbearance of Catherine and Panin, rather than to any repudiation of his attitudes in London. One thing at least was certain: the road to a Russian alliance did not lie through Copenhagen, any more than it lay through Berlin—at least for the present.

In April and May of 1767 there occurred a cluster of interconnected happenings which together marked the end of a phase in the history of British foreign policy. In the middle of April Macartney received the news of his recall. On the twenty-second, Russia and Denmark concluded the provisional *Mageskifte* treaty, though British intelligence in Copenhagen was so poor that it took Gunning three months to discover this fact. On the twenty-eighth, Löwenhielm handed to Goodricke the Swedish draft treaty. On 5 May Breteuil quitted Stockholm for The Hague, leaving only a chargé d'affaires behind him. And on 22 May, Conway wrote to Gunning regretting that "the Prospect of a closer Alliance with Denmark has vanished"—a consequence, he fatuously concluded, of Russian ascendancy in Copenhagen.[29] If, then, he was really still anxious for the Russian alliance, by the middle of May the options open to him had narrowed down to one. The Swedish treaty, in which he had hitherto evinced so tepid an interest, was now the only plank still afloat from the wreck of British diplomacy. To Britain's representatives at the northern courts it seemed an obvious consequence of this situation that Conway should lose no time in climbing on to it. But neither Conway, nor his successor Weymouth, showed any inclination to do anything of the sort. For eighteen months the plank drifted slowly away on the ebb tide of British initiative, and even Goodricke had much ado to keep a hand on it.

(ii)

It is not difficult to draw up a formidable indictment of British foreign policy in the years from 1766 to 1768. The ignorant presumptuousness of ministers' dealings with Denmark, the purblind blundering of Chatham's attempt to enlist the good offices of Frederick to secure the Russian alliance, reflect a grievous misunderstanding of the realities of contemporary continental politics. Conway's thrasonical brags about the power and glory of the British nation, his innocent assumption that any foreign court must esteem it a privilege to be accorded England's alliance, the "empty didactic exhortations" which Catherine found so exasperating,[30] these were no substitute for a foreign policy, and they accorded ill with the oft-repeated excuse that Britain's financial situation was such that even relatively moderate expenditures—let alone a subsidy—were more than the Treasury could be expected to bear. The insistence on the Turkish clause, the constant reiteration of the principle of "no subsidies in peacetime," look like ancient shibboleths which had ceased to have relevance to the times.

> To be positive seldom marks a Greatness of Mind, nor always even a Steadiness; As an ill-placed Obstinacy is generally followed by a late Repentance, and it can never be more so than when a Predilection for some favorite Trifle is allowed to outweigh the most extensive and important Considerations of Policy.[31]

A sober and weighty judgment, this; but it is finely ironical that it should have come from Conway's pen. It was intended as a thrust at Panin; and it would never have occurred to Conway that it applied with even greater force to himself. But apart altogether from these particular issues, it has been argued in general that the search for a continental alliance—inconsequently pursued as it was—was itself a mistake; that the whole alliance system of the middle decades of the century had dissolved into chaos, and that there was no point in trying to revive the dead world of the duke of Newcastle: the right policy was to remember, as Sandwich in his time had remembered, that Britain was an island, and to prepare for the renewal of the struggle with France not by vainly seeking reinsurance on the Continent, but by concentrating on the navy.[32] The balance of forces in Europe was such that a continental war was unlikely in the foreseeable future; and the attempt to counter French ascendancy in the minor courts of Europe was an unthinking conditioned reflex irrelevant to the real interests of the country.

There is force in these arguments; but it is perhaps too easy to forget that there were arguments on the other side. If it be true, as Dr. Langford has written, that in the domestic history of England in the 1760s "the critical factor at every turn is the role of personality,"[33] it is no less true that the personalities of Grafton, Conway, and Weymouth go some way to explaining the weaknesses of British foreign policy. But irrespective of their personalities ministers had a case, and it is well that this should be recognized. On the broadest grounds that case was put, more forcibly than by any English statesman or historian, by Nolcken, when he sent in his report to the *riksdag* of 1769.[34] Nolcken was not unmindful of the apparent weakness and inconsequence of British policy, of the pennywise parsimony of ministers, of their apparent indifference to continental issues which it might have been thought were of essential concern, of the sharp drop in Britain's reputation abroad. But he made the point strongly that "the sounder part of the nation" concurred in the way foreign policy was handled, and that men of all groups and parties—whatever they might say when in opposition—found no reason to diverge from the line chalked out by their predecessors once they had themselves become responsible ministers: he even explained Chatham's mental breakdown by his realization that the measures which he had advocated when out of office were in fact beyond the bounds of practical politics. Bold courses, flashy policies, were forbidden by the parliamentary situation. Ministers certainly foresaw the coming of a new war with France; but they did not think the danger imminent (in which, of course, they proved right), and hence they did not consider the need for continental alliances urgent, however much they might in general desire them. Their much-lamented parsimony was in fact based on a prudent determination to reserve their financial efforts for a real crisis: when that crisis should come, they were confident that they could buy allies at need on better terms than France, having a longer purse; and in the very worst case they calculated that England could deal with a Franco-Spanish attack single-handed. In Nolcken's view, England was strong enough to wage a defensive war alone; and was very unlikely to take offensive action, if only because of the ominous situation in the American colonies. The endless game of ministerial leapfrog, the obsessive preoccupation with electoral politics, which so impressed or depressed foreign observers, obscured the reality of the situation; and as to the much-advertised internal unrest, of which the Wilkes affairs attracted most attention, it was much less serious than foreign diplomats might lead their governments to believe, and would in any case disappear in the event of war.

This was a sober and clear-sighted appraisal: very different from the gloomy reports with which Maltzan, for instance, took care to delight Frederick the Great, and the more remarkable as coming from a minister who was directly concerned with the vain attempts to conclude an Anglo-Swedish alliance. And if we turn from these general considerations to the particular issues which impeded the progress of British diplomacy, Nolcken's observations do not look any the less plausible. It may be that England's argument for retaining the Turkish clause was weaker than Russia's case for deleting it; but for both sides it was really a question of prestige, of refusing to budge from established positions: if Catherine had been willing to make a firm offer of assistance in the event of war in America, or in Portugal, there would have been no difficulty.[35] This she was not prepared to do: aid against the Turks was provided for in her treaties with Prussia and Denmark, and she saw no reason to grant a special dispensation to Britain. Nevertheless, ministers were perhaps entitled to believe, as Frederick the Great also did,[36] that the right way to deal with Russia was to go on saying and demanding the same thing until the Russians became tired and gave way. They were possibly justified in thinking that Russia needed the alliance more than they did. As Panin wrote, she needed it "for spreading our influence to all European affairs, both in peacetime and wartime."[37] And she needed it particularly and specifically in regard to Sweden. When British ministers claimed, as they were never tired of doing, that Sweden was a more important interest to Russia than to England, they may have been tactless, but they were perfectly right: though they blunted the edge of their argument, and involved themselves in contradictions, by simultaneously conceding that

> The first and main object of His Majesty's aim in all the Northern Courts must be the entire overthrow of the French System; and from whatever motive Russia may act, if she forwards and promotes that great and useful work she so far effectually promotes the Interest of Great Britain.[38]

They were right, because a French-dominated Sweden could be used by France as a base for a diversionary attack on Russia; while on the other hand even if both Sweden and Denmark were in the French system, the accession of naval strength which they would provide was probably not beyond the capacity of the British navy to deal with. As English ministers were well aware, it was highly desirable to Russia that there should be an English party in Sweden to hold France in check, since no Swede would wear the Russian colors if he could avoid it. When Goodricke pleaded that the expenditure of a little money in Sweden "would close this back door,"[39] when he wrote that "the Question is not whether it is worth while to bestow money upon Sweden, but the Question is whether it be worth while to bestow it to put off or prevent a new war,"[40] he was in effect (though he did not see it) supporting ministers' case: for the "back door" was the back door to *Russia,*[41] and the only "new war" which money expended in Sweden was likely to prevent was a Swedish attack upon St. Petersburg. It was not entirely unreasonable of ministers to feel that their efforts in Sweden, however small when compared with those of Panin, were not appreciated as they ought to have been: it was open to them to argue that the French system in Sweden had been destroyed, if not by Goodricke's treaty, then at least in consequence of it; and that *thereby* they had made the way clear for Russia.[42] As to subsidies in peacetime, whether experience had proved their inutility or not (as ministers firmly believed) there was certainly some force in the argument that giving a subsidy to one power encouraged demands for similar support from another: they had not forgotten the history of the early fifties.[43] It was certainly no incentive to ministers to be openhanded when they learned from Macartney, as they did in March 1767, that Panin had said that England "might scatter millions in Poland on the one hand, and millions in Sweden on the other," without affecting his determination to stand firm on the Turkish clause.[44] In Sweden *and Poland*? They might well feel that the coupling of the two was a warning signal: from 1763 onwards Panin had been trying to commit England to giving aid in Poland, and the idea was still in his head in 1768.[45] But as Conway rightly said there was no country in Europe with which England had less concern.[46] To oblige Russia Wroughton might be ordered to collaborate with Repnin in Warsaw, and ministers might be willing to associate themselves with declarations in favor of the Dissidents, but further than that no British minister would or could go. Panin's persistent recurrence to the idea of British aid in Poland shows that if there were delusions in Whitehall there were others no less odd in St. Petersburg. As to the suggestion that the old European alliance system was dead, and that ministers ought to have thought out a fresh approach to the country's foreign policy, this is a criticism based on hindsight, and even on that basis is of dubious validity. In 1767 a man might have combed the chancelleries of Europe from one end of the Continent to the other and hardly found a single statesman to endorse it. Most of them earnestly desired the preservation of peace, and sought to preserve it by combinations which would be sufficiently imposing to discourage any aggressor; all—even Choiseul—were determined to keep Germany neutral in any future war; and perhaps the main reason for Frederick's opposition to an Anglo-Russian alliance was his fear that England's connection with Hanover might imperil that neutrality.[47] Choiseul certainly did not think that England was wasting her time in looking for a continental alliance: to

Vergennes he wrote "L'Angleterre voit avec plaisir consolider cette alliance du Nord dans la prévoyance que, s'il arriverait qu'elle fût en rupture avec la France, elle nous embarrasserait, malgré nos alliés, d'une guerre formidable."[48] It might be a matter of comparative indifference to England that Sweden or Denmark, considered as particular cases, should be reincorporated into the French system; but on general principles ministers were bound to resist the extension of French influence to the minor courts. They needed Austria's presence in Italy, as an offset to the preponderance of the Family Compact, with its potential threat to the Mediterranean trade; and they could not stand tamely aside and allow Holland to become a French satellite. Even if their thinking on these points was as wrong as some their critics would maintain, it is unrealistic to expect that they should abruptly break with a tradition of policy which was now nearly a century old. Whitehall had not forgotten Newcastle's argument that "France will outdo us at sea, when they have nothing to fear by land."

But it was precisely because they accepted this argument that it behoved them to accept its consequences also; that is, to make sure that their foreign policy was in fact such as to make the threat of Russian manpower available to them at need. In 1767 and 1768 they still firmly believed that the right way to ensure this was by an alliance. The day would come when they would be disposed to think that this was an advantage which, in the existing state of European politics, could be as well assured by an *entente cordiale*; but that day was only beginning to dawn. Until it arrived the logic of their own policy should have forced them to swallow the fact that if they really wanted the alliance they must pay something for it. There may not have been much wrong with their principles; but it is not much good sticking to principles if what the situation calls for is pragmatism. Despite all Macartney's picturesque eloquence they would not or could not recognize that a new Russia had emerged upon Europe in the course of the two preceding decades; a Russia determined to be treated as one of the great powers, and well able to maintain that pretension; a Russia for whom questions of prestige were almost as important as material advantage.[49] Conway might write of "that haughty Court,"[50] but he remained insensitive to the danger of affronting that hauteur: neither he nor his successors could imagine why for Catherine the inclusion of the Turkish clause in any new treaty seemed to be a one-sided concession which must be balanced by an equivalent. In 1767 neither side for a moment believed that a Russo-Turkish war was imminent; and as long as this situation continued the question of the Turkish clause ought to have been negotiable.[51] Thus the real charge against ministers is a lack of imaginative insight, a failure to understand the minds and motives of the men with whom they had to negotiate. And that failure was made worse by sheer incompetence and pig-headed ignorance. Nowhere had it more serious consequences than in Sweden. Here they were indeed saved from purely local blunders of the type committed by Gunning in Denmark: Goodricke and Osterman were each experts on Swedish politics, and worked in harmony whatever Whitehall might do, while Gunning was a brash ignoramus tramping on the toes of Russian diplomats who knew Danish politics inside out. But Grafton and Conway, having persuaded themselves that Panin's plan provided that Russia should take care of the Exterior in Sweden, took the line that if a subsidy were to be paid at all, it must be Russia that paid it. It may be conceded that it would have been a matter of great difficulty to persuade the House of Commons to agree to a subsidy in peacetime: just how difficult it is impossible to say, since they never risked the attempt. But after 28 November 1766 they can have been left in no doubt as to how Russia would react if they persisted in this attitude: on that day Conway received from Macartney a dispatch in which he conveyed an explicit warning from Panin to the effect that "if he found himself obliged to pay a subsidy to Sweden, which he must do, if We refuse it, He would then engage with us no further, but compose his System as well as he could without us."[52] Conway never seemed to understand that his indifference to the party situation in Sweden made nonsense of Goodricke's treaty, and indeed of his whole mission. They could not afford to let the Caps down; for if they did so they not merely jeopardized the very existence of an "English" party in Stockholm, but they also destroyed that claim to Russia's gratitude which they were never tired of advancing, since the ascendancy of an English party was a vital Russian interest. And if the Russian alliance was deemed to be a major political objective they jeopardized that too, since by the spring of 1767 an Anglo-Swedish alliance was the only remaining approach to their goal—an approach, moreover, which offered good prospects of success.[53] In 1767 and 1768 the center of gravity of British foreign policy had in effect been transferred to Stockholm. They did not see it; did not see that the fortunes of the Caps had become of essential concern to them; did not see, despite Goodricke's efforts to open their eyes, how dubious those fortunes were becoming.

(iii)

If it be true, as Nolcken once reported, that ministers at Westminster were so preoccupied with parliamentary business and the intricacies of group politics that they had little time to attend to the affairs for which they were supposed to be responsible,[54] it is also true that Goodricke was so steeped in Swedish politics that his field of vision was somewhat limited: he tended to judge British policy on the basis of its consequences for Sweden. His job was to keep an English party in being, to maintain it in good fighting trim against the next Diet. Without a subsidy it was going to be difficult to do that: for him a subsidy was therefore common sense. Conway might delude himself that the Senate's demand for a subsidy was put forward only so that they might protect themselves against the accusation of not having made it;[55] but Goodricke knew better. He was under pressure all the time from his Swedish friends.[56] And also from Osterman. His collaboration with Osterman enabled him to appreciate that by the early summer of 1767 the best hope remaining for a Northern System which should include England lay in basing that system on an Anglo-Swedish alliance. The "Great Chain" of which both he and Conway were in the habit of writing should have its first link firmly anchored in Stockholm. Moreover, it seemed to him that England was being presented with a uniquely favorable opportunity. In May 1767 the long-impending recall of Breteuil became an accomplished fact. The queen, the crown prince, the Hats, were all in consternation.[57] France, it seemed, had abandoned the struggle. The stream of French corruption dwindled to a trickle. Choiseul's threats of penalizing Sweden's Mediterranean trade turned out to be hollow.[58] Goodricke appeared to be master of the field.

The opportunity was real enough, but it must be used quickly if it were not to crumble away. Conway's easy assumption that in the absence of a French ambassador there was no cause for disquiet[59] was an assumption which Goodricke well knew to be mistaken. For the sky in Stockholm was darkening ominously. When his discreet attempts to nudge Conway into a more forthcoming attitude proved unavailing, when it became clear to him that he could expect no easing of his task from London, he was forced to look around to see what other expedients he could hit upon to appease and reassure his partisans. A subsidy might be out of the question, but perhaps an acceptable alternative was conceivable. Friesendorff, on a hint from

Osterman, suggested that Sweden might be willing to settle for a lump sum payment of (say) 400,000 rdr.[60] Löwenhielm indicated that he might be prepared to waive a subsidy immediately, if he could be sure of getting it "about the time of the Diet."[61] Neither of these expedients found favor in London. In May Goodricke came up with the idea that the East India Company should undertake an annual payment in return for a guaranteed draft of Swedish recruits for its service. An interesting suggestion, commented Conway,[62] but he feared that it presented difficulties from the Company's point of view. A month later Goodricke recurred to the idea of a loan, this time to be by "a set of merchants," payment of interest and repayment of capital being guaranteed by the British government.[63] But the merchants in question, it appeared, did not find the investment attractive. At this junction the deepening depression of the Cap leaders was momentarily lifted by the arrival in Stockholm of Macartney, on his way home from Russia. His youth, his ebullient self-confidence, his social gifts, charmed Caps and Court alike.[64] His arrival coincided with information from Nolcken that Goodricke was not well seen at home, and that if the alliance with Sweden were made at all, ministers would take care that it should not be Goodricke who made it.[65] How far this report was correct it is impossible to say; but it must have strengthened a feeling that Macartney had not chosen to go home by way of Stockholm simply to see the sights and exchange views with his colleague. It seemed likely that he was to be the next minister to Sweden, and was now reconnoitering the ground. At all events some of the Caps—notably Senators Ribbing and Horn—began to speculate upon such a change. Lovisa Ulrika took the opportunity of venting her spleen on Goodricke by showering attentions upon Macartney; and Ribbing and Horn seem to have hoped that if he returned as minister he might be the means of drawing the queen over to their side:[66] that they should have allowed themselves to entertain such an idea was a significant index to the low state of the Caps' morale. Gregers Juel, who had recently succeeded Schack as Danish minister, observed all this with indignation: to indiscreet Caps who broached the possibility of a change he took occasion to pay emphatic tribute to Goodricke's abilities: from the Caps' point of view, he considered, Goodricke was a "necessity."[67] But whether Macartney was to come back or not, he spoke so warmly in favor of the Swedish alliance, was so loud in his assertions that a subsidy must be paid, and so open in his contempt for Whitehall's ignorance of Europe,[68] that the Senate felt they could do no better than commission him to plead their cause in London.[69] They were not fortunate in their choice of advocate.

Macartney's correspondence with Conway had latterly been of the most acrimonious kind; his intervention produced no effect whatever; and before he had been in England many months he had recanted his opinions and come round to ministers' way of thinking.[70]

Despite the "three weeks of constant dissipation" which celebrated Macartney's visit,[71] the snubs at court to which Goodricke was subjected and the intrigues of some of his clients to have him replaced can hardly have failed to depress his ordinarily resilient temper, however good a face he contrived to put on them.[72] He was making no progress with his negotiation, and perhaps some whisper had reached him of Nolcken's report that the ministry would grudge him the credit of any success: he can hardly have forgotten Grafton's ungracious reception of his earlier treaty. At all events, he began to think of quitting the diplomatic line altogether and trying for a seat in parliament. But the disappointment of his hopes of obtaining a spell of leave from his post put that idea out of the question.[73] A sign of his growing depression had been evident already in April, when he approached Schack, then on the point of quitting the legation in Stockholm, and implored him to ask Bernstorff to let him know if there were likely to be a vacancy in Copenhagen, and in such a case to make representations to the British government in his favor: better a quiet life with his old friends in Denmark than present frustrations in Stockholm.[74] Already he was beginning to fear what might happen to the Caps at the next meeting of the Diet in 1770—if, indeed, they were able to hold out until then. For as the economic crisis deepened he came more and more to fear that it might force the Senate to yield to demands for an Extraordinary Diet, as the Hat Senate had been forced to yield in similar circumstances three years before. It was with these gloomy forebodings in his mind that in September 1767 he produced yet another expedient. His proposal was that if Sweden would conclude an immediate alliance on England's terms, England, Russia, and Denmark should jointly guarantee sufficient financial support to protect the Caps against the retribution which the next Diet would probably bring with it.[75] Osterman, to whom he confided the proposal, was skeptical;[76] but Conway, for once, was prepared to listen: indeed, Goodricke got the impression (probably mistaken) that his plan was "much relished at home."[77] Since England was still represented in St. Petersburg only by a chargé d'affaires, Conway transmitted the plan to Gunning, with instructions to discuss it privately with Saldern.[78]

There, for the moment, the matter rested. But though the idea was not pursued in 1767, it cast long shadows before. For the plan which Goodricke propounded was in effect a blueprint of future British policy: not indeed for 1770, for the Cap régime did not survive so long, but for the Extraordinary Diet of 1769. Goodricke's proposal in fact marks the beginning of a slow swing in British foreign policy in the North: for the first time Conway begins to think in terms of cordial collaboration with Russia as an *alternative* to an alliance, and specifically of cordial collaboration in Sweden. Saldern, for his part, was moving in the same direction: to Gunning he remarked, "Of what consequence was it, whether two such Courts as ours were engaged, or not, by a Scrap of Paper, as he termed it?"; they could and should feel "as much bound in reality, as if They had signed fifty treaties, their interests being the same at all times."[79] Thus Goodricke, in his search for an alternative to a subsidy, had in fact hit upon a solution to ministers' dilemmas, the solution which it was to be his special task to apply. The idea of a Russian alliance, by some route or other (perhaps through Sweden), was certainly not yet dead, and at the end of 1768 Cathcart's arrival in Russia would powerfully revive it. Goodricke himself had not abandoned it. But at least he had adumbrated a different approach. It would need a greater danger than any apparent in 1767 to fuse Anglo-Russian policies into a unity; and such a policy, as Goodricke never ceased to point out, would not be cheap. But events would prove that this was probably the only practicable way forward.

(iv)

Meanwhile the authority and credibility of the Cap Senate, sapped and sopped by the monotonous drip of Conway's refusals, was damaged beyond repair by the consequences of their economic and financial policies. They had come to power with a determination to reverse the inflationary trend which had prevailed since 1757. They wanted cheap food, dearer money, full convertibility of paper; they would improve the balance of payments by stringent legislation forbidding the use of a long list of luxury goods which were mainly consumed by those classes of society which had benefited from the inflation.[80] The Swedish silver daler, which in 1765 fell to nearly 90 marks to the riksdaler *Hamburger banco*, should be brought back if possible to parity—that is, to 36 marks to the riksdaler. On 15 July 1766 the Secret Committee accepted the strategy which the Bank Committee devised with these ends in view. The rate of exchange, which in February had been pegged at 70 marks to the riksdaler, was to be progressively lowered by 4 marks a year until parity was attained; and this policy was to be kept secret, in order to prevent speculation—a stipulation which seems very unlikely to have been practicable. At the same time the amount of paper money in circulation was to be reduced gradually over the next ten years by 21 million silver daler.[81] The plan was thus for a controlled, and therefore reasonably painless, deflation; and for a time the operation looked as though it might succeed: in the late autumn of 1766 the rate was fixed at 66, and for some time seemed likely to stick there. But by the summer of 1767 it proved no longer possible to adhere to the original program. By July 1767 the daler was appreciating at a rate of two to three marks every post-day;[82] by August there was a crisis. The Senate hurried back from its summer holidays to decide what to do, and like most governments in such a situation found that they could not agree: Löwenhielm was for getting the Bank to put the brake on; Rudbeck was for letting the rate float.[83] But by September Rudbeck had changed his mind; and it was at his suggestion, in a desperate attempt to get ahead of the speculators, that the Senate finally agreed to fix the rate at 42.[84] It may well be that by that time the original plan was already wrecked beyond repair; but if not, the decision proved disastrous. The Caps had originally supposed that prices would fall commensurately with the appreciation of the daler; and this did indeed occur in regard to manufactured goods, and particularly bar-iron; but wages, and the cost of raw materials, did not fall at the same rate,[85] so that by the end of 1767 ironmasters were getting no more for their finished product than they were paying for the cost of production. Contracts between iron producers and British importers were made in sterling; and it was alleged that the depreciation of the pound against the daler entailed a loss of £60,000 in 1767.[86] Moreover, the appreciation of the daler produced something like a strike of buyers; and in the expectation that paper money would continue to rise in value men began to hoard it, so that the amount in circulation diminished much more quickly than had been anticipated, and there was a general shortage of cash.[87]

The deflation hit the iron industry especially hard. Though the prices paid for bar-iron in sterling remained constant, and may even have risen, the commission agents who made purchases for their London principals were slow to buy and offered unremunerative prices, with the result that exports dropped dramatically.[88] The *bergsmän*—small operators who smelted the ore and produced the pig-iron for the use of foundries and forges—were also in trouble; for since 1757 the political predominance of the ironmasters (mostly

Hat) had succeeded in preventing the price of pig-iron from rising with the general rise of prices during the inflation, and the *bergsmän* had been driven to accept loans from the manufacturers which put them economically at their mercy: now these loans were being called in, and often the smelters could not repay them.[89] The crisis in the industry was indeed such that it was feared that one-third of the country's forges might be forced to close down.[90] Other industries were also affected: the shortage of circulating medium meant that the Copper Office was unable to pay for the raw copper that was brought to the official weigh-bridges; and the domestic price of raw copper slumped far worse than that of iron: by January 1768, 104 workshops in the Stora Kopparberg had been forced to suspend production.[91] So too with timber: 1767 saw a sharp fall in exports of plank.[92] Thus the well-meant remedies of the Cap economists had produced a financial crisis and a stagnation of trade and industry which made the Hat inflation seem in recollection like a golden era. All those who had borrowed largely during the inflation now found themselves saddled with a burden of debt they could no longer meet. Land is said to have lost a third of its value.[93] Between 1766 and 1768 bankruptcies reached a peak for the century: prominent Hats such as Gyllenborg, prominent Caps such as Adlerberg (Löwenhielm's son-in-law) failed for large sums, though their assets would have been sufficient to meet their liabilities at the prices prevailing in 1765; all the de la Gardies were said to be ruined;[94] even a wealthy man such as Fersen was driven to borrow 150,000 silver daler from Breteuil to keep himself afloat; and many, like Sinclair, were forced to retrench by exchanging life in Stockholm for the rustic autarky of their country estates.[95]

For a time, the Senate confronted the situation with a good measure of vicarious stoicism. They took the line that the ironmasters (though not the *bergsmän*, who were of course the victims of Hat misrule) in fact deserved much of what was happening to them: they had lived beyond their means; or they had bought on credit ironworks which could not be expected to give a reasonable return for the price paid; they were gamblers, economic parasites on the body politic, who had had their good times and must not now complain if they lost their stakes. But as the crisis deepened it became impossible, politically impossible, for the Senate simply to shrug its shoulders and allow things to take their course. Besides, the crisis hit the just as well as the unjust: there were Cap forge-owners, no less than Hat—Rudbeck and Frietzcky among them. They saw very plainly that if things got no better they might be forced into conceding an Extraordinary Diet, of which the upshot would be not only a political defeat but the overturning of the whole program of reform with which they had taken office in 1765. To the end the Caps insisted that their policies were right in principle, though they might somehow have been sabotaged by their political enemies. For they believed, and possibly they had good grounds for believing, that the crisis was deliberately exacerbated by the maneuvers of Hat agents and greedy financiers: for a moment (in March 1767) they even thought of appointing an extraordinary tribunal to uncover these iniquities, and might have done so if Osterman had not dissuaded them.[96] The crucial question soon came to be the level of prices offered to iron manufacturers at the great annual fair at Kristinehamn. Already in July 1766 the Göteborg buyers were refusing to pay more than 5 rdr per skeppund, a price which no longer covered the cost of production; and to meet this situation the Secret Committee, backed by the Bank and the Estimates Office, secretly sent Frietzcky and von Essen to Karlstad, liberally provided with money, with instructions to support a price of at least 6 rdr. The operation was successful, and proved quite cheap: the Göteborg merchants soon awoke to what was happening and offered 6 rdr in their turn.[97] But the forge owners usually sold their bar-iron against payment in three installments—in May, in August, and at Michaelmas—and between each installment in 1767 they found that the exchange had fallen: in May they received their money at the rate of 65-66 marks, in August it was 53-54; at Michaelmas it was expected to be 46-50, but in fact proved less than that.[98] By May 1768 they needed not 6 but 6½ rdr per skeppund if they were to cover the cost of production and transport to Göteborg.[99] The Iron Office, which would normally have intervened to maintain a stable price for iron, was now in no position to take effective action, since the readiness with which it had made loans during the period of inflation, and its inability now to obtain their repayment, had depleted its resources.[100] In August 1767, in an effort to relieve the distress in the mining areas, the Senate decided to distribute to the *bergsmän*, at nominal prices payable in pig-iron, some of the grain which had recently arrived from Russia in part settlement of 300,000 rubles of arrears owing upon an old subsidy treaty;[101] and in November they defied the Bank, began the coining of copper *plåtar*, and made 50,000 copper daler available to cover the smelters' losses.[102] But the problem of the price of bar-iron remained. It must have been with feelings of deep humiliation that the Senate, in October 1767, summoned Finlay, Grill, Tottie, and Lefebure, as the four largest iron exporters, and begged for their advice as to how best to deal with the situation.[103] For these were the very men whom they had hounded in 1765, whom they blamed for the country's economic ills, and who were, one and all, staunch Hats. They can scarcely have been unduly surprised when their appeal produced only a general and noncommittal response. By the end of the year the situation was felt to be desperate: in December Löwenhielm was talking of forcing the Bank to give loans against sound security, and threatening to call an Extraordinary Diet if they refused;[104] in February 1768 the Bank so far relaxed its doctrinaire deflationary policy as to agree to advance up to 150,000 rdr to the ironmasters, and to send a director to Kristinehamn to repeat, if possible, the feat of Frietzcky and von Essen in August 1766.[105] But it proved to be impossible to repeat it. By the middle of March it had become clear that the attempt had failed; and on 12 April Goodricke was reporting that some of the best iron, which used to go to London by way of Göteborg, was still lying unsold.[106] However, this marked the lowest point of the depression. The price of iron in England was rising; and when navigation opened the demand strengthened: by the autumn of 1768 exports of iron had shown a sharp upturn, and Juel could write to Bernstorff at the end of October that the Caps were over the worst, and that the economy was picking up all round.[107] On the whole he was quite right; but the improvement came too late to save the Caps from the consequences of their deflationary policy.

The possible implications of that policy were not lost on those foreign ministers whose task it was to prop up the Cap régime. Juel's dispatches in 1767 are full of details of the economic crisis, and heavy with forebodings of coming electoral disaster. Osterman, left very much to his own devices now that Panin was preoccupied with the problems of Poland, put his hand in his pocket in an effort to offset Hat propaganda; he sent his own agents to the Bergslag; he defrayed the expenses of merchants going to the fair at Kristinehamn. But his counterpropaganda made little impact; his agents returned to Stockholm gloomier than they set out; and the merchants he financed either could not or would not offer remunerative prices.[108] To Goodricke the crisis was both of personal and general concern; personal, because the depreciation of sterling against the daler put him in real difficulties in regard to his own financial position, and in regard to the payment of England's Swedish pensioners;[109] general, because it centered on the iron trade, and thus involved the whole question of Anglo-Swedish commercial relations, of which that trade was the staple. The iron trade, moreover, had in any case reached something of a turning point: in 1765 for the first time British imports of Russian iron exceeded imports from Sweden. The Swedish Iron Office had for years proceeded on the tacit assumption that as far as England was concerned they had the whip hand: as Goodricke put it, they had been "encouraged by the Belief that their Iron is so absolutely necessary to us, that let them make what Regulations they will, we must have it." Now they were on the point of discovering that "the measures taken upon this Doctrine, have raised them up a Rival in Russia, that will in a short time demonstrate the falsity of it to their cost."[110]

The Swedish economic crisis thus presented Goodricke with something of a dilemma. On the one hand was the obligation—which also corresponded with his desire—to improve the terms of Great Britain's trade with Sweden; on the other was the need to save the Caps from the consequences of their economic policies. Ever since his arrival he had hoped that it might be possible to persuade a Cap Senate to relax the discriminatory duties, and remove the outright prohibitions, by which the Hats had sought to foster Swedish industry and shipping. So far he had made little or no impression; and when in August 1766 Conway jogged his memory on this point he could only reply (truthfully enough) that if he pressed the Swedish government to modify its tariff policy he would infallibly strengthen their demand for a subsidy by way of compensation.[111] He resented the discriminatory duties and port dues which penalized the importation of Swedish iron in English ships;[112] he could not understand why the Swedes did not hasten to take advantage of the appreciation of the daler to buy English textiles, which were now not only better but cheaper than their own.[113] He preached salutary doctrines to his Cap friends as occasion offered; and did not hesitate to warn them that if they were not careful they might find that the only iron England would buy from them in future would be the iron for the navy.[114] These home truths and veiled threats enabled his Hat opponents, and even a friendly observer such as Juel, to assert that he used Sweden's predicament to forward England's commercial interests. Up to a point it was true; but Goodricke would have contended that those interests happened to coincide with the best interests of Sweden. What is plainly not true is to suggest that his conduct in the years 1767-68 was determined by that kind of consideration.

It was an unfortunate but undeniable fact that the years after 1765 saw a sharp drop in British imports from Sweden, and particularly in regard to iron: in 1765 England had imported (from all sources) £513,679 worth of bar-iron; in 1766 the figure had dropped to £323,992, and though it recovered to £447,488 in 1768, it did not reach the level of 1765 for the remainder of the decade.[115] The Senate, which blamed the Hat merchants for the failure of bar-iron to command an acceptable price, now began to wonder whether there might not be another and no less sinister explanation for the stagnation of trade. Was it not possible that the merchants of Stockholm and Göteborg had given a hint to their English principals to refuse that *Verlag* without which the ironmasters lacked the capital to carry on their business? Rudbeck put the point to Goodricke, and asked his assistance. It is plain that he did his best to help. He wrote to Sykes of Hull, the biggest importer at the outports, seeking his advice; and explained that Finlay in Stockholm would make advances only to de Geer (the producer of Oreground iron), since other foundries were running at a loss. He wrote to Conway asking him to speak to Macky, the biggest importer in London, and in particular to consult those who contracted for Oreground iron.[116] The replies to his inquiries were neither consistent nor helpful. Macky denied flatly that any orders had been sent from England to refuse advances.[117] Sykes, on the other hand, justified their refusal on the ground of undue risk, and agreed with Finlay's exception in favor of de Geer. Conway for his part found Sykes's answer "judicious," and observed that it convinced him of "the miserable policy of the Sweeds, in the Burthens and Restrictions put on our Trade with them"; adding for good measure that increased trade with Britain would be worth far more to Sweden than "the Receipt of a paultry Subsidy."[118] There was not much comfort for the Caps in this; but Goodricke was prepared to make another attempt to help them: could not the British government ease the position by itself giving a contract to supply iron for the Navy? After all, he added, if the Hats could once persuade the nation that England was going to take *less* iron than in the years before 1765 they would have a damaging political weapon in their hands.[119] This was only too true: Osterman's agent in the Bergslag returned with a report that the animus there against the English was extreme: first they refused a subsidy, and now they stole Sweden's trade.[120] But Goodricke's appeal raised no echo in the Secretary's office, even when it was repeated;[121] and Weymouth remained equally mute when Goodricke urged him at any rate to make trial of 400 tons of the best Värmland iron belonging to "one of our most zealous Friends": the pro-French merchants, it appeared, refused to buy from a Cap producer.[122] But though his efforts thus proved vain, it is clear that Goodricke felt himself bound to exert himself to help his friends out of their difficulties. He realized the cogency of the Caps' arguments for revaluation; though he regretted the precipitate fixing of the exchange rate at 42, and was inclined to believe that if only the Senate would leave the exchange alone, the situation would stabilize itself of its own accord.[123] It was certainly his hope to be able sooner or later to obtain better terms of trade; but this was not his principal objective. Much more important to him was the survival of the Caps in power. He made this quite plain when at the end of 1767 he wrote to Conway, noting with satisfaction a modest increase in British exports to Sweden, and predicting that the trend would continue at an increased rate if only the Caps retained their places; for he then took care to add: "notwithstanding, this is *not* the principal motive of my wishes that we may be able to maintain the Ground we have gained here, but that I am convinced by M. Panin's whole conduct that it is necessary for completing our alliance with Russia."[124] For him, quite as much as for Osterman or Juel, politics took precedence over trade.

(v)

While Conway was reiterating his apologetic *non possumus*, while Weymouth maintained an indifferent silence, the position which Goodricke's efforts had secured was being steadily undermined. From two sides the assault upon it was preparing. On the one hand were the predictable party maneuvers of the Hats; on the other was the growing threat of a revolution which, if it were successful, would make a clean sweep of the Hats and Caps alike. The Hats were active in fomenting discontent in the provinces; their candidates won ominous victories in elections to the Stockholm magistracy.[125] By the middle of 1767 the Caps were losing control of the towns. The objective of the Hat leaders was sufficiently obvious: to force the summoning of an Extraordinary Diet, at the elections for which they might confidently hope to win a substantial majority. Goodricke early foresaw this eventuality if he were unable to conclude the Anglo-Swedish alliance. Bernstorff foresaw it too, and prudently warned Juel to take care to maintain the old friendly relations with Scheffer, Fersen, and other former friends of Denmark.[126] Early in 1768, in an attempt to avoid involvement in the coming *débâcle*, he pressed upon Juel the importance of creating a specifically Danish party in Sweden, which should be independent, financially and otherwise, of Osterman.[127]

The forces working for the overthrow of the Caps might be divided as to their ultimate objectives, but for the moment it suited them to work hand in hand. Each needed the assistance of the other in the immediate future; and it was with a view to cementing the alliance between them that the Hat leaders induced Choiseul, in the spring of 1767, to agree to pay off Adolf Fredrik's debts.[128] In return for this service Lovisa Ulrika, after celebrating the easing of her financial problems by buying new furniture, devoted a great part of the money received to financing the activities of Hat agents.[129] Choiseul's munificence was certainly not prompted by any desire to strengthen the Hats' political position, and still less to refurbish the salons of Drottningholm. Despite the discouragements he received from Breteuil, despite the warnings that no revolution which depended on the king and queen had any security of success, he stuck firmly to his opinion that the only rational policy for France in Sweden was to engineer a monarchical coup d'état. Not for a moment was he prepared to finance a Hat victory at the next elections as an objective in its own right. Such a victory would entail a resumption of the endless drain of money for parliamentary corruption; it was unlikely to be permanent; it might provoke armed intervention by Catherine, after the pattern of events in Poland; and, above all, it would not ensure that Sweden would be at France's disposal in the crisis in Europe which he was doing his best to foment. When in February 1767 the Hat leaders transmitted an appeal for support, Choiseul's answer was a crisp refusal. What Sweden needed, he considered (or at least, what France needed in Sweden), was a monarchy in full command of the armed forces, with the right of appointment to all offices, and with complete control of foreign policy: the Senate should be a purely advisory body; the Estates be restricted to the granting of taxes. It was a constitution which he oddly believed amounted to *monarchie à l'anglaise.*[130] For old times' sake, and upon the principle of *noblesse oblige*, he would not deny some assistance to the most deserving of France's former friends among the Hats;[131] but it was not to them that he now looked for the effecting of his designs. For the moment he appeared to be in no hurry, content to allow the situation to ripen of its own accord; to the state of Swedish politics he affected an indifference which was made the more credible by the fact that over eighteen months were allowed to elapse between Breteuil's departure and the arrival of his successor in Stockholm.[132] But despite this apparent neglect Choiseul never swerved from his purpose, and by the summer of 1767 there were signs that there might not be wanting an appropriate instrument to his hand.

On 24 January 1767, Crown Prince Gustav attained his majority; and from that moment a successor was available if his father should take it into his head to abdicate the throne. Even before then, the prince had begun to make his mark in politics, though his *début* was anything but happy. In November 1766 the Caps' *Ordinance for the Execution of the Laws*, having been accepted by the Estates, was due to receive the royal assent. That assent the king was determined to withhold, and Gustav seized the occasion to provide him with the text of a *dictamen ad protocollum* which, even after it had been considerably toned down, outraged Hats and Caps alike by the rhetorical violence of its language, and its bitter allusions to the humiliations inflicted upon the monarchy in 1756.[133] It was a tactical blunder; but it was also an omen. For the unlucky *démarche* of November was followed by other royal protests on better-chosen occasions and in less exceptionable terms. Such was Adolf Fredrik's *dictamen* against the alliance with England; such his protest against the Senate's violation of its own *Ordinance for the Liberty of Printing*, when it denied him the right to publish the text of his *dictamina*; such was his refusal to sign the disastrous Exchange Ordinance of September 1767, which pegged the exchange at 42; and such, above all, was his powerful demand for an Extraordinary Diet to deal with the economic situation, delivered at the height of the crisis in February 1768.[134] It is not clear that the crown prince was the author of any of these; but it is unlikely that he did not have some hand in them, and virtually certain that his influence stiffened his father's resolution. Certainly the effectiveness of these *dictamina* was immensely increased by the fact that they were usually read on the king's behalf by his son, whose brilliant histrionic gifts ensured that they should be delivered with the maximum incisiveness and dramatic effect. For from 10 March 1767 Gustav, with his father's permission, began a regular attendance at the meetings of the Senate, even in the king's absence. He listened to the proceedings in silence; attentive, watchful, recording his impressions in brief cynical entries in the journal which he began to keep about this time, and relieving the worst of the tedium by adorning its margins with superb doodles of rustic scenes, classical pediments, and votive altars.[135] But if any Senator, catching a glimpse of these innocent diversions, was inclined to dismiss him as a dilettante, he mistook the man with whom he had to do. For in Prince Gustav, as they were soon to learn, not the Cap régime only, but the whole system of government as it had existed since 1720, was to find its most dangerous opponent, and ultimately its master.

The significance of Gustav's emergence as a political force was not lost upon Choiseul. On 28 October 1767 Creutz, the Swedish ambassador in Paris, wrote a private letter to the prince in which he initiated him into Choiseul's desire for a revolution.[136] No news could have been more welcome. By March 1768 Gustav had drawn up the first of many projects for a coup d'état, to be effected by the arrest of the Senate without waiting for an Extraordinary Diet.[137] In May du Prat, the French chargé d'affaires, for the first time let the king and queen into the secret of Choiseul's intentions;[138] at the end of June Gustav enthusiastically accepted a draft plan of action drawn by Choiseul;[139] and by the autumn of 1768 it was generally taken for granted, in Paris and at Drottningholm, that he must be the leader in any attack on the Senate. In September 1768 he undertook a long tour through the mining districts of central Sweden: nominally to improve his knowledge of the country he would one day rule, actually with a view to courting popularity with the *bergsmän* and small forge owners, and to collecting evidence of prevailing hardship which might serve as ammunition against the government.[140] In both respects the tour more than answered expectations; and in November Adolf Fredrik was able to present, to a Senate which received them with indifference, numerous petitions from the distressed mining community.

Though Gustav was undoubtedly shocked by the misery which he observed in the Bergslag, it was not the sufferings of the people, or the economic crisis of the country, which was the main consideration behind his determination to proceed to violence. In 1767 and 1768 Catherine II, in contradiction to Panin's original intention, was drawn into open intervention in Poland upon the pretext of securing toleration for the Dissidents; and the high-handed proceedings of Prince Repnin in Warsaw soon produced a situation which threatened the peace of eastern Europe. Frederick the Great, having vetoed a reasonable compromise on the Dissident question and left Russia to bear the odium of intransigence, was now deeply concerned lest his alliance with Catherine might involve him in these broils. Assuming for once the unwonted role of Satan rebuking sin, he complained loudly that Russia's actions were illegal.[141] This they certainly were; and a climax of outrage was reached when Repnin arranged for the kidnapping of the bishops of Kraków and Kiev, and their removal to Russia. It was these events, more than anything else, which convinced Gustav that a revolution in Sweden was essential. He saw in the fate of Poland a warning of what might be in store for Sweden if the political ascendancy of Russia and England were suffered to continue. Sooner or later, Russian corruption would be backed by threats, threats be made good by force, and Sweden would become, what Poland was becoming, a Russia satrapy.[142] He listened with disgust to the Senate's protracted discussions as to how best they could avoid any meaningful endorsement of Catherine's Polish policy.[143] He had no faith in the possibility of restoring health to Sweden's parliamentary system, no belief in the patriotism of her corrupted politicians: the only hope of salvation, he came to believe, lay in a strong popular monarchy—not, indeed, that constitution based on the separation of powers which was the ideal of physiocrats such as C. F. Scheffer; but rather the "legal despotism" of Mercier de la Rivière, whose book *L'Ordre naturel et essentiel des Sociétés* (London 1767) he read with enthusiasm.[144] He knew that salvation could not come from his easy-going, vacillating father, and still less from his mother, whom no one trusted, and who (ironically enough) was now only half-heartedly in favor of revolution. For Lovisa Ulrika could not forget the fearful crisis of 1756: she would not willingly run that risk again. She had lost hope of ever attaining the kind of monarchy at which she had aimed a decade earlier, and would have been willing to settle for some moderate increase in the prerogative of the type which had formed one of the bases of the Composition. An absolutist régime in which she might one day be her son's subject had increasingly little appeal to her. And so, while Gustav was setting his hopes on a coup d'état, she fell back on the old expedient which had been tried, and had failed, so often in the past: she would get what she wanted by a bargain with the leaders of one party or the other. In 1767 her policy was collaboration with the Hats, and in pursuit of it (if Schack's and Goodricke's reports are to be believed) she even went so far as to effect a reconciliation with Pechlin, one of the terms of which was that he promised to restore to the monarchy all the prerogatives of which it had been stripped in 1756.[145] If Pechlin indeed gave such a promise he never meant to keep it; and if Lovisa Ulrika believed him, she was egregiously deceived. Moreover, the reliance upon the Hats did not prevent her from exploring, with typical inconsequence, the prospect of coming to some sort of arrangement with the Caps also: in the autumn of 1768 it would require all the firmness and tact of Gustav and the French minister to wean her from that idea.[146]

As Gustav clearly saw, most of the leading politicians in either party would enter into agreements with the Court only as a matter of expediency and would keep them only as long as it suited themselves. This was certainly true of Fersen, who was the ablest politician of them all. Now, and to the end of his long career, Fersen was a believer in "liberty," as the Swedes of the eighteenth century understood that term. The fear of absolutism had sunk deep into his mind; a belief in the virtues of parliamentary government, with authority in the hands of the Estates, was a faith to which he clung tenaciously. When, therefore, he was sounded about his attitude to a possible revolution—delicately by Gustav in November 1767, more explicitly in March 1768, until in August du Prat gave him a full exposition of the plan which was proposed—he consistently refused to give the idea his countenance.[147] Any changes must come by parliamentary means; anything approaching an absolutism would have no hope of endorsement by the Estates. Fersen's stubborn refusal to depart from legality represented a serious obstacle; for he was the commander of the Lifeguards, and if the coup were to be carried out by military force his acquiescence, if not his collaboration, seemed to be essential.

Thus in 1768 opposition to the rule of the Caps was split into three distinct elements, and it was difficult to see how any common ground between them could be found. On the one hand Fersen, seeking primarily a Hat victory, and determined to stick to constitutional procedures; on the other Choiseul's plan for a revolution, of which Gustav was now a convinced adherent; in between, the queen, hoping by playing off one party against the other to gain for the monarchy advantages which were never very clearly defined. But though Fersen might remain intransigent, and though the Cap leaders' essential object was to save their political skins, the idea of constitutional change—in the last resort, by revolution, if other means failed—was beginning to make converts in both parties. On the Cap side, for instance, there was the disillusioned Daniel Tilas; on the Hat side, men like Hermansson, Stockenström, Ekeblad, and Hiärne, the last surviving Hat member of the Senate; to say nothing of C. F. Scheffer, who had been advocating reform since 1764, and was now closely linked to the crown prince. All of these would have preferred reform to violence; but some of them, at least, were prepared to contemplate the possibility of violence—if only they could be sure that it would succeed.

Against this shifting background of projects and plots, Hat cabals at Medevi or Åkerö, conspiratorial royalist meetings at Drottningholm, the ministers of Russia, Denmark, and England had to steer their course according to such lights as reached them through their agents, and the more reliable information obtained through Hanoverian intercepts of French dispatches. It is clear that by the summer of 1767 the unyielding attitude of the British government on the question of subsidies, and the increasing improbability that the Caps would be able to rescue themselves by concluding an English alliance, had relegated Goodricke to a subordinate role in the councils of those foreign ministers upon whom the Caps placed their reliance. Despite Bernstorff's desire to establish a separate Danish party in

Sweden, Juel and Osterman maintained the closest collaboration, concerting measures in advance against possible emergencies, framing joint declarations for use at need, and even sharing, in some degree, the expenses of their operations.[148] There were moments, indeed, when Juel appears almost as the senior partner, certainly as the man with the stronger nerve. But is is striking that from these joint activities Goodricke now appears usually to be excluded: a very different situation from that which had obtained in 1765. With little or no money at his command, without a policy to offer, or even an expedient which might do duty for a policy, with his personal prestige shaken by the visit of Macartney and the intrigues of Ribbing and Horn, Goodricke was indeed for the moment in a somewhat forlorn position. Nevertheless, as Juel observed, he was necessary; necessary, because so much depended upon the information supplied by British intelligence; necessary, because he offered the best defense against the accusation that the Caps had sold themselves to Russia; necessary, because the adhesion of Great Britain gave weight to any common resistance to a coup d'état.

In the summer of 1766 the British government had for the first time made the preservation of the Swedish constitution a part of its policy. It had pledged itself to collaborate in measures to resist any attempt to overthrow the established order: "our success in that Point [Conway wrote] promises to be the most effectual Impediment to the Views entertained of overturning all that has been done, by the future Imposition of the royal authority."[149] Once allow the monarchy unfettered control of Sweden's foreign policy, and that policy would be French. So far the situation was clear. What was not clear was the line to take if violent or dubiously constitutional means were used, not to establish an absolutism (or something near it) but merely to bring about the fall of the Cap régime: for instance, by forcing the summons of a Extraordinary Diet. That situation arose in November 1766, when Adolf Fredrik's *dictamen*, and his refusal to sign the *Ordinance for the better Execution of the Laws*, provoked a rumor that he intended to enforce his will by a threat of abdication.[150] For if the king were to abdicate, the summoning of a new Diet must necessarily follow. Neither Goodricke nor Schack took the rumor too seriously; for indeed an abdication while the crown prince was still a minor might have defeated its purpose. But Osterman pressed the British and Danish governments to participate in a minatory declaration, if the king should carry his supposed intention into effect.[151] Conway's response to this application was an unhesitating agreement: henceforward Goodricke was forearmed with authority to join with his colleagues if such a threat were made again.[152] And it appeared likely to be made again. The king's *dictamen* of 9 February 1768—concerted, this time, with the Hat leaders, and at their instigation[153]—was feared to be the preliminary to another attempt at constitutional blackmail of this kind. Juel thought so; Osterman even feared a rising; and together they concocted a declaration, to be delivered if the Senate were forced to concede an Extraordinary Diet.[154] In these circumstances Goodricke felt the need for further instructions. He was already authorized to collaborate with his colleagues against any attempt to change the constitution; he was authorized likewise to join in a declaration against an abdication. But what was he to do if, even without an abdication, the pressure for an Extraordinary Diet proved effective? Was he at liberty to join Osterman and Juel in their declaration?[155] This was a highly pertinent inquiry; and it certainly required an answer. But since Weymouth now sat in Conway's seat, no answer to this—or indeed to any other—question was ever vouchsafed to him. It was an omission which was to have serious consequences ten months later.

There is no doubt that the British government was quite well informed about the progress of Choiseul's plans for a revolution. In September, November, and December 1766, in May and October 1767, Conway confirmed his earlier intelligence.[156] He was not unduly disturbed by it. He was well aware of Choiseul's unwillingness to lay out money simply to secure a Hat majority at the next Diet, and of his doubts whether the king and queen were to be trusted to carry out a coup d'état. In April 1767 he rightly judged that France would be "rather a spectator than an actor in the present scene."[157] His attitude to the prospective danger was therefore one of plaintive deprecation: "it were much to be wished," he wrote, "that the King of Sweden, and the French Party, were not so obstinate in their Project of changing the Constitution."[158] But if he underrated the dangers of the situation, it was mainly because he failed to perceive the implication of the emergence of Prince Gustav as the revolution's destined leader. Those implications did not wholly escape Goodricke's notice, and some of them were fairly conveyed in his dispatches; but till the very eve of the *débâcle* of December 1768 he was to some extent blinded by his fixed idea that the real mover behind any attempt at revolution, in the future as in the past, would be Lovisa Ulrika. The replacement of Conway by Weymouth, however, brought with it a disastrous change for the worse in regard to the flow of intelligence. There is no reason to suppose that by some unfortunate coincidence Weymouth's tenure of the seals was accompanied by the sudden cessation of the Hanoverian intercepts: what happened seems rather to be that Weymouth did not trouble to read them; or if he did, was culpably negligent in passing on the information they contained. During the whole of his period of office as Secretary of State there was a complete stoppage of the secret information which Conway had regularly forwarded to Stockholm. Goodricke was left wholly in the dark about the debate between Choiseul, the Court, and the Hats, at the very time when that debate was moving to a conclusion. And so it fell out that when the crisis broke in December Goodricke found himself thrown upon his own resources, without guidance, without instructions, and without money. No doubt it is true that Weymouth's attention was much engaged by the Middlesex election and the Massacre of St. George's Fields. No doubt his mind was fully exercised in devising arguments against resisting French aggression in Corsica. But it might have been supposed that he could find a little time to pay attention to a situation which was of central importance to the whole strategy of British foreign policy.

By the autumn of 1768 the crisis in Stockholm was approaching more rapidly than Conway had foreseen. The struggle between the Russian troops in Poland and the Confederates of Bar was threatening to involve all eastern Europe. Though French aid to the Confederates was unofficial and ineffective, the nature of the conflict was such that a violation of the Turkish frontier by Russian forces became an increasingly likely possibility: it duly occurred when some of their units crossed the border and burnt the Turkish town of Balta. For some years now Choiseul had been working to incite the Turks to declare war on Russia, and the failure of Vergennes, his minister in Constantinople, to bring about this result had already determined him to send him his recall.[159] But now the prospects began to look more hopeful. In these circumstances it became a matter of increasing urgency for Choiseul to engineer a revolution in Stockholm which by placing control of foreign policy in the king's hands would make it possible for France to impel a Swedish attack on Catherine's northern flank in the event of her involvement in a Turkish war. In June, and again in August, he was writing that the right moment for revolution must be the end of 1768, while Russia's forces were still deeply engaged in Poland;[160] and in October he instructed his new minister to Stockholm, the count de Modène, to try to time a coup d'état to coincide with the Turkish declaration of war which he now confidently hoped for.[161] Prince Gustav, with his gaze fixed constantly on the chaos in Poland, needed no convincing; and Choiseul's arguments appealed with equal force to C. F. Scheffer, who to du Prat urged the additional considerations that Kristian VII of Denmark was wasting his time and depleting his resources by visits to England and France, and that British ministers were far too preoccupied with American problems to be in a position to make trouble.[162]

Goodricke, though he knew nothing of these things, saw very clearly the possible implications of a Turkish war. Whereas he had earlier feared that the Senate might be driven to accept an Extraordinary Diet as a consequence of the economic crisis, by September, under the impression caused by Swedish diplomatic reports from Constantinople, he had come to fear it as a probable result of the outbreak of hostilities on the Russo-Turkish frontier.[163] Sweden had a long-standing defensive alliance with the Turks; and he had no doubt that the Hats would invoke it, as it had been invoked in 1739.[164] The situation had indeed altered since then, for the Swedish-Russian alliance of 1745, renewed for twelve years in 1758, barred any Turkish claim to assistance, since it provided that all engagements contrary to it were null and void.[165] On the whole he did not believe that the Hats really desired another war with Russia; but he did believe that they would urge the international crisis as an irresistible argument for calling the Estates together.

It was with these considerations in mind, and in a last desperate effort to stiffen the Senate to resist such a demand, that on 25 October he decided on his own responsiblity to try to reanimate the negotiations for an Anglo-Swedish alliance.[166] No reply had ever been received from London to the Swedish draft; the expedients he had proposed to Conway had found no favor; he had no new instructions authorizing him to proceed in the matter (despite his assurance to the contrary to Juel),[167] and no expectation of receiving any from Weymouth. But the new French minister, Modène, was expected at any moment, and if anything were to be achieved it must be done before his arrival. In his dispatches he took care to represent the initiative as coming from the Swedish side; but in fact it is clear that it was his own idea.

In the first fortnight of November, then, the sluggish stream of Swedish politics emerged from its backwater, quickened to a freshet, and in the course of the next six weeks mounted to a torrent. On 1 November Goodricke formally opened conversations with Friesendorff.[168] Though Juel thought that he could not have chosen a better moment,[169] the prospects can scarcely have seemed very hopeful. In effect he had nothing new to offer. All he could do was to suggest that the Swedes themselves should propose a suitable alternative to a subsidy; but he was sanguine enough to believe that this might be sufficient to put a temporary spoke in Modène's wheel, and for the moment serve as a bar to an Extraordinary Diet. Lord Rochford, who fortunately had succeeded Weymouth as Northern Secretary on 21 October, seemed to think so too: Goodricke's démarche was commended as "extremely judicious."[170] On 8 November Modène at last arrived. He was not the man the Court had hoped for: Choiseul had originally promised a much bigger gun, in the person of Saint-Priest; but Saint-Priest had been diverted to Constantinople, and the Court had to put up with a minor diplomat whose personal qualities did not endear him to France's friends in Sweden. However, not a moment was lost in initiating him into the business he had been sent to Sweden to do; on the very night of his arrival he was whisked off to Drottningholm and closeted with the queen and Prince Gustav in secret conclave until the small hours of the morning.[171] A week later came the great news which was to transform the situation: the news of the Turkish declaration of war. The Caps received it with consternation; the Court was jubilant: Lovisa Ulrika privately toasted the sultan, and at the next court ball all the women appeared attired as sultanas.[172] Choiseul, of course, was triumphant. In a dispatch to Modène of 4 December he emphasized once again that this was the moment to act; though (a significant anticlimax) he warned him that France could aid Sweden only with money, and not too much of that; he hoped that the expenses for 1769 could be kept down to a million livres. This financial restriction, whether Choiseul realized it or not, compromised the plan of revolution which he would have preferred; for if that revolution came by a coup d'état while the Diet was not sitting Sweden would need massive financial aid in order to put her armed forces in sufficiently good shape to resist armed intervention by Russia. Prince Gustav realized this very well.[173]

The news of the Turkish war, in fact, so far from making the way plain for revolution, brought to a point the divisions between those who might be expected, in greater or less degree, to support it. The nearer the moment of decision, the less agreement among those who approached it. Prince Gustav, with Senator Hiärne, was firmly for a military coup based on the artillery regiments in Stockholm, which were conveniently commanded by Hiärne's relatives, the Ehrensvärd brothers. Lovisa Ulrika hankered for a less hazardous solution, and talked of persuading some Cap Senators to settle for a moderate increase in the prerogative. C. F. Scheffer, Hermansson, and Stockenström, who had originally advocated a coup d'état, allowed themselves to be persuaded by Fersen that the characters of the king and queen must ensure the failure of any such attempt.[174] They were now prepared to contemplate it only as a last resort, if an attempt to force an Extraordinary Diet should fail. The unhappy Modène, sent to Sweden to make a revolution, found himself buffeted by irreconcilable plans for a constitution; from Gustav's side, "legal despotism" *à la* Mercier de la Rivière; from the Hat leaders, a physiocratic separation of powers. Between these conflicting policies he found it increasingly difficult to stick to his orders; and as his resolution weakened those orders grew to seem increasingly impracticable. On 20 November C. F. Scheffer—who only a month earlier had been fixing the day of action as 2 November—together with Hermansson and Stockenström, offered some sort of amends for their change of front by giving Modène a written guarantee that at the next Diet they would carry measures restoring the power of the crown to something like what it had been before 1756.[175] Behind their vacillation, as behind the erosion of Modène's resolution, there undoubtedly lay the determination of Fersen to avoid a coup whose consequences would threaten all his principles. In the face of that determination Gustav himself was at last forced to compromise. Soon after 23 November he abandoned—from necessity, not from conviction—his plan for legal despotism, and drew up the draft of a constitution based upon the division of powers, albeit with a greatly strengthened monarchy: the king should have the right of dissolution, the control of foreign policy would be in his hands, the Senate would be a cabinet responsible both to the Diet and to the crown, and the king would have the power of making ordinances.[176] In exchange, the Hat leaders, including (surprisingly) Fersen, committed themselves to a revolution if the Senate should not have agreed to an Extraordinary Diet by 31 December.[177] But they took immediate steps to avoid having to make good their pledge. The plan they now concerted (which was probably drafted by Scheffer) recurred to the tactic of a threatened abdication. This time the threat was in real earnest. Adolf Fredrik was to make a last demand that the Diet be summoned; and if that demand were refused, was to decline to discharge his royal functions until the Diet had been agreed to. On 9 December the king, queen, and the leading Hats, including Fersen, approved this program. On the following day Scheffer, Hermansson, and Stockenström, joined this time by Senator Hiärne, gave another written promise which went much further than that which they had given earlier: they pledged themselves that the whole executive power should be vested in the crown, and that the Estates should be left only with the power of legislation and taxation.[178] This was, in effect, to accept Gustav's draft constitution; and if it had been carried out it would have fundamentally altered the structure of Swedish politics. But it was a pledge extorted by fear—fear of the counterattack which the Senate was already preparing; and the sequel would show that once victory had been won a Hat-dominated Diet could not be relied upon to make it good.

Of all these tangled debates and nocturnal meetings the foreign ministers had only the vaguest of inklings. They noted, indeed, that the Hats were engaging in vigorous political activity of a kind which strongly suggested that they expected a Diet in the near future;[179] but of Scheffer's plan, of the possibility of abdication, and still less of the possibility of a military coup d'état, they seem to have had no notion. Never had the lack of information from the British intelligence service been more prejudicial to their measures. When Osterman, nervous as usual,[180] proposed that the only way to prevent a Diet (and consequent aid to the Turks) was to devise a joint declaration from the three crowns intimating that they expected that Sweden would remain neutral, Juel and Goodricke concurred in advising that the situation was not yet sufficiently serious to warrant such a step.[181] As to the Cap Senate, they were so free from anxiety for the future that they permitted themselves to take measures which, more than any other single factor, united their enemies in a common program, and thus ensured their own overthrow.

To these measures they were driven by the peculiarities of that constitution which they were now so anxious to defend. It was one of the fundamentals of Swedish liberty that office was a property of which a man might be deprived only if he were found guilty of some misdemeanor.[182] The effect of this principle was that the civil service, local and central, was protected against displacement on purely political grounds. It was entrenched in office; its members in the higher echelons regularly attended meetings of the Diet, where they could and did attack with impunity the measures of their official chiefs. For a whole generation the Hats had been in power, and they had systematically appointed their supporters to offices as they had become vacant. The result was that the civil service was overwhelmingly Hat, and a Cap Senate could do nothing about it if it saw, or believed that it saw, its policies opposed, its measures sabotaged, by civil servants who were its political enemies. Herein lies the basic reason for the fierce antagonism which developed between them in the years 1767 and 1768. But that antagonism was undoubtedly exacerbated by the Senate's desperate determination to carry through its policies, and its increasing indignation when it saw those policies publicly criticized and repudiated by the departments whose business it should have been to carry them out. The provocation was certainly great; but the Senate's response to it was harsh and imprudent. Their anger was concentrated above all on the Exchequer and the College of Mines, both of which took occasion in their reports to paint a black picture of the state of the economy, and implicitly or explicitly to blame it upon the Senate's measures. In April 1768 the Senate was goaded into addressing to the Exchequer a thundering rebuke which charged it collectively with mendacity, partiality, and "a presumptuous and indecent departure from the respectful submission which is at all times due to Us as your superiors"; and went on to inform them that the chancellor of justice had been instructed to institute proceedings against its members. However, having thus relieved its feelings the Senate allowed cooler counsels to prevail, and for the moment nothing further was done in the matter. Encouraged perhaps by this respite the Exchequer College at the end of November compounded its offense by addressing to the Senate another devastating commentary on the economic situation, coupled with a strong protest against the charges which had been leveled against it. At the same time the College of Mines delivered a similar protest against the censures of its conduct which had been voiced in the Senate a few months earlier. Both colleges, moreover, took care to print and disseminate their protests.[183] In the face of this public defiance the Senate clearly felt that it had no option but to assert its authority by making good its threat of legal proceedings. At its meeting on 8 December it decided, by a majority, to prosecute the Exchequer College before a specially constituted branch of the Supreme Court, composed of members handpicked for the purpose; and to entrust the prosecution, not to the proper officer, the chancellor of justice (who unfortunately happened to be that prominent Hat, Stockenström), but to the auditor-general. These measures were of highly questionable legality. The Senate had allowed itself to be hurried into setting up an extraordinary tribunal, in defiance of the resolution of the Diet of 1762, and in flagrant contradiction of the denunciations of such tribunals which they had themselves consistently uttered when in opposition.

It was this decision which precipitated their downfall. For if once such a prosecution were launched there was no knowing into what sort of a political witch-hunt it might not degenerate: they had themselves had bitter experience of the danger in the 1750s. The Hat domination of the civil service was now threatened; their household troops were menaced with proscription.[184] It was a challenge impossible to ignore: on this issue the Hats must fight. From motives of sheer self-preservation they must swallow their differences with the

Court, and trust to the chapter of accidents to extricate them from the constitutional consequences. The effects were immediate: on the following day the leaders of the party met in conclave, composed their differences, and accepted Scheffer's plan for blackmailing the Senate into surrender by the threat of a temporary abdication. Hence the far-reaching written promises given to the Court by Scheffer and his associates on 10 December. The crown prince, with his passion for the French drama, might well have commented, "Tu l'as voulu, Georges Dandin."

All unconscious of the impending danger, the Senate met for business on Monday, 12 December; and the opening moves gave them no great cause for uneasiness. Adolf Fredrik, by the mouth of the crown prince, delivered a weighty protest against the extraordinary tribunal; but the Senate had grown used to the king's protests, and shrugged off this one as it had shrugged off its predecessors. But thereafter events took an unexpected turn. The king caused all officials from the neighboring offices of government to be called into the Senate chamber, and in their presence formally demanded the summoning of an Extraordinary Diet. At that point the crown prince (who was reading the *dictamen*) paused; paused just long enough to tempt Friesendorff to get on his legs to reply. But Gustav was a master of timing; and before Friesendorff had uttered a word he proceeded to deliver the *coup de grâce*. The Senate was informed that until they had agreed to summon a Diet the king would cease to exercise his functions; in the interim he formally forbade the use of his name; and he gave them until Thursday morning to make up their minds whether to submit to his demand.[185]

The surprise was complete; the consternation general.[186] A majority of the Senate was at first for resisting: they argued that abdication was irreconcilable with the constitution; that as the name-stamp could be used to supply the absence of the king's signature, so it could be used wholesale in the absence of the king's person. The possession of the name-stamp was indeed vital to their position; and it was only Friesendorff's quick thinking which forestalled an attempt by Prince Gustav to induce the Chancery to hand it over. The Senate was in fact inclined to stand and fight; or at least to try to call the king's bluff. But when Adolf Fredrik returned to them on the Thursday morning, once again with his son at his elbow to stiffen his nerve, they found it was no bluff. In face of their intransigence the king carried out his threat. Until an Extraordinary Diet was summoned he would suspend the exercise of his royal functions. Alarmed at last, the Senators gathered round him, imploring him to think better of it.

But Gustav whisked him away before he could change his mind, and the Senate was left to contemplate the prospect before them. They did not much relish it. In the course of the afternoon news came in that Gustav was making the round of the Collegia, informing each of them of the king's action, and ordering them in the king's name to take no action without Adolf Fredrik's express command. It seemed that the abdication was no abdication after all: the king was king still—inactive, for the time being, certainly—but giving orders, and expecting that they should be obeyed. By the end of the afternoon the Senate had changed its mind, and by a majority—Ribbing, Kalling, and de Geer alone dissenting—they agreed to inform him that "there was a disposition" to consent to the summoning of a Diet. The crisis seemed over.

But it happened that on that same evening Osterman was giving an official dinner to welcome Modène, and to that dinner the other foreign ministers, the Senate, and also the Hat leaders were invited. Since half of the company was deeply depressed, and the other half as jubilant as good manners would permit, general conversation must have been difficult. Juel took the bull by the horns, and bluntly asked Fersen whether they were now to expect an absolutism.[187] Though the reply was smoothly reassuring, neither he, nor Goodricke, nor Osterman, was prepared to acquiesce in the situation without making an attempt to alter it; and when social obligations had been discharged, the three got down to the business of trying to stiffen the Senate's failing morale. Their exhortations proved effective: by Friday the sixteenth the Senate had recovered its nerve. They would call the king's bluff, and rule with the name-stamp until the next ordinary Diet in October 1770.

This bold resolution ignored one vital factor in the situation: the attitude of the civil service, of those officials whose perquisites they had cut off, whom their measures had driven into bankruptcy, and who were now threatened with quasijudicial proscription. By this time Prince Gustav had completed his tour of the central offices of government, and on the seventeenth the fruits of his activity began to appear. On the morning of that day the Exchequer, the War Office, the Audit Office, and the College of Mines held a joint meeting, of which the upshot was that they refused to recognize the Senate's authority to issue orders. Their example was followed by the Chancery; and on the nineteenth by the Estimates Office, which declined to pay the troops which had been ordered up to preserve the peace of the capital: their officers informed the Senate that they could no longer count on the obedience of the men under their command.

This was the decisive blow; though it was reinforced by the adhesion of the College of Commerce and the Supreme Court to the decision of their colleagues in other offices. The Senate was faced by a general strike of the higher civil service; and in the face of it they could not go on. On 20 December they formally capitulated, and submitted the summons of a new Diet to Adolf Fredrik for his signature; whereupon he graciously consented to resume his constitutional duties. The "Inactivity" was over. The Caps had staked everything on standing fast, and they had lost: lost not merely on the particular issue, but lost also, if the omens spoke true, the election for which both sides now feverishly began to prepare.[188]

The events of the week 12-19 December took Goodricke and his colleagues completely by surprise. They had neither money nor adequate instructions with which to meet the crisis. Against a direct attack on the constitution they were authorized by their governments to concert a joint declaration; against an abdication they were similarly furnished; but both Goodricke and Juel rightly drew a distinction between abdication and "inactivity," and Goodricke, at least, had never received an answer to his inquiry as to how far he might go in resisting an Extraordinary Diet.[189] Well might he write to Rochford that "a Minister has much difficulty to act without instructions where things are come to that Point, that he is not sure, if the Government will subsist in its present state a month longer."[190] Behind the actions of the king he still saw the hand of Lovisa Ulrika; and he was not optimistic about the Hats' ability when in office to preserve the constitution: its fate, he considered, would lie not in their hands but in those of Choiseul, since it was Choiseul who paid them.[191] He was disillusioned by the early collapse of the morale of some of the Cap leaders on whom he had placed his reliance, and especially Friesendorff and Düben (who prudently took to his bed when the crisis began); but his final judgment (in which Juel concurred) was that the Senate had capitulated mainly because they feared they could not rely upon the troops, and had been persuaded of the danger of popular disturbances.[192]

Whatever the explanation, the success of the Court and the Hats in December 1768 was a heavy defeat for England and for Russia. On the day when the Senate surrendered, Juel came to the conclusion that the attack upon it was essentially anti-English and anti-Russian in character, and that it did not imply a threat to the constitution—a verdict which proved correct in the long run, but which was certainly dubious at the time he delivered it.[193] As to Panin, he had no doubt about the implications of what had happened. France's object, he wrote, was to embroil Sweden with Russia, and having thus created turmoil in eastern Europe (from which Choiseul would take good care to keep aloof), to turn, with Spanish assistance, against England.[194] Osterman, for his part, had for some time feared that a Turkish demand for assistance would coincide with a French offer to pay outstanding arrears and provide a new subsidy.[195] If these appreciations were correct, they reinforced the conclusion that in Stockholm, above all other places, England's and Russia's interests went hand in hand. Lord Rochford would be quicker than some of his predecessors to learn that lesson. Goodricke with his wonted resilience would apply it. And as a result most of the ground lost in 1768 would in fact be recovered. The means by which that result was to be achieved were as yet obscure, and nowhere more so than in Whitehall. But it would not take long to perceive that though the Cap surrender was certainly a defeat for England and Russia, it was equally certainly no victory for France. Choiseul had set his hope on a revolution; but no revolution had been vouchsafed to him. He reckoned on a Swedish declaration of war on Russia; but his calculation proved erroneous. The crown prince, after all, had been forced to settle for a second best. Before the year was out he was to realize only too well that the Hats were either unable or unwilling to make good the promises which had induced him to compromise. As Goodricke and Osterman and Juel girded themselves for the coming struggle, the supporters of the Court celebrated their victory; but the event would prove that the resources of the defenders of the constitutional status quo were far from being exhausted. At Christmas 1768 the Court might enjoy its brief illusory moment of triumph; but it would be in a very different spirit that it would confront the Christmas of 1769.

CHAPTER IX

Lord Rochford and the Hat Diet, 1769–1770

(i)

It was in no festive spirit that Goodricke greeted the end of the old year and the opening of the new. In four months the Extraordinary Diet was due to meet in Norrköping; and four months was far too little to give time for the upturn in the economy, already perceptible, to have its effect upon the elections. Without some such recovery, the outlook was undeniably bleak. It was indeed possible to hope that the alliance of Court and Hats which had made possible the success of the Inactivity would break down, once its immediate object had been attained; but the decisive part played by Fersen during the crisis of December had shaken Goodricke's belief that when it came to the fundamental issue of the preservation of "liberty" Fersen could be relied upon to be staunch to the constitution.[1] Though he did not know it, events in January seemed to show that he was right: by the middle of that month, Court and Hats had reached agreement on a plan for constitutional reform which, though it fell short of what Choiseul would have desired, was not too far from the model which Prince Gustav had propounded a few weeks earlier.[2] How far that agreement would hold, how practicable such a reform would prove, once the *riksdag* was assembled—that was, indeed, another question: as with the ill-fated Composition of 1763, it was an agreement reached by party leaders; it could not count on the support of the Hat rank and file; and even between the leaders it was (at least for some of them) no more than a tactical move: experience would very soon prove that for Pechlin, for instance, and also for Fersen himself, it did not represent their real convictions. On the royalist side, Sinclair privately expressed a cynical skepticism.[3] The old mistrust was too deep to be so easily conjured away. And even if the temporary alliance had been as solid as it seemed to be, it did not follow that the consequences which Osterman and Juel apprehended would necessarily ensue: it was one of the basic miscalculations of Russian and Danish policy to suppose that constitutional reform must necessarily entail subservience to France, and the disturbance of the Tranquillity of the North. The British government would begin to grasp this point before many months had passed. Frederick the Great, more realist than any of them, had grasped it already.

Dark though the prospects might seem to be, nothing was to be gained by treating them as hopeless; and Goodricke was not the man to give way to despair. The Senate, it soon became clear, was in no mood for surrender: though some members might for a moment be tempted to put out feelers to the opposition tending to a bargain which would guarantee them a painless retirement, these failures of nerve were transient and untypical. In general their attitude was defiant, their rule more resolute than ever, their clashes with the king sharp and frequent. They did not hesitate to decide disputed elections in their own favor. They were unflinching in their determination to hold the Diet in Norrköping.[4] Until the very moment of the Diet's meeting they acted as became a body in whom was vested *ad interim* the authority which would presently revert to the Estates; nor did they show much sign that they feared the day of reckoning which would come when the Estates resumed it.

No time was lost in organizing the election campaign: their opponents had the start of them, and great efforts would be needed to compensate that disadvantage. It was, indeed, a campaign of unexampled bitterness: Daniel Tilas thought that there had been nothing to compare with it for violence and animosity since the time of King Sigismund.[5] The Caps' Ordinance for the Liberty of Printing had unshackled the press, and both sides took full advantage of the new situation. The Senate on the one hand, the Court on the other, appealed to the electorate with selective and tendentious accounts of the events which had produced the Inactivity; and Esbjörn Reuterholm's *An Explanation to the Swedish Nation*[6] put the Caps' case with a sardonic eloquence and logical cogency which might have been decisive, if the electorate had been accessible to reasoned argument. In this pamphleteering warfare Goodricke, with his command of Swedish, took not only a lively interest but an active part: a pamphlet written to his order, rebutting the Hat argument that Sweden ought to ally with distant powers rather than with her neighbors, sold 2,000 copies in twenty-four hours;[7] and Robert Finlay believed that Goodricke himself was the author of an attack upon him in some unspecified English Gazette.[8] It is not unlikely that he was right. Finlay had been saved from the Caps' vengeance in 1765 by Goodricke's intervention. He had requited that service by consistent opposition to the Caps' economic policy; and he now gave (or was thought to give) powerful financial support to the Hats' electioneering.[9] He might protest to Stakhiev that his motives were purely commercial; that he opposed the Caps because he believed their policies to be disastrous; but to Goodricke he seemed a monster of ingratitude, deaf to the call of patriotism. The British government was therefore urged to bring pressure to bear on iron importers to place no orders with Finlay, and in general to defer any further purchases of Swedish iron until the autumn; and Goodricke wrote to Lord Cathcart in St. Petersburg asking him to investigate the chances of organizing a supply of acceptable bar-iron from Russia.[10] The point seems to have been well taken: in September Juel was reporting that English houses who bought iron through Swedish commission agents had told them to defer settlement until the iron was actually loaded on shipboard, which meant that the forge owners lost six months' interest.[11] As to Finlay, his correspondents in London were already protesting his bills in March, and he was forced to sell some of his forges for a million copper daler (about £20,000) to bolster up his credit.[12] From this time onwards Goodricke hounded Finlay to the bankruptcy and ruin which in 1772 at last satisfied his desire for revenge. As to the general effect of these economic sanctions, Goodricke may have been right when he wrote that they would offset all the bribes and subsidies that Choiseul could offer; but the elections came too early for this strategy to have time to make much effect.

The most powerful weapon, in this election as in its predecessors, was not the press, nor commercial sanctions, but the well-tried expedient of bribery and corruption. It was foreseen that the violence of party feeling, and the obviously labile state of the electorate, would make this an unprecedentedly costly contest; and the event justified the expectation. In 1765 Goodricke and Osterman had been able to capture all ten Stockholm seats for a mere £500;[13] but there was no hope of being able to repeat that feat in 1769. Bernstorff and Panin did not flinch from the prospect. Juel was authorized to draw for up to 150,000 Danish écus (about £20,000). Osterman, pending the receipt of supplies from St. Petersburg, was kept going by mobilizing the financial aid of Russia's allies. Under the terms of the Russo-Danish alliance of 1765, Denmark was bound in the event of a Russo-Turkish war to pay a subsidy in lieu of military aid, and this was now made over to the Russian minister in Copenhagen for forwarding to Stockholm. A similar arrangement existed in regard to Prussia in terms of the treaty of 1764; and Frederick made no difficulty about complying with a request that half the amount due from him be sent to Osterman, though his private comment was that this was money thrown into the sea. By the time the Diet met in April, Osterman may have received, from all sources, something like £150,000; while Juel, if Goodricke's estimate is correct, had a credit for £40,000.[14] This was corruption of a very different order of magnitude from that of 1764-65, when by the "Plan of 31 August" Russia and England had agreed to put up £26,000 between them.[15] But to Osterman and Juel the hope that Lord Rochford might be persuaded to authorize expenditure on anything like an equal basis at first seemed faint indeed; Osterman could hardly forget how slowly and grudgingly Lord Sandwich had dribbled out the £13,000 which England was due to contribute in 1765. Of British Secretaries of State in general both Panin and Bernstorff had a mean opinion, and so far there seemed to be no reason to suppose that Lord Rochford would be any better than the rest of them.

This judgment, however, ignored one important factor which differentiated Rochford from all his immediate predecessors: he was himself a career diplomat, having been successively minister in Turin, ambassador in Madrid, and from 1766 to 1768 ambassador in Paris. No doubt he was something of a lightweight, both as a man and as a minister. He lacked the long administrative experience and business habits of Lord Sandwich, and intellectually he was probably inferior both to Conway and to Weymouth. George III (a benevolent critic) was later to remark of him that though he had "many amiable qualities," he was "not very prudent";[16] and the observation was probably just. He certainly seems to have been prone to verbal indiscretions, the result of a tendency to garrulousness and a natural vivacity of temper. Panin had a poor opinion of him as a drafter of diplomatic documents. But, as Nolcken very soon noticed, he differed from Weymouth in being at least willing to listen; and Chernyshev, the new Russian ambassador to London, thought him a great improvement on his predecessor.[17] Chernyshev was quite right. Rochford's long absence abroad exempted him from the odium attaching to other members of the ministry for their handling of domestic and foreign affairs:[18] it is remarkable that the worst that Junius could find to say about him was to sneer at his inadequate command of French.[19] He brought to the Secretary's office something of which it stood sorely in need: a practical experience of diplomacy. Goodricke had lamented, with good reason, that the lack of such experience disabled successive Secretaries of State from entering into the difficulties and dilemmas of their ministers abroad; and he had envied the good fortune of Osterman, who in Panin had a master as well versed in Swedish politics as himself.[20] Now, for the first time for many years, this want was supplied; and nowhere, perhaps, was the change for the better more obvious than in regard to Sweden. Rochford, it appears, had corresponded with Goodricke during his spell in Paris,[21] so that he cannot have been entirely uninformed about Swedish affairs. In contrast with Weymouth, he gave a prompt and sympathetic attention to Goodricke's dispatches; and, most important of all, he took care that the relevant secret information that came to him should be forwarded to Stockholm without delay: the channel which had been blocked since Conway's departure now flowed freely once more.

Rochford's attitude to expenditure in Sweden was soon defined. He was no more ready than his predecessors to pay a subsidy: to successive eleventh-hour appeals from Goodricke and the Cap Senate he turned a deaf ear.[22] In this he judged wisely; for it is inconceivable that the offer of a subsidy in February or March would have made any difference to the election results, and only a very confident or very desperate Senate would have risked accepting such an offer at a date so near to the meeting of the Diet. In this respect he was a good deal more realistic than Choiseul, who was so afraid of the effect of a possible offer of a subsidy by England that he ordered Modène in that event to take immediate steps to have the entire Senate arrested.[23] Nevertheless, the extent of the credits which he made available to Goodricke gives support to his claim that the refusal of a subsidy was not due simply to parsimony. His view was that French influence must be fought with bribery; that England was entitled to contribute less than Russia or Denmark, as being less immediately concerned; that if France chose to complete the ruin of her finances by inordinately large expenditure, that was no reason to follow her example; but that within these limits fairly generous provision should be available, leaving it to the discretion of the man on the spot to use the money to the best advantage. On 13 January he responded to Goodricke's appeal by sending him a credit for £5,000.[24] On 17 March he allowed him an additional £100 a month appointments, with a further credit which brought the total to £12,000.[25] When

Goodricke informed him that the estimates for expenditure up to the time of the Diet's meeting would be over £30,000, he uttered no remonstrance; and in no instance thereafter did he return a flat refusal to Goodricke's requests for more funds.[26] Goodricke's policy was to "go upon the saving plan," and to husband his resources against the really critical moments; but when those moments came he could be lavish. One such moment came at the end of March, when he drew for the whole of his new credit, and handed over £6,000 to Rudbeck in a single installment.[27] By the end of that month, in fact, Goodricke had spent £12,000 as against the £25,700 of Juel's and Osterman's combined expenditure. On the basis of these figures Panin and Bernstorff were really in no position to grumble about English miserliness.

Panin might dip deep into his (and his allies') pockets, but he had no intention of relying only upon financial inducements. Very soon after the news of the Inactivity reached him he prepared to supplement them by other arguments. Among them, the argument of force, or at least the threat of force. On New Year's day he instructed his minister in Copenhagen to ask Denmark to make military preparations in Norway, and to fit out a squadron capable of making a naval demonstration: for his part, he promised troops on the Finnish frontier, a fleet in the Baltic as soon as navigation should become open, and in the event of war a guarantee of any Danish territorial gains.[28] Bernstorff was all compliance. He was assiduously angling for an Oldenburg family pact, "stretching from the Great Belt to the Pacific," which should include in its terms the immediate implementation of *Mageskiftet*, and the provision by Russia of large supplies of naval stores;[29] and he was in any case much of Panin's opinion as to the desirability of a demonstration *in terrorem*. By February the fitting out of the Danish fleet was under way, and by the end of the month became known in Stockholm. In the event the maneuver rather backfired. The Cap Senate, at first heartened by the news, was soon driven by fear of public opinion into a show of defensive countermeasures, to the extreme annoyance of Juel and Bernstorff;[30] and worst of all, from Bernstorff's point of view, there was no sign whatever of corresponding threatening measures by Russia, the Swedish minister in St. Petersburg having tactfully suppressed all mention of them in his dispatches lest the news should prove damaging to his friends in the Senate.[31] Thus all the odium fell upon Denmark; and Bernstorff was almost equally furious with Panin for producing that situation, and with the Cap leaders for making a pretense of defending their country. The intermezzo had come near to directly involving England also;

for on the news of Denmark's preparations Choiseul had intervened with a threat of war if they were pursued.[32] No British government could remain indifferent in the face of such a prospect, and Rochford immediately assured Bernstorff that he could count on the aid of the British navy if Choiseul should attempt to carry out his threat.[33] He got small thanks for his assurance. Bernstorff remained sourly skeptical. In common with many other statesmen he failed to realize that though England might be unwilling to engage in an expensive war for the sake of the Manila Ransom, or the Canada Bills, or the *cunette* at Dunkirk, or even Corsica, when it came to an issue which was felt to be vital Europe could not count on England's pursuing a policy of appeasement. The danger of a French fleet in the Baltic was certainly an issue of this order. If the fleet which was reported to be fitting out at Brest had really sailed for the Sound, Bernstorff would have found that out soon enough.

These brandishings of arms were only the climax to a more general campaign of menace which began at the time of the Inactivity, and had not reached its end by the time the Diet met. It relied for its effect upon the simultaneous presentation by the representatives of Russia, Denmark, and if possible England and Prussia also, of concerted protests and warnings, couched in terms whose sharpness might vary, but whose essential message was much the same. To those who planned it, this seemed to be a device whose effectiveness was virtually certain. In the sequel it turned out to be a rather humiliating diplomatic fiasco. At various times in the early months of 1769 three such declarations were projected. The first of them was canvassed by Panin immediately after the Inactivity, and would have been a protest against the events leading to the summoning of an Extraordinary Diet. Lord Cathcart, the new ambassador to Russia, obligingly undertook to write to Goodricke enclosing the draft of such a declaration (evidently drawn by Panin himself), together with a letter suggesting that Goodricke might safely sign it without orders.[34] Goodricke was far too wary to do more than forward it to Rochford, and Rochford would have none of it: it was not his policy to "oppose at all events, what may be determined there [in Sweden] contrary to her [England's] wishes."[35] Frederick the Great took much the same line.[36] The projected declaration was quietly dropped; Lord Cathcart was politely rebuked for unsolicited meddling; and the episode closed.

The second declaration was solicited by Friesendorff, and was designed to abort the alleged design of the Hats and the Court to make war on Russia; a design which he represented as having been evidenced by Adolf Fredrik's attempt to delay the sending of pacific instructions to the Swedish minister in Constantinople.[37] What Friesendorff sought was a joint declaration inviting Sweden to use her efforts to help in mediating a peace, to be presented about a month before the Diet was due to meet. Rochford did not much like this;[38] but on 24 February he sent Goodricke a draft declaration, with authority to present it singly or jointly, as might be appropriate. His change of mind was probably caused by the news which had just reached him through his secret intelligence that the Hats were elated by a report that the Turks were thinking of asking for aid from Sweden in terms of the alliance of 1739.[39] Panin contemptuously dismissed Rochford's draft as more of an inquiry than a declaration;[40] but in the event its form made no difference: the news from Constantinople turned out to be untrue; Friesendorff on second thoughts decided that there was no point in making a declaration until the Diet met; and when it met, the declaration was never made at all.

The history of the third declaration was more tangled, and a good deal more significant. It began in January, when Osterman was pressing Goodricke, and Panin was pleading with Frederick, to concert a joint *démarche*, timed to coincide with the election of the *lantmarskalk*, and designed to prevent any attack on the constitution and any French-inspired aggression against Russia. The matter was probably brought to an issue by the unfavorable early election results, and particularly that in Stockholm. On 14 and 15 February Goodricke, Juel, and Cocceji met at Osterman's house to discuss the question.[41] Osterman produced a draft so violently worded that Juel told him it was as good as a declaration of war, and he had to agree to tone it down; the other three put forward drafts more or less in conformity with Osterman's revised version: all demanded assurances that the Tranquillity of the North would be respected; all threatened, in more or less diplomatic terms, the use of force if Sweden should break the peace. But whereas the drafts of Osterman, Goodricke, and Cocceji likewise demanded that no attempt be made to subvert the constitution, Juel's draft, to Osterman's consternation, was silent on this point. Moreover, the passage threatening the use of force in Goodricke's draft was inserted only on Osterman's insistence, and in the face of Goodricke's formal protest; and Cocceji told Osterman that he had no doubt that if Rochford refused to accept the insertion, Frederick would order him to delete the passage of similar import from the Prussian draft.

This was not an auspicious beginning. Goodricke had produced his draft with reluctance, doubting whether it would be allowed at home:

his motives, it is clear, were his belief that it might help the Caps, and above all his feeling that it would be unwise to "break the concert": that concert, after all, represented a Northern System in petto. Frederick was animated by a variety of contradictory considerations:[42] his anxiety to renew his alliance with Russia as soon as possible; his concern for Lovisa Ulrika; his clear-sighted realization that the new Diet would bring neither a Swedish aggression nor an attack on the constitution so serious that Russian intervention would be inevitable. Most complex of all was the position of Bernstorff. For years it had been a cardinal principle of his policy to oppose by every means the least alteration in the Swedish constitution; in pursuing that policy he had since 1765 placed his main reliance on the assistance of Russia; at Panin's behest he had arranged a threatening naval demonstration; and his immediate object, as we have seen, was the perfecting of *Mageskiftet* by the conclusion of an Oldenburg family pact. Yet he accepted the expedient of declarations only with great reluctance, as being dangerous and possibly counterproductive.[43] And the omission in the Danish draft of any mention of the constitution, which Osterman justly found astonishing, seems to have arisen from a transient flash of insight into the realities of politics, and an unwonted concern for the principles of international law. In February he wrote to his minister in St. Petersburg:

> il serait bien difficile, et de fait et de droit, de soutenir la Constitution de la Suède, si toute la Nation estoit unanimement résolue à la changer . . . il ne lui [la Russie] seroit pas plus aisé de forcer d'une Manière durable la Nation entière à une Forme de Gouvernement devenue odieuse à tous ses membres.[44]

Admittedly, it was still a long way to any such unanimity in Sweden. But it was only three years to 1772. And what about that phrase "et de fait *et de droit*"? Bernstorff's doubts became explicit in a letter to Juel on 18 April, when he wrote: "il lui [Kristian VII] paroit très-douteux qu'une Puissance puisse s'attribuer vis-à-vis de l'autre le Droit de défendre et de maintenir une Constitution et des loix qui lui sont étrangères."[45] One can only comment that it was uncommonly late to develop scruples of this sort. In the event it proved uncommonly easy to swallow them. Indeed, at the very moment when Bernstorff was wrestling with this moral problem he was simultaneously behaving as though it did not exist. For while conceding in one breath that the constitution might be none of Denmark's business, in the next he exhorted Juel to do his best to construct a second line of defense for it by making a secret deal with the

Hats: Juel was ordered with all possible secrecy to "ménager . . . une espèce de connexion" with them. Bernstorff was hedging his bets, even to the extent of speculating about the feasibility of a deal with Pechlin.[46] If in the end he agreed to insert a reference to the constitution in the Danish draft declaration, and if he grudgingly consented to its eventual presentation, he did so only on the remarkable condition that Osterman, Goodricke, and Cocceji should give Juel their word of honor that whatever answer came from the Swedish Chancery to the Danish declaration should not be couched in sharper terms than the replies which might be given to their versions: so keenly did he still feel resentment at Panin's leaving him to bear the whole odium of the naval demonstration.[47]

Goodricke's account of the discussions with his colleagues about a concerted declaration reached Rochford on 5 March, nine days after he had sent off to Lord Cathcart his new proposals for an Anglo-Russian alliance. In the circumstances, he was willing to go to some lengths to be agreeable to Russia in Stockholm; and on 17 March he authorized Goodricke to present his draft declaration at his discretion, including the threat of force which had been inserted at Osterman's insistence.[48] But it is most unlikely that Rochford expected ever to have to make that threat good; nor, indeed, that he intended the declaration to mean all that it seemed to mean. As he later explained to Cathcart, it was to apply only to such changes as might have an "immediate" tendency to disturb the Tranquillity of the North. Moreover, at the time he consented to it he confidently counted on concluding the alliance with Russia before any occasion could arise which would necessitate England's intervention; and once the alliance was made he took it for granted that even a Hat Senate would be incapable of mischief.[49] He was well aware that Frederick the Great could not be relied upon to make an issue of changes which left the original constitution of 1720 intact;[50] and Rochford for his part did not regard subsequent accretions to it as important British interests which must at all costs be preserved. On 27 March he received from Cathcart firm information that Russia did not, even in the event of a Hat victory, expect a Swedish attack. About the same time his French intercepts informed him that the Court was above all terrified of getting involved in a war with Russia, which it rightly foresaw would be its ruin.[51] Thus one of the assumptions which had underlain British policy in the North ever since 1766 was revealed as invalid, at least for the moment. The victory of the Court would not necessarily mean an enemy at Russia's back door; Choiseul's hope of a diversion to help the Turks was for the present an illusion. The danger to peace in the North, it was already beginning to be clear, would come from Russia rather than from Sweden: Cathcart was dropping hints, and soon was stating frankly, that constitutional changes in Stockholm might provoke a Russian invasion of Finland, with a partititon treaty with Denmark and Prussia to follow.[52] No doubt the total subversion of the constitution and the establishment of an absolutism would put some substance into the specter which Panin and Bernstorff conjured up; but in March and April 1769 that did not seem a very likely contingency. What then remained, in the way of a British foreign policy towards Sweden? Only the bare bones, the basic anatomy which never changed: first, to counter French influence wherever it threatened to establish itself, or in the alternative make France pay more than she could afford for a minor victory; and secondly, to use collaboration with Russia in Stockholm as a basis for Anglo-Russian friendship, and, if all went well, for an alliance. These implications Rochford faced and accepted: more easily, perhaps, than Goodricke did, who had been conditioned to think in terms of Panin's bogy. And having thus come to terms with reality, Rochford could confront a temporary reverse philosophically, and subsequently spend generously to retrieve it.

Very early in the campaign it became evident to Goodricke that the Caps had only a slender hope of success.[53] In the Estate of Burghers it was soon clear that the Hats would have a landslide victory: anglophile Göteborg did indeed elect the Cap candidates by a substantial majority, but that did not deter the returning officer from declaring the Hats the winners.[54] Stockholm was a plain disaster: whereas in 1765 the Caps had captured all ten seats, in 1769 they could secure only one. By the end of February it was apparent that there would be a massive Hat majority among the Burghers; and Goodricke feared that in the Estate of Clergy there might be a majority for the Court, which would be even worse.[55] Up to the moment when the Diet met, the Cap "operators" confidently counted on retaining the Estate of Peasantry; and they deluded themselves into thinking that their chances were not hopeless in the Nobility also: the parliamentary arithmeticians estimated, only four days before the Diet opened, that here there would be 363 Hats against 353 Caps, with as many as 181 votes "purchasable."[56] But all such calculations mistook the situation. The election of 1769, like that of 1765, was not decided by bribes, or political propaganda, and least of all by the veiled or overt threats of the four powers: it represented something like a real swing of opinion in the political nation; and the number of new members was exceptionally large. The Burghers had been deeply embittered by the Caps' economic policy; the Clergy were anxious to choose men who would extricate them from the embarrassing clash with the Nobility into which zealots such as Serenius had led them in 1766; the Nobility were animated by resentment at Cap retrenchments, by the civil servants' fear of political persecutions, and perhaps—as to some of them—by an uneasy feeling that some modification of the constitution was going to be necessary if it were to be preserved at all. If it came to corruption, after all, the four powers (as Osterman confessed) had ample resources—resources which may indeed have exceeded those available to Modène. This was one of those occasions—as 1765 had been—when the streams of gold were swept back by a tide of national feeling which overflowed the traditional machinery of "influence," or at least reduced it to a position of minor importance. Not, indeed, that such influence was not effectively employed upon occasion: Goodricke noted how with the advent of the Court to Norrköping the universal graciousness of Prince Gustav, the astonishing relaxation of court etiquette in an effort to win over votes, sharply worsened the Caps' chances.[57] Nor were the tactics of Eatanswill left unexploited: on the day before the Peasants were due to elect their Speaker, forty or fifty officers broke into their club, locked up many of the members until next morning, and "carried them in procession to vote, attended by several governors of provinces"; while French "operators," playing upon the Peasants' traditional loyalty to the crown, won over others by feeding them with stories that if the Caps were victorious, Adolf Fredrik would be deposed.[58]

The Diet met at Norrköping on 19 April, in conditions of considerable physical discomfort. There was no room in the little town for the masses of members who converged upon it; foreign ministers jostled for the hiring of houses;[59] the citizens reaped a golden harvest; and members complained of the exorbitance of the rents which they were forced to pay.[60] The inconveniences extended to more serious matters than housing. For the presence of members of the Senate was necessary not only at the Diet, but also in Stockholm for the maintenance of contact with the central offices of government; and there was no way out of this difficulty save to split the Senate into two halves: eight members were to remain in the capital; five were to accompany their sovereign to Norrköping; and it was in the eight, rather than in the five, that the corporate authority of the Senate was considered to be vested. The Caps were paying a considerable price for their insistence on calling the Diet to a provincial town. That decision had been opposed by all the foreign ministers;[61] and the sole advantage that had been expected of it—namely, that the entrenched Hat civil servants would necessarily be absent, since their official duties would keep them in Stockholm—proved illusory: they no more hesitated to desert their civil duties in 1769 than their Cap predecessors had hesitated to desert their military duties in 1760.

Goodricke left for Norrköping in good time, on 8 April, and for some days thereafter it fell to him to do his best to coordinate the tactics of the Cap "operators," along lines which had already been laid down in an elaborate battle-order devised by the four ministers on 24 March.[62] He found the prospects discouraging; and of the Caps' operators he had a poor opinion. However, by the time the Diet opened on 19 April he had the assistance of Osterman and Juel: Cocceji, significantly, was given leave to stay in Stockholm—an arrangement which reflects Frederick's perspicacious prediction that though there would be a rowdy Diet, no hostilities would come of it, and that the whole affair was "un feu de paille qui ne mérite pas qu'on s'en inquiète."[63] Cocceji had, however, given his draft of the famous declaration to Juel, to be handed in when he should deem it appropriate. The appropriate moment, they had all agreed, would be the voting for the *lantmarskalk*. This critical event took place on 22 April. It had been preceded by the unanimous election of Bishop Filenius (a Hat) as Speaker of the Clergy, and the election by a large majority of another Hat as Speaker of the Burghers. From that moment Goodricke, Osterman, and Juel concentrated all their efforts on the crucial election for *lantmarskalk*. It was decided to "risk all upon this point": Osterman and Juel each paid out £10,000, Goodricke, more than £5,000.[64] But two days before it came on they suffered a wholly unexpected blow, when the veteran Hat, Olof Håkansson, was elected Speaker of the Peasants by 86 to 58; and on 22 April came the final catastrophe: in the election to *lantmarskalk* Fersen defeated Rudbeck by 604 to 370. So much for the 181 nobles whom their operators had considered purchasable.

This, then, was the time for action; this the situation in which it had been agreed that the four declarations should be presented; this the crisis for which plans had so long been made. And the result? An anticlimax which was almost ludicrous. Some of the Cap Senate, fearing to exacerbate the party vengeance which now plainly threatened them, begged that no action be taken; others, the rank and file, still hoped that the declarations might cushion their fall. Juel first proposed postponing any action until the composition of the Secret Committee should be known, though only a political innocent (which Juel was not) could now doubt what the composition would be; and subsequently he refused to proceed on the pretext that he was tied by orders not to give a declaration unless the Cap Senate should ask for it: a contingency now conceivable only on the supposition that they had taken leave of their collective senses. By 26 April he had persuaded Osterman to agree with him, arguing that they must avoid inflaming passions to a point which might entail a civil war in which the constitution would be the victim.[65] The truth was that Juel was thoroughly disillusioned with the Cap operators, the Cap Senate, and the Cap party.[66] Already he was beginning to think of defending the constitution by other means: by a reconciliation with moderate Hats, by a Composition of moderates of both parties which should act as a buffer against absolutist dangers and warlike adventures. Only in the most desperate extremity was he now prepared to implement the agreement of 15 February.

Of all the foreign ministers, only Goodricke was still for sticking to the original plan: he was insistent that the declarations be made, and he demanded urgently to know when. As Bernstorff rightly conjectured, he was moved partly by the fact that he was more concerned to save the Caps than to save the constitution; but also by his belief that the plan for a joint *démarche* might lay a foundation upon which an enduring concert of the four powers could be built: upon it might be raised the long-planned edifice of a Northern System.[67] He almost certainly misjudged the effect of any such action upon the fate of his Cap protégés: it was far more likely to have led to their proscription than to their escaping lightly. But the idea of the long-term effects of a quadruple *démarche* had more substance, and he would not abandon it without a struggle. In the meantime, however, the policy of 15 February was irretrievably shattered; and its final ruin was achieved by a characteristic indiscretion of Rochford himself. For on 21 April, the day before the disastrous election of the *lantmarskalk*, Rochford in a conversation with Nolcken remarked "as from himself" that Goodricke had orders in certain circumstances to present a declaration, if it should seem necessary in order to preserve the Tranquillity of the North.[68] Nolcken's dispatch reporting this conversation reached Stockholm on 4 May; it was read in the Senate two days later; and on that same day, as a direct consequence of this revelation, Friesendorff informed all the foreign ministers of his sovereign's intention to make a declaration to the effect that Sweden had no intention of troubling the public tranquillity "in the present conjuncture."[69] The qualification, to be sure, was not without significance, as Goodricke was quick to point out;[70] but there was no escaping the fact that Adolf Fredrik, by getting his blow in first, had secured the moral advantage, that the four powers had been outmaneuvered, and that for the moment their strategy was in total disarray.[71]

(ii)

The election of Fersen as *lantmarskalk* on 22 April was an event of more than local importance. It had implications for the whole system of British foreign policy, and in particular it had unforeseen consequences for Anglo-Russian relations.

When Rochford succeeded Weymouth as Northern Secretary in October 1768 he found himself confronting a new and threatening situation. By this time the British government had virtually written off Corsica, in the belief (which was shared by French critics of Choiseul) that it would prove an acquisition not worth the resources expended upon conquering it. The long-standing controversy about the Manila Ransom, the new dispute about the Falkland Islands, were slowly banking up to the crisis which would culminate in 1771. But the real storm center of Europe lay in the east. French intrigues in Poland, the Inactivity in Sweden, and above all the impending Turkish declaration of war, seemed proof of Choiseul's determination to harass Catherine II, and his recklessness as to the possibility that his policy might produce a general European war involving both Prussia and Austria. Into such a war, if it came, neither France nor Spain would be drawn; for its outbreak would provide the opportunity he had long been seeking: when England's only friend had her hands full, when the American colonies were distracting the British government, that would be the moment for the Franco-Spanish attack upon England.[72] It was no colonial war that he designed; still less a war in Germany on the old lines; but the destruction of England's naval and mercantile ascendancy, to be clinched by that invasion of the British Isles which his agents had been reconnoitering for the past two years.[73]

It was a possibility which ministers faced without undue anxiety. They shared the general belief that the state of French finances made such a war unlikely in the immediate future; they saw with frank astonishment those finances dilapidated still further in vast peripheral expenditures; and they still retained, despite Grenvillian economies and Lord Hawke's administration, a blind faith in the navy's ability to make short work of any Gallispan force that might be brought against it. It would require the Falklands crisis to disabuse them of this delusion, and the efforts of Lord Sandwich to repair it. As for Lord Rochford, he had gone to France with every disposition to avoid exacerbating relations; but he was no Bedfordite, and two years in Paris was sufficient to turn him into "the sworn arch-foe of Choiseul."[74] One eminent historian has called him a "russophil";[75] and no doubt, like most English statesmen of his day, he desired the Russian alliance. But experience was very soon to show that he wanted it on his own terms, and that he would not sacrifice what he considered to be the interests of his country in order to obtain it.

The outbreak of the Turkish war put a new face upon this problem. It was impossible to escape the reflection that if ministers had not stood fast on the Turkish clause they would now have been involved as auxiliaries in a struggle which was no concern of theirs. Costly subsidies, a demand for naval aid in the Mediterranean, a possible deathblow to the ailing Levant trade:[76] such would have been the consequences of compliance. Events had justified their obstinacy; and if ever the negotiation for an alliance was renewed there was not the slightest chance of their budging on this point. But there remained the question whether it ought to be renewed. Frederick the Great could not for the life of him see why they should trouble themselves about it: Russia was already bound to Britain by ties of friendship and commerce which made an alliance superfluous.[77] A decade later Catherine was to meet a British overture with the dry remark that one did not make alliances with powers which were already engaged in war.[78] This, however, was not Rochford's opinion. He was as firmly convinced of the desirability of a Northern System as any of his predecessors;[79] but he reached the not unreasonable conclusion that Catherine's embarrassments, and the evident impossibility of now including Turkey as a *casus foederis*, put him in a strong negotiating position.[80] He wanted an end to the Turkish war as soon as possible, if only for the sake of commerce in the Levant; but while it lasted he felt he had Catherine at a disadvantage.

It so happened that Rochford's accession to office had been preceded in August by the tardy arrival in Russia of an ambassador to succeed the unfortunate Macartney. This was Lord Cathcart, a prosy and precise Scot with a distinguished military career behind him, who now cherished ambitions to succeed where his two predecessors had failed, and bring the Russian alliance safely into harbor. Contemporaries tended to refer to him, without enthusiasm, as "a worthy man," and de Visme (his secretary, until they fell out) felt that "if there was less simmetry and exactness in his way of life I who am debauched should like it better."[81] His hair-raising indifference to the security of his ciphers does not suggest very businesslike habits;[82] his record in Russia shows him to have been somewhat guileless and credulous; but he was laborious, patient, and indefatigable. These estimable qualities were offset by the fact that he was undeniably a long-winded bore, whose conversations and dispatches, though they often concealed substantial nuggets of common sense, enwrapped them in enormous swathes of verbiage. Before his departure he had made an intensive study of all the material in the Secretary's office bearing upon the problem of the alliance;[83] and he therefore arrived in St. Petersburg better primed than his predecessors. Soon after his arrival he received from Weymouth an instruction which formed a remarkable exception to that minister's habitual taciturnity.[84] It included one clear declaration of policy, and one unambiguous warning. Cathcart was given plainly to understand that however desirable the Russian alliance, England could contrive to live without it. And he was warned that in view of the imminence of war with the Turks Panin might well come forward with suggestions for an offset to the Turkish clause. In such an event he was expressly ordered to decline to engage in any discussions along those lines. This instruction Cathcart proceeded without loss of time to disobey. He seems quickly to have succumbed to Panin's frank and cordial manner, and when that minister ventured upon forbidden ground Cathcart did not hesitate to follow him. At a very early stage of their discussions Panin disarmed him by conceding that in view of the likelihood of a Turkish war there was no point in pursuing the argument about the Turkish clause: could they not agree to make a fresh start? To Cathcart, the removal of this long-standing obstacle seemed to alter the whole situation: "I must not conceal from Your Lordship," he wrote, "that they think they have done an immense thing both in the matter and manner of the offer."[85] Panin took care to reinforce the impression by volunteering to send arms and equipment to help Paoli in Corsica, if England would undertake to ship them to their destination.[86] Moved by these evidences of goodwill, Cathcart was soon suggesting that Russia might reasonably ask for a subsidy of half a million rubles, should the Turkish war break out.[87] From Panin's point of view this was well enough, as far as it went, but it was not the equivalent which he was seeking. What he wanted, in return for allowing England to retain the Turkish clause, was a subsidy to Sweden; and he indicated that he would settle for £50,000 a year for not less than eight years. This was a stiff price; but Cathcart had no doubt that it would prove a sound bargain. He accordingly gave Panin's proposals a cordial reception, transmitted them to Rochford buttressed with fifty pages of weighty arguments in favor of their acceptance, and followed this up by dispatch after dispatch, pleading ever more urgently for the acceptance of Russia's terms.[88]

Lord Rochford, however, took a very different view of the matter. He was, of course, delighted that Panin should at last have swallowed the Turkish clause; but he found the rest of Cathcart's budget more than he could stomach.[89] Since the completion of Goodricke's treaty in 1766 a subsidy had been urged as the means to securing an alliance with *Sweden*, which in turn should form the first link in that "great chain" which would ultimately include Russia, Denmark, and (perhaps) Prussia. But now the situation was altered. Panin was now insisting on the Swedish subsidy as a precondition for an alliance with *Russia*, and insisting on it as an equivalent for his surrender on the Turkish clause. This argument Rochford totally rejected. Russia had no right to any such equivalent; he was not prepared to be put in the humiliating position of "buying" the alliance; once England's alliances with Russia and Denmark were concluded a subsidy to Sweden would be unnecessary, for in that case France would be in no position to stir up trouble in the North; and in any case, at a moment when the Caps might well be heading for electoral defeat a subsidy would be unavailing, and would simply be money thrown away. He did indeed add, in a characteristically incautious sentence, that if a Northern System already existed, or were to exist, he *might* be prepared to think again about a subsidy; but certainly he would not pay one as the price of a Russian alliance.[90] He had his own ideas as to the kind of alliance England might be prepared to offer in the existing circumstances, and on 17 February 1769 he forwarded to Cathcart a draft which embodied them. From the *casus foederis* were to be exempted, on the one side, Russo-Turkish wars; and on the other, British wars in the colonies or the Mediterranean region. Duration: twenty years; other powers to be invited to adhere.[91]

These terms, and the language in which Rochford argued for them, make it clear that he felt he need make no concessions. For Panin they were quite unacceptable. Catherine did not for one moment feel that the Turkish war had put her at a diplomatic disadvantage. On the contrary. To her ambassador in London she had written in December: "Endlich fühle sie sich frei und ungeniert . . . man habe die schlafende Katze geweckt, nun gehe es auf die Mäusejagd."[92] Her anxiety was not so much that war with the Turks had at last broken out, but rather lest the offer of English mediation should somehow cozen her into a premature peace.[93] A Hat victory at the forthcoming Swedish elections was certainly an unpleasant prospect; but Panin was reasonably confident that he would be able to prevent its being followed by a Swedish attack. The Danish navy was ready; the Swedish was not. The Finnish frontier lay open to Russian threats. And if the worst came to the worst, if the constitution should really be in danger and an absolutism be established which might be willing to act as Choiseul's tool, Russia would not wait to be attacked: a few divisions would dispose of Swedish forces in Finland, and Catherine's galleys would be in the Stockholm skerries before the fleet at Karlskrona could bend a sail or ship a crew. Rochford's offer of naval aid if Russia should be attacked was poor compensation for the other terms of his proposed treaty, which would have left Catherine committed to give assistance if a colonial dispute should lead to a French invasion of Hanover. But Panin's essential objection was expressed by Filosofoff, his minister in Copenhagen, when he complained to Gunning of "our persisting to treat Russia in the same manner as we did forty years ago, which she was too sensible of her force and superiority to bear."[94]

To Lord Cathcart, Panin's contemptuous reception of Rochford's draft came as a severe disappointment; but being of a persevering character and a sanguine temper he determined to repair the damage by his own exertions. To this end he produced at the beginning of May a series of "Expedients" designed to provide a compromise. His main reliance was upon Rochford's vague hint of a distinction between a subsidy to a general league, and one to a particular power. Panin, it is true, had dismissed the distinction as ridiculous; Cathcart, on the contrary, found it "just," and to his hopeful eye it seemed the presage of an important change in British policy.[95] His one regret was that it had not been thought of earlier. Rochford, one may surmise, soon came to regret that it had been thought of at all. On this insecure foundation Cathcart now built his solution. He would append to Rochford's draft treaty two separate articles, the effect of which would be to transform it (at least in prospect) from a particular to a general alliance. The first of these articles would provide for the accession of Prussia and of Denmark; the second would make it clear that a subsidy was to be paid to Sweden only in consideration of that country's adherence to the general league. Panin gave this proposal a cautious and unenthusiastic reception, being justifiably skeptical as to whether Rochford had really meant what Cathcart supposed him to mean. Still, the second separate article gave him the subsidy he wanted; and after a short hesitation he swallowed his misgivings: on 3 May Cathcart could write jubilantly that his Expedient had been accepted. The alliance seemed as good as made.

Two days later these bright hopes were blasted by the arrival in St. Petersburg of the disastrous reports from Norrköping, and in particular of Fersen's election as *lantmarskalk*. Panin was not slow to draw the logical inference. An Anglo-Swedish alliance, with or without a subsidy, had now become impossible, at least for the present; and since the only quid pro quo for the Turkish clause that he was prepared to consider was a subsidy to Sweden which it was now futile to offer there was no basis remaining upon which a treaty could be made. Thus a domestic political upheaval in Stockholm had wrecked, not only the labors of Lord Cathcart, but the long-term strategy of the British ministry, just when that strategy seemed within sight of success. Nevertheless, Lord Cathcart would not own himself beaten. In quick succession he produced two more Expedients, one of which would even have committed England to assisting Russia in an aggressive war against Sweden. It was labor lost: Panin was not to be appeased. On 20 May he rejected, without explanation, all the Expedients that had been put forward. Even so, it seemed that this might not be his last word. For three days later came an overture, through Saldern, which Cathcart took for an ultimatum. If Rochford would at once put up £50,000 for *bribery* in Sweden; and if he would in addition make to the Northern Courts a plain declaration of England's intention to pursue an anti-French system there, then Panin would be willing to accept Rochford's draft treaty. This overture, together with the record of his diplomatic exertions over the past three weeks, Cathcart transmitted to London by special messenger on 24 May. The packet was a bulky one: seven vast dispatches, eleven lengthy enclosures, a private letter, with hints on the best order in which to read the contents; the whole running to over a hundred folio sheets.[96]

This formidable dossier arrived on Lord Rochford's desk on 13 June; and though the perusal of it may well have been felt by him to be an affliction, the upshot of the matter certainly caused him no pang. At the end of the month he made his attitude perfectly clear; and in one particular, at least, it coincided with Panin's: he had no use whatever for any of Cathcart's ingenious Expedients. In his view, the financial support already afforded to Goodricke was quite sufficient evidence of goodwill. He was not prepared to pledge his assistance in the event of a Russian attack on Finland, and he did not relish Panin's notion of turning that country into a Russian puppet-state. The suggestion that George III could qualify for admission to a Northern System only by making what Rochford described as "a Confession of Faith at Copenhagen and Berlin in order to entitle him to know whether those Courts will condescend to enter into an

Alliance with him" he dismissed (fairly enough) as "very unbecoming to His Majesty's Dignity, as well as perfectly unnecessary": any "extraordinary exertion" must be a consequence, not a precondition, of membership of such a league, and he would not assume previous burdens in order to entitle him to belong to it.[97] To Cathcart he wrote, somewhat tartly,

> it cannot have escaped your Lordship's penetration that Russia may have views in regard to Sweden that may be very politick for her to pursue but that if England was to enter into their full extent would engage us in a warlike system which a commercial nation ought prudently to steer clear of.[98]

The syntax might be cloudy; but the message was clear. And this, for the moment at least, was his last word. On 28 July he declared the negotiation "entirely at an end."[99] Rather than a Russian alliance on such terms he was content to live without one, on the existing basis of friendly cooperation in areas of common concern. If such cooperation should presently ripen into a more formal relationship, well and good; if not, he would support the deprivation with fortitude.

It was entirely consistent with this attitude that he should have given cordial approval to Goodricke's solution to the particular problem of Sweden. In Goodricke's view, the simplest and most effective *riposte* to the Hat victory was for the four powers to unite in a demand that Sweden should join them in a general northern alliance.[100] The ministers of the four powers were already acting in close collaboration; it needed only the development of that collaboration, and the Northern System would virtually create itself. Certainly, if ever this was a feasible road forward, it might appear to be so in the summer of 1769; and until far into the autumn both Goodricke and Rochford continued to hope that something might be achieved along these lines. But in fact the concert was flawed, even in Stockholm, and the confidence less than perfect. Bernstorff was chronically suspicious of England's sincerity, and Juel, though he conceded merit to the idea, thought it came too late.[101] Frederick had no intention of lending his assistance to any plan which might result in a Northern System, least of all if that plan were of English provenance. Panin, though admitting that in other circumstances the idea might have been useful, feared that it might bring as many disadvantages as a Franco-Swedish alliance: France, he thought, would persuade the Senate to accept the proposal in principle; long-drawn negotiations would follow; and the Court would use the interval, with French assistance, to prepare the destruction of the constitution.[102] Goodricke's road may well have been practicable; but unfortunately none of his fellow travelers was willing to take it. As the idea of a great chain had proved abortive, so now a Northern union by instantaneous fusion, with Sweden as the catalyst, turned out to be as delusive as the philosopher's stone.

(iii)

Fersen's election as *lantmarskalk* effectively crushed any lingering hope that the Caps might still make a fight for it. It was followed, according to a pattern which had now become predictable, by sweeping successes for the Hats in the elections to the Secret Committee: of the fifty representatives of the Nobles the Caps secured only three; of the twenty-five Burghers, only four. The Hats, it seemed, had the *riksdag*—and therefore in large measure the state—at their disposal; the Caps, planless, hopeless, appeared to be on the verge of dissolution as an organized political party.[103]

The Hats lost no time in exploiting their triumph. On 2 May "le comique Roi de Stockholm" (by which disrespectful appellation C. F. Scheffer intended that section of the Senate which had remained in the capital) was summoned, in terms of calculated insult, at once to repair to Norrköping.[104] With unexampled speed and sovereign disregard for the accepted procedures the Secret Committee embarked on the congenial task of formulating those quasicriminal charges which provided the necessary legal basis for the Senate's *licentiering*: they had insulted the king; they had set up a commission to judge the Collegia; they had illegally interfered in elections; they had attempted to rule by use of the name stamp and assume sovereignty to themselves. There was some truth in all this, but it was not the essential truth. The criminal charges were merely lip service paid to an etiolated constitutional convention.[105] It was in vain that those Senate members who were in Norrköping met together under Goodricke's presidency to devise arguments in rebuttal of the charges against them:[106] only four of them made any real attempt to defend themselves, and Goodricke for his part had no hope of saving them.[107] Within three weeks the business was completed: of the former thirteen members of the Senate, ten were deprived of office, one (de Geer) had conveniently died, one (Hiärne) was a surviving Hat, and the thirteenth, von Wallwijk, a turncoat loved by neither party, was suffered (though not without difficulty) to escape.[108] It was a real change of government, a single drastic purge, very different from the protracted and piecemeal proceedings of 1765-66. Bishop Serenius drew the appropriate inference, and on the day the *licentieringar* passed the House of Nobility shrugged his shoulders, shook the dust of Stockholm off his feet, and retired to his diocese of Strängnäs, there to meditate (as Tilas maliciously remarked) upon the result of his exertions and the mutability of human affairs.[109] A new Senate was cobbled up with all convenient speed: of the martyrs of 1765-66 only Hamilton, Rudenschöld, and Ekeblad, persuaded with difficulty to resume the office of chancery-president,[110] returned to their places. C. F. Scheffer, with the unhappy experiences of 1761 and 1765 still fresh in his memory, declined to risk another spell of office;[111] but his brother Ulrik was recruited to act as Ekeblad's second-in-command (*rikskansliråd*). On 1 June the Diet broke up from Norrköping, to everyone's relief; on the twenty-seventh it resumed its sessions in Stockholm. Two days earlier Adolf Fredrik re-entered his capital amid scenes of heart-warming enthusiasm. The Inactivity had been endorsed by the verdict of the Nation; Aristocracy lay crushed beneath the royal boot.[112] To royalists of the naiver sort it looked like the dawn of a new era.

Old political hands such as the queen knew better. There were already signs that the Hats could not be relied on to keep the bargain they had made with the Court.[113] The program of action at the beginning of the Diet, which had been agreed on in advance, was not adhered to; the plan that the *licentiering* proceedings should take their rise in a memorandum from the king which would have been a kind of manifesto had been canceled by Fersen.[114] In some ways the Court had not done too badly: the new Senate included at least four members who were avowedly royalists—Sinclair among them—and Ulrik Scheffer was by this time effectively a royalist too.[115] But as long as the Diet was sitting the Senate was of subordinate importance: what mattered was the control of the Estates, above all of the Estate of Nobles, and this depended very much upon the *lantmarskalk*. And the *lantmarskalk* was Fersen; and of Fersen the Court could never be sure. It was no wonder that Lovisa Ulrika took care to keep a tight control of the funds which were at her personal disposal. For by the end of May she had in fact suffered a defeat which in the sequel was to prove decisive. Of the questions which the Diet would have to tackle, two transcended all others in importance. One was the question of the constitution and its possible reform; the other was the question of the finances: upon the solution to these questions even foreign policy was dependent. It had been understood, and in the Court's view firmly agreed, that the constitutional question should take precedence over all others, and should be dealt with as soon as the Diet got down to business. But the order of business of the House of Nobility was the responsibility of the *lantmarskalk*; and Fersen decided that constitutional reform should be not the first but the last item on the Diet's agenda, on the ground—the far from obvious ground—that it would be dangerous for the Diet to continue in session once that problem had been settled.[116] Whether deliberately or not, Fersen's decision sacrificed the best chance of carrying through a moderate constitutional reform while the opposition to it had either not formed, or was in disarray. The Crown Prince saw this very clearly;[117] and other less eminent personages saw it too.[118] The decision had the incidental effect of enforcing the transfer from Norrköping to Stockholm; since in order to frame a plan for the finances access to the books and papers of the Bank was indispensable, and it was not permitted to move them from the capital: this had been one of the few reasons which made a *riksdag* in Norrköping tolerable from the Court's point of view, since it seemed to ensure that finance must take second place to the constitution.[119]

When Fersen came to write his memoirs, he remarked of the Diet of 1769 that its object was to "try to unite the true interests of the country with those of the royal family by the amendment of the fundamental laws and the correction of the abuses which had crept into their application."[120] As a description of the hopes and intentions of men such as C. F. Scheffer and Daniel Tilas this is certainly true; how far it correctly represents Fersen's own policy when the Diet opened is at least questionable, and in the light of his subsequent conduct seems doubtful. It is at least clear that under Fersen's leadership the Hats used their overwhelming victory at the polls with relative sobriety and moderation. Motions to have the displaced members of the Senate subjected to pains and penalties were quietly stifled, to the bitter disappointment of Prince Gustav;[121] no extraordinary tribunals were set up, no odious party persecution indulged in. Despite the violence of party strife there was, after all, a substantial area of common ground between them on matters of policy. They might differ on the need for expenditure on defense, but they were at one in desiring a foreign policy which should keep clear of dangerous involvements. The Hats might lean to France, the Caps to England; but there was no willingness to become France's tool on the one side, or the economic colony of England on the other; and neither was prepared for anything like the control of foreign policy by the Court. So too at home: the Hats' condemnation of their predecessors' economic policy, their attempts to undo it, were directed more against methods than objectives: by this time they were ready to concede that *some* action against the Exchange Control Office had been called for, though they might deplore the violence and illegality of the action which the Caps had taken. In many respects the Hats seemed to have learned from the sharp lessons of 1765-66: while their hold on power remained secure, and until growing weakness made them reckless and irresponsible, there was no return to the bad old days of secrecy, no stifling of the press, no wasteful pampering of Hat industrialists, no scandalous appointments by the Estates. And though not a few men, on both sides, were coming to believe in the desirability of some measure of constitutional—or at least of administrative—reform, there were still very few in either camp who were ready to contemplate the subversion of that parliamentary system under which they had grown up, and by which so many of them had thriven so well.

Of all the foreign statesmen who concerned themselves with Swedish affairs it was Frederick the Great who saw these truths most clearly. The news of the Hat triumph failed to disturb his sense of proportion. Provided that the intoxication of victory did not tempt the Hats to press their advantage too far he did not expect any great harm to be done: they were far too jealous of any increase in the prerogative. As to foreign policy, what did it matter if France were once more to enter into an alliance with Sweden? Swedish territory was wide open to attack from Denmark, from Russia, from himself; and (he might have added, though he did not) any effective military or naval aid from France was liable to be cut off or destroyed by the British navy. Why, then, these flutterings of alarm in Copenhagen, this deep depression over St. Petersburg? What was the Swedish army, what the barely existent Swedish navy, against the potential which could be mobilized on the other side?[122]

These were arguments which were lost on Panin and Osterman, whose confidence had been badly shaken. It was in vain that Fersen spoke reassuringly, both to Osterman and to Goodricke;[123] in vain that Ekeblad disclaimed all aggressive intentions to Stakhiev:[124] Panin remained nervously skeptical. Russian policy must be to fight a rearguard action, standing first on the line of 1766, then on that of 1756, with 1720 as the last ditch; and if the constitution of 1720 itself was threatened she must fight to defend it, even though the Diet should be unanimous for changing it.[125] Early in June Osterman was writing "an incendiary letter" to his colleague in Copenhagen predicting that all was lost, and the constitution in imminent danger.[126]

In Juel's view Osterman was talking alarmist nonsense; but Juel himself was in no position to cast a stone: the correspondence between Bernstorff and his minister in Stockholm was not without evidences of mild hysteria.[127] On the constitutional question the Danish attitude was broadly similar to the Russian, with the addition of the *riksdagsordning* of 1723 to the list of bastions which must be defended to the last—though Bernstorff added that even if these positions were attacked Denmark would fight only in response to a reclamation from her friends in Sweden.[128] It was unfortunate, therefore, that both Bernstorff and Juel should have been in a state of total mental confusion as to who those friends now were. With the Cap leaders they were now thoroughly disgusted; and they permitted themselves to entertain nostalgic daydreams of a return to the good old days when C. F. Scheffer, Fersen, Hamilton, and Ekeblad had been the anchormen of Danish policy in Sweden.[129] After all, Bernstorff had no great objection to the idea of mending his fences with Choiseul, if only Choiseul would not tamper with the Swedish constitution: as Gunning correctly reported, "It is not the Influence of France, but the seeming tendency of it, that gives Umbrage."[130] But the tendency was undeniably there; and it was only long friendship that prevented Bernstorff from admitting that C. F. Scheffer had assimilated a liberal dose of dangerous principles. As to Fersen, they could not make up their minds: if Fersen, the man of 1756, could not be relied upon to stand fast, what resource remained to a perplexed Danish statesman? But by the middle of June Juel had been driven to the conclusion that he could *not* be relied on, and that the only hope, perhaps, was a split in the Hats.[131]

While Juel and Osterman were wringing their hands, Goodricke and Rochford were taking defeat with exemplary British phlegm. Rochford consoled himself with the reflection that however much money he had spent, the French would probably have outspent him, and drew comfort from the thought that he had refused a subsidy, and thus escaped subjecting Britian to "the disgrace of having courted an inconsiderable Power and been baffled in it."[132] As to Goodricke, defeat rather whetted his pugnacity than damped it. Sir Joseph Yorke had written in April: "I am indeed more and more surprised at the spirit and conduct he shews, I am not naturally of a desponding temper, but I believe I should long since have sunk under the weight of the Burthen."[133] But Goodricke was not the man to sink under "Burthens"; he rebounded under them. His analysis of the situation was very similar to Frederick the Great's: he believed that Fersen was too sensible to permit an involvement in the Turkish war, at least for the present; that he was jealous of the Court's popularity; and that he would not be a party to any major alteration in the constitution, whatever France might offer.[134] What worried him was the possibility of a *rapprochement* between Fersen and Denmark, and a renewal of the alignment which had confronted him in 1764, with France, Sweden, and Denmark loosely grouped into a single system.[135] He shrewdly divined the implications of a possible transfer of the Diet to Stockholm, and informed Rochford that he intended to work for it:[136] in the event, Fersen did his work for him, but his instinct proved to be sound.

Goodricke's policy, then, was simply to battle on. He had lost this round, but he had no notion of abandoning the match. Unlike Juel, he never for a moment allowed his dissatisfaction with the Cap leadership to influence his policy. Unlike Osterman, he did not conclude that all that was now open to him was a negative, defensive campaign. He still believed that simultaneous, identical demands by the four powers for Sweden's adhesion to a quadruple alliance would exert a pressure which even a Hat administration would be unable to resist.[137] And he was quite willing to resume the financial battle. Now that the Hats were in power, secret information was much more difficult and expensive to secure.[138] Rochford had agreed that this must be paid for, and had asked for an estimate.[139] In reply Goodricke enlarged the scope of what he considered to be necessary expenditure: he must keep his friends together, he must contribute to the common Chest of Operations, he must provide impoverished Caps with journey money when the Diet was transferred to Stockholm. It was in the nature of things impossible to provide more than a rough estimate for all this, and in any case money by itself would avail nothing unless it was directed to a plan (the quadruple alliance)—but still, a sum of £150,000, divided equally between the three courts, would probably suffice.[140] This was a somewhat staggering sum, and Rochford's three predecessors would certainly have rejected it out of hand; but Rochford took it sufficiently seriously to call a cabinet on it. The result was what might have been expected: since in the government's view Swedish aggression, or the overthrow of the constitution, both seemed unlikely at present, £50,000 was more than they were willing to pay. An extra £5,000, it was intimated, was all the situation seemed to require.[141]

So Goodricke—who can scarcely have had much hope of £50,000—was left to make the best of this financial crumb, and to struggle on as best he might in the hope that something might turn up to improve his position. The move to Stockholm was a useful beginning; and already before the Diet resumed its sessions the something had in fact turned up, more quickly than either Goodricke or Rochford could have expected, in the person of Colonel Carl Fredrik Pechlin.

(iv)

The dramatic vote of 24 August 1761 had excluded Pechlin not only from participating in the remainder of that Diet but also from attendance at the next, no doubt to the relief of the Cap Senate. But now he was back again, active, incalculable, dangerous as an enemy, and scarcely less so as a friend: as Juel observed, after a wary exploratory talk with him in February 1769, "un homme à grands talents, mais ses mauvaises qualités l'emportent sur les bonnes."[142] A prudent respect for those talents had led the Court, on the one hand, and the Hat leaders, on the other, to take care to cultivate him during his interval in the wilderness; and he had made one of the small inner ring of leading Hats who in January 1769 had reached agreement with the Court on the reform of the constitution. They could hardly have selected a worse person for their confidence. Pechlin was as unscrupulous as he was able; ambitious also to form and lead a party of his own, and in consequence jealous of Fersen. But his repeated perfidies were based upon one firm political principle to which he remained remarkably constant. That principle was liberty, as the Swedes of that age understood the term: that is, the virtual sovereignty of the Estates, with all its excesses, abuses and absurdities; and it entailed as a necessary corollary an inflexible resistance to any attempt to modify the constitution as it had developed since 1720, either by a better balance of forces within it, or upon some principle of separation of powers. For tactical reasons he might for a time be willing to work with the Court or the Hats in order to attain a short-term objective; but he could be relied upon to betray them as soon as he saw any prospect of even the most modest increase of the prerogative; and he was scarcely less jealous of any enhancement of the authority of the Senate. Such was the man whom the leading Hats had made a party to their bargain with the Court. By their own action they had made him the master of their dangerous secret: the only question for him, therefore, was how best to use his information to thwart Hats and Court alike.

Already before the Estates assembled in Norrköping he had begun to make his reconnaissances. For this purpose he needed a confidential agent; and he found the man he required in the person of Nils von Oelreich, a political maverick like himself: once a Hat, then a Cap, and now out of business as Censor since the Caps' liberation of the press. Oelreich's first move was to approach Rudbeck with a hint that Pechlin might be willing to change sides in return for the modest sum of 30,000 plåtar (about £4,400), an offer which Rudbeck on the basis of past experience rejected out of hand.[143] But on 22 April came Fersen's election as *lantmarskalk*, and immediately Pechlin took the initiative. On the following day he sent Oelreich to Osterman and laid before him the heads of a treaty of collaboration. His program held out no extravagant expectations. Osterman was firmly told to abandon all idea of averting a *licentiering*: at most it might be possible to save three of the Cap Senate. Pechlin undertook only to try to split the Court from the Hats; to ensure that Sweden's connections with foreign powers should not favor one more than another; and to try to secure the election of "gens nationaux" (whatever they might be) as benchmen. He declined to appear openly against Fersen until the question of the constitution should come up for discussion; he demanded 300,000 d.k.m. (£6,000) as the price of his assistance; he insisted on the strictest secrecy; and he refused to treat with Osterman directly.[144] However, it happened that Juel was with Osterman when Oelreich came to make his proposal, and thus became a party to the intrigue: Goodricke, on the other hand, was for the present kept in ignorance of it as a consequence of Oelreich's insistence on secrecy. Though negotiations about terms seem to have continued for another week, Juel from the beginning had no doubt that Pechlin's offer must be accepted. Bernstorff, for his part, was all eagerness: Pechlin, he wrote, must be secured "at any cost."[145] That he should at the same time have been hoping for an understanding with Fersen—against whose leadership Pechlin's campaign was to be directed—was a significant indication of the disarray into which Danish policy had now fallen.[146]

So the bargain was struck; and during the next two months Pechlin proceeded to prepare his ground, building up within the Hat party a group of followers who could be relied to vote with him in critical divisions. Outwardly he remained a loyal member of the Hat caucus. But it was ominous that he should have separated himself from his colleagues and refused to vote for a motion approving the civil service strike of December.[147] And whatever the feeling of Fersen and his colleagues, the Court, at least, had already begun to suspect his sincerity:[148] Tilas watched his parliamentary maneuvers with growing disquiet.[149] In an effort to conciliate him, Adolf Fredrik asked the Estates to recall from exile a turbulent Pietist preacher who had close political ties with Pechlin; and as late as mid-June Lovisa Ulrika, at Gustav's entreaty, forced herself to a pretense of graciousness towards him;[150] but by that time neither she nor Modène trusted him an inch. Osterman believed that Modène had tried to bribe him with a gift of £10,000;[151] if so, the gift was either not taken, or ill bestowed, and it was decided to have recourse to other methods.

On 27 June Goodricke received from Rochford a French intercept which revealed that it was planned to expel Pechlin from the House of Nobility for ever.[152] This information Goodricke lost no time in passing on to Pechlin. He also communicated it to Osterman and Juel, who used it as a convenient pretext for breaking their promise, and letting Goodricke into the secret of their agreement: by this time they may well have felt that it would be useful to transfer a share of the expenses to English shoulders.[153] Goodricke was perhaps not entirely unprepared for their confidence: he had long ago informed Rochford that he was not without hope that Pechlin might be won over.[154] At all events, his reaction was prompt and practical: he at once advanced £2,000, receiving in return a promise to form a powerful opposition not only to any alteration in the constitution, but also (more important) to any move for a French alliance.[155] Goodricke had contacts of his own which might bring a useful accession of strength to Pechlin's forces,[156] and those forces were now growing so fast that the moment was evidently approaching when he would feel strong enough to break with Fersen. On 12 July there was a violent scene between them, in which Pechlin charged Fersen with risking Sweden's safety for the sake of France.[157] By mid-July Pechlin calculated that he influenced 190 votes in the House of Nobility,[158] and was sure of a majority in the Burghers.[159] By the beginning of August he had openly broken with the Hats, and was voting on the Cap side. His plan now was to set up "a new Party which is to be called the National Party," of which he would be the leader.[160] But for this he needed money—a great deal of money; and towards the end of July he presented Goodricke and his colleagues with his estimate of how much he would require.

What Pechlin was offering was a graduated scale of political objectives, and his financial demands depended upon which of three possible programs the associated courts were willing to pay for. Most radical, and most expensive, was the offer to change the political complexion both of Senate and Secret Committee, and to destroy the whole French system: for this he asked £120,000. Alternatively, to force the Hats to a Composition based on the inclusion of some Caps in the Senate, the preservation of "the actual system of alliance with [Sweden's] neighbours," and the integrity of the constitution: the price for this he put at £72,000. Or finally to form an opposition strong enough to preserve the constitution entire and to prevent "all other violent measures," if need be through breaking up the Diet in confusion as soon as the plan for the finances had been settled: this modest program, he calculated, could be put through for a mere £30,000.[161] On 26 July Goodricke, Juel, and Osterman met at Osterman's house to consider these proposals. Goodricke alone was for the first option, thinking the Hats already so divided that it might be possible. Juel was strongly against: the plan was fantastic, the idea of changing the Secret Committee unprecedented. In this he was certainly right; right also in thinking that Pechlin's unsavory reputation set limits to what he could achieve, and that his first option exceeded them.[162] Osterman concurred with Juel; and in the end all three agreed to recommend the second option to their governments. Pechlin was to be told to expect no firm answer for at least a month; but in the meantime they agreed to give him £2,000 for current expenses, of which sum Goodricke contributed £720, Osterman the remainder.[163] It remained to be seen how the three courts would respond to Pechlin's aggressive salesmanship.

Pechlin's first option found no takers anywhere. It was too expensive even for Russia, and all three courts seem to have considered it as probably unattainable, and in any case much in excess of what the situation required. Bernstorff was not happy with any of the options, considered the third as dangerous (presumably because parliamentary chaos might prepare the ground for a royalist coup), and would have preferred the plan of a Composition as contained in the second.[164] Panin, on the contrary, felt that the second option would bring such anxieties and difficulties as would make it an inadequate return for the expense involved, and therefore plumped for the third.[165] So too did the cabinet in London, who considered that it safeguarded the Tranquillity of the North against disturbance, since it prevented a change in the constitution "which *possibly might* [my italics] be a preparatory step for such a design": it gave them, in short, adequate cover against a risk which Rochford did not consider imminent, and entailed a premium no larger than they were prepared to pay.[166] Even so, it was expensive enough by previous British standards, and was to be a good deal more so before the Diet was over. On 25 August Goodricke was duly authorized to draw for £10,000. Bernstorff and Juel received the news with skepticism: they were sure there was a catch in it somewhere. On the basis of some private computation whose principles defy conjecture Bernstorff calculated that England's share in Pechlin's campaign ought really to be £30,000, rather than £10,000; he doubted the accuracy of Whitehall's arithmetic in regard to the sums actually transmitted; and he accused Goodricke of not using the money he had got—worse, he professed to "know beyond a shadow of doubt" that Goodricke had more than once dissuaded his government from spending money in Sweden. This grotesque distortion of the truth no doubt came to him from his minister in London, who was at this time urging Rochford to make contributions to the common chest in Stockholm far in excess of what had been agreed upon; and it is a fair guess that Rochford evaded his importunities by assuring him that Goodricke saw no need for more.[167] It certainly seems to be true that Goodricke husbanded his resources to good advantage. In these respects he differed markedly from Osterman, who notoriously had to pay for corruption at higher rates than his colleagues or adversaries, was often swindled by his agents, and had to rely at times on temporary loans from Juel, or assistance from Goodricke, to carry him on until the next installment of rubles should arrive.[168] In the matter of providing money Goodricke's preferred method was to pay for services after they had been rendered, and not before. But as usual he had no sooner received one supply than he began to agitate for another. Rochford proved remarkably accommodating. By 27 October he was sanctioning further expenditure to a maximum of £1,800 a month; and on 24 November, as we shall see, he made a final £6,000 available. All in all, the alliance with Pechlin cost the Civil List some £30,000, out of the total of £42,000 expended on this Diet.[169] The reason for this unique openhandedness is clear. Goodricke believed, and he succeeded in getting Rochford to believe, that in Pechlin they had found the only man who could do their business. They were not seriously concerned about possible Swedish aggression; the preservation of the constitution was not an end in itself: what they needed was more vigorous and abler leadership to restore the fortunes of the Caps and topple the Hats from power, or at least prevent them from doing a mischief. The lamentable performance of the Cap operators, the deficiencies of Rudbeck as a leader, made Pechlin, from whatever motives he acted, a man they could not afford to let slip; and his extraordinary achievements in the autumn of 1769 would vindicate that judgment. With Pechlin Goodricke was prepared to go all lengths: hence his preference for Pechlin's first option. The restoration of the Caps to power, if need be by extreme measures, was for him the simple precondition for any constructive policy in the North. The sequel would show that he shared Panin's misgivings about a Composition. But if his government could not afford all that he would have been willing to hazard he would make the best of what he got—and push them into additional expenditure as circumstances should arise.

Pechlin did not wait for the replies from the three courts to begin his operations. With £2,000 in his pocket he made immediate contact with Rudbeck, and presented him with a detailed plan of campaign, to be managed by a small council of himself, Rudbeck, and Ridderstolpe. On the advice of Osterman and Juel the Caps accepted this offer.[170] Pechlin had from the beginning stipulated that any contributions from foreign powers be under the exclusive direction of himself and Osterman, and this was accepted:[171] Goodricke's accounts for the following months show, on the one hand, large payments to Osterman for the main campaign fund, and on the other numerous smaller payments to his own agents, designed for matters in which he was especially interested, or to obtain information (in which he was sometimes more successful than Juel or Osterman), or simply to keep the "English" party steady to its allegiance.[172]

Pechlin had begun his operations against the Hats by maneuvers designed to wreck their plan for the finances. It was an obvious target to choose. Everyone now recognized that something must be done to reduce the supply of paper money, but on the method and the timing of any such operation the economists, the businessmen, and the parliamentarians were all divided and uncertain. Still deeper were the divisions on the question of pegging or unpegging the rate of exchange. On these clashes of opinion (which in part cut across party lines) Pechlin played with great skill; and he took care, in the Secret Committee, to oppose all the equally unpopular solutions to the financial problem which were put forward. Despite his efforts, on 17 and 18 July the finance plan of the Bank Committee was approved by large majorities in the three upper Estates.[173] It provided for the calling in of paper money, to begin at the end of 1770; for the appeasement of the ironmasters and industrialists by lifting the restrictions on loans from the Bank; and for the pegging of the exchange at 48, instead of 42. They thus pursued simultaneously two incompatible ends: on the one hand a realization program, and on the other a policy of mild reflation, designed to encourage industry. Their principal objective was a favorable balance of trade, for most Swedish economists now believed that it was the balance of trade which determined the rate of exchange: hence their policy of credit for exporters, hence their deferment of any reduction in the money supply for eighteen months.[174] But a favorable balance of trade depended in part upon cutting down imports, and especially imports of grain; and the possibility of currency reform depended upon the state's having the financial resources to carry it through. This meant in the first place the prohibition of distilling, for a great part of Sweden's grain consumption went into the production of *brännvin*. And as to the demonetization of paper, the only source from which the Hats had any hope of raising the resources was in reality France.[175] Thus the Hats' plan for financial reform hung essentially upon France's payment of subsidy arrears, and upon the ban upon distilling. It was not a hopeful or a popular program; but it was the best they could devise, and its emphatic endorsement by the three upper Estates permitted them to hope for a moment that they might get away with it. The Caps thought so too, and looked with foreboding at the probable consequences.[176]

This was Pechlin's opportunity. There was nothing he could do about the French arrears, except to demand that any money received from France be applied to the redemption of bank bills, and to no other purpose;[177] but the ban upon *brännvin* offered him a weapon which he was not slow to use. Despite the moral disapprobation of a section of the Clergy, and the strong opposition of the Burghers, the whole Estate of Peasants clung to their long-established right to distill at home.[178] It soon became apparent that the opposition to the ban was too formidable to ignore, and that its political consequences were likely to be serious: early in September C. F. Scheffer was writing that he feared that finance might be the ruin of the Hats, as it had been the ruin of the Caps.[179] By the middle of the month the Nobility had voted to permit distilling for a period of twenty-eight days in the year; soon afterwards they improved this concession to six months; the Clergy and the Burghers then abandoned as hopeless any attempt to control it. An essential prop of the Hat budget had been removed, without thereby removing a growing resentment among the Peasants; and on 19 September Goodricke could write: "we have overturned the whole Foundation of the Secret Committee's plan of finances."[180] They had certainly lopped off one limb of it; and as it happened the other limb was by this time already atrophied also.

It did not need Pechlin's arts to extinguish the Hats' hope of extracting arrears from France. Choiseul had made his attitude perfectly clear in June: when a reform of the constitution had been carried out to his satisfaction, he would be ready to consider another subsidy treaty, but until that had been done any payment of arrears was out of the question.[181] The Hats were reluctant to believe that he meant it; and Modène perhaps gave them more encouragement than was warranted by his orders. At all events, at the beginning of August Ekeblad made another approach through Creutz, Sweden's ambassador in Paris.[182] It is most unlikely that Choiseul would have changed his mind in any case, but as it happened his intransigence was reinforced from an unexpected quarter. At the beginning of June the Court, and the crown prince in particular, had eagerly supported the application for payment of the arrears, for they hoped to use those arrears to carry their plan of constitutional reform through the *riksdag*.[183] Two months later Gustav had changed his mind. He realized now that a refusal to pay arrears could be an effective means to compel the Hats to implement their promises; and he was beginning to suspect that without some such pressure the promises would not be implemented at all. On 2 August, at the very moment when Creutz was ordered to make his application, he sent to Choiseul, through Breteuil (now in Holland), the draft of a suggested French reply, in which Louis XV was made to describe the Swedish application as "incredible."[184] The use of Breteuil as a canal, moreover, sufficiently indicated to Choiseul the Court's opinion of Modène. The effect was all that Gustav could have desired: at the beginning of September Modène was sharply rebuked, and told to remember that he was the ambassador not of Sweden but of France; arrears were again refused; and once more Choiseul made it clear that he would enter into no negotiation until the constitutional issue had been settled.[185] In September, the terms for a French alliance were transmitted to Stockholm, with financial provisions which were generous enough; but though Goodricke wrote alarmed dispatches to the office[186] (one provision of the proposed treaty was his expulsion from Sweden, and a refusal to accept a successor), Choiseul's unvarying insistence on a satisfactory constitutional reform as a prerequisite for any arrangement made it unlikely that it would be arrived at.[187] The arrears question dragged on, however: in December, J. G. Oxenstierna was painfully copying a memorandum on the subject from the Lesser Secret Deputation; but both he and everybody else now realized that it was all a waste of time.[188] The Hats had not been able (as we shall see) to comply with Choiseul's condition precedent; the condition of France's finances in any case made large expenditure unlikely; and the Diet ended with the question left hanging in the air.[189]

In the face of these reverses at home and abroad Fersen attempted a radical revision of his tactics. In mid-August three significant events occurred almost simultaneously. On 16 August Modène informed Fersen that he would stop all financial support unless the question of the constitution was tackled, and added that his resources would be exhausted by the end of September.[190] On the seventeenth a conference of Hat leaders with the Court ended to the satisfaction of both parties, with a firm pledge by the Hats to pursue the "grand objective" of constitutional reform.[191] On the following day Pechlin's operations in the Diet suffered their first serious check.[192] Fersen apparently decided to use this moment to attempt to win over some of the Caps to a revision of the constitution upon a bipartisan basis. He therefore approached the Cap leaders with proposals for a Composition. He offered them five places on the Senate, which in the circumstances was an attractive bait; but in return he asked their support for a plan of reform which was far-reaching, and which may have been more or less identical with that agreed upon at the conference on the seventeenth.[193] The king was to recover those rights to make appointments which he had enjoyed in terms of clause 40 of the Constitution of 1720; he was to regain the right, in conjunction with the Senate, to make alliances; and the *Memorial on the Services* of 1756 (or what remained of it after the Caps' reforms of 1766) was to be revoked. In addition, the king was to acquire the vital right to veto any legislation which changed existing law; the debts of the Court were to be paid; and henceforward (as Reuterholm had predicted already in June) meetings of the Diet would take place only every tenth year.[194] The Cap leaders seem to have consulted only Osterman about this offer. Goodricke had obtained information about the Court's supposed plans which coincided closely with the terms of the Composition,[195] but of the negotiations with Rudbeck and his colleagues he was as yet ignorant; Juel did not report them until 8 September, and was outraged that Osterman should have allowed the Caps to engage in them.[196] Of the course of the negotiations we know nothing, except that they continued for rather more than a fortnight: on 29 August Goodricke was noting that Lovis Ulrika had invited the Cap leaders Horn and Ribbing to stay at Drottningholm,[197] and it is unlikely that their visit (if they made it) was of a purely social nature. But by 15 September Fersen's initiative had clearly failed: on that day Juel could write with satisfaction that the secret talks had come to an end.[198]

Fersen was not prepared to accept that result as final without making another attempt. At the end of September he produced his second plan for a Composition.[199] Once again he offered five seats on the Senate; once again the basis was to be the Constitution of 1720. But this time all changes before and after 1756 were to be rescinded; which meant in fact that the important innovations made *in* 1756 (including the name stamp) were *e silentio* to remain in force, or (if they had been repealed in 1766) were to revive—which was to strike simultaneously at the Court on the one hand, and at the Caps on the other. On the other hand he offered the Caps certain important improvements on his previous version: the veto on changes in the laws was now to be exercised not only by the king, but by king, Senate, *and Estates,*[200] and so too was the control of foreign policy; privileges were to be safeguarded against decisions by a majority of Estates (a point designed to win the support of the Cap Nobility and Clergy); extraordinary courts and commissions were to be forbidden (an old Cap policy); the notion of a ten-year *riksdag* was dropped, so too was the condition that the debts of the Court should be paid; and by a provision which sharply contradicted the trend of the times the old principle that *licentiering* was a matter of criminality was reinforced by entrusting decisions upon it to a special judicial tribunal.[201] These were highly significant concessions; and the fact that Fersen was prepared to make them is perhaps a pointer to his lack of enthusiasm for the radical reform which the Court desired, and to which he had pledged himself in the previous January. His ambivalence on this issue would become still clearer in the constitutional crisis of November.

The Caps were not to be tempted. Pechlin was by this time confident of his ability to block all attempts at reform; and Osterman was solidly behind him.[202] On 6 October Juel informed Bernstorff that Osterman had forced the Caps to break off the negotiations; on the twentieth he was confident that the Composition was dead—at least for this Diet.[203] This time Goodricke seems to have been in the secret; and his views coincided with Osterman's: he was beginning to scent victory in the coming months, and he felt no need to compromise.[204] As to Juel and Bernstorff, it is difficult to establish their attitude, if indeed they were clear about it themselves. Bernstorff was now describing Fersen as the "chef des séducteurs";[205] but both he and Juel changed their minds from week to week as to whether or not a reform based on 1720 was tolerable in view of Denmark's supposedly vital interests.[206] Bernstorff's last contribution to the debate (on 14 October) was fantastic in its remoteness from reality: in the very last resort, he intimated, he would be prepared to accept Fersen's proposals provided that they included a *liberum veto* clause, whereby any future change in the constitution could be blocked by the vote of a single member, and the proposing of any such change (by what might seem a supererogatory precaution) should entail the penalty of death.[207] The fears that Sweden might be threatened with the fate of Poland were perhaps after all not so unjustified as historians of the Lagerroth school would have us believe.[208]

Already, before Fersen's attempt at a Composition had finally stranded, the serious discussion of constitutional reform, hitherto so successfully evaded by the Hats, had been forced upon them. It took its rise in the accident that the post of *justitiekansler*, formerly held by Erik von Stockenström, had become vacant upon his nomination to the Senate. In terms of the Caps' *Ordinance for the Execution of the Laws* the nomination to the vacancy now lay, not with the crown, but with the Estates, and the question arose whether this procedure should now be followed. It was a question which involved not only the possibility of a restoration to the king of a lost prerogative, but also the much wider question of whether that Ordinance could be amended without undergoing a reference to a general election, and endorsement by a following *riksdag.*[209] Here was the opportunity for the Court to open the whole issue of constitutional reform; here too the chance for those who saw Sweden's only hope in a return to the constitution of 1720 *simpliciter* (and were consequently known as "Simplicists") to attempt to apply their remedy. On 25 September it was decided to refer the whole constitutional question to an unwieldly body, comprising the Secret Committee, the Secret Deputation, and the Judicial Deputation, for consideration and report.[210] By 5 October the United Deputations (as this body was called) had almost unanimously voted to restore the nomination of the *justitiekansler* to the king; five days later they voted to rescind the provision of 1766 whereby anyone nominated four times as a candidate for the Senate should be automatically elected: the Caps' Ordinance had thus been overturned in two critical points. From this they turned to more general matters; and on 17 October they accepted and endorsed two memorials by prominent Hats which presented a devastating indictment of the abuses committed by the Estates in the name of the quasisovereign authority which was believed to inhere in them. What the constitution needed, they considered, was some principle of balance; or at the least a separation of the judicial from the legislative power. Certainly what the ordinary subject needed was security against the arbitrariness, the tyranny, the political persecution of an uncontrollable and irresponsibly partisan parliament. The United Deputations set up a committee of five to draft an Act of Security which should be a Magna Carta, Habeas Corpus, and Bill of Rights, all rolled into one.[211]

The Act of Security did indeed try to protect the rights and liberties of the subject, and its provisions shed some light on what "Our

Blessed Liberty" had entailed. It forbade torture, imprisonment without trial, the use of informers, the seizure of private papers (the Wilkes case had not gone unremarked in Sweden), and the setting up of special courts or commissions. Henceforward the legislative and judicial functions were to be kept quite distinct: their confusion was condemned as the very definition of despotism. The Act would therefore have protected the citizen against the malfeasances of his parliamentary representatives, as well as against those of officials; and in particular would have prohibited the meddling of the Estates in judicial decisions, appointments, promotions, rewards, contracts, private grievances, and the ordinary work of the administration. The constitution was to return, in principle, to the basis of 1720, which (it was contended) had in fact included a built-in set of checks and balances which if observed would keep it in equipoise. The Ordinance of 1766 was for the most part to be annulled; but in the final version of the Act the provision for automatic election to the Senate of those nominated four times was restored.

In all this there was little enough of comfort for the Court. No one dared even to touch the issue of a royal veto; nothing about royal influence or control on foreign policy; scarce any real increase in the king's share in appointments. Adolf Fredrik, in a moment of lucid pessimism, had predicted as much before the great debate began;[212] but the crown prince had hoped great things, and Modène had at least pretended to hope them.[213] When the subcommittee was appointed to draw up the Act, Fersen had assured Gustav that a real reform of the constitution would emerge; and on the strength of such assurances had induced Modène to continue subsidizing his party.[214] But the text which came to the *plena* was a shattering disappointment to the supporters of the Court. Rightly or wrongly they believed that the original report of the committee had somehow been sabotaged in transit from the United Deputations to the Estates. Gustav, though he acquitted Fersen of bad faith, believed that he had capitulated to others of his party less honorable than himself; C. F. Scheffer wrote "Je suis outré de dépit contre la corruption lâche et infâme des Ch.[apeaux] et . . . couvert de honte pour l'incapacité ou la mauvaise foy de leurs chefs"; Tilas dismissed it as an Act of Security for the Hat party, no more.[215] Even the morbid suspiciousness of Juel could find little to fasten on: the Act, he wrote, put an end to any danger of real reform.[216] His relief did not prevent him from collaborating closely with Pechlin to defeat it. From an early stage Goodricke was hopeful of success.[217] He had good reason to be so. Pechlin and his allies had fought hard against the majority in the

United Deputations; and his constitutional arguments appealed so effectively to those who saw in the authority of the Estates the only barrier to an autocracy on the one hand, or an aristocracy on the other, that the passage of the Act must in any case have been endangered, even without the massive means of corruption which the three courts had put at his disposal.[218] A critical moment came on 2 November, when Fersen committed the tactical error of dividing the House of Nobles on the question whether they should not first consider the finances, before proceeding to deal with the Act.[219] The debate was tumultuous and protracted; it led to several duels between members of the House; but in the end Fersen carried his point: the finances were to take precedence. Meanwhile Pechlin had used this moment of confusion; and on the same day engineered a resolution of the Estate of Peasants rejecting the Act altogether, and another of the Estate of Burghers postponing consideration of it for this Diet.[220] It is true that two days later the Act was accepted by the Estate of Clergy; and since the resolutions of the two lower Estates were not identical it was still possible that the Act might pass, if the Nobility voted in the same terms as the Clergy to accept it. The friends of reform were still confident of victory.[221] The result came as a profound shock. On 15 November, after a twelve-hour sitting, the Act was thrown out by 457 to 431.[222]

Simplicists and royalists greeted the result with cries of outrage and despair: to them it seemed to signify the triumph of corruption and political immorality, the final degradation.[223] "Before," wrote J. G. Oxenstierna, "one was at least what one was bought to be; but Pechlin has taught our country a higher and finer kind of baseness—that of taking money and betraying all the same." To Goodricke and his allies, on the other hand, it was an enormous triumph. Their expensive investment in Pechlin had paid a bumper dividend. Goodricke wrote in exultation to Rochford, "We have saved the constitution of Sweden"; and Rochford in reply conveyed "H. M.'s highest approbation of your Zeal, Diligence and Activity in carrying through this important point."[224] But the "important point" was not so much the preservation of the constitution (which from the British point of view was simply the battleground on which the engagement was fought out) as the unexpected and demoralizing defeat of the Hats. The Act of Security would in fact have had very little real effect upon the balance of forces within the state. There was little in the Act to change the relations of the king to the Senate and Estates. It would not have brought a royal control of foreign policy one step the nearer. But some of the most damaging malpractices would have been checked or removed; the growing body of moderate men of both parties who desired to preserve the constitution by reforming it would have been strengthened (Tilas believed that some of the more intelligent Caps voted for the Act on 15 November); the disillusionment with the constitution would have been checked. And it was upon such disillusionment that any attempt to subvert the constitution must (at least in part) rely. Ever since the summer of 1766, when the three courts first learned of Choiseul's new course in Sweden, the preventing of any royalist coup d'état had been a common objective which linked them together. The rejection of the Act of Security made an attempt of this sort more, not less likely, for it seemed to bar the way to the only constructive alternative: that is, to reform by agreement of what was admittedly amiss. "Never again," wrote Tilas, "shall we have such an opportunity to place our precious Liberty on an enduring, safe and rational basis."[225] After 1769 it was no longer possible for the Simplicists to believe that their program had any future; and for them all that remained was to turn royalist in the name of patriotism. The Hats themselves, hitherto allies of the crown on the basis of a bargain which they had no intention of keeping, would before very long be forced to the king's party by social developments which the struggle for the Act first clearly foreshadowed. For the Act had been defeated, partly because some Hats in the Nobility defected to the opposition on Pechlinian grounds, partly by corruption, partly by Fersen's incapacity or bad faith, but (and this was what was significant for the future) also by the solid opposition of the Peasants.

Goodricke and his colleagues ought to have been in no doubt as to the real constitutional implications of the Act of Security. The pertinacity and energy with which they worked to defeat it certainly require explanation. As to Russia, Panin had already in 1766 abandoned his original strategy of securing a better balance in the constitution as the best means of preserving it, and the theories of balance which were ventilated in the United Deputations had now no appeal for him. He was no longer interested in constructive reform. No doubt he feared that once reform began it might be impossible to contain it. No doubt Osterman knew, through Pechlin, how far the Hats had committed themselves to the Court in January. Since French supplies for Sweden were now conditional on a reform of some sort, it was reasonable to oppose reform of any sort. Russia had committed large sums to Pechlin, and could not now go back. The success of the alliance with Pechlin changed Panin's attitude from one of flexible defense, with 1720 as the last line of resistance, to one of adamantine opposition to all change.[226]

Bernstorff's policy was dictated by very similar considerations. In 1764 he had been at least prepared to consider C. F. Scheffer's plea for a revision of the constitution. In 1765 he had been ready to concede that the legislation of 1756 was not immutable. Even in 1769 he retained some confidence that his Hat friends were a guarantee against any real danger. But though Scheffer's principles inspired a good deal of the work of the United Deputations, and though the Act was a Hat measure, Bernstorff's constitutional nightmares prevented his grasping its real insignificance. To him it seemed to be the first step towards converting the Swedish constitution into something like the English—and indeed there had been much talk in the United Deputations of the virtues of the English polity. Such a transformation was in his view a risk too great to run: a king in Sweden with the constitutional powers of George III, he considered, would soon become absolute.[227]

These were aspects of the situation which do not seem to have occurred either to Rochford or to Goodricke. They saw the issue in very clear-cut and simple terms. In the constitutional debate they had little interest, provided that the possibility of the king's control of foreign policy was estopped: towards the close of the Diet Goodricke would even support the payment of the Court's debts, on the ground that the splendor and dignity of the crown was an essential feature of the constitution.[228] Their object was the overthrow of the French party and the victory of the English; Pechlin's alliance offered the best hope of that, and once it had been made England must support Pechlin's program, or lose her money. France demanded reform of the constitution; England therefore must resist it: in 1769, as Bernstorff truly remarked, Sweden had become the only place in Europe where England could deal a blow at France, to offset the defeat in Corsica.[229] And, finally, a zealous collaboration with Osterman in Stockholm would demonstrate to Panin once again the sincerity of Rochford's desire for close relations with Russia. That desire was further evidenced by the dockyard facilities which the Admiralty offered to the Russian fleet on its long haul which was to end at Thesmé;[230] as also by well-meaning if embarrassing proffers of British mediation in the Turkish war. But the naval facilities were a short-lived episode; the proffer of mediation more of an irritant than a lenitive, and the attempt in 1770 to hitch a new plan for an alliance to it would prove an unhappy inspiration. The collaboration in Stockholm, on the contrary, had roots in the past and would extend into the future. For a time, between 1766 and 1769, it had seemed that Juel had displaced Goodricke as Osterman's principal partner. But Danish policy in Sweden, despite Bernstorff's total commitment to Russia, had always had private and particular aspects which marked it off from Panin's. For Bernstorff and Juel the return of the Caps to power was almost a matter of indifference.[231] For Goodricke, on the contrary, as also for Osterman, it was the prime tactical objective. Upon this coincidence of view, upon the fact that the maintenance of an English party directly served Russia's interest, was based an intimate collaboration which grew stronger in the course of the next three years. In that relationship it seems that the alliance with Pechlin and the defeat of the Act of Security mark a return to the close association of 1765. Despite the renewal of the Russo-Danish alliance in December 1769, Danish influence in Stockholm would grow weaker and in a year would vanish altogether; but English influence would grow stronger, until in the final phases Goodricke, rather than Osterman, would emerge as the more resolute partner.

(v)

Bitterly disappointed though the Court was with the Act of Security, it had still strained every nerve to secure its passage. Before its defeat, Gustav and Sinclair were doing their best to persuade Modène to finance a coup d'état, to be carried out at the close of the Diet. Modène was not unsympathetic (indeed, after the tumultuous session of 2 November he had opined that what was really needed was a whiff of grapeshot) but he was obliged to tell Sinclair that French financial backing for a coup in the near future was out of the question.[232] Thus the issue of the great debate on the constitution left the Court more embittered and more powerless than ever. The Hats had failed them; and they considered that Modène had failed them too: he had been a great disappointment. Already at Norrköping Gustav had remarked that his presence or absence would make no difference; he was considered to be unbecomingly mean in the matter of hospitality; he played cards distressingly badly; he complained that he was not taken enough notice of at court, and Gustav had to intervene with his mother to do something about it.[233] Barthélémy (his secretary) recalled that Modène "se conduisit pendant tout son séjour en Suède de manière à repousser toute confiance et toute considération."[234] Poor Modène! Choiseul had required of him results which at that time there was no hope of obtaining: neither Breteuil before him, nor Vergennes afterwards, could have done much better in such intractable circumstances. But this was no comfort to Lovisa Ulrika. By Christmas 1769 the Court felt that it had reached the end of the road: of the bright hopes of Norrköping not a rag remained. They could trust now only to time and accident. But for Lovisa Ulrika time was running out faster than she dreamed of.

For Bernstorff and Panin, who had thus saved the Swedish constitution from the grave risk that it might safeguard the liberty of the subject, it seemed logical to entrench this precious palladium of freedom by explicit guarantees. The treaty which Bernstorff had been pressing so eagerly upon Russia since the beginning of the year provided a natural opportunity to do this. When at last, in December, the renewed Danish-Russian alliance was signed, it gave Bernstorff the firm assurance that Paul should be declared of age in 1771, and an undertaking that if he should die before that date the Holstein-Oldenburg exchange should be carried out; the Danish navy was to be supplied by Russia with shipbuilding materials; the Russian navy was to receive from Denmark a much-needed draft of officers and men who had actually seen the sea. And the treaty included a clause which bound both parties to attack Sweden immediately, if the constitution of 1720 should be infringed in the smallest particular, with a guarantee to Denmark (thrust upon the prudishly embarrassed Bernstorff by Panin) of any territorial gains which might accrue to her from resulting hostilities.[235] It is hard to know which partner to this agreement it was that was trying to make the other's flesh creep, or indeed whether either seriously believed in the fatal consequences of *any* alteration in the constitution of 1720: after all, it had stood quite a few alterations already. However that may be, it was a treaty which guaranteed all those abuses which gave the constitution a bad odor and imperilled its survival, and it stands as a monument to the muddle-headed obliquity of Bernstorff, and the indolent cynicism of Panin.

For political realism it compares ill with the parallel treaty between Russia and Prussia, concluded on 23 October 1769. The initiative for a renewal and extension of the alliance of 1764, well before it was due to expire, came from Frederick.[236] He may perhaps have calculated (as Rochford had done) that Catherine's embarrassments would put him in an advantageous negotiating position. If so, the calculation proved erroneous, in the one case as in the other. For Frederick wanted Catherine's guarantee of his succession to the Hohenzollern outpost in Ansbach-Baireuth, and Catherine set a stiff price upon it. Her counterproject would have bound him to join with Russia and Denmark in all measures which might be necessary to avert a Swedish attack upon Russia, and also in all measures which might be necessary to prevent the establishment of the sovereignty of the crown in Sweden.[237] To this Frederick stoutly refused to agree. His attitude to the Swedish constitution was precisely what it had been in 1764, and he saw no reason for changing it. The destruction of the constitution of 1720 was one thing; the recovery by the king of certain powers which had been taken from him since that date was quite another. He was not prepared to concur in any measures which Russia and Denmark might choose to take, or make a *casus foederis* out of any change in the constitution simply because Panin might cry "wolf," and on the strength of it to send his troops into Pomerania.[238] The Russian alliance was oppressive enough already: he was not going to make it more so by the surrender of his judgment to his ally. It was with the idea of warning Catherine that he did not lack alternatives that in August he arranged his celebrated meeting with Joseph II at Neisse. Its effect soon became perceptible: Catherine toned down her demands. She asked now only that Frederick should guarantee certain specific articles in the constitution, and in the event of their violation make a "diversion" in Pomerania.[239] This was at least a precise commitment, which Frederick could interpret for himself; but it was a commitment which covered most of the points where Lovisa Ulrika had hoped for some improvement, and its acceptance in this form undeniably represents something of a concession on Frederick's part. Nevertheless, he took the earliest opportunity after the signature of the treaty to reject a request from Panin that Cocceji should make common cause with Osterman to resist the Act of Security:[240] opposition to the Simplicists was no part of his bargain. For, after all, he professed to be a Simplicist himself.

With constitutional niceties of this sort Goodricke was not much concerned. For him, the defeat of the Act was a springboard for the leap to final victory. Even before the issue of the struggle was decided he was preparing for the possibility of success, and with Pechlin and Osterman planning the next step forward.[241] He was sufficiently sanguine to hope for two things, if the Act were defeated: the restoration of at least some of the Cap Senate; and the orientation of Swedish foreign policy towards England rather than France. Pechlin had offered both already, at a price; and it was in order to put the Caps back into the government that Goodricke extracted a final £6,000 from a complaining, but loyally trustful, Lord Rochford.[242] But it soon proved that the Hats, though badly shaken, were by no means routed: indeed, on 11 November, at a moment when the tide was running strongly against them on the constitutional question, they surprised everyone by carrying their revised finance plan by ten votes in the House of Nobility.[243] Pechlin, however, was by this time cock-a-hoop with his recent successes, and his overconfidence led Goodricke and Osterman into a venture which they would have done better to defer. At Pechlin's suggestion, they concocted a memorial demanding that the Secret Committee should disclose how far the French subsidies had been properly paid, and that it should be forbidden to engage in any negotiations for an alliance until any possible arrears had been made good. This was to touch the Hats on one of their tenderest points; and when the matter was brought forward by a certain Gyllenhaal in the House of Nobility their reaction was impressively vigorous: Gyllenhaal's motion was thrown out by a majority of 123.[244] This was bad enough; but the situation was made worse by the fact that Gyllenhaal's motion had been made without giving Rudbeck preliminary notice, and without informing Juel, who had been excluded from the affair entirely: it was, after all, no great interest of Denmark to substitute an English for a French alliance in Stockholm. The result was an unusually violent explosion from Bernstorff, who condemned both the thing itself and the manner in which it was done: Juel was instructed to tell Rudbeck and Pechlin that he would hold no further communication with them until they promised not to do it again.[245] And though (as he explained) only his old friendship for Goodricke deterred him from *complaining* in London, it did not stop him from *intimating*, and the effect as far as Goodricke was concerned was much the same: he was sharply rebuked for his imprudence, and also for having failed to report the fiasco to which it led.[246] It took a couple of months before the affair was more or less smoothed over; and one has the impression that it left a certain coolness between Osterman and Juel, and an increased intimacy of collaboration between Osterman and Goodricke.

Despite the fate of the Gyllenhaal memorial, there were signs towards the end of 1769 that a shift in Swedish foreign policy was not inconceivable. It became increasingly difficult not to credit the reality of Russian victories in Moldavia; the temporary junction of the Russian and Danish fleets, as the Russian squadron passed Copenhagen on its way to the Mediterranean, provoked nervous reactions in Stockholm; and the Lesser Secret Deputation came to the prudent conclusion that nothing, at least for the moment, should tempt them to give any real assistance to the Turks.[247] It was only with many protestations of peaceable intentions that they permitted themselves to send garrisons and workmen to the defenses of Finland.[248] Pechlin was now for an English alliance, without subsidies: he informed Osterman that "he would not take them if he might."[249] In December, Goodricke broached the idea informally to Fersen, with a view to a more official approach to Ekeblad later; but the response was too cool to encourage him to proceed.[250] Nor would Rochford now have wished it. He was still anxious for a Swedish alliance as the basis for a quadruple system; but a Swedish alliance in isolation might have its dangers: what, he asked himself, if Denmark were once more to ally with France?[251] It was no doubt an absurd speculation, so long as Bernstorff was in power; but by the end of 1769 it was already a question whether he would be in power much longer. If not, it was a fair assumption that he would be succeeded by men who were no friends to Russia, nor even to *Mageskiftet*, or who might even be men of no political principles at all.[252] So the question of a Swedish alliance was allowed to pend, as the question of an Anglo-Russian alliance was also pending; and Ekeblad could congratulate himself on being spared an embarrassment. He had embarrassment enough already, as a result of Fersen's casual remark to Goodricke that he had decided to renew Sweden's treaties with Russia and Denmark, both of which were shortly due to expire.[253] As far as Denmark was concerned, that idea was soon quashed by Bernstorff;[254] but it was not until the middle of December that the chancery-president managed to fend off Osterman's inquiries with a courteous but temporizing reply.[255] Sweden's "system," it appeared, was not to undergo alteration if the Hats had their way; and when the Diet ended the Secret Committee's instruction to the Council prescribed the utmost caution, no innovations, and above all no step which could lead to the country's being drawn into war.[256]

Thus one of Goodricke's hopes was disappointed; and in the event he came no nearer to realizing his other objective of restoring the Caps to office. At the end of October Pechlin had calculated that he could secure a Cap Senate for £18,000; but unfortunately no one at that time had an extra £18,000 to spare.[257] On 7 November Pechlin and Ridderstolpe (described by Goodricke as "at the head of what is called the English party") put forward a comprehensive plan which combined the replacement of the Hat Senate with a revolution in foreign policy: for this political earthquake all they asked was £54,000, paid on the nail.[258] The three ministers agreed to the plan in principle, but decided to take it in financially digestible installments: Goodricke and Juel advanced what they could afford, Osterman borrowed where he could, and it was agreed to pay half the price of each item in advance, and the remaining half after it had been secured.[259] But Juel participated with only tepid interest: much better, he thought, to get the Caps back into the Senate by a Composition.[260] Goodricke and Osterman, on the other hand, were for carrying it by storm; but this proved more difficult than they had anticipated. Osterman in November received only half of the financial support he had expected;[261] it became clear that there would be no time to carry Pechlin's program piecemeal before Christmas, and nobody could face the prospect of the Diet's continuing for long enough to complete it thereafter. Rochford said plainly that he was not prepared to go on paying for what he called "speculative advantages"; and though at the end of the year Osterman received large cash reinforcements, by that time it was too late.[262] There was some talk of Fersen's offering two places on the Senate, if the Caps would agree to be quiet; but it led nowhere, though Bernstorff apparently believed that it might.[263] The Hats were certainly weakening—the Stockholm municipal elections at the end of 1769 went against them, which was an ominous sign[264] —but they were not yet broken: the best the Caps could obtain from a now conciliatory Fersen was a sort of Composition which secured equal pensions to *licentierade* members of the Senate, whether Hat or Cap. In the closing weeks of the Diet Goodricke could report a number of parliamentary successes, and the Hats displayed a significant reluctance to risk divisions; but the foreign ministers' money had run out at last, though fortunately Fersen did not seem to realize it.

Nevertheless, the Diet of 1769 was felt by Goodricke (with some justification) as something of personal triumph: "we have concluded the Diet," he wrote, "in a Manner very different from what was to be expected in the first three months of it, when there was a majority of 240 against us, in the House of Nobles, and three to one in the other Orders."[265] For once Whitehall did full justice to the achievement; and the partial judgment of Sir Joseph Yorke probably fairly reflected informed opinion:

> Our Northern Plenipo has closed his Diet much to his credit and to the mortification of his adversaries. I tell him that he would have made a great figure with the Israelites in Egypt, as he certainly would have help'd them to satisfy their Task Masters by inventing some Method of making Bricks without Straw; it will indeed always redound to his Credit as a Negotiator, that the French made one of the first articles of their entering into more intimate connexions with their party in Sweden, his being recall'd.[266]

There had indeed been a dramatic reversal of fortune within the space of a single year. In Pechlin, Goodricke and Osterman had found a party leader abler and more unscrupulous than Rudbeck or Löwenhielm; and it was Goodricke's merit to convince his government that Pechlin must be supported, and on a scale much exceeding what England had been willing to contemplate before. Apart altogether from financial support, Goodricke had a contribution to make to Pechlin's operations which probably exceeded Osterman's, and certainly exceeded Juel's—the trust he enjoyed among the Caps, his knowledge of their rank and file, his private network of agents: it is significant that in his close collaboration with Osterman it was Osterman who distributed the money to the operators, but Goodricke who procured the secret intelligence and managed the details of negotiation with those who were to be seduced.[267] He was confident, in February 1770, that the same tactics, pursued with the same determination, would at the next Diet restore the triumphant position of 1765, and give to Sweden a Cap Senate and an anglophile foreign policy; certain, therefore, that the working alliance with Pechlin must be continued and strengthened. This was not the opinion of Juel and Bernstorff, who saw Pechlin as the dangerous intriguer rather than as the heaven-sent party chief.[268] But what Bernstorff thought was now of increasingly questionable importance, as his hold on power grew weaker: what mattered was the close union of Osterman and Goodricke behind a common program, and the exemplification through that union of an Anglo-Russian collaboration which was the best substitute for an alliance, and if all went well might even yet be developed into one.

If for England the Diet of 1769 was a modified triumph, for France it was an unrelieved disaster. The revolution which had eluded Choiseul in December 1768 seemed further off than ever. As on the former occasion Fersen had interposed his veto, so now he had contributed, by bad tactics or bad faith, to blast even the modest proposals of the Act of Security, to say nothing of the program of January to which he had pledged himself. Neither France nor the Court could ever wholly trust him again. If the defeat in Sweden had been an isolated incident, it might have been felt to be the less bitter. But indeed it was only the last of a series of reverses. The Turkish war which Choiseul had so recklessly provoked, so far from undermining Catherine's throne, was illustrating it with victories by land, and would shortly add to these the portentous success of Tchesmé; French patronage of the Confederates of Bar had been delayed until it could no longer avail to save either them or France's reputation; a naive attempt to seduce Frederick the Great had ended with a renewed breach of diplomatic relations; and the meeting at Neisse had cast doubt on the reliability of France's Austrian ally. The Family Compact indeed appeared more solid than ever, which from the point of view of French operations in Sweden was just as well: early in 1769 Choiseul was seeking the afforcement of his overstrained secret service fund by the loan of two million dollars from Madrid, and the Spanish minister in Stockholm, the Count de Lascy, was acting as Modène's coadjutor.[269] But even so the Spanish connection was threatened with shipwreck on the rocks of the Falkland Islands. Apart from d'Aranda there was scarcely a statesman outside France who did not regard Choiseul's policies with skepticism and disapproval, and who did not see in his febrile activity the actions of a man who was ready to grasp at any expedient which promised to enhance his credit and prolong his political life. Among such expedients the carrying through of a royalist coup d'état in Stockholm appeared less hopeful than ever.

On 30 January 1770 the Hat Diet (to borrow Fersen's flippant phrase) at last "bored itself to an end,"[270] and the combatants retired to lick their financial wounds, or count their financial gains, as it might happen. Among the latter sort was Pechlin, who virtuously declined a British pension, but did not refuse a gratification from the three ministers of £6,000, together with a present of jewelry for his wife. Yet the Diet's closing days were not wholly taken up with arid party strife and the casting up of the accounts of corruption. They had witnessed one event which was to be of profound significance for the future. For on 20 January there was presented to the Estates the document known as the Memorial of Alexander Kepplerus.[271] Kepplerus's memorial injected into the political debate a new and ominous element. It was a frontal attack upon one of the basic elements of Swedish society. For it demanded, in uncompromising terms, the extension of privileges to the unprivileged orders: that is, it demanded in effect the razing of the whole edifice of social and political discrimination—in appointments, in promotions, in opportunities for advancement. It brought to a point feelings which had been gathering force for the last four or five years, and which had first been apparent at the Diet of 1765. Already in 1762 those feelings had been stirred by a resolution of the House of Nobility not to permit the introduction of any new members until the numbers of the House had fallen to 800: a resolution which denied the ultimate reward of a peerage to the meritorious commoner. The opposition of the Estate of Peasants to the Act of Security had been based on similar resentments: it has been suggested that it was not only that they were determined to preserve the Diet's right to interfere in judicial causes because they saw in that right their best protection against an aristocratic judiciary and a hated officialdom; it was also that they believed that the Act might strengthen the nobility, inasmuch as that it might conceivably strengthen the Council.[272] Rumblings of social discontent could already be heard by those who took the trouble to frequent non-noble clubs: for instance, by Admiral Tersmeden, who was shaken to hear talk which persuaded him that the decline of the Hats was the result of the grievances of the lower orders and the reservation of high administrative posts to members of the first Estate. The company was at no pains to mince its words; and one of those present warned him that the effects would be even clearer at the next Diet.[273]

In so far as this social unrest could be related to party alignments it was clearly in line with the attitudes and policies of the younger Caps: certainly it was hostile to the aristocratic, bureaucratic elements which were so strongly represented among the Hats. But really it was the beginnings of a social struggle which would cut across and transcend the struggle of parties. Since these new pressures came from elements which as a rule tended to vote Cap, it was possible, it was even probable, that Goodricke and Osterman might at the next Diet be able to call upon the support of a strong tide of popular feeling. But it was a question how long they would be able to direct and control it. What is truly remarkable is that Kepplerus's memorial seems to have escaped their attention altogether: in Goodricke's and Juel's dispatches it is not so much as mentioned. And it was a question whether the privileged orders, soon to be under attack, might not be driven to swallow their constitutional principles, and prefer a strong monarchy to the hazards of democracy. Modène, too, missed the possible implications; but his secretary, Barthélémy, began to sniff opportunity on the wind.[274] The next Diet might indeed complete the Cap recovery; but when it came, it might well bring with it consequences and difficulties unforeseen by Goodricke in the euphoria of the spring of 1770.

CHAPTER X

Interlude, 1770–1771

(i)

The Diet was over; the members, dispersed. The political clubs closed their doors, no doubt to the regret of the innkeepers of Stockholm; the exhausted diplomats made up the accounts of corruption, congratulating themselves that with reasonable good fortune it would be three years before the meeting of the next ordinary Diet exposed them to renewed importunities; and the surface of politics in the capital assumed a more tranquil aspect. Goodricke, with obvious relief, predicted a quiet summer.[1] His colleagues seem to have been of the same opinion; for one after another they betook themselves homeward. Count Lascy, the Spanish minister—whose obscure activities on behalf of the French cause had for some time been giving anxiety to Goodricke and the British government[2] —set off for Madrid by way of Paris, there to execute on Lovisa Ulrika's behalf a commission of some importance. Modène was recalled in April, and the legation left in charge of his able secretary, Barthélémy. Gregers Juel spent the summer in Denmark, and so began an absence which was to prove much more protracted than either he or Bernstorff had foreseen.[3] Osterman, whose health engaged Panin's kindly solicitude, was encouraged to drink the waters of some continental spa; though in the event he contented himself with a short visit to the wells of Loka, Medevi being no doubt too closely identified with the Hats to be comfortable.[4] And at the end of February Rochford, with expressions of cordial approbation, acceded to the application for leave which Goodricke had sent in a month earlier.[5]

He was certainly entitled to feel that he had earned it. He had now been twelve years in the North without a break; it was eleven since he had last seen his wife, who seems to have devoted the interval to putting his disordered finances to rights. He had long complained, not without reason, of the financial burden of the Stockholm mission.[6] In February 1769 he had been thinking of retiring from the diplomatic service altogether, and had asked his recall; and though at Rochford's request he agreed to carry on for the time being, he had then pleaded for four or five months' leave when the Diet was over, explaining that Lady Goodricke planned to join him shortly, and that he was anxious to save her an unnecessary journey.[7] But when he sent off this appeal he never expected the Diet to last until the following January, and in the event Lady Goodricke came over in the autumn. Her stay in Stockholm was not without its mortifications, for Goodricke refused to allow her to be presented at Court, since she would be required to kiss the hand of the queen and the princess royal, which was never exacted in England. Rochford approved his decision; Goodricke commented that "in the present situation" it was "of very little consequence whether she goes to Court or not";[8] Lady Goodricke's reactions are not recorded. But one may conjecture that she was not sorry to bring her stay in Sweden to an end.

They left Stockholm on 30 April, traveling by way of Copenhagen to the Hague, where they celebrated the king's birthday with Goodricke's old friend and patron, Sir Joseph Yorke. Sir Joseph thought him "as lively as ever, but grown much older in the 12 years we have been separated, which is in great measure owing to the loss of his upper teeth, which makes his Mouth fall in, and gives a hollowness to the voice"; but though physically he might be somewhat decayed, Sir Joseph found his intellectual teeth as sound and sharp as ever.[9] And so, with an invitation to visit Lord Hardwicke in his pocket, Goodricke returned to those Yorkshire estates which had been rescued by his wife's good management, and resumed for a space that life of a country gentleman which he had not known for a quarter of a century.[10]

He had, however, one important piece of political business to transact. The experience of the effect of French electioneering activity in the period between the last two Diets had convinced him that it was necessary to maintain an effective organization even when the Diet was not sitting, in order to keep the party together in the constituencies, to maintain something like a central office, and to buy proxies in small parcels over an extended period rather than wait till the imminence of the Diet forced their price up. This was also the view of Pechlin, who in March had presented a detailed plan to the ministers of the three courts, with an intimation that their acceptance of it would be a sine qua non for his continued support.[11] The cost to each was estimated at between £2,600 and £2,700 per annum. There was little doubt that Panin would be willing to make the money available;[12] and it was hoped to persuade Bernstorff and Rochford to pay their share. Goodricke carried the plan home with him, and on the way transmitted it to Bernstorff, who indicated that he must first consult Panin; with the predictable result that Denmark agreed to participate.[13] It remained to sell the idea to Rochford; in which less difficulty was encountered than might have been expected. When Goodricke left England in October (this time without Lady Goodricke) he took with him the assurance that the Civil List would provide one-third of the sum required to make the plan effective.[14]

Despite this success, he seems to have returned to his post with some reluctance. He had hoped for permission to stay the winter in England; but the ministry, sensitive to Opposition criticism of diplomats who spent too much time at home, was willing only to give him until the end of October. He might have persisted in a request to be recalled if he could have been assured of a life pension; but no pension, it appeared, happened to be available. His application to be appointed minister plenipotentiary was refused also, on the ground that it might make difficulties with Gunning—who was certainly less deserving of promotion, but had the useful asset of being a friend of Lord Suffolk. All that Rochford would do for him was to grant him a minister plenipotentiary's pay and allowances; and even this was vetoed by George III. It was clear that there was nothing to be got by lingering: by the middle of October he had set out once again for the North.[15]

(ii)

Events did not bear out Goodricke's prediction of a quiet summer. Certainly it was anything but quiet for Lord North's new administration. The last kick of the old Wilkite agitation came in this year, with Brass Crosby's case; and though North's adroit refusal to be baited would soon take the wind out of the Wilkite sails, foreign ministers in London were less impressed by his "absurd stoicism" than by the violence of the demagogues and the press. In foreign affairs too there was much cause for anxiety. It centered at first round the problems created by the presence of the Russian fleet in the Mediterranean. Catherine's ill-found ships had eventually arrived there only because Rochford had been willing to demonstrate goodwill by permitting dockyard and repair facilities in British ports; and perhaps also because they were manned to a considerable extent by British sailors, and commanded by a Scottish admiral. Nevertheless, Rochford was acutely anxious to preserve a correct neutrality, for he feared the effect of possible Turkish reprisals upon England's ailing Levant trade.[16] There seemed for a moment to be a real danger that Choiseul might take the risk of intercepting the Russians on their way to the Aegean, and indeed he was under some pressure from Madrid to do so.[17] Reports came in of French naval armaments in Toulon;[18] and until late in the autumn Count Mercy, the Austrian ambassador to Versailles, was afraid that Choiseul might give way to the temptation to strike some dramatic stroke which would reestablish his weakening position at home.[19] In August Lord Weymouth sent a detachment to the Aegean, ostensibly to protect British trade, but with secret orders to intervene if there were any French attack upon the Russian armament.[20] The sensational Russian victory at Tchesmé on 4 July did something to clarify the naval position, but it also opened up wider perspectives which could not fail to be of concern to a British government. It was followed by Russian victories on land, culminating in the autumn in the capture of Bender. It now seemed likely that Russia might succeed in establishing a foothold both on the Black Sea and in the Mediterranean, that the Turks would be forced to concede free passage of the Straits, and that the trade of the Black Sea would be thrown open, at any rate to Russian shipping. In January 1771 Catherine, in a letter to Frederick the Great, explicitly asserted her claim to the free navigation of the Black Sea for all nations, and to an island in the Aegean as an entrepôt for Russian commerce.[21]

On this question British opinion was divided. The *Annual Register* felt that the opening of the Black Sea "cannot fail to be seriously alarming to most of the commercial states of Europe"; and Rochford agreed that to open it to all nations was "liable to serious objections."[22] Goodricke would later take a more optimistic view: it was the only means, he wrote, to deprive France of her Levant trade, and the effect would be to throw that trade into the hands of England.[23] Cathcart, as might have been expected, minimized the significance of Russian demands. Rochford for his part had no objection to Catherine's making the territorial gains to which her victories might reasonably entitle her; his anxiety was that they should not be of such a nature as to weaken Russia by provoking the opposition of other powers, and in particular of Austria. He was therefore alarmed at the prospect of a Russian annexation of Moldavia, and at the vague plans for the emancipation of Albania and Greece with Russian support. The sooner peace could be restored on decent terms, the better, both for the sake of the Mediterranean trade, and for the sake of Russia herself.[24] And what better way to restore it than by British mediation?

This was an idea which dated back to the very beginning of the war. When hostilities first broke out at the end of 1768, Chernyshev, the Russian ambassador in London, asked for England's good offices in Constantinople. He was much annoyed when Weymouth instructed Murray, the British ambassador to the Porte, to offer not good offices but mediation.[25] There followed a lamentable diplomatic muddle, produced initially by the fact that on this matter, which fell within the province of both Secretaries of State, they did not hold a common language, Rochford's original line being for good offices only. But if there were indeed to be any question of mediation he wanted it to be in England's hands. When therefore Frederick in January 1769 proposed mediation by England and Prussia jointly, Rochford turned it down on the pretext that Russia had not asked for it, but really because he resented Prussian meddling. Frederick, who seems at first to have been genuinely prepared for cooperation, now became jealous in his turn. A struggle between England and Prussia for the mediation began in St. Petersburg. Rochford, warned by Cathcart of Catherine's annoyance at his attitude, then hastily changed his mind, and explained that if a joint mediation was what she wanted, he was prepared to agree to it rather than be left out altogether. Whereupon Catherine took the line that just as mediation was now too late to prevent the war, so also it was too early to end it: there must be Russian victories first. And already it seemed probable that if the moment for mediation should arrive, it would be to Prussia, and not to England, that she would turn. Thus Weymouth and Rochford between them had contrived to bungle it. They had alienated the Turks, they had forfeited some of Catherine's goodwill, and they had snubbed Frederick on the only occasion since 1763 when he had shown some readiness for amicable cooperation.[26]

In August 1770 Rochford made a singularly inept and ill-timed attempt to retrieve these blunders. Even Cathcart now realized that a renewal of the negotiations must probably await the conclusion of peace; but Rochford allowed himself to believe that he could make

English mediation an inducement to persuade Catherine to an alliance. He would bait his offer with territorial advantages which he imagined Catherine would find irresistible; and at one stroke he would trump Frederick's aces by securing both the alliance and the mediation. It was a plan, both in its general conception and its particulars, which bore only a vestigial relation to the realities of politics. The draft which he forwarded to Cathcart on 25 August (with full powers to sign) retained the Turkish clause, but offered in exchange to guarantee any Russo-Turkish peace concluded under English mediation. It promised naval assistance in the event of war not only in the Baltic but in the Mediterranean. Its provisions for mutual assistance would have applied to any attack on any of the lands or possessions of either party, including an attack by a European power upon British possessions beyond the seas: this he justified by the familiar argument that Franco-Spanish activities in America might force England into the position of seeming to be the aggressor in Europe. With vague munificence he explained that he would have no objection to Russia's keeping Azov, Taganrog, the Kuban, and "any other gains on that side"; with more caution he indicated that he would be ready to acquiesce in a limited Russian right of navigation of "the northern and eastern parts of the Black Sea," provided it did not extend to ships of war. And finally he made it clear that the guarantee of any peace concluded under English mediation could not form a part of the treaty, but would be considered as "an obligation of honour."[27]

These were proposals which Catherine could not possibly entertain. As to the mediation, she feared that if she accepted it the Turks would stipulate for the inclusion of France, which she was determined to avoid; she had already made up her mind to try to proceed by direct negotiation; and the only value to her of the British offer was that it enabled her to find a decent pretext for politely deprecating a proposal for Austro-Prussian mediation which the Turks had successfully planted on Frederick and Joseph at the time of their meeting at Neustadt in September.[28] As to the proposed terms of alliance, the obligation to assist England in Europe in what were in origin colonial wars was so burdensome that it was ruled out from the start. A guarantee of any peace with the Turks was no equivalent for the retention of the Turkish clause; for Russia (like England) might find herself "forced" into the position of appearing as the aggressor. And she went out of her way to make the point that there could be no solid basis for an alliance until London recognized that the Turks were a European power, and an element in the European balance.[29]

Negotiations on this unpromising basis dragged on inconclusively from month to month: for long spells they scarcely moved at all. Tempers on both sides were not improved by a well-meaning but futile attempt by Rochford to mediate between Panin and the Czartoryski family in Poland.[30] An increasing preoccupation with the Polish problem was indeed one reason why Panin had little leisure to protract the fruitless debate with Cathcart. The meeting at Neustadt had been a clear warning that the two great powers in Germany were equally concerned at the possible implications of the Polish situation. And it was the danger of an Austro-Russian clash, into which Frederick would have been drawn as Russia's ally, which lay behind the visit of his brother, Prince Henry, to St. Petersburg in October. He took Stockholm on his way, and no doubt transmitted verbal admonitions to his sister to be careful;[31] but his real business was with Catherine, and that business was in effect to coax her into accepting the idea of a partition of Poland, as the best and perhaps the only means to avert a European war.[32] This was more than enough to occupy the time of a statesman of Panin's notorious indolence; but as it happened it came on top of a crisis in a quite different quarter, a crisis which threatened one of the anchors of his Northern System: a crisis in Denmark.

(iii)

Though Choiseul had suspended payment of subsidies to Denmark in January 1768, this was a loss which Bernstorff could support, in view of the security provided by the Russian alliance and the great prize of *Mageskiftet* which now seemed to be within his grasp. But by the close of 1769 there were signs that the ascendancy which he had enjoyed for nearly twenty years might be seriously threatened. The worthless young men whom Kristian VII selected for his favorites were probably essentially apolitical, with no longer views than the advancing of their own fortunes; but it was always possible that in order to defeat Bernstorff's restraining influence they would be willing to enlist such enemies of his political system as Rantzau-Ascheberg, who stood for opposition to *Mageskiftet* and to the Russian alliance, and had an old score against Bernstorff which he was only waiting an opportunity to pay off.[33] Gunning feared the revival of French influence, not least because of the emergence into prominence of General Gähler, who had learned the art of war in the French service.[34] Rochford, too, was uneasy. In February 1770 he feared that Denmark might be on the brink of a crisis: if so, it would be Russia's business to cope with it.[35] In May Gunning for the first time mentioned Struensee, though as yet only in a medical capacity. Panin, with other matters to preoccupy him, was not as yet particularly anxious: court intrigues, after all, could not shake the logic of the Russo-Danish system.[36]

But in the summer of 1770 the Danish Court made a trip to Holstein which marked a turning point. Bernstorff was left behind. But Struensee was of the party, in attendance upon Queen Caroline Matilda, and there was good reason to suppose that his attentions were not purely medical. The enemies of Bernstorff seized their chance. Rantzau-Ascheberg appeared once more at court: within a short time, despite Bernstorff's protests, he was appointed a member of the College of War. It was a direct provocation of Russia: "un acte décisif," wrote von der Asseburg, "et qui, une fois faite, ne connait plus de rémède."[37] But there was more involved than Denmark's relations with Russia: there was also at stake the reputation of Caroline Matilda. The Princess of Wales was not prepared to allow her daughter's good name to be hazarded without making an effort to convince her of the error of her ways. In August she resolutely made her way to Germany, surrounded by a haze of ill-informed speculation, and forced a meeting with Kristian VII and Caroline Matilda at Lüneburg. If her object was to obtain the removal of Struensee, she entirely failed to achieve it: Caroline Matilda had all George III's obstinacy without his sense of what he owed to his position, and maternal exhortations made no impression upon her.[38] But they may well have helped to seal Bernstorff's fate. For most of August Gunning was prostrated by the death of his ill-used wife: there is a gap of a month in his dispatches. Filosoffof, for his part, was in the middle of a nervous breakdown. But even if they had both been in full vigor it would have made no difference. Filosoffof had personally insulted Struensee; and the queen was in no mood to listen to English remonstrances. The news of the ill-success of a Danish expedition against Algiers provided a convenient pretext. On 15 September Bernstorff was relieved of all his offices, and his long reign was over at last.

For Russia, for England, for the Caps in Stockholm, the implications were serious: the Hats, jubilant, at once scented a change of system.[39] In this they were premature: the situation in Copenhagen after Bernstorff's dismissal remained for some months confused. It was possible that the old system might survive its champion; it might even be hoped that Caroline Matilda might still be persuaded not to be foolish. Gunning ventured to suggest that a stiff letter from

George III might help.[40] In fact such a letter had already been written; and it was Goodricke who was entrusted with the task of seeing that it reached its destination, and of reinforcing its effect by some sort of verbal remonstrance.[41] He arrived in Copenhagen on 27 October, having had a talk with Prince Charles of Hesse about the situation on the way.[42] Presumably he delivered the letter; but he was given no chance of conversation with the queen: when he presented himself at court she pointedly avoided speaking either to him or to Gunning. There was nothing for it but to press on to Stockholm, whence he sent home a very gloomy report of the state of affairs in Denmark. It seemed to him uncertain whether Gähler or Struensee would emerge as the dominant figure. Neither was an attractive prospect; and the only gleam of light in a dark business was the hope that foreign affairs might fall to A. S. von der Osten, who had at least had a lengthy spell as minister to St. Petersburg.[43] It was true that opinions as to Osten's political sympathies were hopelessly at variance; it was true that he was disliked both by Panin and by Bernstorff; and the only thing about him upon which all seemed agreed was that his character (as Cathcart temperately put it) was "liable to some weighty objections."[44] But at least he might be better than Gähler, or Struensee, or (worst of all) Rantzau-Ascheberg.

In St. Petersburg the news of Bernstorff's dismissal caused shock and dismay: as Gunning truly remarked, "it will be a grating piece of intelligence for M. Panin."[45] In vain General Warnstedt was sent from Copenhagen to offer emollient explanations. He was not well received; Catherine was not to be appeased.[46] In a personal letter to Kristian VII she did not mince her words: Bernstorff's dismissal was "a precipitate step"; it was a victory for France; it removed a minister for whom personally and politically she had the highest esteem. One could only hope (she concluded ominously) that Kristian's evil councillors did not destroy the *Mageskifte* agreement.[47] Struensee was bold enough to ignore this warning; and when Filosoffof gave Kristian VII a note in which the new ministers were described as a cabal of intriguers, it was contemptuously rejected. There followed, on 3 November, a second, and this time an excoriating letter from Catherine, with an intimation that for the present there could be no talk of implementing *Mageskiftet*.[48] On 15 December Filosoffof left for home, without taking leave; and his going, as A. P. Bernstorff wrote to his uncle, seemed to set the seal on the overthrow of the Northern System.[49]

Already before Filosoffof's departure the Danish Court had received a visit which seemed to reinforce these forebodings. On 22

November Crown Prince Gustav, accompanied by C. F. Scheffer, made his appearance in Copenhagen, en route for Paris, and it was a fair speculation that he would take this unexpected opportunity to fish in troubled waters. He seems to have evaded contact with Struensee, as compromising to his dignity; but he had a long talk with Rantzau-Ascheberg, to whom he mistakenly believed the political future belonged. Rantzau-Ascheberg was prepared for a breach with Russia and a return to the French system, and he may even have held out hopes of financial support for a royalist coup in Stockholm.[50] Gunning reported that Gustav also talked politics with General Gähler, and with Blosset, the French minister.[51] From these discussions no firm commitment could in the nature of things be expected: Struensee was only waiting for the visitors' departure to dismiss all the old Privy Council and establish a régime which should be under his own control—an event which duly took place on 10 December. But when the crown prince left Copenhagen four days earlier he was entitled to feel that the prospects were encouraging.

(iv)

Gustav's trip abroad had been planned for some months. In January the Estates, by way of softening the blow of the rejection of the Act of Security, had voted 100,000 rdr towards the expense of foreign travel by all three of Lovisa Ulrika's sons: the state of Prince Karl's health suggested the desirability of a visit to some continental spa; Prince Fredrik Adolf was to accompany him; but Gustav might leave only after they had returned.[52] It was generally understood that his main objective would be Paris. The Senate hoped that his personal influence might avail to settle the problem of the arrears of subsidy, now more urgently needed than ever. Choiseul was eager for the visit, and in February was urging that it take place as soon as possible.[53] Nothing would have pleased Gustav better. His purpose, as he told C. F. Scheffer, was to enlist French aid to "save Sweden from foreign domination."[54] The experience of 1769 had disillusioned him, if not yet entirely with Fersen, at least with Fersen's colleagues; and he hoped therefore to persuade Choiseul to put France's resources at the disposal of the Court, rather than of the Hats.[55] In Modène he had no confidence at all; and when that minister pressed the importance of preparing a plan for the next Diet, Gustav put him off with vague evasions.[56] But before the time for his departure arrived two other emissaries had appeared in Paris. One was the Spanish minister,

Count Lascy, who at Lovisa Ulrika's behest pressed Choiseul to recall Modène.[57] Choiseul perhaps did not need much persuading; and Modène took his departure, to the queen's vast relief, on 10 July.[58] The other mission was of a more ambiguous character. There was at the Swedish Court a Swiss by the name of Beylon, whom Lovisa Ulrika employed as *lecteur*. Beylon enjoyed the confidence and trust not only of herself but of the whole royal family, whose frequent temperamental clashes he composed with tact, compassion, and a measure of success. He became in fact something like a father confessor to all of them: a situation which proved no sinecure. But Beylon was also the friend of Fersen. He seems to have done his best to reconcile Fersen to the Court, and to have believed that a maintenance of good relations with the Hats was in the Court's best interests. He had since 1767 enjoyed a French pension. It is unclear whether his visit to Paris was at the queen's instance, or at Fersen's;[59] but it appears that when he saw Choiseul in August he either persuaded him, or found it politic to say that he had persuaded him, that France's policy should be to encourage collaboration with the Hats: that is, that it should revert to the line advocated by the unfortunate Modène, and before him by Breteuil—the policy which Choiseul himself had condemned in his famous change of front in 1766.[60] On Beylon's way back from France he met Gustav at Kristianstad, and there gave him an explicit warning that any attempt to prejudice Choiseul against Fersen would not be well received.[61] It must have come as a damper on the prince's spirits; for if Beylon's account of Choiseul's attitude were correct, one object of the expedition, and not the least important, looked unlikely to be within reach.

Soon after quitting Copenhagen, with all the hopes which the discussions there had aroused, Gustav received news which seemed to make it doubtful whether it was worthwhile to go any further. At Brunswick on 5 January 1771 came the shattering intelligence of the dismissal of Choiseul on Christmas Eve. It was not, perhaps, wholly unexpected: Creutz had foreseen the possibility as early as the preceding spring;[62] but to Gustav it came as a thunderbolt. For some time the forces arrayed against Choiseul had been gathering strength for an attack: the *dévots*, Mme du Barry, the opposition to the *parlements*, the men of the King's Secret. For months Choiseul had been playing with the idea of making himself once more indispensable by involving France in war: over the ditch at Chandernagore, perhaps; over the controversy about the Falkland Islands.[63] Count Mercy had more than once used his influence to restrain him.[64] And it was in fact the Falkland Islands question which was the proximate cause of his downfall. The crisis began in September, with the news of Bucarelli's attack upon Port Egmont; it became acute in November; it reached a climax in December; and it caused a shift of power in three capitals.[65] In Madrid, Charles III at the last moment withdrew his support for the bellicose d'Aranda and transferred it to the more pacific Grimaldi; in London, Weymouth, who had been for a hard line towards Spain, resigned in circumstances which mystified contemporaries, and the more diplomatic Rochford was transferred from the Northern to the Southern Secretaryship. In Paris, Louis XV discovered that Choiseul had been carrying on a secret correspondence with Madrid—an activity which he was determined to reserve to himself. He pushed Choiseul to the wall by ordering him to write to Charles III informing him that no consideration would induce France to assist her ally if Spain declared war now. Choiseul declined to obey this order; Louis wrote the letter himself on 23 December; and on the next day Choiseul was dismissed from office, and retired to the accompaniment of unprecedented demonstrations of popular sympathy.[66] Three days earlier Rochford had ordered Harris to quit Madrid. But Harris took care to linger in the suburbs; and from this moment, thanks to Rochford's supple handling, the crisis slowly abated. Before the end of January 1771 Charles III had in effect backed down: Spain did not formally renounce her claims, but England kept Port Egmont. And Choiseul, "the firebrand of Europe," had vanished from the scene, never to return. It was certainly a great event. To Lovisa Ulrika the news was "terrible"; Kaunitz was pained, but not surprised; the Bernstorffs philosophized; Catherine was contemptuous. Only the persuasions of Scheffer prevented Gustav from forthwith abandoning his journey.[67]

The Falklands crisis had repercussions which spread far beyond the immediate issue. First, and least important, it adversely affected Goodricke's personal prospects. Rochford's removal to the Southern Department made it necessary to find a replacement for him in the Northern, and the task did not prove easy. As an interim measure the post was given to Sandwich, but within a month he was transferred to the Admiralty, where his expert knowledge and administrative abilities were urgently required. Lord Suffolk was then thought of; but Suffolk had no French, and a great deal of gout—disabilities which did not deter him from accepting the post six months later, though they disqualified him now. The secretaryship was then offered to Dartmouth, and to Hardwicke, both of whom refused it; whereupon North was forced to make do with that decrepit and impecunious political hack, Lord Halifax.[68] With Hardwicke's refusal Goodricke lost the only chance he ever had of serving under a minister who was both a patron and a friend, and who was, moreover, particularly interested in Swedish affairs. It was a mischance which in the event prevented his ever reaping a fair reward for his exertions.

In the wider international context the crisis made two things very clear: neither France nor England was in a condition to wage a war.[69] The English navy was rotten, and it would take all Sandwich's energy to revive it; the French treasury was empty. Neither Catherine nor Frederick was prepared to be impressed by Rochford's diplomatic success and Spain's humiliation; and if ministers imagined that their display of vigor had caused England's stock to rise in Europe, they were mistaken.[70] Above all, the crisis finally exploded the theory, so dear to Lord Chatham, of the menace of "the formidable League of the South." When it came to the touch, the Family Compact proved a thing of straw.[71] The old argument that a general war was impending, to be provoked by the arch-*boutefeu* Choiseul—an argument which Frederick had been advancing for years—lost most of its credibility, at least until the American colonies revolted. And the whole experience, from England's point of view, must raise serious doubts as to whether a Northern System was so necessary after all. The lesson of the Falklands crisis seemed to be, that England's immediate need was not so much the conclusion of an alliance with Russia, as the repairing and expansion of the navy: Rochford told Masserano, when the question of reciprocal disarmament produced a secondary crisis in the spring, that England could no longer afford to keep so small a fleet as before.[72] As to Russia, Catherine's main concern was now to make peace with the Turks as soon as might be, and her nightmare was a war with Austria which she was being driven to believe could be averted only by Frederick's expedient of a partition of Poland. The danger of a French-inspired attack from Finland could not be neglected, but it no longer seemed so immediate or so menacing. The pattern of European alignments was no longer stable; new partnerships were slowly shaping to meet new situations. And if Sweden were to become less important to Russia, it would follow that it would be less important to England also. After the Falklands crisis the international scene was never quite the same again. Sinclair might console himself for the loss of Choiseul by reflecting that at least France would now be free to give her attention to Swedish affairs without being hampered by an unnecessary war;[73] but within two years the partition of Poland would initiate new lines in French policy also. Old traditions, ingrained habits of thought, still pushed France and England into opposing camps, and not least in Stockholm; and here one final confrontation lay ahead, and Goodricke had his last battle to fight, before the old adversaries attempted—vainly, as it proved—to adjust their policies to the new realities of an altered world; but a slow process of reorientation had already begun. If men still paid lip service to the dogmas of the age of Chatham and Choiseul, that age was already over, however slow they might be to recognize the truth.

In the meantime it was a question whether Louis XV, any more than George III, could find an effective foreign minister, and far from clear what that minister's policy would be, as far as Sweden was concerned. To whom was Gustav now to address himself, if he continued his journey to Paris? De la Vrillière, minister *ad interim*, was a nullity: no man to do the prince's business; the Abbé de Terray was concerned to restore the finances, and unlikely to look favorably upon Swedish applications for monetary aid. In a France which, as Mercy commented to Kaunitz, was "actuellement sans exercise de justice, sans ministère et sans argent"[74] it seemed improbable that anyone would find time or resources for Swedish affairs. And so it proved in the event. Gustav arrived in Paris on 4 February, and by the end of the month had made no real progress. His personal charm captivated everybody, including Louis XV; his intellectual abilities impressed even his adversaries. Lord Harcourt, the British ambassador, hoped that he would visit England, and ventured the wildly improbable surmise that George III would like him.[75] In matters of politics he navigated treacherous waters with remarkable skill and finesse: a letter of condolence to Choiseul, and the frequenting of "republican" salons of such friends of Choiseul as Mme d'Egmont, were balanced by a diamond-encrusted collar for Mme du Barry's lapdog, and his acceptance of her invitation to supper—to the horror and indignation of Maria Theresa.[76] While he collogued with the cognoscenti and paid homage to Rousseau, such negotiation as took place was left to Creutz and Scheffer, assisted by the Spanish ambassador, Fuentes,[77] and it did not advance much. Then, on the night of 1 March, while Gustav was at the opera, came news dramatic, unexpected, and as it proved even more decisive than the fall of Choiseul: the news that on 12 February, after a meal which must have taxed the stoutest constitution, Adolf Fredrik had been taken ill and had expired in a matter of minutes.

Adolf Fredrik's death transformed the whole situation: from Gustav's point of view it retrieved the disaster of the fall of Choiseul. He could now negotiate with all the authority of a reigning monarch. The prospect for a successful coup was no longer subject to the notorious defects of character of Lovisa Ulrika and her husband. It was a moment of opportunity, and it was immediately seized: Scheffer was dispatched to Versailles upon the instant, and Louis XV was woken up to receive the news. His sensibility, his generosity, his friendship, were all engaged; and they combined with traditional French chivalry towards an ally to make that midnight interview decisive: details would remain to be arranged, but from that moment the success of Gustav's mission was assured. Within the next fortnight the great question of the subsidy arrears had been settled: the arrangement of 1764 was to revive; France would pay 1.5 million livres a year, with the first installment falling due on 1 January 1772. In addition, Gustav was to receive 750,000 livres immediately; and was told that France destined a sum of 3 million for the expenses of the coming Diet.[78] Nor was this all: two days after the news of Adolf Fredrik's death Louis offered to put at Gustav's disposal 36 to 38 warships to take him back to Sweden, and if necessary to support him there against any attempt by the Caps to exclude him from the succession in favor of his brother Karl.[79] This offer he prudently referred to the Senate; which in the event concurred with his own opinion that its acceptance would be unwise, since the consequence might be the dispatch to the Baltic of a British squadron of equal or superior strength.[80] And lastly, it was agreed that Modène should be replaced by an ambassador; and at Broglie's suggestion one of France's ablest diplomats, the Count de Vergennes, was selected for the post.[81] Gustav found the choice "admirable"; an opinion which he was later to modify. But his reaction to Vergennes's instructions was highly significant. For those instructions represented a return to the long-standing policy of the "Secret": great prudence; no inciting of a royalist coup; a sharp eye on Lovisa Ulrika; the reconciliation of parties; the limitation of any constitutional change to a return to the Constitution of 1720.[82] Gustav commented that "this was just what I asked for."[83] If he meant what he said, the conclusion must be that when he left Paris on 25 March he was no longer thinking, as he seems to have thought when he set out on his travels, of a revolution by violent means. If so, it is not unlikely that this change of attitude may have been assisted by his contacts with those *philosophes* in Paris with whom it was the fashion to admire the English political system: Gustav's destiny was to be the Patriot King who should compose the nation's discords and unite his people in devotion to the interests of the fatherland. Had not Mme d'Egmont, on hearing the news of Adolf Fredrik's death, at once said to him, "Contentez-vous,

Sire, d'être absolu par la séduction, ne le reclamez jamais comme un droit"?[84]

The probability of his acceptance of some such change of tactics is enhanced by what emerges from his visit to Berlin, whither he betook himself on his way home. Frederick seems to have been favorably impressed by his nephew. He told him frankly that the most he could promise was to order his minister in Stockholm not to work with those opposed to the Court; but he instructed Solms in St. Petersburg to try to persuade Panin that Gustav was not so francophile as might be supposed;[85] he replaced Cocceji in Stockholm by Dönhoff, to Gustav's satisfaction, and ordered Dönhoff to give passive approval if there should be any question of recurring to the "Simplicist" formula of a return to 1720.[86] His immediate concern was to ensure a satisfactory financial settlement for Lovisa Ulrika, but he was, as always, averse to rash proceedings which might imperil the monarchy; and Gustav seems to have given him satisfactory assurances on this head. Altogether, the visit to Berlin was a decided success. It was time to head for home. But before leaving Germany Gustav essayed one other piece of business: he persuaded the Duchess of Brunswick to write to George III asking for the recall of Goodricke and for his replacement by Ralph Woodford, the minister to Hamburg—a garrulous vulgarian whose subsequent career suggests that Gustav may have correctly estimated that he would not be a very formidable adversary.[87] George III was not the man to suffer the interference of his relations in such a matter, and the letter had no effect. Goodricke remained in Stockholm, and proved as dangerous an enemy as Gustav had feared. It was the only failure in a trip which had otherwise paid handsome dividends. On 18 May he landed at Karlskrona; on the thirtieth he returned as king to his capital. One week later Vergennes reached Stockholm. And on 13 June the Diet began.

(v)

The death of Adolf Fredrik found both parties in a position in which their preparations for an election had hardly begun to take shape, though each side suspected the other of planning to use the Falklands crisis to enforce the calling of an Extraordinary Diet.[88] By the time Gustav left Sweden for France, the Court, despite Lovisa Ulrika's conviction of Fersen's bad faith, had reconciled itself to collaboration with the Hats, at least for the time being: they would support the party, but strive to weaken the authority of its leaders.[89] But though Sinclair and Barthélémy were working together, and though some preliminary organization had been agreed on, not much seems to have been done, pending the issue of Gustav's visit to Paris. The Caps had made more progress. They had Pechlin's plan, and Osterman had since the autumn been starting to put it into operation. Then came the news of the fall of Bernstorff. It put a damper upon the none-too-ardent enthusiasm of Rochford. Who could tell whether the new men in Copenhagen would be willing to pay their share of the cost of operations? Would it not be wiser, perhaps, to wait until the situation in Denmark grew clearer, before embarking upon the plan at all? Osterman received these tremors with pardonable exasperation; sent off couriers to St. Petersburg with the news that England had wrecked the plan; and was with difficulty soothed by Goodricke, who assured him that Rochford would come round presently. And so it proved, Rochford explaining apologetically that he had not really changed his mind, but was only being cautious.[90] The Russians had by now become inured to this kind of thing, and the episode passed off without real damage to relations. But Rochford was right to this extent: Juel remained on leave in Denmark, leaving Goodricke and Osterman to get along without him; and the Danish share of expenses showed no signs of being forthcoming. Still, by the end of 1770 Osterman had quietly bought up some thirty proxies; and he and Goodricke added another thirty-five early in the new year. Goodricke was later to comment that if Adolf Fredrik had lived for only three months longer the Hats would scarcely have found a proxy on offer. As it was, his death pushed the price up to triple its former figure.[91]

At first it seemed doubtful whether the Court and the Hats would be able to find the money to buy them. They had no resources immediately available; no news from Paris: on the day after the king's death Barthélémy reported them as being in despair, and urgent appeals went from Sinclair to Gustav to make sure to bring back supplies.[92] Gradually they mobilized their forces: the Stockholm merchants, with Finlay at their head; Grill's Bank; Treasury bills (*statsobligationer*) somewhat rashly made available by Barthélémy.[93] The crisis drove Sinclair and Fersen into closer cooperation; and it was at Fersen's suggestion that the direction of the election campaign was put into Sinclair's hands.[94] They reached agreement, moreover, not only on organization but on principle: "pour faire parade" (as Sinclair confided to Gyldenstolpe) there was to be no attempt to modify the constitution. The way forward, in Sinclair's view, lay along the road which seemed to be serving George III so well: by the creation of a party of King's Friends which should command a majority in the Diet.[95] Thus Sinclair in Stockholm, Gustav in Paris, were thinking along the same lines. For each, the answer to Sweden's troubles lay in a Patriot King who would destroy "the Hydra, Faction."

The Caps confronted the death of Adolf Fredrik in a rather better position. When they met at Goodricke's house on 14 February they had already the beginnings of an organization. Within a week they had defeated, by a timely bribe of £500, a Hat attempt once more to seduce Pechlin; and Osterman secured their access to the secrets of the Hat leaders by the promise of a pension to Senator von Wallwijk.[96] Pechlin's program, as he expounded it to Goodricke, was all that could be wished: an English alliance, without subsidies; no tampering with the constitution.[97] Sinclair conjectured that the Caps would fight the election on the cost of living, the constitutional issue, and the alleged propensity of the new king to wasteful expenditure on luxuries: it was to counter this last charge that Gustav III on Sinclair's advice at once dismissed the French theatrical company which his mother had imported. But there was one other issue in the election which Sinclair did not mention, and which may well have been more important than all the rest: the growing agitation against the privileges of the Nobility. The movement of opinion of which Keplerus's Memorial had been the indicator was given strong impetus in the summer of 1770, when a highly competent candidate for the office of vice-president in the Supreme Court at Åbo was rejected by the Senate on the single ground that this was an office which could be filled only by a person of noble rank. The affair greatly inflamed popular feeling; and in the provinces, especially, seems to have been important in influencing the course of the election.[98] Social tension, the "strife of Estates," was working to the Caps' advantage.

Nevertheless, this election, like all others, could not be won without money. The Cap organizers put the figure at £40,000; Pechlin estimated the total cost of the Diet at £56,000; Panin thought it might well be £95,000.[99] And in 1771 money was not so readily available as in 1769. This time there would be no contribution from Prussia; and it was still uncertain whether any support could be expected from Denmark. In the spring of 1771 a sharp struggle over foreign policy was being fought out in Copenhagen.[100] Osten was trying to bring Denmark back to the principles that Bernstorff had followed; Rantzau-Ascheberg was doing his best to engineer a breach with Russia, an alliance with Sweden, and the adoption of the French system. Struensee was for a middle line: he would stick to the Russian alliance for the sake of *Mageskiftet*, but there was to be no more

Russian interference in Denmark's domestic affairs as in the time of Saldern and Filosoffof; and he was not prepared to squander Denmark's resources on Swedish corruption, nor to sanction any active participation in Swedish party struggles.[101] In this triangular contest Rantzau-Ascheberg's sole success was to obtain the recall (on 30 May) of Juel, and his replacement by the more amenable Guldencrone; but Guldencrone's instructions were wholly in Struensee's spirit: the furthest he was allowed to go in the direction of positive action was to give moral support to Goodricke and Osterman if any attempt were made to overturn the constitution. Struensee was indeed prepared to honor Denmark's obligations under the plan of 1770, and after considerable delay actually paid what was due for that year; but in spite of Osten's remonstrances and Osterman's entreaties that was all; and it was very little.[102] England and Russia must fight the campaign without Danish assistance.

As always, Catherine took care that Osterman should be supplied, even if the supply sometimes came tardily, so that he was reduced to borrowing on his private credit. But this time it was clear that the Turkish war was imposing a strain on Russian finances: already in 1770 Catherine had been driven to look into the possibility of a large loan in Holland or England.[103] Now for the first time Osterman was ordered to observe a prudent economy: he was to try to confine his disbursements to the securing of the two capital points—the preservation of the constitution, and the prevention of Sweden's entering the war. For the rest, he must attempt to ensure that Gustav III gave an Accession Charter similar to that given by his father; and he might try to get some Caps into the Senate, if there seemed a chance of doing so reasonably cheaply. But the line now was moderation: he was to soften, not to exacerbate, party strife, persuading both sides of Russian goodwill; and towards Gustav III he was to observe "extreme discretion," in order not to drive him into the arms of France—a remarkable example of shutting the stable door after the horse had bolted.[104] It was an instruction of the same kind as that which had been sent to him in January 1765: in the one case as in the other Panin opted for caution in the face of a situation which was still unclear.

As to Goodricke, with only the £2,600 provided by the plan to draw on, he at once sent off an appeal to Halifax for reinforcements. Halifax's initial reaction—like the initial reaction of Grafton, Conway, and Rochford before him—was sympathetic: no sense in drawing back now; go *pari passu* with Osterman; but give us some kind of an estimate.[105] As in previous instances, the estimate is sent over; it proves disconcertingly big; a cabinet is held upon it. And this time it fell to

Rochford (Halifax being ill) to deliver the cabinet's decision. It came as a severe disappointment. Goodricke was to be allowed £25,000 and no more; and that sum was to include any money already spent.[106] France, Rochford believed, was as good as bankrupt, and her friends could count on no more than the 750,000 livres (ca. £30,000) already made available to Gustav III, together with the credit already deposited with Grill's bank (which could be realized only at a disastrous loss),[107] and the arrears of subsidy which would not begin to be paid off until January 1772. A supply of £25,000 did not accord too badly with the estimates which Goodricke had forwarded to England on 2 April; but it could hardly be reconciled with his notification on the same date that he and Osterman had between them already laid out £20,000, of which one-third had fallen to Goodricke's share, and it seriously underestimated the resources available to the Hats. They were now approaching the most expensive moment of the campaign: the well-known financial crux of the election of the *lantmarskalk* and of the Secret Committee lay only three or four weeks ahead. On 26 May Goodricke wrote to Halifax expressing the consternation of himself and Osterman at this crippling limitation at a critical moment; and on the same day he dispatched a private letter to Rochford,[108] with whom he evidently considered himself to stand on a more confidential footing, appealing for a reconsideration of the decision. It was a letter which seems to have been written in haste, almost in desperation; and it was not a very wise one. He appealed to his past services: but for the efforts of himself and Osterman, Sweden would have started a war in 1769. He asserted that Vergennes would bring orders to conclude an alliance, if the Caps lost the election. Neither of these assertions was true; and though Goodricke may well have thought so, ministers in London certainly believed they were not. Upon them Goodricke's pleas made no effect whatever. Rochford on 7 June simply replied that £25,000 ought to be more than enough, and any savings on that amount would be considered a meritorious service. A week later, the monoglot Lord Suffolk, who had by this time succeeded to the Northern Secretaryship on Halifax's death, reaffirmed the cabinet's decision in terms which left no hope of any relaxation of the limits it imposed.[109]

The refusal of ministers to budge on this issue was the result of several factors. Their information of the state of French finances came to them mostly from Harcourt, their ambassador in Paris, and as far as it went was correct; but apparently neither Harcourt nor their secret intelligence discovered that Vergennes was to take with him a sum originally agreed to be 3 million livres. Vergennes in the event asked for only 2 million, and in fact set off with only 300,000.[110] But still, Suffolk and Rochford underestimated the amount available to Goodricke's adversaries by a sum difficult to estimate, but certainly very large. Even if they had not done so, however, it is likely that they would have felt it necessary to put a strict curb on Goodricke's expenditure. For on 28 February there had come a weighty intervention from George III himself. In a letter to Lord North he wrote:

> It has ever occurred to Me that the gaining of the Court of Sweden is no real object of this Country, for if after a considerable expence that is effected it will be impossible to keep her Freindship unless a Subsidy is granted for that power cannot subsist without foreign money. Besides as there is no publick mode of obtaining the money that is expended in that corruption it must be taken from my Civil List consequently new Debts incurred and when I apply to Parliament for relieving Me, an odium cast on Myself and ministry as if the money had been expended in bribing Parliament. I therefore think that we ought only to feed the Opposition to France, that that Crown may carry no essential points, and may be drove to spend much greater sums to little purpose.[111]

This was a line of reasoning which Lord North, with his personal devotion to the king, and his eye always on the parliamentary position, would find it hard to resist. It had always been Goodricke's argument that France must spend twice as much as her opponents to achieve the same result; and in the light of ministers' information about the amount France was likely to make available in Stockholm they might well think their allowance to Goodricke adequate. And if it were not, they had no scruple about leaving Russia in the lurch. On the contrary. Rochford was experiencing a mounting sense of injury. The proposals for an alliance which he had transmitted with such optimism in October had elicited no response. No *contre-projet* had been put forward, and Panin made little pretense of working on one. The arguments he had advanced in talks with Cathcart seemed to show unwillingness or incapacity to see the British point of view. Rochford was aware that Russia might find difficulty in pouring out money on the old lavish scale; but if Panin imagined that England, freed from the danger of a conflict over the Falklands, could be relied upon to bail him out, he was very much mistaken.[112] These views were fully shared by Rochford's successor, Suffolk, who crisply dismissed Mussin-Pushkin's appeal for more money for Goodricke, and informed that disconsolate minister that since Sweden was primarily Russia's concern Panin's failure to respond to Rochford's proposals for an alliance did not dispose England to shoulder Russia's obligations.[113] A week later he spelled out to Cathcart his view of the state of Anglo-Russian relations:

> Your Excellency will, I doubt not, feel with me for the Honour of Great Britain in the conduct of that Negotiation.—It should not be committed without a Prospect of immediate success: and neither the situation of Russia, nor the Behaviour of Her Ministers, warrant such an Expectation. It is in vain to attempt to engage their Attention to collateral Matters, while it is engross'd by so urgent and important an Object as a peace with the Porte; And it is unbecoming to attempt it in vain; This alone would be a sufficient Reason for avoiding to press this Subject to the Ministers of the Empress, while they are so anxiously employed on another; But when Your Excellency reflects on the many Delays & Disappointments the Negotiation has met with, & which have not any Excuse, You will see the Necessity for Reserve 'till Advances are made on their Part to renew the Negotiation.[114]

In the meantime, he suggested, Cathcart might do worse than try to curb a tendency to unnecessary prolixity.

Any hopes there may have been in Whitehall of making progress with the alliance were effectively dashed by the limitation imposed upon Goodricke's expenditure. The news of it reached Panin at the very moment when (after eight months) he was sharpening his quill to draft an alternative project. He had told Cathcart in March that Rochford's guarantee was no adequate compensation for the retention of the Turkish clause, but had indicated that he hoped to "point out in the North an equivalent" for Russia.[115] That equivalent, it is reasonable to suppose, could only have taken the form of large English disbursements in Sweden. The restriction to £25,000 thus probably ruled out Panin's expedient at the very moment when he was preparing to put it forward. Once again, as in 1769, the elusive alliance had come to grief on the skerries of Swedish politics. On 5/16 June—a full month before Suffolk's instructions to Cathcart arrived—the empress forbade Panin to pursue the negotiations for an alliance, and this expressly on the ground of England's limitation of supplies to Goodricke.[116] It was the beginning of the end of the long and wearisome pursuit of the will o' the wisp of a Russian alliance. For Rochford's proposals of 1770 were the last ever to be made to Russia by any Secretary of State in peacetime. And from Catherine's point of view there were now other and more urgent matters which must engage her attention: the peace with the Turks, the partition of Poland. What mattered now was not so much the alliance of England as the behavior of Austria and Prussia: the English alliance must wait. It was to wait for nearly a quarter of a century.

Meanwhile the struggle in Stockholm must go on; and if English money was short, Panin could, and did, count himself fortunate that Goodricke was there to make the most of it.[117] The election certainly called forth great, perhaps unprecedented, efforts on both sides: it is doubtful whether any previous contest could match the wide-ranging network of correspondence carried on in the Cap interest by the burgher Johan Westin.[118] Predictions of the result were sharply divergent: there was nothing to indicate such a general swing of opinion as had been evident in 1765 and 1769. Except, that is, in regard to the Burghers, where the Caps were early confident of carrying it, and where the result bore out their confidence. They took seven of the ten Stockholm seats, together with other major towns such as Göteborg, Norrköping, and Gävle.[119] It seemed likely that the Hats would retain control of the Nobility, and perhaps of the Clergy also; but there was no certainty as to the Peasants. Each side was alarmed by stories of the vast sums spent by the other: to Goodricke it seemed that "they spend money as if they had the mines of Peru at their disposal," while Barthélémy wrote to Paris of the "efforts inouïs, répandant l'argent à plusieurs mains, que M. le Chevalier Gooderick et les banquiers fournissent"—a report which would certainly have drawn a wry and toothless smile from that minister, if he had known of it.[120] One result of these financial exertions may well have been the bankruptcy of Goodricke's old enemy Robert Finlay, which Barthélémy reported on 17 May: how far Goodricke had a hand in the protesting of his bills in Holland is obscure; at least he claimed none of the credit, though Barthélémy believed he was at the bottom of it.[121] At all events, when the Diet met on 13 June the outcome of all these efforts was still a matter of conjecture. Barthélémy believed that the Hats could count on a majority of 63 in the Nobility, six in the Clergy, 14 in the Burghers, and almost on unanimity in the Peasants; but the event did not bear out these predictions.[122] Goodricke was much more cautious: he made no precise estimate of party strengths at the time of the Diet's opening. In this he was wise. For the sequel would show that whatever the state of parties on 13 June 1771, the fate of the Diet could not thereby be taken as determined. Much would depend on how far issues were raised which set Estate against Estate, privileged against unprivileged. Much, or more, upon the tactics and skill of the new king. And from Gustav III's point of view a Diet of this uncertain complexion might well offer advantages, and present opportunities for policies of appeasement and the defeat of faction. He was at all events resolved to make the attempt.

CHAPTER XI

Failure of a Mission, 1771–1772

(i)

At the beginning of June, then, Swedish politics were still poised in uncertainty, and no man could be sure to which side the balance would incline. If Gustav III were minded to seize the opportunity which this state of affairs offered to him, he had not much time at his disposal. In a fortnight the crucial divisions which followed the meeting of the Diet would resolve these doubts; and thereby, perhaps, deprive him of the chance to influence the course of events. But if time was short, he did not waste it. Nor did he hesitate about the course to pursue. Within a day or two of his return he had summoned Fersen to meet him, and had extorted his reluctant assistance towards the effecting of a party truce, a "Composition."[1] By 12 June preliminary feelers, including interviews between Fersen on the one hand, and Goodricke and Osterman on the other, had made it possible to arrange a meeting of three party leaders from each side, and with them to hammer out the basis for an agreement; by 27 June negotiations had been successfully completed; and on 1 July, in the presence of the king and his brother Karl, the leaders gave a verbal pledge to abide by it.[2]

The Composition of 1771,[3] after a preamble which recorded Gustav's assurance that he sought no increase in the powers of the crown, pledged the participants to maintain the constitution unaltered; to tender to the king an Accession Charter (*konungaförsäkran*) drawn in precisely the same terms as that which had been signed by Adolf Fredrik in 1751; and to forgo any investigation of the Senate's conduct before the close of the previous Diet. They bound themselves not to permit the country to enter into any engagements with foreign powers save those which entailed no risk of involvement in war, and those which might advantage Sweden's economy. Places for two Caps in the Senate were to be provided immediately, with a promise that four or five more should be contrived for them at the end of the Diet through the voluntary resignation of existing members; and it was further agreed that whichever party might find itself in a majority, one-third of the membership of the committees of the *riksdag* should be guaranteed to the other. Peccant officials were henceforth to be brought to justice in the ordinary courts, and not to be judged on party-political lines by the Estates themselves—a provision which was intended, among other things, to apply to misconduct by magistrates and returning officers in connection with the election. And by a separate, purely verbal understanding, both sides promised that once the vital struggles over the Speakerships of the four Estates had been decided (but not before) neither would have recourse to corruption, least of all from foreign sources.

As a damper upon the rage of party, as the basis for a consensus for national ends, the Composition, despite some obvious defects to be noticed in a moment, was no small achievement; and the willingness of the leaders to accept it, as well as the motives of those who pressed it upon them, certainly require some explanation. Its immediate originator was that old advocate of Compositions, C. F. Scheffer; but it owed its success to the fact that Scheffer's idea had been resolutely adopted by his sovereign. The Composition was indeed Gustav III's personal achievement. As always, his motives were suspect by his contemporaries, and are a matter of controversy among historians. But this at least is clear: he had already begun to see himself in the part of the healer of party strife, who should "rallier tout le monde sous ses drapeaux," and in the process should restore the constitution to its "primitive integrity" and "first good principles": in a word, as the Patriot King.[4] Resembling in all this his contemporary George III, conscious like him of his mission and of his own rectitude, convinced too of the black-heartedness of those who stood in his way, Gustav would find that to annihilate party he must himself become a party leader. But in the case of Gustav III, as in that of George III, any judgment which fails to take account of the strong strain of idealism which informed his program cannot really do justice to it. Of course he calculated that the Composition, by securing something like an even balance of parties, might put him in the position of an arbiter between them. Undoubtedly he was moved by ambition. But it is a purblind appraisal which sees only his superficial insincerity, vanity, and theatricality. Certainly he relished opportunities to strike noble attitudes, and loved to set himself in a historical perspective which even when it was not distorted was hardly relevant to the times: it was idle in 1771 to dream of emulating Gustav Adolf. No doubt he derived enormous satisfaction from making great speeches, and luxuriated in the sonorities of his own superb rhetoric. But still it is true that he believed that it was his duty to rescue his country from a degrading dependence upon foreign powers and the corruption of foreign gold. Many besides himself shared that sense of degradation;[5] none but he seemed to be in a position to take practical steps to end it. He may well have been mistaken in the belief, which had been strengthening in him at least since 1768, that unless drastic measures were taken Sweden was threatened with the fate of Poland,[6] but it is hardly possible to doubt the genuineness of his alarm. With all his affectations and duplicity he was in his way a patriot, even though his enemies might pronounce him a misguided one. It was patriotism, quite as much as ambition, which led him to believe that Sweden needed a stronger and more untrammelled monarchy. On 25 June he addressed the assembled Estates: the first speech from the throne that they had heard for over a hundred years. What he had then to say impressed even hardened parliamentarians; and outside it woke echoes which were slow to die away.

> Born and educated among you, I have from my earliest youth learned to love my country, to hold it for the summit of felicity to be a Swede, and for the greatest honour to be the first citizen of a free people. If by your resolutions the happiness, the independence and the honour of this country be but hastened, stablished and consolidated, I have no more to ask. My utmost wish is to rule over a happy people; the height of my ambition, to guide the steps of a free nation. . . . You have it in your power to be the most fortunate people in the world.[7]

The real passion which lay behind the rhetoric made Gustav III far more dangerous to the constitutionalism of the Age of Liberty than if he had simply been the hypocrite which his enemies believed him to be.

Whatever may have been the case with Gustav III, it is unlikely that the party chiefs entered upon the Composition from any sort of ideal motives. For them it was a question of prudent insurance in good time. The Hats, as the party in power, stood in danger of Cap vengeance for the events of 1769, if they should lose control of the Diet; and the disappointingly small amount of money brought by Vergennes may well have been the final argument which persuaded them of the wisdom of negotiating.[8] As to the Caps, they were a party in opposition with no assurance of becoming the government, and there were solid attractions in the offer of at least a share of power. The Composition incorporated some of their favorite political principles;[9] they feared the odium of refusing; they overestimated the Hats' resources, and knew only too well how strained were their own. But they would certainly have been less amenable to the idea if they had found that the foreign ministers to whom they looked for support were not of the same mind. Here, however, there was little difficulty on either side. Vergennes, indeed, personally disapproved of Composition, as a mere device to prop up the tottering Hats, but ministerially he supported it: his instructions gave him no option.[10] So too with Osterman. Osterman's orders, as we have seen, were to ensure that Gustav gave an Accession Charter identical with his father's; to keep Sweden out of Turkish war; to soften party conflicts; and to try to put some Caps into the Senate if that could be done without too much expense.[11] The Composition seemed to take care of all of these points. As by this time his available funds had shrunk to 9,000 rubles, with all the major expenses still to come, small wonder that he used his best efforts to encourage the Caps to reach an agreement.[12] He and Goodricke did indeed try to extract a promise that half the places on the Senate should go to Caps; but for the moment this was a demand upon which they were in no position to insist.[13]

Goodricke, for his part, was in a rather different situation from that of his colleagues. He had no instructions regarding a Composition; nor was there ever any sign that Rochford or Suffolk appreciated that this was a matter upon which they might be expected to have views. His account of the negotiations, his reports on the subsequent history of the Composition, elicited not a single comment from London. There is but one oblique allusion to it in the letters which reached him in the months that followed: Goodricke might take what line he chose without striking out any responsive spark in the Secretary's office. It seems that from the beginning he was more reluctant to engage than Osterman was; more suspicious, more wary. Though he was so short of money he opposed the idea of a truce to corruption, since that might entail an undesirable negotiation between Osterman and Vergennes, which it was no business of his to bring on.[14] On the whole, he suspected that it was "a *finesse* to discredit us"; and it was partly to avoid falling into that trap that he agreed to participate.[15] It is clear that he was not interested, as Osterman was, in softening party animosities, nor was he anxious to blunt the edge of a possible Cap victory by premature concessions.

The success of the Composition depended upon the calculation that it would prevent the overwhelming preponderance of one party over the other. But even before the final settlement on 1 July the political situation had altered in such a way as to undermine the whole basis of the agreement. The opening of the Diet was immediately followed, in each Estate, by a desperate struggle between the parties to capture the Speakership; and in the three lower Estates the outcome largely depended upon decisions—on party lines—upon the numerous cases of disputed, or double, returns. The result of these violent and often protracted debates came as a shattering blow to the Hats: in the Estate of Burghers the Cap candidate, Sebaldt, on 13 June defeated his rival by 72 to 55; on the following day the Peasants elected the Cap leader Josef Hansson by 84 to 61, despite the fact that it was only a month or so since the Senate had declared him ineligible to sit. The toughest battle of all came in the Clergy; but there too the result was the same: Forssenius, the Cap bishop of Skara, defeated Filenius of Linköping by a single vote (34 to 33). It was true that on the same day the Hats could console themselves with the election as *lantmarskalk* of their amiable but inexperienced candidate Axel Gabriel Leijonhufvud,[16] who defeated Thure Rudbeck by the handsome margin of 523 to 450.[17] But there was now a Cap majority in three of the four Estates; and though it might still be precarious in the Clergy, the Caps would take care that the mere possession of power should render it secure.[18] The immediate consequence was a flagrant breach of the Composition: when the Estates proceeded to choose electors for the all-important Secret Committee the Burghers refused to elect a single Hat; the Clergy chose only four, out of their delegation of twenty-five; and the Nobility retaliated by including only four Caps in their contingent of fifty: so much for the agreement which was to have ensured to the minority one-third of the seats on all committees;[19] so much for Gustav III's hope of presiding over a balance of parties. By the end of June, therefore, the Caps were firmly in control of the Secret Committee. The political pendulum had swung again: Sweden, as d'Aiguillon remarked, seemed to have returned to 1765.[20] In distant Vienna that staunch royalist J. G. Oxenstierna gave a cry of anguish when he heard of the election of Hansson and Sebaldt: "Good God, what fate is in store for our wretched country! Our doom is sealed."[21] He had little doubt of what that doom would be: implicit in the result, he believed, was a Russian alliance and the destruction of Sweden's commerce and industry at England's hands.[22]

By all the old standards it appeared to be a brilliant success for the Anglo-Russian party; and ministers in London were not slow to send Goodricke their congratulations. Yet his own reactions were notably muted: no repetition now of the jubilant trumpetings of 1765. For the closer one looked at it, the more it appeared that this was no ordinary victory. Very large sums had been expended during the first fortnight of the Diet's sitting, fabulous prices were said to have been asked and given for single votes.[23] Osterman had borrowed heavily on his personal credit; Goodricke had drawn for the whole remainder (£2,100) of the £25,000 that had been allowed him.[24] Vergennes had committed 200,000 of the 300,000 livres he had brought with him;[25] but even when supplemented by Gustav III's 750,000 it proved insufficient, so that the king had been driven to the extraordinarily hazardous step of raising a loan of 500,000 livres through the banking house of Horneca of Amsterdam against the security of the first installment of the French subsidy-arrears—though he well knew that those arrears were not his to pledge.[26] It is difficult, perhaps impossible, to give a firm figure for the amount employed on either side; but it seems reasonably certain that the friends of France were in a position to outbid their opponents.[27] It was therefore something of a portent that, except in the election for *lantmarskalk*, where it was generally agreed that French money carried the day, they were nevertheless defeated. The battle was won against the financial odds. Money was not, it appeared, all-powerful; bribery could not be relied upon to turn the scale. This had to some extent been true in the past, but it had never appeared so plainly as now, and it was going to be still more true in the future. New forces were stirring in Swedish politics, beyond the ability of foreign paymasters to harness. The old rules of the game no longer necessarily applied. And Goodricke, contemplating his victory somewhat pensively, had already some glimmering idea of the new difficulties he might have to meet.

The Composition of 1771, like its predecessor, was from the start vitiated by one fatal weakness. It was a pact between aristocratic leaders: in all the discussions which preceded its conclusion not one member of the three lower Estates had been included. This was an omission which was particularly dangerous in the case of the Caps; for the Caps, now as in 1765, were very much the party of the rising middle class; suspicious and resentful both of officialdom and of aristocratic pretensions, enemies to privilege, leaders of the movement to throw down class barriers to advancement and to establish a real equality of opportunity within the (admittedly narrow) limits of *la nation politique*. The hottest Cap partisans were found among such men: parsons and professors such as Kröger,[28] Gadolin, and Wijkman; burgomasters such as Sebaldt and Sundblad; wealthy peasants such as Josef Hansson.[29] Any political bargain which ignored such persons and assumed their assent was likely to run into trouble, irrespective of its content. And the contents of the Composition, as it happened, were by no means to their liking. The agreement to stop corruption, if it had been observed, would have deprived many members of their necessary means of support. They objected also to the clause binding the Estates not to supplant the ordinary courts in the investigation of official delinquencies: was it not this that provided the best safeguard against the tacit solidarity of the official class, which so often had thwarted the ends of justice?[30] Lastly, they felt that the agreement to frame the new Accession Charter in the same terms as the old would have the effect of buttressing that régime of privilege which it was their object to destroy; for the Charter of 1751 had bound the king when making appointments to consider *mainly*—and not, as they wished, *only*—ability and merit.

Goodricke had his ear too close to the ground to remain for long unaware of the feelings in the ranks of the party. His "operators" must very early have told him of the grumbling at the stop of corruption: already at the beginning of July he was noting that disappointed and necessitous members were "ready to follow any new leader that will put himself at their head."[31] Even before the Composition was concluded he predicted—correctly—that it would break both parties; and he shrewdly assessed the probable consequences:

> The great People, on each side, will be in the Administration, and the King will hold the Balance; but the Rest of the Nation, who hate an Aristocratic government, will be discontented, and will make a powerful party at another Diet, if they should be supported by any Court with Money: if not, the King's Authority will gradually gain ground.[32]

In a situation where class animosities and party fanaticism seemed increasingly unamenable to financial arguments (even if he had had the money to give force to them) his chances of saving the non-noble Caps from unwise excesses were slim: he could advise, he could exhort; but he could no longer threaten effectively. On 28 June he summed up the situation without enthusiasm when he wrote, "In short, there is great Confusion; and this will be [the] most extraordinary Diet that ever has been in Sweden."[33]

(ii)

The event speedily bore out these predictions. Within three weeks of the opening of the Diet the three lower Estates had opened a flank attack on the Nobility. There was a standing committee of the *riksdag*, the so-called Despatching Committee (*Expeditions Deputationen*), whose duty it was to collate the resolutions of the Estates and promulgate them for action. On 20 July the three lower Estates resolved to include in the instructions for that Committee a directive that in cases where three Estates had reached concordant decisions, the Committee should at once promulgate them as resolutions of the whole Diet, without waiting for the (possibly dissentient) determination of the fourth. This had already been attempted—and fiercely resented by the Nobility—at the Diet of 1765-66. It would have jeopardized a long-standing constitutional convention that no decision of the Diet could override the privileges of any one of the Estates.[34] It looked like, and probably was intended to be, a device to clear the way for attacks on the Nobility's privileges; and they took it as such. Their reply was to refuse to take any decision on the terms of the instruction for the Committee; which meant in fact (since such an instruction had no force until all the Estates had voted upon it) that the Committee was left without any instruction at all. By these tactics the threat was for the moment parried; but no one could doubt but that in one form or other it would soon come again.[35]

This, however, was a mere preliminary skirmish. What precipitated a major conflict was the affair of the Accession Charter. It was a matter which the party leaders did not expect to cause any difficulty: the Composition, it was supposed, had effectively settled it on the basis of 1751. But when, at the beginning of September, the Secret Committee's subcommittee produced its draft, that draft was found to include three major changes. It bound the king henceforward to reign "continuously"—and thus barred the way to abdication, or to "Inactivity" in the style of 1768. It pledged him always to agree with the Estates of the Realm—and not, as hitherto, with *all* the Estates; which might mean that if the three lower Estates voted to abridge the Nobility's privileges, the king must agree to it. And it laid it down that henceforward the king must make appointments only—

and not "principally"—on the basis of merit and ability. The draft thus represented a party revenge for the events of December 1768; but also, and much more important, another blow for political and social equality between the Estates. It was also, of course, a slap in the face for the men of the Composition, who were served notice that their followers did not consider themselves bound by it.[36]

So began an envenomed struggle which was destined to last six months, which occupied the attention of the Diet to the prejudice of other business of importance, and which did much to weary king and nation of parliamentary government. The longer it lasted, the more intractable it became, as the draft was passed from one committee to another, and then back again for consideration in the *plena* of the Estates; for each transference gave fresh opportunities for adding combustible matter to a fire which was already burning too hot for comfort. In September it was referred to a Grand Committee, similar to that of 1769;[37] and here the representatives of the Burghers demanded that the Charter should include a schedule of privileges for the non-noble Estates, which they were just then busy drawing up; and a move to tack it to the draft was defeated only with difficulty.[38] Dean Kröger then started a fresh hare by proposing an addition making strikes of government officers (as in December 1768) illegal: the lower Estates accepted it with enthusiasm; the Nobility threw it out.[39] Passions were further inflamed by the publication in September of a periodical entitled *The Common Soldier* (*Den ofrälse soldaten*), which gave a scarifying picture of the arrogance and brutality of the aristocratic officer-class, and demanded an increase (which the Estates hastened to grant) in the starvation wages which were paid to the man in the ranks.[40] The Peasants clamored for a curb on the nobility's freedom to buy or exchange crown-land, and a guarantee of equal opportunities for themselves in that matter.[41] The longer the crisis lasted, the bolder the pretensions advanced by the unprivileged Estates. As their solidarity was cemented by the excitements of a common struggle, so the Nobility reacted with increasing vehemence against the threat to their material advantages and social preeminence, and against proceedings which they considered (with some reason) to be a breach of the constitution. Sparrschiöld might cry "We shall stand firm as a rock amid the raging billows, if we take our stand upon the law," but his rock turned to sand when a member of the Clergy could say that "equity [*billighet-en*] was above the law."[42] The young, the hot-headed, the junior officers,[43] the impencunious, and the mischief-makers united in intransigent defense of their privileges, their status, their honor; and their speeches were full as violent, their debates as chaotically tumultuous, as those of their non-noble assailants. The extent of their alarm, the exaggeration of the threat to their position, is shown by the reaction of Carl Bonde, who persuaded himself that his order was menaced with a new *reduktion*.[44] Led by men such as Fredrik Horn, they were by October no longer controllable by their more prudent and experienced leaders. The men of the Composition—Fersen and Karl Sparre on the Hat side; von Essen, Ridderstolpe, and Frietzcky for the Caps—strove vainly to inculcate the virtues of moderation. All these men feared that the strife of Estates, which was tearing the political nation apart, and in which the old party allegiances counted for less and less, must offer opportunities to an ambitious monarch, and must at last disgust the nation.[45] Their arguments fell on deaf ears: it was that old Cap, Josias Cederhielm, who cried, "When it is a matter of our preservation, why should party differences divide us? we are all in the same boat."[46] When Wadenstierna, a moderate Hat, spoke in the nobles' club in favor of accepting the draft Charter, he was lucky to escape with his life;[47] and in the perfervid atmosphere of the crowded House of Nobility the language which caught the votes was that of those who like Liljehorn shouted that they would defend their rights to the death, "sword in hand," and that "one must *vincere aut mori*."[48] By the end of November matters had reached a deadlock. The lower Estates brusquely declined to entertain further representations;[49] the Nobility finally rejected all compromise.[50] The situation called for desperate remedies; and Gustav III came forward to supply them.

On the afternoon of 27 November he summoned Fersen to his presence and asked him to call together the members of the Composition Council (which still continued to meet occasionally) and invite them to consider whether it might not be useful if he were to address a letter of remonstrance to the Estates.[51] The Council duly met; and its Cap members agreed to take soundings with their party. In the meantime, however, the king, never averse to an opportunity for public oratory—mindful too, it may be, of the example of his ideal monarch, Gustav Adolf—had decided for a more attractive procedure:[52] with the assent of the Senate (who would be censured for this by-and-by), and flanked by its four most senior members, he summoned the Speakers of the four Estates, and to them made an eloquent appeal and a tender of his good offices to heal the breach; offering either to serve as a mediator, of if they preferred it to address a *plenum plenorum*. This message he asked them to transmit to their respective Estates. Three of them, with dutiful expressions of gratitude, at first agreed to do so; but Sebaldt, the Speaker of the Burghers, more alert to the constitutional implications than his colleagues, curtly refused to be the bearer of any message, on the undeniably valid ground that any communication from the crown to the Estates must come through the Senate, and be countersigned by them. In this objection the other three hastily concurred.[53] Thus as a result of an error of tactics which may probably be referred to the king's passion for the limelight his initiative was stifled at birth. Not a whisper of it was heard in the three lower Estates; and the Nobility, after a debate lasting twelve hours, decided that it would be improper to discuss it, Fersen's contingent of thirty-odd moderate Hats voting with the Cap majority.[54]

It was a great fiasco, certainly; yet it was not so total as at first sight it appeared. For Gustav III, though denied the chance to speak seasonable words to the Estates, so managed matters as to ensure that they reached a much wider audience, by contriving to get the speech printed in a provincial town.[55] The printer prudently fled the country, out of reach of the rigors of parliamentary justice, but the speech found many readers—to whom it gave no very favorable impression of their legislators, and a correspondingly attractive one of their sovereign.[56]

Such was the posture of affairs when the Estates separated for their Christmas vacation: the Composition as good as dead; the rage of party reinforced and overshadowed by the social struggle; the parties splintered into whirling and uncontrollable atoms; agreement on the Charter further off than ever; and the coronation—which could not take place until the Charter was settled—apparently receding further into the distance with every week that passed.

(iii)

In these cross circumstances, what was a British minister to do? Goodricke had given a reluctant blessing to the Composition: was he now to repudiate it? At the moment of the Diet's opening the objectives to be aimed at seemed clear enough: to complete the reversal of the defeat of 1769 by establishing a Cap control of the Secret Committee, and if possible of the Senate too, and thereby to open the way to the resumption of negotiations for an Anglo-Swedish alliance, which in turn should form the basis for an Anglo-Russian—or at the worst would set a bar to the conclusion of any alliance with France; and, as one aspect of this policy, to take every precaution against any increase in the power of the crown—not from any particular concern for Swedish liberties, but because royal control of foreign policy would imply Sweden's adherence to the French system. But these familiar lines of action had now been blurred and tangled as a result of the shifts of emphasis in Swedish domestic politics. In 1769 Goodricke had opposed, for short-term tactical reasons, any attempt to reform the abuses of the constitution. Whether, if the Act of Security had been carried, it would have enabled the constitution to adapt itself to the strains imposed on it by the strife of Estates may perhaps be doubted; but by 1771 it was becoming clear that by blocking reform he had left a royalist revolution as the only likely alternative to the unbridled power of the Diet. Of this he seems to have had an uneasy consciousness: over a year before he had written, "The only doubt [about backing the Plan of 1770] is, whether, by frequent changes [*sc.* of administration] the Nation may not grow disgusted with the Form of Government, and throw themselves into the hands of the Court of France."[57] According to the old pattern of Swedish politics a Cap victory should have been an effective guarantee that a revolution (and hence a French alliance) would not, indeed could not, happen. But in the event, the more the Caps consolidated their power, the more violent the means they adopted to entrench their ascendancy, the more they manipulated the constitution in order to prosecute social ends, the more likely a revolution became, since the party excesses to which their victory opened the way provided the very soil from which a revolution might spring. In a survey written in September 1772 Goodricke recalled that

> soon after the beginning of the Diet, we [*sc.* Osterman and himself] told them of the fears we had of a change in the Constitution in case they did not conduct themselves with a great deal of Moderation; . . . All our Precautions were rendered useless by some hot-headed People, principally in the Order of Clergy.[58]

This may in part be self-justification, or wisdom after the event;[59] but it is clear that he recognized what political capital Gustav III might be able to make from the situation: when some of the non-noble Cap leaders approached him about supporting their demands for the throwing open of high office to commoners, Goodricke called it "a Point of a very dangerous nature," and advised them to postpone it.[60] It was therefore arguable that the best safeguard against revolution lay not in the full exploitation of victory, but in the line pursued (from whatever motives) by Fersen, by Vergennes, by Osterman, by Gustav III himself: the line of Composition. To secure one's self against a French system and a royalist coup by embracing a policy advocated by the Court, the Hats, and the French ambassador might certainly seem a paradox too extravagant to swallow; and some such feeling had no doubt contributed to Goodricke's evident reluctance to engage in it. By accepting the Composition he had put himself in the position of standing in the way of that total control of the seats of power by the Caps which it was his business (as he saw it) to fight for. The Composition cut across the grain of this Diet; it was the symbol of the old aristocratic monopoly of politics. It was a strong argument against continuing to support it, that it was disliked by precisely those elements (the non-noble Estates, and especially the Burghers) whose confidence and trust in him, carefully built up over the years, now formed his only real asset. In a conversation with Pechlin as early as April, that shrewd judge of the political climate had urged him to act with "the Nation" (by which he meant the non-noble Estates) in opposing both the aristocracy and the crown.[61] Goodricke knew too much about recent Swedish politics not to be skeptical about the effectiveness of Compositions; and experience as well as natural temperament made him a hot partisan. Moreover, one of the terms of the Composition represented the denial of the whole object of his mission: by definition it was no business of his to lend his countenance to an agreement which prescribed a neutral foreign policy. Yet on the other hand the Composition had the backing of most of his party's acknowledged leaders. Rudbeck, von Essen, Ridderstolpe, Frietzcky—these were the respected chiefs, the level heads, the responsible statesmen with whom when the time came he would have to do business, the friends and allies of the last seven years. Was he now to throw them over in favor of the rancorous Serenius, the aged and now half-crazy Nordencrantz, the clerical hotheads such as Kröger and Wijkman, men devoid equally of experience and a sense of responsibility? A party must have leadership if it was to keep together, and it was not among these that a new team of leaders was likely to be found: in 1765-66 it had been in danger of being torn apart by the reckless feuding of men of just this type. It had been difficult enough then, with money at his disposal, to preserve a plausibly united party; now, when he had none, he must hope that the authority of the aristocrats would somehow hold. And, not least, he must for as long as possible keep his policy aligned with Osterman's; for Osterman, though he had less money at his disposal than in the old days, at least had some. Which meant in fact that he must after all stick to the Composition, at least for the present, if only because there was no money for a full-scale party offensive. The refusal of his government to provide him with supplies, once the battles at the beginning of the Diet were over, meant that he was in leading strings to Osterman, that his power to affect the course of events was very limited, that he was deprived of the possibility of striking out a line of his own. For the first time since his arrival in Sweden he was perforce relegated to a subordinate role. His experience, his personal contacts, ensured that he should be consulted,[62] and by his enemies he did not cease to be feared. But for nearly a year England counted for almost as little in Stockholm as Struensee's Denmark. Goodricke faced the last great crisis of his career with his hands tied.

Thus it was that during the summer and autumn of 1771 he consistently followed the policy of moderation. On the great question of the Accession Charter he was firmly behind those members of the Nobility who pleaded for an honorable compromise. The violence of the language of some of the Clergy shocked him, and he did his best to moderate it.[63] In common with many others he suspected that Sinclair was deliberately inflaming the dispute in order to induce a revolutionary situation; and he appealed to Suffolk, urgently but vainly, to send instructions as to what to do if such a situation should arise.[64] Goodricke's own solution to the controversy would have been to persuade the non-noble Estates to drop some of the more obnoxious of their proposals;[65] but of this there was no hope, and he took care not to propose it. And so he found himself in the position, which would have seemed incredible to him six months earlier, of consulting with Fersen about parliamentary tactics; he wrote dispatches commending Fersen's speeches; he noted with satisfaction that Fersen voted with "our Friends."[66] It had indeed now become a nice question who "our Friends" might be; for the lower Estates were flouting his attempts to restrain them, and among the Nobility the attack on privilege had reinforced discontent with the Composition, which in any case had never been relevant to the social struggle. The Hat majority in the House of Nobility refused to follow Fersen any longer; many of them were already looking for succor to the Court. The Cap Nobility was perhaps less insubordinate; but it too reacted to the threat from below, and there are not wanting signs that voting across the party lines occurred. Certainly von Essen and Ridderstolpe now stood closer to Fersen and Wadenstierna than to the mass of their restive supporters. On an issue such as that of Gustav III's appeal to the Speakers—an issue which could be represented as essentially constitutional[67]—voting in the Nobility could still go on predominantly party lines, and on this occasion "our

Friends" clearly meant "the Caps"—though even here they included Fersen's small band of followers; but for most of the time things were not so simple. To Suffolk (who just at this time was transmitting warnings to have nothing to do with Fersen)[68] they must frequently have seemed highly confusing. Yet in this topsy-turvy world, in which Goodricke was lamenting that with a little more money "the Torrent might have been stopt,"[69] he did not lose sight of the traditional objectives of British policy. His anxiety to achieve a quick compromise on the Charter stemmed from his impatience to get the dispute between the Estates out of the way in order to proceed to party measures of a more orthodox sort.[70] Early in September he defined the object of himself and Osterman as being to make another Diet unnecessary for some years to come by establishing the Caps securely in power and committing Sweden to the Anglo-Russian system.[71] He was sympathetic to an appeal from Düben for £5,000-£6,000 to effect the dismissal of ten Hat members of the Senate;[72] he saw in Ekeblad's death in October a great opportunity to put in a chancery-president who could be trusted to take Sweden out of French hands.[73] If the time should come when this kind of policy should clash with the policy of moderation—if the social struggle should be pretermitted, and purely political issues resume their place—the "Componists" would not be able to count with any certainty on Goodricke's continued support. He might, after all, opt for Pechlin's alternative, and rally to "the Nation." For indeed the arguments for the one course or the other had been finely balanced; and "the Nation," once its class objectives seemed secure, could be relied upon to support the English connection. Or so he hoped.

Meanwhile, in marked contrast to the turbid torrent which Goodricke was breasting in Stockholm, scarcely a ripple disturbed the tranquil backwaters of the Secretary's office. "There is so great a calm in this department," wrote Sir Stanier Porten with some complacency, "as to furnish no interesting matter in the dispatches to and from the office, and I may add, there is not one letter in it unanswered."[74] It was in these soothing circumstances that Lord Suffolk, on 14 June, succeeded Lord Halifax as Northern Secretary. Like too many of his predecessors, he was a newcomer to international affairs; but he brought to his office a willingness to learn, considerable shrewdness, and a determination that the work should be done efficiently and thoroughly.[75] Harold Temperley, in a less happily inspired moment, once referred to him as "the arch-Pecksniff of diplomacy," presumably on the basis of a misconception of Suffolk's reaction to the Partition of Poland.[76] But "the masterkey to

Mr Pecksniff's character," we are told, was "a strong trustfulness in sounds and forms";[77] and this was certainly not true of Suffolk, who hated verbiage, and would have considered himself above all as a hardheaded realist. With none of Rochford's volatility and propensity to indiscretion, he said what he meant to say (in English) civilly but frankly; and foreign ministers seem to have respected and trusted him.[78] He was remarkably free from the itch to take action merely for the sake of doing something, was content to allow situations to ripen, but was clear and decided when he believed the moment for action to have arrived. He had a strong sense of the dignity of England, and was accounted more gallophobe than Rochford. It was of course to Rochford, as Southern Secretary, that relations with the Bourbon powers now fell; and in the next twelve months much ink would be spilled in conjectures as to what d'Aiguillon's intentions might be: French aid to the confederates in Poland, possible French attempts to seduce Portugal, French soundings in Berlin, the dragging negotiations over the Canada Bills, French naval maneuvers in the Mediterranean, even for a moment an alarm about a French attack upon India, provided Rochford with plenty to think about.[79] Suffolk's only concern with these matters was their repercussions upon northern Europe; upon the possible participation of Spain in Swedish affairs;[80] upon the money made available to Vergennes and the purposes for which it was intended to be employed. As to this last he was punctual and full in transmitting the secret information that reached him; a service which might have been more valuable to Goodricke if it had been accompanied by the remittance of any countervailing supplies.

But no such supplies were forthcoming. Goodricke was flatly told that he would not get another penny.[81] In Suffolk's view Sweden was of interest to England only as the bridge to a Russian alliance. Of that alliance he saw no prospect for the present. A Northern System seemed as far off as ever—indeed, the Falklands crisis on the one hand, and the Turkish war on the other, suggested that its importance both to England and to Russia had appreciably diminished. For the moment, then, British policy in Sweden must remain in suspense. For more than six months after taking office Suffolk does not seem to have taken the threat of a French victory in Stockholm very seriously. He saw no reason to spend money, as Goodricke urged him to do, to make the Senate completely Cap: the Composition, after all, was supposed to be a safeguard against any Hat predominance.[82] He did not fail to send congratulations upon Goodricke's apparent successes; but when that minister proceeded to correct his misapprehensions he retorted with a prolonged and chilling silence.[83]

At least Goodricke escaped more lightly than Cathcart. Suffolk had already made it perfectly plain that he was not prepared to take the initiative in reviving the negotiations for a Russian alliance, and he lost no time in underlining the point. England, he wrote, valued the possibility of an alliance as highly as ever, but "Importunity is not the means by which [His Majesty] will condescend to obtain it," and Cathcart was told to forbear speculative discussions with Panin on possible expedients.[84] This was an order which it was not in Cathcart's nature to obey. By this time his trust in Panin seems to have been almost absolute; and Panin had only to drop an encouraging word or two and he was all agog, pouring out pages of reflections, speculations, and alternative solutions, in perilous disregard not only of his orders but of Suffolk's already-manifested impatience with his intolerable long-windedness.[85] It was too much. This time he had to do with a Secretary who was indisposed to endure any more of it. On 8 November Suffolk dispatched a sharp rebuke.[86] Three weeks later Cathcart was notified that he was to be recalled—just at the moment, as he lamented pathetically, when the treaty was likely to be signed on the bases he had laid down.[87] It was a delusion which perhaps only Cathcart could have entertained. In selecting Robert Gunning as Cathcart's successor Suffolk took good care to place in St. Petersburg a man of his own type (who happened also to be a personal friend); but it was May 1772 before Gunning could extricate himself from his tangled affairs in Copenhagen and set out, and in the meantime Suffolk had to make do with an ambassador who to the very end (he did not finally quit Russia, to Gunning's extreme exasperation, until 14 August) conducted a kind of private diplomacy in the hope of bringing a treaty home with him.

It was no wonder if in these circumstances Suffolk was confirmed in his policy of waiting upon events; but apart from personal considerations there was much to suggest the wisdom of caution. The domestic situation in Russia gave considerable cause for concern.[88] In August 1771 the Tsarevich Paul was so seriously ill that he was not expected to recover, and it was widely rumored that he had been poisoned.[89] If he should die, European public opinion, mindful of Peter III and Ivan VI, would not have much hesitation in drawing the appropriate conclusions. Catherine was reported to be unpopular with her subjects; the old doubts about the stability of her throne were heard again; the British government had secret information of conspiracies hatching against her.[90] The Russian economy was known to be severely strained by the heavy cost of the Turkish war; the great plague of Moscow came as an additional disaster to a hard-pressed government.[91] The commitment in Poland could neither be abandoned nor, it seemed, carried to a conclusion, and it was fortunate for Catherine that French help for the Confederates was too little, and came too late. Every military advance towards Moldavia brought her nearer to the brink of war with Austria, and the closer she came to that prospect the stronger the pressure on her to accept Frederick's solution of partitioning Poland. All this suggested that Russia might soon be forced to lower her tone and solicit the English alliance; and it suggested also that Catherine's predicament was such as to make her a less eligible ally than before. Only by standing firm on the Turkish clause had ministers escaped involvement in a struggle which was no concern of England; only by their resolute refusal in 1763 to subsidize Russian enterprises in Poland had they avoided the embarrassment, and the guilt, of being accessories in the tragedy which was now approaching its *dénouement*. Suffolk had information of Frederick's plan as early as October 1771, and he put no faith in the credulous Cathcart, who even in May 1772 was prepared to swallow Panin's assurances that there was nothing in it.[92] The indignation with which Suffolk reacted to his information sufficiently refutes the legend that he viewed the matter with cynical indifference.[93] On 31 December 1771 he ordered Cathcart to convey his views to Panin: the object of British policy, he wrote, was the pacification of Poland and an honorable peace for Russia. And that there might be no ambiguity about what he intended by "pacification," he spelled out his meaning in his instructions for Gunning: the maintenance of Stanislaw on the throne, and "the preservation of the Republick entire."[94]

The Partition of Poland, when it came, would represent a significant defeat for Panin, who resisted it to the end and is said to have been willing to sacrifice Russia's conquests in order to avert it;[95] and it was one sign among many of the weakening position of the Panin party at court. The Turkish war was in effect a demonstration of the inadequacy of a Northern System which took little account of Russia's interests in the south, and had scarcely any friends save the empress and himself.[96] The Partition would register the final defeat of his hope of making Poland a vigorous power who might be a useful member of that system. It is true that in Denmark, which after Bernstorff's dismissal had manifested a disinclination to play the part of a Russian satellite, the prospects brightened somewhat with the overthrow of Struensee on 17 January 1772; but the change of régime in Copenhagen reacted adversely rather than otherwise on Anglo-Russian relations, since Suffolk was irritated by Panin's failure to give hearty support to British intervention on behalf of the unfortunate Caroline Matilda.[97] Suffolk would still be ready, in the summer of 1772, to rise to the bait of a Northern System; but it would be for the last time: after 19 August it would cease to play a serious part in the calculations of British statesmen.

(iv)

The Comte de Vergennes was not disposed to take his defeats in June lying down. Though Barthélémy reacted unfavorably to his "froideur, timidité, circonspection," though his biographer noted in him "une sorte de mélancolie résignée," he was after all a diplomat of determination and resource.[98] Choiseul (who had not liked him) said of him on one occasion that he always raised objections to any proposal that was made to him, but never made difficulties about carrying it out; and he was himself reported to have boasted that "he had attacked Russia with success in Constantinople, and that he flattered himself he should have the same good fortune" in Stockholm.[99] He had, indeed, hitherto spent much money to little purpose, but he was in the happy position of having a great deal more at his disposal. The Abbé de Terray might grumble, but by Christmas France had somehow managed to pour into Sweden an amount estimated by d'Aiguillon at 2.4 million livres; and the money was not allowed to lie idle.[100]

Already on 16 July Goodricke had reported that Vergennes was buying up proxies of discontented Caps; and he suspected that his plan was to bribe the Clergy and the Peasants to change their Speakers, abandoning the Burghers as hopeless.[101] This, however, was to underestimate what Vergennes had in mind. He believed that it might be possible to recapture a majority for the Hats not in two but in all three of the non-noble Estates. At the end of August he began to put his plan into operation. Through Sinclair he approached Odelius, the influential secretary to the Peasants, and successfully bribed him; through Fersen he made similar approaches to select Caps in the Clergy and Burghers, who proved equally complaisant. In each case the terms of the bargain were that the recipients, while ostensibly remaining loyal members of the party, would block any attempt to unseat any of the Hats on the Senate.[102] The operation was expensive;[103] but as regards the Clergy and the Burghers it appeared—for a time—to be successful. In the Peasants, however, it provoked a spirited counterattack by Osterman, which led to the eviction on 28 September of the Hat leader, Lars Torbjörnsson; and thereafter neither the machinations of Odelius nor the gold of his paymaster was able to do much damage.[104] The Peasants remained, as before, solidly Cap.

For the social pretensions of the lower Estates Vergennes had no sympathy.[105] He had no wish to foment the strife of Estates, and Goodricke was mistaken in suspecting him of doing so. On the contrary, he condemned the hotheads in the House of Nobility as being likely to do more harm than good; for this did not seem to him to be a situation which could safely be exploited to increase the authority of the crown.[106] This was a matter on which he had no choice but to rely on his own judgment; for his instructions, though apparently explicit, were in reality awkwardly ambiguous. He had been directed to caution Gustav III against *premature* action, and to persuade him to adhere to his promise to rule within the constitution of 1720, "du moins jusqu'à ce qu'il se présente dans la suite des circonstances naturelles d'ajouter quelque accroissement à son pouvoir et son autorité."[107] It was far from clear whether these "natural circumstances" included a rally of frightened aristocrats around the throne. Vergennes deeply distrusted Sinclair's tactics of exacerbating divisions; but he did not fail to note that the zealots in defense of aristocratic privilege were turning into something like a party of King's Friends.

It was not so easy to determine whether the king was in fact their leader. On the whole, Vergennes thought not.[108] Gustav III, from whatever motives, probably started out with a real determination to make the Composition work. In view of d'Aiguillon's attitude during their conversations in Paris he had little room for maneuver. His policy must be to wait upon events, and in the meantime to stick to the conciliatory, "patriotic" posture which he had assumed on his return. This being so, his friends took it upon themselves to do what he was precluded from doing. By the end of September Sinclair and C. F. Scheffer were collaborating in plans to use the strife of Estates to precipitate a crisis. By mid-October Osterman was sure that there was a great plot afoot to produce a parliamentary deadlock, end the Diet without the coronation's having taken place, and so necessitate another which should be more favorably inclined; and in this plot he suspected that Gustav III and Fersen were at least accomplices.[109] The suspicion was certainly unfounded as regards Fersen, and very probably so as regards the king,[110] whose attitude towards enthusiasts such as Liljehorn and Uggla seems to have been faintly contemptuous.[111] It is at all events clear that the Patriot King was really troubled by the Diet's apparent indifference to the welfare of the nation. The harvest had failed; the country was threatened with famine; urgent measures were necessary to avert it; but proposals to take them were met with fiscal, formal, or self-interested objections. One very obvious measure was to prohibit the distillation of *brännvin*. Thanks to a passionate appeal by a merchant named Brandberg, who warned his fellow members that famine might well be followed by revolution, the Burghers did indeed vote for prohibition; but the three other Estates would have none of it: Hats and Caps united in defense of the agricultural interest and what they regarded as a palladium of Swedish liberties.[112] Averting their eyes from the crisis, they returned to the more interesting battle over the Charter. Their indifference filled the cup of the king's exasperation, reinforced his disillusionment with parliamentary government, and no doubt was one reason for his summoning the Speakers on 28 November. The domestic crisis, moreover, coincided with news from Poland which sounded ominously in his ears—the news that King Stanislaw had been kidnapped by Polish patriots. His comment on that event was significant: "Quand on s'écarte des vraies intérêts de son patrie pour des intérêts étrangers, et qu'on sacrifie ses devoirs à des considérations personelles, on mérite tout ce qui peut arriver."[113] Whatever the hazards, this was not a reproach to which he was willing to expose himself.

But the proximate cause of the initiative of 28 November lay, after all, in the strife of Estates. If we may believe the explanation of his action which he later gave to Lovisa Ulrika, he was driven to summon the Speakers by his belief that the non-noble Estates had resolved to carry their draft of the Charter direct to himself. He would then have been confronted with the choice either of signing it, which would have alienated the Nobility, and incidentally have been illegal; or, by refusing to do so, of clashing with "three quarters of my kingdom for the sake of a quarter, who would not have thanked me for it, and were themselves divided." To this impossible dilemma he had been brought by "the imprudence of my friends"—the Fredrik Horns, the Liljehorns—and "the vivacity of their spirits." His offer to the Speakers had been an attempt to escape from this situation; but it also (as he did not fail to add) "coincided with that patriotic spirit which I had made manifest from the opening days of my reign, and was a consequence of my resolution to play the part of a conciliator."[114]

That resolution was now almost exhausted, and the patriotic spirit would direct its appeal henceforward to others than the Componists. The meeting with the Speakers, and its outcome, marked something of a turning point. No longer would he be "a spectator, passive, waiting for things to ripen."[115] His address to the Speakers had contained an implied but unmistakable warning: "Si je ne regardais pas comme le plus grand honneur de régner sur un peuple libre et indépendant, je resterais tranquille spectateur de l'événement, ou je m'assurerais à moi-même, dans l'avenir, une situation plus brillante au dépens de votre liberté."[116] The rejection of his offer meant that that warning would become a policy. It was precisely at this moment of frustration and bitterness that the Duc d'Aiguillon, personally intervening in Swedish affairs for the first time since his accession to office, produced initiatives which were to reinforce Gustav's resentments, and to push him—if he needed pushing—towards revolution.

The Duc d'Aiguillon took charge of French foreign policy in June 1771. His advent was greeted without enthusiasm, especially by France's allies. A man with few friends and many enemies, he had the reputation of being ruthless, obstinate, and an intriguer: the best that Count Mercy could find to say of him was that at least he was better than nothing. But Lord Harcourt thought him a great improvement on Choiseul; and even his enemies conceded that he was a man of ability and intelligence, who applied himself indefatigably to the business of the office.[117] His foreign policy has been severely judged by French diplomatic historians;[118] but in truth he succeeded to no very enviable heritage. Choiseul's gamble of a Turkish war had clearly failed; his house of cards in Poland had collapsed ignominiously, and it fell to d'Aiguillon to evacuate the ruins with as little discredit as possible. Though he was at bottom scarcely less hostile to England than Choiseul,[119] he faced a situation in which France had more urgent concerns than the prosecution of the old quarrel. He saw his main enemy as Russia; and his efforts were from the beginning directed to building barriers against Russian expansion. Above all, to averting the Partition of Poland which he clearly foresaw. The Partition, if it took place, would imply the creation of a *système copartageant* which would revolutionize political alignments and threaten the states of western Europe with a terrible disturbance of the balance of power. No other European statesman saw this danger as early as d'Aiguillon, and none strove harder to avert it.[120] In his attempts to do so he tried to draw closer France's ties with her ally Austria; he made efforts to mend his fences in Berlin; and above all he set himself by all sorts of complaisances to win the goodwill of the chronically suspicious statesmen of London.[121] In March 1772 he took a major initiative in this direction, when he made the explicit suggestion that with a view to preventing Partition England and France should join in a corrdinated *démarche*, France to her ally in Vienna, England to her friend in St. Petersburg.[122] As might have been expected, the overture elicited no favorable response:[123] it would be months before George III and Rochford showed signs of coming round to d'Aiguillon's way of thinking, and even then the implacable gallophobia of British public opinion would bar the way to any progress along that road. In the meantime, the traditional French policy in Sweden now recovered a real relevance: with the Turks on the eve of suing for peace, with the fate of Poland as good as decided, France could not afford to see the last bastion of her historic Eastern System fall into Russian hands. For the first time for thirty years French policy in the North became essentially defensive.[124]

For some months after the opening of the Diet, d'Aiguillon was content to adhere to the policy embodied in the instructions to Vergennes. By late autumn, however, the behavior of the Diet—and probably still more, developments in eastern Europe—had convinced him that France could not afford to wait upon events. In November and December he took steps which between them transformed the situation. Much the most important of them was his secret letter of 10 December to Gustav III.[125] This was a strong exhortation to carry out a "*coup de force*," on the argument that it represented the only alternative to a "Russian-controlled anarchy," and was therefore "indispensably necessary." It represented a major reversal of tactics, a full-blooded return to the policies of Choiseul. Creutz in Paris reinforced the message: there must be an end to "this lamentable Diet . . . Y. M. must beat down his foes by constancy and courage, if you are to induce your allies to new sacrifices."[126] A month later, d'Aiguillon dispatched another letter to the same effect; sent, it was said, "on the express orders" of Louis XV.[127] With the tiresome deviousness inseparable from French diplomacy of the period this vital change of front was for the present not revealed to Vergennes: he might be a member of the King's Secret; but now the duke had a secret of his own. It was no wonder if in these circumstances the ambassador found himself somewhat at a loss in his conversations with Gustav III.[128]

For Gustav III, these communications in effect constituted a statement of the conditions for continued French support. His anger and despair would in any case have disposed him to comply with d'Aiguillon's prescriptions; but there were other, and most pressing, reasons which made it perilous to ignore them. The tenebrous affair of the Horneca loan had from the first been organized on the assumption that France would shoulder the burden of its repayment.[129] The assumption was rash, and already by September Creutz was warning Gustav III that it was untenable: d'Aiguillon was indisposed to oblige. On 27 November the duke wrote to Vergennes making his refusal explicit:[130] the 500,000 livres would be deducted from the first installment of subsidy arrears, due on 1 January 1772. This was catastrophic news: "a thunderbolt," as Ulrik Scheffer remarked; and it produced panic in royalist circles. For it meant that the disreputable transaction with Horneca would no longer be able to be concealed. The political consequences for the king were incalculable; but they would certainly be very grave. Creutz wrote urgently from Paris suggesting that "Y. M. write an affecting letter to the King; a flattering one to Mme du Barry; and a confidential one to the Duc d'Aiguillon."[131] In a desperate scrawl to Creutz, Gustav duly enclosed a letter to Louis XV, promising faithfully not to permit French money in future to be used for Hat party purposes; C. F. Scheffer concocted a memorial for d'Aiguillon; only Mme du Barry, as too indiscreet, was left unsolicited.[132] If d'Aiguillon's object had been to make the royalists in Sweden aware of their need to listen to his counsels he had certainly succeeded. But before any of these dolorous epistles could reach Paris, he had so far relented as to pronounce a suspended sentence. The first installment of the subsidy was now to be paid at the *end* of the first quarter; half a million was to be made available to Gustav III in the meantime, as a loan with which to cover the deficiency. But it was at the same time made clear that the loan must be repaid, and that if it was not, it would be deducted from later installments.[133] Thus the dangerous corner was turned for the moment; but the threat of exposure remained, a sword of Damocles suspended over the king's head. That threat could be removed only in two ways: either by somehow raising the money elsewhere—a highly unlikely eventuality; or by a revolution which would take away the power of the Estates to exact vengeance. There could not be much doubt which alternative d'Aiguillon had in mind.

The duke's encouragement of revolution had as its logical complement the termination of financial support for the Hats. In his letter to Vergennes of 27 November he ordered that all payments to the Hat clubs and to individuals should cease as from 1 January 1772. On 22 December Vergennes duly announced this decision, to the great inconvenience of aggrieved members who had counted on French money for their Christmas holidays.[134] D'Aiguillon later explained that the ban on corruption was not intended to apply to "des engagements particulières," by which it seems that he intended Vergennes' commitments to those Cap members of the Clergy and Burghers whom he had seduced in September;[135] but it bore sufficiently hard upon necessitous members of the Nobility to provoke a violent reaction. The immediate effect was the near-disintegration of the Hat party. No sooner had the Hat club closed its doors than a new club sprang up to take its place. Its members professed their intention to finance themselves without French support, and in sign of their claim to "stand on their own bottom" took the name *Svenska Botten.* Most of them were young, many were junior army officers, all were recruited from that section of the Nobility that was bitterest in the defense of aristocratic privilege, and most rabid against Fersen's leadership: by 2 January they had 117 members; a fortnight later, 210.[136] Vergennes had a poor opinion of them;[137] but behind the rank and file were men with plenty of ability and few scruples. F. C. Sinclair was one of them, Fredrik Horn perhaps another; but their probable founder was Jacob Magnus Sprengtporten:[138] a man who was destined to play a leading part in the preparations for revolution. For, in varying degrees, and with more or less ardor, this was plainly a club of royalists—the first organized party which the Court had possessed since 1765. In *Svenska Botten* the cause of privilege was finally transmuted into the cause of the king; and it was not long before Vergennes (despite the ban on corruption) was privily making contributions to its upkeep. Gustav III was a contributor almost from the beginning.[139] D'Aiguillon had indeed transformed the situation. He had committed the king in principle to revolution; and he had provoked the creation of a rallying point for those elements to whom a desperate monarch would most naturally turn for assistance. If by stopping corruption he had in the meantime left Osterman master of the Diet, that was a price he could afford to pay. His main concern was that France's money should be usefully employed; and if corruption should once again offer tangible rewards, he would not be so doctrinaire as to decline it.

(v)

The Christmas recess did nothing to resolve the deadlock over the Charter. By the third week of January it seemed that the situation which Gustav III had foreseen, and which by his appeal to the Speakers he had hoped to avert, was actually upon them; that the three lower Estates would in fact present their draft to the king for his signature, that the Nobility would follow their example, and that Gustav III might be placed in the intolerable situation of having to choose between them.[140] No one wanted this to happen; and there was a growing feeling, extending over the whole spectrum of politics and shared by all the foreign ministers, that desperate efforts must be made to avert a total breakdown. For, as Gustav III wrote, "Nous sommes enfin parvenus au point que, dans peu, l'anarchie réelle, la guerre civile ou un ordre parfait naîtra de tous ces désordres,"[141] The first hopeful sign came when the Despatching Committee sent back the draft to the Grand Committee for reconsideration; and the next, when the Judicial Committee presented a draft bill to make strikes of officials illegal. If this bill were to pass, it would remove any pretext for mentioning the matter in the Charter, and so meet one of the Nobility's objections. On 8 February, accordingly, they made no difficulty about declaring their willingness to support it.[142]

This however, was but a small advance: great issues of principle still divided the Estates, and the bitter animosity between them might well prove resistant to attempts at settlement. Other methods therefore became necessary; and behind the scenes maneuverings and intrigues supplemented the efforts of those such as Rudbeck who sought to reach some compromise in the Grand Committee. One such attempt came from the side of the Court. It seems to have originated in Sprengtporten; but it had the support of Gustav III, and also of Vergennes. Though the line of approach varied from time to time, its consistent purpose was to win over one of the non-noble Estates by offering inducements which they would be unable to resist. Two Estates would then be ranged against two; the king, professing his adherence to the constitution, would use the resulting deadlock as a pretext to dissolve the Diet (which he had no legal power to do), and would defer the summoning of another for twelve years. The first attempt was to be made upon the Clergy, and the bait to be offered to them was the ennoblement of the sons of the most prominent of them.[143] This was linked to a proposal to remove the limitation on the numbers of members of the House of Nobility which had been imposed in 1762,[144] by permitting persons ennobled since 1761 to sit as proxies for other families. But when a motion to this effect was moved in the House of Nobility on 12 February it was defeated by 57 votes, and as a consequence the scheme was abandoned.[145] Despite this setback, however, the attempt to seduce leaders of the lower Estates made progress: Gustav III triumphantly reported that he had bribed Wijkman and Sundblad to support a distinctly shady transaction whereby he had acquired one of Jennings's houses for Lovisa

Ulrika;[146] and he noted with satisfaction the appearance at Court of such formerly inveterate enemies as Wijkman, Gadolin, and Melin.[147] Through Vergennes he put himself in touch with Stockholm burghers ambitious to acquire noble land. There seemed to be a real basis for a bargain between the crown and the lower Estates: if they could be assured of royal support for the redress of their social grievances they might not prove too nice about insisting on limitations of the prerogative. Already at the beginning of February Gustav III was foreseeing that they might try to secure his support by constitutional concessions.[148] It was a speculation which in 1789 would pay a dividend.

For the moment, however, such prospects were obscured by the action of Osterman. Osterman had decided that the main obstacle to any settlement was Sinclair; and that obstacle he proceeded to remove by the only method likely to be effective with a person of Sinclair's character. Sooner or later, and certainly as soon as the affair of the Charter was out of the way, the Caps would move to unseat some or all of the remaining Hat members of the Senate. The bribe which Osterman offered, and which on 11 February Sinclair accepted, was a promise that when that purge occurred Sinclair would be spared, and would in addition be appointed to the lucrative post of governor-general of Pomerania; the immediate quid pro quo was that his friends were instructed to refrain from factious opposition to the bill making strikes of officials illegal.[149] The motives which led him to accept this offer are not clear: by his friends it was contended that the object of his maneuvers was to destroy the political predominance of the Hat aristocracy, typified by his personal enemy Fersen, and to build a purified royalist party in its place.[150] But the most likely explanation is simply that he acted from motives of self-interest; and indeed in a letter to his friend Nils Philip Gyldenstolpe he confessed as much; "Tout va au Diable [he wrote], et me confirme qu'il est temps de songer de soi-même."[151] For the moment his defection remained a secret; but the cessation of his machinations may perhaps have done something to make possible the settlement of the question of the Charter.

On 22 February the Estate of Nobility took into consideration a suggestion which had been referred to the *plena* by the Grand Committee, and which seems to have emanated from Rudbeck.[152] It proposed as a basis of settlement that the ban upon strikes of officials be omitted, since that matter was now to be the subject of separate legislation; and that the special interests of the Nobility be safeguarded by appending to the Charter a memorial, signed by the Speakers of all four Estates, purporting that nothing in the Charter was to be construed as infringing the privileges of any one of them. It was a proposal which plainly involved an almost total capitulation by the Nobility. It made no mention of the king's obligation to rule continuously; it dropped the demand that a decision of the Diet must rest on a vote by *all* Estates; it left appointments to be made only on a basis of merit and ability; it abandoned the Nobility's attempt to preserve a special position in regard to the acquisition of crown land; and it incorporated no particular guarantee of the Nobility's privileges. Those who argued for its acceptance insisted that such a Charter made no real difference to the legal position; that the Nobility's rights were in any case protected by the fundamental laws of the constitution; that the changes were purely verbal rather than material. Which was exactly what the lower Estates had been maintaining for the past five months, although it is most unlikely that they really thought so. The critics of the proposal had thus an easy task, and in the great debate had undeniably the better of the argument. But the big guns on either side kept up a rolling fire to cover surrender: Fersen and Wadenstierna, on the one hand; all the leading Caps on the other: von Essen, Frietzcky, Rudbeck, Pechlin, Nackreij, Durietz. A main argument was that the situation was so serious that the interests of a single Estate must not be allowed to stand in the way of reconciliation. Famine in the country, and small prospect of relief; plague on the Russian border; a massive debt and a budget deficit which there was little chance of filling;[153] the fear of civil disturbances. No one mentioned the danger of royalist revolution; but it cannot have been far from the thoughts of the leaders. What all were conscious of, what was alluded to time and again in debates about this time, was the venomous press campaign against the Nobility, the "universal hatred" with which they found themselves regarded.[154] The power and determination of the lower orders had been seen already in their carrying the election of Sundblad to the office of *justitiekansler,* though this was eminently one of those "high offices" hitherto reserved to the Nobility; and in this appointment they had felt it prudent to concur.[155] The Cap leaders feared to alienate their intransigent followers still further; and there was widespread defeatism on both sides: as Ridderstolpe remarked, no doubt it would have been better to insist on their own draft, "but it is not in our power."[156] It was left to that indiscreet and fractious Cap, Gyllensvan, to sum up this feeling of helplessness when he said:

> It is true that if the Nobility had now the same influence upon the other Estates as formerly, when we were able to do jobs for our fellow-citizens—to provide a living for this man, commercial advantages for that, a farm

> and tillage to a third—then our Yea or Nay might still have some effect. But now, when every section of them is in possession of the country's wealth, they feel their strength, and we stand here powerless.[157]

For ten years the tide of social egalitarianism had been creeping up on them, and now they stood in danger of being overwhelmed. The bitter-enders fought remorselessly throughout two long *plena*, and it was not until 2 a.m. on the second day that the work of the tellers was completed, after Sprengtporten had led a phalanx of 77 members in signing an irregular protest against surrender.[158] When the result was at last announced, the advocates of capitulation were found to have carried the day by 359 to 327. The other Estates jubilantly accepted a formula which in effect gave them all they had demanded; and on 4 March Gustav III, with ostentatious indifference, affixed his signature to a Charter which he did not trouble himself to read.

So ended this bitter and protracted struggle. Osterman received the order of Alexander Nevsky from a grateful empress, together with a further 100,000 rubles, "to bring the Diet to an end."[159] And the three lower Estates, flushed with their triumph, could turn their attention to the congenial task of advancing their interests and persecuting their enemies. Above all, to the replacement of the remaining Hat Senators by men of their own party. The crisis over the Charter had scarcely been resolved before it was succeeded by another, not less violent, and equally grievous to men of moderation: a crisis over the Senate. This was a matter of central importance both to Gustav III and to Goodricke. To Goodricke, because a Senate wholly in Cap hands might have the collective nerve to break away from the French system and risk the loss of the French arrears; and because the displacement of the Hats would entail the appointment of a chancery-president who was a friend of England. To Gustav III, on the other hand, the preservation of as many as possible of the existing members was a matter of both political and personal concern. Even though by this time d'Aiguillon cared little or nothing for the fate of the Hats as a party, they were the guarantee of Sweden's fidelity to France. They might be very dubious supporters of a royalist revolution, but at least they were men with whom Gustav III was accustomed to work, and with some of whom (Nils Bielke, Ulrik Scheffer) he stood upon a basis of close friendship; while a Cap Senate would be composed of men who to him were either almost unknown or positively distasteful. In Ulrik Scheffer he had an enthusiastic supporter of his plans for revolution: a man, moreover, who was well seen by d'Aiguillon, even though Vergennes might dislike him. Goodricke might have made up his mind to put in Joakim von Düben as chancery-president; but Gustav III was not less determined that the office should go to Scheffer.

At the end of February the situation regarding the Senate was that the Caps had already three members out of the total of sixteen: two recalled in August in terms of the Composition; one admitted in October in consequence of Ekeblad's death. The Composition had laid it down that places should be made available for three more; and by January Gustav III had persuaded three tractable Hats to retire if satisfactory pensions could be guaranteed to them.[160] On 5 March he called the Composition Council together and offered these terms to the Caps, with the additional proviso that there should be no further removals: the terms of the Composition, he considered, had now been honestly fulfilled. But the Cap representatives, well aware that the mass of their party regarded them as Laodiceans or worse, did not risk accepting this offer. They turned for advice to Goodricke and Osterman; and the advice they received was to be content with four or five places, if they could get them.[161]

As far as Goodricke was concerned the advice was a matter of tactics rather than conviction. There is little doubt that he wanted a clean sweep of all the Hat Senators. In October he had strongly supported Düben's appeal for English money to effect it: as all the Caps had been turned out in 1769, so should all the Hats be removed in 1772. This was the line taken by the zealots of the non-noble Estates; and that in itself was one reason why he should prefer it. But Osterman was strongly for moderation, and not only because he was short of money. Goodricke consequently found himself in a delicate and at times embarrassing situation between his Russian colleague and the Cap militants: in January, when Osterman had tried to discipline his following by threatening to stop supplies, Goodricke had "not ventured to approve" so unpopular a measure, and had been forced to take refuge in an anodyne appeal for party unity.[162] But though, as he told Suffolk, he would have followed a different policy if he had been in Osterman's position,[163] he found himself obliged to keep in step with the party's paymaster. He might dislike moderation, but there were prudential reasons which for the moment seemed to enforce it. He knew by this time of Vergennes' earlier bribing of Odelius, and of some members of the Clergy; and he feared that if the Caps were too exigent the result might be to set two Estates against two, and thus prevent any removals at all.[164] If that should happen, farewell to the hope of making Düben chancery-president.

It was reasons such as these which led him, in March and again in April, to join Osterman in urging the Cap leaders to limit their demands to from three to five additional places. At the end of March the three Senators whose conditional resignations Gustav III had secured did in fact resign; and their places were taken by Funck, Ribbing, and Düben.[165] At the beginning of April, Gustav III entered into an extraordinary negotiation with Osterman and Goodricke which amounted to bargaining about the composition of his own government with the representatives of the two powers whom he feared and detested. Surprising concessions were made on both sides. The king agreed that Düben should be chancery-president, with Ridderstolpe as *rikskansliråd*; another Cap was to be admitted as a supernumerary member; Caps were to be appointed to provincial governorships as they fell vacant. But on the other hand Ulrik Scheffer was to remain in the Senate; the Caps were to be content with only two further places; and at the next Diet there were to be no dismissals save for high crimes and misdemeanors.[166] Gustav III must have felt it to be profoundly humiliating; but Goodricke regarded it as a great success. And so it was, in one vital aspect: the appointment of Düben to take charge of foreign affairs.

For these delicate negotiations the three lower Estates cared not at all. While Osterman and Goodricke were displaying sweet reasonableness, the appropriate deputations had framed their indictment against all the remaining Hat Senators. It was a truly deplorable document, which magnified mistakes, misjudgments, petty irregularities, into enormous crimes against the constitution; but it served the purpose of those who drew it as well as if it had disclosed peculation or high treason. For it recommended an almost total change of government: ten Senators were to be censured; seven of them to be dismissed. On 11 April these recommendations came to the *plena* of the lower Estates. Great efforts were made to soften or reject them.[167] In March, Vergennes, reduced to the extreme of irritability by his efforts to fend off assaults on his pocket—he complained that he was treated as though he were a cashier in Grill's bank[168]—had predicted with gloomy relish that nothing could save the Hat Senators, and had recommended bribing two of them to resign, in the faint hope that this might be sufficient to appease their adversaries.[169] But he roused himself now, opened his purse strings, and successfully bribed Sundblad and Westin.[170] The members of the Clergy who had taken his money in September remained true to their bargain; but Odelius, alarmed by the news that his dealings with Vergennes had leaked out, prudently returned the money destined for him.[171] Nevertheless, Vergennes had more allies than he could have reckoned on. The Cap leaders themselves pleaded for mercy; and the astounding spectacle was seen of Russian money coming to the assistance of French corruption.[172] It was all to no avail. Intoxicated by the fiery oratory of the clubs the Estates voted—by large majorities in the Peasants and Clergy, by 68 to 41 in the Burghers—to accept the recommendations. Seven Senators were to be dismissed; and the three who were simply to be censured included—significantly—the turncoat von Wallwijk and the defector Sinclair, who thus reaped the firstfruits of his desertion. Ten days later the Secret Committee completed the bargain by voting to send him as governor to Pomerania.[173]

The dramatic votes of 11 April caused consternation and bewilderment. Gustav III felt himself betrayed by Sinclair on the one hand and the Cap Componists on the other;[174] Vergennes professed himself to have lost all faith in human nature.[175] The Cap leaders, humiliated and apologetic, sought a meeting with Fersen in which they attempted to excuse themselves, and even undertook to reinstate four of the evicted—a promise which they certainly lacked the power to keep.[176] Goodricke's feelings well reflect the confusion of the moment. The vote of 11 April had at least demonstrated that on this issue there was no danger of a deadlock: that argument for moderation, at all events, had been exploded. But its place had been taken by another: the fear that the violence of the militants might provoke the king to risk a coup d'état. Goodricke's immediate reaction, then, was to declare himself "extremely apprehensive."[177] Gustav III and Vergennes, he believed, were holding back a supply of money; and assuredly for some important enterprise.[178] Yet for all that it was impossible for him to suppress a feeling of excitement and triumph at the result: "We have carried more than we asked, without spending one farthing."[179] The Hats were crushed; Sinclair, that dangerous intriguer, was to be removed to a safe distance, and with his removal went a fear that the anti-Componists among the Caps might perhaps find in him a new leader;[180] above all, Düben was now chancery-president. To a man of Goodricke's temperament there was something inspiriting in the situation: "If we maintain our Superiority till the conclusion of the Diet, I flatter myself to be able to make any alliance with Sweden which the King may judge to be a proper foundation for a Northern System, to which, it appears, both Russia and other powers would accede."[181]

Though the three lower Estates had thus decided the fate of the Senate, it still remained to debate the question in the House of

Nobility. A vote here could now make no difference; but it offered an opportunity to Componists, Hats, and royalists to stand up for political decency and elementary justice. On 25 April, in a great debate marked by splendid eloquence, speaker after speaker tore the flimsy rags of pretext from the recommendations of the deputations and exposed their pettiness and their malice.[182] Scarcely anyone on either side considered the accused to be in any real sense guilty; none believed that even if they were so they deserved to lose their offices. The Cap leaders declared their disapproval in principle of any total change in administration, and urged that if there must be dismissals they be limited to two or three;[183] Gyllensvan conjectured that the main crime of the accused might well be their connections with the aristocracy, and offered the unpopular suggestion that it might be prudent to sacrifice them as a measure of appeasement.[184] The Hats, conveniently unmindful that they had swept way an entire Cap Senate in 1769, thundered against the malignity which used trivial errors to ruin well-meaning statesmen. Modern historians of the Age of Liberty have sometimes made the point that before it reached its end men had come to accept a two-party system in which governments naturally changed with changing parliamentary majorities, and that the convention that it was necessary to prove criminality before displacing a Senator was already recognized to be a hollow sham; and they are apt to adduce in support of this contention the remark of John Jennings in 1769, when he demanded the dismissal of the Cap Senate on the simple ground that "the country needed another government."[185] But there was absolutely no sign of any such feeling among the Nobility on 25 April. No one asserted the need, no one pointed out the logic, of a homogeneous Senate to match the party majority in the Estates: on the contrary, speaker after speaker on both sides professed belief in a mixed administration drawn from each party. The principles of parliamentarism were less well established than some historians have been disposed to imagine: the Nobility, it is clear, suffered under the disadvantage of not having read the works of Fredrik Lagerroth. What they did feel, and feel very strongly, was that a ruthless purge of this sort had sinister implications for that liberty which the constitution—in theory, though too often not in practice—was supposed to guarantee. As Fersen put it in a memorable passage: "We are now struggling to deprive each other of offices . . . from this we may go further, and take away men's property; and at last we may come to take away their lives: so it is, when the law is not scrupulously observed."[186] This great debate was indeed a kind of swan song of the Age of Liberty; the last protest against developments which could scarcely be reconciled with the ideals which had inspired the men of 1720. And the result was proportionably depressing. Many members must have been unwilling to be parties to a decision which could have no practical effect except still further to feed the animosity of the enemies of the aristocracy; many had gone home, dispirited. In a House distinctly thinner than for the last divisions upon the Charter, the recommendations of the deputations were accepted, the resolutions of the lower Estates endorsed, by 277 to 272.

(vi)

It took almost a month before the vacancies on the Senate could be filled; and when at last its numbers were made up it did not present a very impressive appearance. Again and again, out of the three candidates for each place put forward by the electors, the man selected by the king declined to accept appointment; the most notable example being Ridderstolpe, who however at last capitulated to the entreaties of both friends and enemies, and resigned himself to his fate. The history of the last few years strongly suggested that membership of the Senate carried with it more of responsibility than of power, that tenure of office was likely to be short, and that its termination might only too probably carry with it censure, disgrace, and no adequate *solatium* in the way of pension. As one member of the Nobility put it, *vestigia terrent*.[187] So it happened that the Cap Senate, with the honorable exception of Ridderstolpe and perhaps Falkengrén, was recruited from men of untried abilities and second-rate importance in the party. Moreover, since the electors for the Nobility happened all to be Hats, they were able after protracted bargaining to force one member of their party—Falkenberg—into the triads of candidates; and to Goodricke's chagrin Gustav III appointed him, and not Ridderstolpe, to be *rikskanslíråd*. As it happened, it was an appointment which was justified on its merits; but it took some of the gilt off the great victory of 25 April.

Despite these rubs, that victory had for Goodricke been decisive. This time there was no apprehension discernible in his reaction: he was frankly triumphant. Never since 1739 had the Caps been in such an apparently unassailable position, not even in the spring of 1765.[188] He appeared now to be presented with the opportunity for which he had been working for the last eight years: at last, he might think, the objective of his mission was within his grasp. He could no longer afford a constrained and reluctant moderation: the Composition was dead; the favorable moment must at all costs be seized. After the end of April he threw in his lot with "the Nation," with those militant elements whom Osterman was powerless to hold in check: if Sweden was ever to be wrested from the hands of France it was upon such persons that he must rely for assistance. Osterman's attempts to constrain his followers to be reasonable had recoiled on his own head: in March he had actually stopped payments to the Burghers and the Peasants, only to be told that they could do very well without him; in June he was reduced to the desperate expedient of dismissing his "operators" and taking new ones.[189] Goodricke was happily exempt from such mortifications by the very fact that he had no money to give, and he could swim with the tide of democracy unperturbed by any consideration that he had hitherto spent lavishly to dam it back. In the summer of 1772, for the first time since the beginning of this Diet, he pursues his own course; he ousts Osterman from the position of authority which his financial power had secured to him; he emerges as the leader and counselor of the rude mass of the party. As Gustav III wrote: "C'est Milord Rosbiff qui s'est maintenant emparé des rênes du gouvernement; aussi paraît-il être le maître au train que prennent les affaires."[190] The adoption of this course entailed the risk that the violence of his followers and allies might precipitate a revolution. But he probably told himself that with any luck he might bring off an alliance with Sweden, and that Russia's adhesion to it might be obtained, before a royalist coup could prevent it; or, alternatively, that the Caps would be so vigilant that there would never be any revolution at all. Even if it came, even if as its consequence any Anglo-Swedish treaty became so much waste paper, what did it matter provided that in the meantime the accession of Russia had given England the alliance she had sought for so long? On 28 April, in the same dispatch in which he reported the vote in the House of Nobility, he urged that no time be lost in sending him full powers to negotiate a defensive treaty on the model of Conway's instructions of 1767, so that the whole business might be finished before the end of the Diet.

Lord Suffolk's response to this appeal was prompt, vigorous, and surprisingly positive. On 21 May he reported that a Cabinet had been held at which it was decided that Goodricke be authorized to proceed; on the twenty-eighth he sent off his instructions by Messenger.[191] He made some practical suggestions for modifying the terms of 1767; and he intimated that though subsidies in peacetime might be out of the question, England might possibly be willing to pay "a tempting price for actual succours" in wartime: in the last resort Goodricke was empowered to offer Sweden a subsidy in case she were involved in war as a consequence of the alliance, the precise amount being left to him to negotiate, but not to exceed £100,000 a year. No Secretary of State hitherto had been prepared to go so far.[192] Suffolk was indeed ready to go even further. At the same time as he sent off his instructions to Goodricke, he drafted those which Gunning was to take with him to St. Petersburg.[193] They took as their starting point the eviction of the Hat Senate, news which for Suffolk, as for Goodricke, clearly constituted a major transformation of the situation. Gunning was instructed that if "the late change of circumstances in Sweden" turned out to have removed one of the main difficulties in the way of an alliance with Russia, he was not debarred from listening to any proposal Panin might have to make, nor even from "proposing to improve the opportunity, for framing a comprehensive Northern Alliance"; and he was immediately to inform Panin of the orders which were being sent to Goodricke. And since the alliance with Russia must always be the basis of any Northern System, "you will give more or less attention to other treaties, which may be proposed to you, according to the relation they may bear to that alliance, and their importance to that System." Lastly, and most surprisingly, "If in discussing the terms of such treaties, any subsidy to be paid by us *alone* [my italics] shall be proposed, you will report the proposition to us, but without encouraging any expectations that we shall agree to it." Suffolk had thus modified his attitude on three points: he was now prepared in certain circumstances to take the initiative in resuming negotiations with the Russians; he was prepared to consider "other treaties"—which could only mean a treaty with Denmark, a power with whom only three months before he had been on the brink of war;[194] and by implication he did not dismiss the possibility of paying subsidies in peacetime to the Scandinavian powers, provided Russia were willing to contribute her share. Thus for Suffolk the political developments in Sweden provided the impetus for a final effort to secure the Russian alliance: as the fall of the Cap Senate in 1769 had ruined the chances of that alliance, so the fall of the Hats in 1772 had revived them. The instructions to Gunning plainly show that Suffolk had little doubt that this time they would succeed: Russia had many times urged an Anglo-Swedish alliance as the basis for an extended system; Catherine had "expressed the desire that His Majesty should guarantee the dominions of Sweden even against herself"; everything for which Panin had expressed a wish had now been adopted.[195] A fortnight later came a report from Cathcart which reinforced this optimism: according to Cathcart, Panin agreed that the success in Sweden had been much greater than anticipated; agreed that there should now be an Anglo-Swedish alliance, with a guarantee to Sweden against her neighbors; agreed that it was now probably obtainable without a subsidy; and he had added that such an alliance was "capable, if improved," of providing a basis for an Anglo-Russian treaty. He had later intimated (as so often before!) that he was considering offering a quite fresh project, probably to coincide with the conclusion of peace with the Turks.[196] No wonder that Suffolk told Goodricke that "the Manner in which the Court of Russia considers the present Opportunity in Sweden is exactly such as we expected. What Count Panin wishes us to do upon it corresponds entirely with what you are already directed to negotiate."[197]

This, alas, was wishful thinking: Suffolk for once failed to take Cathcart with the necessary pinch of salt. When Gunning arrived in St. Petersburg he was astonished to meet with a chilly reception. Panin was cold and reserved; his only comment on the proposed Anglo-Swedish treaty was an indifferent "It is an expedient," and he saw little chance of carrying it as long as France continued to pay the subsidy-arrears. As to an Anglo-Russian alliance, he "did not see his way clear at present."[198] He pointedly omitted to instruct Osterman to assist Goodricke in his negotiations: a further supply of 50,000 rubles was indeed dispatched to him, but as Goodricke ruefully noted they were not available for this purpose.[199] The event would prove that Panin was wise not to risk his money.

The project which Goodricke presented to Düben in July was for a defensive alliance for ten years, limited (as far as Great Britain was concerned) to "the King's possessions in Europe."[200] It bound each party to assist the other with six ships of the line, or alternatively with up to 6,000 men, the expense to be borne (in contradistinction to the project of 1767) by the *partie requérante* rather than the *partie requise*. It contained a dangerously elastic clause which pledged the *partie requérante* to try to ensure that at the conclusion of peace the *partie requise* should receive full compensation, or be restored to the state "où il étoit *ou auroit dû être*" (my italics) before the war—a clause which might have involved England in a campaign to recover St. Petersburg. Russia was to be invited to accede. Finally, by a last revival of the bright hopes of 1764-65, a separate trade treaty was to be negotiated: pending its conclusion each was to enjoy most-favored-nation treatment by the other, with the necessary exception for French rights in Wismar under the Franco-Swedish treaty of 1741.

Goodricke later added an assurance that though England would not give subsidies in peacetime, the question of subsidies in time of war might be a matter for negotiation once the treaty was signed.[201]

To this proposal Düben made four objections: it was difficult to reconcile with the Franco-Swedish convention of 1764; England was more likely to be involved in war than Sweden was; the treaty would be at variance with Sweden's pacific policy; and it would entail the loss of French subsidies without any compensation.[202] Suffolk found these "cavils" unreasonable. He seems to have been sincerely convinced that the terms he was offering were liberal, and genuinely surprised that they should be considered unacceptable. It was precisely because England was more likely to be involved in war than Sweden that he had proposed that the cost of aid be borne by the *partie requérante*; the prospect of a subsidy in wartime offset the refusal to pay one in peacetime; the loss of French money (more often promised than paid!) would be amply compensated by securing the Tranquillity of the North; and as to the "pacifick plan" of Sweden's foreign policy, that plan would be "more secure, because more respected, than at present, when protected by the naval power of this great kingdom, which is always actuated by the Desire of preserving the Ballance of Power among her Neighbours, not by that of aggrandizing herself."[203]

These arguments may have seemed extremely cogent in London, but they made little impression in Stockholm. However much Düben and his supporters may have wished to throw off the "French yoke," they dared not risk it on these terms. Sweden had once already felt the effects of the loss of the French subsidies, as a consequence of Goodricke's treaty of 1766, and the financial situation in 1772 was not such as to permit a repetition of that experience unless some compensation were made available. Goodricke realized this very well: from the beginning he was not hopeful of success.[204] As early as 5 May Düben had confided to him that there would be grave difficulties as long as France continued to pay the arrears. The warning was repeated at intervals by the most zealous friends of England, notably by Serenius.[205] It might perhaps have been possible to carry the treaty by judicious bribery in the Secret Committee; but that way too was barred. Not only would Suffolk not give a subsidy, he refused absolutely to spend any money at all to secure a treaty which in his view any sensible Swede ought to be glad to accept.[206] In this situation the only chance remaining was that France might be provoked by the dismissal of the Hat Senate, or by the knowledge of Goodricke's negotiations, to stop her supplies, and that the Secret Committee in their anger might throw material considerations to the winds and retort by concluding the alliance. This was what Düben hoped for at the beginning of the negotiation; and this was the last-ditch position which Goodricke took up at the end of it.[207]

D'Aiguillon declined to oblige him by falling into that trap. The dismissal of the Hat Senate provoked no immediate reaction in Paris: d'Aiguillon's methods were more subtle and more effective than Praslin's heavy hand in 1766. He met the situation by suggesting to Creutz (who duly passed it on to Düben) that France had no objection to Sweden's allying with her neighbors if she thought proper: an alliance with Russia, for example, would be unexceptionable, though naturally France could hardly be expected to view a connection with England with indifference.[208] Creutz supplemented this information with the conjecture (which was not wholly without foundation)[209] that France, finding her alliance with Austria cooling, might well be seeking to improve relations with St. Petersburg. The handful of Hats in the Lesser Secret Deputation in panic besieged Vergennes with demands that he modify or disavow the reports from Paris;[210] but they need not have excited themselves: d'Aiguillon was not really ready to give his blessing to a Russo-Swedish connection, as his subsequent actions would demonstrate. His object was to wreck Goodricke's negotiation, and by tempting the Swedes into substituting for it a negotiation with Osterman, to gain time: time for the plans for a revolution to become effective. The maneuver was brilliantly successful. The Caps, disheartened by Suffolk's intransigence, began to direct their attention to concluding a treaty with Russia. Goodricke was not surprised: what do we offer, he wrote, to offset France's 1.5 million livres a year?—a guarantee against Russia! But if they can ally with Russia themselves, what reason have they to accept it, especially since it seems that such an alliance would not forfeit the French arrears?[211]

The idea of renewing the old Russo-Swedish alliance of 1758 was of course not new. Osterman had brought it up in December 1769, had received a put-off from Ekeblad, and had then allowed the matter to drop. In August 1771, however, it was unexpectedly revived by a memorial presented to the Secret Committee by a certain Sorbon, contemptuously described by Ulrik Scheffer as "un épicier de Mariestad."[212] The Cap leaders disavowed it; and Osterman was taken completely by surprise. However, when he reported it to his government and asked for instructions, he was ordered to encourage the initiative, and Catherine minuted that if he could secure the alliance he would be rendering her an outstanding service.[213] Thereafter no more was heard of it until in mid-July "a leading Cap" tentatively inquired of Goodricke whether England would be averse to acceding to such an alliance.[214] The Caps had taken d'Aiguillon's lure. On 16 July the proposal for a Russian alliance was taken into consideration by the Lesser Secret Deputation, which decided that in view of France's reaction to Goodricke's treaty of 1766 the best thing Sweden could do would be to inform d'Aiguillon and see how he took the information. France, they innocently surmised, must surely take such an intimation as a sign of Swedish confidence and goodwill.[215] On 27 July Düben wrote to Creutz, substantially in terms of this resolution;[216] and the Lesser Secret Deputation waited hopefully for a response to their meek enquiry. They were not left long in uncertainty. On 4 August the Senate heard a report from Creutz which must have come as a rude shock. Having tempted Sweden into a negotiation with Russia, d'Aiguillon now adroitly changed his tune. Creutz was informed that in view of that negotiation France proposed to defer payment of the third quarter's installment of arrears until any treaty which might emerge had been forwarded to Paris and received d'Aiguillon's *nihil obstat.*[217] Thus he had contrived to use the question of the subsidy to make an alliance with Russia as difficult as an alliance with England. Nevertheless, Osterman went ahead with his negotiations; Goodricke shrugged his shoulders and resigned himself to waiting for his treaty until after the end of the Diet—a highly uncertain prospect; and Suffolk, still unaware of the success of d'Aiguillon's tactics, accepted the change of plan with a reasonably good grace: as between one method of proceeding to the Russian alliance and another, he did not much care which.[218] Indeed, from England's point of view the change of plan had positive advantages. It transferred to Russia the intractable problem of subsidies; it saddled Panin not only with the Interior, but with the Exterior also.

But it meant the end of Goodricke's last attempt to reach the great goal of British foreign policy by way of Sweden. When first he came to Stockholm nobody had thought of the possibility of coming at a Russian alliance by this route, and without his zeal and activity the chance of doing so would hardly have presented itself. At the time of his appointment the ends which Lord Sandwich had had in view had been altogether more modest. But by the beginning of August 1772 scarcely one of the hopes with which he had set out in 1764 still remained alive. His draft treaty might stipulate for naval aid, might envisage a commercial treaty to follow, but these provisions, once so interesting to England, were now mere window dressing, as he very well knew. It was vain to talk of naval aid when, as he wrote, "the Swedes cannot equip six men of war of the line: they want stores of all sorts."[219] With what confidence could he look forward to a trade treaty, at the very moment when his friends in the Burghers were demanding higher protective duties against English leather?[220] And as to the larger hope, the inflexible British attitude on subsidies, and now even on bribery, had destroyed forever the prospect of using an English System in Stockholm as an avenue to St. Petersburg. The British government accepted the situation without repining. On 11 August Suffolk washed his hands of Sweden in words which have a valedictory ring:

> if, after all, there is no chance of concluding [the Anglo-Swedish treaty], but by a blind Profusion of previous Expence, Sweden must continue to enjoy, in a state of the most dangerous Dependency, the miserable Comfort that arises from the precarious Emoluments of a Connection with France; and submit to the almost daily risk of seeing her Liberties and Constitution subverted by French intrigues.[221]

Never again would a Secretary of State be tempted to look upon Stockholm as the fulcrum of British diplomacy.

For Goodricke, the disappointment must have been hard to bear, on personal grounds: he was unlikely, at the age of sixty-four, to have another such opportunity of commending himself to the favor of his sovereign; small hopes, now, that his soliciting of the Order of the Bath would meet with much attention.[222] But it was not only on personal grounds that he regretted the outcome; for to the end he believed that the expenditure from which Suffolk and his predecessors had shrunk would have proved a sound investment. As he wrote to Gunning,

> Ten thousand pounds more bestowed on the Diet would have made both the treaties. . . . We have been often enough given to understand that if we go on with them [*sc.* Russia] in Sweden they will make an alliance with us. Our Court cannot therefore be surprised at Mr Pannin's receiving the communication of my instructions with indifference; because the only thing Russia desires of us was not in them. I do not enter into the reasonableness of their desiring it or of our refusing it but the fact is so.[223]

It is just possible that he was right; but his masters had other views. And since things were as they were, he made the best of the situation as so often before, if not cheerfully then at least without bitterness. But it meant that his mission had now really only one *raison d'être* remaining: the defeat of French influence at Stockholm. Yet even here the triumph of the English party could not ensure the adoption of English policies: the Senate, the chancery-president, the Secret Committee, the lower Estates, might all be friends of England, but their dependence on French subsidies constrained them, in spite of everything, to maintain good relations with France.[224] The initial victory of 1765 in the event had proved more exploitable, from England's point of view, than the final triumph of 1772. The best that Goodricke could now hope for was that he might be the agent for arranging England's accession to a Russo-Swedish alliance. And that hope proved as delusive as the other. For time had run out: Osterman was chaffering and negotiating in a house already falling about his ears.

(vii)

Gustav III was now committed to making a revolution as a virtual condition of Louis XV's continued support. But in January, when this situation was made more or less explicit, he had still no clear idea of how this was to be done. In interviews with Vergennes towards the end of the month he hinted that he might be thinking of a revolution by force, but even so no immediate move was contemplated: the Estates had so far done nothing to make it imperative, though he would not answer for what he might do if they provoked him.[225] Vergennes, still in the dark as to d'Aiguillon's real wishes, gave no encouragement, and for the moment no more was heard of the possibility of violent measures. For indeed the king was by no means certain that he preferred the *coup de force* that Louis XV had recommended, or that he had the means to carry it through. A revolution by semilegal methods—for instance, by parliamentary maneuvers and snap divisions—was still a conceivable alternative. By the end of February the debates on the Charter demonstrated that the crown had nothing to hope from the Componists, who made no fight at all to save the king's right to abdicate. There remained, then, as the only alternative to violence, the manipulation of the Estates in such a way as to demonstrate the futility of their proceedings and their incapacity to govern; and, as an initial maneuver, to endeavor to bring about the deadlock situation of two Estates against two. These plans were taken sufficiently seriously for d'Aiguillon to accept them as possible alternatives to a military coup: at the end of February he indicated that France "as a final sacrifice" would be prepared to put up 400,000 livres to support at least some of them, though he prudently made it a condition that no money should be paid over until success had been achieved.[226]

In the event, he was not called upon to make good his promise. Nevertheless, the mere fact that some members of the lower Estates were prepared to entertain the idea of a bargain revealed that the issue of privilege, the social struggle, was beginning to take precedence over the preservation of the constitution—not only for the needy officers of *Svenska Botten*, but also for the wealthy burghers of Stockholm: equality was beginning to look more important even than "Our Blessed Liberty." An obscure episode at the end of April made this clear. It arose out of Sinclair's defection. On 25 March Fersen passed on to Vergennes information, obtained at second-hand through Frietzcky, that Sinclair had agreed to support the Caps; information which confirmed suspicions which Gustav had felt for some time.[227] At the beginning of April C. F. Scheffer was ordered to interview Sinclair and demand an explanation; and his report, though not conclusive, was sufficiently unfavorable to convince the king (at least for the moment) that he had been betrayed.[228] On 26 April, six days after the Secret Committee had voted to appoint Sinclair governor-general of Pomerania, Gustav summoned him to his presence and told him what he thought of him. There followed an unexpected sequel. Sinclair had managed to build up a personal following in the lower Estates; and on 27 April two emissaries from this group came to Scheffer to inquire whether he was really in disgrace. On receiving an affirmative answer they asked whether Gustav would be willing to reward them in return for any service they could render him. In the course of the next two days they promised that the new Senate should be composed of men agreeable to the king; adding that they had broken with the Cap leaders, and intended also to sever their links with Sinclair, whose attempts to manipulate them they were beginning to resent, and who in any case, now that he was out of favor, was in no position to do their business for them. For they had indeed a remarkable offer to make. They would be willing to restore to the crown an authority so extensive as to leave to the Estates no more than the control of taxation and finance: all the executive power should be in the king's hands, together with a veto on legislation. In return for this staggering concession, which went far beyond a simple return to the original constitution of 1720, they asked, implicitly or explicitly, royal support for their program of social equality, and a cash reward of 6 million daler (ca. £120,000), to be paid after this constitutional revolution should have been completed—an event which they seem to have expected shortly after the coronation on 29 May.[229] To the extreme chagrin of C. F. Scheffer the negotiation came to nothing;[230] possibly because Gustav disrelished the social implications, but almost certainly because Vergennes declined to promise the very large sum of money that was required.[231] Nevertheless, the affair left its traces. At the beginning of May Gustav could discern "un escadron démocratique," a "Third Party," among the mass of the Caps in the Burghers;[232] and there may well be truth in the Court's belief that such men hoped to get in ahead of the Nobility in making a deal with the crown.[233] And though by this time Gustav had transferred his interest to a solution by violence, the breakdown of the negotiation did not mean that the alternative expedient was wholly abandoned. French intercepts revealed a plan to "slip into some of the Acts towards the Conclusion of the Diet" a clause giving the king more votes on the Senate and a *votum decisivum* on foreign policy;[234] and until as late as the first week of August Goodricke reckoned with the possibility that Gustav might try to effect a revolution by "throwing himself on the affection of his people."[235]

Nevertheless, in the first half of May Gustav III finally committed himself to solving his problems by a military coup. To this conclusion he was led by a variety of considerations. The most important of them was probably the *licentiering* of the Senate.[236] To Gustav III it implied a revolution in foreign policy: a breach with France, and probably vassalage to Sweden's hereditary enemy Russia. The negotiations for the Partition of Poland were in their concluding stages; the final treaty would be signed on 5 August. The moral seemed plain; the menace imminent. If Sweden were to escape it the Caps must be overthrown before the complications of the Polish question had been tidied up, and above all before Catherine's negotiations with the Turks at Focsany had been brought to a successful conclusion. The respite might well be very short. Gustav could not foresee Orlov's petulant rupture of the congress, nor did he realize that Catherine had her hands too full with problems both foreign and domestic to contemplate predatory enterprises against Sweden unless she were actually driven to them.[237] It is understandable that he should have felt a sense of urgency and of desperation. Parliamentary intrigue was too slow a method to meet the crisis, and might well be too unreliable a method also. Moreover, the fall of the Hat Senate, and the vindictive persecution by the Caps of their political enemies, had brought to the king a recruit whose adherence meant much to him, in the person of Axel von Fersen.[238] Sickened by the abuses of parliamentary absolutism when committed by his political adversaries, alarmed by the progress of "democracy," the old Whig now despaired of "liberty," and was ready to rally to the king as the last bulwark against chaos and degradation.[239] In the sequel Fersen's support proved no more than passive, and at the hour of decision he took care to keep well out of the way; but for the moment it seemed important.

It was all very well to decide to attempt a coup, but if decision were to issue in action two things were necessary. One was a practicable plan; and the other was the money to carry it out. And just at this juncture a plan was provided for him. Its author was J. M. Sprengtporten, now the unchallenged leader of *Svenska Botten*: jealous, atrabilious, but extremely efficient, who would have preferred, if he could have had his choice, a bicameral parliament on the English model.[240] Sprengtporten was a Finn, and the commander of a detachment of light dragoons stationed at Borgå; and his plan was to engineer a rising in Finland, seize the great fortress of Sveaborg, and with the troops thus placed at his disposal to sail over to Stockholm and topple the rule of the Estates by force. The admiral on the Sveaborg station, Henrik Trolle, discontented and disillusioned also, undertook to organize the necessary transport; the Sveaborg garrison constituted the largest concentration of troops in the kingdom, apart from those around Stockholm; and Sprengtporten had some grounds for hoping that it could be persuaded to follow him. The Guards officers in Stockholm were for the most part crypto-royalists; non-commissioned officers everywhere had grievances which could be exploited; and all felt themselves threatened by the prospect of a reduction in the strength of the armed forces, which the Caps, in a characteristic spirit of economy, were believed to be intending. The weak point in Sprengtporten's plan was its reliance upon favorable winds to waft him over to Sweden; and it was probably this element of uncertainty that led him, some time in May, to engraft upon his plan another scheme quite extraneous to it, and independently conceived. It emanated from J. K. Toll, a resourceful and ingenious officer who faced the prospect of being deprived of a livelihood as the result of the Secret Deputation's stripping him of an office bestowed upon him by the Hat Senate in 1769.[241] Toll's plan was to duplicate the rising in Sveaborg with a similar rising in Kristianstad, in the far south. Prince Karl was to be admitted to the conspiracy, and was to be sent to Skåne on the pretext of meeting Lovisa Ulrika, then due to return to Sweden after a sojourn in Berlin. He was to use his presence there at the time of the rising to collect troops, ostensibly to suppress it, but in fact to reinforce it. If then the winds should drive Sprengtporten off course, he was to make his landfall at Norrköping, whither the southern rebels would march to meet him; or in the last resort was to steer for Karlskrona, which Toll also engaged to win over. The rising in Kristianstad was to be effected by Captain Abraham Hellichius, then stationed in that fortress, a man with grievances whom Toll was confident of persuading; and it was to take place eight days after Sprengtporten had seized Sveaborg. Essentially Toll's plan was a measure of reinsurance, at best a diversion; it was peripheral to the real decision, which must come in Stockholm; it was to take place in an area notoriously Cap in sympathy; it would require great management and address in Prince Karl if he were to play his part effectively; and above all it was geared to a timetable which might only too easily be upset. All in all, it probably entailed more risks than it averted; and in the sequel it was the direct cause of the revolution's taking a quite different course from that which the planners had intended.[242]

The adoption of a definite plan of revolution made it necessary to end the absurd situation of Vergennes' being in ignorance of his minister's policy, since he might be called upon to supply considerable sums at very short notice. A start with the process of enlightenment had indeed been made as early as 23 February, when d'Aiguillon replied to his reports of conversations with the king by sending him a new directive. Unfortunately its phrasing was almost as Delphic as his original instructions. He was told that the situation was now such that "possibly" only force could provide a remedy. But on the other hand his attention was called to the "inconvenience" of premature action: his conduct therefore must be circumspect; he was to continue to give Gustav III counsels of moderation, "mais sans contredire les mesures que vous aurez lieu de juger qu'il se propose à son but."[243] It is not surprising that this nicely balanced injunction should have had its effect on the ambassador's never overcheerful temper: in March he was complaining that "mes pauvres nerfs sont dans une contraction qui n'est pas peu douloureuse," and was gloomily asking "pour quoi agir, lors que l'inactivité est le seul bon parti à prendre?"[244] On 20 May, however, his nerves received a salutary shock; for on that day he was given all the details of Sprengtporten's plot and asked to provide 65,000 livres immediately for necessary expenses.[245] His reactions show how confusing he found d'Aiguillon's instructions of 23 February: he hesitated, excused himself, was persuaded, and at length grudgingly promised the money on condition that his part in the affair be kept secret, and that he be given a receipt stating that the money was for "an object of the first importance." Fortunately for his peace of mind it turned out that he had guessed right: on 11 June d'Aiguillon sent his approval, and added that he would be willing to contribute up to 600,000 livres if it should be necessary:[246] subsequent orders which arrived on 1 August expressly authorized him to make that amount available, starting with an initial advance of 200,000.[247] So now at last Vergennes knew where he stood. He was still anything but openhanded—he made no large financial contributions until two days before the revolution; but at least he was cured of moderation: Gustav III might write to Louis XV assuring him that he did not aspire to unlimited power;[248] but Vergennes would now have none of such half-measures, and still less Sprengtporten's bicameral English constitution: he robustly advised Gustav III to make himself absolute, and to impose his absolutism by force.[249]

The necessary preparations now began to be set in motion. Troop reviews and maneuvers were held just outside the capital, with Prince Karl as their commander; and the king, by way of winning the goodwill of the army, manifested a demonstrative (and unwonted) interest in these martial exercises. It had originally been planned that the revolution should come off in the middle of July, and as late as the ninth Vergennes was reporting that Gustav was still for striking a blow in Stockholm on the twenty-fourth;[250] but Henrik Trolle in Finland had promised more than he could perform, and lack of transports necessitated a postponement. Nevertheless, on 9 June Toll had started for Skåne, to coach Hellichius in his part and reconnoiter Karlskrona; and Sprengtporten's younger brother was sent over to Finland to prepare the ground there. As for Gustav III, once the reviews and maneuvers were over, he betook himself to the spa at Loka, there to excogitate, with C. F. Scheffer's assistance, the constitution which should embody the principles of the revolution.

Many of these proceedings had not gone unremarked by Goodricke, and all were very soon known in Whitehall. Never, perhaps, was the remarkable efficiency of the Hanoverian interception service more brilliantly illustrated than in the years 1771-72.[251] The standard of security was extremely high: Suffolk on the one hand, Goodricke on the other, seem to have been most careful to safeguard their source of information. Until the very eve of the revolution neither Vergennes nor d'Aiguillon had any idea that their correspondence was opened and deciphered; and even when they were forced to realize that there was a leak they attributed it to indiscretion or British espionage in Paris. They therefore continued to use the ordinary posts, only rarely employing couriers; with the result that their most vital secrets came into the hands of George III, were passed on by him to Suffolk, and were expeditiously forwarded to Goodricke. The state of Hat finances, the scandal of the Horneca loan, the parliamentary intrigues of the spring of 1772—all this was known to Goodricke in detail; and the substance of a dispatch from Vergennes might on occasion reach him almost as early as Vergennes received d'Aiguillon's reply to it. He had for some months been well aware that some design or other was in contemplation;[252] but it was not until 16 July that he received from London certain information of its real nature.[253] On that day, by a Messenger dispatched in such haste that Rochford committed the grave imprudence of sending unciphered copies of his originals,[254] Goodricke learned of the plan to seize Sveaborg and descend upon Stockholm; and though his information did not mention Sprengtporten's name, he had no difficulty in guessing it.[255] Five days later, another Messenger brought an allusion—too vague to be intelligible to Rochford, and apparently equally obscure to Goodricke—to Toll's design upon Kristianstad:[256] it was not until tidings of the outbreak there reached Stockholm that Goodricke realized that this was the "southern mine" to which Rochford's source had made reference. Further supplementary information reached him on 28 and 31 July; in particular a copy of Gustav III's letter to Louis XV of 17 June, disclaiming any intention of making himself absolute.[257]

Thus Goodricke was put in possession, in good time, of the broad outlines of what was really the kernel of the king's plan; and it was left to him to take measures to defeat it. He had to observe the most rigorous discretion if he were not to betray the source of his information: only Osterman and Düben seem to have been given all the details. There was a general disposition, both in London and in Stockholm, to consider the idea of a revolt in Finland and a descent upon Stockholm as "extravagant" and scarcely practicable: the real danger, it was believed, was of a coup in the capital.[258] This turned out to be a correct assessment; but though it might be easy to identify the danger, it was much less easy to take effective precautions against it. Such precautions would normally be authorized by the Senate or by the Secret Committee; but Sprengtporten himself was a member of the Committee, and the king regularly attended meetings of the Senate. In any case, as Goodricke lamented, he had no authentic paper which he could take the risk of producing in order to bring home to the Caps the seriousness of their situation.[259] However, it seemed obvious that Sprengtporten was the man to watch, and Osterman immediately offered to "set half a dozen spies" upon him, and to send an agent to Sveaborg to find out what was afoot there.[260] But since the main danger was thought to lie in Stockholm, and since Sprengtporten was identified as the king's chief agent and organizer, it seemed sensible if possible to get him well out of the way. A pretext for doing so, and for other precautionary measures, was found in the appearance of a broadsheet entitled *The Dominion of the Kingdom of Darkness,* which in inflammatory language charged the government with indifference to the sufferings of a starving people. On 21 July von Essen produced this to the Secret Committee, represented it as being evidence of dangerous unrest, and persuaded them to take vigilant action. A battalion of the Uppland Regiment, stationed near the capital, was to be held ready to march; local authorities were instructed to keep a sharp lookout for signs of disaffection; Rudbeck (since February, governor of Stockholm) was sent down to the southern provinces, ostensibly to inspect the docks at Karlskrona; and in his absence the security of the capital was entrusted to the able and ruthless hands of Pechlin—much to the concern of Gustav III, who vainly tried to block the appointment. Most important of all, Sprengtporten was ordered to go to Finland to investigate reports of unrest alleged to be caused by shortages of salt. The Caps seem to have thought that they had now done all that the situation required; but Goodricke was by no means satisfied that these measures were adequate.[261] Certainly the decision to send Sprengtporten to Finland played straight into his hands, for it neatly solved the problem of how he was to get there without attracting too much attention, and Suffolk was later to condemn it as a blunder.[262] Moreover, it revealed to Sprengtporten that he was under suspicion. To throw the Caps off the scent, therefore, he made a great parade of begging to be allowed to decline the commission; stood on his right as a member of the Nobility not to be precluded by official duties from attendance at the Diet; urged that at least his place on the Secret Committee should not be held to have been vacated: in short, played his comedy so well that the Nobility rallied to the defense of the privileges of their order, and voted to support him; and it was only at that stage that he declared, with a great show of submission, that he did not venture to delay compliance with the Secret Committee's orders any longer.[263] On 29 July he sailed for Finland. He reckoned on being in control of Sveaborg by 4 or 5 August. The rising in Kristianstad was to take place eight days after that. The Cap leaders, as they drifted away from the Diet for shorter or longer respites on their country estates, might think that there was now no great cause for uneasiness. But though they did not know it, the revolution had begun.[264]

In Finland, through no fault on the part of Sprengtporten, it began exceedingly ill.[265] From start to finish the winds and weather did their best to ruin his enterprise. He could not reach Finland till 4 August; nor rally his light dragoons until the twelfth; and it was only by dint of hard rowing (the wind being, as always, contrary) that he was able to bring a small detachment of thirty-three men to Sveaborg on the night of 15-16 August. Once arrived, his boldness and address enabled him to seduce the garrison: Sveaborg was in his hands by the afternoon of the sixteenth, and the more important centers in western Finland soon afterwards; but his timetable was now in hopeless disarray. The transport on which he had counted was not ready; it was not until 23 August that he could embark his men, not until the twenty-eighth that the winds allowed him to sail, not until the thirtieth that he made his landfall in Sweden at Sandhamn. By that time Gustav III's revolution was already eleven days old, and Sprengtporten's real contribution to it was confined to the organization he had left behind him in Stockholm.[266]

If the northern half of the plan was thus fatally delayed, the southern half went off with fatal punctuality. Sprengtporten was not so lacking in foresight as not to realize that he might encounter unexpected delays, and he believed that before leaving for Finland he had made sure that Hellichius should not move in Kristianstad until the signal came from Sveaborg; but by some misunderstanding Prince Karl on 27 July gave the order to Toll to prepare the rising for 12 August, and in obedience to it the coup was effected without trouble in the early dawn of the appointed day.[267] A "deserter" was allowed to "escape" from the fortress to carry the news to Prince Karl, who at once proceeded to collect troops with a view to marching on Kristianstad. He lost no time in dutifully informing the Senate of the measures he was taking to restore their authority; but at the same time he dispatched Lieutenant Boltenstierna to the king, with a private letter sewn into the sole of his boot. So far all had gone smoothly; but on the very morning of the rising a quite unexpected complication had presented itself in the person of General Rudbeck, who turned up outside Kristianstad, all unsuspecting, and found to his astonishment that admission was denied him, that the sentry purported to be acting on the king's orders and was not to be moved by invoking the respectable authority of the Estates, and that no explanations were forthcoming from those in command. It did not take him long to draw the correct inferences: without loss of time he set off hotfoot for Stockholm; on 16 August he arrived there with his disquieting news; on the following morning he communicated it to the Senate and the Secret Committee.

The Senate could no longer be in any doubt about the gravity of the situation. Goodricke's warnings had proved true: the king was engaged in a conspiracy to overthrow the constitution, and it was obvious that Prince Karl was an accessory to it. No news yet had come of Sprengtporten's activities in Finland; the rising in Skåne could probably be contained, and might well have been designed to distract attention from the real point of danger in Stockholm. It was upon Stockholm, therefore, that they concentrated their activity, there that they took their real countermeasures. As usual in time of crisis the Burgher cavalry of the city was ordered to patrol the streets at night; detachments of the Uppland and Södermanland Regiments were ordered up to Stockholm; the command of all the armed forces in the city was placed in the hands of Senator Kalling, who of all his colleagues was personally the most odious to Gustav III. It was a question whether these measures were sufficient: Goodricke and Osterman are said to have pressed for the king's immediate arrest,[268] and it seems certain that this step was considered. But apparently they judged it more prudent to defer this extreme measure until they had more troops at their disposal; and the Uppland Regiment would not reach Stockholm until midday on the nineteenth. They therefore delayed for one day; and that delay was decisive. Before the troops could arrive the revolution was completed, and the king was master of his capital.

The news from Kristianstad was almost as unwelcome to Gustav III as to his adversaries; for it forced him to attempt what the planners had never contemplated as a possibility: the making of a revolution on his own, single-handed, without the possibility of timeous aid either from Finland or the South. Rudbeck's arrival pushed him to the wall. It was now obvious that the Senate would suspect him; and any doubts he might have had on that score were removed when on 17 August he was confronted with a copy of his own letter to Louis XV of 17 June: some careless or crypto-royalist Cap had evidently betrayed Goodricke's confidence. On that day and the next Gustav received warnings from two independent sources that the Senate was only waiting the arrival of the Uppland Regiment to arrest him.[269] On the eighteenth came the news that Sprengtporten would be hopelessly delayed. His closest friends and political collaborators—the Scheffers, Nils Bielke—were away at their country houses; and so too was that prudent aristocrat Fersen. The king could turn for counsel or practical aid only to a handful of officers: Major von Saltza; Captain König; Admiral Tersmeden, recently appointed to the command of the Stockholm naval base. But really he must rely upon himself. Only he could now make the revolution. And it must be made at once if it were to be made at all.

Something, no doubt, could be done by distributing money; and Vergennes at last made large sums available for bribing common soldiers and underofficers. One may question whether they were really needed. For it was personality rather than gold that ensured the success of the enterprise. In the twenty-four hours between the evening of the eighteenth and that of the nineteenth Gustav III displayed a steadiness of nerve and a capacity for physical endurance of which his enemies can hardly have believed him capable, together with a talent for dissembling and a histrionic ability which they knew only too well. He believed that his life was in danger; but on the evening of the eighteenth the routine of the court proceeded with much liveliness and an appearance of perfect normality: numerous guests invited to supper, including all the Senate; a dress rehearsal of the new opera *Thétis och Pélée;* political friends and enemies making up their parties of *quadrille;* and the king gracious, affable, talking at ease, manifesting not the least symptom of nervous strain under the keen scrutiny of his enemies. When the evening was over and the guests dispersed, he rode out to inspect the Burgher patrols: their goodwill might be valuable tomorrow. He was not in bed until 3 a.m.; rose at 6; made his last preparations and gave his last orders; and by 10 was inspecting the parade at the Artillery headquarters. Thence he went to the Arsenal; thence back to the castle, with an ever-growing number of royalist officers accompanying him. The officers and underofficers of the Guards had been ordered to attend at the orderly room in the castle courtyard, and were awaiting his arrival. He went in and addressed them; at first with visible nervousness, but gradually with assured eloquence. He told them of the danger that threatened himself; denounced the "aristocratic" rule of the Estates; gave them a written assurance that he had no intention of making himself absolute; and invited them to renounce their allegiance to the Estates and take an oath of loyalty to himself. There followed a dreadful minute of silence: the tension in the orderly room was so great that one officer fainted. At last someone cried "Yes! God save your Majesty!" and the crisis was over: with one single exception all the officers followed that example, and subscribed the oath which he tendered to them. Out in the castle courtyard the palace guard had just been relieved; the old and new guard stood facing each other. To them now the king went out and repeated his appeal; and this time it was responded to without hesitation. A guard was now set upon the chamber in the palace where the Senate was in session;[270] its members were informed that they were under arrest; arrangements were made to provide them with lunch; and subsequently they were removed to comfortable confinement in the palace.

With that, in the space of less than an hour, the revolution was in effect over; a revolution orderly, bloodless, and in the sequel marvellously magnanimous towards the vanquished. What followed was in the nature of a triumphal procession, as the king rode round his capital to assure himself of one critical position after another. The white handkerchief he had tied around his arm as a token now broke out everywhere, the enthusiasm was universal, the great waves of cheering echoed across the water to Skeppsholm, where Tersmeden had been practising persuasions upon the sailors; and by the time Gustav arrived on a visit of inspection they had already learned to sing the song of triumph which, with prophetic inspiration, Bellman had published only two days before.[271] The once-powerful Secret Committee discreetly dispersed itself, unbidden. The advance of the Uppland Regiment was halted outside the city. Of all the Cap leaders only Rudbeck tried to organize resistance in Stockholm; while Pechlin, slipping away just in time to avoid arrest, made for Jönköping in the vain hope of raising resistance there. For the king, the labors of the day were by no means over: the foreign ministers had to be given reassurances and explanations; elaborate care was taken to inform the wives and families of the imprisoned Senators that no harm should come to them; innumerable urgent letters had to be written—to Louis XV, to Lovisa Ulrika, to his brothers; not until the small hours was he able to retire in the conviction that the revolution was secure. For the first and last time in his life he had shown that he was everything that his most devoted admirers believed him to be.

In spite of superficial appearances, this was not really a military coup. No one, then or later, has disputed the overwhelming popularity of the revolution; not only in Stockholm but even in such traditionally Cap areas as Skåne.[272] The handful of men and officers who followed the king on 19 August could hardly have imposed his rule upon a people unwilling to receive it.[273] The revolution succeeded because it could draw strength from the weariness, the impatience, the resentment, of the mass of ordinary citizens; because they were willing to rid themselves of a régime which had itself become a kind of absolutism wielded by a coterie of party politicians; and because they were ready to respond to Gustav's offer of something which—though it was ominously vague at crucial points—they hoped might be better. They were not concerned with the fact—and it was a fact—that the Age of Liberty represented a kind of constitutionalism which was very advanced for its time: they saw only the inability of the Estates to discharge effectively those executive functions which they had usurped to themselves, the shameless corruption of their members, the infringements by partisan bodies of those elementary civil rights which the Act of Security of 1769 had been designed to safeguard.

Of the events of 19 August Goodricke was in the nature of the case condemned to be a passive spectator, powerless to avert the overthrow of the party he had supported and the constitution which he had made such efforts to defend. If the Senate and the Secret Committee would not make a fight for it there was nothing he could do to help them; for he had neither money to dispense nor instructions to guide him. On receipt of the first clear warning from London Goodricke had asked urgently for fresh instructions.[274] They were indeed sent to him, and with very little delay;[275] but they were not particularly helpful: the main considerations must be "the Safety of our Friends, and the preservation of the Constitution," and Goodricke hardly needed Suffolk to tell him that; but they also added: "and whatever personal Hazards the King of Sweden's desperate Behaviour may, in the upshot of things, possibly expose him to, I am sure it will never appear that they have been encouraged by your means." This was no doubt a creditable attitude, but it was nullified by the accident that the instructions had not reached Stockholm when the revolution took place. Still less had any supply of money. It was not until 30 August that George III, by that time informed of events in Kristianstad, authorized a credit of £15,000,and this only if "the States and Senate seem firm": otherwise "the Caps cannot expect any assistance from hence after having so little counteracted the intrigues of the Court, though so timely warned from hence."[276] Osterman was in no better case than his colleague: though he had asked for fresh instructions and more money on 22 July, it was not until 24 August that Panin found time to reply to him.[277] Only the Danish minister was in the possession of instructions appropriate to the occasion; but as these envisaged action in concert with Osterman, and Osterman would not act without instructions, Guldencrone might as well not have had any instructions at all.

After the arrest of the Senate had made the success of the coup probable, Gustav III had sent a courteous but pressing invitation to the foreign ministers to come to the palace for their own security, and to remain there until the situation again became normal. Only after the invitation had been repeated did Goodricke and Osterman reluctantly accept it. They ate the dinner which was provided for them in glum silence, while Vergennes exulted in the success of the day:

not until the morrow were they permitted to send couriers to their governments with a report of the disaster. For disaster it seemed at that moment to be. Whatever England's policy in Sweden might have been, it was now irretrievably in ruins. The English party was dead; and there would be no resurrection. For Catherine II, this was perhaps the most severe reverse of her reign. For France, on the other hand, it was a transient moment of triumph, and Vergennes and d'Aiguillon would each in the future claim the sole honor of it for himself.[278] It would not be long before the triumph was shown to be illusory, and indeed irrelevant; but for the moment it had an electric effect on French morale.

As to Goodricke, that "vieillard vif, spirituel et malin" of Barthélémy's description,[279] the revolution swept away at one stroke the labor of the last eight years. In the new world that followed the revolution there would be no scope for his peculiar talents as party leader, parliamentary organizer, and discreet paymaster: had not the king decided that "the hated names of Hats and Caps" should be forever proscribed? The role he had played for so long, and often under such handicaps, was now played out. Through no fault of his own his mission had ended in total failure at all points: no hope now of an alliance; no prospect of using Swedish politics to bind Russia closer to England; Vergennes victorious, and Sweden for the foreseeable future a client of France. Though he would linger on in Stockholm for several months yet, after 19 August it was full time for him to be gone.

Tranquillity Preserved, 1772–1773

The revolution of 19 August 1772 was an event in the history of England, no less than in that of Sweden. It was not simply that it had obvious consequences for Anglo-Swedish relations. It marked the end of a quite distinct period in the history of British foreign policy, for it dealt the final blow to the assumptions upon which that policy had been founded since 1763.

After the Peace of Paris the essential objective of successive administrations in regard to foreign affairs was the preservation of peace: a policy which coincided with the wishes of the great majority of Englishmen. It is not remarkable that this should have been so. After all the great wars—after the War of the Spanish Succession, after the Napoleonic wars, after 1918—there follows a revulsion, an imperious desire for a period of quiet. And so after the two great wars of the mid-eighteenth century men wished to forget about Hanover, to enjoy the great gains which the Seven Years War had brought to England, to exploit British commercial and mercantile supremacy undisturbed; and they were deeply perturbed by the huge increase in the National Debt which had been the price of victory. The overriding concern of successive Secretaries of State, therefore, was to devise means whereby the dear-bought peace might be safeguarded. A generation of experience had led them to believe that in the immediate future, as in the past, the only real threat to it would come from France. France, bound to Spain by the Family Compact, linked to Austria by alliance, confronted them with something that England lacked—with a "system"; and it seemed natural to them that they should seek to neutralize that system by constructing, in opposition to it, a system of their own, its equal or superior in strength. In itself this was neither a pusillanimous nor unintelligent policy, though undeniably it could on occasion appear so; and the fact that the men who pursued it were on the whole of second-rate abilities does not invalidate it: Chatham could do no better. To Frederick the Great, to Choiseul, it seemed an entirely rational response to the situation in which England found herself. British statesmen were looking above all for a deterrent; and they trusted to a balance of forces in Europe to provide it. But the old system of King William was gone beyond recall, though it took them some time to acknowledge that fact; Prussia, for reasons good or bad, was not prepared to cooperate: there remained only Russia, the new Great Power, the victor of Kunersdorf, the "natural ally" as well on economic as on political grounds. It happened, moreover, that Russia too was at this time concerned to create a bloc of powers with a view to securing her ascendancy in the Baltic and expanding her influence in central Europe. Here was a system already in the making—Panin's Northern System—which might provide England with the European counterweight for which her statesmen were looking; and though for as long as the hope of regaining Austria remained they viewed it doubtfully, they gradually came to accept it as a possible solution to their problem. And this remained true even after it became clear that a Northern System would not, as Chatham had hoped, provide the bridge to a reconciliation with Prussia. Nevertheless the Northern System, however they might feel about it, really only interested them as an element in—or a road to—the alliance with Russia which from 1763 to 1773 appeared to be the only way out of their difficulties. They saw that alliance essentially as an insurance: insurance against another European war; and it was their misfortune that, by an apparent inconsequence which was the despair of British representatives abroad, they felt bound to jib at the cost of the premium.[1]

Within this basic pattern of policy Anglo-Swedish relations soon came to assume a quite unexpected importance. When Goodricke arrived in Stockholm in 1764 his mission was seen as no more than a relatively insignificant local action in conformity with the broad strategy of Whitehall: the objective was no more than to preserve the Tranquillity of the North, to prevent French troublemaking in an economically sensitive region, to ensure that Choiseul should not have the Swedish navy at his disposal. Goodricke himself was soon to urge, as a main argument for spending money on Sweden, that such expenditure might "prevent another war." But quite soon his mission developed in such a way as to make Sweden a major factor in Anglo-Russian relations, and therefore in the whole strategy of British policy. As the endless negotiations in St. Petersburg drifted on inconclusively, year after year, with growing frustration and irritation on either side, it seemed increasingly likely that the way out of the impasse might lie through Stockholm, and that the prize which eluded Buckinghamshire, Macartney, and Cathcart might be secured by active British intervention in Swedish domestic politics. An Anglo-Swedish alliance might provide the ground on which an alliance with Russia could be built: Russia might prove complaisant to British demands in return for adequate financial contributions to Swedish corruption, or in exchange for a subsidy to the Swedish government. This was no illusory calculation. More than once Panin made it clear that Russia would accede to any defensive alliance which England might conclude with Sweden. Goodricke's treaty of 1766 was certainly intended to be the preliminary to such an alliance; Suffolk's offer to the Caps in 1772 was made with a view to the subsequent adhesion of Russia. The policy in fact came tantalizingly close to success: it is possible that only the fall of the Caps in May 1769 prevented the conclusion of an Anglo-Russian alliance. Thus Goodricke's mission became central to British foreign policy in the postwar decade, though hitherto its importance has escaped the notice of English historians. If it had not been so, ministers would hardly have admitted the strife of Swedish parties to be an important British interest, nor would they have considered the preservation of the Swedish constitution to be a legitimate call upon the Civil List. It was Goodricke who brought home to them the relevance of these things; it was his energy, insight, and skill in using his opportunities which made it possible to think of Sweden as the ladder from which they might reach up to grasp the prize for which they were groping.

From about 1771 the arguments for the foreign policy which ministers had pursued since the peace began rapidly to lose their force, though by 19 August 1772 they had not yet been wholly abandoned. It did not greatly matter that both in London and St. Petersburg men came increasingly to feel that no great harm would be done if in view of the difficulties about the terms of an alliance they were to content themselves with an entente. On both sides there was a vague confidence that in an emergency they would behave as allies, whatever the formal position; though Panin by the end of the sixties was probably more skeptical about England's value as an ally than British public opinion was about the value of friendship with Russia, and though it is true that Russian designs in the Balkans, and above all Russian claims to domination of the Black Sea and to free passage through the Straits, were already undermining the readiness of ministers to afford amicable cooperation in this area. But what really mattered was the progressive erosion of the assumptions upon which the desire for an alliance, or even for an entente, had been based. Those assumptions were first challenged by the Falkland Islands crisis. That crisis had produced no great evidence of Russian goodwill; but on the other hand it had brought the fall of Choiseul, and had plainly revealed France's real fear of war in the immediate future: the Family Compact, it seemed, was a good deal less solid than had been supposed. And, not least, it had confronted ministers with the most alarming evidence of the unfitness of the British navy to meet an emergency. For the first time since 1763 it became a question whether the securing of a continental deterrent ought not to take second place to the maintenance of a fleet competent to deal with the combined navies of France and Spain.

A year later, the very fundamentals of British foreign policy were shaken by the Partition of Poland. In the first place, as Lord Cathcart with unusual insight was the first to point out, the Partition for all practical purposes destroyed Russia's usefulness as an ally in Europe: after it was complete, Russia's access to the battlefields of Germany was cut off by the annexations of Frederick the Great.[2] And in the second place, it meant that the whole theory of securing the peace of Europe by the construction of a bloc of friendly or allied powers capable of balancing "the formidable League of the South" had become a political irrelevance. Not only had the French system become for the moment a good deal less formidable, but there now existed in Europe a new system independent of any other alignments, whether French or English: the *système copartageant.* It was this new system, and no other, which now appeared to menace the European balance; and into it England had neither the wish nor the power to insinuate herself. D'Aiguillon, on the one hand, George III and Rochford on the other, saw clearly what had happened; Vergennes would see it a little later; and to all of them occurred the same revolutionary idea: the idea that the logical response to the new constellation of forces was an Anglo-French entente. In this situation it was hardly surprising that the pursuit of the Russian alliance petered out in the spring of 1773. When Suffolk made it clear that England would in no circumstances guarantee the territorial integrity of Russia's acquisitions in Poland, he dealt the prospects of alliance a mortal blow. And any hope of obtaining it finally expired under the impact of his attitude to the Swedish revolution.

Seen from this point of view, the revolution of 19 August appears as the legacy of an age that was gone. Choiseul's policy had triumphed; but Choiseul was politically dead, and his policies seemed to have died with him. Though d'Aiguillon might boast, though Versailles might be jubilant, it was an almost pointless victory; since the sequel would show that France dared not exploit it, and above all since it threatened to bring France and England into collision at the very moment when d'Aiguillon was hoping to range them in a common front against the predatory monarchs of the East.

These broad international considerations do something to explain the fortitude with which George III and his ministers reacted to the overthrow of their policies and their partisans in Stockholm.[3] For Catherine it was a humiliating defeat, coming at a moment when she was already beset by grave difficulties, and when her morale was temporarily shaken; for Panin it meant the end of his dream of a Northern System. In London, ministers took it much less tragically, and their adjustment to the altered circumstances was creditably quick and clear-sighted. They wasted no time in lamentations over the victory of France in the final round of the long duel in Stockholm. The sting of defeat did not upset their judgment. What disturbed them was not the thing itself, but the consequences which might flow from it: consequences of infinitely greater concern to them than the loss of Sweden. Both Suffolk and Rochford realized quite quickly that the revolution confronted them with the possibility—indeed, the probability—of a European war on the largest scale. Once Catherine was clear of the Turkish war she would seek to restore her influence in Stockholm; she would demand the restoration of the constitution of 1720; and if need be she would use force. France would feel bound to come to the aid of Gustav III; Russia would call upon her allies Denmark and Prussia for assistance, and would probably get it; France would invoke the Family Compact. No longer was Sweden the nodal point of British diplomacy: it had become a tinderbox which might precipitate a major conflagration of unforeseeable extent.

In this situation ministers instinctively reverted to the basic principle of their policy: the preservation of peace. Their position in regard to Sweden now returned to that from which Goodricke had started in 1764; their object once more became the preservation of the Tranquillity of the North. As early as 8 September Suffolk laid it down that though England had been ready to work with Russia to *prevent* a revolution in Sweden, it by no means followed that she would be ready to help Catherine *overthrow* it. In November he ordered Gunning to declare plainly to Panin that if Russia began an aggressive war against Sweden England would remain neutral.[4] The long Anglo-Russian collaboration in Stockholm was broken, and it was broken for good. The situation was now such that it required only the dispatch of a French fleet to the Baltic to touch off an explosion; and that could certainly be predicted if Russian troops crossed the Finnish frontier. In the face of this imminent danger Suffolk's policy was to keep the peace by threatening France with a squadron of superior force, and to restrain Russia by persuading Catherine that if she attacked Sweden a French fleet would be allowed to sail without interference from England. His fellow-Secretary Rochford, engaged (with George III's approval) in secret diplomatic exchanges designed to lead to some sort of entente with France, went much further: he would even have been willing to encourage d'Aiguillon to rescue Gustav III by the dispatch of French troops in a French convoy, if only he would be quick about it. So utterly had the perspectives altered in the space of a few months. In the event, Sweden was saved by Catherine's nervousness and Gustav III's emollient diplomacy; the clandestine attempt at a rapprochement with France broke down on justified fears of the strength of British gallophobia; and ministers were left to face an isolation more total and more hopeless than anyone in the sixties could have foreseen, and which was certainly not their wish—nor, perhaps, their fault. In this new and bleaker world Sweden presented neither opportunities, nor any features of interest, to the cabinet in London. When next a Secretary of State actively intervened in Scandinavian affairs it would be to discharge the function which d'Aiguillon had been forbidden to discharge in 1773, and to rescue Gustav III from the attacks of his neighbors. Meanwhile, for a decade and a half, Stockholm became a legation as unimportant as Copenhagen, and less important than Lisbon. But from 1764 to 1772 it had been far otherwise.

For Goodricke, the revolution meant the drastic curtailing of his field of activity, the enforced distancing from former political friends, almost the disappearance of a way of life. The old frequenters no longer came to his door; information, and above all information on foreign affairs, was no longer easy to come by now that it was confined to the king and a small circle of his confidential ministers;[5] above all, there was now no scope for an expert in parliamentary management, since there was no longer any parliament: after its dissolution in September 1772 the Diet was not to meet again till 1778. When in January 1773 Gustav III, with ill-requited magnanimity, released Pechlin from the prison to which he had been consigned after 19 August, Goodricke realized well enough that Pechlin's day was over, and gracefully evaded his solicitation of a present.[6] He was under no illusions about the new constitution, and shrewdly pointed out the loopholes for arbitrary action which lay half concealed behind the façade of constitutional monarchy.[7] For a little while he permitted himself to hope that all was not quite lost, and tentatively suggested that it would be convenient to be able to draw for a few thousands to rally discontent;[8] but Suffolk gave him no encouragement. He did enough, nevertheless, to provoke the anger of Gustav III and his new chancery-president, Ulrik Scheffer. Nolcken in London reported that Goodricke was making every effort to alarm his government; Scheffer and Vergennes denounced him as a fomenter of disorder, an intriguer "avec les gens les plus vils et les plus bas"; pressing appeals were sent to d'Aiguillon asking him to make representations in London to obtain his recall.[9] But as the chance of an immediate counterrevolution grew fainter, and above all as Gustav III came increasingly to pin his hopes upon England as the only power capable of deterring Catherine from aggression, the old antagonisms died away surprisingly quickly, on both sides. By February 1773 Nolcken was informed that Goodricke's conduct was so much improved that his recall was no longer desired; by March Scheffer was calling him "the best *Cheval de Bataille* for making any impression on the Court of Great Britain."[10] Goodricke for his part was by this time upon so good a footing with Scheffer "that I could easily and privately negotiate through his interest with the King of Sweden," and was inquiring what his government's attitude would be to a proposal for an Anglo-Swedish alliance. And Suffolk expressly authorized him to keep these conversations secret from Osterman.[11] Changed days indeed.

Change for Goodricke in other ways also; for in February 1773 came news which transformed his personal situation. That same George Fox Lane who had married Lady Goodricke's half-sister in 1731, and had been instrumental in giving Goodricke a start in 1758, was now dead; and on his death Bramham Park, and a great part of his estates in Yorkshire, passed to Lady Goodricke. After a lifetime of more or less precarious financial circumstances Goodricke found himself a very rich man. For fifteen years now, with only one short interval of leave, he had been exiled in the North; and he would soon be sixty-five. In its way it had been a good life, and he had clearly enjoyed himself: enjoyed his profession, and probably enjoyed life in Sweden too, despite occasional hankerings after a return to Copenhagen or a transfer to St. Petersburg. But now he was free to close the chapter, to take his ease as a country gentleman, to go into parliament as he had long wanted to do, and perhaps (if he could find workmen competent to do the job) to install at Bramham Park and Ribston those incomparable Swedish stoves of which he wrote with such enthusiasm.[12] His health at this time was not good: he had been suffering from eyestrain, and in May was attacked by an obstinate bleeding at the nose (attributed by Sir Joseph Yorke to "a violent scorbutic habit")[13] which seemed for a few days to threaten his life. On all accounts it was time to quit the field and go into winter quarters. Lord Suffolk put a warship at his disposal to take him to England; on 10 July he quitted Sweden forever; in November he finally retired from the diplomatic service.

If he had expected much recognition for his services when he got home he was destined to be disappointed. They made him a privy-councillor; but no more was heard of George III's promise to bear him in mind for the Order of the Bath. As in the beginning, so at the end of his career, his stock does not seem to have been very high in London. Foreigners had always been at a loss to understand why. The hatred and fear with which his adversaries in Stockholm regarded him—Breteuil, Modène, Vergennes, and (till circumstances altered) Schack—must certainly be regarded as in the nature of a tribute; and as to the representatives of friendly courts, the testimony is unanimous that he was an exceptionally able minister. The impression he made during his stay in Copenhagen was never effaced; and Bernstorff to the end of his life retained his admiration for the minister and his affection for the man. Gregers Juel's verdict was equally positive. As for Panin, he paid Goodricke repeated and emphatic tributes: he told Cathcart in 1769

> that he knew something of men and politics, and was acquainted with Sir John Goodricke as a Minister, and assured me that he knew no situation more difficult than Sir John was [in], nor any man more equal to it, by the Ability and Zeal, Integrity, Resources and Prudence of which he was possessed.[14]

It was an estimate which competent judges in England would on the whole have been very ready to accept. Sir Joseph Yorke considered him "the Person best versed in the Finances of Europe of any Man I have ever met with, and the readiest at Expedients for improving them."[15] Of all the Northern Secretaries under whom Goodricke served there was only one—Lord Weymouth—who did not at one time or another convey his praise and approbation in terms which must have satisfied any man's vanity, if Goodricke had been (which he was not) a vain man; and of them all it was Lord Rochford—who as a former diplomat was perhaps better qualified to pronounce a judgment than any of the others—who rated his services most highly. In 1769 he told Chernyshev: "C'est le meilleur de tous les ministres que nous avons près des Cours étrangères; on peut tout lui confier . . . l'argent excepté."[16] It was certainly an important reservation; and it may perhaps provide the explanation for his country's failure to reward him as might have been expected—though only two months later Rochford was writing to assure Panin that "the greatest justice is done to his abilities, experience *and integrity.*"[17] But it seems more likely that even if Chernyshev reported Rochford correctly this was not the whole explanation: the age was not overnice in these matters, and Rochford himself was suspected of using his position to engage in stockjobbing. It was Goodricke's misfortune throughout his life that he lacked influential friends: as he wrote to Hardwicke

> A foreign minister has continued need of the patronage of somebody at home both for his own and the publick affairs; I endeavour, as much as I am able, to obtain that of the minister with whom I correspond, but the misfortune is that I generally lose him before I can get acquainted with him.[18]

Macartney was launched by Lord Holland and married a daughter of Lord Bute; Gunning was the personal friend of Lord Suffolk; Sir Robert Murray Keith was a member of "The Gang," an inner circle of convivial young ministerialists serving under Lord North. Goodricke had few or none of these advantages: Sir Joseph Yorke was abroad; the second Lord Hardwicke had little influence; Charles Yorke he does not seem to have known; and otherwise there was only his Yorkshire neighbor Lord Galway. It was significant that the individual whom he had to employ to bring his solicitation of the Red Ribband to the attention of ministers was a political nobody.

If he felt these disappointments he did not show it; he was never one to molest his masters with complaints, or badger them for favors. He slipped easily and good-humoredly into private life, apparently well content with its satisfactions. Away up on his Yorkshire estates he found, perhaps, a new meaning for the Tranquillity of the North. He sat as an independent ministerialist for Pontefract from 1774 to 1780, and again for Ripon from 1787 until his death; in 1788 (in his eightieth year) he was made a commissioner of the Board of Trade. His interest in economic questions remained lively, and he watched with satisfaction the progress of the Industrial Revolution in the West Riding. To the very end of his life he maintained an intermittent correspondence with Lord Hardwicke. His health recovered; and his first fit of the gout did not appear until 1777: induced, he believed, by "a moderate indulgence in Scarborough waters."[19] It was indeed a long and vigorous old age: perhaps as good a reward for his labors as could be wished. He died on 3 August 1789, at the age of eighty-one, having lived long enough to see the reputation of his country restored to what he believed it ought to be. No entry in the *Dictionary of National Biography* commemorates his name; but the history of British foreign policy is incomplete—and in part unintelligible—without the record of his achievement.

Notes

Notes

CHAPTER I
THE ROAD TO STOCKHOLM

1. Public Record Office SP 75/104/1, Holdernesse to Wynantz, 10 March 1758 (hereafter PRO sources cited by collection number only).

2. For this episode, see Torgny Höjer, "Christopher Springer och principalatsfrågan vid 1742-3 års riksdag"; Bertil Boëthius,*Magistraten och Borgerskapet i Stockholm, 1719-1815,* pp. 218-25.

3. For the progress of this affair, see SP 95/100 and 95/101/1-43, 59-65, 395-98; C.G. Malmström, *Sveriges politiska historia från konung Karl XII:s död till statshvälfningen 1772,* III:254, 278, 319-21, 350-55, 429-30; *Handlingar ur v. Brinkmanska Archivet på Trolle-Ljungby,* ed. G. Andersson, II:172-73; E. R. Adair, *The Exterritoriality of Ambassadors in the Sixteenth and Seventeenth Centuries,* p. 225.

4. SP 95/101/100-101, 164-65. At least one of them was said to be a Jacobite. For Swedish contacts with the Jacobites, see Claude J. Nordmann, "Jakobiterna och det svenska hovet 1745-6," pp. 408-16.

5. *Riksrådet Anders Johan von Höpkens skrifter,* ed. Carl Silfverstolpe, II:268 (hereafter Höpken).

6. For some explanation of this state of affairs, see H. S. K. Kent, *War and Trade in Northern Seas. Anglo-Scandinavian Economic Relations in the Mid-Eighteenth Century*, passim.

7. For Springer in England, see Stig Rydberg, *Svenska studieresor till England under Frihetstiden,* pp. 98 ff.

8. Springer's correspondence, or a good deal of it, is in SP 101/93.

9. *The Grenville Papers,* ed. W. J. Smith, II:272, note 1.

10. SP 95/101/113.

11. For Gedda, see Gunnar Olsson, *Hattar och Mössor. Studier över partiväsendet i Sverige 1751-1762* (hereafter Olsson); and his own account of his services in SP 101/93/145.

12. SP 95/103/242-44 (or 1745 according to Gedda himself: SP 101/93/145).

13. SP 95/101/112-13.

14. HMC *Weston-Underwood,* p. 221; *Calendar of Home Office Papers (1760-65),* p. 238. Gedda's correspondence is mainly in SP 95/101-4; some also in SP 75; some in SP 101/93.

15. SP 95/102/232.

16. For the value of Gedda's "Journals of the Diet," see Olsson, pp. 47, 57-59. For a hostile (Cap) judgment on Gedda, see the anonymous Pro-Memoria (Spring 1764) in BM Add. MS 35,885, fo. 82.

17. SP 75/107/237; SP 95/104/7-8.

18. For the origins of Swedish parties, and their connection with foreign policy, see Göran Nilzén, *Studier i 1730-talets partiväsen.*

19. Claes Frietzcky, e.g., who was a typical Cap, admired England as being "a free people, full of industry and ideas about economics": "Pro Memoria 1799," printed in M. J. Crusenstolpe, *Portefeuille,* V:95. For the Caps' English orientation, see the comments in Tom Söderberg, *Den namnlösa medelklassen. Socialgrupp två i det gamla svenska samhället,* p. 241.

20. Malmström, III:419.

21. An admiring courtier recorded that he was able to look gracious even when viewed from the rear: A. L. Hamilton, *Anteckningar till svenska historian under Gustaf III:s regering,* p. 10.

22. "Too vehement not to be sincere, she often thereby revealed plans she had better have kept hidden. Magnanimous, generous, splendour-loving, proper, courteous, keen-witted, a good friend to her friends, her society was agreeable, her information extensive though ill-ordered, her ambitions limitless": Hamilton, p. 11.

23. For Lovisa Ulrika's political ideals and principles, see Olof Jägerskiöld, *Hovet och författningsfrågan 1760-1766,* passim (hereafter Jägerskiöld); for her biography, the same author's *Lovisa Ulrika.* For a critical review of the former, see Sven Ulric Palme, in *Historisk tidskrift,* 1944.

24. SP 95/102/154, 159. For the relations between the old Caps and the supporters of the Court, and the difficult question of party nomenclature, see Olsson, chap. 3.

25. SP 95/103/89.

26. Though it was now some nineteen years since his last visit.

27. SP 95/103/53, 68-70.

28. SP 95/103/89.

29. SP 95/103/62, 100-104.

30. SP 95/103/97-99, 106.

31. Gunnar Carlquist, *Carl Fredrik Scheffer och Sveriges politiska förbindelser med Danmark åren 1752-1765,* p. 178.

32. Höpken, I:60-62; SP 95/103/56, 62, 68-70.

33. Philip C. Yorke, *The Life and Correspondence of Philip Yorke, Earl of Hardwicke,* III:126-27; Albert von Ruville, *William Pitt Earl of Chatham,* II:184-85.

34. Yorke, III:129.

35. SP 75/104/32-34.

36. G. E. C. *Complete Baronetage,* II:137.

37. *Dictionary of National Biography,* s.v. "Bingley."

38. What follows is based on the Galway Papers, 12779-81 (unfoliated) in the University of Nottingham Library.

39. For Selwyn, see J. H. Jesse, *George Selwyn and His Contemporaries,* I:31. It would be piquant if he was identical with the MP known to the French as "Selvins," who declined to act as their agent in England because they did not offer enough: P. Coquelle, *L'Alliance Franco-Hollandaise contre l'Angleterre 1735-1788,* p. 145.

40. Lord Bingley was one of the group of Tory magnates responsible for building Cavendish Square: Sir John Summerson, *Georgian London,* pp. 89, 105, 110.

41. Romney Sedgwick, *The House of Commons, 1715-1754,* II:48; Sir Lewis Namier and John Brooke, *The House of Commons, 1754-1790,* II:509-10.

42. PRO Chatham Papers, 30/8, vol. 33, fos. 42-43.

43. 32 *Commons Journals* 484 has an entry for the year 10 October 1754-10 October 1755 recording that Goodricke was paid £500 due to him for arrears on his appointments.

44. See note 42.

45. His only son married a girl from Namur, and for some years lived in Groningen: Namier and Brooke, II:509-10.

46. Galway MSS 12780.

47. Add. MS 35,425, fo. 171, Goodricke to Lord Royston 17 May 1760.

48. BM Egerton MS 1755, fos. 27-28. The same volume also contains a MS in his hand headed "Considerations on the Memorial," dealing with Flemish linens, and another entitled "Extract of a Letter from Amsterdam 17 April 1755," concerning exports from Silesia to Holland, and the routes they followed: *ibid.,* fos. 29-30, 127 ff.

49. Add. MS 35,425, fos. 142, 167: Goodricke to Royston 25 March and 27 October 1759.

50. F. de Martens, *Recueil des Traités et Conventions conclus par la Russie,* IX (X):275.

51. Add. MS 35,425, fos. 139-40, 170, 199: Goodricke to Royston, 25 March 1759, 17 May 1760, 11 April 1761.

52. SP 95/103/153.

53. SP 75/104/3-7.

54. SP 75/104/9-12.

55. Yorke, III:129.

56. Riksarkivet, Stockholm (hereafter RA), Diplomatica, Anglica. Nolcken to Kanslipresidenten (hereafter KP), 29 May 1764, reporting Yorke.

57. Mitchell wrote that Goodricke, "the General [Yorke]told me, was a man of most excellent parts. The only proof I had of this [was]that the Knight seemed to be a humble admirer, and swore to everything the General said": BM Add. MS 6,867, fo. 78.

58. Yorke also commented on the length of the dinner: Yorke, III:202; and Mitchell noted that he seemed not pleased because Frederick talked all the time: Add. MS 6,867, fo. 83.

59. *Politisches Correspondenz Friedrichs des Grossen* (hereafter *Pol. Corr.*)XXIII:268, Frederick to Lovisa Ulrika, 1 February 1764.

60. SP 75/104/15-17, 22, Goodricke to Holdernesse, - April 1758, 28 April 1758.

61. SP 75/104/23-26, 39-41, 42-45, 50-53, Goodricke to Holdernesse, 16, 19, 23 May, 3 June 1758; SP 75/104/29-31, Holdernesse to Goodricke, 30 May 1758.

62. *Ibid.*

63. Höpken, I:60-62. Lovisa Ulrika later contended that Adolf Fredrik had done all in his power to oppose the refusal of Goodricke, with the result that she had received a letter of thanks from George II, and a promise to champion her cause. This letter, she alleged, she had subsequently burnt: *Riksrådet och Fältmarskalken m.m. Grefve Fredrik Axel von Fersens Historiska skrifter,* ed. R. M. Klinckowström III:276 (hereafter Fersen). If ever this letter existed it is most unlikely that it contained any such promise.

64. BM Egerton MS 2701, fo. 172, Woodford to Gunning, 9 September 1772: "Good God, what society, what hopes and expectation from this Ct—either as to advantage, or amusement . . . as to living here—I am already in the Dumps." Things were no better in Fredrik V's time: Dudley Cosby in 1764 found that there was no such thing as "a sensible conversible society": HMC *Weston-Underwood,* p. 373; Gleichen in 1759 found that "L'ennui est aussi épais que l'eau qu'on boit": *Souvenirs de Charles-Henri baron de Gleichen,* ed. P. Grimblot, p. xv.

65. RA Diplomatica, Danica, Sprengtportens brev till KP, Faxell to KP, 20 October 1763.

66. See, e.g., SP 75/108/42, 102; 113/212.

67. See, e.g., SP 75/104/167-70; 107/5-23; 108/70, 73-4; Add. MS 34,425, fos. 140, 157. The archive of the Swedish minister in Copenhagen, Ungern-Sternberg, contains some evidence of Goodricke's concern with these matters: Uppsala Universitets Bibliotek (UUB) F 367, Neutralitet till sjöss (unfoliated). For the most recent treatment of these problems see Kent, pp. 130-61.

68. SP 75/108/93, 191: 115/26-28; Kent, pp. 112-29.

69. In a private letter to Schack, of February 1766, Reventlow wrote: "Je suis aussi flaté du souvenir de Mr le chevalier Goodrick, qu'édifié des sentimens qu'il conserve pour une cour et pour une nation qui l'ont vu partir avec bien du regret . . . il n'y a guerre moyen d'avoir plus haute idée de ses talens et meilleure opinion de son caractère que je l'ai": *Udvalgte Breve Betaenkninger og Optegnelser af J. O. Schack-Rathlous Arkiv 1760-1800*, ed. Th. Thaulow, p. 334 (hereafter *Schack-Rathlous Arkiv*).

70. *Correspondance ministérielle de Comte J. H. E. Bernstorff, 1751-1770* ed. P. Vedel, II:311 (to Juel, 16 March 1767) (hereafter *Corr. Min.*).

71. RA Diplomatica, Danica, Sprengtporten to KP, 6 May 1764.

72. "Charlotte Dorothea Biehls historiske Breve," ed. J. H. Bang, pp. 370-71; BM Egerton MS 2697, fo. 31, Woodford to Gunning, 29 January 1768; E. Holm, *Danmark-Norges Historie under Kristian VII*, I:i:106, E. S. F. Reverdil, *Struensee og Hoffet i Kjöbenhavn 1760-1772* pp. 80-82, 102.

73. Add. MS 35,425, fos. 134-35, Goodricke to Royston, 25 March 1759.

74. Add. MS 35,425, fo. 180; SP 75/111/164.

75. E.g., BM Stowe MS 260, Breteuil to Praslin (intercepted) 16 November 1764.

76. In Add. MS 32,285 are a number of translations, in Goodricke's unmistakable hand, of deciphers of intercepted Swedish diplomatic papers, mostly from the period around 1716.

77. He furnished Lord Royston, whose appetite for information on Scandinavia seems to have been inexhaustible, not only with journals of the Diet, but with much other material on Sweden: UUB F 386, 2 March 1759; Add. MS 35,425, fos. 134-37, 150-52, 191, 220-21. For examples of his sure grasp of how Swedish institutions worked, see, e.g., SP 75/111/18; 108/226-31. And compare the concurring judgment of Olsson, pp. 150-51.

78. SP 75/104/46, 69-71, 91-92; 110/39, 179; 111/49, 126. Among them was John Fenwick, a Stockholm merchant, whose brother Goodricke persuaded the government to appoint as British consul at Elsinore: SP 95/134: "Narrative of Mr Jno Fenwick's situation, and the principal causes of it," 14 November 1767; SP 75/110/27; 116/182.

79. E.g., SP 75/104/55; 107/31.

80. SP 75/110/10-13, 16; 111/74; 115/149.

81. SP 75/104/144-46.

82. SP 75/107/35-38, 43-46, 53-54, 66-69.

83. Van Marteville's cipherer had originally written £2,000 instead of £20,000.

84. SP 75/107/43-46.

85. SP 75/107/66-69.

86. SP 75/107/157-59.

87. Höpken, I:124: "des vues particulières, des schismes, de la mésintelligence, du désordre et un pillage des fonds publics qui ne connaissait ni bornes ni décence."

88. *Ibid.*, I:135; and for his opinion of French policy in February 1759, II:370. Gedda defined Höpken's attitude to France as "en un mot, être attaché à la France, sans en être l'esclave": SP 95/103/322, 23 May 1760. Nevertheless, Choiseul thought it worthwhile to maintain a private correspondence with Höpken behind the back of d'Havrincour, his minister in Stockholm: Lars Trulsson, *Ulrik Scheffer som Hattpolitiker. Studier i Hattregimens politiska och diplomatiska historia,* pp. 409-10.

89. SP 95/101/365, 368, 395-98.

90. For Höpken and the invasion scheme, see Höpken, I:149, II:551, 594-95; Carlquist, p. 217.

91. Höpken's letter is in Höpken, II:557-62; Ungern-Sternberg's comment in SP 75/107/70-73.

92. SP 75/107/70-73. The risks Höpken ran were seen in the scandal and recriminations provoked by a story that state-secretary Carleson was secretly negotiating with Goodricke: Carlquist, pp. 214-15. Höpken's contacts with Goodricke leaked out, all the same, perhaps through the Danish minister in Stockholm, von der Asseburg: *ibid*, p. 236.

93. SP 75/107/161, 167.

94. SP 75/107/169-73, 195-99.

95. SP 75/107/169-73.

96. [F. W. von Ehrenheim], *Tessin och Tessiniana*, p. 190.

97. There is no good study of Pechlin: the only book about him seems to be Hj. Lindeberg, *En ränksmidare. Strödda blad ur 1700-talets partistrider.*

98. Pechlin was a Holsteiner. For his imperfect command of Swedish, see Claes Frietzcky's "Pro Memoria, 1799," printed in Crusenstolpe, *Portefeuille*, II:101; *Handlingar rörande Skandinaviens historia*, XVI:230.

99. Gunnar Sundberg, "Lantpartiet vid riksdagen 1760-2." For what follows, see also Olsson, pp. 137-54, *id.*, "Krisuppgörelsen mellan hattpartiet och Carl Fredrik Pechlin 1760"; Malmström, V:24-34; Fersen, III:282-84; Höpken, I:106-8, 111; SP 75/108/157-60, 193, 212; 110/1-4. Adam Horn (an old Cap) wrote of a coalition between "the old Patriot party which is called the King's party and our new brethren who are called French malcontents": Adam Horn to [C. Springer] 27 January 1761, SP 101/96/6.

100. SP 75/110/1-4. The French ambassador, d'Havrincour, reported that Pechlin had secured the election of a majority hostile to the Senate by bribing with English money; Olsson, "Krisuppgörelsen," p. 20. There seems no foundation for the statement.

101. Jägerskiöld, pp. 19-20; Fersen, III; 321; SP 75/110/10-13, 16; *Pol. Corr.* XX:128, 182, 217.

102. SP 75/110/19-21; Fersen, III:320. Newcastle's London agent, Magens, jeopardized the secrecy of the transaction by sending a credit on the Stockholm firm of Finlay & Jennings, though Jennings, as a pillar of the Hats and a member of the Secret Committee, was the last man who should have been given any inkling of the transmission of money to Sweden: SP 75/110/91; SP 101/93/11-12. This blunder was to be repeated in 1764 (see below, chap. 3). News of the transaction was somehow leaked in London: as Bute believed, through Springer: SP 75/113/84, Bute to Goodricke, 9 March 1761. In the autograph narrative which Lovisa Ulrika drew up for Prince Henry of Prussia upon his visit to Sweden in 1770, she said that the £5,000 [*sic*] was given on condition not only of using it to stop the war, but also of receiving an English minister in Stockholm: RA Kungl. arkivet 259. There seems to be no other evidence to support this, and it is probably a deliberate distortion.

103. For all this, see Olsson, "Krisuppgörelsen," esp. pp. 35-43.

104. Cf. the drastic judgment of Bernstorff, who was Ekeblad's political friend and protector: "Une crainte excessif qui approche de la pusillanimité, jointe a une indolence inconcevable, fait le fond du caractere de ce ministre": *Corr. Min.*, II:106 n. 1.

105. Malmström, V:31-34.

106. SP 75/110/200-3.

107. SP 75/110/155-59, Goodricke to Holdernesse, 22 February 1761. Choiseul was so desperate for peace that he authorized Breteuil, his ambassador in Russia, to spend a million livres in bribing Russian ministers, in order to obtain it: *Recueil des Instructions données aux ambassadeurs de France: Russie*, pp. 163-74. Choiseul to Breteuil, 18 December 1760.

108. Malmström, V:78-79; Fersen, III:296-97, 300; Carlquist, p. 256.

109. SP 75/111/84-87, Goodricke to Bute, Most Secret, 15 September 1761; cf. Carlquist, pp. 269-70.

110. SP 75/111/108-11, 118, 197.

111. For the difficulty of making peace without being sure of the success of the approach, see Gustaf Bonde, "Oförgripliga tanckar om medel att erhålla freden," in Carl Trolle-Bonde, *Anteckningar om Bondesläkten. Riksrådet Grefve Gustaf Bonde,* I:255-59.

112. SP 75/113/127, Goodricke to Bute, 3 April 1762. The decision to appeal to her was taken on 27 March 1762: Jägerskiöld, p. 88. The draft of her letter to Frederick, asking him to appoint someone to treat for peace, is in RA Kungl. arkivet (unfoliated).

113. Printed in *Sverges traktater med främmande magter,* VIII: 831-34.

114. SP 75/104/14, Goodricke to Holdernesse, 27 March 1758.

115. "It is a kind of drawn Battle between the two parties . . .": Goodricke to George Grenville, 22 January 1762: SP 75/113/190.

116. SP 75/115/103, Goodricke to Holdernesse, 20 September 1763.

117. SP 75/108/199-200.

118. SP 75/110/29-30, Holdernesse to Goodricke, 27 January 1761.

119. SP 101/93/9, John Springer to [C. Springer], 24 February 1761.

120. SP 101/93/14, A. Ramsay to [C. Springer], 10 April 1761.

121. SP 75/110/179; 111/43, Goodricke to Holdernesse, 9 May, 18 August 1761; cf. SP 101/93/13, 28, Ramsay to [C. Springer], 7 April, 3 November 1761. Hedman wrote to Christopher Springer, 17 July 1761: "God forgive England, that for Ceremony's sake only it did not send a Minister, when earnestly requested to do it. Had it complyed with our moving request, We had at this Juncture liberated ourselves, Effectually crushed this Hellish French faction, been in alliance with Britain and on the eve of a general peace": SP 101/93/17.

122. SP 75/113/3-5.

123. SP 75/113/68-70, Goodricke to Bute, 13 February 1762.

124. For this episode, SP 75/113/3-5, 38-39, 60, Bute to Goodricke, 5 January, 9 February, 23 February 1762; SP 75/113/31-34, 43-44, 55, 68-70, Goodricke to Bute, 19, 30 January; 6, 13 February 1762. SP 101/93/34, Ramsay to [C. Springer], 30 January 1762.

125. *Bernstorffske Papirer. Udvalgte Breve og Optegnelser vedrørende Familien Bernstorff i Tiden fra 1732 til 1825,* ed. Aage Friis I:301-2 (hereafter *Bernstorffske Papirer*); SP 75/115/78, Goodricke to Halifax, 16 August 1763.

126. Gunnar Castrén, *Gustav Philip Creutz,* p. 192.

127. SP 75/115/14-16, Goodricke to Halifax, 12 February 1763.

128. SP 75/115/88.

129. UUB F 386 has the original, with Goodricke's endorsement of receipt.

130. SP 75/115/102, 104.

131. SP 75/115/98-100, Goodricke to Sandwich, 20 September 1763.

132. RA Diplomatica, Danica, Sprengtportens brev till KP. Faxell to KP, 22 September 1763.

133. SP 75/115/107. Goodricke's dispatch of 20 September arrived on 30 September; Sandwich replied on 7 October.

134. SP 75/115/109-15. The Franco-Swedish alliance of 1754 was due to expire in 1768. For the question of the French arrears, and the French offer, see Malmström, V:225-26; Lars Trulsson, *Ulrik Scheffer som Hattpolitiker,* pp. 466-74; SP 75/115/138, Goodricke to Holdernesse, 8 November 1763; SP 101/93/167, [Gedda] to [Holdernesse], 6 December 1763. Lovisa Ulrika's confidant and principal agent, F. C. Sinclair, was expecting an Extraordinary Diet in February 1764: RA Sjöholms arkivet, Gyldenstolpske samlingen, Sinclair to N. Ph. Gyldenstolpe, 17 October 1763.

135. RA Riksrådets protokoll i utrikes ärenden, 3 October 1763 (hereafter RRPUÄ); Diplomatica, Danica, Faxell to KP, 13 October 1763.

136. SP 75/115/116-18. Goodricke to Sandwich, 11 October 1763.

137. SP 75/115/122-26.

138. He had grounds for his suspicion: this tactic had already been suggested in the senate: RRPUÄ, 9 May 1763.

139. SP 91/72/176, Buckinghamshire to Sandwich, 14 October NS 1763. Solms, the Prussian minister at St. Petersburg, thought that Panin was genuinely alarmed at the French proposals to Sweden, and believed that "il sera très nécessaire de prendre un concert, pour prévenir ce coup!": *Sbornik Imperatorskago Russkago Istoricheskago Obschchestva,* (hereafter *SIRIO*), 22:127: Solms to Frederick, 4/15 October 1763. Russian pressure to send Goodricke was again reported by Buckinghamshire on 28 October NS, but this dispatch did not reach Sandwich until 7 December: SP 91/72/203.

140. He died 5 October 1763.

141. For all this, see my *Macartney in Russia.*

142. *The Despatches and Diplomatic Correspondence of John, Second Earl of Buckinghamshire,* ed. A. D'Arcy Collyer, II:10-11, 18, Halifax to Buckinghamshire, 1 March, 5 April 1763 (hereafter, *Buckinghamshire Despatches*). For Catherine's unreasonable demands for more, *SIRIO,* 48:319; for her exploitation of England's desire for an alliance to extort promises about Poland, *ibid.,* p. 324; for her evasion of requests for a statement of her intentions, *ibid.,* p. 486.

143. SP 91/71/253-54, Halifax to Buckinghamshire, 24 June 1762.

144. *SIRIO,* 48:568, 572; SP 91/72/79-84, Buckinghamshire to Halifax, 22 August NS 1763.

145. *Additional Grenville Papers, 1763-1765,* ed. J. R. G. Tomlinson, p. 318.

146. SP 91/72/106 ff., Sandwich to Buckinghamshire, 2 September 1763.

147. See, e.g., Add. MS 32, 288 fo. 83, A. R. Vorontsov to Golitsyn, 3 December 1763 (intercepted); Sandwich's comment of 17 February 1764 (to Buckinghamshire) SP 91/73/67; HMC *Lothian,* pp. 181-82, Buckinghamshire to Lady Suffolk, 30 March 1764; Martens IX (X):219; *Grenville Papers,* II:240; *Buckinghamshire Despatches,* II:119, Sandwich to Buckinghamshire, 20 December 1763.

148. SP 91/72/180-81.

149. Sandwich could rely on an intercept of a rescript to Gross (the Russian minister in London), which revealed that Catherine believed that Goodricke was being sent to Stockholm to oblige her; and he lost no time in telling Gross that this was the case: SP 91/107, Catherine to Gross, 13/24 February 1764; Gross to Catherine, 19/30 March 1764 (intercepts); and see Michael F. Metcalf, *Russia, England and Swedish Party Politics 1762-1766,* pp. 46, 69.

150. SP 75/115/142-48, Goodricke to Sandwich, 12 November 1763.

151. SP 75/115/156-59, 160-63, Goodricke to Sandwich, 29 November 1763. Such, at least, was the account Goodricke sent to the office. It did not in all respects tally with the account Faxell sent to Stockholm, and it seems likely that Goodricke permitted himself at least one significant editorial omission; for it is certain that he did in fact give Faxell a note on 10 November, and not a mere memorandum of the conversation: RA Diplomatica, Danica, Faxell to KP, 10 November 1763.

152. RA Diplomatica, Danica, Faxell to KP 23 November 1763. For Goodricke's nervousness, *ibid.,* same to same, 4 December 1763.

153. See Faxell's enormous dispatch of 1 December 1763.

154. RA Diplomatica, Danica, Faxell to KP, 4 December 1763; and cf. the survey of foreign affairs presented by the Senate to the Diet of 1765: RA Riksdagen, Sekreta propositionen, Utrikes, 1765, fo. 59, and appendix document Ff.

155. RRPUÄ, 22 November 1763.

156. SP 75/115/171-73. Sandwich was not being excessively prickly: the same point held up Sweden's resumption of diplomatic relations with Prussia: SP 75/113/280; *Pol. Corr.*, XXIII:178, 251.

157. Rigsarkivet, Copenhagen (hereafter DRA), Tyske kansliets udenrigske Afdelning (hereafter TKUA), Sverige B 150, Schack to Bernstorff, 13, 24 January 1764.

158. RA Diplomatica, Danica, Sprengtporten to KP, 15 April 1764.

159. DRA TKUA Sverige B 150, Schack to Bernstorff, 20 April 1764.

160. RRPUÄ, 6 February 1764. I owe this reference to the kindness of Prof. Michael Metcalf.

161. SP 95/104/12, Goodricke to Sandwich, 18 February 1764.

162. SP 95/104/42-43; RA Diplomatica, Danica, Sprengtporten to KP, 15 April 1764.

163. SP 95/104/33-6, Sandwich to Goodricke, 30 March 1764: Add. MS 35,367, fos. 19-20.

CHAPTER II
A DIPLOMATIC REVOLUTION

1. Carlquist, p. 226. Bernstorff realized it too: *Correspondance entre le comte Johan Hartvig Bernstorff et le duc de Choiseul, 1758-1766* p. 137 (hereafter *Bernstorff-Choiseul Corr.*).

2. For the connexions between the origins of the Hats and foreign policy, see Göran Nilzén, *Studier i 1700-talets partiväsen;* Sven Ulric Palme, "Befolkningsutvecklingen som bakgrund till partiomvälvningen 1738. Ett socialhistoriskt försök."

3. Höpken recorded that one of Lovisa Ulrika's grievances against him was that he did not approve of her desire to conquer Norway; and that she once said to C. F. Scheffer "that a king could not be said to have reigned gloriously unless he had made conquests": Höpken, I:40.

4. There is a good statement of France's Baltic policy in *Recueil des Instructions données aux Ambassadeurs de France, Danemark,* pp. 158-67: instructions for Ogier, 8 August 1753.

5. *Sverges traktater,* VIII:512-17, 533-34, 537-53, 553-62, 580-81.

6. P. Vedel, *Den aeldre Grev Bernstorffs Ministerium,* pp. 6-7; Beth Hennings, *Gustav III som kronprins,* pp. 215-16 (hereafter Hennings); Nilsson, "Blad ur konung Gustaf III:s och Sofia Magdalenas giftermålshistoria," IV (1877): 314 ff.

7. *Konung Gustaf III:s efterlemnade och femtio år efter hans död öppnade papper,* ed. E. G. Geijer, I:29-30, 32 (hereafter *Gustavianska Papperen*).

8. For the treaties establishing the Armed Neutrality, see *Sverges traktater,* VIII:772-79, 787-95, 801-8.

9. See, e.g., Höpken, II:571-73, Höpken to Ulrik Scheffer, 17 April 1759; and in general Kent, pp. 135-41; Vedel, *Den aeldre Grev Bernstorffs Ministerium,* pp. 34-38, 66, 72; Carlquist, pp. 143, 179-81, 185; Trulsson, pp. 297-99.

10. Jägerskiöld, p. 219.

11. France spent at least 1,400,000 livres on the Diet of 1760-62: Olsson, *Hattar och Mössor,* p. 229.

12. Alfred Bourguet, *Etudes sur la politique étrangère du Duc de Choiseul,* pp. 32-33; *Mémoires du Duc de Choiseul,* ed. F. Calmettes, p. 243.

13. Jägerskiöld, pp. 49-50; Trulsson, pp. 444, 474; Malmström, V:218.

14. For Choiseul's opinion on naval and colonial strength as the criterion of great-power status, see Alfred Bourguet, *Le Duc de Choiseul et l'alliance espagnole,* p. 159; for French

ideas on the balance of power, Gaston Zeller, "Le Principe d'équilibre dans la politique internationale avant 1789," pp. 24-37; for his idea that England was a danger to Europe, Bourguet, *Etudes sur la politique étrangère du Duc de Choiseul,* pp. 45, 66, 114; and see M. S. Andersson, "Eighteenth-Century Theories of the Balance of Power," pp. 192-94.

15. Bourguet, *Choiseul et l'alliance espagnole,* pp. 229-50; Louis Blart, *Les Rapports de la France et de l'Espagne, aprés le Pacte de Famille jusqu'à la fin du ministère du Duc de Choiseul,* p. 79; G. Lacour-Gayet, *La Marine militaire de la France sous la règne de Louis XV,* p. 412.

16. R. Konetzke, *Die Politik des Grafen Aranda. Ein Beitrag zur Geschichte des spanisch-englischen Weltgegensatzes im 18. Jahrhundert,* p. 17; J. F. Ramsey, *Anglo-French Relations 1763-1770,* pp. 149-50.

17. In 1762 Ulrik Scheffer, the Swedish ambassador in Paris, wrote: "The most humiliating thing is that they consider us as annihilated and practically reduced to complete anarchy; from which they conclude that we are neither dangerous nor deserving of support": C. T. Odhner, *Minne af Riksrådet m.m. Grefve Ulrik Scheffer,* pp. 31-32.

18. Höpken, II:602; and cf. *ibid.,* I:111.

19. RA Malmström avskrifter, Breteuil to Praslin, 12 February 1764. Breteuil's official instruction of 8 October 1763, printed in *Recueil des Instructions, Suède,* pp. 402-6, has nothing about the new policy.

20. E. Amburger, *Russland und Schweden 1762-1772. Katharina II, die schwedische Verfassung und die Ruhe des Nordens,* pp. 50-56; Malmström, V:231, n. 2. Frederick the Great took the opportunity to advise Peter to strengthen the Swedish monarchy, and advised Lovisa Ulrika to use Russian assistance: G. Olsson, "Fredrik den Store och Sveriges författning," p. 350.

21. Fersen, III:327, 329; Amburger, pp. 57-58.

22. Fritz Arnheim, "Beiträge zur Geschichte der nordischen Frage in der zweiten Hälfte des 18. Jahrhunderts," p. 430.

23. *Buckinghamshire Dispatches,* I:105, 110-11.

24. *Recueil des Instructions, Russie,* p. 240: instructions for Bausset, 18 December 1763; *Correspondance ministérielle du Comte J. H. E. Bernstorff, 1751-1770,* II:154, n. 2 (hereafter *Corr. Min.*).

25. Amburger, pp. 67-68. Lovisa Ulrika sent, through Frederick the Great, a warning to Catherine of the threat of domestic disturbance if she undertook her projected trip to Livonia, and it was in fact canceled: *Pol. Corr.,* XXIII:329, 377.

26. Vedel, pp. 249-51; "Grev v.d. Ostens Gesandtskaber," pp. 615-16.

27. Arnheim, "Beiträge zur Geschichte der nordischen Frage," p. 430.

28. As the Danish minister in Russia, Haxthausen, assured Schack soon after her accession would be the case: *Schack-Rathlous Arkiv,* p. 271: Haxthausen to Schack, 13/24 August 1762.

29. *SIRIO,* 48:8: Report of College for Foreign Affairs, with Catherine's MS annotations, 2 July 1762.

30. *SIRIO,* 48:70. For a detailed analysis of Russian policy in Sweden from 1762 to 1764, see Metcalf, pp. 12-37.

31. The following summary of Panin's policy conflates the resolutions of the October Conference and the rescript to Osterman which arose out of it: *SIRIO,* 51:1 ff., 4 ff; cf. "Ostens Gesandtskaber," p. 569, and see Metcalf, pp. 22-24, 31.

32. Axel Brusewitz, ed., *Frihetstidens grundlagar och konstitutionella stadgar,* p. 23.

33. SP 91/73/93-94, Buckinghamshire to Halifax, 22 August 1763; cf. *SIRIO,* 48:568, 572. The proposal was thus for a balance of parties, rather than a balance of forces within the constitution: presumably it was phrased like this because Panin had (legitimate) doubts

about British interest in the Swedish constitution. But from Sandwich's point of view there must have seemed little sense in aiming at a balance of parties: what England wanted in Sweden, if anything, was not to balance the French party, but to overthrow it.

34. Fersen, III:328; Amburger, p. 50.

35. *Pol. Corr.*, XXIII:115-16.

36. *Pol. Corr.*, XXIII:162, 219, 260, 317.

37. The secret article is printed in Niklas Tengberg, *Om kejsarinnan Catharina II:s åsyftade stora nordiska alliance*, appendix A. For fresh light on the genesis of the Russo-Prussian alliance, see H. M. Scott, "Frederick II, the Ottoman Empire and the Origins of the Russo-Prussian Alliance of April 1764," pp. 153-76.

38. *SIRIO*, 51:49; Metcalf, pp. 44-45.

39. Aa. Friis, *Bernstorfferne og Danmark*, II:149-50.

40. Carlquist, pp. 125, 148.

41. *Correspondance de Bernstorff et Choiseul*, pp. 26-27; Vedel, pp. 142-72.

42. "Grev Adam Gottlob Moltkes efterladte Mindeskrifter," ed. C. F. Wegener, pp. 316-17, for Fredrik V's prayers.

43. In 1754 he wrote to Wedel-Frijs, "It is a Danish System, and not an English or a French, that it is appropriate for Denmark to follow": Friis, II:198; and cf. *Corr. Min.*, II:105; Vedel, p. 21.

44. *Corr. Min.*, II:122-29, instructions for Osten, 7 April 1763. He changed his opinion of Catherine later, and they ended in mutual admiration and respect: Friis, II:210.

45. *Corr. Min.*, II:109-10; "Ostens Gesandtskaber," pp. 558-59, 615-16; Arnheim, II:443.

46. *Corr. Min.*, II:158, Bernstorff to Schack, 26 November 1763.

47. *Corr. Min.*, II:107, and cf. II:3, 6-7.

48. As Goodricke saw: SP 75/113/152, Goodricke to Bute, 4 May 1762.

49. Carlquist, pp. 251, 270; Jägerskiöld, pp. 49-50, 78.

50. Compare A. P. Bernstorff's judgment on Choiseul: *Bernstorffske Papirer*, I:447; with Höpken's: Höpken, I:147; and Gleichen's: Gleichen, *Souvenirs*, p. 26.

51. *Correspondance de Bernstorff et Choiseul*, p. 14.

52. *Corr. Min.*, II:62, 83: Puysieulx in 1750 would have done better, he thought. For France and this crisis, see *Correspondance de Bernstorff et Choiseul*, p. 227 n.; *Bernstorffske Papirer*, I:420-25, 453-55. For Choiseul's snubbing of Bernstorff, *Bernstorffske Papirer*, II:659-60; *Correspondance de Bernstorff et Choiseul*, p. 182; for d'Havrincour's suspicions of Denmark, *Schack-Rathlous Arkiv*, p. 288; Höpken, II:613.

53. For the arrears question, see *Corr. Min.*, II:160, n. 2; Barthélémy, pp. 241-44, 246-47.

54. *Corr. Min.*, II:85-86, Bernstorff to Haxthausen, 8 September 1762.

55. *Ibid.*, II:114-15, Bernstorff to Schack, 19 February 1763.

56. *Corr. Min.*, II:133-42, instruction for Gleichen, 10 June 1763.

57. *Corr. Min.*, II:175-76, Bernstorff to Gleichen, 30 June 1764; *Ibid.*, II:177-78, Bernstorff to Schack, 25 August 1764; Barthélémy, pp. 246-47.

58. "Ostens Gesandtskaber," p. 618; Carlquist, pp. 303-5.

59. Carlquist, pp. 303-5; Metcalf, pp. 45-46.

60. *Corr. Min.*, II:158, n. 3.

61. *Corr. Min.*, II:164-66 and n. 1, Bernstorff to Osten, 12 March 1764; SP 91/73/79; "Ostens Gesandtskaber," pp. 576-84; C. W. von Düben, now Swedish ambassador in St. Petersburg, commented that the offer over Poland was significant of Bernstorff's desire to propitiate the empress: RA Diplomatica, Muscovitica, von Düben to KP, 2/13 April 1764.

62. For a selection of such opinions, see Roberts, *Swedish and English Parliamentarism*, pp. 38-39, to which may be added Höpken's judgment in 1757: "Quand le Roi est regardé comme nul, les Etats peu considérés, le sénat un objet d'envie, de haine et de critique, dès

lors il n'y a point de gouvernement, ni d'obéissance, et l'un et l'autre forment la chaîne et les liens de toute société: Höpken, I:136.

63. Hennings, pp. 126-27; Jägerskiöld, p. 136.

64. Hennings, pp. 113-16, 269; RA Malmström avskrifter, Breteuil to Praslin, 12 February 1764.

65. For the history of the Composition, see [S. Piper], "Pro Memoria, 1771" (RA Stavsundsarkivet, Smärre enskilda arkiv), pp. 7-9; Jägerskiöld, pp. 64-72, 102-15, 118, 125-36, 141, 151-57; Fersen, III:29, 305-15.

66. Adam Horn, for one, was said by Lovisa Ulrika to have consistently opposed a Composition: Fersen, III:316, n. 1. The Caps later professed that they entered the Composition reluctantly, and for tactical reasons: Metcalf argues that they did so simply as "clients of the Court": Metcalf, pp. 103, 119.

67. Fredrik Lagerroth, "En frihetstidens lärobok i gällande svensk statsrätt."

68. Olof Jägerskiöld, "C. F. Scheffer och 1750-talets författningskris," pp. 193-94.

69. Jägerskiöld, *Hovet och författningsfrågan*, pp. 151-52. Cf. RA Stavsundsarkivet, "Pro Memoria, 1771"; pp. 8-9; RA Sjöholmsarkivet, Gyldenstolpske samlingar, F. C. Sinclair to N. Ph. Gyldenstolpe, 7 July 1763.

70. Quoted in M. J. Crusenstolpe, *Portefeuille*, I:108.

71. DRA TKUA Sverige B150, Schack to Bernstorff, 24 April 1764.

72. Printed in Tengberg, *Om kejsarinnan Catharina II:s åsyftade stora nordiska alliance*, appendix B; Jägerskiöld, pp. 153-57.

73. Jägerskiöld, pp. 138-41. Metcalf (pp. 28-29) argues that the memorandum ascribed to Löwenhielm in fact rather represents the views of the Composition.

74. See Palme's review of Jägerskiöld, in *Historisk tidskrift*, (1944), pp. 181-87, Jägerskiöld's reply, pp. 314-16, and Palme's rejoinder, pp. 317-18. Palme (p. 187) dismissed the whole policy of Composition as "the vain and hopeless attempt of a politically foolish, hysterical and ambitious woman to steer the course of events to suit herself, without having adequate solid resources for doing so."

75. SP 75/104/13-14, 15-17; 110/192.

76. SP 75/104/69-71, 91-92.

77. SP 75/107/31.

78. Add. MS 35,425, fo. 152.

79. SP 75/113/92-93, Goodricke to Bute, 2 March 1762.

80. SP 75/107/12; and cf. *ibid.*, 108/199-200.

81. SP 75/110/185; 111/51.

82. SP 75/115/109.

83. SP 101/93/6, Adam Horn to [C. Springer], 27 January 1761.

84. For a contrary view, see Metcalf, pp. 98-100, 103, 119.

85. DRA TKUA, Sverige C 321, Bernstorff to Schack, 14 November 1763.

86. Add. MS 35,425, fo. 175, Goodricke to Lord Royston, 19 July 1760.

87. SP 75/111/192.

88. SP 75/113/294; 115/5, 60, Goodricke to Halifax, 16 November 1762, 15 January, 25 June 1763.

89. Martens, IX (X):221; cf. SP 91/73/281, 310-13, Sandwich to Buckinghamshire, 3, 21 August 1764.

90. SP 91/73/5, Buckinghamshire to Sandwich 9 December NS 1763.

91. SP 91/73/33, Sandwich to Buckinghamshire, 20 January 1764.

92. SP 91/73/55-56, 72-74, 134-35, 141-42, Buckinghamshire to Sandwich, 17 January, 24 January, 31 March, 3 April 1764.

93. SP 91/72/138, Buckinghamshire to Sandwich, 20 September NS 1763.

94. SP 91/72/231, Buckinghamshire to Sandwich, 23 November NS 1763.

95. Panin minutes in the spring of 1764 his opinion that "en agissant sagement et avec fermeté on pourrait certainement amener l'Angleterre à payer une partie des pertes subies dans les affaires de Pologne": Martens, IX (X):224; and cf. *SIRIO*, 22:277-82, Solms to Frederick, 13/24 July 1764. For a different interpretation of these exchanges, see H. M. Scott, "Great Britain, Poland and the Russian Alliance, 1763-1767," pp. 53-74, where he argues that in 1763 England missed the best chance of the Russian alliance (at a price of a subsidy of £100,000 a year and support in Poland!) that was ever to be offered, and that Panin, so far from holding all the trumps, felt it necessary to solicit England's alliance.

CHAPTER III
THE OVERTHROW OF THE "FRENCH SYSTEM"

1. It was of course common form for ministers to complain of the particularly high cost of living in their place of residence, but in the case of Stockholm the complaints were well founded.

2. G. F. Gyllenborg was glad in 1770 to move in to the Old Town from Södermalm, which he described as "neither town nor country, and has the inconveniences of both without the compensations of either": G. F. Gyllenborg, ***Mitt lefverne 1731-1775. Självbiografiska anteckningar***, p. 84.

3. The present Gustav Adolfstorg.

4. SP 95/104/35.

5. RA AVPR 10, Osterman to Catherine, 16/27 April 1764; SP 95/104/46.

6. For the Nienburg intercepts, and their importance for Sweden, see Helle Stiegung, *Den engelska underrättelseverksamheten rörande Sverige under 1700-talet*; Bengt Petersen, " 'The Correspondent in Paris'–en engelsk informations-källa under 1700-talet," pp. 387-89. Petersen considers that it took about a month for intercepts of French dispatches from Stockholm to reach London.

7. SP 95/104/68-96, Goodricke to Sandwich, 11 May 1764.

8. SP 95/104/66-67. Sandwich to Goodricke, 22 May 1764.

9. SP 95/104/97-99, Sandwich to Goodricke, 19 June 1764.

10. Metcalf, p. 32.

11. SP 95/104/54-57, 59-62, Goodricke to Sandwich, 1 May, 4 May 1764.

12. SP 95/104/68-76, 11 May 1764.

13. Though Goodricke did not know it, Löwenhielm had already been promised a pension from Russia: *SIRIO*, 51:296, Osterman to Panin, 19/30 March 1764; AVPR 10, same to same, 8/19 June 1764.

14. For the attitude of the Caps to Höpken, SP 95/104/74-76, Goodricke to Sandwich, 11 May 1764; for Lovisa Ulriks's ban on him, *ibid*., fo. 80, Goodricke to Sandwich, 15 May 1764.

15. AVPR 10, Osterman to Catherine, 14/25 September 1764.

16. The possibility of cooperation between Höpken and Goodricke was a long-lived fear, shared at various times by the queen, Schack, and Breteuil: RA Kungl. arkiv 259, [Gyldenstolpe] to "Lorier," 10 February 1764, "Lorier" to "Breton," 24 February 1764; DRA TKUA Sverige B 150, Schack to Bernstorff, 24, 28 February, 20 April, 24 July 1764; RA Malmström avskr., Breteuil to Praslin, 12 February 1764; and cf. SP 95/104/11-12, 21-23, Goodricke to Sandwich, 24 January, 28 February 1764.

17. Add. MS 35,885, fos. 91-98 (undated). The case for conjecturing that the queen herself may have been the author, or have guided the pen that wrote it, lies in its general resem-

blance to her remarks to Goodricke in the course of their secret interview on 3 July (for which see below), and in particular that on that occasion she used the argument (also used in the "Pro Memoria") that Sweden had always been anglophile when the monarchy was strong.

18. SP 95/104/83, Goodricke to Sandwich, 18 May 1764.

19. RA Kabinettet för utrikes brevvexling, KP to Ulrik Scheffer, 8 May 1764.

20. *Pol Corr.*, XXIII:268, n. 1, Lovisa Ulrika to Frederick, 6 January 1764. Frederick replied drily: "Vour trouverez Le Sr Godric un homme fort peu civilizé, et ses Supérieurs des Gens moins Traitables que Jacques Rosbiff": RA Kungl. arkiv, 259, N. Ph. Gyldenstolpe to C. W. von Düben, 24 February 1764.

21. The identification of Borcke with the "Lorier" of the secret correspondence in RA Kungl. arkiv 259 seems to me virtually certain.

22. SP 95/104/101-4, Goodricke to Sandwich, 8 June 1764. Goodricke had considered Rudbeck as "one of our principal champions" as early as 30 June 1761: SP 75/110/231-35; and see *ibid.*, 110/185, 12 May 1761.

23. On 20 June she distinguished Osterman, Goodricke, and Cocceji, alone among the diplomatic corps, by inviting them to attend a review of the Stockholm militia: AVPR 10, Osterman to Catherine, 22 June 1764.

24. SP 95/104/93-97, Goodricke to Sandwich, 1 June 1764; Buckinghamshire, *Correspondence*, II:188-90, Goodricke to Buckinghamshire, 6 June 1764.

25. So at least it would appear from *SIRIO*, vol. 57.

26. SP 95/104/93-97, Goodricke to Sandwich, 1 June 1764.

27. SP 95/104/112-14, Goodricke to Sandwich, 15 June 1764. The original French is in SP 95/104/202-9, in Goodricke to Sandwich, 28 July. The memorial reached Goodricke just before he wrote his dispatch of 8 June: *ibid.*, 104/101 4. On the constitutional question, the Memorial ran that "the design is only to re-establish the Royalty in it's rights and prerogatives, that are founded in Law; to regulate the functions and duties of the Senate, and to put just limits to the Power of the States."

28. SP 95/104/142, Goodricke to Sandwich, 3 July 1764. He had taken care to concert with Osterman what he should say to the queen at the interview: AVPR 10, Osterman to Catherine, 25 June/6 July 1764.

29. *Buckinghamshire Correspondence*, II:201-2.

30. RA Diplomatica, Anglica, Nolcken to KP, Apostille, 6 November 1764.

31. SP 95/104/66-67, Sandwich to Goodricke, 22 May 1764.

32. SP 95/104/80-81, Goodricke to Sandwich, Most Secret, 15 May 1764. The amount was rumored to be 300,000 livres: Goodricke deduced that this portended an early meeting of the Diet.

33. SP 91/73/187, Buckinghamshire to Sandwich, 23 May 1764 (Sandwich received this dispatch on 18 June). Buckinghamshire was to change his mind more than once on the question of the supposed financial straits to the empress: *Buckinghamshire Correspondence*, II:232; SP 91/74/131.

34. BM Stowe MS 258, fos. 168-69, Sandwich to [?], 19 June 1764; HMC *Weston-Underwood*, p. 367, Edward Sedgwick to Weston, 20 July 1764; SP 91/73/282, Sandwich to Buckinghamshire, 3 August 1764; *Buckinghamshire Correspondence*, II:217-18, Sir J. Yorke to Buckinghamshire, 14 August 1764; *Pol. Corr.*, XXIII:456, Frederick to Rohd, 6 August 1764. Sandwich was still nervous about this possibility in June, and was only reassured by Stormont's dispatch from Vienna of 19 June: Frank Spencer, *The Fourth Earl of Sandwich. Diplomatic Correspondence 1763-1765*, pp. 168, 172 ff. (hereafter Spencer). Metcalf argues (pp. 50-51) that Panin exploited these alarms to put pressure on England in regard to the negotiations for an alliance, and that they may have provoked the launching of his "Northern System."

35. For the Turks Island and logwood-cutting disputes, see Nolcken's apt comments in RA Dipl. Angl., Nolcken to KP, 24 July 1764; for Sandwich's fear of popular reaction if England did not take a stiff line on them, see Spencer, pp. 197-99. For the view that Sandwich was the only minister capable of facing a war, HMC *Stopford-Sackville*, I:95, Lord George Sackville to General Irwin, 22 August 1764.

36. *Pol. Corr.*, XXIII:288, 338, Frederick to Rohd, 24 February 1764; to Michell, 14 April 1764.

37. *Grenville Papers*, II:171-74, 290-92, Egmont to Grenville, 3 December 1763, 16 April 1764.

38. SP 95/104/106, Sandwich to Goodricke, 22 June 1764.

39. SP 95/104/105-6, Sandwich to Goodricke, 22 June 1764.

40. SP 95/104/97-99, Sandwich to Goodricke, 19 June 1764.

41. SP 91/73/192-93, Sandwich to Buckinghamshire, 19 June 1764.

42. SP 95/104/132-35, Sandwich to Goodricke, 6 July 1764. As late as November, Lovisa Ulrika was inquiring pointedly whether Goodricke had received any reply to her "Pro Memoria": SP 95/105/111-13, Goodricke to Sandwich, 13 November 1764.

43. SP 95/104/165-67.

44. SP 95/104/157-61, Goodricke to Sandwich, 13 July 1764.

45. SP 95/104/190-97, Goodricke to Sandwich, 28 July 1764.

46. *Ibid.*, Löwenhielm is presumably "the great man mentioned in my despatch of 6 June." But Goodricke does not seem to have written any dispatch on 6 June, though he did send one on 8 June. If it is to this that he meant to allude, then the person referred to is Rudbeck, which the context makes unlikely. However, in Add. MS 35,885, fos. 99-101, there is Goodricke's draft of the dispatch of 28 July, and here he writes of "the great man" mentioned in his dispatch of 12 June. If this is what was intended, the reference is to Löwenhielm.

47. Rudbeck's estimate to Osterman was 60,000 plåtar as soon as the summoning of the Diet was proclaimed, of which 20,000 were to go to Sinclair: AVPR 10, Osterman to Catherine 20/31 July 1764. A plåt was worth about 3/-.

48. SP 95/104/190-97. A livre was worth 10d: HMC *Weston-Underwood*, p. 368, Edward Sedgwick, 24 July 1764; cf. Malmström, V:198-99, which gives £1 as equivalent to 23.40 livres.

49. Spencer, pp. 214, 218.

50. SP 95/104/245-48, Sandwich to Goodricke, 11 September 1764.

51. BM Stowe MS 260, fos. 41 ff., Praslin to Breteuil (intercepted), 15 July 1764. Sandwich transmitted this information to Goodricke on 17 August: SP 95/104/181-82.

52. *Grenville Papers*, II:434-35.

53. SP 95/104/249-53, Goodricke to Sandwich, 31 August 1764. The estimates were drawn up by Rudbeck: SP 95/107/27-30, Goodricke to Sandwich, Private, 2 July 1765.

54. For further discussion of this, see below.

55. SP 95/104/256-57, Sandwich to Goodricke, 18 September 1764.

56. SP 95/104/279-82, Sandwich to Goodricke, 21 September 1764.

57. SP 91/74/18-20, Sandwich to Buckinghamshire, 18 September 1764; SP 95/104/279-82, Sandwich to Goodricke, 21 September 1764.

58. AVPR 10, Osterman to Catherine, 27 August/7 September 1764.

59. DRA TKUA Sverige B 150, Schack to Bernstorff, 7 September 1764. Breteuil reported Schack as "au désespoir," fearing that the decision portended reforms of the constitution: RA Malmström avskr., Breteuil to Praslin, 7 September 1764.

60. SP 95/104/267-69, Goodricke to Sandwich, 4 September 1764.

61. SP 95/104/59-62, Goodricke to Sandwich, 4 May 1764.

62. AVPR 10, Osterman to Catherine, 30 April/11 May 1764.

63. *Buckinghamshire Correspondence*, II:188-90, Goodricke to Buckinghamshire, 6 June 1764.

64. SP 95/104/121-25, Goodricke to Sandwich, 15 June 1764; Add. MS 35,885, fos. 99-101, Goodricke to Sandwich (draft), 28 July 1764.

65. SP 95/104/249-53.

66. SP 95/104/256-57, 279-82, Sandwich to Goodricke, 18, 21 September 1764.

67. SP 91/74/18-20, Sandwich to Buckinghamshire, 18 September 1764.

68. SP 95/104/279-82, Sandwich to Goodricke, 21 September 1764.

69. SP 95/105/32-34, Goodricke to Sandwich, 12 October 1764.

70. SP 91/74/111-15, Buckinghamshire to Sandwich, 17 October 1764.

71. SP 95/105/16-18, Sandwich to Goodricke, 12 October 1764.

72. SP 95/105/13-15, Goodricke to Sandwich, 21 September 1764; received 8 October. They gave the money to Rudbeck on the understanding that he should pretend it was his own, with the idea of avoiding a flood of solicitations.

73. AVPR 10, Osterman to Catherine 1/12 October, reporting his request to Goodricke not to give a definite answer; *ibid.*, same to same, 15/26 October, reporting dispatch of Goodricke's Messenger, and the answer Goodricke alleged him to carry. Osterman's version is supported by the undoubted fact that Goodricke did keep the Messenger until the twenty-second, though there was no obvious reason for doing so, apart from the reason which Osterman alleged.

74. SP 95/105/35-36, Sandwich to Goodricke, 6 November 1764.

75. SP 95/105/37-39, Sandwich to Goodricke, 9 November 1764.

76. *SIRIO*, 57:50, Panin to Osterman, 28 October (OS) 1764.

77. In September 1766, Macartney paid 25,000 rubles in presents at a cost of £5,326.0.9, excluding brokerage, which would make the ruble worth about 4/3d: SP 91/75/255.

78. For Jennings & Finlay see K. Samuelsson, *De stora köpmanshusen i Sverige*, passim; Kent, pp. 33-34; K.-G. Hildebrand, "Foreign Markets for Swedish Iron in the 18th Century," p. 30; Arndt Öberg, *De yngre mössorna och deras utländska bundsforvanter 1765-1769*. pp. 44-45, 75; Carl Forsstrand, *Skeppsbroadeln. Minnen och Anteckningar från Gustav III:s Stockholm*, pp. 10, 17, 29 n. 1.; *Svenskt biografiskt lexikon*, XVI (for Finlay), XX (for Jennings). For earlier references by Goodricke to them, SP 75/108/93; 113/65-66; 115/38-39. Colonel Ramsay had written to Christopher Springer already in 1761 urging him to take care that any English minister in Stockholm should avoid contact with them, as being "entirely Frenchified": Jennings's father, he added, "betrayed both Col. Guydickens and you." If Springer passed on the message to Holdernesse then, it seems to have been forgotten: SP 101/93/28, Ramsay to Springer, 3 November 1761.

79. SP 95/105/47, Goodricke to Sandwich, 16 October 1764.

80. SP 95/105/230-31, Goodricke to Phelps, 7 December 1764.

81. Finlay, unlike Jennings, had not turned Lutheran, and so could play no part in politics: SP 95/106/39-40.

82. Jennings is said for a time to have written Pechlin's speeches, since Pechlin could not write or speak Swedish correctly: Hj. Lindeberg, *En ränksmidare*, p. 76. Finlay, too, was Pechlin's brother-in-law.

83. SP 95/105/47. Goodricke had, however, no objection to using the services of Jennings & Finlay as intermediaries between himself and his wife's half-sister in the matter of his brother-in-law's will: RA Dipl. Anglica, Nolcken to KP, 24 September 1764.

84. UUB F 386, Sandwich to Goodricke, 14 December 1764.

85. SP 95/105/230-31, 237, Goodricke to Phelps, 7, 11 December 1764; *Buckinghamshire Correspondence*, II:266, Goodricke to Buckinghamshire, 14 December 1764.

86. SP 95/105/79-81, Sandwich to Goodricke, 20 November 1764; SP 95/105/82-83, Robert Macky to Jennings & Finlay, 20 November 1764. Macky had saved the firm by

advancing £25,000 at the time of the commercial crisis of 1763. For Jennings's definance, SP 95/106/39-40, Goodricke to Sandwich, 15 January 1765.

87. SP 91/74/111-15, Buckinghamshire to Sandwich, 17 October 1764. Cf. Bodley MS Eng. hist. c. 62, fos. 19-20, Buckinghamshire to Goodricke, 17 October (NS) 1764.

88. Panin had made the same point to Solms, the Prussian minister in St. Petersburg, observing that some replacement for the French subsidy must be found, and England must pay for it: *SIRIO*, 22:277-82. Frederick the Great predicted that England would refuse, and that since neither Prussia nor Russia would be able to pay enough, Sweden would in the end fall back on France: *Pol. Corr.*, XXIV:15-16, Frederick to Solms, 18 October 1764. He had made exactly the same point to Lovisa Ulrika in January: *Pol. Corr.*, XXIII:260, Frederick to Lovisa Ulrika, 22 January 1764.

89. *Buckinghamshire Correspondence*, II:241; SP 91/73/281, 310-13, Sandwich to Buckinghamshire, 3, 21 August 1764.

90. SP 91/74/131, Buckinghamshire to Sandwich, 6 November (NS) 1764.

91. SP 91/74/118-21.

92. SP 91/74/107-8, 118-21, 128-29, Sandwich to Buckinghamshire, 13, 20, 30 November 1764; BM Stowe MS 260, fos. 30-31, Sandwich to Buckinghamshire, 21 December, 1764; cf. SP 95/105/77-79, Sandwich to Goodricke, 20 November 1764; UUB F 386, Sandwich to Goodricke, 14 December 1764.

93. See, e.g., *Pol. Corr.*, XXIII:444, n. 4, Cocceji to Frederick, 13 July 1764.

94. As Lovisa Ulrika put it in her Memorial to Goodricke: "Care was taken to make it the foundation of agreement, that the enterprise of the Reform should be absolutely independent of all foreign Politicks: the Contractors even engaged themselves to one another, to keep off all influence of Foreign Powers in these Operations": SP 95/104/112-21, Goodricke to Sandwich, 15 June 1764.

95. RA Malmström avskr., Breteuil to Praslin, 27 November 1764.

96. DRA TKUA Sverige B 150,Schack to Bernstorff, 7, 11, 18 September 1764.

97. *Ibid.*, Schack to Bernstorff, 2 October 1764.

98. RA Malmström avskrifter, Excerpter ur danska ministrarnas i Petersburg depescher, Osten to Bernstorff, 2 October 1764.

99. *Corr. min.*, II:184, Bernstorff to Osten, 27 October 1764. Though A. G. Moltke, for one, still thought the Russian terms were such as Denmark could not accept, and had perhaps been framed with a view to their rejection: *Bernstorffske Papirer*, II:357, Moltke to Bernstorff [6 November 1764].

100. DRA TKUA Sverige B 150, Schack to Bernstorff, 9 October 1764.

101. "Egenhändig uppsats af RiksRådet Grefve C. Fr. Scheffer, angående tillståndet i Riket, näst före början af 1765 års riksdag," *Handlingar rörande Skandinaviens historia*, XVI.

102. DRA TKUA Sverige B 150, Schack to Bernstorff, 30 October 1764; RA Malmström avskr., Breteuil to Praslin, 22 October 1764.

103. DRA TKUA Sverige B 150, Schack to Bernstorff, 30 October 1764.

104. DRA TKUA Sverige B 150, Schack to Bernstorff, 13 November 1764. RA Hemliga rådsprotokoll i flere slag af ärenden, 1761-1766, 12 November 1764: cf. *ibid.*, 30 January 1765; UUB F 386, Sandwich to Goodricke, 14 December 1764.

105. RA Malmström avskr., Breteuil to Praslin, 9 November 1764.

106. *Pol. Corr.*, XXIV:53, Cocceji to Frederick, 13 November 1764.

107. SP 95/105/111-12, Goodricke to Sandwich, 13 November 1764; cf. AVPR 10, Osterman to Catherine, 5/16 November 1764.

108. RA Malmström avskr., Breteuil to Praslin, 9 November 1764; DRA TKUA Sverige B 150, Schack to Bernstorff, 9 November 1764.

109. DRA TKUA Sverige B 150, Schack to Bernstorff, 13 November 1764.

110. *Pol. Corr.*, XXIV:8, Frederick to Solms, 9 October 1764.

111. SP 95/104/275, Goodricke to Sandwich, 11 September 1764. Goodricke seems to have seen Scheffer's letter, or a copy of it.

112. SP 95/104/213-16, Goodricke to Sandwich, 10 August 1764. For the French version of the arrears question, see RA Dipl. Gallica, Franska regeringens noter till Ambassadören Grefwe Creutz, 1766-83, Choiseul to Creutz, 6 June 1766.

113. SP 95/104/265, Goodricke to Sandwich, 7 September. The rejection of the French offer was thus not, as Frederick the Great supposed, the reason for the decision to summon an Extraordinary Diet: *Pol. Corr.*, XXIV:8, Frederick to Solms, 9 October 1764.

114. SP 95/105/60, Goodricke to Sandwich, 22 October 1764.

115. RA Dipl. Gallica, KPs brev til F. U. von Friesendorff, 1764-66, KP to Friesendorff, 9, 16 November 1764; text of Breteuil's declaration is in *Sverges Traktater med främmande Magter*, VIII:886-88.

116. Cf. SP 95/105/60, Goodricke to Sandwich, 22 October 1764.

117. SP 95/105/60, Goodricke to Sandwich, 22 October 1764. The Senate, in the review of foreign affairs presented to the next Diet, argued (implausibly) that there was no danger that France would stop payment of arrears, if Sweden declined to renew the alliance in 1768: RA Mindre Sekreta deputationen, Sekreta Proposition, Utrikes, 1765., fo. 33.

118. Osterman received his 50,000 rubles on 22 November—in time to influence the decision—but he does not seem to have used them: this was after all preeminently an English interest: SP 95/105/129-31, Goodricke to Sandwich, 23 November 1764.

119. For a sketch of the relations between Senate and Estates, see M. Roberts, *Swedish and English parliamentarism in the Eighteenth Century*, pp. 16-20.

120. SP 95/105/120-21, Goodricke to Sandwich, 16 November 1764.

121. SP 95/105/203-7, Breteuil to Praslin (intercepted), 16 November 1764.

122. *Ibid.*, where Breteuil wrongly attributes the protest to "du Bentzel"; SP 95/105/120-21, Goodricke to Sandwich, 16 November 1764.

123. SP 95/105/94-95, 132-34, Goodricke to Sandwich, 6, 23 November 1764.

124. He offered him 50,000 livres: SP 95/106/4-6, Sandwich to Goodricke, Separate and Most Secret, 4 January 1765. BM Stowe MS 260, fos. 47-48, 54-57, Breteuil to Praslin (intercepted), 28 September, 16 November 1764; SP 95/105/43-44, Breteuil to Praslin (intercepted), 9 November 1764; AVPR 10, Osterman to Catherine, 9 November 1764. For Löwenhielm's view, as expressed to Cocceji, *Pol. Corr.*, XXIV:48, Cocceji to Frederick, 6 November 1764.

125. SP 95/105/134, Goodricke to Sandwich, 23 November 1765; cf. HMC *Weston-Underwood*, p. 380, Edward Sedgwick to Weston, 25 December 1764. For Goodricke's account of the final vote, SP 95/105/215-17, 30 November 1764; and cf. DRA TKUA Sverige B 150, Schack to Bernstorff, 27 November 1764; RA Malmström avskr., Breteuil to Praslin, 27 November 1764.

126. DRA TKUA Sverige B 150, Schack to Bernstorff, 27 November 1764.

127. RA Diplomatica, Gallica, KP to Friesendorff, 30 November 1764. *Sverges Traktater*, VIII:888-89.

128. RA Diplomatica, Anglica, Nolcken to KP, 1 January 1765.

129. RA Malmström avskr., Breteuil to Praslin, 28 June 1764; AVPR 10, Osterman to Catherine, 21 May/1 June, 15/26 June 1764.

130. SP 95/105/9-11, Goodricke to Sandwich, 21 September 1764; AVPR 10, Osterman to Catherine, 25 September 1764.

131. SP 105/108-10, 120-21 Goodricke to Sandwich, 13, 16 November 1764; AVPR 10, Osterman to Catherine, 15/26 October 1764.

132. Metcalf, pp. 101-2.

133. SP 95/105/103-5, Goodricke to Sandwich, 9 November 1764.

134. *Pol. Corr.*, XXIV:53.

135. SP 95/105/132-34, Goodricke to Sandwich, 23 November 1764.

136. Cf. Juel's report of an occasion when Adolf Fredrik stormed out of the Senate in "one of those moments of vivacity which are natural to him, and put him into a kind of fury which even the Queen does not venture to resist": DRA TKUA Sverige B 160, Juel to Bernstorff, 12 May 1767.

137. RA Kungl. arkivet 259, Lovisa Ulrika to Frederick, 12 February 1765: "At the moment when I had most to hope for, everything went against me." For a later (1771) account by a Court partisan of the queen's motives during this crisis, see RA Stavsunds arkivet, "Pro Memoria, 1771," fos. 14-17; for a contemporary one, RA Kungl. arkiv 259, N. Ph. Gyldenstolpe to C. W. von Düben, 30 November 1764.

138. AVPR 10, Osterman to Catherine, 19/30 November 1764.

139. RA Malmström avskr., Breteuil to Praslin, 27 November 1764.

140. DRA TKUA Sverige B 150, Schack to Bernstorff, 27 November 1764.

141. RA Kungl. arkiv. 259, [N. F. Gyldenstolpe] to C. W. von Düben, 30 November 1764; Malmström, V:248, n. 2. Lovisa Ulrika's real opinion of Osterman was expressed in a letter to Frederick (undated: ?January 1765) where she calls him "une bonne dupe," who "croit bonnement tout les conte de peau danne que l'on lui fait et les rend fidellement à Sa **Cour** cest un malheur que meme cette Cour a fait dun ministre aussi bornée"[*sic*]: RA Kungl. arkiv 259.

142. AVPR 10, Osterman to Catherine, 26 November/7 December 1764.

143. *Ibid.* For a discussion of the various versions of this manifesto, and its significance, see Brolin, Exkurs III, pp. 435-37; Metcalf, p. 109.

144. DRA TKUA Sverige B 150, Schack to Bernstorff, 3 July 1764.

145. AVPR 10, Osterman to Catherine, 8/19 June 1764.

146. DRA TKUA Sverige B 150, Schack to Bernstorff, 7 September 1764.

147. *Ibid.*, 18 September 1764.

148. *Ibid.*, 21 September 1764.

149. BM Stowe MS 260, fos. 47-48, Breteuil to Praslin, 28 September 1764.

150. RA Malmström avskr., Breteuil to Praslin, 22 October 1764; cf. SP 95/105/60, Goodricke to Sandwich, 22 October 1764. But in the same dispatch Breteuil mentioned that he had in fact spent the relatively insignificant sum of 17,000 livres on the Stockholm election.

151. AVPR 10, Osterman to Catherine, 20/31 July, 15/26 October 1764.

152. For the Stockholm elections in general, see Brolin, pp. 25-31, 52, 107, 138-40; Bertil Boëthius, *Magistraten och Borgerskapet i Stockholm 1719-1815*, pp. 303-7, 333. For Goodricke's reports on the progress of the election, SP 95/104/274-75; 105/13-15, 21-23, Goodricke to Sandwich, 11, 21, 28 September.

153. For Kierman, see Brolin, pp. 67-69, 404. Goodricke reported that Kierman's family were offering as much as £120 to burgomasters for their interest: SP 95/104/274-75, Goodricke to Sandwich, 11 September 1764.

154. AVPR 10, Osterman to Catherine, 15/26 October 1764.

155. DRA TKUA Sverige B 150, Schack to Bernstorff, 9 November 1764.

156. SP 95/105/121, Goodricke to Sandwich, 16 November 1764.

157. SP 95/105/124-27, Goodricke to Sandwich, 20 November 1764. A Swedish crown was worth about 5/-: Malmström, V:241, n. 1.

158. DRA TKUA Sverige B 150, Schack to Bernstorff, 30 October, 9 November 1764.

159. *Ibid.*, 30 October 1764, reporting (skeptically) Breteuil.

160. *Ibid.*, 9 November 1764. The only basis for the story was that Goodricke had raised the possibility of Sweden's floating a loan on the English money market, guaranteed by the

British government: Sandwich had replied that there might be no objection, once the French system had been overthrown: SP 95/104/283-84, Goodricke to Sandwich, 14 September 1764; 95/105/5, Sandwich to Goodricke, 5 October 1764. Adolf Fredrik seems to have believed that England planned "to ruin all the Swedish Manufactures, and to introduce their own"—a suspicion much nearer to the truth: SP 95/105/122, Goodricke to Sandwich, 16 November 1764.

161. See UUB F 279, "Handlingar till Sveriges politiska historia, 1756-1772," fos. 462 ff. The Hats also made play with stories that Prussia wanted to buy Swedish Pomerania, and that Russia was blockading Swedish ports: Amburger, p. 115.

162. *Buckinghamshire Correspondence*, II:184, Sir Joseph Yorke to Buckinghamshire, 15 May 1764.

163. His last petition to retire to England was drawn on 27 July 1764, and was enclosed in Goodricke's dispatch of 28 July: SP 95/104/210-11: in reply he got a pretty cool *nihil obstat: ibid.*, 104/220-21.

164. SP 95/105/51-53, Goodricke to Sandwich, 16 October 1764.

165. RA Kabinettet för utrikes brevvexling, KP to Nolcken, 16 October 1764; RA Dipl. Angl., Nolcken to KP, 6 November 1764.

166. RA Dipl. Danica, Sprengtporten to KP, 25 October 1764.

167. RA Dipl. Danica, Sprengtporten to KP, 11, 18 November 1764.

168. RA Dipl. Angl., Nolcken to KP, 15, 22 January 1765.

169. RA Dipl. Angl., Nolcken to KP, 12 March 1765; RA Ekebladska samlingen., Bref till Claes Ekeblad, vol. II, Charles Gedda to Claes Ekeblad, 18 February 1765.

170. Trolle-Bonde, *Anteckningar om Bondesläkten*, I:103; RA Dipl. Angl., Nolcken to KP, 12, 29 March 1765. His pension of £200 per annum seems to have been continued. As late as October Nolcken reported that Gedda still had free access to the Secretary of State's office, and that his letters continued to be forwarded to him in the diplomatic bag: Nolcken to KP (Private), 4 October 1765.

171. SP 95/105/217-18, Goodricke to Sandwich, 30 November 1764.

172. SP 95/105/129-31, Goodricke to Sandwich, 23 November 1764.

173. Add. MS 35,425, fo. 138, Goodricke to Royston, 25 March 1759.

174. SP 95/105/73-76, Goodricke to Sandwich, 30 October 1764.

175. *Buckinghamshire Correspondence*, II:252-53, Goodricke to Buckinghamshire, 9 November 1764.

176. SP 95/105/241-42, Goodricke to Sandwich, 18 December 1764; AVPR 10, Osterman to Catherine, 10/21 December 1764.

177. SP 95/105/241-42, Goodricke to Sandwich, 18 December 1764.

178. SP 95/105/235-36, Goodricke to Sandwich, 11 December 1764.

179. SP 95/105/92-93, Goodricke to Sandwich, 6 November 1764.

180. AVPR 10, Osterman to Catherine, 10/21 December 1764.

181. SP 91/74/163, Buckinghamshire to Sandwich, 4 December (NS) 1764. *SIRIO*, 57:57, Panin to Osterman, 31 October, 11 November 1764.

182. AVPR 10, Osterman to Catherine, 3/14 December 1764, with Panin's comment that such things could not be helped. Frederick the Great had applauded Panin for refusing, and instructed Solms to tell Panin that he would never get anything worthwhile out of the existing English ministry: *Pol. Corr.*, XXIV:38, Frederick to Solms, 7 November 1764.

183. *Pol. Corr.*, XXIII:162, Frederick to Lovisa Ulrika, 31 October 1763.

184. RA Malmström avskr., Breteuil to Praslin, 21 December 1764. But he also conceded that he was the best head at the Court's disposal.

185. AVPR 10, Osterman to Catherine, 29 October/9 November 1764.

186. SP 95/105/102-5, 129-31, Goodricke to Sandwich, 9 November, 23 November 1764; AVPR 10, Osterman to Catherine, 29 October/9 November 1764.

187. AVPR 10, Osterman to Catherine, 10/21 December 1764.

188. AVPR 10, Osterman to Catherine, 23 October/3 November 1764. C. W. Von Düben in St. Petersburg had warned her as early as August 1764 that Catherine would never tolerate this: RA Kungl. arkiv 259, C. W. von Düben to N. Ph. Gyldenstolpe, 20/31 August 1764.

189. DRA TKUA Sverige B 150, Schack to Bernstorff, 30 October 1764.

190. SP 95/105/243-44, Goodricke to Sandwich, 18 December 1764; AVPR 10, Osterman to Catherine, 3/14 December 1764. The members were Sinclair and Col. Ribbing, for the Court; Rudbeck, Funck, Durietz, Ridderstolpe, and Gyllensvan, for the Caps.

191. SP 95/105/246-47, Goodricke to Sandwich, 25 December 1764; AVPR 10, Osterman to Catherine, 10/21, 17/28 December 1764; RA Malmström avskr., Breteuil to Praslin, 21 December 1764. For a detailed account of Cap finances, Goodricke's and Osterman's contributions, and the problem of Sinclair, see Metcalf, chap. 5 and passim.

192. This is the general thesis of Jägerskiöld in his *Hovet och författningsfrågan*, pp. 183-84, and his *Lovisa Ulrika*, pp. 240 ff.

193. *Pol. Corr.*, XXIV:80, Frederick to Lovisa Ulrika, 27 December 1764.

194. RA Malmström avskr., Breteuil to Praslin, 11 January 1765.

195. DRA TKUA Sverige B 152, Schack to Bernstorff, 11 January 1765.

196. RA Malmström avskr., Breteuil to Praslin, 11 January 1765; intercepted and its substance forwarded to Goodricke in SP 95/106/60-64, Sandwich to Goodricke, Separate and Secret, 12 February 1765. For a benevolent view of the queen's policy, see Jägerskiöld, *Hovet och författningsfrågan*, pp. 259-62, 264-65, 268-73.

197. SP 95/106/23-24, Goodricke to Sandwich, 8 January 1765.

198. AVPR 10, Osterman to Catherine, 11/22 January 1765; SP 95/106/32-34, Goodricke to Sandwich, Most Secret, 11 January 1765; and see Metcalf, p. 116.

199. RA Malmström avskr., Breteuil to Praslin, 20 January 1765.

200. *SIRIO*, 57:126 ff., rescript for Osterman, 29 November/9 December 1764.

201. RA Malmström avskr., Breteuil to Praslin, 11 January 1765.

202. SP 95/106/36-38, Goodricke to Sandwich, 15 January 1765: Metcalf, pp. 114-17.

203. RA Malmström avskr., Breteuil to Praslin, 20 January 1765. Goodricke had already reported that Sinclair had given 7 proxies to the Gyllenborgs: SP 95/106/32-34, 11 January 1765.

204. *Tessin och Tessiniana*, p. 207.

205. DRA TKUA Sverige B 152, Schack to Bernstorff, 29 January 1765.

206. RA Malmström avskr., Breteuil to Praslin, 20 January 1765.

207. SP 91/73/295-99, Sandwich to Buckinghamshire, 14 August 1764; SP 91/74/58, same to same, 12 October 1764; SP 91/74/142-43, Buckinghamshire to Sandwich, 13 November NS 1764; RA Kabinettet för utrikes brevvexling, KP to Düben, 23, 30 November 1764; AVPR 10, Osterman to Catherine, 19/30 November 1764.

208. *SIRIO*, 57:126 ff., rescript for Osterman, 29 November/9 December 1764.

209. AVPR 10, Osterman to Catherine, 11/22 January 1765. But Goodricke reported that if Stakhiev (shortly expected as coadjutor to Osterman) had been declared persona non grata in Sweden, Catherine might have taken action: SP 95/106/51-53, Goodricke to Sandwich, 22 January 1765.

210. SP 95/106/95-97, Goodricke to Sandwich, 29 January 1765.

211. SP 95/106/92, Goodricke to Sandwich, 25 January 1765. The Caps won 52 out of the 58 benches, and made a clean sweep of the electors: SP 95/106/95-97.

212. Goodricke's list included 7 Hats among the 50 representatives of the Nobility, and four members of the Court party: SP 95/106/80 ff., in Goodricke to Sandwich, 2 February 1765.

213. Metcalf's detailed analysis makes it clear that Breteuil had at his disposal far more

money than Goodricke and Osterman combined, and that he actually spent more than they did; his conclusion is that "the Hats' utter defeat had cost more than the Caps' total victory," and that foreign money had little influence on the composition of the Diet of 1765-66: Metcalf, pp. 140-41.

214. Soon after arriving in Sweden, Goodricke detected three sections of the Hats: one, led by Fersen; another, by General Ehrensvärd; a third, consisting of the Gyllenborg family: SP 95/104/80, Goodricke to Sandwich, 15 May 1764.

215. Brolin, p. 47 and passim; Tom Söderberg, *Den namnlöse medelklassen. Socialgrupp två i det gamla svenska samhället*, pp. 169-73.

216. AVPR 10, Osterman to Catherine, 24 September/5 October 1764, reporting Breteuil's conversation with Löwenhielm.

217. One reason for this may be that Osterman, until the very end of the year, was hamstrung by lack of clear instructions. DRA TKUA Sverige B 152, Schack to Bernstorff, 1 January 1765. Bernstorff clearly considered the election results as an English, and not a Russian, victory: DRA TKUA England C 267, Bernstorff to Bothmer, 16 February 1765.

218. DRA TKUA Sverige B 152, Schack to Bernstorff, 1 February 1765.

219. BM Stowe MS 260, fos. 54-57, Breteuil to Praslin (intercepted), 16 November 1764.

220. DRA TKUA Sverige B 150, Schack to Bernstorff, 7 August 1764.

221. RA Malmström avskr., Breteuil to Praslin, 26 October 1764.

222. DRA TKUA Sverige B 150, Schack to Bernstorff, 10 July 1764; and cf. *ibid.*, same to same, 28 September 1764.

223. DRA TKUA Sverige C 321, Bernstorff to Schack, 13 October 1764. A similar eulogy, with orders to do everything possible in Goodricke's favor, was sent to Bothmer, the Danish minister in London: DRA TKUA England C 267, Bernstorff to Bothmer, 13 October 1764.

224. DRA TKUA Sverige B 150, Schack to Bernstorff, 23 October 1764.

225. DRA TKUA Sverige B 152, Schack to Bernstorff, 1 January 1765.

226. For Nebb's pasties, see Nils Erdmann, *Carl Michael Bellman. EnKultur- och karaktärsbild fran 1700-talet*, p. 132.

227. DRA TKUA Sverige B 152, Schack to Bernstorff, 29 January 1765.

228. *Tessin och Tessiniana*, p. 207.

229. SP 95/105/46, Goodricke to Sandwich, 16 October 1764; Brolin, p. 302. And see SP 95/134, "Narrative of Mr Jno Fenwick's situation, and the principal causes of it," 14 November 1767.

230. Add. MS 35,367, fo. 300, Sir Joseph Yorke to Lord Hardwicke, 31 May 1765.

231. SP 95/106/56, Sandwich to Goodricke, 8 February 1765; HMC *Weston-Underwood*, pp. 382-83: "Sr J G has work'd Miracles at Stockholm": Edward Sedgwick to Weston, 21 February 1765.

232. RA Dipl. Angl., Nolcken to KP, 4 December 1764.

233. Bodley MS Eng. hist. c. 62, Sandwich to Goodricke, Private, 27 November 1764.

CHAPTER IV
LORD SANDWICH IN SEARCH OF A POLICY

1. SP 95/106/1-3, Sandwich to Goodricke, 4 January 1765.

2. Probably on 23 or 24 January: Osterman did not mention Sandwich's refusal in his dispatch of 22 January; Goodricke acknowledged the arrival of the letter on 25 January: AVPR 9, Osterman to Catherine, 11/22 January 1765; SP 95/106/87-89, Goodricke to Sandwich, 25 January 1765.

3. SP 95/106/89, Goodricke to Sandwich, 25 January 1765.

4. SP 107/104/18-22, Gross to Catherine, 24 December/4 January 1765 (intercepted and deciphered).

5. SP 95/106/4-6, Sandwich to Goodricke, Separate and Most Secret, 4 January 1765.

6. SP 95/106/13-15, Sandwich to Goodricke, 15 January 1765.

7. SP 95/106/18-20, Goodricke to Sandwich, 4 January 1765.

8. SP 95/106/13-15.

9. SP 95/106/100-103, Sandwich to Goodricke, 19 February 1765.

10. *SIRIO*, 57 no. 1099, rescript to Gross, 13/24 November 1764; *ibid*., p. 124, Panin to Osterman, 5/16 December 1764.

11. *SIRIO*, 57:126 ff., rescript to Osterman, 9/20 December 1764.

12. For Panin's Northern System, see below.

13. *SIRIO*, 57, no. 1099.

14. PRO N[orthern] I[reland], T 2513, Sandwich to Macartney, 15 January 1765.

15. SP 95/106/100-103, Sandwich to Goodricke, 19 February 1765.

16. SP 91/75/75-77: Sandwich to Macartney, 26 February 1765.

17. SP 91/74/32, 34, 42-47, Buckinghamshire to Sandwich, 31 August, 4 and 8 September 1764; SP 95/105/129-31, Goodricke to Sandwich, 23 November 1764.

18. SP 91/73/294, Buckinghamshire to Sandwich, Most Secret, 20 July 1764.

19. SP 91/74/42-47, Buckinghamshire to Sandwich, Most Secret, 8 September 1764.

20. SP 91/73/111-15, Buckinghamshire to Sandwich, 17 October 1764.

21. SP 95/105/92-93, Goodricke to Sandwich, 6 November 1764.

22. SP 95/105/253-54, Goodricke to Sandwich, 31 December 1764.

23. SP 91/75/19-20, Buckinghamshire to Sandwich, 1 January 1765.

24. SP 95/104/256-57, 105/98-99, Sandwich to Goodricke, 18 September, 30 November 1764; SP 91/74/120, Sandwich to Buckinghamshire, 20 November 1764; BM Stowe MS 260, fos. 30-31, same to same (draft), 21 December 1764.

25. SP 107/104/18.

26. *SIRIO*, 22:116, Solms to Frederick, 29 August/ 9 September 1763; and see Frederick's comment, *Pol. Corr.*, XXIII, 133 (to Solms, 27 September 1763).

27. SP 91/74/42-47.

28. SP 95/106/18-20, Goodricke to Sandwich, 4 January 1765.

29. For Sandwich's attitude to Denmark, see SP 75/117/223, Sandwich to Cosby, 20 November 1764; SP 95/105/100-102, Sandwich to Goodricke, 30 November 1764; and Roberts, "Great Britain, Denmark and Russia, 1763-1770," pp. 236-67.

30. Gross reported that Sandwich was prepared to pay Russia a subsidy of 500,000 rubles a year for the duration of any war with the Turks, if Russia would do the same in the case of an Anglo-Spanish war: this seems so improbable that Gross must have misunderstood him.

31. SP 107/104-18. "He approved your Intention of making Denmark an Active, and Sweden a passive, power,"

32. PRO NI T 2513, Sandwich to Macartney, 15 January 1765.

33. SP 95/106/170-74, Sandwich to Goodricke, 9 April 1765.

34. *SIRIO*, 57, no. 1083, Panin to Osterman, 31 October/11 November 1764.

35. Cf. DRA TKUA Sverige B 152, Schack to Bernstorff, 8 March 1765, and *ibid*., same to same, 19 March 1765, where he writes that the only parties possible in Sweden are a French and an English: "dans toutes les familles depuis la première noblesse jusques aux Paysans les plus pauvres, l'amitié ou la Haine pour Elles succéda depuis tant de générations qu'on ne connoit presque en Suède que ces deux Cours-là dès qu'il s'agit d'Intérêts politiques; chaque Particulier pour ainsi dire croit sa Fortune attaché à la leur, et les choses en sont venues au Point qu'on sçait et qu'on se dit assez publiquement qu'un tel est Pensionnaire de la France ou de l'Angleterre."

36. SP 95/105/253-54, Goodricke to Sandwich, 31 December 1764.

37. As Goodricke wrote: "I cannot but allow Mr Panin's notions with regard to each Nation forming her own party to be right enough; but he would have obtained more from our Court if he had declared at once—we will spend £15,000 if you will spend as much and in case these £30,000 will not do the business I will engage the Empress to add what more shall be necessary—by this way we should have been brought in, but the talking of an unlimited sum frighted our Ministry from entering into the Plan": PRO NI T 2513, Goodricke to Macartney, 21 June 1765.

38. For this see Roberts, *Macartney in Russia*, passim, and *idem*, *Splendid Isolation* passim.

39. See the historiographical discussion in Knud Rahbek-Schmidt, "Wie ist Panins Plan zu einem Nordischen System entstanden?", pp. 406-22. And see David M. Griffiths, "The Rise and Fall of the Northern System: Court Politics and Foreign Policy in the First Half of Catherine II's Reign," pp. 549-53; and Metcalf, pp. 46-63.

40. Sabathier de Cabres, *Catherine II, sa Cour et la Russie*, p. 80.

41. *SIRIO*, 22:316-17, Solms to Frederick, 7/18 September 1764.

42. *Corr. min.* II:188, Bernstorff to Osten, 1 December 1764; SP 91/75/52, Sandwich to Macartney, 19 February 1765.

43. *Buckinghamshire Correspondence*, II:183, Sir J. Yorke to Buckinghamshire, 15 May 1764.

44. *SIRIO*, 22:168, Solms to Frederick, 25 November/6 December 1763.

45. *Pol. Corr.*, XXIII, 226, XXIV, 126, Frederick to Solms, 23 December 1763, 19 February 1765, when he wrote that he could not comply with Panin's request that he renew his alliance with England without "prostituting myself in the eyes of Europe."

46. *Pol. Corr.*, XXIII, 385, Frederick to Solms, 14 May 1764.

47. *SIRIO*, 22:241, Solms to Frederick 17/28 April 1764, reporting Panin's exposition of his System; *SIRIO*, 57, no. 1089, rescript to Gross, 10/21 November 1764.

48. *SIRIO*, 22:271-72, Solms to Frederick, 13/24 July 1764; *Pol. Corr.*, XXIII, 486, Solms to Frederick, 25 August 1764.

49. Spencer, p. 88, Sandwich to Count William Bentinck, 18 October 1763.

50. "Mr Grenville said [to George III], the greatness of the King of Prussia's situation could never be but temporary; that England and France, being the two greatest powers of Europe, would ever be courted by Russia and Prussia, and in proportion as the one got in closer alliance with France, it would throw the other into the scale of England": *Grenville Papers*, II:533 (17 December 1764); for Sandwich's views to the same effect, SP 91/73/33, Sandwich to Buckinghamshire 20 January; and Spencer, p. 130.

51. As Sir Joseph Yorke put it: "I am sure however that without we do preserve a certain influence upon the Continent, we cannot maintain the Peace we always fight for and purchase": HMC *Weston-Underwood*, pp. 364-65, Sir J. Yorke to Weston, 25 May 1764.

52. ***The Annual Register***, 1765, p. 6: "In short, Europe seems, in general, to wear a much more serene appearance, than from history there is any reason to judge she ever did."

53. RA Mindre sekreta deputationen, Riksdagsberättelser 1765, Baron G. A. von Nolckens riksdagsberättelse, fos. 70-75.

54. Richard Rigby, e.g., whose remarks in Amsterdam were reported by Thulemeyer to Frederick, *Pol. Corr.*, XXIII, 458, Frederick to Solms, 6 August 1764.

55. SP 91/74/120, Sandwich to Buckinghamshire, 20 November 1764.

56. SP 91/74/114, Buckinghamshire to Sandwich, 17 October 1764.

57. Spencer, p. 169.

58. BM Stowe MS 260, fos. 115-17, Sandwich to Stormont (draft), 8 January 1765.

59. As Frederick clearly saw: *Pol. Corr.*, XXIV, 253 (to Rohd, 16 July 1765); and see A. R. von Arneth, *Geschichte Maria Theresias*, VIII:7, 9, 12-13, 17, 20-21, 119-20.

60. SP 91/72/231-32, Buckinghamshire to Sandwich, 23 November 1763; *ibid.*, 72/237, 74/3-4 Sandwich to Buckinghamshire, 20 December 1763, 7 September 1764; BM Stowe MS 260, fo. 127, Sandwich to Macartney (draft), 15 January 1765.

61. RA Dipl. Angl., Nolcken to KP, 12 October 1764; SP 90/83/43, 52-55, 72-75, 92-93/116-18, for this affair.

62. BM Stowe MS 260, fo. 117, Sandwich to Stormont (draft), 8 January 1764.

63. SP 91/74/131, Buckinghamshire to Sandwich, 6 November 1764.

64. SP 95/106/18-20, Goodricke to Sandwich, 4 January 1765.

65. SP 95/106/82-83, Goodricke to Sandwich, 2 February 1765.

66. PRO NI T 2513, Goodricke to Macartney, 1 February 1765.

67. SP 95/104/165-67, Sandwich to Goodricke, 3 August 1764.

68. SP 95/104/231-33, 241-44; 105/86-91.

69. SP 75/117/227-29, Memorandum on the State of the Danish Navy. It appears from an endorsement that Bothmer supplemented the memorandum with verbal information.

70. SP 75/117/230-31, Sandwich to Cosby, 30 November 1764.

71. SP 75/118/68-79, Cosby to Sandwich, 23 February 1765.

72. SP 91/74/118, Sandwich to Buckinghamshire, 20 November 1764.

73. SP 91/75/26-29, Sandwich to Macartney, 15 February 1765 (my italics).

74. *Svenska Flottans Historia*, II:187.

75. SP 95/105/56-59, Goodricke to Sandwich, 20 October 1764. Goodricke listed Aleppins, Shaloons, Norwich stuffs, Coventry ribbons and Tammies, Scotch and Irish linens, Hardware of all sorts, cotton velvets and other Manchester goods, cabinet ware and all sorts of furniture, Hats, stockings and knit waistcoats, and breeches.

76. Staffan Högberg, *Utrikeshandel och sjöfart på 1700-talet. Stapelvaror i svensk export 1738-1808*, pp. 28-29.

77. Arndt Öberg, *De yngre mössorna och deras utländska bundsförvanter 1765-1769*, pp. 48-60.

78. Boëthius and Heckscher, p. lvi; Kent, p. 59.

79. Hildebrand, 'Foreign Markets for Swedish Iron,'' p. 12; Kent, p. 80; Högberg, p. 150.

80. Kent, pp. 11, 76.

81. *Ibid.*, p. 34.

82. SP 95/134, Navy Board to Admiralty, 23 June 1769.

83. Though in 1761 the Navy Board refused to buy Öregrund iron because it considered the price too high. It seems to have been temporarily forced up because Jennings & Finlay, and C. & C. Grill, had between them effected a corner in it: K.-G. Hildebrand, *Fagerstabrukens historia*, I:124-25.

84. Swedish pitch and tar were "of such high quality that even heavily subsidised imports from America could not drive them out of the English market": Kent, p. 80, and *ibid.*, p. 83, for their being necessary to the navy.

85. *Ibid.*, p. 34.

86. For *Jernkontoret*, see Bertil Boëthius and Åke Kromnow, *Jernkontorets historia*, vol. I.

87. K. Samuelsson, *De stora köpmanshusen i Stockholm 1730-1815*, p. 10: Öberg, pp. 42-44.

88. Samuelsson, p. 74.

89. SP 95/115/97-98, Goodricke to Rochford, 11 August 1769. Hildebrand, however, suggests that this generally accepted picture may need some modification: *Fagerstabrukens historia*, I:187-88.

90. SP 95/105/180-84 (statistics from the Board of Trade, December 1764); Elizabeth Boody Schumpeter, *English Overseas Trade Statistics, 1697-1808* pp. 17-18; Boëthius and Heckscher, p. lvi; Höpken, II:678, n. 1; Erik Zettersten, *Om allmänna handels Historien och Wetenskapen*, p. 252.

91. Dr. Solander had in 1764 attempted to attract Matthew Boulton: see *Calendar of Home Office Papers (1760-65)*, pp. 414, 420-21, 517, 527, 601; RA Diplomatica Anglica, Nolcken to KP, 19 April, 12 July 1765; Kabinettet för utrikes brevvexling, KP to Nolcken, 22 March. The famous exploit of C. B. Wadström, who stole the secret of making Solingen blades, was to justify the anxiety of British officials; for this, see Ellen Hagen, *En frihetstidens son. Carl Bernhard Wadström.*

92. Kent, pp. 110-11.

93. SP 95/105/140-83, Hillsborough to Sandwich, 10 December 1764.

94. The defective records of the Board of Trade, as revealed by this investigation, probably led to the issue of a circular in January 1765 reminding all English diplomats of their duty to return trade statistics: SP 95/106/16.

95. SP 95/105/139, Sandwich to Goodricke, 14 December, 1764.

96. Öberg, passim. Having persuaded himself that Sandwich's main interest in Sweden was economic, it seemed clear to Öberg that he must have sent Goodricke instructions on the basis of Hillsborough's report. And as he apparently did not notice the brief postscript in which Sandwich transmitted that report on 14 December, he ingeniously constructed a "missing" instruction from Sandwich, supposed to have been sent at about the New Year, to which Goodricke's dispatch of 1 February was the answer. It seems highly unlikely that such instruction ever existed anywhere outside Öberg's imagination (Öberg, p. 87).

97. SP 95/106/65-67, Goodricke to Sandwich, 1 February 1765.

98. SP 95/106/72-75, Goodricke to Sandwich, Most Secret, 1 February 1765.

99. SP 95/106/223, Goodricke to Sandwich, 9 April 1765.

100. SP 107/104/29-34, Osterman to Gross, 24 December/4 January 1765, (intercepted and deciphered).

101. BM Stowe 260, fo. 164, Gross to Sandwich, 14 February 1765.

102. SP 95/106/100-103, Sandwich to Goodricke, 19 February 1765.

103. *SIRIO*, 57:420, Panin to Osterman, 7/18 February 1765.

104. *Pol. Corr.*, XXIV, 139, n. 5, Solms to Frederick, 19 February 1765.

105. *SIRIO*, 57:420, Panin to Osterman, 7/18 February 1765.

106. SP 95/106/106-7, Sandwich to Goodricke, 19 February 1765.

107. It may not have been without significance that on 16 February Sandwich received word from Buckinghamshire that Russia would spend a further 50,000 rubles in Sweden if the prospects seemed to warrant it: SP 91/75/38-39. Under-Secretary Weston was profoundly skeptical about the chances of getting a treaty without a subsidy: HMC *Weston-Underwood*, p. 384. So was Catherine II, who commented on Osterman's report that Goodricke had been ordered to obtain a treaty without a subsidy, "apparemment pour leurs beaux yeux": *SIRIO*, 57:232, 8 April [OS] 1765. Goodricke remained optimistic: he wrote privately to Macartney that he was confident he could carry the treaty provided he had enough money for bribery: "I see plainly that this last [Russia] is determined to pull down the French in Sweden and will take it ill of us if we do not concurr as heartily as they expect . . . it is vain to reason with them about the difference between what comes out of the King's private purse and what is granted by parliament": PRO NI T 2513, Goodricke to Macartney, 12 April 1765. But he was mistaken in believing that Russia's *main* object in Sweden was to overturn the French party: SP 95/106/142: to Sandwich, 8 March.

108. SP 95/106/163-64, 248-49, Goodricke to Sandwich, 14 March, 30 April 1765: contrast Metcalf, p. 211.

109. Öberg, p. 91.

110. SP 95/106/72-75, Goodricke to Sandwich, Most Secret, 1 February 1765.

111. SP 91/75/202-3, Sandwich to Macartney, 9 April 1765.

112. SP 95/106/250-52, Goodricke to Sandwich, 4 May 1765.

113. *SIRIO*, 22:387, Solms to Frederick, 8/19 July 1765. Macartney had already correctly reported that Catherine was much irritated by France and Austria: BM Stowe 260, fos. 193-98, Macartney to Sandwich, 1/12 March 1765.

114. SP 91/75/302, Macartney to Sandwich, 19/30 July 1765; 76/188-90, Macartney to Grafton, 8/19 August 1765; "Ostens Gesandtskaber," pp. 593-94; *SIRIO*, 20:215-18, 222, 229; SP 90/84/227, Burnet to Grafton, 7 September 1765; SP 91/76/250, Macartney to Grafton, 9/20 September 1765.

115. SP 95/106/170-74, Sandwich to Goodricke, 9 April 1765.

116. SP 95/106/250, Goodricke to Sandwich, 4 May 1765.

117. *Ibid.* Macartney had already reported receiving hints that an English concession on the Turkish clause might facilitate his own commercial negotiations: BM Stowe 260, fos. 193-98.

118. SP 95/106/248-49, Goodricke to Sandwich, 30 April 1765: the text of the treaty of 1741 is enclosed in Goodricke to Sandwich, 4 May 1765, SP 95/106/267-69. Sandwich conveniently forgot that the treaty of 1720 had expired in 1738.

119. SP 95/106/251, Goodricke to Sandwich, 4 May 1765. This idea was much canvassed by anti-English elements, including the king: SP 95/105/122, Goodricke to Sandwich, 16 November 1764.

120. RA Diplomatica, Anglica, Nolcken to KP, 17 May 1765, 14 June 1765; SP 95/107/33-34.

121. RA Kabinettet för utrikes brevvexling, KP to Nolcken, 2 July 1765; SP 95/107/33-34, Goodricke to Sandwich, 5 July 1765.

122. *Calendar of Home Office Papers, 1760-65*, pp. 553-54, Sandwich to the Lords of Trade, 29 May 1765.

123. BM Stowe 261, fo. 135, Hillsborough to Phelps, 7 May [*sic: sc.* June] 1765.

124. *Calendar of Home Office Papers*, p. 558, Lords of Trade to Sandwich, 11 June 1765.

125. BM Stowe 261, fo. 66, Cabinet Minute in Sandwich's hand, 12 June 1765; cf. Ian R. Christie, "The Cabinet during the Grenville Administration 1763-1765," p. 89.

126. SP 95/106/304-6, Sandwich to Goodricke, 14 June 1765, enclosing a précis of England's treaties with Sweden, 1654-1720 (fos. 309-10).

127. SP 95/107/27-30, Goodricke to Sandwich, 2 July 1765. He had received full powers already, on 25 April: SP 95/106/243.

128. SP 95/106/251, Goodricke to Sandwich, 4 May 1765.

129. SP 95/107/38-39, Goodricke to Sandwich, 9 July 1765.

130. SP 95/106/251-54, Goodricke to Sandwich, 4 May 1765.

131. Goodricke had warned Sandwich on 1 February that France would stop payment if Sweden did not renew the alliance in 1768: SP 95/106/72-76.

132. SP 91/75/19-20, Buckinghamshire to Sandwich, 1 January NS 1765; SP 91/75/57-59, 220, Macartney to Sandwich, 18/29 January, 28 March/8 April 1765; cf. UUB F 386, Macartney to Goodricke, 28 May 1765.

133. Breteuil had reported that Russia had promised to pay the French arrears if Sweden would abandon France. This dispatch was intercepted and deciphered by the Secret Office, and may well have influenced Sandwich: SP 95/106/279-82, Sandwich to Goodricke, 28 May 1765.

134. UUB F 386, Macartney to Goodricke, 28 May 1765.

135. They were as wholeheartedly in favor of bounties on exports of Swedish manufactures as ever the Hats had been: see *SRARP*, XXIV:604-8.

136. SP 95/106/274-76, 277-78, Goodricke to Sandwich, 7 May 1765, Sandwich to Goodricke 24 May 1765; RA Kabinettet för utrikes brevvexling, KP to Nolcken, 10 May, 9 June 1765; Diplomatica, Anglica, Nolcken to KP, 31 May, 14 June 1765; Riksrådets proto-

koll i utrikes ärenden, 8 July 1765. Goodricke lost no time in reassuring Ekeblad: SP 95/107/38-39.

137. SP 95/107/33-34, Goodricke to Sandwich, 5 July 1765.

138. SP 95/107/43-44, Goodricke to Sandwich, 16 July 1765; and cf. *ibid.*, fo. 39, same to same, 9 July 1765.

CHAPTER V
THE CAPS AND THE COURT

1. Gyllenborg, *Mitt lefverne*, pp. 59-60.

2. See, e.g., Lagerroth, "Det frihetstida statsskickets utvecklingsmöjligheter."

3. See, e.g., Landberg, *Sveriges riksdag*, I:vii.

4. Daniel Tilas, *Anteckningar och brev från riksdagen 1765-1766*, pp. 44, 207 (hereafter Tilas, I).

5. [Anders Nordencrantz] *Tankar om Krig i gemen och Sveriges Krig i synnerhet*, I:76-77.

6. *Ibid.*, I:43-44.

7. *Ibid.*, I:117, 123.

8. AVPR 9, Stakhiev to Panin, 2/13 May 1765; SP 95/106/72-75, Goodricke to Sandwich, Most Secret, 1 February 1765.

9. See, e.g., [Esbjörn Christian Reuterholm], *Uplysning för svenska Folket om Anledningen, Orsaken och Afsigterne med urtima Riksdagen 1769*, p. 62.

10. DRA TKUA Sverige B 154, Schack to Bernstorff, 6 September 1765.

11. RA Malmström avskr. Fransiska Minister-berättelser, Breteuil to Praslin, 13 September 1765.

12. Schack wrote that the Cap party "s'est même acquis la confiance de la plus grande partie de la Nation": DRA TKUA Sverige B 153, Schack to Bernstorff, 17 May 1765. For the popular rejoicings, see Tilas, I:15.

13. [Nils von Oelreich], *En gammal mans Instruction För sin Son N. N. då han år 1765 första gången bewistade Riks-Dagen.*

14. For this, see [Anders Nordencrantz] *Ursprungliga orsaker, hwarföre Rikets goda Lagar haft så elak wärkställighet* [1765], printed in his *Undersökning om De rätta Orsakerna til den Blandning som skedt af Lagstiftande och Lagskipande, Redofordrande och Redoskyldige Magternes Gjöromål*, pp. 226 ff.

15. Hilding Eek, *Om Tryckfriheten*, p. 162.

16. He proposed among other things the representation in the Diet of all owners of landed property, and a one-year term of office for magistrates: Metcalf, p. 152.

17. [Nordencrantz], *Undersökning om De rätta Orsakerna til den Blandning som skedt af Lagstiftande och Lagskipande, Redofordrande och Redoskyldige Magternes Gjöromål*, p. 143.

18. DRA TKUA Sverige B 150, Schack to Bernstorff, 21 December 1764.

19. For the circumstances of this pamphlet's production (in which Goodricke may have been involved) see the discussion in Metcalf, pp. 150-53. For the suspicion that Goodricke had a hand in it, Tilas, I:27.

20. Söderberg, p. 186; for Chydenius, Georg Schaumann, *Biografiska Anteckningar om Anders Chydenius.*

21. Birgitta Eriksson, *Bergstaden Falun*, p. 244. Even in the Estate of the Nobility a high proportion of those attending (831 out of 1,161) had no landed property: Jan Liedgren, "Ridderskapet och adeln vid riksdagarna 1719 och 1765-66," p. 40.

22. Crusenstolpe, *Portefeuille*, II:107.

23. Karl Petander, *De nationalekonomiska åskådningarna i Sverige sådana de framträda i litteraturen*, vol. I., *1718-1765*, p. 249; Schaumann, p. 83.

24. The Russian minister Stakhiev laid stress on this, as one of their weaknesses: AVPR 9, Stakhiev to Panin, 2/13 July 1765.

25. Crusenstolpe, *Portefeuille*, II:97-98. Frietzcky wrote of him, many years afterwards, that "he had a fine voice, and the gift of speaking in the House of Nobility, but found it difficult to keep his presence of mind when surprised by a speaker of the opposite party . . . ; his friends had to give him a hand with the motions, so that he should not miss the point."

26. For drastic examples of how far this hatred extended, see Johan Gabriel Oxenstierna, *Ljuva ungdomstid. Dagboken för åren 1766-1768*, pp. 126, 143; and Tessin's judgment in *Tessin och Tessiniana*, p. 394.

27. SP 95/106/68, Goodricke to Sandwich, Secret, 1 February 1765.

28. Malmström, V:251-54; RA Sekreta Propositionen, Inrikes, 1765.

29. Malmström, V:266-68, 333-35, 361.

30. Boëthius and Kromnow, *Jernkontorets historia*, I:588, 595, 600-601.

31. Malmström, V:381; Boëthius and Kromnow, I:579.

32. Malmström, V:352-59: Boëthius and Kromnow.

33. Malmström, V:279-80; C. T. Odhner, *Minne af Riksrådet m.m. Grefve Ulrik Scheffer*, p. 42; Gunnar Castrén, *Gustav Filip Creutz*, pp. 211-12.

34. Hamilton, p. 17. Ordinances against luxury had been of frequent occurrence for the last three decades: a convenient list of them appears as an appendix to Niklas Tengberg, *Om Frihetstiden. Några anmärkningar*, App. B.

35. Nils Erdmann, *Carl Michael Bellman. En kultur- och karaktärsbild från 1700-talet*, p. 337. And see the hilarious debate on women's clothing in *SRARP*, XXV:74-82, 86-99.

36. For the controversy over *brännvin* see Evers, *Den svenska brännvinslagstiftningens historia*, II:6, 32, 34-46. Grain imports had reached a peak in 1764.

37. The ordinance is printed in Brusewitz, *Frihetstidens Grundlagar och konstitutionella stadgar*, pp. 451-57. For the party background to it, see Olle Stridsberg, "Hattarnas och mössornas ställningstaganden till tryckfrihetsfrågan på riksdagarna 1760-62 och 1765-66"; and Eek, pp. 163-64. And see the Memorials of Cederström and Schönberg, in *SRARP*, XXIV, Appendix, pp. 28-36, 44.

38. Boëthius and Kromnow, I:193.

39. *Ibid.*, i: 246.

40. Malmström, V:270-73. For Kierman's sharp tongue, see Höpken, I:486.

41. Boëthius and Kromnow, I:505-8.

42. Robert V. Eagly, "Monetary Policy and Politics in Mid-eighteenth Century Sweden," pp. 751-54.

43. Malmström, V:273.

44. *Ibid.*, V:319-20.

45. SP 95/107/170-72, 175-76, 214, Goodricke to Grafton, 15, 18 October, 12 November 1765.

46. *SRARP*, XXV:13, 17.

47. Malmström, V:392-93.

48. Tilas, I:59; *En Stockholms krönika i C. G. Gjörwells brev*, ed. Otto Sylwan, p. 21. Even Chydenius was in favor of severity: had not Achan, he inquired, been stoned for much less?: Schaumann, *Chydenius*, p. 120.

49. *SRARP*, XXXI:191-204, 255-60, 263-82; and see Frietzcky's admission in Crusenstolpe, *Portefeuille*, II:98.

50. DRA TKUA Sverige B 154, Schack to Bernstorff, 2 August 1765.

51. *Ibid.*, Sverige B 152, Schack to Bernstorff, 1 February 1765.

52. Crusenstolpe, *Portefeuille*, I:117 (25 February 1765).

53. DRA TKUA Sverige B 153, Schack to Bernstorff, 25 June 1765.

54. *Ibid.*, 9 July 1765.

55. RA Malmström avskr., Breteuil to Praslin, 28 June 1765; cf. SP 95/107/35-36, unsigned draft to Goodricke, 26 July 1765. Breteuil's version is not supported by Stakhiev's own report of the conversation in question; but he would hardly have risked so explicit a criticism in a dispatch to his government: see AVPR 10, Stakhiev to Panin, 27 June/8 July 1765, and AVPR 9, same to same, 2/13 May 1765. Stakhiev's instructions are in *SIRIO*, 57: 135.

56. AVPR 9, Stakhiev to Panin, 2/13 May 1765.

57. Fersen, III:338-42.

58. This charge, like the preceding, rests upon Breteuil's report of what Lovisa Ulrika alleged that Stakhiev had said to her; but it may well be more or less true.

59. Assuming that Breteuil's stories of such demands were accurate: Osterman does not seem to have reported them: RA Malmström avskr., Breteuil to Praslin, 20 January, 20 April 1765. Schack probably had them from Breteuil: DRA TKUA Sverige B 152, Schack to Bernstorff, 18, 25 January 1765.

60. *SIRIO*, 57:202, rescript to Osterman, 17 March OS 1765.

61. AVPR 9, Osterman to Catherine, 5/16 May. Panin's comment was written on Osterman to Catherine, AVPR 9, 22 April/3 May 1765. On the pardon, see SP 95/106/245-47, Goodricke to Sandwich, 30 April 1765.

62. AVPR 9, Osterman to Catherine, 11/22 February 1765.

63. DRA TKUA Sverige B 155, Schack to Bernstorff, 18, 22 October 1765.

64. SP 95/106/198, Goodricke to Sandwich, 26 March 1765. Even before the Diet opened, Schack believed that Goodricke was inciting the Caps to violence: DRA TKUA Sverige B 152, Schack to Bernstorff, 1 January 1765.

65. SP 95/106/87-89, Goodricke to Sandwich 25 January 1765.

66. SP 95/106/204-205, Goodricke to Messrs Clifford, 26 March 1765. Claes Grill, too, though only lightly inculpated in the Kierman affair, was sufficiently frightened to refuse for a time to continue to act as Breteuil's banker—to the ambassador's no small embarrassment, since all supplies from France had passed through his hands: SP 95/106/229, Sandwich to Goodricke, 30 April, relaying French intelligence.

67. SP 95/106/124-26.

68. DRA TKUA Sverige B 152, Schack to Bernstorff, 8 March 1765. It was probably on the basis of this dispatch that Malmström based his assessment of the position: Malmström, V:247.

69. DRA TKUA Sverige B 152, Schack to Bernstorff, 19 March 1765.

70. BM Stowe MS 260, fos. 193-98, Macartney to Sandwich, 1/12 March 1765.

71. UUB F 386, Macartney to Goodricke, 28 May 1765.

72. Trolle-Bonde, *Anteckningar om Bondesläkten. Riksrådet Carl D. Bonde*, I:159-60, S. Bergensköld to Carl Bonde, 26 March 1765.

73. SP 95/106/319-21, Goodricke to Sandwich, 11 June 1765.

74. SP 95/107/4-5, Goodricke to Sandwich, 18 June 1765.

75. SP 95/106/170-74, 302-303; 107/25-26.

76. SP 95/106/295-97; 107/74-75, Goodricke to Sandwich, 21 May 1765; Goodricke to Grafton, 6 August 1765.

77. SP 95/107/107-108, Goodricke to Grafton, Separate and Secret, 27 August 1765.

78. SP 95/106/143-46, 286, 319-21, Goodricke to Sandwich, 5 March, 13 May, 11 June 1765.

79. UUB F 386, Macartney to Goodricke, 28 May NS 1765; *SIRIO*, 57:235, rescript to Osterman, 8/19 April 1765.

80. RA Malmström avskr., Breteuil to Praslin, 1 March 1765; SP 95/106/155-58, Goodricke to Sandwich, 13 March 1765; Tilas, I:25. See the debate in *SRARP*, XXIV:59-71. The Nobility's decision was, however, overridden by the concordant vote of the three lower Estates: see *Bondeståndets riksdags protokoll*, X:68.

81. SP 95/106/283-86; Tilas, I:65.

82. SP 95/106/300-301, Goodricke to Sandwich, 23 May 1765.

83. SP 95/107/40, Goodricke to Sandwich, 16 July 1765.

84. SP 95/106/328-30, Goodricke to Sandwich, 14 June 1765; RA Malmström avskr., Breteuil to Praslin, 19 June 1765; *SRARP*, XXIV:184-204; Tilas, I:83.

85. DRA TKUA Sverige B 150, Schack to Bernstorff, 7 December 1764.

86. *Ibid.*, 4 December 1764.

87. *Ibid.*, 14 December, 18 January 1764-65; cf. *ibid.* B 152, Schack to Bernstorff, 5 February 1765; DRA TKUA Sverige C 322, Bernstorff to Schack, 28 January 1765.

88. Malmström, V:287.

89. RA Kungl. ark, 259, Lovisa Ulrika to Frederick, 12 February 1765; Fersen, III:338-40.

90. Russian policy towards the Court was reiterated in the instruction which reached Osterman at the end of December: *SIRIO*, 57, no. 1099.

91. RA Malmström avskr., Breteuil to Praslin, 20 January 1765.

92. *Ibid.*

93. *SIRIO*, 22:358, Solms to Frederick, 26 January 1765; *SIRIO*, 57:202, rescript to Osterman, 17/28 March 1765. Goodricke had the same fear: SP 95/106/116-18, Goodricke to Sandwich, 15 February 1765.

94. RA Malmström avskr., Breteuil to Praslin, 11 January 1765; Metcalf, p. 145; and see Jägerskiöld's comment: *Hovet och författningsfrågan*, p. 271.

95. SP 95/106/326-27, Sandwich to Goodricke, 25 June 1765, relaying the intercept of Breteuil to Praslin, 31 May 1765.

96. RA Kungl. arkivet 259, Frederick to Lovisa Ulrika, 3 March 1765; cf. *SIRIO*, 22: 358, Solms to Frederick, 26 January 1765.

97. RA Kungl. arkiv 259, Frederick to Lovisa Ulrika, 26 January 1765.

98. *Pol. Corr.*, XXIV:115, same to same, 5 February 1765.

99. RA Kungl. arkiv 259, Frederick to Lovisa Ulrika, 27 December 1764.

100. *Ibid.*, same to same, 3 March 1765.

101. *Pol. Corr.*, XXIV:89, same to same, 5 January 1765; RA Kungl. arkiv 259, same to same 25 April 1765.

102. *Pol. Corr.*, XXIV:237, Frederick to Solms, 27 June 1765; cf. *ibid.*, 108, 134, 140 n. 2.

103. Printed in *SRARP*, XXIV, Appendix, pp. 11-12; the debate in *ibid.*, p. 37. The discussion in Metcalf, pp. 171-77, which is based on fresh evidence, supplants Malmström, V: 263 and Jägerskiöld, p. 280. See also Tilas, I:16-17.

104. RA Malmström avskr., Breteuil to Praslin, 16 February 1765; DRA TKUA Sverige B 152, Schack to Bernstorff, 15 February 1765.

105. DRA TKUA, Sverige B 152, Schack to Bernstorff, 22 February 1765.

106. SP 95/106/111-12, Goodricke to Sandwich, 8 February 1765. Cederhielm, all the same, professed himself to be "English," as against "Russian," and Goodricke had apparently believed him: *ibid.*, 106/72-76, Goodricke to Sandwich, Most Secret, 1 February 1765.

107. PRO NI T 2513, Goodricke to Macartney, 15 February 1765.

108. RA Stavsundsarkivet. "Pro Memoria 1771," fo. 18.

109. *SIRIO*, 57:420; *Pol. Corr.*, XXIV:142 n. 1.

110. SP 95/106/150-54, Sandwich to Goodricke, 29 March 1765; RA Malmström avskr., Breteuil to Praslin, 1 March 1765.

111. *Pol. Corr.*, XXIV:142 n. 1, Cocceji to Frederick, 22 February 1765.

112. SP 95/106/143-46, Goodricke to Sandwich, 5 March 1765; *Pol. Corr.*, XXIV:211 n. 1, Cocceji to Frederick, 17 May 1765.

113. *SIRIO*, 57:232.

114. *Ibid.*, p. 202.

115. *Ibid.*, p. 208.

116. SP 95/106/237-39, Goodricke to Sandwich, 19 April 1765.

117. *SIRIO*, 57:232, Catherine to Panin, 12/23 April 1765.

118. *Pol. Corr.*, XXIV:204, Catherine to Frederick, 4/15 May 1765.

119. *Ibid.*, XXIV:194 n. 3, Solms to Frederick, 30 April NS 1765.

120. RA Malmström avskr., Breteuil to Praslin, 21 June 1765; *SIRIO*, 57:429, Osterman to Catherine, 10/21 June 1765. Frederick professed himself "désolé" by her "fâcheuse conduite": *Pol. Corr.*, XXIV:211 n. 1.

121. SP 95/106/326-27, Sandwich to Goodricke, 25 June 1765, relaying intercept of Breteuil to Praslin, 31 May 1765.

122. RA Malmström avskr., Breteuil to Praslin, 19 June 1765.

123. *Pol. Corr.*, XXIV:246 n. 3. Whereupon Frederick (*ibid.*, 246) gave her up as incorrigible.

124. This was an idea which dated back to 1763. Panin mentioned it again to Osten in June 1765: RA Tengberg avskr., Osten to Bernstorff, 4/15 June 1765.

125. *SIRIO*, 57:269, Panin to Osterman, 28 May/8 June 1765; cf. *ibid.*, p. 231, Panin's note, 8/19 April 1765.

126. SP 95/106/68-70, 319-21, Goodricke to Sandwich, 1 February 1765, 11 June 1765; SP 95/106/279-82, Sandwich to Goodricke, 28 May 1765, relaying French intelligence from the end of April; DRA TKUA Sverige B 152, Schack to Bernstorff, 19 February 1765.

127. DRA TKUA Sverige B 152, Schack to Bernstorff, 18 January 1765; RA Malmström avskr., Breteuil to Praslin, 20 January, 20 April 1765.

128. *SIRIO*, 57:269, rescript to Osterman, 28 May/8 June 1765.

129. Schack wrote that Stakhiev "vit pour ainsi dire depuis son Retour de Petersbourg, de façon qu'on ne le voit presque nulle part et pas même chez lui": DRA TKUA Sverige B 153, Schack to Bernstorff, 16 April 1765; and cf. Fersen, III:342.

130. DRA TKUA Sverige B 153, Schack to Bernstorff, 14 June 1765. RA Malmström avskr., Breteuil to Praslin, 28 June 1765.

131. *Ibid.*; and SP 95/107/35-36, unsigned draft to Goodricke, 26 July 1765, relaying French intelligence.

132. AVPR 10, Stakhiev to Catherine, 27 June/8 July 1765.

133. Tilas, I:100-101; SP 95/107/13-15, Goodricke to Sandwich, 25 June 1765. Stakhiev professed to be unable to decide whether the Caps had really any plan for reform or not, and urged that their leaders ought to be compelled to formulate one. Two months earlier he had advised Panin that an attack be mounted against the Senate the moment the business of Kierman was disposed of: AVPR 9, Stakhiev to Panin, 2/13 July, 2/13 May 1765.

134. DRA TKUA Sverige B 154, Schack to Bernstorff, 5 July 1765; BM Stowe MS 261, fo. 12, Breteuil to Praslin (intercept), 8 March 1765.

135. SP 95/106/319-21, Goodricke to Sandwich, 11 June 1765.

136. Tilas, I:100-101; Jägerskiöld, p. 301; Metcalf, pp. 188-89.

137. The incident caused an open breach between Osterman and Stakhiev, and each wrote home complaining of the other. Stakhiev remained in Sweden for another six years, a perennial thorn in Osterman's side, periodically raising his hopes by talk of his recall; but he never ventured an initiative of this sort again: see *Pol. Corr.*, XXIV:266, Cocceji to Frederick, 16, 19 July 1765; SP 95/107/107-109, Goodricke to Grafton, Separate and Secret, 27

August 1765; AVPR 10, rescript to Osterman, 30 July [OS] 1765; AVPR 9, Catherine to Osterman [undated].

138. *Danske Tractater 1751-1800*, pp. 183-200. The treaty cost Denmark a great deal of money in bribery, including 20,000 rubles to Princess Dashkova: "Ostens Gesandtskaber," p. 601.

139. *Pol. Corr.*, XXIV:180 n. 1, Borcke to Frederick, 20 April 1765; SP 75/118/222, Titley to Sandwich, 30 July 1765.

140. SP 95/106/23-24, Goodricke to Sandwich, 8 January 1765; *ibid.*, 29-31, Sandwich to Goodricke, 29 January 1765; *SIRIO*, 57: 155, Panin to Korff, 14/25 January 1765.

141. *Danske Tractater*, p. 200: Secret Article II.

142. *Pol. Corr.*, XXIV:99-100, Frederick to Solms, 19 January 1765.

143. *Corr. min.*, II:195, Bernstorff to Osten, 31 January 1765.

144. E.g., DRA TKUA Sverige B 154, Schack to Bernstorff, 2 July 1765.

145. *Corr. min.*, II:195, Bernstorff to Osten, 31 January 1765.

146. DRA TKUA Sverige B 152, Schack to Bernstorff, 1 January 1765.

147. DRA TKUA Sverige C 322, Bernstorff to Schack, 28 January 1765; Sverige B 152, Schack to Bernstorff, 5 February 1765.

148. *SIRIO*, 57:186, Panin to Korff, 21 February/4 March 1765.

149. RA Malmström avskr., Breteuil to Praslin, 17 May 1765; SP 95/106/235-36, Goodricke to Sandwich, 16 April 1765; PRO NI T 2513, Goodricke to Macartney, 12 April 1765. For the alarmed reactions in the Senate, see RRPUÄ, 13 May 1765.

150. Bernstorff had genially urged Schack not to be cold to "our friends" (*sc.* the Hats), but at the same time to use "des ménagements de propos et de politesse pour le ministre russe et ses opérations": *Schack-Rathlous Arkiv*, p. 183; and see his letter in *Bernstorffske Papirer*, II:453.

151. DRA TKUA Sverige B 154, Schack to Bernstorff, 3 September 1765.

152. *Danske Tractater*, pp. 201-2, Secret Article III. Russia and Denmark agreed to preserve the "gesätzmässige Regierungs-Form" unaltered, and to safeguard "die in Betracht der National Freyheit und deren Reichs-Immunitäten so heilige, als für die Nachbarn wichtige und unveränderliche Constitution' from 'Zerrüttung." Titley reported that Bernstorff would have preferred the absolute suppression of this article, and gave way only when Panin insisted: PRO SP 75/118/111-12, Titley to Sandwich, 2 April 1765; and this seems to be correct: *SIRIO*, 57:186, 196.

153. DRA TKUA Sverige B 153, Schack to Bernstorff, 28 June 1765; cf. *ibid.*, B. 150, Schack to Bernstorff, 30 March 1764.

154. RA Malmström avskr., Breteuil to Praslin, 3 May 1765; "M. Schack me vanta beaucoup de ce clause, qui selon M. Bernstorff lie les mains à Russie."

155. Schack had been ordered to plead no instructions, if questioned on this point: *Corr. min.*, II:225.

156. DRA TKUA Sverige B 153, Schack to Bernstorff, 7 May 1765. The rescript communicating the news of the treaty had not explained this point: *SIRIO*, 57:200.

157. *Corr. min.*, II:211, Bernstorff to Osten, 6 April 1765.

158. *Corr. min.*, II:225-27, Bernstorff to Schack, 27 July 1765.

159. DRA TKUA Sverige B 154, Schack to Bernstorff, 9, 20 August 1765.

160. DRA TKUA Sverige B 152, Schack to Bernstorff, 4 January, 1 February 1765.

161. DRA TKUA Sverige B 152-53, Schack to Bernstorff, 22 February, 21 May 1765.

162. RA Kungl. arkiv. 259, Lovisa Ulrika to Frederick, 12 August 1764.

163. DRA TKUA Sverige B 153, Schack to Bernstorff, 21 May 1765.

164. *Ibid.*

165. *SIRIO*, 57:238, rescript to Korff, 24 April/5 May 1765.

166. *Corr. min.*, II:215-18, Bernstorff to Schack, 1 June 1765.

167. *Ibid.*, II:223, Bernstorff to Schack, 22 June 1765; RA Malmström avskr., Breteuil to Praslin, 14 June 1765, 5 July 1765; SP 95/197/6-8, Sandwich to Goodricke, 2 July 1765; "Ostens Gesandtskaber," pp. 636-39. Sinclair was however promised 20,000 Danish crowns: DRA TKUA Sverige B 154, Schack to Bernstorff, 2 July 1765.

168. Initial moves had been made already in mid-June.

169. DRA TKUA Sverige B 154, Schack to Bernstorff 9 July 1765; Tilas, I:96.

170. BM Add. MS 35,425, fo. 242, Goodricke to Hardwicke, 28 August 1765.

171. RA Malmström avskr., Breteuil to Praslin, 26 July 1765; SP 95/107/74-77, Goodricke to Grafton, Most Secret, 6 August 1765.

172. SP 95/107/27-30, 52-54, Goodricke to Sandwich, 2, 23 July 1765. At Panin's request, Macartney wrote to reinforce this appeal: SP 91/75/300-301, Macartney to Sandwich, 15/26 July 1765.

173. DRA TKUA Sverige B 154, Schack to Bernstorff, 26 July 1765.

174. *Ibid.*, same to same, 2 August, Apostille; 3 August 1765.

175. SP 95/107/69-71, Goodricke to Grafton, Secret, 2 August 1765; DRA TKUA Sverige B 154, Schack to Bernstorff, 6 August 1765.

176. DRA TKUA Sverige B 154, Schack to Bernstorff, 2, 3 August 1765.

177. *Ibid.*, same to same, 20 August 1765; SP 95/107/47-48, Grafton to Goodricke, 9 August 1765.

178. BM Stowe MS 261, fo. 10, Ogier to Breteuil, 12 March 1765 (intercepted); SP 95/106/181-85, 326-27, Sandwich to Goodricke, 9 April, 25 June 1765.

179. DRA TKUA Sverige B 154, Schack to Bernstorff, 10 September 1765.

180. *Ibid.*, Schack to Bernstorff, 24, 27 September 1765.

181. DRA TKUA Sverige B 160, Juel to Bernstorff, 9 October 1767.

182. DRA TKUA Sverige B 154, Schack to Bernstorff, 10, 13 September 1765.

183. *Corr. min.*, II:230-34, Bernstorff to Dreyer, 31 August 1765; cf. SP 75/118/229-30, 236-37, Titley to Grafton, 13, 17 August 1765.

184. *Corr. min.*, II: 230-34, 242-43, Bernstorff to Dreyer, 31 August, 21 September 1765. The amount demanded by Catherine was 50,000 rubles: *SIRIO*, 57:302, 373, 409, 432. Macartney commented that he wished his own court would pay up with as good a grace: Bodley MS Eng. hist. c. 62, fos. 24-25, Macartney to Goodricke, 20-31 December 1765. Osterman was ordered to keep the payment a secret from Schack: *SIRIO*, 57:432, Panin to Osterman, 6/17 January 1766.

185. RA Malmström avskr., Breteuil to Praslin, 29 March 1765.

186. SP 95/106/298-99, Sandwich to Goodricke, 7 June 1765, relaying French intercepts.

187. DRA TKUA Sverige B 154, Schack to Bernstorff, 11 October 1765; cf. *ibid.*, same to same, 21 May 1765; *SRARP*, XXIV:423-27.

188. For these alarms, see Tilas, I:119, 121, 125.

189. SP 95/107/74-77, Goodricke to Grafton, 6 August 1765.

190. SP 95/107/82-83, 90-92, Goodricke to Grafton, 16, 20 August 1765: for the debates in the House of Nobility, see *SRARP*, XXIV:344-414, Appendix pp. 97-105; for those in the Estate of Peasants, *Bondeståndets riksdagsprotokoll*, X:181-91.

191. SP 95/107/37.

192. RA Malmström avskr., Breteuil to Praslin, 20 August 1765. Frederick the Great, for his part, thought their departure would be no great loss: *Pol. Corr.*, XXIV:277.

193. SP 95/107/87-89, Goodricke to Grafton, 19 August 1765.

194. The Nobility voted to reject the Committee's report, 375 to 353.

195. SP 95/107/111-13, Goodricke to Grafton, 28 August 1765.

196. RA Malmström avskr., Breteuil to Praslin, 18 October 1765; cf. Tilas, I:159.

197. SP 95/107/74-77, Goodricke to Grafton, 6 August 1765.

198. *SIRIO*, 57:382, rescript to Osterman, 15 October OS 1765.

199. DRA TKUA Sverige B 154, Schack to Bernstorff, 6 September 1765.

200. SP 95/107/142, Grafton to Goodricke, 4 October 1765.

201. SP 95/107/189-90, Goodricke to Grafton, 28 October 1765.

202. Metcalf, p. 149.

203. DRA TKUA Sverige B 154, Schack to Bernstorff, 13 September 1765. SP 95/107/133-35, 136-37, Goodricke to Grafton, 10, 13 September 1765. For Breteuil's contemptuous assessment of them, see RA Malmström avskr., Breteuil to Praslin, 13 September 1765. Schack thought poorly of them, too.

204. SP 95/107/138-40, Goodricke to Grafton, 13 September 1765.

205. SP 95/107/72-73.

206. Olof Nilsson, 'Blad ur Konung Gustaf III:s och Drottning Sofia Magdalenas giftermålshistoria,' V:133-8; Hennings, pp. 150-151.

207. *SIRIO*, 57: 228, 425; SP 75-118/136, Titley to Sandwich, 23 April 1765.

208. *SIRIO*, 57:266, 271; UUB F 386, Macartney to Goodricke, 28 May 1765; SP 91/75/252-53, Macartney to Sandwich, 31 May NS 1765.

209. SP 95/106/181, Sandwich to Goodricke, Private and Secret, 9 April 1765; 107/10-12, Goodricke to Sandwich, Private, 21 June; PRO NO T 2513, Goodricke to Macartney, 27 September 1765.

210. SP 95/106/235-36, Goodricke to Sandwich, 16 April 1765.

211. SP 95/106/322-25, Sandwich to Goodricke, 25 June 1765, transmitting French intelligence.

212. SP 95/107/108-10, Goodricke to Grafton, 27 August 1765.

213. SP 95/107/118, Goodricke to Grafton, 30 August 1765; Fersen, III: 335-38, 338-40; PRO NI T 2513, Goodricke to Macartney, 29 August 1765.

214. *Corr. min.*, II:237, Bernstorff to Schack, 14 September 1765.

215. DRA TKUA Sverige B 155, Schack to Bernstorff, 8 October 1765.

216. *Gustavianska papperen*, I:46, Gustav to Nils Bielke, 20 September 1765; RA Malmström avskr., Breteuil to Praslin, 27 September 1765; SP 95/107/164-65, Grafton to Goodricke, 25 October; 107/190-91, Goodricke to Grafton, 28 October 1765.

217. *SIRIO*, 57:384, Osterman to Panin, 17/28 October 1765.

218. *Corr. min.*, II:245-46 n. 1.

219. DRA TKUA Sverige B 155, Schack to Bernstorff, 3 December, 6 December 1765.

220. SP 95/109/110, Goodricke to Grafton, 18 February 1766.

221. DRA TKUA Sverige B 154, Schack to Bernstorff, 24 September; B 155 same to same, 8 October, 5 November, 20 November 1765.

222. *Ibid.*, B 154, same to same, 13 September; B 155, same to same, 8 October 1765.

223. *SIRIO*, 57:381, Panin to Osterman, 15 October [OS] 1765; cf. SP 95/107/223-25, Goodricke to Grafton, 19 November 1765.

224. DRA TKUA Sverige B 155, Schack to Bernstorff, 8 November, 3 December 1765.

225. Gyllenborg, *Mitt lefverne*, p. 68.

226. *SIRIO*, 57:410, Catherine's note on Report from Osterman, 18/29 November 1765.

CHAPTER VI
THE ROCKINGHAMS AND GOODRICKE'S TREATY

1. *Memoirs and Correspondence of George, Lord Lyttelton*, II:683.

2. J. E. Tyler, "John Roberts, M.P., and the first Rockingham Administration," p. 554,

memorandum by John Roberts; cf. RA Dipl. Angl., Nolcken to KP, 2 August 1765.

3. HMC *Weston-Underwood*, p. 390.

4. *Memoirs of the Marquis of Rockingham and his Contemporaries*, I:193.

5. *Ibid.*

6. "The ramming Austria deeper with France and kindling a new War by unnecessary alliances are things I can neither answer to my God nor to my conscience': *Correspondence of George III*, I:124, and cf. *ibid.*, 120; *Autobiography and Political Correspondence of Augustus Henry, third Duke of Grafton* (1898), pp. 83-84; *The Jenkinson Papers*, p. 376.

7. E.g., SP 75/118/196-97, Grafton to Titley, 29 July 1765; and cf. RA Dipl. Angl., Nolcken to KP, 26 July 1765; Kabinettet för utrikes brevvexling, KP to Nolcken, 1 August 1765.

8. RA Dipl. Angl., Nolcken to KP, 3 September 1765.

9. *Pol. Corr.*, XXIV:383, 385.

10. For the negotiations, see SP 90/84/184-86, 247, 274, 282; 85/5, 22-23; Mitchell's instructions are dated 25 April 1766; he did not arrive in Berlin until 7 June: SP 90/85/101-4, 105.

11. SP 95/107/62-65, Goodricke to Grafton, Secret, 30 July 1765.

12. SP 95/107/37, unsigned draft to Goodricke, 26 July 1765.

13. SP 95/107/56-58, Conway to Goodricke, 10 August 1765; *Correspondence of George III*, I:178-79, Conway to the king, 10 August 1765; BM Egerton MS 982, fo. 6, George III to Conway, 11 August 1765, where he refers to "the oeconomical &, I may say injudicious ideas of this country in the time of peace."

14. SP 95/107/93-94, 97-100, Goodricke to Conway, 23 August 1765; Goodricke to Grafton, 26 August 1765.

15. SP 95/107/97-100.

16. SP 95/107/116-17, Goodricke to Grafton, 30 August 1765. The "oeconomy" was not imaginary: George Grenville boasted that under his administration the Secret Service money "was by a great deal less than under any other minister," and the statistics bore him out: *Grenville Papers*, III:143-45.

17. SP 95-107-95-97, Grafton to Goodricke, 10 September 1765.

18. This had been the basis of Goodricke's appeal for money.

19. SP 95/107/162-64, Grafton to Goodricke, 25 October 1765.

20. For this, see Roberts, *Macartney in Russia*, pp. 24-29.

21. SP 95/107/141-42, Grafton to Goodricke, 4 October 1765.

22. SP 95/107/181, Goodricke to Grafton, 18 October 1765.

23. SP 95/107/196-99, Grafton to Goodricke, 16 November 1765.

24. SP 95/107/141-42, Grafton to Goodricke, 4 October 1765; SP 91/76/235-39, Grafton to Macartney, 29 September 1765. Macartney pursued this line on his own account, within the limits of the means at his disposal: he offered Panin first 6,000 and then 10,000 rubles for Swedish corruption, in the hope of persuading him to be complaisant about art. 4 of the commercial treaty: SP 91/76/333, Macartney to Grafton, 5/16 November 1765. Goodricke told Macartney that he was not surprised that Panin should reject his offer: by Russian standards the amount was trivial: PRO NI T 2513, Goodricke to Macartney, 12 December 1765.

25. Cf. his failure to show any interest, when Titley hinted that there might be changes in Danish policy in the offing: SP 75/118/173-74, Titley to Sandwich, 4 June 1765; SP 75/118/186, Sandwich to Gordon, 24 June 1765.

26. SP 75/118/261-63, Grafton to Titley, 12 November 1765.

27. SP 75/118/229-30, Titley to Grafton, 13 August 1765.

28. *Corr. min.*, II:256-58, Bernstorff to Asseburg, 5 December 1765; DRA TKUA England C 267, Bernstorff to Bothmer, 27 November 1765. Bothmer's instructions of 11 October, it is perhaps pertinent to note, had laid down that any advances for a closer relationship must come from the English side.

29. SP 91/76/278-79, Macartney to Grafton, 13/24 December 1765. Panin seems to have taken the British overture in Copenhagen seriously: *SIRIO*, 57:432, Panin to Osterman, 6/17 January 1766.

30. RA Tengberg avskr., Asseburg to Bernstorff, 27 December 1765.

31. SP 75/118/287-91, Titley to Grafton, 21 December 1765. Macartney sent a similar warning: SP 91/76/383, Macartney to Grafton, 20/31 December 1765.

32. SP 95/106/279-82, Sandwich to Goodricke, 28 May 1765. Macartney had earlier informed Sandwich that Panin "almost owned to me, that if England made a subsidiary engagement with that Kingdom [Sweden], Russia could not be a party to it," but would pay two or three times the amount in bribes: SP 91/75/220-23, Macartney to Sandwich, 9 April [NS] 1765.

33. SP 95/107/212-13, Goodricke to Grafton, 5 November 1765.

34. SP 95/107/221-22, Grafton to Goodricke, 6 December 1765.

35. SP 91/76/353-55, Grafton to Macartney, 24 December 1765; and cf. *ibid.*, 77/21-22.

36. Roberts, *Macartney in Russia*, pp. 28-29.

37. E.g. SP 95/109/9, Grafton to Goodricke, 24 January 1766; SP 95/109/101-2, same to same, 28 February 1766, where Grafton writes: "You will observe, Sir, that the whole of this is thoroughly consistent with that Scheme which Monsr Osterman opened to you by Monsr Panin's Orders, and by which Russia was to take Sweden upon herself"; and SP 95/109/158, where he writes that Osterman "must recollect that M. Panin, in opening his Plan to Sir George Macartney, as also to you, through him, proposed that Sweden was to be secured by the means of Russia . . . "; and cf. 91/77/21-22, Grafton to Macartney, 28 February 1766.

38. SP 95/109/100-101, Grafton to Goodricke, 28 February 1766: "When I find, by the whole of the correspondence, that what His Majesty has expended in Sweden, has been at the Instigation of the Czarina, and that you have been repeatedly instructed to intimate this to Her Imperial Majesty's Minister, I did not expect, that you would admit a Claim of Obligation from thence on that Account."

39. SP 95/197/196-99, 200-201, Grafton to Goodricke, 16 November 1765.

40. UUB F 386, Grafton to Goodricke, 3 January 1766.

41. This emerges clearly from his letter to Macartney of 24 December in which he informed him that Grafton was only waiting for the return of the Messenger from Russia to take into consideration the affair of a subsidy treaty: PRO NI T 2513, Goodricke to Macartney, 24 December 1765. And Panin wrote to Osterman that he was glad to hear that Goodricke's hopes of a subsidy for Sweden had substance: this assessment of the prospects must clearly have come from Goodricke to Osterman: *SIRIO*, 57:432, Panin to Osterman, 6/17 January 1766.

42. SP 95/107/270-73, Goodricke to Grafton, 24 December 1765; Metcalf, p. 222.

43. SP 95/109/15-18, Goodricke to Grafton, 3 January 1766; Metcalf, p. 223.

44. SP 95/109/9 ff., Grafton to Goodricke, 24 January 1766.

45. SP 95/109/111-13, Goodricke to Grafton, 18 February 1766.

46. PRO NI T 2513, Goodricke to Macartney, 15 November, 22 November 1765.

47. Osterman made this point strongly to Panin: *SIRIO*, 57:414, 1/12 December 1765.

48. SP 95/109/57-60, Goodricke to Grafton, 18 January 1766.

49. RA Kabinettet för utrikes brefvexling, KP to von Friesendorff, Apostille particulière, 11 January 1765.

50. RRPUÄ, 4 January 11 February, 17 March, 12 April, 15 May, 29 July, for Senate debates on this issue.

51. SP 95/107/153-54, Grafton to Goodricke, relaying French intelligence, 15 October 1765; SP 95/107/220, same to same, 6 December 1765.

52. SP 95/107/179-80, Goodricke to Grafton, Secret, 25 October 1765; RA RRPUÄ, 21, 28 October, 4 November 1765.

53. SP 95/107/211-12, Goodricke to Grafton, Secret, 5 November 1765; RA Diplomatica, Gallica, KP:s brev till F. U. von Friesendorff, 22 October, 26 November 1765; *Pol. Corr.*, XXIV: 379, Cocceji to Frederick, 29 November 1765.

54. RA Kabinettet för utrikes brefvexling, KP to von Freisendorff, 17 December 1766; SP 95/107/259, Goodricke to Grafton, 17 December 1765; RA RRPUÄ 20, 23 December 1765: cf. Tilas, I:168.

55. RA Kabinettet för utrikes brefvexling, KP to Friesendorff, 24 December 1765; cf. BM Add. MS 35,444, fos. 36-37, which gives Löwenhielm's report to Senate of his interview with Breteuil.

56. SP 95/107/261-65, Goodricke to Grafton, Most Secret, 20 December 1765.

57. SP 95/109/26-28, Goodricke to Grafton, 21 January 1766.

58. RA RRPUÄ, 23 January 1766.

59. *Ibid.*, 20 December 1765; RA Riksens ständers brev, no. 131, Secret Committee to Senate 20 December 1765.

60. RA RRPUÄ, 10 January, 21 January 1766.

61. *Ibid.*, 21 January 1766.

62. *Ibid.*, 21 January 1766.

63. *Ibid.*, 13, 16 December 1765; *Sverges traktater*, VIII:896, prints the Chancery's answer, of 12 December 1765. And cf. Tilas, I:198-201.

64. RA RRPUÄ, 16 December 1765.

65. SP 95/107/261-65, Goodricke to Grafton, 20 December 1765. A month later, the Chancery College presented the Senate with the result of its own researches in the matter, and was obliged to concede that France had not consistently observed her obligations: RA RRPUÄ, 28 January 1766.

66. RA RRPUÄ, 20 December 1765.

67. *Ibid.*, 7 January 1766.

68. RA Malmström avskr., Breteuil to Praslin, 6 December 1765.

69. SP 95/107/264, 280-85, Goodricke to Grafton, 20 December, Separate and Secret; 24 December 1765. On 20 December 1765 Goodricke wrote of Löwenhielm: "His View is to govern the Senate and augment his own Importance, by showing that whatever Party he serves shall be the uppermost." Schack shared Goodricke's suspicions: DRA TKUA Sverige B 155, Schack to Bernstorff, 17 December 1765.

70. SP 95/109/23-25, Goodricke to Grafton, Secret, 14 January 1766; Metcalf, pp. 224-25.

71. SP 95/109/41-43, Grafton to Goodricke, 11 February 1766, relaying Breteuil's dispatches of 3 and 10 January 1766: RA Malmström avskr., Breteuil to Praslin, 3, 10 Jamuary 1766.

72. RA RRPUÄ, 21, 22, 23 January 1766.

73. SP 95/109/129-31, Goodricke to Grafton, Most Secret, 7 March 1766.

74. Schack reported that Löwenhielm had many enemies among the Caps, and that Osterman was struggling hard in his favor: DRA TKUA Sverige B 156, Schack to Bernstorff 17 January 1766. And cf. Tilas, I:185-86, 213.

75. RA Malmström avskr., Breteuil to Praslin, 3, 10, 17 January 1766. SP 95/109/23-25, 47-48, Goodricke to Grafton, 14, 28 January 1766.

76. SP 95/109/20-21, Goodricke to Grafton, 7 January 1766.

77. SP 95/109/64-65, Goodricke to Grafton, 31 January 1766. Goodricke wrote to Sir Joseph Yorke on 5 February 1766: "I did all I could to keep the £2000 sent me by the Messenger for the call that I foresaw would be upon me at the time of signing the treaty,

and even declared . . . that I would give out no more till that was done, but unluckily the Russian Minister was also without money at that moment, and as I saw that the whole depended upon one point's being carried against us in the Secret Committee I was obliged to go on till they had left me nothing for the treaty itself": Add. MS 35,444, fos 41-42.

78. Fersen's memorial, dated 20 December 1765, is enclosed in Goodricke's dispatch of 28 January 1766: SP 95/109/49-57. For the effect of Fersen's arguments on Clergy and Burghers, *ibid.*, 109/70-71. And see the very similar arguments of Ulrik Scheffer: Trulsson, pp. 508-9.

79. *Calendar of Home Office Papers*, pp. 553-54.

80. In his overture to the Senate on 2 December 1765.

81. SP 95/107/238-39; 109-37, Goodricke to Grafton, 3 December 1765, 21 January 1766.

82. It seems not unlikely that he deliberately refrained from reporting discouraging information on this topic: Metcalf, p. 229.

83. SP 95/109/57-60, Goodricke to Grafton, 28 January 1766.

84. The course of the negotiations appears from RA Diplomatica, Anglica, Konferensprotokoll II, 1719-1766; Svenska Beskickningarnas memorial, 1729-82; RRPUÄ; Mindre sekreta deputationens expeditioner 1766; Riksens ständers brev 1765-1766 uti utrikes ärenden; SP 95/109/64-65, 73-75, Goodricke to Grafton, Secret, 31 January 1766, same to same, 6 February 1766.

85. RA Kabinettet för utrikes brevvexling, KP to Nolcken, 24 December 1765.

86. Goodricke reported that Breteuil had offered 300,000 daler to members of the Burghers on the Secret Committee to reject it: SP 95/109/47-48, Goodricke to Grafton 28 January 1766.

87. KP's note in SP 95/109/76-77, Goodricke to Grafton, Separate, 6 February 1766. On 28 March Grafton transmitted a reply to the Swedish Note promising justice to those to who had suffered injury, and giving an assurance that in future the most scrupulous attention would be paid to the rules of international law: any more precise stipulation must, however, depend on whether a defensive alliance was concluded or not: SP 95/109/127-28; RA RRPUÄ, 18 April 1766.

88. RA Kabinettet för utrikes brevvexling, KP to Nolcken, 6 February 1766.

89. Text in SP 95/109/79-80; printed in *Sverges Traktater*, VIII:893-95.

90. When the Russian minister congratulated him on the treaty, Grafton replied "que la nouvelle de la signature du traité en question leur était des plus indifférentes": Amburger, p. 166.

91. SP 95/109/100-101, Grafton to Goodricke, 28 February 1766.

92. SP 95/109/40-41, Grafton to Goodricke, 11 February 1766.

93. Ratifications were exchanged on 21 March 1766: RA RRPUÄ, 19, 21 March 1766.

94. SP 95/109/137-39, Goodricke to Grafton 18 March 1766.

95. The limitation to Europe, which Professor Metcalf seems to regard as a significant concession by Goodricke, was surely no more that an underlining of the obvious: even Grafton can hardly have expected Swedish forces to be sent to Coromandel or the Caribbean: Metcalf, p. 226.

96. SP 95/109/73-75, 137-39.

97. PRO NI T 2513, Goodricke to Macartney 27 March 1766.

98. SP 95/109/20-21, 38-39, Goodricke to Grafton, 7 January 1766; Grafton to Goodricke, 7 February 1766.

99. SP 95/109/159-60, Grafton to Goodricke, 15 April 1766; 109/119-20, 185-87, 190-91, 198-99, Goodricke to Grafton, 4, 18 March, 6, 13 May 1766; RA RRPUÄ, 9, 12 May 1766. Grafton's parsimony naturally provoked unfavorable comment in diplomatic circles: DRA TKUA Sverige B 156, Schack to Bernstorff, 21 March 1766.

100. SP 95/109/259-60, Goodricke to Conway, 20 June 1766.

101. Add. MS 35,444,fo. 71, Goodricke to Sir Joseph Yorke, 26 July 1766.

102. SP 95/109/101-2, 158, Grafton to Goodricke, 28 February, 11 April 1766.

103. *SIRIO*, 57:272, 411, 414.

104. "There is no observation truer than what your Excellency makes in your kind letter . . . of the necessity there is that some of those who direct foreign affairs, should have been foreign ministers themselves as is the case in all other countries but ours. . . . One of the things that has both vexed and surprised Russia is that we affect to have no interest at all in any transactions in the North, we are continually telling her that we would have nothing to do in Sweden but to oblige her, that we make an alliance in Denmark to please Russia and now at this moment that we send Sir And. Mitchell to Berlin for the same reason. This manner is not engaging": Add. MS 35,444,fos. 62-63, Goodricke to Sir Joseph Yorke, 25 March 1766.

105. PRO NI T 2513, Goodricke to Macartney, 27 March 1766. On this point, see D. B. Horn, "The Diplomatic Experience of Secretaries of State."

106. *SIRIO*, 57:490, Panin to Gross, 27 March [OS] 1766; cf. *ibid.*, p. 470, Gross to Panin, 17/28 March 1766.

107. DRA TKUA England C 267, Bernstorff to Bothmer, 22 March 1766; and see Add. MS 35,444,fo. 61, where Goodricke transmits Bernstorff's favorable opinion to his friend De La Val at the Hague.

CHAPTER VII
THE END OF THE CAP DIET

1. RA Kab. f. utr. brevvexling, KP to Friesendorff, 21 January 1766; RRPUÄ, 24 January 1766; SP 95/109/61-64, Goodricke to Grafton, 31 January 1766.

2. RRPUÄ, 12 February 1766; DRA TKUA Sverige B 156, Schack to Bernstorff, 29 April 1766; SP 95/109/169-70, Goodricke to Grafton, 8 April 1766.

3. SP 95/109/175-77, Goodricke to Grafton, 15 April 1766; RRPUÄ, 29 April, 5, 9 May 1766; DRA TKUA Sverige B 156, Schack to Bernstorff, 29 April 1766.

4. Choiseul; *Mémoires*, pp. 383-93.

5. *Correspondance entre Bernstorff et Choiseul*, pp. 234-37.

6. Ogier had been highly esteemed in Copenhagen: he was known as "Ogier the Dane": *Bernstorffske Papirer*, I:335, A. P. Bernstorff to A. G. Bernstorff, 15 April 1766.

7. *Correspondance entre Bernstorff et Choiseul*, pp. 234-37, Choiseul to Bernstorff, 15 April 1766.

8. *Ibid.*, pp. 238-48, Bernstorff to Choiseul, 24 May 1766.

9. *Recueil des instructions, Danemark*, pp. 177 (22 April 1766), and 180-84 (14 October 1766).

10. *Recueil des instructions, Suède*, pp. 407-13.

11. For a discussion of the relationship between Choiseul's policy and that of the Secret, see Lennart Sjöstedt, "Le Secret du Roi, hertigen av Choiseul och Sverige," pp. 399-406; Hell Stiegung, "Le Secret du Roi och Sverige. Ett genmäle," pp. 289-97; Hennings, pp. 281-83.

12. Hennings, p. 282.

13. *Ibid.*, Sjöstedt, p. 404; Stiegung, "Le Secret du Roi och Sverige," pp. 294-95.

14. Hennings, p. 283. In fact Breteuil did not leave Sweden until the following spring.

15. RA Diplomatica, Gallica, Franska regeringens noter till ambassadören Grefwe Creutz 1766-1783, 25 May, 6 June; cf. RRPUÄ, 3 June, 23 June; SP 95/110/13-18, Goodricke to Conway, 1 July 1766; 109/228, Conway to Goodricke 13 June 1766.

16. RRPUÄ 23, 30 June; 1, 9, 21, 28 July; 5, 11 August; SP 95/110/9-12, 21-22, 47-66, 84-86: Goodricke to Conway, 1, 8, 26 July, 26 August 1766; DRA TKUA Sverige B 157, Schack to Bernstorff, 27 June, 18 July 1766. And see Tilas, I:335-36, and his sardonic comment to J. G. Lillienberg on 18 July: "And so we are now, praise the powers, free from the French alliance, we have become a great and glorious people, we are now independent, we can now take our economic measures and be prosperous again. I and some others sat, as scared as rabbits, lest the gentlemen in question should come up and plank all 12 millions on the table before we had managed to complete this admirable proceeding, for what is such a bagatelle in comparison with independence. And we can no doubt safeguard ourselves with the precaution of forbidding our Senate ever again to enter into such a negotiation. Hallelujah! Who now would not be a Cap, who is not now an Englishman, who now does not lend his ear to – – – [Sir John Goodricke?]. Goddam the fransh Dogg" (*sic*): *ibid*., pp. 460-61.

17. RRPUÄ, 4, 15 September 1766; SP 95/110/95-97, 101-2, Goodricke to Conway, Secret, 5, 9 September 1766; DRA TKUA Sverige B 158, Schack to Bernstorff, 6, 9 September 1766.

18. RA Kab. för utr. brevvexling, KP to Creutz, 3 October 1766; SP 95/110/141-43, Goodricke to Conway, Secret, 7 October 1766; Tilas, I:394-95.

19. Fersen, III:353; *Tessin och Tessiniana*, p. 388.

20. SP 95/110/97, Goodricke to Conway, Secret, 5 September 1766.

21. SP 95/109/248-49, Conway to Goodricke, 28 June 1766.

22. DRA TKUA Sverige B 157, Schack to Bernstorff, 18 July 1766.

23. *Tessin och Tessiniana*, p. 405; Tilas, I:69; cf. *ibid*., pp. 43, 162, 203-8.

24. Tilas, I:43, 45, 75, 380-81.

25. For the background to Hoffman's rebellion, see Malmström, V:364-65.

26. SP 95/109/221-22, Goodricke to Grafton, Separate and Secret, 23 May 1766; DRA TKUA Sverige B 157, Schack to Bernstorff, 20 May 1766.

27. DRA TKUA Sverige B 157, Schack to Bernstorff, 6 June 1766; SP 95/109/243-44, Goodricke to Grafton, 10 June 1766; SP 95/109/228, Grafton to Goodricke 13 June 1766; *Corr. Min*., II:274-75, Bernstorff to Schack, 24 May 1766.

28. SP 95/110/28-30, 92-93, Goodricke to Conway, Secret, 13 July 1766, 2 September 1766.

29. Malmström, V:366 ff.; SP 95/109/223-25, 229-31, Goodricke to Grafton, 27, 30 May 1766; Tilas, I:281-83.

30. Tilas, I:295, 315-16, 361; *SRARP*, XXV:394-97, 456-70, 527-40.

31. SP 95/110/8, Goodricke to Conway, 1 July 1766.

32. See his speech in *SRARP*, XXV:386 ff.

33. SP 95/109/232-34, 239-42; 109/231, Goodricke to Grafton, 21 May, 6 June 1766.

34. SP 95/109/223-25, 232-34, 239-42, Goodricke to Grafton, 27, 30 May, 6 June 1776; DRA TKUA Sverige B 157, Schack to Bernstorff, 30 May, 3 June 1766; *SRARP*, XXV:399, 407, 429; Tilas, I:297, 298.

35. See above; and Tilas, I:100-101, 105-6, 108.

36. She told Serenius "I am myself and the third party, with my friends": *ibid*., p. 158.

37. For a full account of Russian policy on the constitutional issue, see Metcalf, chap. 7.

38. DRA TKUA Sverige B 156, Schack to Bernstorff, 15 April 1766.

39. *Ibid*., Sverige B 157, Schack to Bernstorff, 5 June 1766.

40. See above; DRA TKUA Sverige B 157, Schack to Bernstorff, 17 June 1766; *Corr. Min*., II:275-80, Bernstorff to Schack, 28 June 1766.

41. DRA TKUA Sverige B 156, Schack to Bernstorff, 15 April 1766.

42. *Ibid*., Sverige B 157, Schack to Bernstorff, 17 June, 19 August 1766.

43. *SIRIO*, 67:47, Osterman to Panin, 4/15 August 1766; *ibid.*, p. 60, Panin to Osterman, 19/30 August 1766; Tilas, I:255, 361-62, 371, 374-75, 484. DRA TKUA Sverige B 157, Schack to Bernstorff, 19 August 1766; *ibid.*, Sverige B 158, Schack to Bernstorff, 2 September 1766; SP 95/110/90-91, Goodricke to Conway, 2 September 1766.

44. *SIRIO*, 67:132, Panin to Osterman, 30 September/11 October 1766.

45. DRA TKUA Sverige B 158, Schack to Bernstorff, 9 September 1766.

46. Text printed in Brusewitz, *Frihetstidens grundlagar och konstitutionella stadgar*, pp. 213-14.

47. UUB F 514, C. F. Scheffer to Crown Prince Gustav, 27 August 1766.

48. For the extent of the Russian capitulation to Danish objections, see *SIRIO*, 67:47, 60, Osterman to Panin, 4/15 August; Panin to Osterman, 19/30 August 1766. Osterman seems to have tried to overcome Bernstorff's opposition by alleging that the Caps agreed with him. It seems unlikely; but the course of events is obscure: see Metcalf, pp. 192-202.

49. My italics, quoted in Metcalf, p. 201.

50. As C. F. Scheffer pertinently pointed out: UUB F 514, Scheffer to Crown Prince, 27 August 1766.

51. Hennings, pp. 299-303.

52. See above, and SP 95/107/243-45.

53. SP 95/109/71-72, Goodricke to Grafton, Secret, 6 February 1766.

54. Tilas, I:222, 275.

55. SP 95/109/157-58, Grafton to Goodricke, Secret, 11 April 1766.

56. Tilas, I:277.

57. SP 95/109/196-97.

58. SP 95/109/206-8.

59. Tilas, I:305.

60. SP 95/109/251, Goodricke to Conway, 17 June 1766: "There is certainly no honester man in our Party than this new Senator, who has directed our Clubs, and been in all our secrets."

61. Tilas, I:426 (7 October 1766); SP 95/110/136-38, Goodricke to Conway, 7 October 1766.

62. SP 95/110/150-51, Goodricke to Conway, Secret, 14 October 1766.

63. SP 95/110/236-37, Goodricke to Conway, 23 December 1766.

64. Goodricke had gloomily predicted, in October 1765, that it might last till Easter: SP 95/107/195, Goodricke to Grafton, Private, 29 October 1765. It finally ended on 15 October.

65. SP 95/110/77, 126, Goodricke to Conway, 12 August, 26 September 1766. All the same, Osterman told Goodricke that he had spent £9,000 in July and August: *ibid.*, 105-7, Goodricke to Conway, 16 September 1766.

66. SP 95/109/227, Conway to Goodricke, 13 June 1766; 109/265-67, Goodricke to Conway, 27 June; 110/26-27, same to same, 11 July; SP 91/77/138-41, Conway to Macartney, 15 July; SP 95/110/33-35, Conway to Goodricke, 1 August; SP 95/110/79-80, Goodricke to Conway, 19 August 1766.

67. SP 95/110/105-7, Goodricke to Conway, Separate and Secret, 16 September 1766; 110/124-26, same to same, Most Secret, 26 September 1766; 110/140, same to same, 7 October 1766; 110/134-35, Conway to Goodricke, 17 October 1766; 110/144-46, Conway to Goodricke, 24 October 1766.

68. Goodricke's consolidated accounts for the Diet, in SP 95/110/180-82, Goodricke to Conway, 7 November 1766; 110/183, Most Secret, same to same, 8 November 1766 (on pensions); 110/216, Conway to Goodricke, 19 December 1766. The figures given for "Secret and Special Service" in 32 *Commons Journals*, pp. 555-99, give the allocation to Good-

ricke, for the period October 1764 to October 1766, as totalling no more than £5,555. It seems very probable that Goodricke had to find considerable sums out of his own pocket: he wrote to De la Val on 10 October 1766: "our appointments, which amount to 1,983£ a year, are soon spent in such a country as this; I have had a present this year, otherwise I should not have held out so far. You Southern people can have no idea what extravagant fellows we are in the North; we are not content with simple fare and ordinary good French wines, but we must have Champagne and Burgundy, and above all sweet wine at the Desert: all these are loaded with prodigious duties so that a bottle of good Champagne comes to about 5 shillings sterling in the cellar": Add. MS 35,444, fo. 98.

69. SP 91/77/221-22, Macartney to Conway, 25 July/5 August 1766. The figure of half a million rubles was a round number, and according to Osterman's information to Goodricke the correct figure was £88,880; SP 95/110/175, Goodricke to Conway, 7 November 1766, calculated at the rate of 4/6 to the ruble.

70. For Gyllensvan and von Essen, see Tilas, I:23, 185. For a more favorable view of von Essen, see Frietzcky's 'Pro Memoria, 1799," in Crusenstolpe, *Portefeuille*, II:98-99.

71. Tilas, I:128.

72. *Ibid.*, pp. 396, 401. "Mice" is an untranslatable pun: the Swedish for Cap is "Mössa"; the Swedish for mice is "möss".

73. *Ibid.*, p. 424.

74. *Ibid.*, p. 147.

75. *Ibid.*, p. 358.

76. *Ibid.*, p. 248.

77. *Ibid.*, p. 308. Schack suspected that Goodricke inspired this move, though there seems no evidence for it: DRA TKUA Sverige B 157, Schack to Bernstorff, 20 June 1766.

78. SP 95/110/36-37, Goodricke to Conway, 22 July 1766; DRA TKUA Sverige B 157, Schack to Bernstorff, 25 July 1766.

79. Breteuil wrote in November 1766: "M. Löwenhielm est mécontent des Bonnets, il hait la Russie, il a été négligé par le Mn Anglais qui l'a cru perdu et qui surement y a travaillé, il veut plaire à la Reine de Suède, il est bien avec moi": RA Malmström avskr.

80. Tilas, I:430, 434-38.

81. DRA TKUA Sverige B 158, Johnn to Bernstorff, 19 September 1766.

82. SP 95/110/114-16, Goodricke to Conway, 19 September 1766. On the same day he wrote to De la Val: "You will see by the inclosed despatch that we are in hopes to finish the Diet soon; if now we stay till everybody had a mind to end it, we may continue it these two years": Add. MS 35,444, fo. 91.

83. See the debate in the House of Nobility, *SRARP*, XXVI:380-96.

84. See Fersen's gloomy summary of the situation in *Handlingar ur v. Brinkmanska Archivet på Trolle-Ljungby*, II:184-85.

85. UUB F 386, Macartney to Goodricke, 15/26 September 1766.

86. UUB F 386, Conway to Goodricke, 14 November 1766.

CHAPTER VIII
DRIFT, DEFLATION, AND DEFEAT

1. RA Riksens ständers brev 1765-66 uti utrikes ärenden, 13 October 1766; RRPUÄ 24 October 1766; 9 March 1767: cf. SP 95/110/99-100, 201-3; RA Malmström avskr., Breteuil to Choiseul, 14 November 1766.

2. SP 95/110/9-12, Goodricke to Conway, 1 July 1766. For Swedish approaches to Denmark, RRPUÄ 20 February, 3 March, 14 April, 15 May 1766; DRA TKUA Sverige B 156,

Schack to Bernstorff, 15 February, 14 March, 15 April 1766 (No. 1); B 157, 16 May 1766; *Corr. min.*, II:266-69, Bernstorff to Schack, 1 March 1766; SP 95/109/162, Goodricke to Grafton, 1 April 1766.

3. New taxation amounted to 274,063 silver daler a year. Tilas commented: "And that's all. We'll then be out of debt and entering the Golden Age. Hallelujah!": Tilas, I:420, 439.

4. SP 95/110/154, Goodricke to Conway, 17 October 1766. Danish diplomats also thought the budgetary situation sound: DRA TKUA Sverige B 158, Johnn to Bernstorff, 17 October 1766; *ibid.* B 159, Schack to Bernstorff, 11 November 1766; *ibid.*, B 160, Schack to Bernstorff, 16 January 1767. For Serenius in the Secret Committee, Tilas, I:425-26.

5. *Pol. Corr.*, XXIV:152.

6. For details of this scheme, SP 95/109/175, 188-89, 226, 245-46, 261; RRPUÄ, 1 July 1766.

7. For the Genoa Loan, Tilas, I:258; SP 95/110/7-8, 29, 120-22, 126-27, 142.

8. SP 95/110/199-203, Goodricke to Conway, 7 November 1766.

9. For this preliminary fencing, RRPUÄ 9, 23 February; 2, 9 March; 13, 14, 27 April 1767; SP 95/112/7-10, 25, 30, 35, 45; BM MS 2969, fos. 164, 217, 239, Goodricke to Gunning, 13 January, 1 March, 2 April 1767.

10. RRPUÄ, 25 April; UUB F 478, Gustav III's Dagbok 1767-1769, 25 April; Goodricke's comment in SP 95/112/112-16, 15 May 1767.

11. SP 95/112/93-102: received 15 May 1767.

12. SP 95/112/107-8, Conway to Goodricke, 22 May 1767.

13. E.g., RA Dipl. Anglica, Nolcken to KP, 23 May 1767.

14. Nolcken's complaints in *ibid.*, Nolcken to KP, 10 July, 4 August 1767; Maltzan's in *Pol. Corr.*, XXVI:221 n. 4.

15. Goodricke seems to have been particularly ill-served: at least two important communications went from Weymouth to Gunning and to Cathcart: SP 75/120/27-31; SP 91/78/18-24.

16. SP 91/77/190-91, Macartney to Conway, 4 July 1766.

17. *SIRIO*, 67:29.

18. SP 91/77/320, Conway to Macartney, 19 December 1766.

19. Even more remarkable than Pitt's real plans were the designs attributed to him in Louis XV's secret correspondence. D'Havrincour told Louis XV that Pitt aimed "1.° d'entrer dans la ligue du Nord et, de concert avec la Russie et la Prusse, de forcer la Suède à y accéder aussi, à défaut, de lui déclarer la guerre; 2.° de détacher définitivement le nouvel empéreur d'Allemagne de la France, enfin de favoriser un partage de la Pologne entre la Russie et la Prusse": P. Coquelle, *L'Alliance Franco-Hollandaise contre l'Angleterre* 1735-1788, p. 199.

20. SP 90/85/166, 204, 216, Mitchell to Conway, 17 September, 8, 25 November 1766; *ibid.*, 175-78, 189, 223-28; 86/1-2, Conway to Mitchell, 30 September, 24 October, 4 December 1766, 2 January 1767.

21. SP 91/78/45, Conway to Macartney, 13 March 1767; RA Dipl. Angl., Nolcken to KP, 28 May 1767.

22. SP 91/78/30, Macartney to Conway, 26 January/6 February 1767.

23. SP 75/120/132, in Gunning to Conway, 4 May 1767.

24. SP 75/119/130-32, Titley to Grafton, 13 May 1766; *ibid.*, 251 Gunning to Conway, Most Secret, 2 September 1766.

25. SP 75/119/144-48, 292-96, 412-15, Conway to Titley, 13 June; to Gunning, 30 September; to Titley, 19 December 1766. And see, for what follows, Roberts, "Great Britain, Denmark and Russia, 1763-1770," pp. 248-52.

26. SP 75/120/13-14, Gunning to Conway, 17 January 1767; *Corr. min.*, II:306.

27. He was also afraid of alienating France since France was one of the guarantors of the treaty of 1750 with Sweden: Vedel, *Den aeldre Grev Bernstorffs Ministerium*, pp. 286-88.

28. SP 95/110/217, Conway to Goodricke, 19 December 1766.

29. SP 75/120/140, Conway to Gunning, 22 May 1767.

30. *SIRIO*, 67:286: "They load everything on to us," she minuted, "and it is enough to make one really angry that they act so weakly and blindly."

31. SP 91/77/267, Conway to Macartney, 30 September 1766.

32. P. Langford, *The First Rockingham Administration*, p. 88; cf. Spencer, pp. 60-61; but contrast Sir Herbert Butterfield, "British Foreign Policy, 1762-1765," p. 131.

33. Langford, p. 3.

34. RA Mindre sekreta deputationen, Ministerrelationer, G. A. von Nolckens riksdagsberättelse, 1769 (R 3478).

35. For a discussion of the Turkish clause, and of the possibility of Russian aid in America or Portugal, see Roberts, *"Splendid Isolation," 1763-1780*, pp. 27-30, 41-44.

36. *Pol. Corr.*, XXXI:529, Frederick to Finckenstein, 12 November 1767.

37. *SIRIO*, 87-179, Panin to Chernyshev, 27 October/7 November 1768.

38. SP 75/119/418, Conway to Titley, 19 December 1766.

39. SP 95/197/270-73, Goodricke to Grafton, 24 December 1765.

40. BM Add. MS 35,425, fo. 246, Goodricke to Hardwicke, 25 March 1766.

41. Though this was not the view of Sir Joseph Yorke, who wrote that if France had Sweden at her disposal "they would be very troublesome at *our* back door [my italics] and oblige us to divide our forces, more than would be agreeable if we were at war with the whole House of Bourbon. It is upon this account that I think Sweden worth our attention": Add. MS 35,369, fo. 10 (to Hardwicke, 31 January 1769).

42. "Our Treaty [of 1766] will prove, if followed, not a Wound only but a Mortal Blow to the French Interests in Sweden, by which the Field is now open for Russia to take what Walk She pleases; 'tis the great Scene of her Ambition; She is Principal in the Cause; and tho' His Majesty wishes, and is now endeavouring, to promote a close Union with that Court, He must still consider His, but as a secondary Interest there, and look upon any Alliance he can conclude with Sweden but as a Link of that Great Chain which must, if formed, infallibly remain in the Hands of Russia, and serve her Purposes chiefly . . . ": SP 91/77/319, to Macartney, 19 December 1766.

43. Even Chatham declared (24 October 1766) "that he would not advise to pay for or even court foreign alliances": *Correspondence of John, fourth Duke of Bedford*, III:349.

44. SP 91/78/39, Macartney to Conway, 2/13 February 1767; received 10 March.

45. *SIRIO*, 87:111, rescript to Ivan Chernyshev, July OS 1768; cf. SP 91/77/296, Macartney to Conway, 12/23 October 1766.

46. SP 91/77/321, Conway to Macartney, 19 December 1766.

47. Cf. von Arneth, *Geschichte Maria Theresias*, VIII:106-7. Frederick told Solms that he would ally with England only on conditions which did not bind him to upset the peace of Germany: *Pol. Corr.*, XXV:70 (7 March 1766).

48. L. B. de Marsangy, *Le chevalier de Vergennes. Son ambassade à Constantinople*, II: 304-5, 21 April 1766. Frederick the Great was of the same opinion: "l'Angleterre ne jouera qu'un chétif rôle en Europe, sans être fortifiée d'alliances": and again, "les ministres anglais, n'importe de quelque parti qu'ils soient, se voient dans la nécessité de s'y procurer aussi des amis," *Pol. Corr.*, XXVI:305, 314, to Maltzan, 11 September, 10 November 1767.

49. See, e.g., SP 91/76/320, Macartney to Grafton, 5/16 November 1765; *ibid.*, 77/225-26, Macartney to Conway, 1/12 August 1766.

50. SP 75/119/285, Conway to Titley, 30 September 1766.

51. As late as 23 April 1768, Robert Wood, one of the undersecretaries of state, minuted

"Nothing more improbable than that the Turks should be engaged in an offensive war with any Power in Christendom": SP 103/63/360.

52. SP 91/77/304, Macartney to Conway, 20/31 October 1766.

53. Panin told Macartney that if there seemed a chance of concluding an Anglo-Swedish alliance, even without a subsidy, "He would not only order Count Osterman to forward it, to the utmost of his Power, but would endeavour to persuade the Empress to accede to it": SP 91/78/8-11, Macartney to Goodricke (copy), 22 December/2 January 1766/7, in Macartney to Conway, s. d.; and Osterman told Schack that he had no doubt that Russia would do so: TKUA Sverige B 158, Promemoria by Schack, 2 October [November] 1766.

54. RA Dipl. Angl., Nolcken to KP, 3 July 1767.

55. SP 95/112/20-24, Conway to Goodricke, 20 February 1767.

56. See, e.g., SP 95/109/253, Goodricke to Conway, 17 July 1766.

57. C. F. Scheffer lamented it as "énigmatique et incomprehensible": UUB F 514, Scheffer to Crown Prince, 21 July 1767.

58. RRPUÄ, 26 November 1766; SP 95/110/221-23, Goodricke to Conway, 2 December 1766; 112/7-10, same to same, 13 January 1767.

59. SP 95/112/44, 162-65; SP 75/120/206.

60. SP 95/110/206-7, Goodricke to Conway, 18 November 1766; *SIRIO*, 67:208, Osterman to Panin, 14 November [NS] 1766.

61. SP 95/112/30, Goodricke to Conway, 17 February 1767; RRPUÄ, 16 February 1767.

62. SP 95/112/105-6, Goodricke to Conway, 5 May 1767; 112/118-19, Conway to Goodricke, 5 June 1767.

63. SP 95/112/137-40, Goodricke to Conway, 23 June 1767.

64. RA Kabinettet för utrikes brevvexling, KP to Nolcken, 23 June 1767; RA AVPR, Osterman to Catherine, 8/19 June 1767.

65. DRA TKUA Sverige B 161, Juel to Bernstorff, 12 June 1767.

66. *Ibid.*, Juel to Bernstorff, 12, 16 June 1767. Baron Frederick Ribbing had been Adolf Fredrik's choice as Senator in place of Rudenschiöld, and Goodricke's initial verdict on him was, "There is certainly no honester man in our Party than this new Senator, who has directed our clubs, and been in all our secrets": SP 95/109/251, 17 June 1767.

67. DRA TKUA, Sverige B 161, Juel to Bernstorff, 19 June 1767. Bernstorff agreed with him: in his Instruction for Diede von Fürstenstein (18 July 1767) he remarks that it was only in Sweden that British policy was active, thanks to the "génie" of Goodricke: *Corr. min.* II:329-32.

68. He told Juel "il étoit obligé d'avouer que le Ministère Anglois actuel qui connoissoit parfaitement l'Intérieur du Royaume, n'entendoit goutte à la politique du dehors": DRA TKUA Sverige B 161, Juel to Bernstorff, 3 July 1767.

69. *Ibid.*, SP 95/112/132-35, Goodricke to Conway, 19 June 1767.

70. RA Dipl. Angl., Nolcken to KP, 6 November, 18 December 1767, Apostille; 18 March 1768, Enskilt Apostille.

71. BM Egerton MS 2696, fo. 298, Goodricke to Gunning, 30 June 1767.

72. Helped (commented Juel) by "les Ménagements sans Nombre que Mr de Goodricke observe et dont il tire aussi habilement de fréquents avantages": DRA TKUA Sverige B 161, Juel to Bernstorff, 19 June 1767.

73. BM Add. MS 35,425, fos 249-50, Goodricke to Hardwicke, 19 June 1767.

74. DRA TKUA Sverige B 160, Schack to Bernstorff, 10 April 1767.

75. SP 95/113/187–88, Goodricke to Conway, 15 September 1767.

76. SP 95/113/25-26, Goodricke to Conway, 5 January 1768.

77. SP 95/112/192-93, 201-2, Conway to Gunning, 23 October 1767; BM Egerton MS 2696, fo. 412, Goodricke to Gunning, 13 November 1767. To a less sanguine reader than Goodricke, Conway's reply to him looks distinctly tepid: SP 95/112/201-2 (27 October 1767).

78. SP 75/120/206, Conway to Gunning, 23 October 1767; BM Egerton MS 2696, fos. 427-28, Goodricke to Gunning, 8 December 1767.

79. SP 75/120/219-23, Gunning to Conway, 7 November 1767.

80. For a defense of their program, see [Esbjörn Christian Reuterholm] *Uplysning för swenska Folket om Anledningen Orsaken och Afsigterne med Urtima Riksdag.*

81. Boëthius and Kromnow, I:579.

82. DRA TKUA Sverige B 161, Juel to Bernstorff, 10 July 1767.

83. *Ibid.*, 21 August, 15 September 1767.

84. SP 95/112/172-74, 186, Goodricke to Conway, 11 August, 15 September 1767.

85. BM Egerton MS 2696, fo. 358, Goodricke to Gunning, 25 September 1767. They seem however to have dropped six months later: on 24 March 1768 Fredenheim was writing to Bishop Mennander that food prices and rents had dropped by half since 1765, and that a civil servant's wage was now worth having, since its purchasing power had risen: *Fredenheims och Mennanders brefvexling*, pp. 60, 67.

86. *SRARP* XXVII:220: speech of Eric Linderstedt (a Cap).

87. Boëthius and Kromnow, II:11; Öberg, pp. 106-7.

88. Imports from Sweden for 1761-65 averaged £242,000 a year; for 1766-70, £179,000 a year, imports of bar-iron from all sources were in 1765, £513,697; in 1766, £323,992; in 1767, £365069 and in 1768, £447,488, which suggests that the decline affected Russian iron also: E. B. Schumpeter, *English Overseas Trade Statistics, 1697-1808*, pp. 18, 51.

89. Öberg, pp. 116-21.

90. DRA TKUA Sverige B 161, Juel to Bernstorff, 14 August 1767.

91. Birgitta Ericsson, *Bergstaden Falun 1720-1769*, p. 249; Öberg, p. 109. In 1763 the price per skeppund of raw copper was 275 silver daler; by 1768 it had dropped to 110.

92. Schumpeter, p. 51: the figures given apply to all types of timber imports.

93. DRA TKUA Sverige B 161, Juel to Bernstorff, 5 June 1767: SP 95/113/47, Goodricke to Weymouth, 1 March 1768.

94. Carl Trolle-Bonde, *Anteckningar om Bondesläkten. Riksrådet och Riksmarskalken Carl D. Bonde samt hans närmaste Anhöriga*, pp. 140-41.

95. DRA TKUA Sverige B 161, Juel to Bernstorff, 16 October 1767; Gyllenborg, *Mitt lefverne*, p. 70; Samuelsson, *De stora köpmanshusen*, p. 228; Nils Erdman, *Carl Michael Bellman*, pp. 217-18. A. J. von Höpken wrote to Tessin: "L'ennui, la tristesse, la désolation de tous les habitants, le déperissement du commerce et de tout ce qui est rélatif, tout cela m'a forcé à précipiter mon départ": Höpken, I:332, 28 December 1767.

96. DRA TKUA Sverige B 161, Juel to Bernstorff, 21 August 1767. For the supposed machinations of Hat merchants, see SP 95/112/159-61, 211-12, Goodricke to Conway, 4 August, 20 October 1767.

97. Tilas, I:317, 340; Boëthius and Kromnow, II:2.

98. SP 95/112/172-74, Goodricke to Conway, 11 August 1767.

99. SP 95/113/60, Goodricke to Weymouth, 12 April 1768.

100. Boëthius and Kromnow, II:16.

101. DRA TKUA Sverige B 161, Juel to Bernstorff, 21 August 1767.

102. Öberg, p. 113.

103. DRA TKUA Sverige B 161, Juel to Bernstorff, 23 October 1767.

104. *Ibid.*, Juel to Bernstorff, 8 December 1767.

105. ***Ibid.*** B 162, Juel to Bernstorff, 16 February 1768; SP 95/113/47, Goodricke to Weymouth, 1 March 1768; Boëthius and Kromnow, II:201.

106. SP 95/113/60, Goodricke to Weymouth, 12 April 1768.

107. DRA TKUA Sverige B 162, Juel to Bernstorff, 28 October 1768.

108. *Ibid.*, B 161, Juel to Bernstorff, 2 October, 20 November 1767.

109. SP 95/112/5, 145, 166-67, Goodricke to Conway, 9 January, 7 July, 18 August, 1767; SP 95/134, no. 48, Goodricke to Conway, Private, 27 October 1767.

110. SP 95/112/40, Goodricke to Conway, 17 March 1767. Goodricke had been saying this in his dispatches for some time: cf. SP 95/109/235-36, to Grafton, Separate, 3 June 1766.

111. SP 95/110/73, Goodricke to Conway, 3 August 1766.

112. SP 95/113/169-70, Goodricke to Rochford, 27 December 1768.

113. SP 95/110/74-76, Goodricke to Conway, 8 August 1766.

114. DRA TKUA Sverige B 161, Juel to Bernstorff, 23 October 1767, 27 November 1767; *ibid.*, B 162, Juel to Bernstorff, 7 June 1768; SP 95/113/93-95, Goodricke to Weymouth, 26 July 1768.

115. Schumpeter, p. 51; cf. Öberg, p. 111. The figures probably include quantities of plate-iron, illegally imported under the pretext of its being extra-broad bar-iron: see *Calendar of Home Office Papers, 1766-69*, pp. 24-25.

116. SP 95/112/227-28, Goodricke to Conway, 11 November 1767.

117. SP 95/112/229-30, Conway to Goodricke, 11 December 1767.

118. SP 95/113/1-2, Conway to Goodricke, 1 January 1768.

119. SP 95/113/44-46, Goodricke to Weymouth, 23 February 1768.

120. DRA TKUA Sverige B 161, Juel to Bernstorff, 20 November 1767; cf. SP 95/112/221-22, Goodricke to Conway, 10 November 1767.

121. SP 95/113/57-58, Goodricke to Weymouth, 29 March 1768.

122. *Ibid.*, 68-70, Goodricke to Weymouth, 10 May 1768. This was scarcely true in general: after all, Senator de Geer was among the staunchest Caps.

123. See his luminous and particular account in SP 95/134, no. 39, Goodricke to Conway, Private, 4 September 1767; SP 95/113/97, Goodricke to Weymouth, 9 August 1768; BM Egerton MS 2696, fos. 327, 357-58, Goodricke to Gunning, 11 August, 25 September 1767.

124. SP 95/112/245, Goodricke to Conway, 15 December 1767.

125. DRA TKUA Sverige B 160, Schack to Bernstorff, 3, 24 March 1767; SP 95/112/46, Goodricke to Conway, 24 March 1767; Boëthius, *Magistraten och Borgerskapet*, p. 344. On the Court's efforts to win over the burghers, RA AVPR 10, 28 December/8 January 1767/8, Osterman to Catherine II.

126. SP 95/112/32-34, Goodricke to Conway, 24 February 1767; BM Egerton MS 2696, fo. 208, Goodricke to Gunning, 1 March 1767; *Corr. min.* II:309-11, instruction for Juel, 16 March 1767; DRA TKUA Sverige C351, Bernstorff to Juel, 9 January 1768.

127. DRA TKUA Sverige C 351, Bernstorff to Juel, 9 February 1768.

128. UUB F 514, C. F. Scheffer to Prince Gustav, 6 April 1767; SP 95/112/60-62, Goodricke to Conway, 28 April 1767; Hennings, pp. 292-93.

129. RA Stavsundsarkivet, "Pro Memoria 1771," fos. 23-24; DRA TKUA Sverige B 161, Juel to Bernstorff, 11 August 1767; *ibid.* B 160 same to same 1 May 1767, for the furniture.

130. For Choiseul's views see *Recueil des instructions, Suède*, pp. 416-23; Fersen, III:373-74 (Choiseul to du Prat, 27 June 1768); RA Malmström avskr., Choiseul to du Prat, 14 August, 16 October 1768; Hennings, p. 293.

131. E.g., RA Malmström avskr., Choiseul to du Prat, 8 May, 28 August 1768.

132. UUB F 509, Creutz to Prince Gustav, 18 October 1767.

133. For the circumstances of its composition, see Hennings, pp. 288 ff.; UUB F 414, Konung Gustaf III:s egenhändiga Skrifter. Memorier och Bidrag till konungens egen historia, 1756-1778, no. 9; UUB F 417, Gustav to Adolf Fredrik, 12 October 1766; to Lovisa Ulrika, 13 October 1766. For the reactions, SP 95/112/65-68, Goodricke to Conway, 27 November 1766; DRA TKUA Sverige B 159, Schack to Bernstorff, 28 November 1766 (where Schack described it as "d'une force terrible"); *Corr. min.*, II:300.

134. For these see Malmström, VI:21, 26, 30; SP 95/113/39-43, 109-11.

135. UUB F 478, Gustav III:s Dagbok.

136. UUB F 509.

137. UUB F 414, no. 10; Fersen, III:40-41; Hennings, pp. 309-11.

138. Hennings, pp. 313-15.

139. *Ibid.*, p. 316.

140. *Ibid.*, pp. 323-24; SP 95/113/105, Goodricke to Weymouth, 9 September 1768.

141. *Pol. Corr.*, XXV:293, Frederick to Solms, 7 November 1766. He took care to secure a Russian guarantee against loss as a result of Polish complications: *ibid.*, XXVI:33-35, 61 ff. 119-20, 165; For Frederick's policy regarding the Dissidents, see Ambrose Jobert, "Le Grand Frédéric et la Pologne," pp. 230-31, which is based on W. Konopczyński, *Frydryk Wielki a Polska* (Poznań 1947).

142. For Gustav's strong feelings about Poland, see UUB F 478, Gustav III:s Dagbok, 19 August 1767, 28 November 1768; *Gustav III:s och Lovisa Ulrikas brevvexling*, I:117, 148-50.

143. For Osterman's pressure on Löwenhielm to make a declaration in favor of the Dissidents, RA AVPR 10, Osterman to Catherine, 5/16 March 1767. The Senate debated the Polish question on at least fourteen occasions between June 1766 and August 1767: RRPUÄ, passim.

144. Hennings, pp. 300-303.

145. DRA TKUA Sverige B 160, Schack to Bernstorff, 10 February 1767; SP 95/112/26, Goodricke to Conway, 10 February 1767.

146. UUB F 414, no. 18, Gustav to Sinclair, 8 November 1768.

147. Fersen, III:40-41, 373-74, 377-79; *Gustav III:s och Lovisa Ulrikas brevvexling*, I:150; RA Stavsundsarkivet, "Pro memoria 1771," fo. 25; RA Malmström avskr., du Prat to Choiseul, 7 September 1768; Hennings, pp. 306-8, 312, 314, 318.

148. E.g., DRA TKUA Sverige C 351, Bernstorff to Juel, 9 January, 9 February 1768; Sverige B 162, Juel to Bernstorff, 22 March, 19 April 1768; Rusland B 96, Dreyer to Bernstorff, 29 February/11 March 1768.

149. SP 95/110/83, Conway to Goodricke, 9 September 1766.

150. SP 95/110/184-85, 192-93, Goodricke to Conway, 8, 10 November 1766; DRA TKUA Sverige B 159, Schack to Bernstorff, 10, 11, 14 November 1766. Bernstorff, deeply shocked, wrote that "c'est à mon gré une idée si hardie, si téméraire, et si criminelle que je ne l'aurais pas supposée même aux plus fanatiques des enthousiastes de la Cour": *Corr. min.*, II:299-300. Catherine II merely scribbled on Osterman's dispatch: "Then he may go to the devil": *SIRIO*, 67:204. Frederick the Great dismissed the idea as "absurd," and rebuked Cocceji for retailing it to Solms: one more "coq-à-l'âne" of this kind, and he would be recalled: "Gardez-vous bien de ne plus faire de pareils micmacs": *Pol. Corr.*, XXV:333, 335.

151. *SIRIO*, 67: 204, 217.

152. SP 95/110/216, Conway to Goodricke, 19 December 1766.

153. DRA TKUA Sverige B 162, Juel to Bernstorff, 19 February 1768; *ibid.* C 351, Bernstorff to Juel, 13 February, 12 March 1768; Malmström, VI:30, 33.

154. DRA TKUA Sverige B 162, Juel to Bernstorff, 5, 15 February 1768.

155. SP 95/113/40-43. He also asked urgently that he might be informed what money France had sent, or was to send, to Sweden: to this also he received no answer. Goodricke had told Schack in January 1767 that he was authorized to resist an Extraordinary Diet, but clearly he felt he had gone too far in doing so: DRA TKUA Sverige B 160, Schack to Bernstorff, 13 January 1767.

156. SP 95/110/83, 172-74, 227-29; 112/108, 203.

157. SP 95/112/42, Conway to Goodricke, 3 April 1767.

158. SP 95/113/108, Conway to Goodricke, 22 May 1767.

159. In June 1766 Vergennes was informed that to secure a Turkish declaration of war, Louis XV "Ne met pas de bornes à la dépense et vous autorise à y employer l'argent que vous croirez nécessaire, que vous mettrez sur vos frais extraordinaires, en me prevenant de chaque somme que vous dépenserez": Marsangy, *Le Chevalier de Vergennes. Son ambassade à Constantinople*, II:319.

160. Fersen, III:373-74; RA Malmström avskr., Choiseul to du Prat, 14 August 1768.

161. RA Malmström avskr., Choiseul to Modène, 16 October 1768.

162. RA Malmström avskr., du Prat to Choiseul, 23 September 1768, with enclosures.

163. SP 95/113/110-11, Goodricke to Weymouth, 23 September 1768; and *ibid*. 123-24, same to same, 25 October 1768.

164. SP 95/113/136-38, Goodricke to Rochford, 22 November 1768.

165. SP 95/113/138-40, Goodricke to Rochford, 19 November 1768.

166. SP 95/113/123-24, Goodricke to Weymouth, 25 October 1768.

167. DRA TKUA Sverige B 162, Juel to Bernstorff, 8 November 1768.

168. SP 95/113/125-27, Goodricke to Rochford, 1, 8 November 1766; UUB F 478, Gustav III:s Dagbok, 3 November 1768; BM Egerton MS 2697, fo. 298, Goodricke to Gunning, 8 November 1768; RRPUÄ, 3 November 1768. Löwenhielm had died in March, and had been succeeded as chancery-president by Friesendorff.

169. DRA TKUA Sverige B 162, Juel to Bernstorff, 8 November 1768.

170. SP 95/113/19, Rochford to Goodricke, 2 December 1768.

171. *Gustavianska Papperen*, I:75-8, Gustav to C. W. von Düben; Hennings, pp. 331-32.

172. DRA TKUA Sverige B 162, Juel to Bernstorff, 22 November 1768.

173. Hennings, p. 324.

174. UUB F 414, no. 18; Hennings, p. 334-35.

175. For Scheffer's plan for a revolution on 2 November, UUB F 514, Scheffer to Gustav, 20 October 1768; For Gustav's criticism of the written promise, as vague and inadequate, UUB F 414, no. 20.

176. Jonas Nordensson, "Kronprins Gustavs författningsprojekt 1768," pp. 493-97.

177. UUB F 414, no. 18.

178. Hennings, p. 342; Malmström, VI:59.

179. DRA TKUA Sverige B 162, Juel to Bernstorff, 25 November 1768; SP 95/113/141-43, Goodricke to Rochford, 6 December 1768.

180. Juel's verdict on Osterman was, "C'est un très honorable et galant Homme, mais il m'embarrasse presque toujours par la Manière douteuse, craintive et circonspecte au delà de toute expression, dont Il me parle sur les affaires un peu épineuses": DRA TKUA Sverige B 162, Juel to Bernstorff, 5 January 1768.

181. SP 95/113/141-43, Goodricke to Rochford, 6 December 1768; DRA TKUA Sverige B 162, Juel to Bernstorff, 6, 9 December 1768.

182. For what follows, see Roberts, *Swedish and British Parliamentarism*, pp. 14, 19-21.

183. Malmström, VI:40-43, 56-58.

184. For the fears of a young civil servant on this score, see J. G. Oxenstierna, *Ljuva ungdomstid*, p. 170.

185. Hennings, pp. 343-44; Malmström, VI:60-61; Fersen, III:40-43; SP 95/113/144-47.

186. UUB F 478, Gustav III:s Dagbok, 12 December 1768.

187. DRA TKUA Sverige B 162, Juel to Bernstorff, 16 December 1768.

188. For a full narrative of the crisis, see Malmström, VI:60-80. Goodricke's account of it is in his dispatches of 13, 16, 18, 20 December 1768: SP 95/113/144-47, 148-51, 152-54, 157-58. See also BM Egerton MS 2697, fos. 318, 319-20, Goodricke to Gunning, 16 December 1768, 1 January 1769; Juel's account is in DRA TKUA Sverige B 162, Juel to Bernstorff, 16, 20 December 1768. For a contemporary account of the civil service strike, Oxenstierna,

Ljuva ungdomstid, pp. 172-73; for a later account by a Cap, see [Reuterholm], *Uplysning för swenska folket*, pp. 35-40.

189. DRA TKUA Sverige B 162, Juel to Bernstorff, 16 December 1768: they thought, all the same, of presenting a joint declaration, but Friesendorff begged them to hold their hands: *ibid*.

190. SP 95/113/144-47, Goodricke to Rochford, 13 December 1768.

191. SP 95/113/157-60, Goodricke to Rochford, 20 December 1768.

192. BM Egerton MS 2698, fos. 3-4, Goodricke to Gunning, 1 January 1769; DRA TKUA Sverige B 162, Juel to Bernstorff, 16, 20 December 1768.

193. DRA TKUA Sverige B 162, Juel to Bernstorff, 20 December 1768.

194. *SIRIO*, 87:253, Panin to Osterman, 31 December 1768.

195. DRA TKUA Sverige B 162, Juel to Bernstorff, 6 December 1768.

CHAPTER IX
LORD ROCHFORD AND THE HAT DIET

1. Goodricke described him (to Rochford, 3 January 1769) as "Our greatest enemy, and the most dangerous man in Sweden . . . A man of profound Dissimulation and of a sanguinary Temper, who took away the Lives of those who opposed his measures in 1756, and who is now forming a Party to govern more absolutely than he did then. His Language is that of Liberty; at the same time we know him to have entered into the Scheme of those who accelerate the Subversion of the present form of Government": SP 95/114/104.

2. RA Stavsundsarkivet, "Pro memoria 1771," fos. 17-19; UUB F 514, Bref från . . . Carl Scheffer [to Gustav III], 19 Jan. 1769; *Gustavianska Papperen*, I:84; Hennings, pp. 352-53.

3. RA Sjöholms arkivet, Gyldenstolpske samlingen, Bref ifrån . . . Sinclair till N. P. Gyldenstolpe, 4 January 1769: "Pour moi, je vous ai déjà marqué, que la route me désolait; j'entrevois, que ce n'est que le vieux penchant pour l'indépendance à l'égard de Mamma, qui l'a [i.e., Gustav] fait prendre."

4. SP 95/114/32, Rochford to Goodricke, 17 March 1769; Malmström, VI:85-87.

5. Daniel Tilas, *Anteckningar från riksdagen 1769-1770* (hereafter Tilas, II), p. 9. Juel wrote privately to Schack: "Bon Dieu, quel pais que la Suède! La haine, la fureur et les intrigues absorbent actuellement tout autre sentiment": *Schack-Rathlous Arkiv*, p. 274.

6. [Reuterholm], *Uplysning för Swenska Folket*. Malmström doubted whether the usual attribution to Reuterholm is correct, and his doubts seem to be confirmed by Osterman: AVPR 104, Osterman to Catherine II, 13/24 November 1769.

7. SP 95/114/200, Goodricke to Rochford, 12 April 1769. Goodricke made it his business to read Swedish political pamphlets,"most of them fit only for waste paper at the end of the year." "Nevertheless," he added,"this pamphlet learning is not to be neglected by those who will know the temper of the times": BM Add. MS 35,425, fo. 252, Goodricke to Hardwicke, 1 March 1768.

8. AVPR 75, Stakhiev to Panin, 1/12 May 1769.

9. For Finlay's electioneering activities, SP 95/113/165-68; 114/109-10, 136-37.

10. DRA TKUA Sverige B 163, Juel to Bernstorff, 10 January 1769; SP 95/114/114-18, Goodricke to Rochford, 24 January 1769; UUB F 386, Cathcart to Goodricke, 31 March 1769. Osterman likewise urged Panin to delay the resumption of grain exports (due in settlement of Russia's subsidy arrears to Sweden) until after the elections: AVPR 104, Osterman to Panin, 4/15 February 1769; cf. *SIRIO*, 87:333.

11. DRA TKUA Sverige B 164, Juel to Bernstorff, 8 September 1769.

12. *Ibid*., B 163, Juel to Bernstorff, 17 March 1769.

13. SP 95/114/103, Goodricke to Rochford, 3 January 1769.

14. DRA TKUA Sverige B 163, Juel to Bernstorff, 31 January, 10, 28 February, 3 March 1769; *SIRIO*, 87:263, 350, 356; *Pol. Corr.*, XXVII:65, 160; SP 91/80/188-92.

15. See above. Actual expenditure was at first on a much more modest scale: by the end of March Osterman and Juel had spent (according to Goodricke's estimate, which is unlikely to have been too low) no more than £25,700: SP 95/114/149, 155-56, 186-87. But there must have been heavy spending in the next three weeks, if Juel's statement is correct that he began the Diet with only 159,350 d.k.m. in the account (about £3,187): DRA TKUA Sverige B 164, Juel to Bernstorff, 12 December 1769.

16. *Correspondence of George III*, III:370. Sir Joseph Yorke, however, said of him that he was "universally esteemed as a plain dealer": BM Add MS 35,370, fo. 16. Horace Walpole's judgment was: "Lord Rochford was a man of no abilities, and of as little knowledge, except in the routine of office; but he meant honestly, behaved plausibly, was pliant enough to take whatever was offered to him, and too inoffensive to give alarm or jealousy to any party": Horace Walpole, *Memoirs of the Reign of George III*, III:248.

17. Martens, *Recueil des traités et conventions*, IX (X):280; and cf. *SIRIO*, 97:350. For his "vivacity," RA Dipl. Angl., Nolcken to KP, 20 June, 22 July 1769; and cf. *ibid.*, Nolcken to KP, 11 November 1768.

18. As Nolcken noted: RA Dipl. Angl., Nolcken to KP, 30 December 1768.

19. *The Letters of Junius*, ed. C. W. Everett, p. 190 n. 1.

20. BM Add MS 35,444, fos. 62-63, Goodricke to Sir J. Yorke, 25 March 1766. See in general D. B. Horn, "The Diplomatic Experience of Secretaries of State," Of ten Northern Secretaries between 1761 and 1782 only Rochford, Sandwich, and Stormont had any experience; of eight Southern Secretaries, only Rochford and Richmond.

21. SP 95/114/137, Goodricke to Rochford, 15 February 1769, where he writes of an exchange of letters in 1767.

22. For these appeals, see SP 95/114/114-18, 144, 156-57; for Rochford's final rejection of them (after taking Cabinet opinion), *ibid.*, 39-40 (24 March 1769). Goodricke was well aware of the risk the Senate would run by accepting a subsidy so near to the meeting of the Diet: *ibid.*, 122-23 (3 February 1769).

23. J. F. Ramsey, *Anglo-French Relations 1763-1770*, p. 199, citing Choiseul to Modène, 24 January, 5 February 1769.

24. SP 95/114/149; SP 95/134 [? Phelps] to Goodricke, 13 January 1769.

25. For detailed accounts of Goodricke's credits and expenditure, see SP 95/116/417-23.

26. Rochford had more room for maneuver than his predecessors: in the spring of 1769 parliament voted to pay the Civil List debt: BM Add. MS 35,369, fo. 24, Sir J. Yorke to Hardwicke, 21 March 1769.

27. SP 95/114/161; 116/418. Even Panin testified to Goodricke's having used his resources to the utmost advantage: SP 91/80/190.

28. *SIRIO*, 87:246, Panin to Filosoffof, 21 December/1 January 1768/69.

29. DRA TKUA Rusland C 180, Bernstorff to Scheel, 23 February 1769; *Corr. min.*, II: 383-90, 409, 413 n. 1; *SIRIO*, 87: 335, 415.

30. DRA TKUA Sverige B 163, Juel to Bernstorff, 28 February: 12, 24, 31 March 1769; Sverige C 351, Bernstorff to Juel, 12 March, 8 April 1769.

31. *Ibid.*, Sverige B 163, Juel to Bernstorff, 31 March 1769, no. 2.

32. *Corr. min.*, II:380-81; SP 75/122/77-78, Gunning to Rochford, 7 March 1769.

33. SP 75/122/12-13, 23-24, Rochford to Gunning, 14 April, 9 May 1769; *SIRIO*, 87:415.

34. UUB F 386, Cathcart to Goodricke, 16/27 December 1769.

35. SP 95/114/13-14, Rochford to Goodricke, 31 January 1769; and in identical terms to Cathcart, 13 January 1769: SP 91/80/3-4.

36. *Pol. Corr.*, XXVIII:26, Frederick to Solms, 10 January 1769.

37. Though in actual fact the Senate itself had taken a resolution in this sense on 20 January: UUB F 478, Gustav III:s dagbok, 20 January 1769; SP 95/114/107-8.

38. He had already ordered his ambassador at Constantinople to offer mediation (an offer which had been received coldly by Panin), and he felt that he could not now invite the good offices of a third power: SP 95/114/14, Rochford to Goodricke, 31 January 1769.

39. SP 95/114/21-24, Rochford to Goodricke, 24 February 1769.

40. SP 91/80/129.

41. What follows is based on the reports of Goodricke and Juel, which do not agree in detail: SP 95/114/139-47; DRA TKUA Sverige B 163, Juel to Bernstorff, 15 February, 11 April 1769.

42. He later produced an amended draft of his own: *Pol. Corr.*, XXVIII:150 (28 February 1769).

43. DRA TKUA Sverige C 351, Bernstorff to Juel, 21 February, 1 April, 8 April 1769.

44. DRA TKUA Rusland C 180, Bernstorff to Scheel, 23 February 1769 (no. II).

45. *Ibid.*, Sverige C 351, Bernstorff to Juel, 18 April 1769.

46. *Ibid.*, Sverige C 351, Bernstorff to Juel, 11 February 1769 (nos. I and II). Not without some effect: see C. F. Scheffer's letter to Schack, 24 February 1769, assuring him that in the event of victory the Hats would recur to their old policy of close union with Denmark: *Schack-Rathlous Arkiv*, p. 382.

47. DRA TKUA Sverige C 351, Bernstorff to Juel, 18 April 1769.

48. SP 95/114/31-32; cf. SP 91/80/151-52.

49. SP 91/81/22-25, Rochford to Cathcart, 6 June 1769.

50. SP 95/114/33-34, 50-51.

51. SP 91/80/168-70, Cathcart to Rochford, 28 February NS 1769. Solms reported similarly on the same day: *Pol. Corr.*, XXVII:183. Already in January Panin had written to Chernyshev, "In actual fact I do not in the least despair of restraining Sweden from war even without English subsidies, only we need not disclose this hope to the English Court": *SIRIO*, 87:299. Frederick had discounted the possibility equally early: *Pol. Corr.*, XXVIII:37 (to Solms, 16 January 1769); SP 95/114/43, Rochford to Goodricke, 28 March 1769.

52. SP 91/80/121, 168-70, 200, Cathcart to Rochford, 31 January NS, 28 February NS, 13 March NS 1769.

53. SP 95/112/32, Goodricke to Conway, 24 February 1767.

54. SP 95/114/137, Goodricke to Rochford, 15 February 1769.

55. SP 95/114/137-38, Goodricke to Rochford, 15 February 1769; BM Egerton MS 2698, fo. 54, Goodricke to Gunning, 15 February 1769.

56. SP 95/114/202, Goodricke to Rochford, 14 April, 1769.

57. SP 95/114/203-6, Goodricke to Rochford, 19 April 1769: "the Prince Royal during the three days he has been here hath walked the Streets like a candidate for an election, having people with him, who can tell him the names of those he meets, and speaking to all without Distinction." Gyllenborg recalled in his memoirs how "King and people were like a happy family of parents and children in each other's company. There was a similarly complete liberty in society, all embraced with the same good nature, joy was depicted in every countenance": Gyllenborg, *Mitt lefverne*, p. 77.

58. SP 95/114/208-10; 115/3-4, Goodricke to Rochford, 22, 29 April 1769; and cf. Tilas, II:13-15; *Gustavianska Papperen*, I:89-91, for similar exploits by the Caps.

59. Goodricke, getting in early, managed to obtain one for £25 a month on the outskirts, "Very commodiously placed for having Couriers without any Body knowing it," as well as a private room in town for secret interviews; but Modène was summarily evicted from his, since it was needed for the use of the Estates: SP 95/134, Goodricke to Porten, 12 April 1769; cf. Tilas, II:10.

60. SP 95/134, Goodricke to Porten, 12 April 1769; SP 95/114/160-61, Goodricke to Rochford, 7 March 1769; RRPUÄ, I., 6 February 1769; *Fredenheims och Mennanders brefvexling*, p. 88; *Amiral Carl Tersmedens Memoarer*, V:7, 10-14.

61. SP 95/113/183, Goodricke to Rochford, 30 December 1768.

62. *Ibid*., 114/176-80.

63. *Pol. Corr.*, XXVIII:26, to Solms, 10 January 1769; *ibid*., 180,293, to Cocceji, 13 March 1769, 30 April 1769.

64. SP 95/114/208-10, Goodricke to Rochford, 22 April 1769.

65. DRA TKUA Sverige B 163, Juel to Bernstorff, 22, 26 April 1769; SP 75/122/117-18, Gunning to Rochford, 6 May 1769.

66. DRA TKUA Sverige B 163, Juel to Bernstorff, 15 April 1769.

67. *Ibid*., Sverige C 351, Bernstorff to Juel, 2 May 1769; Sverige B 163, Juel to Bernstorff, 27 April 1769; BM Egerton MS 2698, fo. 119, Goodricke to Gunning, 26 April 1769; SP 95/115/1-2, Goodricke to Rochford, 26 April 1769.

68. RA Dipl. Angl., Nolcken to KP, 21 April 1769: cf. *ibid*., same to same, 28 March 1769.

69. RRPUÄ 1769, I; cf. *SRARP*, XXVII:57, 60.

70. SP 95/115/18-21, Goodricke to Rochford, 10 May 1769.

71. Compare Nolcken's report of Rochford's reaction: RA Dipl. Angl., Nolcken to KP, 26 May 1769; and SP 95/115/55-57, Rochford to Goodricke, 26 May 1769.

72. Cf. *Pol. Corr.*, XXVII:418, Frederick to Rohd, 2 November 1768, and *SIRIO*, 87: 299, Panin to Chernyshev, 2 January OS 1769.

73. M. C. Morison, "The Duc de Choiseul and the Invasion of England, 1768-1770."

74. See RA Kabinettet för utrikes brevvexling, Cirkulär, 15 January 1771. For his moderation on first going to France, *Chatham Corr.*, III:113, Shelburne to Chatham, 18 October 1766; *Bedford Corr.*, III:390-1, Rigby to Bedford, 12 September 1767.

75. D. B. Horn, *British Public Opinion and the First Partition of Poland*, pp. 3,9.

76. In the last third of the century not more than an average of 27 British ships a year went to the Levant, compared with some 600-700 to Russia: M. A. Anderson, "Great Britain and the Russian Fleet, 1769-70," p. 149. And see A. C. Wood, *A History of the Levant Company*, pp. 140, 151-61, 166.

77. *Pol. Corr.*, XXVIII:59 (to Maltzan, 23 January 1769); 77 (to Solms, 30 January 1769); 92-93 (to Maltzan, 6 February 1769).

78. I. de Madariaga, *Great Britain, Russia, and the Armed Neutrality of 1780*, p. 132.

79. *Pol. Corr.*, XXVII:507-8, Maltzan to Frederick, 2 December 1768. He told Maltzan that he could "take it as a barometer for the future, that he would not remain in the ministry without forming an alliance with the Northern powers, and that if he did not succeed, I could be assured that his views had not prevailed."

80. Choiseul and Rossignol (France's consul in St. Petersburg) concurred in the view that Catherine's position was now extremely weak: *SIRIO*, 141:482, 519.

81. BM Egerton MS 2697, fos. 259-60; cf. *ibid*., 2701, fos. 6, 8, 95. For other judgments see, e.g., HMC *Laing*, II:466; *Pol. Corr.*, XXVII:73 n., where Maltzan, writing what Frederick wanted to hear, described him as having neither great gifts of intelligence nor of character.

82. See the comments of Gunning (his successor in St. Petersburg) in 1772: SP 91/90/206; 91/41-42, 141.

83. PRO SP Foreign Treaty Papers, 63, has a large collection of documents bearing on the alliance, 1763-71, with annotations by Cathcart: see especially fos. 37-62 ("Principles of the Alliance") and fos. 353-75 (Memorandum by Cathcart, 23 April 1768, with comments by Robert Wood).

84. SP 91/79/18-24, Weymouth to Cathcart, 30 September 1768.

85. SP 91/79/415-16, Cathcart to Rochford, 12/23 December 1768.

86. SP 91/79/283, Cathcart to Weymouth, 12/23 October 1768. Rochford declined this

embarrassing offer, and suggested financial aid instead: *ibid.*, 79/44-45, Rochford to Cathcart, 11 November 1768.

87. A suggestion which reached Swedish ears, and caused a painful impression: RA Kabinettet för utrikes brevvexling, KP to Ribbing, 6 October 1768; *ibid.*, KP to Nolcken, 7 October 1768; RA Dipl. Musc. Ribbing to KP, 3/14 October 1768.

88. SP 91/79/219-68, Cathcart to Weymouth, 7/18 October 1768; *ibid.*, 280-81, 287, 351, 368, 405, 407-12.

89. SP 91/79/48-49, 50-53, Rochford to Cathcart, 25 November 1768.

90. Rochford's arguments can be collected from his letters to Cathcart: SP 91/80/1-4 (12 January 1769); 21-23 (17 January); 70-80 (17 February).

91. SP 91/80/70-98, Rochford to Cathcart, 17 February 1769.

92. Karl Stählin, *Geschichte Russlands von den Anfängen bis zur Gegenwart*, II:503. So much for Choiseul's egregious expectations, relayed by Creutz to Lovisa Ulrika, that "the least reverse will precipitate her from her throne" (23 August 1768): Fersen, III:377-79.

93. Note by Catherine on Chernyshev's dispatch of 3 May NS 1769: *SIRIO*, 87:349.

94. SP 75/122/79, Gunning to Rochford, 7 March 1769.

95. UUB F 386, Cathcart to Goodricke, 31 March NS 1769.

96. SP 91/81/58-165.

97. SP 91/81/185-89, Rochford to Cathcart, 30 June 1769.

98. BM Add. MS 9242, fo. 53, Rochford to Cathcart, 28 July 1769.

99. SP 91/81/240-43.

100. SP 95/115/7-8, Goodricke to Rochford, 3 May 1769; BM Egerton MS 2698, fo. 127, Goodricke to Gunning, 6 May 1769.

101. DRA TKUA Sverige B 163, Juel to Bernstorff, 16 June 1769.

102. *SIRIO*, 87:446, Panin to Osterman, 6/17 June 1769.

103. RA Riksdagsjournaler, G. Reuterholm, Dagbok öfwer början af 1769 års riksdag, fo. 74; Tilas, II:14, 25.

104. UUB F 514, Scheffer to Gustav, 29 April, 1769; *SRARP*, XXVII, 30-31; Appendix, pp. 4-5.

105. For the *licentiering*, see *SRARP*, XXVII:67-124; and in general, L. Linnarsson, *Riksrådens licentiering. En Studie i frihetstidens parlamentarism*, pp. 280-328.

106. RA Tessinska samlingen. Brev till C. G. Tessin, VI. Fr. Sparre to Tessin, 11 May 1769.

107. SP 95/115/22-24, Goodricke to Rochford, 10 May 1769.

108. For van Wallwijk, see G. Ehrensvärd's verdict, in *Dela Gardieska Archivet*, XV:66; Tilas, II:47-8, 60; UUB F 514, C. F. Scheffer to Gustav, 25 April 1769.

109. Tilas, II:52.

110. RA Ekebladska samlingen, Bref till Claes Ekeblad, vol. 2 (VI), Fersen to Ekeblad, 12, 25 May 1769.

111. Tilas, II:65; RA Skrifvelser till C. F. Scheffer, V. Schack to Scheffer, 18 June 1769.

112. Tilas, II:63; Oxenstierna, *Dagboks-Anteckningar,* p. 33.

113. RA Stavsundsarkivet, "Pro Memoria, 1771," fos. 30-35.

114. Adolf Fredrik's intended memorandum is in UUB F 433.

115. The four were Nils Bielke, Sinclair, J. F. von Schwerin, and Ulrik Bark.

116. Malmström, VI:123.

117. UUB F 414, Gustaf III:s egenhändiga skrifter, no. 28.

118. E. g., Oxenstierna: *Dagboks-Anteckningar*, p. 61.

119. "Pro Memoria, 1771," fo. 35. Though Modène wrote bravely to Choiseul on 24 May that he expected a successful reform of the constitution, once the finances had been adjusted, and the end of the Diet by September: RA Malmström avskr.

120. Fersen, III:46.

121. Hennings, p. 357. Choiseul had urged moderation, and would have liked to see Reuterholm exempt from *licentiering*, as being a man of sincere convictions: Malmström, VI: 116, n. 1.

122. *Pol. Corr.*, XXVIII:331 (to Goltz, 18 May), 369 (to Prince Henry, 12 June), 394 (to Cocceji, 23 June).

123. *SIRIO*, 87:433, Panin to Osterman, 11/22 May 1769; SP 75/112/119-20, Gunning to Rochford, 13 May 1769; SP 95/115/25-27, Goodricke to Rochford, 13 May 1769.

124. RA AVPR 75, Stakhiev to Panin, 1/12, 20/31 May 1769.

125. *SIRIO*, 87:446, Panin to Osterman 6/17 June 1769; cf. *Pol. Corr.*, XXIX:4-5, Solms to Frederick, 18 July 1769.

126. DRA TKUA Sverige B 164, Juel to Bernstorff, 9 June 1769 (cf. B 163, same to same, 17 May); Sverige C 351, Bernstorff to Juel, 17 June.

127. On 29 April Bernstorff wrote to Juel: "Il ne s'agit plus de conserver le commandement aux bonnets, ils l'ont laissé échapper, ni de combattre le système de la France, il triomphe, les Anglais l'ont voulu. [!] . . . Il n'est plus question que de sauver la constitution et la liberté de la Suède. . . . Il faudra, s'il est possible, capituler avec les chefs du parti français et s'arranger avec eux aux meilleures conditions possibles": II:397-98.

128. DRA TKUA Sverige C 351, Bernstorff to Juel, 1 April 1769, and cf. same to same, 17 June 1769 (no. II).

129. For Danish approaches to the leading Hats, see DRA TKUA Sverige C 351, Bernstorff to Juel, 29 April, 6 May, 24 June 1769; Sverige B 164, Juel to Bernstorff, 6 June, 30 June.

130. SP 75/112/119-20, Gunning to Rochford, 13 May 1769.

131. DRA TKUA Sverige B 164, Juel to Bernstorff, 24 June 1769. Beth Hennings misread this dispatch when she wrote: "Man gjorde sig alltså nu rent av förhoppningar på att Fersen helt övergivit alla reformplaner" (Hennings, p. 360). In fact, Juel had said exactly the opposite.

132. SP 95/115/52-54, Rochford to Goodricke, 9 May 1769.

133. BM Add. MS 35,369, fo. 28, Sir Joseph Yorke to Lord Hardwicke, 4 April 1769.

134. SP 95/114/213-14; 115/4-5, Goodricke to Rochford, 26 April, 29 April 1769.

135. SP 95/115/28-29, Goodricke to Rochford 20 May 1769; BM Egerton MS 2699, fo. 78, Goodricke to Gunning, 20 May 1769. He was right to worry: Juel's dispatch of 17 May shows that he was thinking in these terms—and taking care that Goodricke should not know of it: DRA TKUA Sverige B 163.

136. SP 95/115/10-11, Goodricke to Rochford, 6 May 1769.

137. SP 95/115/7-8, Goodricke to Rochford, 3 May 1769; BM Egerton MS 2698, fo. 127, Goodricke to Gunning, 6 May 1769. Osterman and Juel professed to agree with him, and to urge their governments accordingly, but though Juel thought that it might do good if the plan for such a demand were allowed to be known, neither he nor Osterman was willing to make it: DRA TKUA Sverige B 163, Juel to Bernstorff, 6 May 1769.

138. SP 95/115/8, Goodricke to Rochford, 3 May 1769.

139. SP 95/115/57, Rochford to Goodricke, 26 May 1769.

140. SP 95/115/53-55, Goodricke to Rochford, 13 June 1769.

141. SP 95/115/70-71, Rochford to Goodricke, 28 July; SP 91/81/189, Rochford to Cathcart, 30 July 1769.

142. DRA TKUA Sverige B 163, Juel to Bernstorff, 21 February 1769.

143. RA Riksdagsjournaler, G. Reuterholm, Dagbok öfwer början af 1769 års riksdag, fos. 50, 63.

144. DRA TKUA Sverige B 163, Juel to Bernstorff, 26 April 1769.

145. DRA TKUA Sverige C 351, Bernstorff to Juel, 2 May 1769.

146. *Ibid.*, Bernstorff to Juel, 6 May 1769.

147. Tilas, II:57; *SRARP*, XXVII:155.

148. Already on 20 April Gustav wrote to C. F. Scheffer, "Pechlin betrays us, they say, or will betray us, in the great question. So much the worse for him": *Gustavianska Papperen*, I:91.

149. Tilas, II:68, 72, 75.

150. Hj. Lindeberg, *En ränksmidare,* p. 96; *Gustav III:s och Lovisa Ulrikas brevväxling*, I:175-76.

151. SP 95/115/48, Goodricke to Rochford, 6 June 1769. Osterman had good grounds for thinking so: on 11 August Rochford relayed a French intercept containing the information "that Monsr de Modène having strong suspicions of Colonel Pechlin has order'd an offer to be made him of one hundred thousand Dalers to quit the Diet, and go to his Regiment, and will look on this as a Test of his Intentions. In case of his Refusal, M. de Modène proposes to employ that sum to carry his exclusion from the House of Nobles for ever": SP 95/115/76.

152. SP 95/115/62, Rochford to Goodricke, 9 June 1769.

153. SP 95/115/66-68, Goodricke to Rochford, 27 June 1769; DRA TKUA Sverige B 164, Juel to Bernstorff, 27 June 1769.

154. SP 95/115/7, Goodricke to Rochford, 6 May 1769.

155. SP 95/115/66-68.

156. See, e.g., Reuterholm, Dagbok, fos. 53, 92, 95.

157. *Ibid*., fos. 103-4.

158. A figure which tallies significantly, perhaps, with the Cap operators' calculation of 181 purchasable votes.

159. Reuterholm, Dagbok, fos. 77, 81, 123.

160. SP 95/115/74-75, Goodricke to Rochford, 11 July 1769; cf. Reuterholm, Dagbok, fo. 109 (22 July 1769). Tilas dated his open adhesion to the Caps to as early as 20 July: Tilas, II:83.

161. SP 95/115/91-93, Goodricke to Rochford, 28 July 1769; DRA TKUA Sverige B 164, Juel to Bernstorff, 28 July 1769. Their accounts of Pechlin's terms show small discrepancies. Reuterholm on 22 July succinctly summarized Pechlin's options as (i) crushing the Hats entirely; (ii) attaining parity with them; (iii) cutting the Diet short: Reuterholm, Dagbok, fo. 110.

162. DRA TKUA Sverige B 164, Juel to Bernstorff, 28 July 1769.

163. *Ibid*., Juel offered to contribute £600, but Osterman told him to keep it for his own private operations.

164. DRA TKUA Sverige C 351, Bernstorff to Juel, 5 August 1769. He characteristically added that if only Juel could induce Fersen to enter into a Composition with the three crowns on the basis of preserving 1756 and 1766, that would be better than a Cap victory. He was to change his mind about Compositions before very long.

165. *SIRIO*, 87:478, Panin to Osterman, 25 August/5 September 1769. So too did Gustaf Reuterholm, who commented that if it were adopted they would soon have to fight the battle over again: Reuterholm, Dagbok, 23 July, fo. 116.

166. SP 95/115/80-82, Rochford to Goodricke, 25 August 1769.

167. DRA TKUA Sverige C 351, Bernstorff to Juel, 12 August; 2, 23 September 1769; B 164, Juel to Bernstorff, 22 August; 12 September, 3 October 1769.

168. *Ibid*., Sverige B 163, Juel to Bernstorff, 17 May 1769; Sverige B 164, same to same, 14 July 1769; SP 95/115/129-30, Goodricke to Rochford, 15 September 1769.

169. SP 95/115/80-82, 94-95, 98-100, and the full schedule of Goodricke's expenditures in SP 95/116/417 ff. Cf. The draft memorandum (by Porten?) of 19 October, in SP 95/134.

170. DRA TKUA Sverige B 164, Juel to Bernstorff, 1 August 1769.

171. Reuterholm, Dagbok, fos. 109, 116.

172. See his accounts in SP 95/116/417 ff.

173. SP 95/115/81-83, Goodricke to Rochford, 18 July. It is typical that Goodricke should have appreciated the significance of the economic problem: by Juel it was hardly so much as mentioned.

174. P. G. Andréen, "Det svenska 1700-talets syn på banksedlar och pappersmynt," p. 18; Boëthius and Kromnow, II:34-35; Malmström, V:131.

175. In July Hope of Amsterdam had informed their correspondents in Sweden that they would not lend money on prospective French subsidies; *Pol. Corr.*, XXIX:16, to Thulemeier, 6 August 1769; in the same month Grills in Amsterdam failed owing to accepting bills drawn upon them in Sweden—to Rochford's jubilant satisfaction: SP 95/115/75, 78-79, 88-89.

176. Gustaf Reuterholm commented in his journal that if the plan went through "then all interests will be so satisfied that the cohesion of the [Hat] party will thereby be redoubled. It could happen that in order to consolidate it they may evade the constitutional issue, hand over the decision on alliances with foreign powers to the King and Senate, obtain agreement to not summoning the Estates again for six or ten years"—the first mention of an idea which was soon to appear again—" and then put a quick end to the Diet": Reuterholm, Dagbok, 23 July, fo. 117.

177. SP 95/115/94-96, Goodricke to Rochford, 2 August 1769.

178. Malmström, VI:126-7; A. Evers, *Den svenska brännvinslagstiftningens historia*, II: 58-72. J. G. Oxenstierna, who was among those who thought *brännvin* a necessity, commented sardonically that presumably the best way to make Sweden happy, and to economize, would be to order everyone to go naked, and prohibit food and drink: *Dagboks-Anteckningar*, p. 48.

179. UUB F 514, Scheffer to the Crown Prince, 4 September 1769.

180. SP 95/115/133, Goodricke to Rochford, 19 September 1769. The Secret Committee frankly admitted as much: *SRARP*, XXVII:25; and cf. Jennings' remarks, *ibid.*, 47.

181. Ramsey, p. 202. Rochford conveyed this information to Goodricke on 4 August: SP 95/115/72-73. G. Castrén, *Gustav Philip Creutz*, pp. 222-23.

182. Hennings, p. 361.

183. Hennings, p. 359.

184. UUB F 414, nos. 27, 28.

185. SP 95/115/88-89, Rochford to Goodricke, relaying a French intercept; DRA TKUA Sverige B 164, Juel to Bernstorff, 5 September 1769; Hennings, p. 363; Amburger, p. 217.

186. SP 95/115/129-30, 131-33, 139-40, 146-47, Goodricke to Rochford, 15, 19, 26, 29 September 1769.

187. Ekeblad realized very well that it was hopeless: RA Kab. f. utr. brevvexling, KP to Creutz, 29 September 1769.

188. Oxenstierna, *Dagboks-Anteckningar*, p. 75.

189. SP 95/115/216-19; 117/70-72, Goodricke to Rochford, 1 December 1769, 6 March 1770; DRA TKUA Sverige B 164, Juel to Bernstorff, 26 December 1769; B 165, same to same, 19 January, 2, 9 February 1770.

190. RA Malmström avskr., Modène to Fersen, 16 August 1769.

191. Malmström, VI:136; SP 95/115/105-7, Goodricke to Rochford, 22 August 1769.

192. At the beginning of August, Assessor Arvid Virgin had published a pamphlet *En patriots tankar om grundlagens nödvändiga förbättring* which castigated successive governments' indifference to the keeping of faith with individuals, and proposed that resolutions of the Estates be unalterable save with the agreement of all four Estates (which had been the Caps' policy in 1766) *and* of the King. The Caps seized on this, led by Pechlin, as a typical Hat at-

tempt to undermine the constitution by giving the King a veto. Virgin was fined 300 d.s.m. It was rumored that Virgin wrote at Lovisa Ulrika's orders: Malmström, VI:128-30; Tilas, II:95-8; *SRARP*, XXVII:289-309; SP 95/115/99.

193. DRA TKUA Sverige B 164, Juel to Bernstorff, 8 September 1769; cf. SP 95/115/105-7, Goodricke to Rochford, 22 August 1769; Hennings, p. 363. Malmström (VI:136) confuses this proposal with Fersen's second attempt, a few weeks later.

194. Goodricke had also reported this plan on 2 August: SP 95/115/94-95.

195. See the copy, endorsed "18 Aug. 1769," in Add. MS 35,609, fos. 25-26.

196. DRA TKUA Sverige B 164, Juel to Bernstorff, 8 September.

197. SP 95/115/117-18, Goodricke to Rochford, 22 August 1769.

198. DRA TKUA Sverige B 164, Juel to Bernstorff, 15 September 1769.

199. Annexed to DRA TKUA Sverige B 164, Juel to Bernstorff, 6 October 1769, and printed in Niklas Tengberg, *Om Kejsarinnan Catharina II:s åsyftade stora nordiska alliance*, Appendix 1.

200. Which was precisely what Virgin had been prosecuted for proposing.

201. It was only a month or so since an anonymous author had written: "I accept, with the most profound respect, the resolution of the Estates, and I believe them to possess an inalienable right to declare that their plenipotentiaries [*sc.* the Senate] have forfeited their confidence, *even if they have committed no positive fault* [my italics], if the welfare of the realm so demands," *Den svenska Fatburen*, no. 20, 1 August 1769.

202. SP 95/115/146-47, Goodricke to Rochford, 29 September 1769.

203. DRA TKUA Sverige B 164, Juel to Bernstorff, 6, 20 October 1769.

204. SP 95/115/146-47.

205. DRA TKUA Sverige C 351, Bernstorff to Juel, 16 September 1769.

206. Contrast Juel's dispatches of 26 September, 3 and 6 October (TKUA Sverige B 164) and Bernstorff's instructions of 7 and 14 October (TKUA Sverige C 351).

207. DRA TKUA Sverige C 351, Bernstorff to Juel, 14 October 1769.

208. See, e.g., *SRARP*, XXVII:119, 295, 307.

209. This was the procedure laid down by the Ordinance for any change in the fundamental laws; but the Hats argued that it was a provision which applied to the Ordinance itself: the election of 1769, on this view, had been a verdict of the electorate, rejecting the Ordinance, and it was now open to the *riksdag*, if so disposed, to modify or rescind it: *SRARP*, XXVII:419, 425, 430, App., 140.

210. For the constitutional debate in the United Deputations and the Estates, see Fredrik Lagerroth, *Frihetstidens författning*, pp. 615-30; K.-E. Rudelius, "Författningsfrågan i de förenade deputationerna 1769"; Gunnar Kjellin, *Rikshistoriografen Anders Schönberg. Studier i riksdagarnas och de politiska tänkesättens historia*, pp. 172-201; Erik Fahlbeck, "Studier öfver frihetstidens politiska ideer," pp. 31-56, 104-26; [Anders Nordencrantz], *Undersökning af De rätta Orsakerna til den Blandning som skedt af Lagstiftande och Lagskipande, Redofordrande och Redoskyldige Magternas Gjöromål*; Tilas, II:126-30, 133-46, 159-61.

211. A draft is printed in *SRARP*, XXVIII, Appendix pp. 50-57.

212. RA Malmström avskr. Modène to Choiseul, 7 September 1769.

213. Hennings, p. 365; *Gustav III:s och Lovisa Ulrikas brevväxling*, I:189.

214. Malmström, VI:143 and n. 1.

215. UUB F 414, Memoir, 11 November 1769; UUB F 514, C. F. Scheffer to Gustav, 29 October 1769; RA Ericsbergsarkivet, Fr. Sparres dagbok, 10 November 1769; Tilas, II:152-53. For a discussion of the episode, see Malmström, VI:142-44 (who maintains that the Act did represent a real watering-down of the Deputations' intentions), and Hennings, p. 368 (who holds that there was no substantial difference, and that Gustav had been deluding himself, and had taken altogether too sanguine a view of the committee's intentions).

216. DRA TKUA Sverige B 164, Juel to Bernstorff, 20 October 1769.

217. SP 95/115/138-39, 146-49, Goodricke to Rochford, 26, 29 September, 3 October 1769; cf. RA AVPR 76, Osterman to Catherine, 19/30 September 1769.

218. His arguments are recapitulated (and approved) in Lagerroth, *Fribetstidens författning*, pp. 619-20, 625-30.

219. *SRARP*, XXVIII:1-23; possibly, as Malmström suggested, under the combined pressure of the "easy-credit" wing of his party and that section of it which disliked any sort of reform: Malmström, VI:142. Tilas, II:159-62.

220. Tilas, II:161; RA Malmström avskr, Modène to Choiseul, 10 November 1769; SP 95/115/184-86, Goodricke to Rochford, 3 November 1769; 115/187-88, Goodricke to Weston, 3 November 1769; RA AVPR 104, Osterman to Catherine, 23 October/3 November 1769, which suggests that Fersen hoped to cool party passions by diverting attention to finance, but perhaps also to induce Caps who did not usually live in Stockholm and had come up for the division on the constitution, to return home. He thought it likely also that some Caps, not having eaten all day, were too lazy or hungry to await their turn to vote, and that some, having gone off to dinner, did not return. If so, they enjoyed their dinner: Oxenstierna noted in his journal that "There was drinking at the club on a scale I never saw before. You could see the Nobility, sitting round reeking punch-bowls, hoarsely reaffirming their staunchness and swearing to defend law, fatherland and liberty at the very moment when they appeared to be taking leave of their senses": *Dagboks-Anteckningar*, p. 58.

221. RA Ericsbergsarkivet, Fr. Sparres dagbok, 14 November 1769: Oxenstierna, *Dagboks-Anteckningar*, p. 60.

222. Tilas, II:165-68; *SRARP*, XXVIII:63-90.

223. Tilas, II:165-68; Oxenstierna, *Dagboks-Anteckningar*, pp. 59-61.

224. SP 95/115/200-204, Goodricke to Rochford, 17 November; 115/101-2, Rochford to Goodricke, 15 December 1769.

225. Tilas, II:168.

226. Though both Osterman and Juel seem seriously to have regarded Rappe's memorial to the United Deputations (which urged an act to safeguard the liberties of the citizen) as a plan to change the constitution: RA AVPR 104, Osterman to Catherine, 9/20 October 1769; DRA TKUA Sverige B 164, Juel to Bernstorff, 20 October 1769.

227. DRA TKUA Rusland C 180, Bernstorff to Scheel, 11 November 1769; cf. Sverige B 164, Juel to Bernstorff, 21 November 1769.

228. SP 95/117/45, Goodricke to Rochford, 2 February 1770: "Liberty," he wrote, "is best preserved by decent Behaviour to the King, by Subordination, and a Respect of Government, and the Support of the Dignity of the Crown, is as real a part of the Form of Government, as any other Branch of the Constitution"—a view which would hardly have commended itself to Bernstorff or Juel.

229. SP 75/122/218, Gunning to Rochford, 23 September 1769.

230. For this, see M. S. Anderson, "Great Britain and the Russian Fleet, 1769-70."

231. DRA TKUA Rusland C 180, Bernstorff to Scheel, 4 November 1769.

232. RA Malmström avskr., Modène to Choiseul, 10, 13 November 1769; UUB F 414, Mémoire, 11 November 1769 (no. 29); *Gustav III:s och Lovisa Ulrikas brevväxling*, I:190.

233. *Gustavianska Papperen*, I:94; *Gustav III:s och Lovisa Ulrikas brevväxling*, I:168, 183; RA Tessinska samlingen, Fr. Sparre to Tessin, 24 April 1769; Oxenstierna, *Dagboks-Anteckningar*, p. 11.

234. *Mémoires de Barthélémy 1768-1819*, p. 8.

235. *Danske Tractater 1751-1800*, pp. 302-10. For the antecedent discussions, *Corr. min.*, II:369, 383-90, 409, 413, 417, 425; *SIRIO*, 87:335, 415, 510-11; and in general, Vedel, *Den aeldre Grev Bernstorffs Ministerium*, pp. 338-44.

236. *Pol. Corr.*, XXVIII:50-4, to Solms, 21 January 1769.

237. *Ibid.*, XXVIII:344, Solms to Frederick, 9 May 1769.

238. *Ibid.*, XXVIII:406 ff., to Solms, 28 June 1769.

239. *Ibid.*, XXIX:90-91, 102. The text of the third secret article, concerning the Swedish constitution, is printed in Fersen, III:468; Catherine's original draft is in A. Geffroy, *Gustave III et la Cour de France*, I:39-42. For a general survey of Frederick's attitude to the Swedish constitution, see G. Olsson, "Fredrik den store och Sveriges författning," pp. 338-61.

240. *Pol. Corr.*, XXIX:170, to Solms, 29 October 1769.

241. SP 95/115/171-74, 179-81, 189-91, Goodricke to Rochford, 24, 27 October, 7, 14 November 1769; DRA TKUA Sverige B 164, Juel to Bernstorff, 27 October 1769.

242. SP 95/115/98-100, Rochford to Goodricke, 24 November 1769.

243. RA AVPR 104, Osterman to Catherine, 7/18 November 1769; *SRARP*, XXVIII:43-61; Tilas, II:165; RA Ericsbergsarkiv, Fr. Sparres dagbok, 11 November 1769; cf. Oxenstierna, *Dagboks-Anteckningar*, pp. 66-67.

244. DRA TKUA Sverige B 164, Juel to Bernstorff, 1 December 1769; Tilas, II:183-85; *SRARP*, XXVIII:148-79. Ostensibly the debate turned on constitutional issues, questions of foreign policy being reserved to the Secret Committee, and the *plenum* debarred from meddling with them.

245. DRA TKUA Sverige C 351, Bernstorff to Juel, 9 December 1769.

246. SP 95/117/3, Rochford to Goodricke, 5 January 1770; 117/41, Goodricke to Rochford, 2 February 1770; BM Egerton MS 2699, fos. 20-21, Goodricke to Gunning, 6 February 1770; DRA TKUA Rusland C 180, Bernstorff to Scheel, 30 December 1769, 10 February 1770; Sverige B 164, Juel to Bernstorff, 6 March 1770.

247. RA Kab. f.u.b., KP to Nolcken, 3 September 1769; KP to Creutz, 4 July, 19 September, 12 December 1769; cf. SP 95/134, Goodricke to Murray, 17 November 1769; RA Malmström avskr., Modène to Choiseul, 20 October 1769. For the difficulty of securing publicity in Sweden for Russian victories, RA AVPR 75, Stakhiev to Coll. of Foreign Affairs, 2/13 October 1769.

248. RRPUÄ, II, 325.

249. SP 95/115/146-47, Goodricke to Rochford, 29 September 1769.

250. SP 95/115/211, 216-19, Goodricke to Rochford, 28 November, 1 December 1769; DRA TKUA Sverige B 164, Juel to Bernstorff, 1, 5, 8 December 1769.

251. SP 95/117/4, Rochford to Goodricke, 5 January 1770. Goodricke was acting against his instructions: see *ibid.*, 115/90-91, Rochford to Goodricke, 24 October 1769.

252. Rochford was no doubt influenced by the alarming (perhaps alarmist) reports from Gunning: see, e.g., SP 75/122/228, 239-45, 252, Gunning to Rochford, 24 October, 25 November, 16 December 1769. For the forces working against Bernstorff and his policy, see E. Holm, *Danmark-Norges Historie under Kristian VII*, I:199-256.

253. SP 95/115/216-19, Goodricke to Rochford, 1 December 1769: "a finesse," in Frederick's opinion: *Pol. Corr.*, XXIX:287-88, to Cocceji, 8 January 1770.

254. DRA TKUA Sverige B 164, Juel to Bernstorff, 26 December 1769.

255. *Ibid.*, Juel to Bernstorff, 8, 15 December 1769; SP 95/115/224, 228-30, Goodricke to Rochford, 12, 19 December 1769; RA Kab. f.u.b., KP to Creutz, 8 December, KP to Ribbing, 8 December 1769; RRPUÄ 1769, II, 404, 7 December 1769.

256. RA Kab. f.u.b., Cirkulär, 12 March 1770; KP to Ribbing, 16 March 1770; DRA TKUA Sverige B 165, Juel to Bernstorff, 9 February 1770.

257. DRA TKUA Sverige B 164, Juel to Bernstorff, 27 October 1769.

258. SP 95/115/189-91, Goodricke to Rochford, 7 November 1769.

259. SP 95/115/204, Goodricke to Rochford, 17 November 1769.

260. DRA TKUA Sverige B 164, Juel to Bernstorff, 21 November 1769.

261. *Ibid.*, same to same, 28 November 1769; SP 95/115/209-11, Goodricke to Rochford, 28 November 1769.

262. SP 95/115/101-2, Rochford to Goodricke, 15 December 1769; DRA TKUA Sverige B 164, Juel to Bernstorff, 29 December 1769.

263. DRA TKUA Sverige C 351, Bernstorff to Juel, 30 December 1769.

264. RA AVPR 104, Osterman to Catherine II, 5/16 December 1769.

265. SP 95/117/43, Goodricke to Rochford, 2 February 1770.

266. BM Add. MS 35,369, fo. 123, Sir J. Yorke to Hardwicke, 20 February 1770.

267. SP 95/115/195-96, Goodricke to Rochford, 14 November 1769.

268. DRA TKUA Sverige B 165, Juel to Bernstorff, 9 January 1770: "cet homme dangéreux et difficile."

269. Vera Lee Brown, *Studies in the History of Spain in the Second Half of the Eighteenth Century*, p. 38.

270. *Tersmedens memoarer*, V:35.

271. For Kepplerus's Memorial, see Gunnar Kjellin, 'Kring Alexander Kepplerus' memorial," pp. 276-91; Göran von Bonsdorff, "En finländsk insats i frihetstidens statsrättsliga diskussion. King Alexander Kepplerus' Memorial . . . ," pp. 321-57. And cf. *Bondeståndets riksdagsprotokoll, 1769-1770*, Appendix 58, for a peasant Memorial of similar tendency.

272. See Erland Alexandersson, *Bondeståndet i riksdagen 1760-1772*, pp. 107, 165, 175; though I do not find much support for this view in the debates of the Estate of Peasants.

273. *Tersmedens memoarer*, V:33-34.

274. RA Malmström avskr., Barthélémy to Choiseul, 10 July 1770.

CHAPTER X
INTERLUDE

1. SP 95/117/105-6, Goodricke to Rochford, 24 April 1770. Nolcken thought so too, and snatched three weeks leave on the strength of it: RA Dipl. Anglica, Nolcken to KP, 10 July 1770.

2. See, e.g., SP 95/114/170-71, Goodricke to Rochford, 14 March 1769; 117/198-99, same to same, 13 November 1770.

3. Helle Stiegung, "Bröderna Scheffer, Gustav III och den danska politiken åren 1770-1772," p. 96.

4. *SIRIO*, 97:41, Panin to Osterman, 25 March OS 1770; RA AVPR 104, Osterman to Panin, 17/28 April 1770; *ibid.*, Stakhiev to Catherine II, 18/29 June 1770.

5. SP 95/117/30-31, Goodricke to Rochford, Private, 30 January 1770; 117/46, Rochford to Goodricke, 27 February 1770.

6. E.g., BM Add. MS 35,425, fo. 201, Goodricke to Hardwicke, 1 March 1768.

7. SP 95/114/128-30, Goodricke to Rochford, Private, 15 February 1769; 114/188-89, same to same, 28 March 1769.

8. SP 95/115/155-56, Goodricke to Rochford, Private, 6 October 1769; cf. *ibid.*, 115/92.

9. "I have met few people so quick and so clear as he is, and any Minister he serves under may make great use of him": BM Add. MS 35,369, fo. 167, Sir J. Yorke to Hardwicke, 3 July 1770. During his spell in Copenhagen Goodricke had suffered from asthma, but there is no sign that it bothered him in Sweden: RA Dipl. Danica, Sprengtporten to KP, 29 September 1763.

10. Nolcken reported that he spent most of his leave in Yorkshire, and came to town only four days before his departure: RA Dipl. Anglica, Nolcken to KP, Apostille particulière, 16 October 1770.

11. Summary of the plan in SP 95/117/77-79, Goodricke to Rochford, 20 March 1770; copy of Goodricke's memorandum on it in *ibid.*, 116/436-39; full text in French, endorsed by Edward Weston "Recd from Sir John Goodricke 6 Sep. 1770," in *ibid.*, 116/440-42.

12. Catherine agreed almost at once: *SIRIO*, 97, rescript to Osterman 19 July OS 1770.

13. SP 75/123/59, Gunning to Rochford, 12 May; DRA TKUA Sverige C 351, Bernstorff to Juel, 12 May; Sverige B 165, Rosencrone to Bernstorff, 4 August 1770.

14. SP 91/85/74, Rochford to Cathcart, 25 August; SP 95/117/166, Rochford to Goodricke, 19 October 1770.

15. RA Dipl. Anglica, Nolcken to KP, 5 October, 16 October 1770; SP 95/117/165-66, Rochford to Goodricke, Private, 19 October 1770; *ibid.*, 157-58, Goodricke to Rochford, 4 October 1770.

16. *Calendar of Home Office Papers* (1766-69), pp. 498-99; RA Dipl. Anglica, Nolcken to KP, 8 May 1770; SP 91/84/31-32, 41, 45, 50, 57, 65, 97; and in general, Anderson, "Great Britain and the Russian Fleet," passim.

17. SP 91/82/160-61, Rochford to Cathcart, 24 October 1769, relaying secret intelligence from Paris.

18. Bodley MS Eng. hist. c. 62, Robert Walpole to Goodricke, 8 January 1770; *Calendar of Home Office Papers* (1770), pp. 48-49.

19. *Correspondance secrète du Comte de Mercy-Argenteau avec l'Empéreur Joseph II et le prince de Kaunitz* (hereafter *Mercy-Kaunitz Corr.*), II:380.

20. *Calendar of Home Office Papers* (1770), p. 58. Cathcart was ordered not to reveal the secret instructions to Panin: this order he disobeyed; SP 91/85/63-65, Rochford to Cathcart, 25 August; *ibid.*, 86/44, Cathcart to Rochford, 8/19 October 1770.

21. *Pol. Corr.*, XXX:461-62.

22. *Annual Register*, 1770, p. 6; SP 91/86/70-73, Rochford to Cathcart, 30 November 1770. And cf. Shelburne's speech on 22 November, 1770, in *Parliamentary History*, XVI:114.

23. BM Egerton MS 2701, fo. 223, Goodricke to Gunning, 16 October 1772. Favier, incidentally, agreed with him: P. de Ségur, *Politique de tous les cabinets*, I:340, and cf. *ibid.*, II:162, and H. Uebersberger, *Russlands Orientpolitik in den letzten zwei Jahrhunderten*, p. 284.

24. SP 91/82/286, Rochford to Cathcart, 24 November 1769: cf. *Pol. Corr.*, XXIX:498, for Frederick's similar feelings about Moldavia.

25. Martens, IX (X):280; SP 91/79/34, Weymouth to Murray (copy), 20 December 1769.

26. SP 90/88/3-4, Rochford to Mitchell, 27 January 1769; SP 91/80/, 101-3, 194, 251, Rochford to Cathcart, 24 February, 4 April, 5 May 1769; 81/25-26, same to same, 6 June 1769; *ibid.*, 80/208-10, 236, Cathcart to Rochford, 17 March [OS], 24 March/4 April 1769; 81/183-85, same to same, 22 May/2 June 1769; *Pol. Corr.*, XXVIII:2, 25, 83, 174, 385; XXIX:492-93.

27. SP 91/85/59-72, 105-6, Rochford to Cathcart, 25 August, 14 September 1770.

28. *SIRIO*, 20:275, Frederick to Catherine, 14 September; *ibid.*, pp. 279-80, Catherine to Frederick, 28 September 1770; *SIRIO*, 97:150; *Pol. Corr.*, XXX:215-18, Catherine to Frederick, 9 October 1770; *Oeuvres posthumes de Frédéric* II, V:54.

29. SP 91/86/81-84, Cathcart to Rochford, 29 October/9 November 1770; Panin's answer (28 October [OS]) and Cathcart's notes to him in SP 91/100-55, Cathcart to Rochford, 14/25 November 1770. Catherine when it suited her took a different line about the Turks: at the end of 1770 Austria was asserting, Catherine denying, that they were part of Europe: Uebersberger, pp. 316-18, citing *SIRIO*, 97:391 ff.

30. Konopczyński, "England and the First Partition of Poland," p. 8; SP 91/85/167-69, Rochford to Cathcart, 2 October 1770; 85/219-20, Cathcart to Rochford, 7/18 September 1770; *SIRIO*, 97:44, 54.

31. By way of correcting his ideas, Lovisa Ulrika wrote a holograph narrative justifying her actions since 1764: RA Kungl. Ark. 259, undated.

32. *Grefwe Hårds Berättelse om . . . Prins Henrics resor*, p. 24.

33. Erik Arup, "Rantzau-Ascheberg," pp. 9-19.

34. SP 75/122/239-45, 252, Gunning to Rochford, 25 November, 16 December 1769.

35. SP 91/83/148, Rochford to Cathcart, 23 February 1770.

36. *Ibid.*, 84/82, Cathcart to Rochford, 23 March/3 April; SP 75/123/50, 53, Gunning to Rochford, 5 May, 12 May 1770.

37. Asseburg, *Denkwürdigkeiten*, pp. 424-29; cf. *Bernstorffske Papiren*, I:623; *SIRIO*, 97:104, Panin to Filosoffof, 15 July OS 1770.

38. For an account of the meeting, and the reasons for its failure, BM Egerton MS 2698, fos. 274-75, Woodford to Gunning, n. d.; E. S. Reverdil, *Struensee og Hoffet i Kjöbenhavn 1760-1772*, pp. 125-26.

39. SP 95/117/164, Tullman to Rochford, 28 September 1770.

40. SP 75/123/156-57, Gunning to Rochford, 6 October 1770.

41. As appears from SP 75/123/154 and 175.

42. *Bernstorffske Papiren*, II:114. Goodricke hoped to meet Bernstorff in Pinneberg, but missed him. Bernstorff was not sorry: "I like the Chevalier very much; but what could I have said to him?": *ibid.*, I:652.

43. SP 95/117/181-84. Goodricke to Rochford, Private and Secret, 30 October 1770.

44. SP 91/86/201, Cathcart to Rochford, 7/18 December 1770.

45. SP 75/123/133-35, Gunning to Rochford, 18 September 1770.

46. RA Dipl. Muscovitica, C. Ribbing to KP, 1/12 October 1770; RA Tengberg avskr., Scheel to Kristian VII, 2 October 1770; *SIRIO*, 97, Panin to Filosoffof, 21 October OS 1770.

47. Substance in SP 91/86/156-62, Cathcart to Rochford; a more explicit threat in *SIRIO*, 97:158, Note to Scheel, 17 October [OS]; and see *ibid.*, 13:44, Catherine to Fru Bielke, 8 October OS 1770. Ditlev Reventlow thought the letter badly composed, and predicted that it would be quite ineffective: *Bernstorffske Papiren*, III:187-88.

48. Holm, "Styrelsen af Danmark-Norges Udenrigspolitik under Struensee," pp. 360-62.

49. *Bernstorffske Papiren*, I:658-59.

50. Stiegung, "Bröderna Scheffer," pp. 89-92; Hennings, pp. 382-83; *Gustav III:s och Lovisa Ulrika brevvexling*, I:232, 239.

51. SP 75/123/185, Gunning to Rochford, 1 December 1770.

52. Hennings, p. 374. In the event, Fredrik Adolf accompanied Gustav.

53. A. Geffroy, *Gustave III et la Cour de France*, I:107-9, Creutz to Gustav, 9 February 1770.

54. *Gustavianska Papperen*, I:115, Gustav to C. F. Scheffer, 5 March 1770.

55. RA Malmström avskr., Barthélémy to Choiseul, 19 October 1770; cf. Fersen, III:49.

56. *Gustav III:s och Lovisa Ulrikas brevvexling*, I:202-4.

57. UUB F 525, Lascy to Beylon, 12 April; RA Ekebladska samlingen, Lascy to Ekeblad, 4 April 1770.

58. *Gustav III:s och Lovisa Ulrikas brevvexling*, I:205; BM Egerton MS 2699, fo. 86, Tullman to Gunning, 29 May 1770.

59. For the missions of Lascy and Beylon, see Helle Stiegung, *Ludvig XV:s hemliga diplomati och Sverige 1752-1774*, pp. 107, 109.

60. In reality, Choiseul at the time of his fall had not made up his mind about his Swedish policy: Stiegung, *Ludvig XV:s hemliga diplomati*, p. 136.

61. RA Malmström avskr., Barthélémy to Choiseul, 30 November 1770.

62. Hennings, p. 376.

63. L. Blart, *Les Rapports de la France et de l'Espagne après le Pacte de Famille jusqu'à*

la fin du Ministère du Duc de Choiseul, pp. 92 ff.; R. Konetzke, *Die Politik des Grafen Aranda*, pp. 36-44.

64. *Mercy-Kaunitz Corr.*, II:373, 375.

65. For the Falklands crisis, see M. H. Nieto, *La Cuestión de las Malvinas*, esp. pp. 200-15, and, in general, J. Goebel, *The Struggle for the Falkland Islands*.

66. Blart, pp. 158-200; Konetzke, pp. 47-48.

67. *Gustav III:s och Lovisa Ulrikas brevvexling*, I:245; *Mercy-Kaunitz Corr.*, II:383; *Bernstorffske Papiren*, I:676; *SIRIO*, 13:63.

68. *George III Corr.*, II:205-11. The difficulties prompted the king to suggest that Rochford combine both departments and become sole foreign secretary: a foreshadowing of the change which he was to carry through in 1782.

69. See the comments of Count Bentinck in *Archives de la maison d'Orange-Nassau*, I: 224-25.

70. Compare the comments of David Hume: *Letters of David Hume*, II:241-42.

71. *Correspondence of James Harris, first Earl of Malmesbury*, I:76-79, Harris to Rochford, 14 February 1771.

72. Goebel, p. 382.

73. RA Sjöholmssamlingen, Sinclair to Gyldenstolpe, 28 January 1771.

74. *Mercy-Kaunitz Corr.*, II:387: 17 March 1771.

75. SP 78/282/76, 137-38, for Harcourt's reactions: cf. those of Charles of Hesse and Bernstorff: *Bernstorffske Papiren*, I:661; II:120.

76. A. von Arneth and A. Geffroy, *Marie Antoinette. Correspondance entre Marie-Thérèse et le Cte. de Mercy-Argenteau*, I:147, 156; Hennings, pp. 385-88. On Gustav's letter to Adolf Fredrik of 11 February, reporting the letter of condolence to Choiseul, is however the endorsement "not sent": UUB F 414 No. 37.

77. UUB F 414 No. 38, Gustav to Adolf Fredrik, 15 February 1771.

78. *Gustavianska Papperen*, I:127; Geffroy, I:124; G. D'Albedyhll, *Skrifter af blandadt, dock mest politiskt och historiskt Innehåll*, II:161-63, 170-71. Creutz's relation 1771 (20 May) in RA MSD, fos. 13v-16, gives a full account of the negotiation on arrears.

79. D'Albedyhll, II:166-68; *Gustavianska Papperen*, I:194. Karl had personal connections with the Caps, and they hoped for a time to play him off against his brother; but Karl never seriously lent himself to such ideas: see Gustaf Iverus, *Hertig Karl av Södermanland, Gustav III:s broder*, pp. 26, 45-46, 48-49.

80. RA Kabinettet f. u. brevvexling, KP to Creutz, 9 April 1771.

81. L. Bonneville de Marsangy, *Le Comte de Vergennes. Son ambassade en Suède 1771-1774*, II:45. Louis XV had at first thought of sending Breteuil. Gustav and Scheffer, believing Breteuil to be an adherent of Fersen, enlisted d'Aiguillon and Broglie to persuade Louis to change his mind: Stiegung, *Ludvig XV*, p. 175. Gustav also succeeded in preventing Lascy's removal from Stockholm to St. Petersburg: Stiegung, "Bröderna Scheffer," p. 100 n. 49.

82. Marsangy, *Le Comte de Vergennes*, II:62-63 (henceforward simply Marsangy).

83. UUB F 414 No. 41. This must have been a preliminary draft: Vergennes' final instructions, as Malmström pointed out (Malmström, VI:204-6) were not written until after Gustav had left France: they are printed in *Recueil, Suède*, p. 432.

84. Geffroy, I:124.

85. Panin was not much impressed: SP 91/87/248-9, Cathcart to Halifax, 20/31 May 1771.

86. *Pol. Corr.*, XXXI:109, 127-28, 156-58; Marsangy, II:78.

87. Gustav wrote to the Duchess (who passed it on to George III) that Goodricke "se conduit comme si j'étais l'ennemi juré et déclaré de son maître": *George III Corr.*, II:249-50.

88. SP 95/117/189-90; 118/2-6; RA Sjöholmssamlingen, Sinclair to Gyldenstolpe, 28 January 1771.

89. "Pro Memoria 1771," fos. 51-54; RA Malmström avskr., Barthélémy to Choiseul, 10 Aug. 1770; Stiegung, *Ludvig XV*, pp. 146-47, 149.

90. SP 95/117/166, 202-3, Rochford to Goodricke, 19 October, 4 December; 117/196-97, Goodricke to Rochford, 13 November 1770.

91. SP 95/118/2-5, 96.

92. RA Malmström avskr., Barthélémy to de la Vrillière, 12 February 1771; "Pro Memoria 1771," fos. 55-58; Fersen, III:52-53; *Gustavianska Papperen*, I:122.

93. At the close of the preceding Diet, the Estates had deposited 1,500,000 livres with Grill's bank, to pay off an earlier loan by Louis XV to Adolf Fredrik and Lovisa Ulrika.

94. *Gustavianska Papperen*, I:123; DRA Dept. f.u.A., Rosencrone to Osten, 22 February 1771.

95. RA Sjöholmssamlingen, Sinclair to Gyldenstolpe, 1 March 1771.

96. C.T. Odhner, *Sveriges politiska historia under . . . Gustaf III:s regering* (hereafter Odhner, *Gustaf III*), I:19.

97. SP 95/118/128, Goodricke to Halifax, 23 April 1771.

98. Malmström, VI:191-93; SP 95/117/125-26, Tullman to Rochford, 15 June 1770. For the effect on the elections, Gjörwell, *En Stockholmskrönika ur C. G. Gjörwells brev*, p. 34, Gjörwell to Ehrensvärd, 5 February 1771.

99. SP 95/118/148-50, Goodricke to Halifax, 19 February 1771; *SIRIO*, 97:211. Goodricke's information was that the Hat merchants subscribed 200,000 copper daler (£1 = ca. 50 daler); that Grill advanced 150,000 daler; that Gustav III brought home 750,000 livres (£1 = 25 livres): a total of £37,000. But this was an underestimate. In the course of the spring Barthélémy released 500,000 daler in *statsobligationer* (which, however, realized only 60% of their nominal value); and Grill advanced, not 150,000 daler but 3,500,000—which would add another £43,000 to Goodricke's figure. Stiegung, *Ludvig XV*, pp. 191-95. When the campaign opened Goodricke and Osterman had their respective contributions to the Plan of 1770, or £5,200 at the most; at the beginning of March Osterman was sent 100,000 rubles (£25,000), which was later fixed as a maximum for Goodricke also. It is clear that he and Osterman were heavily outspent.

100. See Holm, "Styrelsen af Udenrigspolitik under Struensee," pp. 342-408; Stiegung, "Bröderna Scheffer," pp. 93-101; *Bernstorffske Papiren*, I:698-99, III:137-38.

101. SP 75/124/72-76, 152-57, Gunning to Halifax, 23 March, 4 April 1771.

102. *Ibid.*, 63, Gunning to Halifax, 5 March; DRA Dept. f.u.A. Sverige II, Rosencrone to Osten, 12, 30 April, 24 May 1771. For Goodricke's anxiety about Denmark's share, and his strong desire for Juel's return, BM Egerton MS 2700, fos. 111-12, Goodricke to Gunning, 22 March 1771. A month later he was commenting: "Blessed be he who expecteth nothing, for he shall not be disappointed": *ibid.*, fo. 131, same to same 3 April.

103. *SIRIO*, 97:32, 86; RA Dipl. Muscovitica, Ribbing to KP, 6/17 August 1770.

104. *SIRIO*, 97:212, 276. Goodricke commented, and Osterman agreed, that if this were to be the limit of Russian objectives they need not have spent as much as they had: SP 95/118/169, Goodricke to Halifax, 4 June 1771.

105. SP 95/118/36-37, 42-44, 67-68, Goodricke to Halifax, 12, 13, 26 February 1771; UUB F 386, Halifax to Goodricke, 1 March 1771.

106. SP 95/118/122-25, Rochford to Goodricke, 7 May 1771.

107. "Pro Memoria 1771," fos. 55-58; [J. F. Schartau], *Hemliga Handlingar hörande till Sveriges Historia efter Konung Gustaf III:s Anträde till Regeringen*, II:64-65, Ulrik Scheffer to Creutz, 16 April 1771.

108. SP 95/118/153-56, Goodricke to Halifax, 26 May; 118/157-58, Goodricke to Rochford, Private, 26 May 1771. On the back of Rochford's instruction of 7 May Goodricke scribbled notes for his appeal to Rochford, ending: "Que les cours devroient determiner: De

deux choses L'une, ou de ne point travailler en Swede [*sic*] ou de faire la Depense necessaires [*sic*] puisque leurs Ministres se font des ennemis malapropos & entrent dans des Engagemeņs qui Les menent tres Loin & qu'ils ont de la peine a tenir": UUB F 386. Sir Joseph Yorke also regretted the limitation upon expenditure: Add. MS 35,444, fo. 133 (to Cathcart, 27 July 1771).

109. SP 95/118/151-52, Rochford to Goodricke, 7 June; 118/161-62, Suffolk to Goodricke, 14 June 1771.

110. See, e.g., SP 78/282/151, Harcourt to Halifax, 27 March 1771; and SP 95/118/143-44, Sedgwick to Goodricke, 31 May 1771: "Pro Memoria 1771," fo. 61.

111. George III, *Corr.*, II:222.

112. UUB F 386, Rochford to Goodricke, 29 March (received 17 April); SP 95/118/125, same to same, 7 May 1771.

113. SP 95/118/161-62, Suffolk to Goodricke, 14 June 1771. But this scarcely justifies Odhner's judgment that England, like Denmark, was "indifferent" to the outcome of the election: Odhner, *Gustaf III*, I:16.

114. SP 91/87/235-36, Suffolk to Cathcart, 21 June 1771.

115. SP 91/87/130-33, 202, Cathcart to Halifax, 15/26 March, 29 April/10 May 1771.

116. *Ibid.*, 87/267-70, 88/4-11, 60-62, Cathcart to Halifax, 31 May/11 June, 17/28 June, 5/16 July 1771.

117. *SIRIO*, 97:p. 276, Panin to Osterman, 10 May OS 1771.

118. His election correspondence is in UUB W-n 978.

119. AVPR 76, Osterman to Catherine II, 8/19 April 1771; SP 95/118/119-21, Goodricke to Halifax, 16 April 1771.

120. SP 95/118/119-21, 172-74, Goodricke to Halifax, 16 April, 11 June 1771; Marsangy, II:53: cf. *Hemliga Handlingar* [Schartau], III:64-65, Ulrik Scheffer to Creutz, 16 April 1771.

121. RA Malmström avskr., Barthélémy to de la Vrillière, 10, 17 May; SP 95/118/139-40, Goodricke to Halifax, 14 May 1771.

122. RA Malmström avskr., Barthélémy to de la Vrillière, 24 May 1771.

CHAPTER XI
FAILURE OF A MISSION

1. Stig Hallesvik, *Axel von Fersen och gustaviansk politik* (hereafter *Axel von Fersen*), p. 29; Helle Stiegung, *Ludvig XV:s hemliga diplomati och Sverige 1752-1774*, p. 231; Fersen, III:59-63; "Pro Memoria, 1771," pp. 96-100; Malmström, VI:216-17.

2. For the soundings and negotiations, Fersen: UUB F 379 (von Essen's journal, in UUB F 379); *Gustavianska Papperen*, I:138-39; SP 95/118/178, Goodricke to Halifax, 14 June 1771; Amburger, pp. 237-39.

3. One version of it is printed in Fersen, III:399-406. See also SP 95/119/25-26, Goodricke to Suffolk, 9 July 1771; Stig Hallesvik, "Partimotsättningarna vid 1771-2 års riksdag som bakgrund till Gustav III:s statskupp" (hereafter *SVT*), pp. 399-400; Malmström, VI:222-23.

4. The term seems first to appear in Sweden in April 1772, but the idea was already well established: Gunnar Kjellin, "Gustaf III, Den Patriotiske Konungen," pp. 330-32, 326; Birger Sallnäs, 'England i den svenska författningsdiskussionen 1771-72," p. 29.

5. A splendid example is Höpken's commemorative eulogium over Tessin, delivered on 25 March 1771: *Höpken*, I:238.

6. Though it is as well to remember that he seems to have been exceptionally well informed on Polish affairs: better, e.g., than Louis XV: Stiegung, *Ludvig XV:s hemliga diplomati*, pp. 219-26.

7. *SRARP*, XXIX:25-26. Goodricke noted on 28 June: "The King gains ground every day": SP 95/119/12, to Rochford.

8. Stiegung, *Ludvig XV:s hemliga diplomati*, p. 150, and n. 69; "Pro Memoria, 1771," p. 64; Malmström, VI:215. Six months later, when French corruption seemed to have been cut off, Fersen was reported to have told a discontented Hat that he had accepted the Composition precisely because he foresaw that this was going to happen: SP 95/120/8-10, Goodricke to Suffolk, 14 January 1772.

9. Hallesvik, *SVT*, pp. 399-400.

10. Fersen, III:64-65; Stiegung, *Ludvig XV:s hemliga diplomati*, p. 233; Hallesvik, *Axel von Fersen*, p. 29.

11. Odhner, *Gustaf III*, I:21; RA Tengberg avskr., Scheel to Osten, 17 May, 30 July 1771.

12. *SIRIO*, 97:374; Amburger, p. 237; H.-J. Bull, *Friedrich der Grosse und Schweden in den Jahren 1768-1773* p. 60, citing Dönhoff to Frederick, 5 July 1771.

13. Fersen, III:61-64; SP 95/118/177-80, Goodricke to Halifax, 14 June 1771.

14. SP 95/118/182-83, Goodricke to Halifax, 18 June 1771.

15. SP 95/118/177-80, Goodricke to Halifax, 14 June 1771. Vergennes, noting that his attitude was harder than Osterman's, suspected that his real object was to ruin Sweden's trade for England's benefit; and he conjectured (improbably enough) that funds to effect that purpose might have been placed at his disposal by unspecified commercial interests: RA Malmström avskr., Vergennes to d'Aiguillon, 17 June, 15 July 1771; P. de Véou, "Un chapître inédit des Mémoires de Barthélémy: La Révolution suèdoise de 1772," p. 281.

16. Fersen had resisted all the king's entreaties to stand.

17. RA AVPR 76, Osterman to Catherine, 3/14, 10/21, 17/28 June 1771; SP 95/118/174, Goodricke to Halifax, 11 June 1771; Malmström, VI:217-22.

18. It took them until 3 July, and involved unseating eight Hats: Tengberg, *Konung Gustaf III:s första regeringstid till och med 1772 års statshvälfning* (hereafter *Gustaf III*), pp. 38-43. Vergennes believed that Osterman and Goodricke gave 160,000 daler (*ca.* £3200) to three members to change sides, but he was certainly mistaken: Odhner, *Gustaf III*, I:30.

19. SP 95/119/10-12, Goodricke to Rochford, 28 June 1771. The Secret Committee consisted of 50 of the Nobility and 25 each of the Clergy and the Burghers: the Peasants were not represented. Voting in the Committee was by Estates, not by head, so that the Caps had now a secure majority.

20. RA Malmström avskr., D'Aiguillon to Vergennes, 26 July 1771.

21. Oxenstierna, *Dagboks-Anteckningar*, p. 173. And cf. Gustav III's comment: *Gustav III:s och Lovisa Ulrikas brevvexling* (hereafter *G III och LU*), II:1.

22. Oxenstierna, *Dagboks-Anteckningar*, p. 177.

23. SP 95/118/181-83, Goodricke to Halifax, 18 June 1771; 119/10-12, Goodricke to Rochford, 26 June 1771; Amburger, p. 241.

24. SP 95/118/174, 181-83, Goodricke to Halifax, 11, 18 June 1771; 119/30-31, Goodricke to Suffolk, 12 July 1771, at which date Osterman had received no further supplies since March: for several months Panin left him without instructions: *SIRIO*, 97:374,436.

25. Marsangy, II:83-84, Vergennes to de la Vrillière, 11 June 1771; *ibid.*, 100-101, Vergennes to d'Aiguillon [June 1771].

26. Hallesvik, *Axel von Fersen*, p. 86, for a schedule of Vergennes' disbursements. For the Horneca loan, see most recently Stiegung, *Ludvig XV:s hemliga diplomati*, pp. 191-95, 241-52. British ministers soon knew about it, though they did not at first realize that the borrower was not the Swedish government, but the king. Information on French supplies to Sweden was early and on the whole accurate: UUB F 386, Rochford to Goodricke, 2, 9, 12 July, 27 August 1771.

27. Goodricke certainly felt that he and Osterman could not match the expenditure on the other side: SP 95/118/181-83, 119/25-29, 32-34.

28. For an explanation of Kröger's antiaristocratic feelings, see Frietzcky's "Pro Memoria, 1799," in Crusenstolpe, *Portfeuille*, II:102.

29. On Hansson's social and financial position, see Sten Carlsson, "Sverige under 1760-talet," p. 27.

30. SP 95/119/27, Goodricke to Suffolk, 9 July 1771. For the suspicion of officialdom, see Kenneth Awebro, *Gustaf III:s räfst med ämbetsmännen 1772-1779*, chap. 2.

31. SP 95/119/21, 25-29. Goodricke was referring particularly to the impecunious members of the Nobility, who felt the pinch as much as any commoner.

32. SP 95/119/4-5, Goodricke to Halifax, 2 June 1771; cf. *ibid.*, fo. 29, Goodricke to Suffolk, 9 July 1771: "It seems as if the French . . . would make use of the King in order to form a new party under pretence of assisting His Majesty; and by uniting all the great families on both sides with the Court, to prevent, as far as possible, any opposition to their projects."

33. SP 95/119/12, Goodricke to Rochford, 28 June 1771.

34. And it was, in fact, a contravention of the *riksdagsordning* of 1723, which was accounted a fundamental law: see Wadenstierna's argument in *SRARP*, XXIX:523.

35. The Committee did in fact issue an instruction to the Secret Committee, on the vote of the three lower Estates, and in defiance both of the Estate of Nobility and of the constitution, whereat the Nobility's members protested and withdrew: *ibid.*, 626-28 (23 November).

36. Malmström, VI:233-36.

37. It comprised the Secret Committee, the Secret Deputation, and twenty-five members of the Estate of Peasants.

38. It was significant that the Burghers gave Osterman no advance information of their intention to put forward a demand for privileges: DRA Dept. f. u. A., Guldencrone to Osten, 24, 27 September 1771; Malmström, VI:244.

39. Malmström, VI:241-43; Tengberg, *Gustaf III*, pp. 59-60. Frietzcky believed that Sinclair put Kröger up to it, in order still further to envenom the conflict: Odhner, *Gustaf III*, I:37.

40. *SRARP*, XXIX:348-58. It was only one of many antinoble pamphlets. This particular storm was allayed by an intimation from the *Justitiekansler* that he was preparing to prosecute.

41. Malmström, VI:244. This was an old controversy. It had been settled in favor of the Peasants in 1765; but that decision had been overturned in 1769: Sten Carlsson, "Bondeståndet i Norden under senare delen av 1700-talet," pp. 44-45, 48.

42. *SRARP*, XXIX:411; Tengberg, *Gustaf III*, p. 63; Malmström, VI:245. This spirit was not confined to one side: it was Fredric Horn who said "that he felt in his bones another law, which was in conflict with the written law": *SRARP*, XXIX:651.

43. Vergennes wrote: "C'est un ameutement de la jeunesse": Hallesvik, *SVT*, p. 387.

44. Carl Trolle-Bonde, *Anteckningar om Bondesläkten. Riksrådet och Riksmarskalken Grefwe Carl D. Bonde samt hans närmaste Anhöriga*, I:275.

45. As Frederic Horn put it: "If this coldness increases, it could at last be difficult to preserve the constitution; and it may end with something more than verbal fencing": *SRARP*, XXIX:632.

46. *SRARP*, XXIX:351; cf. *ibid.*, 425, 452-53.

47. Hallesvik, *SVT*, p. 387.

48. *SRARP*, XXIX: 463, 650. See the tremendous debate on 17 October, which began at 9:00 AM and finished at 3:00 the following morning. It turned to a large extent upon the question whether or not the Charter was to be considered a fundamental law and how far the "Parliament Act" clause of the Ordinance of 1766 applied to it: *SRARP*, XXIX:399-470.

49. The Estate of Peasants resolved "that they would not be burdened with any further Extracts from the Minutes of the Nobility on this subject": *SRARP*, XXIX:651-52.

50. *SRARP*, XXIX:695-96 (4 December).

51. Fersen had already suggested to Goodricke that a possible expedient might be a royal *dictamen* to the Senate: SP 95/119/160-61, Goodricke to Suffolk, 19 November 1771.

52. Possibly on the suggestion of C. F. Scheffer: Odhner, *Gustaf III*, I:50-51.

53. Fersen, III:74-76, for his account; *ibid.*, 408-12, for Gustav's version to Lovisa Ulrika; *GIII och LU*, II:95-96, for her blistering comments; Schartau, *Hemliga Handlingar*, III:204-10, for text of the speech; Véou, "Un chapître inédit," p. 294; RA AVPR 112, Osterman to Panin, 11/22 December 1771; DRA Dept f. u. A., Guldencrone to Osten, 27 November 1771.

54. *SRARP*, XXIX:656-87. UUB F 514, C. F. Scheffer to Gustav III, 1 December 1771.

55. Y. Rosander, "Några brev från Gustav III," p. 434, prints Gustav's letter to Sinclair, 10 December 1771, which makes clear that he arranged for publication; though to his mother he denied responsibility: Fersen, III:410.

56. Malmström, VI:261, n. 1.

57. SP 95/117/79, Goodricke to Rochford, 20 March 1770.

58. SP 95/122/16, Goodricke to Suffolk, 8 September 1772.

59. As it certainly was when he added: "We urged this as a reason for the . . . preserving of some of the Senators who were most in the King's Favour." For his attitude to the question of the Senators, see below.

60. SP 95/119/34-35, Goodricke to Suffolk, 16 July 1771.

61. SP 95/118/128, Goodricke to Halifax, 23 April 1771.

62. Sir Joseph Yorke reported (no doubt relaying information from Goodricke himself) that he was "advised with by more than one party": Add. MS 35,370, fo. 18 (to Hardwicke, 24 February 1772).

63. SP 95/119/149-50, Goodricke to Suffolk, 5 November 1771.

64. SP 95/119/125-27, Goodricke to Suffolk, 15 October; 119/138-39, same to same, 25 October 1771.

65. SP 95/119/161, Goodricke to Suffolk, 19 November 1771.

66. SP 95/119/114-15, 130-31, 160-61, Goodricke to Suffolk, 8, 18 October, 19 November 1771.

67. Eric Linderstedt (a Cap), with obvious *Schadenfreude*, read extracts from the Hats' constitutional Bible, *Ärlig Svensk*, to prove their impropriety in attempting to discuss the matter: *SRARP*, XXIX:677.

68. SP 95/119/142-43, Suffolk to Goodricke, 15 November 1771.

69. SP 95/119/134, Goodricke to Suffolk, 22 October 1771.

70. SP 95/119/149-50, Goodricke to Suffolk, 5 November 1771.

71. SP 95/119/86-87, Goodricke to Suffolk, 3 September 1771.

72. SP 95/119/102-103, Goodricke to Suffolk, 20 September 1771.

73. SP 95/119/120, 126, Goodricke to Suffolk, 11, 15 October 1771. No agreement could be reached on a successor, and for the time being Ulrik Scheffer, as *rikskanslіråd*, managed foreign affairs *ad interim*.

74. Add MS 35,610, fo. 6, Porten to Hardwicke, 13 July 1771.

75. To his friend and undersecretary William Eden he wrote insisting on "great steadyness, accuracy, punctuality, attention, secrecy, activity and habits of discretion": Add. MS 34,412, fo. 174, 21 June 1772.

76. Harold Temperley, *Frederic the Great and Kaiser Joseph*, p. 263. The misconception probably rests on an uncharacteristically casual phrase in which Suffolk referred to "the terms and quantum of this curious transaction": SP 90/91/114, Suffolk to Harris, 5 June 1772.

77. *Martin Chuzzlewit*, chap. 2.

78. See, e.g., the very favorable judgment of the Danish minister Diede von Fürstenstein: DRA Dept. f. u. A., Diede to Osten, 3 April 1772.

79. SP 78/283 ff. contains a mass of correspondence on these matters. For Franco-Prussian approaches, SP 90/90/150, 175, 202.

80. For the anxiety about Spain, Add. MS 24,157, fos. 7, 195, Instructions for Grantham, 23 May 1771; Rochford to Grantham, 1 November 1771.

81. SP 95/119/142-43, Suffolk to Goodricke, 15 November 1771.

82. SP 95/119/116-18, Suffolk to Goodricke, 25 October 1771.

83. Goodricke's urgent appeal for instructions, which arrived on 11 November, and his crushing rebuttal of Suffolk's criticisms of 25 October, which arrived on 30 November, were answered first on 13 December with "I have nothing particularly in command from His Majesty in Answer to them": SP 95/119/138-39, 153-57, 165-66. Goodricke evidently felt this treatment: on 6 March NS 1772 Cathcart wrote sympathetically: "The accident you mention of the Having not [been] so much as acknowledged has happened to me not long ago: I believe it is a novelty in Office . . . ": UUB F 386.

84. SP 91/88/63-64, Suffolk to Cathcart, 16 August 1771.

85. SP 91/88/109-12, 167, 204-5, 216-17, Cathcart to Suffolk, 20/31 August, 23 September/4 October, 4/13 October, 18/29 October 1771.

86. SP 91/88/192-93, Suffolk to Cathcart, 8 November 1771.

87. SP 91/88/220-23, 239, Suffolk to Cathcart, 29 November, 10 December 1771; 89/5-12, Cathcart to Suffolk, 23 December/3 January 1771/2.

88. See Cathcart's gloomy report to Rochford, 31 December/11 January 1770/71: SP 91/86/230-36.

89. Marsangy, II:142-43, Vergennes to d'Aiguillon, 15 August 1771. The event produced excited speculation by Gustav III as to the possibility of Catherine's recognizing his succession to Holstein-Gottorp if Paul should die: UUB F 414, Gustav III to Mörner, September 1771.

90. SP 91/90/93, Suffolk to Gunning, Most Secret, 24 July 1772, referring to information conveyed verbally to Gunning before his departure. Cf. Ribbing's reports of popular risings: RA. Kab. f. u. Brevvexling, KP to Ribbing, 2 August 1771.

91. From 1769 the state debt increased at the rate of 2 million rubles a year, and the government began printing paper money: David R. Ransel, *The Politics of Catherinian Russia: The Panin Party*, p. 230.

92. SP 90/90/167-68, 91/37 Burnet to Suffolk, 26 October 1771, 15 February 1772; *ibid.*, 91/54, 111, Harris to Suffolk, 7 March, 23 May 1772; SP 91/88/267; 89/116, Suffolk to Cathcart, 31 December 1771, 20 March 1772; SP 91/90/20-21, Cathcart to Suffolk, 24 April/5 May 1772. Cathcart was not convinced that it was impending until June, when he found it "most extraordinary and incomprehensible": *ibid.*, 90/72-74, to Suffolk, 1/12 June 1772.

93. See, e.g., SP 91/92/119-21, Suffolk to Gunning, 26 March 1773, where he refuses to guarantee the integrity of Russia's annexations; and see, in general, Wolfgang Michael, *Englands Stellung zur ersten Teilung Polens*.

94. SP 91/90/8, draft instructions for Gunning, 27 May 1772.

95. Asseburg, p. 413; David M. Griffiths, "The Rise and Fall of the Northern System: Court Politics and Foreign Policy in the First Half of Catherine II's Reign," p. 556.

96. Ransel, pp. 136, 145, 197-98.

97. SP 91/89/138-39, Suffolk to Cathcart, 7 April 1772.

98. Barthélémy, p. 22; Marsangy, II:389.

99. Geffroy, I:132; SP 95/119/134, Goodricke to Suffolk, 22 October 1771.

100. Stiegung, *Ludvig XV:s hemliga diplomati*, p. 234 n. 6.

101. SP 95/119/32-34, Goodricke to Suffolk, 16 July 1771.

102. Rosander, pp. 428-29, Vergennes to Sinclair, 31 August 1771.

103. SP 95/119/118, Suffolk to Goodricke, 25 October 1771; Hallesvik, *Fersen*, p. 86.

104. SP 95/119/106-7, 118, 130-31, Goodricke to Suffolk, 24 September, 18 October, Suffolk to Goodricke, 1, 25 October 1771; DRA Dept. f. u. A., Guldencrone to Osten, 1 October 1771.

105. RA Malmström avskr., Vergennes to d'Aiguillon, 10, 15 August 1771.

106. SP 95/119/130-31, Goodricke to Suffolk, 18 October 1771; Stiegung, *Ludvig XV:s hemliga diplomati*, p. 235.

107. *Recueil des instructions données: Suède*, pp. 434, 439.

108. Hallesvik, *Fersen*, p. 32.

109. *SIRIO*, 97:450, Osterman to Panin, 14 October 1771. Goodricke seems to have written to Cathcart to the same effect: SP 91/88/230.

110. The letter from Gustav to Sinclair cited by Rosander as proof of his complicity does not support this conclusion: all Gustav had said was that the Hats "me craignent plus qu'ils ne craigne les bonnets": Rosander, pp. 430-31.

111. *G III och LU*, II:101 ("Le fameux Lilliehorn et un M. Uggla, qu'on nomme Ridderskapets och Adelns klockare . . . ").

112. See, e.g., *SRARP*, XXIX:93, 116-26, 149-52, 567-77. Some ironical member of the chancery scribbled on the back of a letter from KP to Ribbing: "Och sedan få vi bröd och salt/Ty herren hafver oss skänkt Sebalt" ("So now we'll all get bread and salt/Since God Almighty has sent us Sebaldt") RA Kab. f. u. brevvexling, KP to Ribbing, 28 February 1772. A. Evers, *Den svenska brännvinslagstiftningens historia*, II:89-95: after the revolution, Gustav forced a prohibition through the Diet in a matter of three days: *ibid.*, p. 103. For his indignation, see *G III och LU*, II:54.

113. *G III och LU*, II:65 (to Lovisa Ulrika, 29 November 1771).

114. *Ibid.*, II:98-104 (to Lovisa Ulrika, 27 December 1771).

115. *G III och LU*, II:99.

116. *Collection des écrits politiques et littéraires de Gustave III*, I:90.

117. SP 78/283/31 (to Rochford, 9 July 1771); and see *Pol. Corr.*, XXXI:219 n. 2, Sandoz Rollin to Frederick, 1 July 1771. For other estimates, less favorable, *Mercy-Kaunitz Corr.*, II:384-85, 391; R. Konetzke, *Die Politik des Grafen Aranda*, p. 72; Abbé Georgel, *Mémoires pour servir à l'histoire des événements de la fin du dix-huitième siècle*, I:150, 190-91.

118. See, e.g., Duc de Broglie, *Le Secret du Roi. Correspondance secrète de Louis XV avec ses agents diplomatiques*, II:372-85; Alexis de Saint-Priest, *Etudes diplomatiques et littéraires*, I:255-73, 283.

119. The espionage with a view to an invasion of England continued: G Lacour-Gayet, *La Marine militaire de la France sous la règne de Louis XV*, p. 456.

120. See Konopczyński, "England and the First Partition of Poland," pp. 10, 28.

121. See, e.g., SP 78/283/148, 150, 269; 284/20, 35; *Corr. of George III*, II:260, 285.

122. Fraguier, p. 610; *Pol. Corr.*, XXXI:445 and n. 2. Panin and Kaunitz were expecting this move: *SIRIO*, 118:20, Panin to Golitzin (draft) 10 February OS 1772.

123. See SP 78/284/304, Rochford to Harcourt, 10 April 1772.

124. Goodricke was worried by rumors of an attempt to construct a Franco-Austrian Northern System, to include both Sweden and Denmark: SP 95/119/44-46, 98-99.

125. Stiegung, *Ludvig XV:s hemliga diplomati* p. 252.

126. *Gustavianska Papperen*, I:192.

127. Marsangy, II:186-87.

128. See, e.g., his letter to d'Aiguillon of 24 January 1772, in Marsangy, II:179-82.

129. UUB F 514, C. F. Scheffer to Gustav III, 13 July 1771.

130. Marsangy, II:152.

131. *Gustavianska Papperen*, I:192.

132. UUB F 414, nos. 54, 56; Geffroy, I:147. Ulrik Scheffer reinforced these pleas two days later: Schartau, III:79.

133. Stiegung, *Ludvig XV:s hemliga diplomati*, pp. 248, 251; Marsangy, II:155. Rumors that d'Aiguillon intended to defer payment for the first installment were current in Paris as early as 10 November: SP 78/283/232, Blaquière to Rochford. Goodricke knew about it on 24 December: SP/95/119/191-92; cf. *ibid.*, 120/6-7, Suffolk to Goodricke, 25 January 1772.

134. SP 95/120/1-3, Goodricke to Suffolk, 7 January 1772; DRA Dept. f. u. A., Guldencrone to Osten, 3 January 1772; Barthélémy, p. 16.

135. Stiegung, *Ludvig XV:s hemliga diplomati*, p. 253.

136. Gustav III wrote: "ils sont tous horriblement fâchés contre le C. de Fersen": *G III och LU*, II:117; *Gustavianska Papperen*, I:144; AVPR 17, Osterman to Panin, 2/13 January 1772.

137. He thought them "gens qui ont plus de courage et d'enthousiasme que de lumières et connoissances d'affaires," and that they consisted mainly of people conspicuous only for their debts: Stiegung, *Ludvig XV:s hemliga diplomati*, p. 257; Hallesvik, *Fersen*, p. 79.

138. For conflicting accounts of the responsibility for founding *Svenska Botten*, see Fersen, III:71; "Pro Memoria, 1771," pp. 75-76; *Ur J. M. Sprengtportens papper*, VIII:17-18; *En Stockholmströnika ur Gjörwells brev*, p. 38 (Gjörwell to Ehrensvärd, 2 January 1772).

139. Malmström, VI:268; Hallesvik, *Fersen*, p. 45; *Ur J. M. Sprengtportens papper*, p. 19.

140. *SRARP*, XXX:53-64, 22 January 1772.

141. *G III och LU*, II:135.

142. *SRARP*, XXX:98. Pechlin's argument for acceptance was significant: he urged it "in the position in which the Nobility now stands in relation to the other Estates": *ibid.*, 97.

143. *Gustavianska Papperen*, I:167-69; Marsangy, II:185-86; Malmström, VI:270-72.

144. In 1762 the Nobility had resolved that no new creations should be permitted to sit until the number of peers had fallen to 800.

145. *SRARP*, XXX:109-36.

146. *G III och LU*, II:133.

147. *Ibid.*, II:144-45.

148. *Ibid.*, II:134; cf. "Pro Memoria, 1771," pp. 67-70, 91-95.

149. SP 95/120/28-29, Goodricke to Suffolk, 11 February 1772. The idea of sending him to Pomerania had occurred to Guldencrone some months earlier: DRA Dept. f. u. A., Guldencrone to Osten, 22 October 1771.

150. Hallesvik, *Fersen*, pp. 65-66, 71.

151. RA Sjöholmsarkivet, Gyldenstolpske samlingen, 12 February 1772. The correct date must be 13 February, since Sinclair refers to the debate of 12 February as taking place "hier."

152. For the debates of 22 and 24 February, *SRARP*, XXX:165-236, 237-89.

153. For the serious financial crisis, see *SRARP*, XXX:469-85.

154. E.g., *SRARP*, XXX:113, 115, 125.

155. *SRARP*, XXX:81: carried by 302 to 288. Sundblad in the event declined the appointment.

156. *SRARP*, XXX:250.

157. *SRARP*, XXX:274.

158. *SRARP*, XXX:276-79; AVPR, 11, Osterman to Catherine II, 17/28 February 1772.

159. *SIRIO*, 118:35, 39; SP 95/120/71-73, Goodricke to Suffolk, 31 March 1772.

160. SP 95/120/53-55, 58-60, same to same, 10, 17 March 1772.

161. *Ibid.*, 120/9, same to same, 14 January 1772.

162. *Ibid.*, 120/24, same to same, 4 February 1772.

163. *Ibid.*, 120/53-55, same to same, 10 March 1772.

164. *Ibid.*, 120/58-60, same to same, 17 March 1772.

165. SP 95/120/58-60, same to same, 17 March 1772.

166. SP 95/120/76-78, same to same, 7 April 1772.

167. UUB F 514, C. F. Scheffer to Gustav III, 6 April 1772. There seems no ground for the suggestion that Gustav and Vergennes in the end ensured that the recommendation should not be seriously resisted: *Mémoires historiques . . . de Hordt* [*sc.* Hård], II:235.

168. UUB F 525, Vergennes to Beylon, 13 March 1772; *Gustavianska Papperen* I:148, same to same, 25 February 1772.

169. UUB F 525, Vergennes to Beylon, 12 March 1772.

170. Hallesvik, *Fersen*, p. 60.

171. Rosander, pp. 435-36, Vergennes to Sinclair, 12 April 1772.

172. Fersen, III:428. Osterman is said to have spent 12,000 écus.

173. SP 95/120/98, Goodricke to Suffolk, 21 April 1772; Fersen, III:80-81.

174. UUB F 414, no. 57, Gustav III to Ridderstolpe, 13 April 1772. Sprengtporten's comments in *Gustavianska Papperen*, I:152-53; C. F. Scheffer's in UUB F 514, (to Gustav III, 20 April 1772).

175. *Gustavianska Papperen*, I:152-53, to Beylon, 12 April 1772.

176. Fersen, III:430, Fersen to Gustav III, 22 April1772; RA Malmström avskr., Vergennes to d'Aiguillon, 14 April 1772.

177. SP 95/120/90-91, Goodricke to Suffolk, 14 April 1772.

178. *Ibid.*, 120/99, same to same, 21 April 1772.

179. *Ibid.*, 120/89, same to same, 14 April 1772.

180. *Ibid.*, 120/98-100, same to same, 21 April 1772.

181. *Ibid.*

182. *SRARP*, XXX:491-569.

183. E.g., Ridderstolpe, Frietzcky, von Essen: *SRARP*, XXX:513, 548, 553.

184. *SRARP*, XXX:540.

185. *SRARP*, XXVII:70.

186. *SRARP*, XXX:546.

187. *SRARP*, XXXI:79: Leijonanckar, 20 May. For the difficulties about filling the Senate, RA AVPR 13, Osterman to Catherine, 27 April/8 May, 4/15, 11/22, 18/29 May 1772; SP 95/120/136-37, 140-46, Goodricke to Suffolk, 19, 26 May 1772.

188. A Cap is reported to have said to Schönberg: "We are now so firmly in the saddle that no mortal power can unseat us": A. Fryxell, *Berättelser ur svensk historia*, 42:105.

189. Hallesvik, *Fersen*, p. 75; Odhner, *Gustaf III*, I:79, 86, 97.

190. *G III och LU*, II:233-34 (to Lovisa Ulrika, 7 July 1772); Fersen, III:85.

191. SP 95/120/116, 122, 124-30, Suffolk to Goodricke, 21, 28, 29 May 1772. Rochford at this time remarked to the Danish minister that this seemed the moment for Russia to "reprendre son grand plan" in Sweden: DRA Dept. f. u. A., Diede to Osten, 22 May 1772.

192. Though someone in the office (Sir Stanier Porten?) had suggested it in a draft memorandum of 19 October 1769: SP 95/134.

193. SP 91/90/5-8, Suffolk to Gunning, 27 May 1772.

194. On the question of the treatment of Caroline Matilda.

195. SP 91/90/43, Suffolk to Gunning, 12 June; SP 95/120/149, Suffolk to Goodricke, 16 June 1772.

196. SP 91/90/28-30, Cathcart to Gunning, 8/19 May: this reached Suffolk on 10 June, and probably influenced his letters to Gunning and Goodricke of 12 and 16 June.

197. SP 95/120/149, Suffolk to Goodricke, 16 June 1772.

198. SP 91/90/90-92, 105, Gunning to Suffolk, 19/30 June, 22 June/3 July 1772.

199. SP 95/120/207, Goodricke to Suffolk, 14 July 1772; RA AVPR 11, 5 June [OS?] 1772.

200. SP 95/121/10-23, Goodricke to Suffolk, 21 July, received 3 August 1772.

201. SP 95/121/28, Goodricke to Suffolk, 21 July 1772: his language was commended as "very able and judicious": *ibid.*, 121/54, Suffolk to Goodricke, 4 August 1772.

202. SP 95/120/199/200; 121/24-28, Goodricke to Suffolk, 7, 21 July 1772.

203. SP 95/120/205-6, Suffolk to Goodricke, 28 July 1772.

204. SP 95/120/168-70, 175-76, 185-87, 200, Goodricke to Suffolk, 9, 16, 23 June, 7 July. Osterman asked him if he expected to carry the treaty without money: he replied that he did not, but that he meant to try.

205. SP 95/120/112-13; 121/10-12, Goodricke to Suffolk, 5 May, 21 July 1772.

206. SP 95/120/166, Suffolk to Goodricke, 26 June 1772; SP 91/90/65-66, Suffolk to Cathcart, 30 June 1772.

207. SP 95/120/113; 121/125-27, Goodricke to Suffolk, 5 May, 14 August 1772.

208. SP 95/120/161, 168-70, Goodricke to Suffolk, 5, 9 June 1772. Goodricke actually saw two letters from d'Aiguillon to Düben, of 4 and 14 May, to this effect; Suffolk confirmed their authenticity on 16 June: *ibid.*, 120/149.

209. *Recueil des instructions données: Russie*, pp. 286-300, Instructions for Durand, 24 July 1772; cf. SP 78/285/311, Blaquière to Rochford, 12 August 1772.

210. SP 95/120/188, Goodricke to Suffolk, 23 June 1772.

211. SP 95/120/169-70, Goodricke to Suffolk, 9 June 1772.

212. SP 95/119/76-77, 96-97, Goodricke to Suffolk, 23 August, 13 September 1771; *SIRIO*, 97:400, Osterman to Panin, 19/30 August 1771; Schartau, III:72.

213. *SIRIO*, 97:436, Panin to Osterman, 8 September OS 1771; UUB F 386, Cathcart to Goodricke, 21 September 1771.

214. SP 95/120/207-209, Goodricke to Suffolk, 14 July 1772.

215. RA Mindre Sekreta Deputationen, Expeditioner (1772), 16 July.

216. Schartau, III:92-95.

217. RA RRPUÄ (1772), fo. 397 (3 August); Kabinettet f. utr. brevvexling, Ulrik Scheffer to Creutz, 4 August 1772.

218. SP 95/121/43-44, Suffolk to Goodricke, 4 August 1772.

219. BM Egerton MS 2701, fo. 151, Goodricke to Gunning, 26 August 1772. He had earlier forwarded to Suffolk the translation of a report to the Diet of the state of the navy in 1771, which bore this out: SP 95/121/79-87 (4 August 1772).

220. *SRARP*, XXXI:495 (12 August): debate on an extract from the Burghers' minutes of 22 July.

221. SP 95/131/54, Suffolk to Goodricke, 11 August 1772.

222. SP 95/134, Goodricke to Hopkins, 21 July 1772.

223. BM Egerton MS 2701, fo. 70, Goodricke to Gunning, 17 July 1772.

224. As Ulrik Scheffer had predicted in September 1771: Schartau, III:75 (to Creutz, 17 September 1771).

225. Marsangy, II:179-82, Vergennes to d'Aiguillon, 24 January 1772; Malmström, VI:268.

226. Helle Stiegung, *Den engelska underrättelseverksamheten rörande Sverige under 1700-talet*, p. 54.

227. UUB F 525, Fersen to Vergennes, 25 March 1772. On 7 March he had written "Je marche environné de trahisons et de perfidies, et je ne puis rien dire de plus"; on 17 March he knew that Sinclair was not to be dismissed, and was to be sent to Pomerania: *G III och LU*, II:162, 171.

228. UUB F 514, C. F. Scheffer to Gustav III, 3 April 1772.

229. Hallesvik, *SVT*, pp. 395-96.

230. *Ibid.*, p. 397.

231. Stiegung, *Ludvig XV:s hemliga diplomati*, p. 259: the most Vergennes was willing to promise was 600,000 livres (ca. £24,000).

232. *G III och LU*, II:200-201.

233. "Pro Memoria, 1771," fos. 67-70, must refer to this episode, despite the date ascribed to its composition; and cf. a similar passage at fos. 91-95, which refers to December 1771.

234. UUB F 386, Rochford to Goodricke, 12 May 1772.

235. BM Egerton MS 2701, fo. 93, Goodricke to Gunning, 3 August 1772; SP 95/121/47-49, Suffolk to Goodricke, 4 August 1772.

236. Already after the vote in the lower Estates Ulrik Scheffer had urged Gustav to "seize the tiller with a Herculean arm": Odhner, *Minne af Riksrådet m.m. Ulrik Scheffer*, p. 50.

237. During the closing months of 1772 Catherine is described as "utterly bewildered and sunk in indolence"; "Government business came to a complete standstill": Ransel, *Politics of Catherinian Russia*, p. 234.

238. For Gustav's reluctant recognition that he must secure Fersen, *Gustavianska Papperen*, I:160, Gustav III to C. F. Scheffer, 21 April 1772.

239. On 22 April Fersen wrote to Gustav III: "Si tout est précaire dans ma malheureuse patrie, si les intérêts les plus sacrés de l'Etat sont sujets au changement; si les engagements les plus solennels sont altérables, les vertus de notre respectable Monarque ne le seront assurément pas, et serviront tôt ou tard de ralliement à son peuple": Fersen, III:432.

240. For Sprengtporten's plan, see *Ur J. M. Sprengtportens papper*, passim.

241. For Toll's plan, see his memoirs in *Dela Gardieska Archivet*, XIV:191-248.

242. For the best account of Toll's rising, and the precarious nature of the enterprise, see G. Iverus, *Hertig Karl av Södermanland*, pp. 56-80.

243. Marsangy, II:188-89.

244. UUB F 525, Vergennes to Beylon, 12, 16 March 1772.

245. Marsangy, II:208-10, Vergennes to d'Aiguillon, 21 May 1772; Véou, "Un chapître inédit," pp. 275, 299-301.

246. Marsangy, II:222.

247. Stiegung, *Ludvig XV:s hemliga diplomati*, pp. 263-65.

248. Marsangy, II:220-21, Gustav III to Louis XV, 17 June 1772.

249. *Ibid.*, II:230; *Gustavianska Papperen*, I:185-86.

250. RA Malmström avskr., Vergennes to d'Aiguillon, 9 July 1772.

251. For an account and an analysis of its achievements, see Stiegung, *Den engelska underrättelseverksamheten*, passim.

252. SP 95/120/33, 51/52, Suffolk to Goodricke, 6, 24 March; 120/142, 163, Goodricke to Suffolk, 26 May, 5 June 1772: UUB F 386, Rochford to Goodricke, 12 May 1772.

253. SP 95/120/179-80, Rochford (*vice* Suffolk) to Goodricke, 3 July 1772; *Correspondence of George III*, II:363-64.

254. Much to George III's annoyance: *ibid.*, II:364-65.

255. SP 95/121/1-4, Goodricke to Suffolk, 19 July 1772.

256. SP 95/120/181-84, Rochford to Goodricke, 7 July 1772; Add. MS 34,412, fos. 177-78, Suffolk to W. Eden, 5 July 1772; *Correspondence of George III*, II:365-66.

257. SP 95/121/128-32, Goodricke to Suffolk, 18 August 1772.

258. So Suffolk, on 5 July, Rochford, on 7 July. Goodricke reported Osterman and Düben as agreeing with him "that the project was as extravagant a one as could be imagined, and they could neither of them conceive how it could be put in execution": SP 95/121/1-4.

259. SP 95/121/5-7, Goodricke to Suffolk, 21 July 1772.

260. SP 95/121/1-4, Goodricke to Suffolk, 19 July 1772.

261. SP 95/121/5-7, Goodricke to Suffolk, 21 July 1772.

262. SP 95/121/113-14, Suffolk to Goodricke, 21 August 1772. Goodricke's defense does not accord too well with his dispatch of 21 July, though there may well have been a considerable measure of truth in it: he wrote, "As to his being sent to Finland, in the manner he was, I can assure your Lordship, that both Count Osterman and I expressed our Dislike to it, but the Members of the Secret Committee were grown so ungovernable, when we had no Money to give them, that they were not to be guided, neither in this, nor in many other Affairs of great importance to the Preservation of their Liberties, tho' we strongly represented to them the Danger they were in": SP 95/122/15-16, Goodricke to Suffolk, 8 September 1772.

263. *SRARP*, XXXI: 389-400, 409. The debate gives an indication of how narrow was the circle of Caps to whom Goodricke's information had been confided. Only Frietzcky spoke for sending Sprengtporten to Finland; while Grönhagen, Nackreij, and even Pechlin argued for the inalienable right of a member of the Diet to neglect his duty to the state, whether civil or military.

264. For an evaluation of contemporary and near-contemporary accounts of the revolution, see Herman Schück, *Gustav III:s stasvälvning i berättande källor och äldre litteratur.* The best account (which is followed here) is still that in Malmström, VI:344-91.

265. There is a detailed account of Sprengtporten's adventures and misadventures in Suolahti, *Sprengtporten's Statskupp och andra Essayer*, pp. 7-100.

266. See the copy of his instructions for Major von Saltza, *Gustavianska Papperen*, I:184-85.

267. For a detailed account, see Iverus, *Hertig Karl*. Goodricke's account is in SP 95/121/128-32 (to Suffolk, 18 August 1772).

268. Goodricke says nothing in his dispatches of giving any such advice.

269. *Tersmedens memoarer*, V:75: one warning came from Tersmeden himself, who had it from a clerical member of the Secret Committee. The king told him that he had been warned already.

270. There is a story that the Senate were just approving the minute ordering Senator Funck to take command against the rising in Skåne, when a member asked what the commotion was in the courtyard below; and von Wallwijk, who was looking out of the window, drily replied that it looked as though the king was amending the minute.

271. *Tersmedens memoarer*, V:86.

272. Iverus, *Hertig Karl*, p. 74.

273. Though immediately after the success of the revolution Gustav III took care to spread the rumor that Sprengtporten and his forces had arrived: Schück, *Gustaf III:s statsvälvning*, pp. 21, 23.

274. SP 95/121/5-7, Goodricke to Suffolk, 21 July 1772.

275. SP 95/121/50-51, Suffolk to Goodricke, 4 August 1772.

276. *Correspondence of George III*, II:384, the king to Suffolk, 30 August 1772.

277. *SIRIO*, 118:202.

278. D'Aiguillon went so far as to claim that the first thing that Vergennes knew about the plan for a revolution was after it had succeeded: *Mémoires d'Aiguillon*, p. 163.

279. *Mémoires de Barthélémy*, p. 28.

EPILOGUE
TRANQUILLITY PRESERVED

1. For a more extended discussion of the difficulties of British foreign policy during the period, see Roberts, "*Spendid Isolation.*"

2. SP 91/90/145, Cathcart to Suffolk, 23 July 1772. Thus by a curious irony Partition secured *one* long-standing French objective: it interposed a barrier between Russia and Europe.

3. For a detailed examination of the crises provoked by the revolution, and of British policy in particular, see Roberts, "Great Britain and the Swedish Revolution, 1772-3," pp. 286-347.

4. SP 95/121/169-72, Suffolk to Goodricke, 8 September 1772; SP 91/91/124, Suffolk to Gunning, 10 November 1772.

5. SP 95/122/20; 123/36, 124-25; though it seems that till as late as February 1773 Goodricke normally had access to the books of the Bank.

6. SP 95/123/20-21.

7. SP 95/121/162-65; 122/77-79.

8. SP 95/122/31-32.

9. RA Diplomatica, Gallica, Brev till Creutz, 29 September 1772; AE Suède, 262/204, 233; RA Kab. f. utrikes brevvexling, KP to Creutz, 16 September 1772.

10. RA Diplomatica, Anglica, KP to Nolcken, 19 February; Gallica, KP to Creutz, 26 March 1773.

11. SP 95/123/16-17, 33-34, 39, 45-46, 49-50.

12. BM Egerton MS 2696, fo. 299, Goodricke to Gunning, 30 June 1767.

13. Add. MS 35, 370, fo. 13.

14. SP 91/80/233.

15. Add. MS 35, 369, fo. 137 (to Hardwicke, 10 April 1770).

16. Martens, IX (X):275.

17. SP 91/80/249: my italics.

18. Add. MS 35, 425, fo. 281.

19. Add. MS 35, 425, fo. 281.

Bibliography

Bibliography

MANUSCRIPT SOURCES

London

The Public Record Office (PRO)

State Papers, Foreign. Denmark. SP 75/104, 107-8, 110-11, 113, 115-27.
State Papers, Foreign. France. SP 78/282-89, 313, 323.
State Papers, Foreign. Prussia. SP 90/82-94.
State Papers, Foreign. Russia. SP 91/71-94.
State Papers, Foreign. Sweden. SP 95/101, 103-24, 134.
State Papers, Foreign. SP 101/93. Letters of Sir John Goodricke. Letters and Dispatches, 1758-1763.
State Papers, Foreign. 103. Treaty Papers. 63.
State Papers, Foreign. SP 107/104. Copies. Foreign Ambassadors (Intercepted. Also Translations and Extracts).
Chatham Papers. 30/8. Vols. 33, 84, 88.
Bliss transcripts from Riksarkivet, Stockholm. 31/13/2.

British Museum (BM)

Add. MS 6810. Mitchell Papers. Letter-book, 1764-1770.
Add. MS 6829. Mitchell Papers. Letters from Ambassadors, 1756-69.
Add. MS 9242. Coxe Papers. Correspondence of Lord Rochford with Lord Shelburne, 1766-1773.
Add. MS 21,501. Sweden. Drafts and Précis.
Add. MS 24,157-59. Grantham Papers.
Add. MS 32,258. Decyphers of Diplomatic Papers. France, I. 1650-1774.
Add. MS 32,285. Decyphers of Diplomatic Papers. Sweden, I. 1716-1818.
Add. MS 32,288. Decyphers of Diplomatic Papers. Russia.
Add. MS 33,024. Newcastle Papers. Diplomatic Correspondence 1761-1767.
Add. MS 33,764. Situation of Russia, Written by Sir G. Macartney.
Add. MS 34,412. Auckland Papers. Lord Suffolk's Letters to W. Eden.

Add. MS 35,367, 35,369-70. Hardwicke Papers. Correspondence of the 2nd Earl of Hardwicke with Sir J. Yorke.
Add. MS 35,385. Hardwicke Papers. Correspondence of Charles Yorke with Sir J. Yorke.
Add. MS 35,425. Hardwicke Papers. Political Correspondence of the 2nd Lord Hardwicke with the Duke of Newcastle and Sir John Goodricke, 1754-1782.
Add. MS 35,444. Hardwicke Papers. Diplomatic Letter-book of Sir J. Yorke, 1756-1772.
Add. MS 35,502. Hardwicke Papers. Diplomatic Letter-book of Sir R. Gunning, 1772-75.
Add. MS 35,503-5. Hardwicke Papers. Diplomatic Letter-book of Sir Robert Murray Keith, 1772-74.
Add. MS 35,609-10. Hardwicke Papers. General Correspondence of 2nd Earl of Hardwicke.
Add. MS 36,800. Letters of Sir W. Lynch.
Add. MS 37,054. Letter-book of Henry Shirley, 1767-68.
Add. MS 38,199, 221, 339. Liverpool Papers.
Add. MS 38,348. [fos. 199 ff. have "Hints about the Turkey Treaty"]
Add. MS 46,490. Auckland Papers. Supplementary.
Add. MS 51,388. Holland House Papers.
Egerton MS 1755. Bentinck Papers.
Egerton MS 2696-2701. Gunning Papers.
Stowe MS 252. Commercial Relations with Russia, 1732-1765.
Stowe MS 259-61. Phelps Correspondence.

Belfast

The Public Record Office of Northern Ireland (PRO NI)

T 2513/1-2. Macartney Papers (photostats).

Oxford

The Bodleian Library

Bodley MS Eng. hist. c. 62. Correspondence of Sir John Goodricke.
Bland Burges Papers. Transcripts of political papers of Col. Burges and Sir James Burges [contains "Observations on the nature of the Connection which has hitherto subsisted between Great Britain and Russia . . . "].

Nottingham

Nottingham University Library

Galway Papers, 12779-81.

Copenhagen

Rigsarkivet (DRA)

Tyske Kansliets udenrigske Afdelning (TKUA)

Sverige B 149-50, 152-60. Gesandtskabs-Relationer . . . fra Envoyé Extraordinaire Joachim Otto von Schack.
Sverige B 161-65. Gesandtskabs-Relationer . . . fra Envoyé Extraordinaire Gregers Juel.

Sverige C 322-25. Envoyé Extraordinaire Joachim Otto von Schacks Gesandtskabs-Arkiv. Ordrer, til Dels med Bilag, 1765-67.
Sverige C 351. Envoyé Extraordinaire Gregers Juels Gesandtskabs-Arkiv. Ordrer, til Dels med Bilag. 1767-April 1770.
England C 267. Envoyé Extraordinaire Hans Caspar von Bothmers . . . Gesandtskabs-Arkiv 1764-1767.
Rusland B 96. Gesandtskabs-Relationer . . . fra Envoyé-Extraordinaire og Ministre-plenipot. Achatz Ferdinand v.d. Asseburg, Legationsraad Christoph Vilhelm Dreyer, og Envoyé Extraordinaire Grev Christian Scheel.
Rusland C 180. Envoyé-Extraordinaire Grev Christian Scheels Gesandtskabs-Arkiv 1768-70. Ordrer, til Dels med Bilag m.m.
Department for udenriges Arkiv 1771-1848.
England II. Depescher 1772-73.
Sverrig II. Depescher 1771. Rosencrone/Guldencrone.
England I. Ges. Arkiver. Ordrer 1771-1777.

Paris

Archives du Ministère des Affaires Etrangères (AE)

Correspondance politique. Angleterre. Vols. 500-502.
Suède. Vols. 262-63.

Stockholm

Riksarkivet (RA)

Kungl. Arkivet 259. Drottning Lovisa Ulrika. Anteckningar och utgångna brev. Lovisa Ulrikas hemliga korrespondens 1764-1766.
Diplomatica. Anglica. Engelska beskickningens memorial och noter, 1729-82.
Anglica. Konferensprotokoll, II. (1719-1766).
Anglica. Nolckens brev till kanslipresidenten 1764-1770.
Anglica. Nolckens brev till kanslipresidenten 1771-1772.
Anglica. Nolckens brev till Kongl. Maj:t 1769-1771.
Anglica. Nolckens brev till K. M:tt 1771-72.
Anglica. Nolckens depescher 1773.
Danica. Sprengtportens brev till kanslipresidenten 1763.
Danica. Sprengtportens brev till kanslipresidenten 1763-65.
Gallica. Franska Regeringens Noter till Ambassadören Grefve Creutz, 1766-87.
Gallica. Kanslipresidentens brev till F. U. von Friesendorff, 1764-66.
Gallica. Brev till Ambassadören Gref Creutz. (Vols. 461-62).
Muscovitica. K. W. von Dübens brev till kanslipresidenten, 1763-66.
Muscovitica. Baron Karl Ribbings brev till kanslipresidenten, 1766-73.
Muscovitica. Baron F. von Nolckens Depescher 1773.
Kabinettet för utrikes brevväxling (Presidentskontoret). Koncept. 1764-1773.
Svenska beskickningar till G. von Nolcken (Vols. 436-37).
Upplösta chifferbrev (Vol. 438).
Rådsprotokoll. Riksrådets Protokoll i utrikes ärenden 1763-1772. (RRPUÄ)
Hemliga rådsprotokoll i flere slags ärenden 1761-1776.
Riksdagen. Riksens ständers brev 1765-1766 uti Utrikes Ärenden.

Riksens ständers brev 1769-70. Utrikes Ärenden.
Mindre sekreta deputationen. Sekreta propositionen. Utrikes. 1765.
Mindre sekreta deputationen. Sekreta proposition. Utrikes-ärende. 1769-70.
Mindre sekreta deputationen. Sekreta proposition. Utrikes. 1771-72.
Mindre sekreta deputationens expedition 1766.
Mindre sekreta deputationens expeditioner åren 1771-72.
Mindre sekreta deputationen. Ministerberättelser. 1765-66. G. von Nolckens riksdagsberättelse. 1765.
Mindre sekreta deputationen. Ministerrelationer. Grefve G. Creutz' riksdagsberättelse. 1769.
Mindre sekreta deputationen. Ministerrelationer. G. A. von Nolckens riksdagsberättelse. 1769.
Mindre sekreta deputationen. Ministerrelationer. C. Ribbings sekreta riksdagsberättelse. 1769.
Mindre sekreta deputationen. Ministerrelationer. 1771-72. G. Creutz.
Mindre sekreta deputationen. Ministerrelationer. 1771-72. C. Ribbing.
Mindre sekreta deputationen. Ministerberattelser. 1771-72. G. von Nolckens riksdagsberättelse. 1771.

Riksdagsjournaler. G. Reuterholms Dagbok öfwer början af 1769 års riksdag.
Ekebladska samlingen. Bref till Claes Ekeblad. Vol. II.
Ericsbergsarkivet. Fredrik Sparres samling. Fredrik Sparres dagbok 1769-70.
Schefferska samlingen. Skrivelser till C. F. Scheffer, Vols. IV-VI.
Skrivelser till Ulrik Scheffer.
Sjöholmsarkivet. Gyldenstolpske samlingen. Bref ifrån riksrådet och Gen. Gouv. Gref Sinclair, till Hans Excel. Kon. Gouv. Gref N. P. Gyldenstolpe, åren 1763-1773.
Stavsundsarkivet. Smärre enskilda arkiv. [S. Piper], "Pro Memoria, 1771."
Tessinska samlingen. Brev till C. G. Tessin.
von Dübenska samlingen. Vol. 14. Handlingar rörande kanslipresident J. von Düben d. y.
Avskriftsamlingen. N. Tengbergs avskriftsamlingen. Excerpter ur danska ministrarnas i Petersburgs depescher 1762-1772.
N. Tengbergs avskrifter ur främmande arkiv. Excerpter ur danska ministrars i Stockholm depescher 1762-1772.
C. G. Malmström. Fransiska Minister Berättelser 1764-72.
Microfilm. Arkhiv vneshnei politik Rossii (AVPR), MID SSSR (Old and New Series). (I am indebted to Professor Michael Metcalf for kindly excerpting and translating these for me.)

Uppsala

Uppsala Universitets Bibliotek (UUB)

F. 211. Gyldenstolpske handlingar, 1762-1787.
F. 279. Handlingar till Sveriges politiska historia, 1756-1772.
F. 367. Neutralitet till sjöss. 1757-1760.
F. 377. Riksrådet och Generalgouvernören Grefve Carl Sinclair. Bref och conjunctur skrifter under riksdagen 1765.
F. 379. Claes Frietzckys papper, 1756-1771.
F. 386. Letters of Sir John Goodricke.
F. 414. Konung Gustaf III:s egenhändiga skrifter, Memoirer och Bidrag till konungens egen historia, t. I. 1756-1778.
F. 478. Gustav III:s Dagbok 1767-1769.
F. 514. Bref från Grefve Carl Fredrik Scheffer, 1762-86, I.

F. 525. Bref till Jean Franc. Beylon.
W-n. 978. Bref till Ålderman John Westin den äldre angående riksdagsmanna valen 1771.

PRINTED SOURCES

(The place of publication of books, unless otherwise indicated, is London)

"Aktstykker og Breve til Belysning af Grev Ostens politiske Stilling og Danmark-Norges Forhold til Sverige 1772-1773." *Dansk Magazin*, V Raekke, 4 Bind. (Copenhagen 1900).

Albedyhll, G. d': *Skrifter af blandadt, dock mest politiskt och historiskt, Innehåll*, II. (Nyköping 1810).

Albemarle, George Thomas, Earl of: *Memoirs of the Marquis of Rockingham and his Contemporaries*, I-II. (1852).

Algarotti: *Letters of Count Algarotti to Lord Hervey . . . containing the state of the Trade, Marine, Revenues and Forces of the Russian Empire*, I-II. (1769).

Archives ou correspondance inédite de la maison d'Orange-Nassau. 5th Series, ed. F. J. L. Krämer, I. 1766-1779. (Leyden 1910).

Arneth, A. d', and Geffroy, A.: *Marie-Antoinette. Correspondance secrète entre Marie-Thérèse et le Cte de Mercy-Argenteau*, I. (Paris 1875).

Asseburg: *Denkwürdigkeiten des Freiherrn Achatz Ferdinand von der Asseburg.* (Berlin 1842).

Barthélémy: *Mémoires de Barthélémy 1768-1819*, ed. J. de Dampierre. (Paris 1914).

Bedford: *Correspondence of John, fourth Duke of Bedford*, ed. Lord John Russell, III. (1846).

Bernstorff: *Bernstorffske Papirer. Udvalgte Breve og Optegnelser vedrørende Familien Bernstorff i Tiden fra 1732 til 1835*, ed. Aage Friis, I-III. (Copenhagen 1882).

——: *Correspondance ministérielle du Comte J. H. E. Bernstorff, 1751-1770*, ed. P. Vedel, II. (Copenhagen 1882).

——: *Correspondance entre le comte Johan Hartvig Ernst Bernstorff et le duc de Choiseul.* 1758-1766. (Copenhagen 1871).

Biehl: "Charlotte Dorothea Biehls historiske Breve," ed. J. H. Bang. *Historisk Tidsskrift*, III Raekke, 4 Bind. (Copenhagen 1865-66).

Boëthius, Bertil, and Heckscher, Eli: *Svensk handelsstatistik 1637-1737* (Stockholm 1938).

Bonde, Count Trolle-: *Anteckningar om Bondesläkten. Riksrådet Grefve Gustaf Bonde*, I. (Lund 1898).

——: *Anteckningar om Bondesläkten. Riksrådet och Riksmarskalken Grefwe Carl D. Bonde, samt hans närmaste Anhöriga*, I-II. (Lund 1895).

Bondeståndets riksdagsprotokoll, ed. Sten Landahl, 10-11. 1765-1770. (Stockholm 1973-75).

Brefvexling rörande Sveriges historia från åren 1772-1780, ed. L. Manderström. (Stockholm 1854).

Breve fra slutningen af det 18de århundrede, ed. L. Koch. *Dansk Magazin*, V Raekke, 3 Bind. (Copenhagen 1893).

Broglie, Comte de: *Correspondance secrète du Comte de Broglie avec Louis XV*, I-II, ed. D. Ozanam and M. Antoine. (Paris 1961).

Broglie, Le Duc de: *Le Secret du Roi. Correspondance secrète de Louis XV avec ses agents diplomatiques 1752-1774*, I-II. (Paris 1878).

Brusewitz, Axel, ed.: *Fribetstidens grundlagar och konstitutionella stadgar.* (Stockholm 1916).

Buckinghamshire: *The Despatches and Correspondence of John, Second Earl of Buckinghamshire, Ambassador to the Court of Catherine II of Russia 1762-1765*, I-II, ed. A. D'Arcy Collyer. *Camden Society*, 3rd Series. (1900, 1902).

Burke, Edmund: *The Correspondence of Edmund Burke*, II., ed. Lucy S. Sutherland. (Cambridge 1960).

Calendar of Home Office Papers, 1760-1765, 1766-1769, (1878-79).

Carlsson, Ingemar: *Frihetstidens handskrivna politiska litteratur. En bibliografi.* (Göteborg 1967).

Cavendish: *Sir Henry Cavendish's Debates of the House of Commons during the thirteenth Parliament of Great Britain*, ed. J. Wright. (1841).

Chatham: *Correspondence of William Pitt, Earl of Chatham*, ed. W. S. Taylor and J. H. Pringle, III. (1839).

Choiseul: *Mémoires du Duc de Choiseul*, ed. F. de Calmettes. (Paris 1904).

Corberon: *Un diplomate français à la Cour de Cathérine II. 1775-1780. Journal intime du Chevalier de Corberon.* (Paris 1901).

Crusenstolpe, M. J.: *Portfeuille*, I-V. (Stockholm 1837-45).

D'Aiguillon: *Mémoires du ministère du duc d'Aiguillon*, ed. J. W. G. Soulavie. (Paris 1790).

Danske Tractater 1751-1800. (Copenhagen 1882).

Dela Gardieska Archivet, ed. P. Wieselgren, 19 Vols. (Lund 1831-42), Vols. XII, XIV, XV.

"Depeche af 12 (23) April 1767 fra Gehejmraad C. v. Saldern og Generalmajor Filosofof til den russiske Regering," ed. Edvard Holm. *Dansk Magazin*, V Raekke, 3 Bind. (Copenhagen 1893).

Engeström, Johan von: *Historiska Anteckningar och Bref från åren 1771-1805 af Johan von Engeström*, ed. E. V. Montan. (Stockholm 1877).

Falkenskiold: *Mémoires de M. de Falkenskiold*, ed. P. Secretan. (Paris 1826).

Fersen, Fredrik Axel von: *Riksrådet och Fältmarskalken m. m. Grefve Fredrik Axel von Fersens Historiska Skrifter*, ed. R. M. Klinckowström, III. (Stockholm 1869).

Fredenheim: *Fredenheims och Mennanders brefväxling*, ed. Henrik Schück (Stockholm 1901).

Frederick II: *Oeuvres posthumes de Frédéric II, Roi de Prusse*, V-VI. (Berlin 1788).

——: *Politisches Correspondenz Friedrichs des Grossen*, 46 Vols. Vols. XX-XXXIII. (Berlin 1879-1939).

George III: *The Correspondence of George the Third from 1760 to December 1783*, ed. Sir John Fortescue, I. (1927).

Georgel, Abbé: *Mémoires pour servir à l'histoire des événements de la fin du dix-huitième siècle*, I. (Paris 1820).

[Gestrin, Johan] : *Mörksens Rike och Wäldigheter, tecknad til Åminnelse af warande hunger och dyr Tid, år 1772.* (Stockholm 1772).

Gjörwell, C. G.: *En Stockholmskrönika ur C. G. Gjörwells brev*, ed. Otto Sylwan. (Stockholm 1920).

Gleichen, Charles-Henri: *Souvenirs de Charles-Henri Baron de Gleichen*, ed. Paul Grimblot. (Paris 1868).

Grafton: *Autobiography and Political Correspondence of Augustus Henry, third duke of Grafton*, ed. W. R. Anson. (1898).

Grenville: *The Grenville Papers*, ed. W. J. Smith, II-IV. (1852).

——: *Additional Grenville Papers 1763-1765*, ed. J. R. G. Tomlinson. (Manchester 1962).

Gustav III: *Collection des écrits politiques et littéraires de Gustave III*, I. (Stockholm 1803).

——: *Konung Gustaf III:s efterlemnade och femtio år efter hans död öppnade papper*, ed. E. G. Geijer, I-III. (Uppsala 1843).

——: *Gustav III:s och Lovisa Ulrikas brevväxling*, ed. Henrik Schück, I-II. (Stockholm 1919).

Gyllenborg, Gustaf Fredrik: *Mitt lefverne 1731-1775. Självbiografiska Anteckningar*, ed. Gudmund Frunck. (Stockholm 1885).

Hamilton, Adam Ludvig: *Anteckningar till svenska historien under Gustaf III:s regering.* (*Svenska memoarer och brev*, IV., ed. Oscar Levertin). (Stockholm 1901).

Handlingar rörande Deras Excellencers Herrar Riksens-Råds Licentierande wid Riksdagen år 1772. (Stockholm 1772).

Handlingar rörande Skandinaviens Historia, II, XVI. (Stockholm 1817, 1831).

Handlingar ur v. Brinkmanska Archivet på Trolle-Ljungby, ed. Gust. Andersson I-II. (Örebro 1859-65).

Harris, James: *Diaries and Correspondence of James Harris, first Earl of Malmesbury . . . , edited by his grandson*, I. (1844).

Hemliga Handlingar hörande till Sveriges Historia efter Konung Gustaf III:s anträde till Regeringen, ed. J. F. Schartau, I-III. (Stockholm 1882-85).

Historical Manuscripts Commission Reports (HMC): Aitken (1891)
Carlisle (1897)
Earl of Dartmouth, III (1896)
Laing, II (1925)
Lonsdale (1893)
Lothian (1905)
Stopford-Sackville, I (1904)
Various, VI (1909)
Weston-Underwood (1885).

Historiska Handlingar, II-IV. (Stockholm 1862-64).

Hume, David: *Letters of David Hume*. (Oxford 1932).

Hård: *Grefwe Hårds Berättelse om Hans Kongl. Höghets, Prins Henriks Resa till Swerige och Ryssland, åren 1770 och 1776; med mera*. (Stockholm 1790).

———: *Mémoires historiques, politiques et militaires de M. le Cte de Hordt*, I-II. (Paris 1805).

Höpken, Anders Johan von: *Riksrådet Anders Johan von Höpkens Skrifter*, ed. Carl Silfverstolpe, I-II. (Stockholm 1890).

Jenkinson: *The Jenkinson Papers*, ed. Ninetta S. Jucker. (1949).

Junius: *The Letters of Junius*, ed. C. W. Everett. (1927).

Keith, Sir Robert Murray: *Memoirs and Correspondence . . . of Sir Robert Murray Keith*, ed. Mrs. Gillespie Smyth. I. (1849).

Louis XV: *Correspondance secrète inédite de Louis XV sur la Politique étrangère*, ed. E. Boutaric, I-II. (Paris 1866).

Lyttelton: *Memoirs and Correspondence of George, Lord Lyttelton*, ed. Robert Phillimore. (1845).

Martange: *Correspondance inédite du Général-Major de Martange*, ed. Charles Bréard. (Paris 1898).

Martens, F. de: *Recueil des Traités et Conventions conclus par la Russie avec les Puissances étrangères*, IX (X). (St. Petersburg 1892).

Mercy-Argenteau: *Correspondance secrète du Comte de Mercy-Argenteau avec l'Empéreur Joseph II et le prince de Kaunitz*, ed. A. d'Arneth and J. Flammermont, II. (Paris 1891).

Moltke, Adam Gottlob: "Grev Adam Gottlob Moltkes efterladte Mindeskrifter," ed. C. F. Wegener. *Historisk Tidsskrift*, IV Raekke, 2 Bind.

Nordencrantz, Anders: *Tankar om Krig i gemen och Sveriges Krig i synnerhet*, I-II. (Stockholm 1767, 1772).

———: *Undersökning om de rätta Orsakerna til den Blandning som skedt af Lagstiftande och Lagskipande, Redofordrande och Redoskyldige Magternas Gjöromål . . .* (Stockholm 1770).

[Oelreich, Nils von] : *En gammal mans Instruction för sin son N. N. då han år 1765 första gången biwistade Riks-Dagen*. (Stockholm 1765).

Osten: "Grev v. d. Ostens Gesandtskaber." *Historisk Tidsskrift*, IV Raekke, 1 Bind. (Copenhagen 1869-70).

Oxenstierna, Johan Gabriel: *Dagboks-Anteckningar af Johan Gabriel Oxenstierna åren 1769-1771*, ed. Gustaf Stjernström. *Skrifter utg. av svenska litteratursällskapet*, 2. (Uppsala 1888).

——: *Ljuva ungdomstid. Dagboken för åren 1766-1768*, ed. Inga Estrabaut. (Uppsala 1965).

Parliament: *The History, Debates and Proceedings of both Houses of Parliament . . . from the year 1743 to the year 1774.* (1792).

——: *A Complete Collection of the Protests of the Lords*, ed. J. E. Thorold Rogers, II. (Oxford 1875).

Poniatowski: *Correspondance inédite du Roi Stanislas-Auguste Poniatowski, 1764-1777*, ed. C. de Moui. (Paris 1875).

Recueil des Instructions données aux Ambassadeurs de France: *Angleterre* III. (Paris 1965).
Danemark (Paris 1895).
Russie IX (2) (Paris 1890).
Suède (Paris 1885).

Rosander, Yngve: "Några brev från Gustav III och Charles Gravier de Vergennes till Fredrik Carl Sinclair under riksdagen 1771-1772." *Historisk tidskrift*. (Stockholm 1959).

Ryder: *The Parliamentary Diaries of Nathaniel Ryder, 1764-7*, ed. P. D. G. Thomas, *Camden Miscellany*, XXIII. (1969).

Saint-Priest, François-Emmanuel Guignard, Comte de: *Mémoires. Règnes de Louis XV et de Louis XVI*, I. (Paris 1929).

Sandwich: *The Fourth Earl of Sandwich: Diplomatic Correspondence 1763-1765*, ed. Frank Spencer. (Manchester 1961).

——: *The Private Papers of John, Earl of Sandwich*, ed. G. R. Barnes and J. H. Owen, I. *Navy Records Society*. (1932).

Sbornik Imperatorskago russkago istoricheskago obshchestva. (St. Petersburg 1867-1916). (Vols. XIII, XX, XXII, XLVIII, LI, LVII, LXVII, LXXXVII, XCVII, CXVIII, CXLI).

Schack: *Udvalgte Breve, Betaenkningar og Optegnelser af J. O. Schack-Rathlous Arkiv 1760-1800*, ed. Th. Thaulow and J. O. Bro Jørgensen. (Copenhagen 1936).

Schumpeter, Elizabeth Boody: ***English Overseas Trade Statistics 1697-1808.*** (Oxford 1960).

Ségur, P. de: *Mémoires Souvenirs et Anecdotes par M. le Comte de Ségur*, I-II. (Paris 1890).

Sprengtporten: *Ur J. M. Sprengtportens papper.* (*Svenska memoarer och Brev*, VIII, ed. Henrik Schück). (Stockholm 1904).

Sverges traktater med *främmande Magter*, VIII, ed. Bertil Boëthius. (Stockholm 1922).

Sveriges Ridderskaps och Adels Riksdagsprotokoll från och med år 1719, ed. Sten Landahl, XXIV-XXXI. (Stockholm 1958-1970).

Tersmeden, Carl: *Amiral Carl Tersmedens memoarer*, ed. Nils Erdmann, IV-V. (Stockholm 1918).

Tessin, Carl Gustaf: [F. W. von Ehrenheim], *Tessin och Tessiniana*. (Stockholm 1819).

Thulemeyer: *Depeches van Thulemeyer 1763-1788. (Werken uitgegeven door het Historisch Genootschap [gevestigd te Utrecht]*, III Series, no. 30). (Amsterdam 1912).

Tilas, Daniel: *Anteckningar och brev från riksdagen 1765-1766*, ed. Olof Jägerskiöld. (*Kungl. Samfundet för utgivandet av handskrifter rörande Skandinaviens historia*. Handlingar, del 2). (Stockholm 1974).

——: *Anteckningar och brev från riksdagen 1769-1770*, ed. Olof Jägerskiöld. (*Kungl. Samfundet för utgivandet av handskrifter rörande Skandinaviens historia*. Handlingar, del 3). (Stockholm 1976).

Véou, P. de: "Un chapître inédit des Mémoires de Barthélémy: La Révolution suèdoise de 1772," *Revue des Etudes Historiques*, CIV. (Paris 1937).

[Virgin, Arvid]: *En patriots tankar om grundlagens nödvändiga förbättring*. (Stockholm 1769).

Walpole, Horace: *The Letters of Horace Walpole, fourth earl of Oxford*, ed. Mrs. Paget Toynbee, V. (Oxford 1904).

——: *Memoirs of the reign of George III*, ed. Sir Denis Le Marchant. (1845).

SECONDARY AUTHORITIES

Adair, E. R.: *The Exterritoriality of Ambassadors in the sixteenth and seventeenth centuries.* (1925).

Alexandersson, Erland: *Bondeståndet i Riksdagen 1760-1772.* (Lund 1975).

Amburger, Erich: *Russland und Schweden 1762-1772. Katharina II, die schwedische Verfassung and die Ruhe des Nordens.* (Berlin 1934).

Anderson, M. S.: *Britain's Discovery of Russia 1553-1815.* (1958).

——: "Eighteenth-Century Theories of the Balance of Power," in *Studies in Diplomatic History. Essays in Memory of David Bayne Horn.* (1970).

——: "Great Britain and the Russian Fleet, 1769-70," *Slavonic and East European Review,* XXXI. (1952-53).

Andréen, P. G.: "Det svenska 1700-talets syn på banksedlar och pappersmynt," *Historisk tidskrift.* (Stockholm 1956).

Annual Register, The. (1763-1773).

Arneth, Alfred Ritter von: *Geschichte Maria Theresias,* VIII. (Vienna 1877).

Arnheim, Fritz: "Beiträge zur Geschichte der nordischen Frage in der zweiten Hälfte des 18. Jahrhunderts," *Deutsche Zeitschrift für Geschichtswissenschaft,* II-V, VII. (1889-92).

Arup, Erik: "Rantzau-Ascheberg," *Historisk Tidsskrift,* VIII Raekke, 4 Bind, Tillaegshaefte. (Copenhagen 1913).

——: *Studier i engelsk og tysk Handelshistorie.* (Copenhagen 1907).

Awebro, Kenneth: *Gustaf III:s räfst med ämbetsmännen 1772-1779.* (Uppsala 1977).

Bakhrushin, Sergei V., and Skazkin, Sergei D.: "Diplomacy," in *Catherine the Great. A Profile,* ed. Marc Raeff. (New York 1972).

Bamford, P. W.: "French Shipping in Northern European Trade, 1660-1789," *Journal of Modern History.* (1954).

Barral, Comte de: *Etude sur l'histoire diplomatique de l'Europe de 1648 à 1791.* (Paris 1880).

Barthélémy, E. de: *Histoire des relations de la France et du Danemarck sous le Ministère du Comte de Bernstorff.* (Copenhagen 1887).

Behre, Göran: *Underrättelseväsendet och diplomati. De diplomatiska förbindelserna mellan Sverige och Storbritannien 1743-1745.* (Göteborg 1965).

Blart, Louis: *Les Rapports de la France et de l'Espagne après le Pacte de Famille jusqu'à la fin du Ministère du Duc de Choiseul.* (Paris 1915).

Boëthius, Bertil: *Magistraten och Borgerskapet i Stockholm 1719-1815.* (Stockholm 1943).

——: "Swedish Iron and Steel, 1660-1955," *Scandinavian Economic History Review,* VI. (Stockholm 1958).

Boëthius, Bertil, and Kromnow, Åke. *Jernkontorets historia,* I-II. (Stockholm 1947, 1968).

Bonsdorff, Göran von: "En finländsk insats i frihetstidens statsrättsliga diskussion. Kring Alexander Kepplerus' Memorial angående privilegier för de ofrälse stånden," *Svenska litteratursällskapet i Finland: Historiska och litteraturhistoriska studier,* 27-28. (Helsingfors 1952).

Bourguet, Alfred: *Le Duc de Choiseul et l'alliance espagnole.* (Paris 1906).

——: *Etudes sur la politique étrangère du Duc de Choiseul.* (Paris 1907).

Boyson, V. F.: *The Falkland Islands.* (Oxford 1924).

Brandt, Otto: *Caspar von Saldern und die nordeuropäische Politik im Zeitalter Katharinas II.* (Erlangen-Kiel 1932).

——: "Das Problem, der 'Ruhe des Nordens' im 18. Jahrhundert," *Historische Zeitschrift,* 140. (1929).

Brolin, Per-Erik: *Hattar och mössor i borgareståndet 1760-1766.* (Uppsala 1953).

Brown, Vera Lee: *Studies in the History of Spain in the second half of the eighteenth century. Smith College Studies in History,* 15:1-2. (Northamptom, Mass. 1930).

Bull, H.-J.: *Friedrich der Grosse und Schweden in den Jahren 1768-1773.* (Rostock 1936).
Butterfield, Sir Herbert: "British Foreign Policy, 1762-5," *Historical Journal*, VI. (Cambridge 1963).
Cabres, Sabathier de: *Cathérine II, sa Cour et la Russie.* (Berlin 1862).
Campbell, John: *A Political Survey of Britain.* (1774).
Carlquist, Gunnar: *Carl Fredrik Scheffer och Sveriges politiska förbindelser med Danmark 1752-1765.* (Lund 1920).
Carlsson, Sten: "Bondeståndet i Norden under senare delen av 1700-talet," in *Grupper och Gestalter.* (Stockholm 1964).
——: "Sverige under 1760-talet," in *Från Fattigdom till överflöd*, ed. Steven Koblik. (Stockholm 1973).
Castrén, Gunnar: *Gustav Philip Creutz.* (Stockholm/Borgå 1917).
Chalmers, George: *An Estimate of the Comparative Strength of Britain during this present and Four Preceding Reigns.* (1782).
Colenbrander, H. T.: *De Patriottentijd*, I. ('s Gravenhage 1897).
Coquelle, P.: *L'Alliance Franco-Hollandaise contre l'Angleterre 1735-1788.* (Paris 1902).
Corwin, E. S.: *French Policy and the American Alliance of 1778.* (Princeton, N. J. 1916).
Christie, Ian R.: "The Cabinet during the Grenville Administration, 1763-1765," *English Historical Review* (1958).
Critical Review, The. Vols. 29-38. (1770-1774).
Eagly, Robert V.: "Monetary Policy and Politics in mid-eighteenth century Sweden," *The Journal of Economic History*, 29 (1969).
Edler, P. J.: *Om börd och befordran under Frihetstiden.* (Stockholm 1942).
Eek, Hilding: *Om Tryckfriheten.* (Stockholm 1942).
Ellis, K. L.: "British Communications and Diplomacy in the Eighteenth Century," *Bulletin of the Institute of Historical Research*, XXXI. (1958).
Elmroth, Ingvar: *Nyrekryteringen till de högre ämbetena 1720-1809.* (Lund 1962).
Erdmann, Nils: *Carl Michael Bellman. En Kultur- och karaktärsbild från 1700-talet.* (Stockholm 1899).
Eriksson, Birgitta: *Bergstaden Falun 1720-1769.* (Uppsala 1970).
Evers, Artur: *Den svenska brännvinslagstiftningens historia*, II. (Lund 1930).
Fahlbeck, Erik: "Studier öfver frihetstidens politiska ideer," *Statsvetenskaplig tidskrift.* (Stockholm 1915-16).
Fitzmaurice, Lord: *Life of William Earl of Shelburne*, I. (1912).
Flammermont, Jules: *Les correspondances des Agents diplomatiques étrangers en France avant la Révolution.* (Paris 1906).
Flassan, J. B. P. G.: *Histoire générale et raisonnée de la Diplomatie française*, VI-VII. (Paris 1811).
Forsstrand, Carl: *Skeppsbroadeln. Minnen och Anteckningar från Gustav III:s Stockholm.* (Stockholm 1916).
——: *Storborgare och stadsmajorer.* (Stockholm 1918).
Fraguier, Bertrand de: "Le Duc d'Aiguillon et l'Angleterre (juin 1771-avril 1773)," *Revue d'Histoire diplomatique*, XXVI. (Paris 1912).
Friis, Aage: *Bernstorfferne og Danmark. Bidrag till den danske Stats politiske og kulturelle Udviklingshistorie 1750-1835*, I-II. (Copenhagen 1903, 1919).
Fryxell, Anders: *Berättelser ur svensk historia*, 42. (Stockholm 1873).
Geffroy, A.: *Gustave III et la Cour de France*, I. (Paris 1867).
Geijer, Erik Gustaf: *Samlade skrifter*, V. (Stockholm 1854).
Gerhard, Dietrich: *England und der Aufsteig Russlands.* (Munich and Berlin 1933).
Goebel, Julius: *The Struggle for the Falkland Islands: A Study in Legal and Diplomatic History.* (New Haven, Conn. 1927).

Griffiths, David M., "The Rise and Fall of the Northern System: Court Politics and Foreign Policy in the First Half of Catherine II's Reign," *Canadian Slavic Studies*, IV. (1970).

[Grimblot, P.] : *La Cour de la Russie il y a cent ans, 1725-1783*. (Berlin 1858).

Hagen, Ellen: *En frihetstidens son. Carl Bernhard Wadström*. (Stockholm 1946).

Hallesvik, Stig: *Axel von Fersen och gustaviansk politik 1771-1779*. (Göteborg 1977).

——: "Partimotsättningarna vid 1771-2 års riksdag som bakgrund till Gustav III:s statskupp," *Statsvetenskaplig tidskrift*. (1962).

Hennings, Beth: *Gustav III som kronprins*. (Stockholm 1935).

——: *Gustav III. En biografi*. (Stockholm 1957).

Hildebrand, Karl-Gustaf: *Fagerstabrukens historia*, I. (Uppsala 1957).

——: "Foreign Markets for Swedish Iron in the 18th Century," *Scandinavian Economic History Review*, VI. (Stockholm 1958).

Hjelt, A. J.: *Sveriges ställning till utlandet närmast efter 1772 års statshvälfning*. (Helsingfors 1887).

Hjärne, Harald: "Sverige inför Europa 1772," in *Ur det förgångna*. (Stockholm 1912).

Holm Edvard: "Caspar von Saldern og den dansk-norsk Regering," *Historisk Tidsskrift*, IV Raekke, 2 Bind. (Copenhagen 1870-72).

——: *Danmark-Norges Historie under Kristian VII*, I. (Copenhagen 1902).

——: "Styrelsen af Danmark-Norges Udenrigspolitikk under Struensee," *Historisk Tidsskrift*, IV Raekke, 2 Bind. (Copenhagen 1870-72).

Holmberg, Nils: "Oderhandeln, Preussen och svenska Pommern vid mitten av 1700-talet. Ett historiskt perspektiv," *Scandia*, XIV. (Lund 1941).

Horn, David Bayne: *British Public Opinion and the First Partition of Poland*. (Edinburgh 1945).

——: "Rank and emolument in the British Diplomatic Service 1689-1789," *Transactions of the Royal Historical Society*. (1959).

——: *Sir Charles Hanbury Williams and European Diplomacy*. (1930).

——: "The Cabinet Controversy on Subsidy Treaties in Time of Peace, 1749-50," *English Historical Review*, XLV. (1930).

——: "The Diplomatic experience of Secretaries of State," *History*. (1956).

Högberg, Staffan: *Utrikeshandel och sjöfart på 1700-talet. Stapelvaror i svensk export och import 1738-1808*. (Stockholm 1969).

Höjer, Torgny: "Christopher Springer och principalatsfrågan vid 1742-43 års riksdag," *Studier och handlingar rörande Stockholms historia*, I. (Uppsala 1938).

Iverus, Gustaf: *Hertig Karl av Södermanland. Gustav III:s broder*. (Uppsala 1925).

Jacobsohn, Ljubow: *Russland und Frankreich in den ersten Regierungsjahren der Kaiserin Katharina II, 1762-1772*. (Berlin 1929).

Jesse, J. H.: *George Selwyn and his Contemporaries*, I-IV. (1882).

Jobert, Ambroise: "Le Grand Frédéric et la Pologne," *Revue historique*. (Paris 1950).

Jägerskiöld, Olof: *1721-1792*. (Vol. II:2 of *Den svenska utrikespolitikens historia*, ed. Nils Ahnlund et al.) (Stockholm 1956-59).

——: "C. F. Scheffer och 1750-talets författningskris," *Historisk tidskrift*. (Stockholm 1939).

——: *Hovet och författningsfrågan 1760-1766*. (Uppsala 1943).

——: *Lovisa Ulrika*. (Stockholm 1945).

Kaeber, Ernst: *Die Idee des europäischen Gleichgewichts in der publizistischen Litteratur von 16. zum Mitte des 18. Jahrhunderts*, I. (Berlin 1906).

Kaplan, Herbert: *The First Partition of Poland*. (New York and London 1962).

Kent, H. S. K.: *War and Trade in Northern Seas. Anglo-Scandinavian Economic Relations in the Mid-Eighteenth Century*. (Cambridge 1973).

Kirchner, Walther: *Commercial Relations between Russia and Europe, 1400 to 1800*. (Bloomington, Indiana 1966).
Kjellin, Gunnar: "Kring Alexander Kepplerus' memorial," *Historisk tidskrift*. (Stockholm 1955).
——: "Gustaf III, Den Patriotiske Konung," in *Gottfried Carlsson, 18. 2. 1952*. (Lund 1952).
——: *Rikshistoriografen Anders Schönberg. Studier i riksdagarnas och de politiska tänkesättens historia*. (Lund 1952).
Konetzke, Richard: *Die Politik des Grafen Aranda. Ein Beitrag zur Geschichte des spanisch-englischen Weltgegensatzes im 18. Jahrhundert*. (Berlin 1929).
Konopczyński, Władysław: "England and the first Partition of Poland," *Journal of Central European Affairs*, VIII. (1948).
——: "Polen och Sverige i det adertonde århundradet," *Historisk tidskrift*. (Stockholm 1925).
Lacour-Gayet, G.: *La Marine militaire de la France sous la règne de Louis XV*. (Paris 1910).
Lagerroth, Fredrik: "Det frihetstida statsskickets utvecklingsmöjligheter," *Scandia*. (Lund 1966).
——: "En frihetstidens lärobok i gällande svensk statsrätt," *Statsvetenskaplig tidskrift*. (Stockholm 1937).
——: *Frihetstidens författning. En studie i den svenska konstitutionalismens historia*. (Stockholm 1915).
——: *Frihetstidens maktägande ständer, 1719-1772*, I-II, in *Sveriges Riksdag*, I Series, Vols. V-VI. (Stockholm 1934).
Landberg, Georg: *Den svenska riksdagen under den gustavianska tiden*, in *Sveriges Riksdag*, I Series, Vol. VII. (Stockholm 1932).
Langford, P.: *The First Rockingham Administration*. (Oxford 1973).
Leijonhufvud, Sigrid: *Ur svenska herrgårdsarkiv*. (Stockholm 1902).
Liedgren, Jan: "Ridderskapet och adeln vid riksdagarna 1719 och 1765-6" (Studier över den svenska riksdagens sociala sammansättning), *Skrifter utgivna av statsvetenskapliga föreningen i Uppsala*, VII. (Uppsala 1936).
Lindeberg, Hj.: *En ränksmidare. Strödda blad ur 1700-talets partistrider*. (Stockholm 1928).
Linnarsson, Lennart: *Riksrådens licentiering. En studie i frihetstidens parlamentarism*. (Uppsala 1943).
Macartney, Sir George: *An Account of Russia*. (1768).
Macfarlane, Robert: *The History of the Reign of George the Third*. (1770).
Madariaga, Isabel de: "The use of British Secret Funds at St. Petersburg, 1777-82," *Slavonic and East European Review*, XXXII. (1954).
——: *Great Britain, Russia and the Armed Neutrality of 1780*. (1962).
Malmström, Carl Gustaf: *Smärre skrifter rörande sjuttonhundratalets historia*. (Stockholm 1889).
——: *Sveriges politiska historia från konung Karl XII:s död till statshvälfningen 1772*, III-VI, 2nd ed. (Stockholm 1893-1901).
Marsangy, Louis Bonneville de: *Le Chevalier de Vergennes. Son ambassade à Constantinople*, II. (Paris 1894).
——: *Le Comte de Vergennes. Son ambassade en Suède 1771-1774*. (Paris 1898).
Martelli, George: *Jemmy Twitcher. A Life of the Fourth Earl of Sandwich*. (1962).
Marx, Karl: *Secret Diplomatic History of the Eighteenth Century*, ed. Lester Hutchinson. (1929).
Mauduit, Israel: *Considerations on the Present German War*. (1760).
Mellander, Karl: *Johan Christopher Toll som militär och politiker under Gustav III*. (Stockholm 1933).

Metcalf, Michael F.: *Russia, England and Swedish Party Politics 1762-1766. The Interplay between Great Power Diplomacy and Domestic Politics during Sweden's Age of Liberty*. (Stockholm and Totowa, N.J. 1977).

——: "Russia, England and the Younger Caps on the Eve of the Riksdag of 1765-6." (M.A. thesis, University of Stockholm 1972).

Michael, Wolfgang: *Englands Stellung zur ersten Teilung Polens*. (Hamburg and Leipzig 1890).

Morison, M. C.: "The Duc de Choiseul and the Invasion of England 1768-1770," *Transactions of the Royal Historical Society*, 3rd Series, IV. (1910).

Namier, Sir Lewis, and Brooke, John: *The House of Commons, 1754-1790*. (1964).

Nielsen, Yngvar: "Gustav den III:s norske Politik," *Historisk Tidsskrift*, II Raekke, 1 Bind. (Kristiania 1877).

Nieto, Manuel Hidalgo: *La Cuestión de las Malvinas. Contribución al estudio de las relaciones hispano-inglesas en el siglo XVIII*. (Madrid 1947).

Nilsson, Olof: "Blad ur Konung Gustaf III:s och Drottning Sofia Magdalenas Giftermålshistoria," *Historiskt bibliotek*, ed. C. Silfverstolpe, IV-VI. (Stockholm 1877-79).

Nilzén, Göran: *Studier i 1730-talets partiväsen*. (Stockholm 1971).

Nordensson, Jonas: "Kronprins Gustavs författningsprojekt 1768," *Statsvetenskapliga studier till statsvetenskapliga föreningens i Uppsala tjugofemårsdag*. (Uppsala 1944).

Nordmann, Claude J.: "Jakobiterna och det svenska hovet 1745-6," *Historisk tidskrift*. (Stockholm 1959).

Öberg, Arndt: *De yngre mössorna och deras utländska bundsförvanter 1765-1769. Med särskild hänsyn till de kommersiella och politiska förbindelserna med Storbritannien, Danmark och Preussen*. (Uppsala 1970).

Odhner, Clas Teodor: *Minne af Riksrådet m.m. Grefve Ulrik Scheffer*. (Stockholm n.d.).

——: *Sveriges politiska historia under Konung Gustaf III:s regering*, I. (Stockholm 1885).

Olsson, Gunnar: "Fredrik den Store och Sveriges författning," *Scandia*, XXVII. (Lund 1961).

——: *Hattar och mössor. Studier över partiväsendet i Sverige 1751-1762*. (Göteborg 1963).

——: "Krisuppgörelsen mellan hattpartiet och Carl Fredrik Pechlin 1760," *Scandia*. (Lund 1960).

Palme, Sven Ulric: "Befolkningsutvecklingen som bakgrund till partiomvälvningen 1738. Ett socialhistoriskt försök," *Scandia*. (Lund 1960).

——: Review of Olof Jägerskiöld, *Hovet och författningsfrågan*, in *Historisk tidskrift*. (Stockholm 1944).

Partiers Ursprung och ***Wärken i Swcrige***. [Anon.] (Stockholm 1769).

Petander, Karl: *De nationalekonomiska åskådningarna i Sverige sådana de framträda i litteraturen*, I. 1718-1765. (Stockholm 1912).

Petersson, Bengt: "Ludvig XV:s hemliga diplomati—några reflexioner," *Scandia*. (Lund 1962).

——: "The Correspondent in Paris—en engelsk informationskälla under 1700-talet," *Scandia*. (Lund 1961).

Potiemkine, M., ed: *Histoire de la Diplomatie*, I. (Paris 1946).

Przezdziecki, R.: *Diplomatic Ventures and Adventures. Some Experiences of British Envoys at the Court of Poland*. (1953).

Raeff, Marc, ed.: *Catherine the Great: A Profile*. (London and New York 1972).

Rain, Pierre: *La Diplomatie française d'Henri IV à Vergennes*. (Paris 1945).

Ramsey, J. F.: *Anglo-French Relations, 1763-1770: A Study of Choiseul's Foreign Policy*. (Berkeley, Calif. 1939).

Ransel, David L.: *The Politics of Catherinian Russia: The Panin Party*. (New Haven, Conn. and London 1975).

Reddaway, W. F.: "Macartney in Russia, 1765-67," *The Cambridge Historical Journal*, III. (Cambridge 1931).

[Reuterholm, Esbjörn Christian] : *Uplysning för Swenska Folket om Anledningen, Orsaken och Afsigterne med Urtima Riksdagen 1769.* (Stockholm 1769)

[Reverdil, E. S. F.] : *Struensee og Hoffet i Kjøbenhavn 1760-1772*, trans. L. Moltke. (Copenhagen 1859).

Richmond, Sir H.: *Statesmen and Sea Power.* (Oxford 1941).

Ritter, Gerhard: *Frederick the Great. An Historical Profile.* (1968).

Roberts, Michael: "Great Britain, Denmark and Russia, 1763-1770," in *Studies in Diplomatic History. Essays in Memory of David Bayne Horn*, ed. Ragnhild Hatton and M. S. Anderson. (1970).

——: "Great Britain and the Swedish Revolution, 1772-3," in *Essays in Swedish History.* (1967).

——: *Macartney in Russia.* Supplement 7 to *English Historical Review.* (1974).

——: *"Splendid Isolation," 1763-1780.* (Reading 1970).

——: *Swedish and English Parliamentarism in the Eighteenth Century.* (Belfast 1973).

——: Review of Arndt Öberg, *De yngre mössorna och deras bundsförvanter*, in *English Historical Review.* (1972).

Rudelius, Karl-Elof: "Forfattningsfrågan i de förenade deputationerna 1769," *Statsvetenskaplig tidskrift*, XXXVIII. (Stockholm 1935).

Ruville, Albert von: *William Pitt, Earl of Chatham*, III. (1907).

Rydberg, Stig: *Svenska studieresor till England under Frihetstiden.* (Uppsala 1951).

Sahlberg, Gardar: *Gustaf Fredrik Gyllenborg. Hans lif och diktning under Frihetstiden.* (Stockholm-Uppsala 1943).

Saint-Priest, Alexis de: *Etudes diplomatiques et littéraires*, I-II. (Paris n.d.).

Sallnäs, Birger: "Det ofrälse inslaget i 1772 års revolution," *Historisk tidskrift.* (Stockholm 1954).

——: "England i den svenska författningsdiskussionen 1771-2," *Vetenskaps-Societeten i Lund. Årsbok 1958-9.* (Lund 1959).

——: *Samuel Åkerhielm d.y. En statsmannabiografi.* (Lund 1947).

Samuelsson, Kurt: *De stora köpmanshusen i Stockholm 1730-1815.* (Stockholm 1951).

Schaumann, Georg: *Biografiska Anteckningar om Anders Chydenius.* (*Skrifter utgivna av Svenska Litteratursällskapet i Finland*, LXXXIV). (Helsingfors 1908).

Schiern, F.: "Bidrag til Oplysning af Katastrofen den 17de Januari 1772," *Historisk Tidsskrift*, IV Raekke, 2 Bind. (Copenhagen 1870-72).

Schmidt, K. Rahbek-: "Problems connected with the last Polish Royal election. A Study in the Development of Panin's Northern System," *Scando-Slavonica*, II. (1956).

——: "The Treaty of Commerce between Great Britain and Russia 1766. A Study on the Development of Count Panin's Northern System," *Scando-Slavonica*, I. (1954).

——: "Wie ist Panins Plan zu einem Nordischen System entstandet?" *Zeitschrift für Slawistik*, II. (Berlin 1957).

[Schönberg, Anders] : "Om Förbund, mellan Stater," *Gjörwells Statsjournal*, II. (Stockholm 1768).

Schück, Herman: *Gustav III:s statsvälvning i berättande källor och äldre litteratur.* (Stockholm 1955).

Scott, H. M.: "Frederick II, the Ottoman Empire and the Origins of the Russo-Prussian Alliance of April 1764," *European Studies Review.* (1977).

——: "Great Britain, Poland and the Russian Alliance, 1763-1767," *The Historical Journal*, 19. (Cambridge 1976).

Sedgwick, Romney: *The House of Commons, 1715-1754.* (1970).

Ségur, P. de: *Politique de tous les cabinets de l'Europe pendant les règnes de Louis XV et Louis XVI*, I-III. (Paris 1824).

Sheridan, Charles Francis: *A History of the late Revolution in Sweden: containing an Account of the Transactions of the Three last Diets in that country . . .* , 2nd ed. (1783).

Sjöstedt, Lennart: "Le Secret du Roi, hertigen av Choiseul och Sverige 1766-1770," *Scandia.* (Lund 1962).

Spencer, Frank: "The Anglo-Prussian Breach, 1762," *History.* (1956).

———: "Russian Masts and American Independence," *Mariners Mirror,* 44. (1958).

Stählin, Karl: *Geschichte Russlands von der Anfängen bis zur Gegenwart,* II. (Berlin 1930).

Stavenow, Ludvig: *Frihetstiden. Dess epoker och kulturlif,* 2nd ed. (Göteborg 1907).

———: *Om rådsvalen under Frihetstiden. Bidrag till svenska riksrådets historia.* (Uppsala 1890).

Stiegung, Helle: "Bröderna Scheffer, Gustav III och den danska politiken åren 1770-1772," *Vetenskaps-Societeten i Lund. Årsbok 1963.* (Lund 1963).

———: *Den engelska underrättelseverksamheten rörande Sverige under 1700-talet. En studie i Londonkabinettets politiska spionage med särskild hänsyn tagen till åren 1770-1772.* (Stockholm 1962).

———: "Le secret du roi och Sverige. Ett genmäle," *Historisk tidskrift.* (Stockholm 1953).

———: *Ludvig XV:s hemliga diplomati och Sverige 1752-1774.* (Lund 1961).

Stridsberg, Olle: "Hattarnas och mössornas ställningstaganden till tryckfrihetsfrågan på riksdagarna 1760-2 och 1765-6," *Historisk tidskrift.* (Stockholm 1953).

Summerson, Sir John: *Georgian London,* 3d ed. (1978).

Sundberg, Gunnar: "Lantpartiet vid riksdagen 1760-2," *Historisk tidskrift.* (Stockholm 1953).

Suolahti, Gunnar: *Sprengtportens statskupp och andra essayer.* (Stockholm-Helsingfors 1919).

Svenska Fatburen, Den: *Sjätte öpningen.* No. 20, 1 August 1769. (Stockholm 1769).

Svenska Flottans Historia. Örlogsflottan i ord och bild från dess grundläggning under Gustav Vasa fram till våra dagar, II. (Malmö 1942).

Svenskt biografiskt lexikon. Vol. 16, art. Robert Finlay (by Birgitta Lager); Vol. 20, art. John Jennings (by Staffan Högberg).

Swahn, W.: *Beylon, Sveriges store okände.* (Stockholm 1925).

Söderberg, Tom: *Den namnlösa medelklassen. Socialgrupp två i det gamla svenska samhället.* (Stockholm 1956).

Tankar om Alliancer, Och hwilka kunna wara för Swerige de förmånligaste. (Stockholm 1771).

Tegnér, Elof: *Bidrag till kännedomen om Sveriges yttre politik närmast efter statshvälfningen 1772* (*Valda Skrifter,* V). (Stockholm 1904).

Temperley, Harold: *Frederic the Great and Kaiser Joseph,* 2nd ed. (1968).

Tengberg, Niklas: *Konung Gustaf III:s första regeringstid till och med 1772 års statshvälfning.* (Lund 1871).

———: *Om Frihetstiden. Några anmärkningar.* (Stockholm 1867).

———: *Om kejsarinnan Catharina II:s åsyftade stora nordiska alliance.* (Lund 1863).

Trulsson, Lars: *Ulrik Scheffer som Hattpolitiker. Studier i Hattregimens politiska och diplomatiska historia.* (Lund 1947).

Tyler, J. E.: "John Roberts, M.P., and the first Rockingham Administration," *English Historical Review,* LXVII. (1952).

Uebersberger, Hans: *Russlands Orientpolitik in den letzten zwei Jahrhunderten.* (Stuttgart 1913).

Valentin, Hugo: "Det sociala momentet i historieskrivningen om 1772 års statshvälfning," *Scandia.* (Lund 1941).

———: *Frihetstidens riddarhus. Några bidrag till dess karakteristik.* (Stockholm 1912).

Vedel, P.: *Den aeldre Grev Bernstorffs Ministerium.* (Copenhagen 1882).

Whitworth, Sir Charles: *State of the Trade of Great Britain*. (1766).

Wood, Alfred E.: *A History of the Levant Company*. (Oxford 1935).

Wraxal, Nathaniel A.: *A Tour through some of the Northern Parts of Europe*. (1775).

Yorke, Philip C.: *The Life and Correspondence of Philip Yorke, Earl of Hardwicke*, III. (Cambridge 1913).

Zeller, Gaston: *Histoire des Relations internationales*, III. *Les Temps modernes*, II. *De Louis XIV à 1789*. (Paris 1955).

——: "Le principe d'équilibre dans la politique internationale avant 1789," *Revue historique*, CCXV. (Paris 1956).

Zetterström, Erik: *Om allmänna Handels Historien och Wetenskapen*. (Stockholm 1769).

Index

Index